Standard Encyclopedia of

Pressed Glass

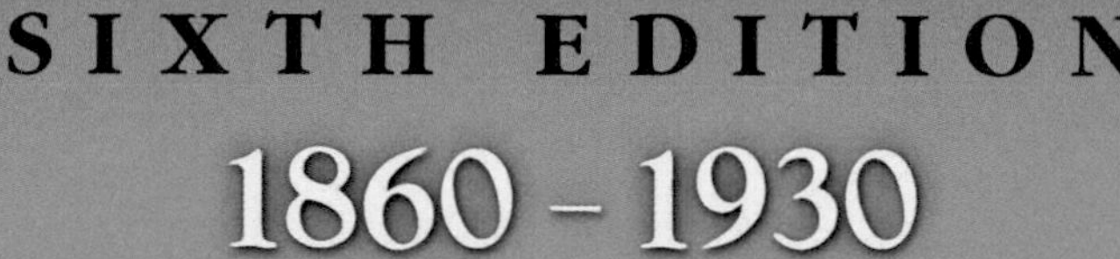

SIXTH EDITION

1860 – 1930

Identification & Values

Mike Carwile

COLLECTOR BOOKS

A Division of Schroeder Publishing Co., Inc.

Front cover: Greentown Squirrel pitcher, chocolate glass, $600.00. Rebecca at the Well compote, crystal, $800.00. Carriage novelty bowl, amber, $135.00.

Back cover: Bakewell Waffle pitcher, crystal, $1,500.00. Alligator toothpick holder, crystal, $175.00. Fiddle Bottle, amber, $300.00.

Cover design by Beth Summers
Book design by Beth Ray

COLLECTOR BOOKS
P.O. Box 3009
Paducah, Kentucky 42002-3009

www.collectorbooks.com

Mike Carwile
180 Cheyenne Drive
Lynchburg, VA 24502
Email: mcarwile@jetbroadband.com
Phone: 434-237-4247
If you would like a reply by mail,
please include a self-addressed stamped envelope.

The current values in this book should be used only as a guide. They are not intended to set prices, which vary from one section of the country to another. Auction prices as well as dealer prices vary greatly and are affected by condition as well as demand. Neither the author nor the publisher assumes responsibility for any losses that might be incurred as a result of consulting this guide.

Searching for a Publisher?

We are always looking for people knowledgeable within their fields. If you feel that there is a real need for a book on your collectible subject and have a large comprehensive collection, contact Collector Books.

Contents

A Personal Thank You

I first and most importantly
want to thank God,
and to thank my mother,
Carolyn J. Carwile (1927 – 2007),
for introducing me to Him.
It's been well worth it Mom.

Dedication

I'd like to sincerely thank Gary and Sharon Vandevander for graciously allowing me into their home on numerous occasions to photograph many of the fine pieces from their collection to show in this edition, especially the nice cover photos.

Acknowledgments

A work of this magnitude just couldn't be accomplished without the help of many people who contributed time, information, and photos of their glass.

A special thanks to those who permitted me to photograph their collections or show their photos. These include Green Valley Auctions Incorporated located in Mt. Crawford, Virginia, and their photographer William H. McGuffin; Winfred Huff; Joe Brooks; Steve and Radka Sandeman; Dave and Vickie Peterson; Mike Wonders; and Jean C. Loomis, author of *Krys-tol, Krys-tol, Krystol*.

In addition, a special thanks also goes to Siegmar Geiselberger from Germany for his continued support in sending me the *Pressglas-Korrespondenz* in print and/or CD format, and Don Watley.

And finally, I want to acknowledge all those who offered their help and kindness by sending photos, information, and suggestions for the current edition: John and Rae Ann Calai, Philip Hergatt, Valerie Caudill, Al and Debbie Barrett, Bill and Phyllis Burch, Don and Becky Hamlet, Don and Dorene Ashbridge, Cindy Blais, Emma H. Crane, Mary Crum, Richard and Merri Houghton, Linda Zucker, Martha W. Cope, Ronald E. Noble, James Edward Dial, Merlin Brose, Ted Friesner, James S. Wilkins, Samantha Prince, Alice Miller, Larry Enriques, Gerald Reed, Joyce Power, Mr. and Mrs. Lloyd Howard, Daniel Ruth, Bill Holmeide, Herman Gaffney, Frank Smith, Gregory Ferguson, Maggie Ramey, William and Patsy Roberts, Virginia Radcliffe, June Hanekrat, Mr. and Mrs. Brian Stout, Alice Widtfeldt, Billy Wilson, Larry Wilson, Judy Chaney, Steve and Jo Ann Burke, Geof. and Jill Patterson, Barbara Dunkley, Myra Dreitzer, Dave Cotton, Tom Darden, Tom McCartney, Lorelei Howard, Rebecca Bowen, Jerry W. Holley, E. J. Parsons, Charla Holtschneider, Mr. and Mrs. Lance Hilkene, Doug and Dustin Siska, Cathy Dahms, Jeanette Drumm, Emily Thompson, Larry Landis, Mary Hamition, Pat Bennett, Todd Kuwitzky, John and Elizabeth Sherwood, Harriet Arklie, Martin C. Puyear, Paula Dochney, Teri Comer, Pat Yourdon, Brian Stout, Judy St. John-Belt, Charlotte's Web, Don Bailey, Steve and Deb Barney, Charlan Ledbetter, Thomas and Valerie Schneider, Wayne Ritt, Joan Wilson, Ken and Shirley Rose, Jeanette Drumm, Ray Stocks, Roy Manno, Bill Delano, Howdy and Shirley Sanders, Kris Shiner, Don and Jane Henson, Gail Wheatley, Julian Penrod, Charlotte Brady, Susan Parker, John Howe, Lori Cheche, Dan and Marie Dusek, Gweneth Smith, Colleen Mailly, Ray Stutsman, Designofthetime, Greg Dilian, Ossie Perry, Kathy Bowlin, Cliff and Ann Stephan, Joshua Wilson, Bruce and Darcy Hill, Lyle Bennett, Lise-Anne Pilon-Delorus, Linda Reid, J.C. Wilson, Dennis Crouse, Noreen and Gil McGurl, Rose at Clovis Antiques, and a special thanks to James Wilkins, Jerey W. Holley, and Scott Shuford of the Dallas Auction Galleries for so many rare item photos.

My thanks also goes out to anyone I may have overlooked. I appreciate the contributions each and every one of you has given to this edition.

Introduction

American pressed glass had its beginning in 1821 when J. P. Bakewell received a patent to produce glass furniture knobs. Before that time glass was blown, financially often beyond the reach of most, simple in design by necessity, and limited in availability. With the Bakewell patent, others quickly followed and within a few years, pressed tableware was being produced in vast amounts and in shapes previously unheard of. America's pressed glass industry was on its way.

Other makers and other patents soon followed but in the 1860s an urgent military need for available lead forced the glass industry into a bind that lasted until William Leighton Sr., developed a soda-lime formula for Hobbs, Brockunier, eliminating the need for lead in glass production. Finally, glass could be pressed easily and was thinner and more adaptable to detailing, permitting patterns never before possible. Within a decade pressed glass was at its zenith and companies still bound to the old ways of flint glass began to pass from the scene, replaced by a wave of vital new concerns. Plants sprouted where there was a supply of natural gas in western Pennsylvania, Ohio, West Virginia, Maryland, and Indiana. Hundreds of patterns and dozens of shapes with elaborate geometric, animal, fruit, and flora designs poured into the marketplace in crystal and sparkling colors.

By the 1890s problems in the glass industry had mounted. Labor disputes, depletion of some of the gas supply, a national depression, all forced a rethinking of production methods. Soon combines like that of U.S. Glass (15 companies joining together) and National (19 companies) were organized. The impact on the marketplace was rewarding, with increased production, reworked moulds, and re-issued patterns, all allowing full mileage from every glass pour. New patterns and treatments were offering cased, ivory (custard), and opalescent glass treatments that remain very collectible today.

By early 1900, production again suffered. The number of quality producers dwindled due to fires, financial failures, or various other reasons. The answer was new blood with new ideas, and companies like Northwood, Fenton, Millersburg, Imperial, and Cambridge brought iridized, gilded, enameled, and stained wares to intrigue new interest from buyers.

By the end of the 1920s with a national depression looming, quality declined. This, coupled with a trend toward reproduction of early pressed items and the arrival of full-machine moulding, changed the industry forever. Sixty years of quality hand-pressed glass seemed doomed as Depression glass became the norm, and the golden age of American pressed glass ended.

A Special Note to Readers

As this book has continued to grow with additional patterns and information, I've had to make a few editorial decisions to keep this book a managable size. I considered removing the Commemorative and Advertising section; however, many readers and collectors continue to enjoy the patterns in this category.

To reduce page count, I removed many plain or obscure-patterned items. I also removed photos that were out of focus making it difficult to properly see the pattern. Too, most all individual credits have moved into the general acknowledgment section.

Photos in this book are from a variety of sources, and most come from readers and collectors like you. For this reason, the color of photo backgrounds will vary; when these photos have the backgrounds removed, some variations in the coloring of the glass will occur. I want you to understand why these variations occur, and I feel it is a small price to pay, especially for hard-to-find or rare patterns that I want to share with you.

Hopefully, you will notice a definite upgrade in the quality of photographs of glass displayed in this book. I will continue to collect photographs for future publications as this work progresses. Fortunately, I have been able to personally photograph individual collections and have received a number of higher quality photos from various collectors. If you have any early pressed glass that dates from 1860 to 1930 and can supply a high quality clear photo, I would certainly appreciate hearing from you, either through my email or my address provided in the front of this publication.

My goal is to provide you with excellent quality photographs and information to make pattern identification easier and enjoyable, whether to identify patterns for your family and friends, or as a collector of early American pattern glass (EAPG).

Further, I encourage readers and collectors to personally contact me if you can provide information to update or correct information I have provided herein. To do so, please provide any and all documented reference information that pertains to manufacturer, date of production, colors produced, and pieces made. I will then gladly include this information in future editions to make your collecting experience more knowledgeable, factual, and enjoyable.

Pattern Attribution

Researchers and writers of books about American glass patterns are often criticized for their conclusions, but the reader should be aware of all the pitfalls in placing a pattern or group of patterns with a single maker.

Glass companies opened and closed with some regularity, and they moved to other locations at will. Combines like U.S. Glass and National absorbed companies, controlling their production, often moving moulds from one member-factory to another. Finally, blanks were sold to other concerns to be stained, gilded, or decorated, with these concerns then advertising and selling the glass as their own, and never giving credit to the glassmaker.

All of these things have clouded the history of glass and so mistakes were often made in the identification of a pattern's true maker. Granted, in the last decade, research has gained ground, and while all of us do our best to be as accurate as possible, some mistakes do occur, and some patterns linked to one maker also may have been made by others. So I hope the reader won't judge too quickly. Every year more facts are learned, more company catalogs appear, more company glass ads surface, and more general information is confirmed or discounted.

As I've said in previous editions, I use several methods for attribution that include identifying glass shards, comparing with other patterns for similarity, and researching old glass catalogs and advertisements. In addition I take a long look at those researchers who have gone before me and compare one writer's ideas with another's, and that is why I produce succeeding editions of all my books. Again, if you have additional information or can attribute any pattern in this edition to a specific maker, please share your knowledge with me so that I can improve my books with each new edition.

Shapes

Below are some of the common shapes you find in pressed glass, but certainly nowhere near all of them. Specialty pieces, many vase shapes, novelty shapes, and others can be found. Here are the ones you will encounter most often.

Berry Set — has one large bowl (usually 8" - 9") and six individual small bowls.

Bread Plate — may be round or oblong. Usually larger than a regular plate.

Cake Stand — a flat plate shape on a stem. If found without the stem it is considered "plate" not a stand.

Carafe — a water bottle that doesn't come with a stopper.

Celery Vase — a tall holder for stalks of celery. May be flat based or on a stem.

Compote — a stemmed vessel usually meant to hold fruit (large) or jelly (small), or just be decorative.

Cruet — a stoppered bottle that holds liquids such as oil.

Decanter — a bottle to hold spirits. Can have many shapes but comes with its own stopper. Depending on the type of spirits, it can be found with wine glasses, goblets, clarets, or champagne glasses.

Ice Cream Set — like the berry set, this one is shallow and has the edges of the bowl turned up and slightly inward.

Jam Jar — a receptacle for jam. Has a lid that is slotted for its own spoon. Also known as a mustard jar when holding mustard or horseradish.

Nappy — a one-handled piece, meant to hold mints, jam, nuts, etc.

Pickle Dish — a long, narrow flat dish used to hold pickles.

Punch Set — consists of a punch bowl, a standard or base, matching cups (often 12, but may be as few as six), and occasionally a large underplate.

Salt Dip — a small flat salt holder that is usually put at each place setting. Can be a master salt or individual salt dip.

Sandwich Tray — a large plate, usually with a center handle.

Shakers — usually means salt and pepper shakers although there is a larger shape that is a sugar shaker.

Spill — Used to hold small slivers of wood or rolled paper wands used to light oil lamps.

Syrup — a handled container for syrup. Has a metal lid and pouring spout.

Table Set (Basic) — usually has four parts: covered butter dish, a covered sugar holder, a creamer, and a spooner (spoon holder).

Table Set (Extended) — everything in the basic table set in addition to bowls, celery vase, pickle and relish dish, cruet, syrup, water set, toothpick holder, and various other shapes.

Toothpick Holder — just what the name implies. A small receptacle, handled or not, to hold toothpicks.

Water Set — consists of a water pitcher and six matching tumblers. The pitcher may be a squat design, a tall tankard, a pedestal based one, or a standard shape (usually has a collar base). Tumblers can be of standard size, tall (called lemonade tumblers), or squat.

Glass Companies

Adams and Company, Pittsburgh, Pennsylvania, c. 1851 - 1891. Joined U.S. Glass Co. in 1891 as Factory A.

Aetna Glass and Manufacturing Co., Bellaire, Ohio, 1880 - 1891.

American Flint Glass Works, Wheeling, West Virginia, 1840s.

Anchor Hocking Glass Co., c. 1904 to present. Began as Hocking Glass Co., and in 1906 Ohio Flint Glass Co. merged with it.

Atterbury and Company, Pittsburgh, Pennsylvania, 1850s.

Bakewell, Pears and Company, Pittsburgh, Pennsylvania. Began as Bakewell, Payn and Page Co. (Pittsburgh), 1808. Still operating in the 1870s.

Beatty, Alexander J. and Sons, Steubenville, Ohio, 1879. Moved to Tiffin, Ohio, and joined U.S. Glass in 1892 as Factory R.

Beatty-Brady Glass Co., Steubenville, Ohio, 1850; Dunkirk, Indiana, 1898. Joined National Glass in 1899.

Beaumont Glass Co., Martins Ferry, Ohio, 1895. In 1905 joined Hocking Glass Co., which became Anchor Hocking Glass Co.

Beaver Falls Cooperative Glass Co., Beaver Falls, Pennsylvania, 1879. Became Beaver Falls Glass Co., 1887.

Bellaire Goblet Co., Bellaire, Ohio, 1879; Findlay, Ohio, 1888. Joined U.S. Glass in 1891 as Factory M.

Belmont Glass Co., Bellaire, Ohio, 1866; still operating in 1888.

Boston and Sandwich Glass Co., Sandwich, Massachusetts, 1825 - 1889.

Boston Silver Glass Co., East Cambridge, Massachusetts, 1857 - 1870s.

Brilliant Glass Works, Brilliant, Ohio, 1880. Moved to LaGrange in 1880 and merged with Novelty Glass Works, 1889.

Bryce, McKee and Co., Pittsburgh, Pennsylvania, 1850. Became Bryce, Walker and Co. in 1854.

Bryce, Walker and Co., Pittsburgh, Pennsylvania, 1855. Became Bryce Brothers in 1882.

Bryce Brothers, Pittsburgh, Pennsylvania, 1882. Moved to Hammondsville, Pennsylvania, 1889; joined U.S. Glass in 1891 as Factory B. Moved to Mt. Pleasant, Pennsylvania, in 1896 and was still operating in 1952.

Bryce, Higbee and Co. (Homestead Glass Works), Pittsburgh, Pennsylvania, 1879. Became J. B. Higbee Glass Co. c. 1900 at Bridgeville, Pennsylvania, and was still operating in 1911.

Buckeye Glass Co., Wheeling, West Virginia, 1849; moved to Bowling Green, Ohio, in 1888. Closed c. 1903. See Excelsior Glass Works for their other factory.

Cambridge Glass Co. (National Glass Co.), Cambridge, Ohio, 1901; closed 1958.

Glass Companies

Campbell, Jones and Co., Pittsburgh, Pennsylvania, 1865. Became Jones, Cavitt and Co., 1883.

Canton Glass Co., Canton, Ohio, c. 1883; Marion, Indiana, 1883. Joined National Glass in 1899.

Central Glass Co., Wheeling, West Virginia, 1863. Joined U.S. Glass in 1891 as Factory O; became Central Glass Works later.

Central Glass Co., Summitsville, Indiana. Joined National Glass in 1899; survived and was still operating in 1924.

Challinor, Taylor and Co. (Challinor, Hogan Glass Co.), Pittsburgh, Pennsylvania, 1866; Tarentum, Pennsylvania, 1884. Joined U.S. Glass as Factory C in 1891.

Columbia Glass Co., Findlay, Ohio, 1886. Joined U.S. Glass in 1891 as Factory J.

Cooperative Flint Glass Co., Beaver Falls, Pennsylvania, 1879 - 1937.

Crystal Glass Co., Pittsburgh, Pennsylvania, 1879; Bridgeport, Ohio, 1882. Burned in 1884. Moved to Bowling Green, Ohio, 1888. Joined National Glass Co. in 1899; reorganized by 1906; closed in 1908.

Cumberland Glass Co., Cumberland, Maryland. Joined National Glass Co. in 1899.

Curling, R. B. and Sons (Curling, Price and Co.), Pittsburgh, Pennsylvania, 1827; became Dithridge and Sons, 1860.

Dalzell, Gilmore, and Leighton Glass Co. (Dalzell Brothers and Gilmore), Brilliant, Ohio, 1883; went to Wellsburg, West Virginia, in 1888. Joined National Glass, 1899.

Dithridge and Co. (Ft. Pitt Glassworks), Pittsburgh, Pennsylvania, 1860; went to Martins Ferry, Ohio, in 1881; New Brighton, Pennsylvania, in 1887 and became Dithridge and Sons.

Doyle and Company, Pittsburgh, Pennsylvania, 1866. Joined U. S. Glass, 1891 as Factory P.

Dugan Glass Co. (Indiana Glass Co.), Indiana, Pennsylvania, 1892. Dugan/Diamond became Diamond Glass Company, 1913 - 1931.

Duncan, George and Sons, Pittsburgh, Pennsylvania, 1874; became George A. Duncan and Sons and George Duncan's Sons. Joined U.S. Glass in 1891 as Factory D. Became Duncan and Miller Glass Co. in 1903, closed in 1955.

Eagle Glass and Mfg. Co., Wellsburgh, West Virginia.

East Liverpool Glass Co., East Liverpool, Ohio, 1882 - 1883. In 1889 Specialty Glass Co. started there.

Elson Glass Works, Pittsburgh, Pennsylvania, c. 1870s.

Evansville Glass Co., Evansville, Indiana, 1905.

Excelsior Glass Works (Buckeye Glass Co.), Wheeling, West Virginia, 1849; moved to Martins Ferry, Ohio, 1879. Burned in 1894.

Fairmont Glass Co. joined National Glass in 1899.

Fenton Art Glass Co., Martins Ferry, Ohio, and Williamston, West Virginia, 1906 to present.

Findlay Flint Glass Co., Findlay, Ohio, 1889; failed shortly thereafter.

Fostoria Glass Co., Fostoria, Ohio, 1887; Roundsville, West Virginia, 1891. Added factory at Miles, Ohio, in 1910. Closed in 1986.

Franklin Flint Glass Co., Philadelphia, Pennsylvania, 1861. Operated by Gillinder and Sons.

Gillinder and Sons, Philadelphia, Pennsylvania, 1861. Moved to Greensburg, Pennsylvania, in 1888. Joined U.S. Glass as Factory G in 1891.

Greensburg Glass Co., Greensburg, Pennsylvania, 1889. Joined National Glass in 1899.

Heisey, A. H. Glass Co., Newark, Ohio, 1895; closed in 1957.

Higbee, J. B. Glass Co., Bridgeville, Pennsylvania, 1900; still operating in 1911.

Hobbs, Brockunier and Co. (Hobbs, J. H. Glass Co.), Wheeling, West Virginia, 1863. Joined U.S. Glass as Factory H in 1891; dismantled shortly thereafter.

Imperial Glass Co., Bellaire, Ohio, 1901 - 1984.

Indiana Glass Co., Dunkirk, Indiana, 1897.

Indiana Tumbler and Goblet Co., Greentown, Indiana, 1853. Joined National Glass in 1899; burned in 1903.

Iowa City Flint Glass Co., Iowa City, Iowa, 1880 - 1882.

Jefferson Glass Co., Steubenville, Ohio, 1901; to Follansbee, West Virginia, in 1907; still operating in 1920s.

Jenkins Glass Co., Greentown, Indiana, 1894.

Jones, Cavitt and Co., Pittsburgh, Pennsylvania, 1884.

Kemple, John E. Glass Co., Kenova, West Virginia; East Palestine, Ohio, 1945 - 1970. Reproduced McKee patterns from old moulds.

Keystone Tumbler Works, Rochester, Pennsylvania, 1897. Joined National Glass in 1899.

King, Son and Co., Pittsburgh, Pennsylvania, 1864 as Johann, King and Co.; became King Glass Co., c. 1879.

King Glass Co., Pittsburgh, Pennsylvania, c. 1879. Became U.S. Glass Factory K in 1891.

Kokomo Glass Co., Kokomo, Indiana, 1899.

LaBelle Glass Co., Bridgeport, Ohio, 1872; burned in 1887; sold in 1888 to Muhleman Glass Works, LaBelle, Ohio.

Lancaster Glass Co., Lancaster, Ohio, c. 1915.

Libbey, Wh. H. and Sons, Co., Toledo, Ohio, c. 1899.

McKee and Brothers, Pittsburgh, Pennsylvania, c. 1853; moved to Jeannette, Pennsylvania, 1889. Joined National Glass in 1899. Was McKee Glass Co. by 1904.

Millersburg Glass Co., Millersburg, Ohio, 1909 - 1912.

Model Flint Glass Co., Findlay, Ohio, 1888; to Albany, Indiana, between 1891 and 1894. Joined National Glass in 1899; failed c. 1903.

National Glass Co., Pittsburgh, Ohio, 1898 - 1905.

New England Glass Co. (New England Glass Works), Cambridge, Massachusetts, 1817. Became W. L. Libbey and Sons in 1880.

Nickel Plate Glass Co., Fostoria, Ohio, 1888. Joined U.S. Glass as Factory N in 1891.

Northwood Glass Co., Indiana, Pennsylvania (became part of Dugan Glass Co., c. 1896). Joined National Glass in 1899. Became Harry Northwood Glass Co. in 1910 at Wheeling, West Virginia. Failed c. 1923.

Novelty Glass Co., LaGrange, Ohio, 1880. Moved to Brilliant, Ohio, 1882. Joined U.S. Glass in 1891 as Factory T. Moved to Fostoria, Ohio, in 1892 and burned in 1893.

Ohio Flint Glass Co., Lancaster, Ohio. Joined National Glass in 1899.

Pittsburgh Glass Works, Pittsburgh, Pennsylvania, 1798 - 1852. Became James B. Lyon Glass Co. Associated with O'Hara Glass Co., Pittsburgh. Joined U.S. Glass in 1891.

Portland Glass Co., Portland, Maine, 1864.

Richards and Hartley Flint Glass Co., Pittsburgh, Pennsylvania, 1866; Tarentum, Pennsylvania, 1884. Joined U.S. Glass in 1891.

Ripley and Co., Pittsburgh, Pennsylvania, 1866. Became U.S. Glass Factory F in 1891.

Riverside Glass Co., Wellsburg, West Virginia, 1879. Joined National Glass in 1899.

Robinson Glass Co., Zanesville, Ohio, 1893. Joined National Glass in 1899; burned in 1906.

Rochester Tumbler Co., Rochester, Pennsylvania, 1872. Joined National Glass in 1899.

Royal Glass Co., Marietta, Ohio. Joined National Glass in 1899.

Specialty Glass Co., East Liverpool, Ohio, 1889 - c. 1898.

Steiner Glass Co., Buckhannon, West Virginia, 1870s.

Tarentum Glass Co., Tarentum, Pennsylvania, was operating in 1894; still operating in 1915.

Thompson Glass Co., Uniontown, Pennsylvania, 1889 to 1898.

Union Flint Glass Works, Pittsburgh, Pennsylvania, 1854. Moved to Bellaire, Ohio, in 1880; Martins Ferry, Ohio, in 1880; sold to Dithridge Flint Glass Works in 1882. New plant at Martins Ferry; to Ellwood, Pennsylvania, in 1895. Became Northwood Co. in 1896.

Westmoreland Glass Co. (Westmoreland Specialty Co.), Grapeville, Pennsylvania, 1889.

West Virginia Glass Co., Martins Ferry, Ohio, 1861. Joined National Glass in 1899.

Windsor Glass Co., Pittsburgh, Pennsylvania, 1887.

Decoration Definitions

Enameling: A hand-painted design used to add emphasis to the pattern of the glass.

Engraving: Glass design is cut into the piece by a copper wheel and differs from etching (frosting) which is done using a pattern sheet and either acid or sand.

Flashing: Often confused with staining, flashing is actually a thin layer of glass applied to the original glass, often altering the color.

Frosted: A clouding of the glass by treating it to an acid etching or by abrasion from a rough agent such as sand.

Gilding: A light application of gold decoration, often seen on edges, as a banding, or decorating the design of a glass item.

Goofus: A special treatment that combines gilding and enameling to cover the entire pattern. Added to the backs of bowls or plates and to the underside of lamp bases, it was sealed but can be removed by wear or scraping.

Staining: A thin coat of paint that is applied to glass, usually in a heat-application treatment. Colors are primarily ruby, lemon, amber, or pink (this color is also called Maiden's Blush or cranberry).

American Table Glass Factories

I am including this list of table glass factories that was composed in 1985 by the late William Heacock and he states: "These are factory listings, not company listings. Frequently a single factory would go through a number of different owners or reorganizations."

I hope the information will be helpful in some way to collectors of glass and will add to all the information about pressed glass factories in this country. I am happy to share Mr. Heacock's efforts with readers. My former co-author Bill Edwards helped Mr. Heacock assemble portions of this listing, and I thank him for allowing me to carry it forward into this edition.

Mike Carwile

A

Adams and Company, Pittsburgh, Pennsylvania (1851 – 1935) (originally known as Adams, Macklin & Co.). Joined USG in 1891. Making percolator tops in 1935. Patterns: Liberty Bell (1876), King's Crown (1890), Moon & Star (Palace), possibly Horseshoe (Good Luck).

Aetna Glass and Manufacturing Co., Bellaire, Ohio (1880 – 1889). Patterns: Adonis Swirl (formerly Gonterman Swirl), Hobnail-In-Square, Jumbo covered figural fruit bowl, possibly Butterfly Handles (journal quote), Goddess of Liberty epergne, Aetna's No. 300.

American Glass Company, Anderson, Indiana (1889 – 1890). Started by former Buckeye manager John F. Miller, this new factory was a manufacturer of opalescent, decorated, cut, and engraved tableware, lamps, etc. in the style of Buckeye, Northwood, etc. The factory was closed about a year after it began operations in mid-1889. It then became the Hoosier Glass Co., a manufacturer of prescription ware.

Atterbury and Company, Pittsburgh, Pennsylvania (1858 – 1902?). Patterns: Basket Weave (pitcher has snake handle), Ceres (Medallion), Atterbury Lily, many milk glass covered animal dishes, possibly Raindrop, Atterbury Waffle.

B

Bakewell, Pears and Co., Pittsburgh, Pennsylvania (1807 – 1880?) (had four different names) 1880 last patent. Patterns: Argus (Thumbprint), Bakewell Cherry, Arabesque, Icicle, Ashburton, Bakewell Victoria.

A.J. Beatty & Sons, Steubenville, Ohio (1845 – 1890); Tiffin, Ohio (1890 – 1891), joined USG. The Steubenville factory was also absorbed by U.S. Glass but never operated. Mr. A.J. Beatty also involved in Brilliant and Federal Glass factories, among others. Patterns: Beatty Rib, D&B with V-Ornament, Beatty Waffle, Over-all Hobnail, Orinoco. A July 1888 journal lists their No. 87 new opalescent line, as well as No. 79 crystal set, plain or engraved.

Beatty-Brady Glass Co., Dunkirk, Indiana (1898 – 1907); Indiana Glass Co. (1907 – present). Patterns: Loop and Jewel, Shrine, Late Butterfly, Flower Medallion, Narcissus Spray, Rocket, Rayed Flower, Bethlehem Star, Star Band, Whirled Sunburst in Circle, Double Pinwheel, Nogi, Togo, Gibson Girl.

Beaumont Glass Co., Martins Ferry, Ohio (1898 - 1902); Grafton, West Virginia (1903 - 1906); Morgantown, West Virginia (1913 - recent). Grafton factory became Tygart Valley Glass Co. Percy Beaumont went to Union Stopper Co., Morgantown, West Virginia, in 1906, and then opened his own lamp shade factory in that town about 1913. Patterns: Decorated only until 1899 (X-Ray, Esther); Flora, Beaumont's Columbia, Widmer, Acorn salt & pepper, Seaweed cruet, Inside Ribbing.

Bellaire Goblet Co., Bellaire, Ohio (1876 - 1888); Findlay, Ohio (1888 - 1891), joined USG-M. Factory manager, John Robinson, opened Robinson Glass Co. at Zanesville, Ohio. Patterns: Queen's Necklace, Gargoyle goblet, Bellaire, Daisy & Cube, Log and Star, Pig & Boxcar match holder, Bellaire Basketweave, Corset toothpick, Turtle salt, and many other novelty design goblets.

Belmont Glass Company, Bellaire, Ohio (1866 - 1890); Belmont Glass Works (listed under this name in 1888). The firm reportedly chipped molds for Crystal, Gillinder, and Fostoria. Patterns: Dewberry (early), Royal (figured woman's head), Belmont #100 (Daisy & Button on pedestal stem), No. 444 line released July 1888, described as a full line in both plain and engraved.

Boston and Sandwich Glass Co., Sandwich, Massachusetts (1825 - 1888). Patterns: A variety of lacy glass in early years, much opal ware and art ware in later years.

Brilliant Glass Works, Brilliant, Ohio (1880 - 1882). Factory burned in 1882, rebuilt and leased to Dalzell Bros. & Gilmore (1883 - 1884). Purchased by Central in 1884, operated by them as second factory until late 1886. Sold again in 1888 by new firm which moved equipment and molds to Greensburg, Pennsylvania, in 1889. Reopened as prescription ware factory in 1894, burned down in 1895. Patterns: see Greensburg Glass Co. A July 1888 journal states Brilliant was offering Winona and Melrose, and a new line Aurora. Some of these molds were also used later at Huntington, also possibly at Royal Glass Co., Marietta, Ohio.

Bryce Brothers, Pittsburgh, Pennsylvania (1850 - 1835). Had three other names, joined USG in 1891 as Factory B, closed during Depression. Patterns: Harp, Diamond Point, Tulip with Sawtooth, Strawberry, Thistle, Jacob's Ladder, Atlas, Panelled Daisy, Ribbon Candy, Wooden Pail, Roman Rosette, Pleating, Diamond Quilted (No. 1108), Argent, Derby, Pittsburgh, Wheat & Barley, Rose in Snow. Bryce Bros., Mt. Pleasant, Pennsylvania (1896 - present), became part of Lenox Corp. in 1965. Patterns: specialized in production of stemware.

Buckeye Glass Company, Martins Ferry, Ohio (1879 - 1896). Harry Northwood worked there in 1887. Factory burned down in February 1896. Patterns: Acorn, Reverse Swirl (Opalescent, Speckled). Trade journal of 6/28/88 reports the firm released seven new lines in "common crystal" and "opalescent, with glass feet." The latter could be the controversial Northwood Hobnail, which was listed by BB in 1890.

C

Cambridge Glass Co., The, Cambridge, Ohio (1901 - 1958). Originally built by newly formed National Glass Company but opened as an independent concern. Purchased by A.J. Bennett in 1910. Patterns: Star-of-Bethlehem, Cambridge Ribbon, Marjorie, Chelsea, Bordered Ellipse, Alexis, Big X pitcher, Stratford, and many others.

Campbell, Jones & Co., Pittsburgh, Pennsylvania (1863 - 1886); Jones, Cavitt & Co., Ltd. (1886 - 1891). Factory burned down in January 1891. Revi incorrectly indicates factory closed in 1895. Some molds acquired by U.S. Glass. Patterns: Currant, Rose Sprig, Panelled Dewdrop, Dewdrop with Star, Argyle, Button and Oval Medallion (Russian), Barley.

Canton Glass Co., Canton, Ohio (1883 - 1903?), joined National Canton Glass Co., Marion, Indiana (1898 - recent), branch plant which also joined National, listed in 1899 ads. Patterns: Jumbo, Hercules figural stem lamp, Kingfisher toothpick, acquired Paden City molds in the 1950s, some National molds during takeover (re-organized in 1904 in Marion as an independent). Later patterns include many from National: Kingfisher toothpick, Domino shakers, Eagle & Leaf vase.

Central Glass Co., Wheeling, West Virginia (1863 - 1939), joined USG-O Central Glass Co., Summitville, Indiana (1898 - 1900), joined National in 1899. The West Virginia firm began as Osterling & Henderson Co. and was closed down by USG in 1893, reopened as an independent in 1896. Moved to Indiana in 1898 to be closed after National merger. West Virginia factory opened again as a new company sometime after 1900, carrying same old name. Patterns: U.S. Coin, Log Cabin, Open Plaid, Cabbage Rose, Leaflets (with reclining cat finial), Wheat in Shield, Picture Window. Patterns from Indiana unknown. Main design from last Wheeling firm was their Krys-Tol line of Chippendale pattern, many etched stem lines.

Challinor, Taylor & Co., Tarentum, Pennsylvania (1866 - 1893). Earlier known as Challinor, Hogan Glass Co., at Pittsburgh. Joined USG as Factory C, burned down in 1893. Patterns: Oval Panel, Flower & Panel, Blockade, Hobnail with Bars, Double Fan, Opaque Scroll, Sanborn, Majestic Crown, Scroll with Star, Flying Swan.

Columbia Glass Company, Findlay, Ohio (1886 - 1892), joined USG in 1891. Patterns: Heavy Gothic, Broken Column, Henrietta, Radiant, Puss in Slipper, Dog Vase, Double Eye Hobnail, Bamboo Beauty, Shell on Ribs, Old Columbia, Banquet, Pointed Jewel, Climax.

Co-Operative Flint Glass Co., Ltd., Beaver Falls, Pennsylvania (1879 - 1937), earlier called Beaver Falls Co-Operative Glass Co. Patterns: Co-Op's Columbia, Eulalia (Currier & Ives), Madoline, Jeweled Moon and Star, Co-Op's Rex (Fancy Cut toy set), Sunk Daisy, Ivy-in-Snow, Sheaf and Block, Art Navo, Famous, Magna, Dewberry.

Crystal Glass Co., Pittsburgh, Pennsylvania (1868 - 1890). Other companies used this name or similar names, including the rebuilt La Belle Glass Works in 1888. Patterns: Frosted Eagle, Polar Bear, Pinafore (Actress?), a swan pattern of unknown description.

Crystal Glass Co., Bridgeport, Ohio (1888 - 1908). A reopened La Belle Glass Works, operated by Ed Muhlemann (later of Imperial Glass Co.), joined National in 1900, closed in 1908, probably never reopened. Patterns: Beaded Swirl and Lens, Big Button, Clematis (Flower and Pleat), Block and Lattice, Bullseye & Arrowhead.

D

Dalzell Brothers & Gilmore (1884 - 1888), Wellsburgh, West Virginia; Dalzell, Gilmore & Leighton Co. (1888 - 1902), Findlay, Ohio, joined National in 1900, closed in 1902. Patterns: Onyx ware, Klondike pattern, Dalzell's Columbia, Bringing Home the Cows, Bicycle Girl, Retort, Deer and Oak Tree, Eye Winker, Paragon, Double Fan, Wellsburg, Magnolia, Racing Deer pitcher, Serrated Teardrop, Plume and Fan, Bulging Bars wine, Three Birds pitcher, Quaker Lady, Teardrop & Cracked Ice, Ivanhoe.

Dithridge and Co., Pittsburgh, Pennsylvania (circa 1850 - 1903), started as R.B. Curling Co., ended as part of Pittsburgh Lamp, Brass and Glass Co. Patterns: Versaille, Astoria, Roses & Ruffles, mostly opal table and novelty lines, lamps, syrups, shakers, etc.

Doyle and Co., Pittsburgh, Pennsylvania (circa 1866 - 1891), USG-P Atterbury designed for them in 1870. Patterns: Red Block, Picket Band, Stippled Grape & Festoon, Grape & Festoon with Shield, Panelled Forget-Me-Not, Hobnail with Thumbprint Base, Doyle's Shell.

Dugan Glass Co., The, Indiana, Pennsylvania (1904 - 1913); Diamond Glass-Ware Company (1913 - 1931). Formerly The Northwood Co., which merged into National (1890 - 1904). Patterns: Many carried over from former owners; Maple Leaf, Inverted Fan & Feather, Shell, Beaded Ovals in Sand, Argonaut Shell, Circled Scroll, Quilted Phlox.

Dugan Glass Company, Lonaconing, Maryland (1914 - 1915); Lonaconing Glass Company, Lonaconing, Maryland (1915 - 1916?). Started by Thomas Dugan after he left Indiana, Pennsylvania, in Nov. 1914, leaving five months later due to friction. The name was then changed to Lonaconing Glass Co. Patterns: Reissued old molds from some National factories, including Melrose (Brilliant/Greensburg), Circular Saw (Riverside), Cadmus (Beaumont), and National Prism (a pattern advertised by National in 1903).

George Duncan & Sons, Pittsburgh, Pennsylvania (1874 - 1892), USG-D Factory began as Ripley & Co. in 1866 but name changed in 1874 when Mr. Ripley established new firm by this name elsewhere in Pittsburgh. Factory burned in 1892. Patterns: Many also by USG, molds may have been relocated to other factories after factory burned down: Swirled Column, Three Face, Squared Shell and Tassel, Berkeley, Swag Block, Snail, Double Snail, Zippered Block, Maltese Cross, Late Block, Gonterman.

George Duncan's Sons & Co., Washington, Pennsylvania (1894 - 1900); Duncan & Miller Glass Co. (1900 - 1955). Patterns: Flowered Scroll, Grated Diamond & Sunburst, Starred Loop, Teepee, Quartered Block, Quartered Diamonds, Button Arches, King Arthur, Sunflower Patch, many others.

E

Eagle Glass & Mfg. Co., The, Wellsburg, West Virginia (1890s - still in business in 1913). Patterns: Maker of mostly novelties, lamps, vanity items, salt shakers, toothpicks, etc., mostly in milk glass (decorated).

East Liverpool Glass Co., East Liverpool, Ohio (1882 - 1883), burned after opening, patterns preserved by local library. Patterns: East Liverpool (K4, 69), reportedly Beaded Swirl & Disc (Pet Sal), probably based on this same library (however the latter is proven U.S. Glass).

Elson Glass Co., The, Martins Ferry, Ohio (1882 - 1894); West Virginia Glass Mfg. Co. (1894 - 1900), joined National. Patterns: Elson Block IOU, a variant of Daisy & Button, West Virginia Optic, "Pandora" (trade journal listing), Scroll with Cane Band, Gem, Opalescent Fern, Polka Dot.

Evansville Glass Co., Evansville, Indiana (1903 - 1908?). Trade journals of 1904 indicate six new lines of tableware were displayed. Only Fernette pattern attributed to date. Firm also operated a separate bottle factory. Last trade notice found is from early 1907. Molds probably sold to other firms.

F

Federal Glass Co., Columbus, Ohio (1901 - 1978). Patterns: Got molds from National, USG, Co-Op, McKee, etc. Beaded Triangle pitcher, D & B with V-ornament pitcher, Stars & Stripes (Jenkins), Kansas (USG), Boxed Star (Jenkins), Peacock Feather (USG).

Fenton Art Glass Co., The, Williamstown, West Virginia (1907 - present). Patterns: Butterfly and Berry, Honeycomb with Clover, Waterlily with Cattails, Orange Tree.

Findlay Flint Glass Co., The, Findlay, Ohio (1888 - 1891). Patterns: Findlay #19, Pillar, Findlay's Dot, Spur Hobnail, Drawers toothpick holder, Elephant Head mustard with lid, Squash castor set, Pichereau ink well, Butterfly toothpick.

Fostoria Glass Company, Fostoria, Ohio (1887 - 1891); Moundsville, West Virginia (1891 - 1986). Diverse manufacturer of pressed and blown glass tableware, lamps, decorated opal specialties, blown stemware, cut glass, etched and engraved ware, and much, much more. Acquired by Lancaster-Colony. Factory closed in 1986. Some molds moved to Indiana Glass Co. Patterns: Cameo (Apple and Grape in Scroll), Diamond Window, Captain Kidd (Red Block copy), Brazilian, Fostoria's Atlanta, Lorraine, Victoria, Hartford, Alexis (these five names used by other firms); and many others.

G

Gillinder & Sons (1861 - 1891). Philadelphia and Greensburg, Pennsylvania, factories originally called Franklin Flint Glass Co., Philadelphia, Pennsylvania (second factory at Greensburg, Pennsylvania, joined in 1891, as factory G). Patterns: Classic, Westward Ho, Ruffles, Barred Star, Daisy & Button with Thin Bars.

Greensburg Glass Co., Greensburg, Pennsylvania (1889 - 1892); Greensburg Glass Co., Ltd. (1893 - 1898); Greensburg Glass Co. (1901 - 1937), sold to L.E. Smith, started by Brilliant Glass Co., re-organized with new management and new patterns in 1893. Closed in late 1898, joined National Glass in 1900, factory sold in 1901. Operated until L.E. Smith Glass Co. took over and operated as a second factory location. Patterns: Aurora, Florida (Sunken Primrose), Melrose, Murano, Tacoma, Corona (molds on last two moved to McKee in 1902).

H

A.H. Heisey Glass Co., Newark, Ohio (1895 - 1957). Patterns: Ring Band, Winged Scroll, Locket on Chain, Greek Key, Punty Band, Plain Band, Fandango, Fancy Loop, Pineapple with Fan, Continental, Kalonyal, Touraine.

Bryce, Higbee & Co., Homestead, Pennsylvania (1879 - 1906); J.B. Higbee & Co., Bridgeville, Pennsylvania (1907 - 1916). Patterns: Cut Log (Ethol), New Era, Flora, Sheraton, Sprig, Grand, Homestead, Drum toy set, Panelled Thistle, Hawaiian Lei, Style, Perkins, Alfa.

Hobbs, Brockunier & Co., Wheeling, West Virginia (1845 - 1891), joined USG. Hobbs Glass Co. (reorganized under John Hobbs in August 1888), started as Barnes, Hobbs & Co., a "partnership limit on the old firm" expired on 12/31/1887. Patterns: Leaf & Flower, Viking, Goat's Head, Blackberry, Hobnail, Mario, Hobb's Block, Hexagon Block, Wheeling Peachblow (Coral), Daisy & Button.

Huntington Glass Company, The, Huntington, West Virginia (1891 - 1897). Started up by old New Brighton stockholders, bought molds from Greensburg Glass Co. in 1894. President Addison Thompson moved to new factory at Marietta, Ohio (see Royal Glass Co.). Patterns: Pearl, Huntington, others from Greensburg molds (Aurora, Winona, Brilliant).

I

Imperial Glass Company, The, Bellaire, Ohio (1902 - 1984). Listed in October 1902 trade journals as independent with 56 pots, 16 more than Fostoria Glass. Patterns: Octagon, File, Nu-Cut pressed ware, carnival glass tableware.

Indiana Glass Co. (see Beatty-Brady Glass Co.)

Indiana Tumbler & Goblet Co., Greentown, Indiana (1894 - 1903). Joined National in 1901, burned down in 1903. Patterns: Austrian, Holly Amber, Dewey, Teardrop & Tassle, Herringbone Buttress, Cactus, Cord Drapery, Leaf Bracket, Pleat Band (all known as Greentown glass).

J

Jefferson Glass Company, Steubenville, Ohio (1901 - 1907); Follansbee, West Virginia (1907 - 1933). Several owners and reorganizations. Ads for firm still appeared as late as 1936, possibly selling remaining stock of bankrupt firm. Patterns: Tokyo, Ribbed Thumbprint, Chippendale, Ribbed Drape, Jefferson Optic, Follansbee, Jefferson Colonial, Diamond with Peg, some Button Arches, Dolly Madison, Swag with Brackets, concentrated on lighting ware after 1910.

K

King, Son & Co., Pittsburgh, Pennsylvania (1864 - 1880); King Glass Company, The (1880 - 1935), joined USG-K, joined U.S. Glass in 1891. Closed during the Depression after Pittsburgh flood. Patterns: Panelled Grape Band, Bleeding Heart, Frosted Ribbon, King's No. 500, Double Arch King's Centennial Thumbprint, Picket, Jumbo wall match holder.

Kokomo Glass Co., The, Kokomo, Indiana (1901 - 1905); D.C. Jenkins Glass Co. (1906 - 1932). Patterns: Panelled Grape, Sunburst, Grape Jug, Cherry with Thumbprint, Thistleblow.

L

La Belle Glass Co., Bridgeport, Ohio (1872 - 1888), Harry Northwood here from 1884 to 1888. Factory closed April 1888 due to exaggerated reconstruction costs of burned and rebuilt factory. Sold in September 1888 to Capt. Ed Muhleman, becoming Crystal Glass Works. Patterns: Queen Anne, Actress, Bamboo, a copy of Hobbs Hobnail, opalescent sets.

Lancaster Glass Co., The, Lancaster, Ohio (1908 - 1937). A new firm established by Lucien Martin (formerly at Hobbs, Fostoria, National, and Hocking Glass Co.) at the closed Ohio Flint Glass Co. plant. Factory absorbed by Hocking Glass Corp. in 1937. Patterns: Rustic Rose, Stippled Fans, Pogo Stick, Panelled Oak, Carnation, reissued McKee's Kansas and Beaded Triangle, also made many unnamed patterns (FGM catalog).

Lonaconing Glass Co., Lonaconing, Maryland (1915 - 1919?), see Dugan Glass Co., Lonaconing, Maryland.

M

McKee & Bros., Pittsburgh, Pennsylvania (1864 - 1888); McKee & Bros., Jeannette, Pennsylvania (1888 - 1900); National Glass Company, McKee & Bros., Jeannette, Pennsylvania (1900 - 1904); McKee-Jeannette Glass Co., Jeannette, Pennsylvania (1904 - 1910); McKee Glass Company, Jeannette, Pennsylvania (March 1910 - 1952). Patterns: Belleflower, Excelsior, Eugenie, Barberry, Panelled Hexagons, Comet, Yale, Dragon, Germanic, Champion, Carltec, Britannic, Heart Band, Lenox, Lone Star, Sunbeam, Majestic, Tappan toy set, Sultan toy set, Wild Rose with Bowknot, Geneva, imitation cut "tec" patterns, Prescut lines.

Millersburg Glass Co., Millersburg, Ohio (1909 - 1912), became Radium Glass Co., then sold to Jefferson Glass Co. in 1913. Some molds sent to Jefferson's Canadian factory. Patterns: Ohio Star, Country Kitchen, Hobstar & Feather, Millersburg Flute, carnival glass novelties.

Model Flint Glass Co., Findlay, Ohio (1888 - 1894); Model Flint Glass Co., Albany, Indiana (1894 - 1900); National Glass Co., Model Flint Glass Works (1900 - 1902). Patterns: Bevelled Star, Heck, Wreath & Shell, Shepherd's Plaid, Model's Peerless, Midway, Twist toy set.

N

National Glass Company, The (1900 - 1904). Announced in fall 1899, nineteen factories joined. Some burned down, others were closed by National. In 1904 the merger accepted defeat and leased or sold the remaining factories, as well as the one built by them at Cambridge. In 1908 the parent company went into receivership.

Member factories:

1. **Beatty-Brady Glass Works,** Dunkirk, Indiana.
2. **Canton Glass Works,** Marion, Indiana.
3. Central Glass Works, Summitville, Indiana.
4. Crystal Glass Works, Bridgeport, Ohio.
5. **Cumberland Glass Works,** Cumberland, Maryland.
6. Dalzell, Gilmore & Leighton Works, Findlay, Ohio.
7. **Fairmount Glass Works,** Fairmount, West Virginia.
8. Greensburg Glass Works, Greensburg, Pennsylvania.
9. **Indiana Tumbler & Goblet Works,** Greentown, Indiana.
10. Keystone Glass Works, Rochester, Pennsylvania.
11. **Model Flint Glass Works,** Albany, Indiana.
12. **McKee & Bros. Glass Works,** Jeannette, Pennsylvania.
13. **The Northwood Glass Works,** Indiana, Pennsylvania.
14. **Ohio Flint Glass Works,** Lancaster, Ohio.
15. **Riverside Glass Works,** Wellsburg, West Virginia.
16. Robinson Glass Works, Zanesville, Ohio.
17. **Rochester Glass Works,** Rochester, Pennsylvania.
18. **Royal Glass Works,** Marietta, Ohio.
19. West Virginia Glass Works, Martins Ferry, Ohio.

All in boldface were still in operation in 1902. The numbers on each factory were used in a special advertisement coding for ordering patterns. The Greentown and Marietta factories burned shortly afterward. The Cambridge Factory was built the following year, but opened as an independent concern. Patterns and factory numbers: S-Repeat (13), The Prize (12), Reward (15), Delos (6), Vulcan (12), Cord Drapery (8), Hobble Skirt (15), and many others.

New Brighton Glass Company, New Brighton, Pennsylvania (1888 - 1891), went bankrupt in early 1891. Stockholders started up a new factory at Huntington Glass. Local New Brighton investors reopened abandoned factory as a maker of prescription ware, but factory failed soon after. Patterns: A Paradise pattern is mentioned in trade journals, also colored tableware (research pending).

New England Glass Co., East Cambridge, Massachusetts (1818 - 1888); W.L. Libbey & Son Co., Toledo, Ohio (1888 - present), now known as The Libbey Glass Co. Patterns: Maize, Washington Centennial, Huber, Mitre Diamond, Union, Vernon, Reeded, Philadelphia.

New Martinsville Glass Mfg. Co., New Martinsville, West Virginia (1900 – present), now called Viking Glass Co. Patterns: NM Carnation, Japanese Iris (Rebecca), NM Lorraine, Frontier, Florene, Leaf & Star, reissued many Higbee molds when Ira Clark came to NMG from Higbee.

Nickel Plate Glass Co., The, Fostoria, Ohio (1888 - 1891), USG-N, started up in June 1888. Patterns: Frosted Circle, Richmond, Akron Block, Fluted Ribbon, Fostoria pattern, N.P. Thumbprint.

Northwood Glass Works, The, Martins Ferry, Ohio (1888 - 1890); Northwood Glass Co., The, Elwood City, Pennsylvania (1890 - 1895); The Northwood Co., Indiana, Pennsylvania (1896 - 1904), joined National; H. Northwood & Co., Wheeling, West Virginia (October 1902 - 1924). Patterns: Royal Ivy, Royal Oak, Leaf Umbrella, Quilted Phlox, Louis XV, Alaska, Fluted Scrolls, Wild Bouquet, Maple Leaf, Inverted Fan & Feather, Peacock at the Fountain, Singing Birds, Argonaut Shell, S-Repeat, Crystal Queen. Many of these patterns were continued in production by National and Dugan/Diamond.

O

O'Hara Glass Co., Ltd., Pittsburgh, Pennsylvania (1848 - 1891). USG-L, originally called J.B. Lyons, joined U.S. Glass in 1891. Patterns: O'Hara Diamond (Sawtooth & Star), Cordova, Prism Column, Pennsylvania Hand, Daisy in Diamond.

Ohio Flint Glass Co., Dunkirk, Indiana (1893 - 1899); Lancaster, Ohio (1899 - 1908). Firm began in Bowling Green, Ohio, at a leased factory while new one built at Dunkirk. A fire destroyed factory in Indiana, so another new plant was built at Lancaster. The brand new factory was almost immediately absorbed by National Glass and was expanded. Managers operated independently after National became holding company in 1904. Closing in 1908, the factory reopened later that year as a new tableware firm, the Lancaster Glass Co. Then later absorbed by Hocking Glass Corp. in 1937 (see Lancaster Glass). Patterns: Belle, Ada, Chippendale (Jefferson and Central also made this), other Krys-Tol line patterns (Kenneth and Gloria).

P

Paden City Glass Mfg. Co., Paden City, West Virginia (1916 - 1951), started up with many Higbee molds. After closing, many molds went to Canton Glass, Marion, Indiana, and to Viking Glass Co., New Martinsville. Patterns: Tree, Higbee Pineapple (#206), Estelle (Higbee Colonial), Inna, Etta, Webb, later DG era patterns like Penny Line, Crow's Foot, Gadroon, Largo, etc.

Pittsburgh Lamp, Brass & Glass Co., Pittsburgh, Pennsylvania (12/1901 - 1926). Three manufacturers (Dithridge, Kopp Lamp & Glass, Pittsburgh Lamp & Brass) which made mostly lamps, but some tableware in opal and satin colors in early years. Became Kopp Glass Inc., with remaining factory in Swissvale by 1926. Patterns: continued lines of Dithridge and Kopp's famous ruby "red satin" (possibly Open-Heart Arches).

Portland Glass Co., The, Portland, Maine (1864 - 1874). Patterns: Tree of Life, Loop & Dart with Round Ornament. Has been unfortunately credited with many other lines which were made much later by other firms.

R

Richards & Hartley Glass Co., Tarentum, Pennsylvania (1866 - 1893?), became Factory E of U.S. Glass in 1891, factory sold to Tarentum Glass Co. in 1894. Patterns: Loop & Dart with Diamond Ornaments, Hanover, Thousand Eye, Hartley, Russian, Three Panel, D&B with Crossbars, Oval Loop, Oregon, Clover, Bar & Diamond.

Ripley & Co., Pittsburgh, Pennsylvania (1874 - after 1902), USG-F (see also George Duncan & Sons for earlier firm by this name). Joined USG in 1891, closing date uncertain. Patterns: Scalloped Swirl (York Herringbone), Mascotte, Nail, Roanoke, Teardrop & Thumbprint, Dakota.

Ripley & Co., Connellsville, Pennsylvania (1910 - 1918), office in Pittsburgh, Pennsylvania. Made tableware until about 1915, factory became Capstan Glass Co. in 1918 (jars and bottles). Patterns: Iverna and others.

Riverside Glass Co., Wellsburg, West Virginia (1879 - 1907), joined National but re-emerged as an independent. Closed in 1907, reopened later as Crescent Glass Co., a manufacturer of automobile lenses and blown tumblers. Patterns: Empress, Esther, Croesus, X-Ray, Victoria, America, Double Daisy (Riverside's Chrysanthemum?), Box-in-Box.

Robinson Glass Co., Zanesville, Ohio (1893 - 1900). Started by former Columbia manager, John Robinson. Joined National and immediately closed. Molds moved to Ohio Flint and later Cambridge factory. Patterns: Vera (Faggot), Monroe, Zanesville.

Royal Glass Company, Marietta, Ohio (1898 - 1903). Started up by Huntington Glass President Addison Thompson, joined National Glass in 1900. Factory reportedly burned down in 1903. Patterns: a No. 314 "figured" pattern is mentioned in trade journals for 1902, another "imitation cut" pattern in 1901. Probably continued production of some Brilliant/Greensburg/Huntington molds.

S

L.E. Smith Glass Co., Mt. Pleasant, Pennsylvania (1908 - present). Originally a gold and silver decorating company, started making glass by 1912. Mr. Smith severed his connection with firm in 1912, moving over to Westmoreland Specialty Co. Oddly, no factory name change ever occurred. By 1929, firm was operating Greensburg factory as a subsidiary. Mt. Pleasant factory still in operation today, a division of Libbey-Owens. Patterns: Decorated Rock Crystal and Chippendale with gold, early patterns unknown, much Depression tableware in color.

T

Tarentum Glass Company, Tarentum, Pennsylvania (1894 - 1918). A new concern reopening old Richards & Hartley factory with entirely new lines, burned in 1918. Patterns: Manhattan, Albany, Atlanta (Royal Crystal), Columbia (Heart with Thumbprint), Hartford, Peerless (Frost Crystal), Virginia, Victoria, Portland, Georgia, many of these with names used by other factories.

Thompson Glass Co., Ltd., Uniontown, Pennsylvania (1889 - 1895). Acquired by National in 1901, reopened briefly by George Fry, brother of H.C. Fry, of Patterson-Fry Specialty Co., a glass decorating firm. Patterns: The Summit, Tile, Truncated Cube, Bow Tie.

Tygart Valley Glass Co., Grafton, West Virginia (1906 - 1926). A reorganized Beaumont Glass Co., originally continued production of tableware, stationers' goods. By 1918 made bottles, jars, and tumblers. Factory burned in 1926 and company moved to Washington, Pennsylvania.

United States Glass Co., Pittsburgh, Pennsylvania (1891 - 1963). A consolidation of factories. Most were closed by the time the Great Depression ended, with only the Glassport and Tiffin factories remaining in operation until 1963. The Glassport factory was destroyed by a tornado and the Tiffin factory became Tiffin Art Glass Co. (dismantled in 1985).

Member factories:

A. **Adams & Co.,** Pittsburgh, Pennsylvania.
B. **Bryce Bros.,** Pittsburgh, Pennsylvania.
C. **Challinor, Taylor & Co.,** Ltd., Tarentum, Pennsylvania.
D. **George Duncan & Sons**, Pittsburgh, Pennsylvania.
E. **Richards & Hartley**, Tarentum, Pennsylvania.
F. **Ripley & Co.,** Pittsburgh, Pennsylvania.
G. **Gillinder & Sons,** Greensburgh, Pennsylvania.
H. **Hobbs Glass Co.,** Wheeling, West Virginia.
J. **Columbia Glass Co.**, Findlay, Ohio.
K. **King Glass Co.,** Pittsburgh, Pennsylvania.
L. **O'Hara Glass Co.,** Pittsburgh, Pennsylvania.
M. **Bellaire Goblet Co.,** Findlay, Ohio.
N. **Nickel Plate Glass Co.,** Fostoria, Ohio.
O. **Central Glass Co.,** Wheeling, West Virginia.
P. **Doyle & Co.,** Pittsburgh, Pennsylvania.
R. **A.J. Beatty & Sons,** Tiffin, Ohio.
S. **A.J. Beatty & Sons,** Steubenville, Ohio (non-operating).
T. **Novelty Glass Co.**, Fostoria, Ohio.

New factories built: Glassport, Pennsylvania, and Gas City, Indiana.

V

Valley Glass Co., Beaver Falls, Pennsylvania (1889 only), formerly Whitla Glass Co. Patterns: Probably Monkey, opal glass novelties, and condiments.

W

Westmoreland Specialty Co. (1892 - 1923); Westmoreland Glass Co., Grapeville, Pennsylvania (1923 - 1985). Began in 1889 to 1892 as The Specialty Glass Co., East Liverpool, Ohio. Grapeville factory closed in 1985. Patterns: Pillow & Sunburst, Late Swan, Westmoreland's No. 15 (Cut Log copy), Shell & Jewel, Late Westmoreland, High Hob, Flute & Crown, English Hobnail, Cane Medallion, Indian Sunset, Wellington, Flickering Flame.

West Virginia Glass Co., The (see Elson Glass Company).

Whitla Glass Company, Beaver Falls, Pennsylvania (1887 - 1890). Closed January 1890 by bankruptcy, became Valley Glass Company. Patterns: Started by John Whitla who also started New Brighton Glass Co.

Patterns

Acorn

Dated about 1870, shapes include a pitcher, goblet, table set, celery vase, egg cup, covered compote, and an open compote. Some researchers credit Boston and Sandwich Glass for this pattern. The goblet was reproduced.

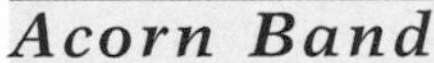

Acorn Band

There are some variations in this pattern made by the Portland Glass Company. A similar design accredited to Boston and Sandwich Glass is called Panelled Acorn Band. Shapes include a table set, celery vase, egg cup, compotes, flat or footed sauces, goblet, wine, water pitcher, covered compote, covered bowls, open bowl, and stemmed dessert.

Actress

This collection of similar designs is attributed to Adams & Company and known as Pinafore, Theatrical, or Goddess of Liberty as well as Jenny Lind or Annie. Shapes include many sizes of bowls, a table set, cake stand, candlesticks, celery vase, cheese dish, covered and open compotes, goblet, jam jar, pickle dish, water set, milk pitcher, platter, relishes, salt, and dresser tray. All subjects deal with the theater or actors. The lettered relish has been reproduced and is often seen with the late Imperial logo: "I" superimposed over a "G." Other shapes have been reproduced in various colors, including the shakers in blue, amber, and crystal.

Ada

Made by Cambridge Glass Company (#2577 pattern) and Ohio Flint Glass as their (#808 pattern), Ada dates to 1898 and was made in more than 100 shapes including a table set, water set, berry set, cruet, shakers, compotes, pickle dish, celery vase and dish, goblet, wine, and syrup. The design is well balanced and interesting.

Adam's Apollo Lamp

Made by Adams & Company of Pittsburgh, this lamp is part of a line called Apollo. Different base designs and colors, as well as different fonts came in several sizes from 8" to 13". The example shown is 11⅞" tall and has a leaf cutting on the font. Colors are blue, amber, canary, or crystal.

Adonis

Made by McKee & Brothers in 1897, Adonis is also known as Washboard or Pleat and Tuck. In addition to clear, examples in canary and blue glass are known. Shapes are berry sets (beaded rim), table sets, cake plate, cakc stand, celery vase, covered compotes, open jelly compote, plates in both 8" and 10" sizes, relish tray, shakers, and syrup.

African Shield

Made by the Sowerby Glass Company of England, this pattern is well known to carnival glass collectors. Its only shape seems to be the squat vase shape shown that is 2⅞" tall and has a top diameter of 3½". Originally a wire flower holder fit into the top ot the vase.

Alabama

From U.S. Glass in 1890 and the first of the States series, Alabama is also called Beaded Bulls-Eye and Drape by some collectors. It is found in clear, green, or ruby in table sets, tall celery vase, both covered and open compotes, covered honey dish (rare), nappy, water set, syrup, and three sizes of relish dishes.

Alaska (Northwood)

This well-known pattern was made in both crystal and opalescent glass, beginning in 1897 through 1912. It is found in berry sets, water sets, table sets, a rose bowl, a jewelry tray, as well as several novelty pieces. Besides the opalescent colors, clear or emerald green glass is known and pieces are often decorated with enamel flowers.

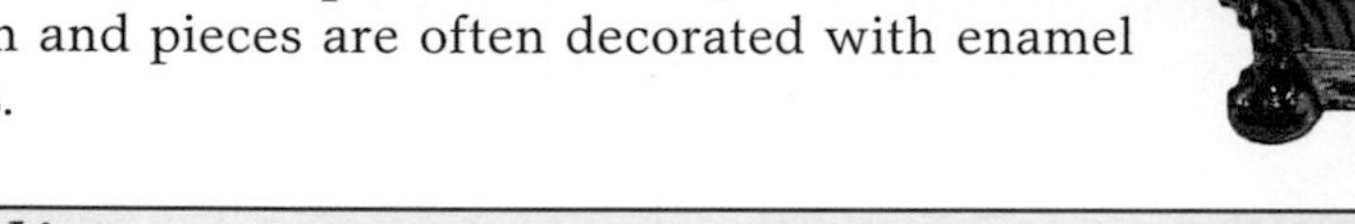

Aldine

This pattern is also known as Beaded Ellipse and is credited to McKee in 1900 (some references also credit it to Cambridge as its #2519 and to Imperial as its #261 in 1910). It is found in crystal with some rare items found in chocolate glass. Shapes include a table set, covered bowl, water set, wine, pickle dish, and a celery dish.

Alexis

This was first shown as Fostoria's #1630 Alexis pattern (1909 – 1925) and then in only the goblet shape from D.C. Jenkins as their #23 goblet. Shapes from Fostoria are many and include bowls, a table set, tall celery vase, celery tray, catsup bottle, champagne, claret, cocktail, cordial, ice bowl and plate, custard (two styles), decanter, egg cup, finger bowl, goblet, relish jar, ice tea set with plates, water set (three size pitchers), mayonnaise plate and bowl, syrup, nasturtium vase, nut bowl, olive tray, cruets (three sizes), pickle tray, tankard pitcher, salt shakers, sherbets (high or low), sugar sifter, sweet pea vase, toothpick holder, water bottle, wine, whiskey tumbler, and a wine tumbler. The toothpick holder was reproduced in 1980 for founders of the Fostoria Glass Society of America.

Alligator

This interesting 3" tall toothpick holder sits atop an alligator, although it has a bit of resemblance to a salamander as some think. Made in the late 1800s, it can be found in crystal, amber, blue, and milk glass (referred to as Opal to some collectors.)

All-Over Diamond

This U.S. Glass (Duncan's #356) pattern is also known as Diamond Splendor. It is found in an extended table service including egg cup and wines, in crystal or ruby stain.

Almond (U.S. Glass)

U.S. Glass Company's #5601 pattern is found in a wine decanter with matching tray and stemmed wines. It is shown in clear and was also available with gold trim and may have been made in emerald green glass. The design should not be confused with Diamond Thumbprint which is sometimes called simply Almond, which was made by Bryce, Bakewell, and also U.S. Glass in 1891. It is also known as Mirror and Fan.

Almond Thumbprint

This is attributed to Bryce, Bakewell (1865); Bakewell, Pears (1868); and then U.S. Glass in 1891. Shapes include a table set, champagne, celery vase, high or low covered compotes (5", 7", 10"), a cordial, cruet (two styles), decanter goblet, punch set, water set, salt dip (master or individual), covered sweetmeat, and a wine. It is found in crystal, milk glass, or blue.

Amaryllis (Northwood)

This was primarily a bowl pattern designed for a goofus treatment. Some pieces are plain crystal and show the design well. The example shown is an 8" bowl with scalloped edges. This is a Northwood pattern and some pieces are so marked. It is also known as Tiger Lily.

Amazon

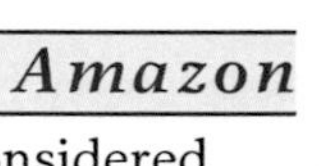

Amazon was made by U.S. Glass primarily in crystal (all colors are considered rare). This pattern is also called Sawtooth Band by some collectors. Shapes are many and include a banana stand, both oval and round covered bowls, table set, celery vase that may be flat or footed, child's toy table set, champagne, claret, goblet, wine, both open and covered compotes, water set, egg cup, syrup, vase, and master and individual salt dips. Covered bowls have "lion" handles and finials.

Amberette

This pattern was first made by George Duncan and Sons in 1885 and then by U.S. Glass in 1892. It is also known as Panelled Daisy and Button or Ellrose (without the amber stain). Shapes include covered or open bowls in two sizes with flat or collared bases, finger bowl, table set, butter pat, cake stand, celery tray or vase, cruet, gas shade, olive dish, pickle dish, milk pitcher, water set, bread or dinner plates, sauces, and salt shaker.

American Beauty

Mistakenly called a Northwood pattern, this is actually Cooperative Flint's La France, made in 1909; some collectors also call this pattern Rose and Sunbursts. Shapes include a table set, water set, berry set, and jelly compote (shown). The pattern is pictured in a 1909 Butler Brothers ad next to Northwood's Gold Rose pattern, which likely explains the mistaken identity in years past.

Angel's Crown

In the 1890s Dalzell, Gilmore & Leighton made a series of jelly tumblers and jars in Finlay, Ohio, and this jar is one of the designs attributed to them. It has a winged angel sitting on top of a crown with the usual interior paneling found on most of these pieces. The idea was to turn the jelly out into a saucer so that the interior design was moulded into the jelly mound. Many companies made similar wares.

Angelus

Apparently the moulds for the Huntington line from Huntington Glass Company (1892 – 1896) were retooled to form this Angelus line of glass (according to Heacock). Shapes include a table set, celery vase, pickle dish, waste bowl, water set, and a wine. Montgomery Ward advertised both lines from 1892 to 1896 with the Angelus examples not showing the diamond-point filling that the Huntington line had.

Angular

Made in the 1880s (McKee & Bros.), this rather plain design depends on the handles for its name. Shapes are a table set, water set, and covered compote. Surely some of the pieces in this design were etched but I haven't seen them. It is also known as Berlin.

Anthemion

Anthemion was from the Model Flint Glass Company in 1890. It is found in an extended table service that includes a berry set, table set, and water set.

Ape with Basket

Credited to the Tiffin Glass Company in 1886, this very rare toothpick holder, unlike all the Monkey pieces, is a true ape. The holder is a basketweave pattern and is held in place by the wire frame and wire bands.

Apple Tree

Apple Tree was made by the Fenton Art Glass Company in 1912 as its #1561 pattern and is found mostly in carnival glass in water sets. In other types of glass only the vase whimsey (sometimes with a straight top and sometimes like the spittoon top shown) is known. Colors for this vase shape are crystal, royal blue, moonstone (semi-opaque white), milk glass, ebony, and jade green opaque.

Appomattox

Found on many dressers in the early 1920s, these mirrors were made in a host of designs and materials. The example shows a back that imitates Jasperware while the handle is a fine, pressed glass wand that would please any lady.

Aquarium

Made by U.S. Glass after 1891 and possibly as late as 1909, this favorite of collectors is reported in the water pitcher shape only, in clear, amber, and emerald green. The pattern is very realistic with fine mould work and is well worth the search.

Aquarius Lamp

This fine lamp was likely made by Adams and Company, circa 1880s. It has been reported in six sizes in amber, blue, and the vaseline shown. Two sizes of footed finger lamps are also known. It is a nice addition to any collection.

Aquatic

This interesting ball footed pitcher with its shell like motif has not been attributed to a maker that I know of. I'm assuming that at least a matching tumbler was made but I have not seen one to date. It is found in crystal.

Arcadia Lace

This is Jenkins #202 pattern from 1927. Shapes include a table set, water set, berry set, vase, plates, and other shapes.

Arch and Forget-Me-Not Bands

Found only in clear glass, this familiar pattern dates to the 1880s but the maker seems to be unknown at this time. Shapes are a berry set, table set, and water set, as well as a covered jam jar.

Arched Fleur-de-Lis

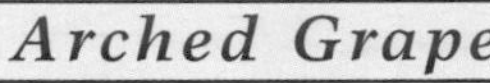

This is a Bryce, Higbee pattern found in crystal or ruby stained glass like the mug shown. Other shapes include a table set, water set, shakers, a vase, banana stand, cake stand, 7" bowl, jelly compote, handled olive dish, square plate, relish, sauce, toothpick holder, and a wine. Most often seen is the pedestal-based vase shape.

Arched Grape

This pattern is from Boston and Sandwich Glass (1870s) and is also attributed to Burlington Glass of Canada. Finials are clusters of grapes and leaves, and shapes include a table set, celery vase, champagne, covered compote, goblet, water set, wine, and flat and footed sauces.

Arched Ovals

This pattern was first made by Ripley, sometimes called Optic or Concaved Almond, and was made as U.S. Glass #15091 after 1891 to 1919. It is found in clear or ruby stain. Shapes include a berry set, table set, water set, cake stand, celery vase, goblet, mug, plate, open or covered compotes, relish, shakers, syrup, sauce, wine, and toothpick holder. Other treatments were gilded, rose flashed, or emerald green.

Argent

Argent, made by Bryce, then U.S. Glass, is also known as Clear Panels with Cord, or Rope Bands. Shapes include a water set, table set, compote, celery vase, cake stand, and a platter. Both the sugar and compote shapes can be found open or with lids.

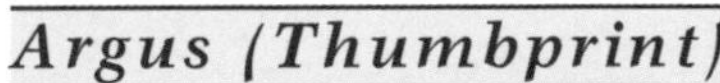

Argus (Thumbprint)

Argus was made by Bakewell, Pears and Company in 1870; by King, Son & Company in 1875; and McKee & Brothers in 1865. It is also known as Concave Ashburton and has been reproduced by Imperial Glass and Fostoria for the Henry Ford Museum (pieces are marked HFM). Shapes known are ale glass, beer glass, bitters bottle, bowls (open or covered), table set, celery vase, champagne, high or low covered compotes, open compote, cordial, decanter, egg cup, jelly glass, goblet, honey dish, oil lamp in two sizes, mug, paperweight, pickle jar, water set, punch set, salt dips, and wine.

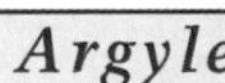

Argyle

Argyle is also known as Squared Daisy and Diamond and was made by Jones, Cavitt and Company in 1888. Shapes include a water set and goblets.

Army Hat

This novelty powder jar was made by Paden City Glass in the 1920s and is found mainly in crystal but other colors have been reported. It is 1" tall and measures 3½" across the top.

Arrowhead

Also called Anderson, this pattern's maker is unknown. Production was in the 1895 – 1905 era and both crystal and canary are known. Shapes include a table set, pickle dish, compote, celery dish, but certainly other shapes probably exist. The design is a good one.

Arrowhead-in-Oval

This pattern was made by Higbee in 1890 and is also known as Madora. Shapes include a plate, sherbet, handled basket, cake stand, celery, toy table set, punch set, water set, and berry set.

Art

Art, sometimes called Job's Tears or Teardrops and Diamond Block, was made by Adams & Company in the 1870s and then by U.S. Glass in the 1890s, in both clear and ruby stained. Shapes are a 10" fruit basket, berry set, table set, cake stand, covered and open compotes in several sizes, cracker jar, cruet, banana dish, goblet, mug, water set, relish, and wine. The compote was reproduced in milk glass by L. E. Smith.

Artichoke

This Fostoria pattern (#205) from 1891, is also known as Frosted Artichoke when it has the acid etched treatment. Shapes include 7" and 8" bowls, a rose bowl, covered compote, open compote, table set, cake stand, cruet, finger bowl, oil lamp, syrup, water set, shakers (rare), tankard pitcher, tray, and a vase. If you find a goblet, none of them are old. All goblets were reproduced by L. G. Wright.

Ashburton

This pattern was made by New England Glass in 1869; Bakewell, Pears in 1875; Bryce, Richards in 1854; and U.S. Glass after 1891. Shards are reported at Burlington in Canada also, and Boston & Sandwich is also reported to have made this pattern. Colors are primarily crystal, with amber, amethyst, aqua, canary, green, and milk glass all considered rare. Shapes are many and include an ale glass, bitters bottle (shown), carafe, bowl, table set, celery vase, champagne, claret, open compote, cordial, decanter, egg cup, goblet, lamp, mug, water set, sauce, wine. Many shapes have several variations and some pieces are engraved.

Ashman

There appears to be much confusion about this pattern, with some collectors calling it Cross Bar or Crossroads, but it isn't the same as either of these. Ashman is reported to be from Adams & Company in 1886. All pieces of Ashman are square in shape and are found in clear, amber, or blue. Shapes include a bread tray, bowl, table set, cake stand, open or covered compotes, goblet, water set, relish, water tray, wine, and pickle jar. It was reproduced in various shapes by Westmoreland.

Atlanta

This pattern was advertised as Westmoreland's #228 in 1908. It can be found in table sets, jelly compote, goblet, salt shakers, celery vase, berry set, syrup, wine, toothpick holder, and lamp shade (electric or gas sizes). The primary design seems to be the hobstar in an oval, bordered by a wreath of leaves. It was also made by Federal in 1914.

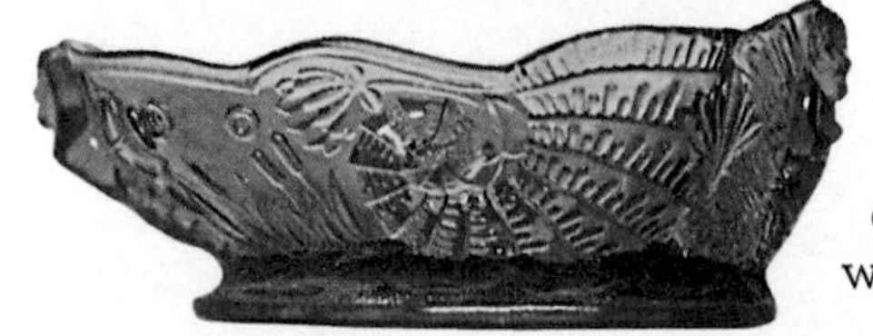

Atlantis

Shown is an interesting bowl shape, approximately 6" long and 2¾" wide. The coloring is a fine blue and the design is one of two Neptune-like figures at each end with a cornucopia and drifting seaweed on the sides. It can also be found in amber.

Atlas

This is not the same Atlas pattern as that from Bryce, and later U.S. Glass; it is attributed to Atterbury in the 1870s. It is a well-designed compote with a toga-draped figure holding up the bowl. The treatment is opal or milk glass opaque.

Atlas (Bryce)

Also known as Cannon Ball, Bullet, Knobby Bottom, or Orbed Feet, this pattern is attributed to Bryce Brothers (1889) and U.S. Glass (1891). It is found in crystal, etched crystal, or ruby stain. Shapes include covered and open bowls (5", 6", 7", 8"), finger bowl, table set, hotel table set, cake stand (8", 9", 10"), celery vase, covered or open compotes (5", 7", 8"), cordial, goblet, jam jar, mug, milk pitcher, water set, salt shakers (single, master), sauce (flat or footed), syrup, toothpick holder, water set, wine, and whiskey tumbler.

Atlas (Northwood)

This is one of the earlier Northwood patterns to carry the famous trademark N in a circle. This pattern is actually a bit scarce, but can be found in crystal, gilded crystal, or as the example shown, with a Maiden-Blush stain, in an extended table service and a water set.

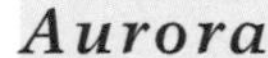

Aurora

Aurora was made by Brilliant Glass and then Greensburg Glass (1888) and is also called Diamond Horseshoe by some collectors. Shapes include a table set, cake stand, compotes, cordial, wine, salt shaker, pickle dish, and bread plate. The design is often difficult to distinguish from one shape to another.

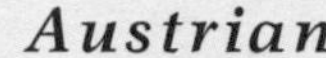

Austrian

This pattern, also called Finecut Medallion or Western, was first made at the Indiana Tumbler and Goblet Company (Greentown) and in 1897 at Indiana Glass in Dunkirk, Indiana, and Federal Glass in 1914. Austrian can be found in clear, amber, canary, occasionally green, and rarely in chocolate glass, Nile Green opaque, and cobalt blue. Shapes include a banana stand, berry set, table set, child's table set, child's mug, compotes, cordial, goblet, nappy, water set, punch set, shakers, wine, and both a rose bowl and vase in three sizes.

Azmoor

This was Ohio Flint Glass pattern #45, first advertised in 1904. The glass is fine and the design bold and impressive. Shapes are many and include a table set, punch set, 8½" oval relish, handled nappy, small deep bowl, cruet, tumbler, and a water pitcher. The design was pictured as shown here or with the center pinwheel pattern reversed.

Aztec

Aztec was part of McKee & Brothers' (1903 – 1927) "tec" grouping of patterns found in crystal or ruby stained glass. Shapes include a table set, berry set, celery bowl, pickle dish, water set, punch set, water bottle, cordial, goblet, claret, champagne glass, wine, and rose bowl. The punch set production was continued by McKee-Jeannette until 1950. The butter dish, creamer, punch bowl, punch cup, and toothpick holder were reproduced.

Aztec Sunburst

This pattern, also called Sunburst, was made by McKee in 1910 and can be found in bowls, a table set, celery vase, shakers, a quart pitcher, half gallon pitcher, 8" saucer, cracker bowl, rose bowl, compotes (7", 8", 9"), salver, handled nappy, pickle dish, celery tray, berry, creamer and open sugar, tall compote, vase, sweet pea vase, tall cake plate, and the tall footed rose bowl. This pattern has been reproduced in colors.

B

Baby Animals

This mug with a cat in a basket and a baby bear on a drum is found in two sizes (the large size has a flower in the base). It was more than likely made in the 1890s and the small size has been reproduced in colors by Mosser Glass and in carnival glass in 1977.

Baby Face

Baby Face was made by McKee and Brothers in 1880 (Geo. Duncan made a similar pattern called Three Face), and can be found in both clear and frosted glass. Shapes include a table set, celery dip bowl, celery vase, champagne, covered compote in four sizes, open compote in two sizes, cordial, goblet, water pitcher, and wine.

Baby Mine

From the Enterprise Manufacturing Co. in Akron, Ohio, this circa 1883 elephant novelty container is used as a toothpick holder and match safe, but may have actually been a mustard container when first produced. Colors are crystal and amber. This item has been reproduced in colors.

Bakewell Waffle

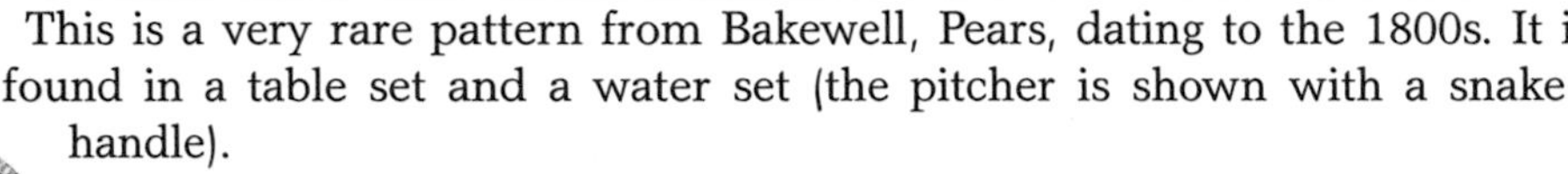

This is a very rare pattern from Bakewell, Pears, dating to the 1800s. It is found in a table set and a water set (the pitcher is shown with a snake handle).

Balky Mule

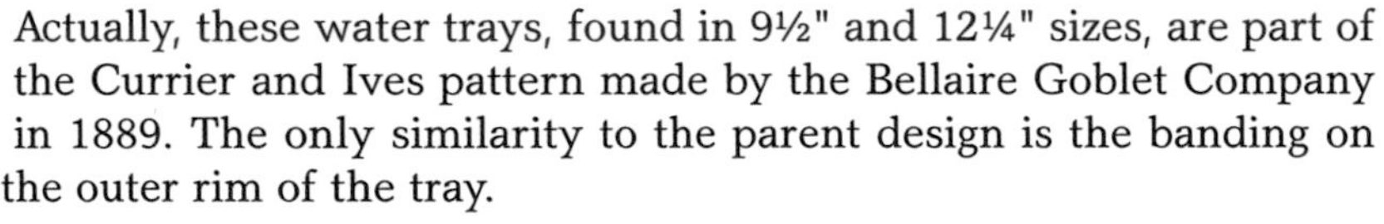

Actually, these water trays, found in 9½" and 12¼" sizes, are part of the Currier and Ives pattern made by the Bellaire Goblet Company in 1889. The only similarity to the parent design is the banding on the outer rim of the tray.

Ball and Bar

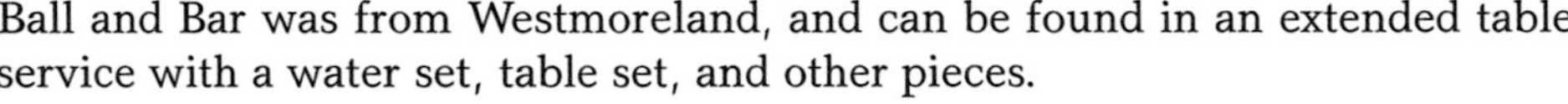

Ball and Bar was from Westmoreland, and can be found in an extended table service with a water set, table set, and other pieces.

Ball and Swirl

The mug shown was made by Beatty & Sons, as well as McKee Brothers (1894). Other shapes include a table set, shakers, a celery vase, 6" plate, cordial set, syrup, footed jelly, cake stand, and candlesticks. Colors are clear, ruby stain, opaque white, and marigold carnival glass.

Baltimore Pear

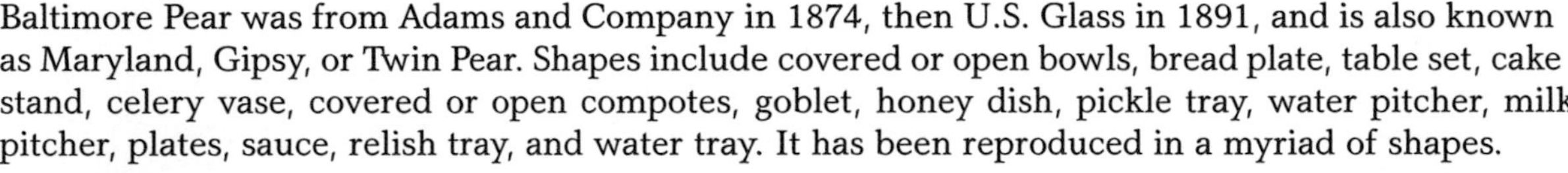

Baltimore Pear was from Adams and Company in 1874, then U.S. Glass in 1891, and is also known as Maryland, Gipsy, or Twin Pear. Shapes include covered or open bowls, bread plate, table set, cake stand, celery vase, covered or open compotes, goblet, honey dish, pickle tray, water pitcher, milk pitcher, plates, sauce, relish tray, and water tray. It has been reproduced in a myriad of shapes.

Bamboo Beauty

This seldom-seen U.S. Glass pattern from 1891 was made in a rare table set, berry set, and water set. Factory ads show the table set with two sizes of trays that do not match, so perhaps these weren't meant to be part of the pattern. Only clear pieces of Bamboo Beauty have been seen by me, and some appear to have once had gold trim at the top. This was originally from Columbia Glass Company as the #150 line.

Band and Diamond Swirl

This 6" vase shape was from U.S. Glass, made in 1898, and shown in one of its ads as part of a vase assortment. It was the company's #16048 pattern and can be found in clear, amber, or emerald green with gold trim.

Banded Base

Banded Base was first made by Beatty & Sons in 1886 as its #1215 tumbler pattern and then as U.S. Glass pattern #860 in 1891. While there may well be other shapes in this pattern, the catalog from U.S. Glass shows only the tumbler. The example shown has gilding on the banding.

Banded Buckle

Banded Buckle, first a product of the Sandwich Glass Company and later made by other factories after 1870, is known in flint and non-flint glass. Shapes are table sets, berry sets, egg cup, goblet, water set, footed salt dip, high and low open compotes, wine, and cordial. A similar pattern called Buckle without the banding is known.

Banded Diamond with Peg

This is a variant of the regular Diamond with Peg pattern, with an actual band circling the piece, which has been painted, not just a painted band in itself. It was made first by McKee Glass in 1894 and then by Jefferson Glass after 1900. In 1913 Jefferson began marking its items "Krys-tol." Shapes known are a table set, toothpick holder, berry set, and water set. Pieces can be found in both clear and ruby stained. The example shown is a tumbler.

Banded Finecut

The shapes in this pattern seem to be limited to the one-handled nappy (either round or hexagonal shape), 8" bowl, a goblet, and a wine. The example shown has a beautiful wheel-cut design in the base that adds greatly to the overall pattern.

Banded Fleur-De-Lis

Originally called Imperial's #5, this pattern is well known to carnival glass collectors by that name. It is shown in crystal in a 1909 Imperial catalog in a berry set (flat or footed), cake stand, jelly compote, egg cup, water set, milk pitcher, syrup, shakers, celery vase, table set, and the footed cake stand shown. Only a celery vase and bowls are reported in carnival glass.

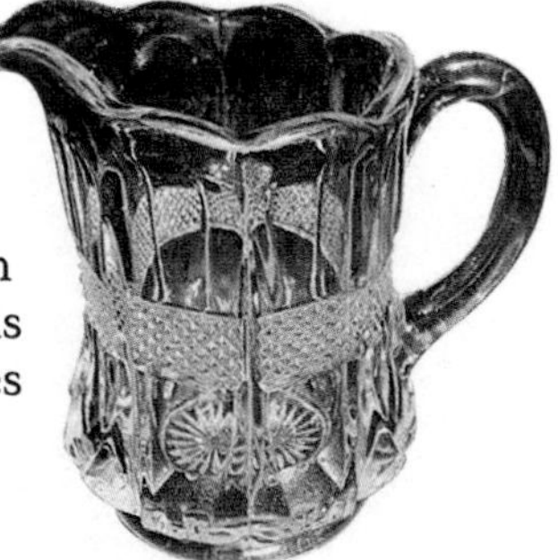

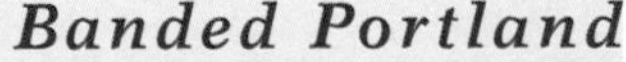

Banded Portland

Also known as Virginia or Portland with Diamond Point, this U.S. Glass pattern (15071) was a Gillinder as well as Richards and Hartley pattern. It is found in an extended table service and a wide variety of other shapes in crystal, green, or rose flashed or ruby stain.

Banded Raindrops

Found in crystal, amber, opalescent blue, and milk glass, this pattern is also called Candlewick; the maker is unknown. Shapes include a table set, water set, covered compote, cup and saucer, goblet, 7½" and 9" plates, square relish dish, shakers, sauce, and wine.

Banded Star

This pattern was made by King, Son & Company in 1880. Shapes include a table set, water set, celery vase, sauces, high or low covered compotes, individual creamer and sugar, and pickle dish. It is also known as Footed Lobe or #500.

Banner

This collectible butter dish was made by Bryce Brothers for the 1876 Centennial and later as a U.S. Glass novelty. (A rare flag shield bread tray with Miss Liberty's head was made in 1891 that is similar in design.) It is found in clear, blue, and amber.

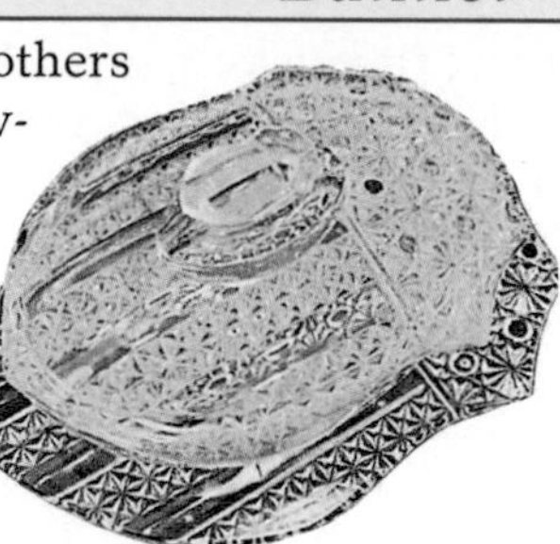

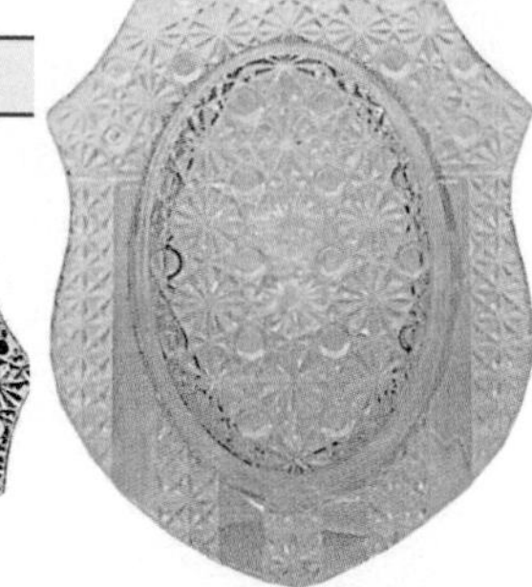

Bar and Block

Bar and Block is also known as Nickel Plate's Richmond or Akron Block and was reissued by U.S. Glass in 1891. There are many variations of this pattern, all listed under the same name(s). The pitcher shown is always called Bar and Block and other shapes include a table set, tumbler, celery vase, finger bowl, shakers, mustard jar with lid, and wine.

Bar and Diamond

This pattern, made by Richards and Hartley (U.S. Glass in 1891) and also known as Kokomo, Richards and Hartley Swirl, or Zippered Swirl, is found in both clear and ruby stained glass. Shapes include compotes, a sugar shaker, decanter, shakers in two styles, cruet, tray, toy table set, hand lamp, wine, celery vase, and a full table set. On some pieces the swirl is reversed.

Barberry

Barberry was reported to have been made by Boston and Sandwich Glass in the 1860s and then by McKee Glass in the 1880s. Shapes include a table set, wine, cordial, celery vase, cake plate, egg cup, goblet, footed sauce, syrup, sauce, covered bowls, covered compote, bowls (open), 6" plate, tumbler (footed), pitcher, and a cup plate.

Barley

This pattern's maker is unknown, but may be Campbell, Jones & Company of Pittsburgh in the late 1870s. It can be found in clear and rare colors that include amber. Shapes include round or oval bowls, a table set, cake stands, celery vase, covered or open compotes on high or low stands, cordial, vegetable dishes, honey dish, jam jar, pickle castor, pickle dish, water set, plates, platter, flat relish dish, relish wheelbarrow in two sizes, sauce, bread tray, and wine. It is also called Indian Tree or Sprig.

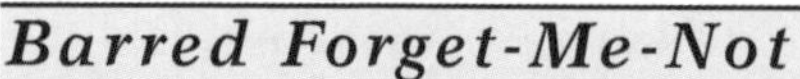

Barred Forget-Me-Not

This Canton Glass pattern in crystal, amber, blue, apple green, or canary dates to 1883. Shapes include a table set, water set, cordial, wine, goblet, pickle dish with square handles, bowls, and the two-handled plate shown.

Barrelled Thumbprint

The original name was Challinor's Thumbprint made by Challinor, Taylor, Ltd., of Tarentum, Pennsylvania, in 1882. Shapes reported are a table set, water set, berry set, celery vase, goblet, pickle dish, salt shakers, water bottle, wine, and nappy in 4", 4½", 6", and 8" sizes.

Barry Plate

Apparently this was made to honor the work of St. Bernard dogs in their Swiss rescue missions (the named dog, "Barry," saved 40 people before being killed himself). The plate has a frosted center and is 10" in diameter.

Basket Epergne

In the late 1800s affluent homes centered their dining room table with elaborate pieces like the one shown here, a tall standard with a shallow bowl on top and stems that held six small baskets. Handles and arms or stems are hand applied. The bowl usually held grapes or fruit while the baskets held mints or nuts.

Basketweave

Made around the mid-1880s, this pattern is found in crystal, amber, canary, apple green, blue, and some items in milk glass. Shapes include berry sets, waste and finger bowls, a table set, covered or opened compotes (both high and low), a cordial, egg cup (double or single), goblet, mug, milk pitcher, pickle dish, water set, cake plate, footed or flat salt dip, sauce, saucer, syrup, water tray, and a wine. Recent information given to me places this at Boston and Sandwich Glass Company.

Basketweave and Medallion Lamp

This well-designed, very attractive piece is found in two sizes, a hand lamp and the table lamp shown. It seems to have been made only in crystal and if readers have more information, I would like to hear from them.

Bassettown

This pattern, first made by Geo. Duncan and Sons in 1898 and also known as Duncan #40, is found in crystal or ruby-stained crystal. Shapes include a table set, water set, berry set, punch set, stemmed celery vase, pickle dish, celery dish, and possibly other shapes.

Beacon #410 Innovation

This pattern is from the McKee Glass Company in the mid-1920s and features the vase shown, two sizes of square vases, a sugar and creamer set, handled basket, fernery, oval orange bowl, fruit compote, 12" footed tray, several footed bowl shapes, and several flat novelty bowls. It was advertised in clear, jade, or opalescent glass, and I've heard of the handled basket in carnival glass.

Bead and Scroll

This well-known pattern from Riverside Glass is found in clear, blue, frosted, ruby stained, cobalt, emerald, and amber glass, many times with gold trim. Shapes are a water set, goblet, jelly compote, toothpick holder, table set, berry set, salt shakers, and a rare child's toy table set.

Bead Column

Some have ventured a guess that this is a D.C. Jenkins Glass Company pattern. I do know it was made in the 1905 – 1910 period and can be found in a table set as well as a water set. Albany is also a possible maker. Shown is a spooner.

Beaded Acorn Medallion

Beaded Acorn Medallion is also known as Beaded Acorn and was made in 1869 by the Boston Silver Glass Company (shards are also reported from the Boston & Sandwich site) as a companion pattern to the Beaded Grape Medallion pattern. It is found in only crystal; shapes include a fruit bowl, table set, champagne, covered compote (high or low), egg cup (shown), goblet, honey dish, lamp, pitcher, plate, oval relish dish, open salt, sauce, or a wine.

Beaded Arch Panels

This pattern, attributed to Burlington Glass Works of Canada in 1890, is also known as Archaic Gothic or simply Beaded Arch. Shapes are a table set, goblet, and handled mug. Pieces are found in clear or cobalt blue.

Beaded Band

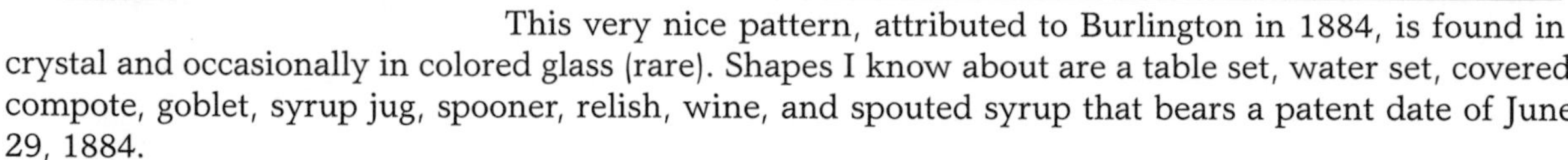

This very nice pattern, attributed to Burlington in 1884, is found in crystal and occasionally in colored glass (rare). Shapes I know about are a table set, water set, covered compote, goblet, syrup jug, spooner, relish, wine, and spouted syrup that bears a patent date of June 29, 1884.

Beaded Cable

Here is the well-known Northwood footed rose bowl, best known in carnival glass, in custard glass with nutmeg stain.

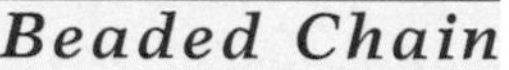

Beaded Chain

Also known as Looped Cord, this easy-to-recognize pattern can be found in a table set, celery vase, plate, sauce, relish, water set, and the goblet shown. The pattern dates to the late 1870s.

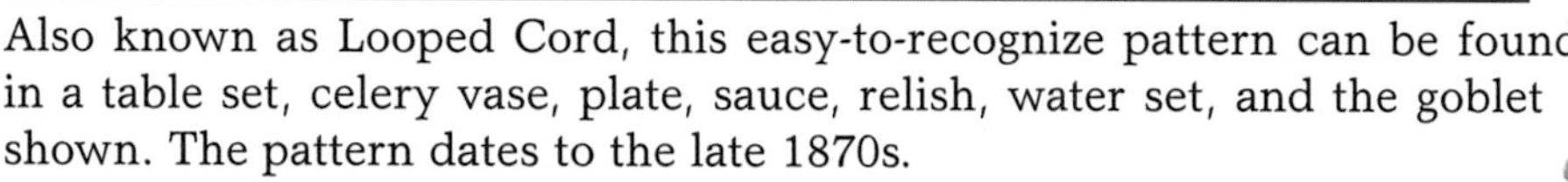

Beaded Coarse Bars

Beaded Coarse Bars is found in table sets, water carafe, mug, goblet, pickle dish, and salt shakers, but other shapes may exist. This ribbed pattern is much like so many others made in the 1890 – 1910 era of pressed glass.

Beaded Comet Band

This pattern was made at Albany, Indiana, by Model Flint Glass in 1893 and is also known as Ways' Beaded Swirl. It is found in crystal and ruby-stained glass and is also known in carnival glass (rare) as Beads and Bars. Crystal shapes include a berry set, 10" plate, table set, cruet, and pickle dish, but the carnival examples are a nut bowl (from the spooner) and a rose bowl.

Beaded Dart Band

This Geo. Duncan & Sons pattern of 1882 (its #600) is found in crystal, blue, vaseline, amber, and ruby stain (goblet only). Shapes include a table set, goblet, oval dish (7", 8", and 9"), and the beautiful pickle castor shown.

Beaded Ellipse and Fan

This U.S. Glass pattern from 1905 is found in table sets, water sets, and other table pieces, including the plate shown.

Beaded Grape

Beaded Grape was made by U.S. Glass Company in 1899 and possibly Burlington Glass in Canada in 1910, in clear, emerald green, and gold trimmed. It is also known as California. Shapes include a table set, cake stand, cordial, compotes, toothpick holder, 6" vase, wine, round or square bowls, round or square water sets, pickle dish, sauces, shakers, berry set, and bread plate.

Beaded Grape Medallion

This pattern is credited to the Boston Silver Glass Company in 1869 (shards have been found at Boston and Sandwich Glass) and was made in clear crystal. Shapes include a flat bowl, a table set, cake stand, castor set, celery vase, champagne, covered high or low compotes, open compote, cordial, oval bowl, egg cup, goblets, honey dish, pickle dish, pitcher, 6" plate, relish dish, salt dip, master salt dip, sauce, and a wine. The goblet was reproduced and embossed under the base with an "R" and three stars inside a shield.

Beaded Medallion

This pattern, also known as Beaded Mirror, was made by Sandwich Glass in the early 1870s, then supposedly by National Glass in 1901 at the Dalzell plant. It can be found in a water set, table set, jelly compote, egg cup, open salt, relish, sauce, and possibly a goblet. Apparently found in clear glass only.

Beaded Oval Medallion

Other than the name, which was supplied by its owner, no other information has been reported to me on this nice pitcher. One can assume by the blank oval panel that it might possibly be found with etching in the medallion. Vaseline is the only color reported to me and I can suspect that a tumbler may have been made and possibly other shapes as well.

Beaded Panel and Sunburst

Beaded Panel and Sunburst was made by Heisey (its #1235) in 1898 in clear and color stained. Shapes include a table set, hotel creamer and sugar, bowls, berry bowls, nappy, celery vase, celery tray, toothpick holder, plate, cruets in three sizes, pickle tray, spoon tray, salt dip, shakers (three shapes), punch set, water set, carafe, wine, whiskey tumbler, water sets in two sizes, compotes in five sizes, cake stand, and oil jug.

Beaded Shell

Called simply Shell by opalescent glass collectors and Beaded Shell by carnival glass people, this pattern was also made in crystal, colored glass, and decorated glass. The Dugan Glass Company is the maker. Shapes include a berry set, table set, water set, mug, cruet, shakers, toothpick holder, a cruet set, and compotes. Shown is a green master berry bowl with gilded beading.

Beaded Stars and Mums

This is another of Northwood's Verre D'or patterns, and is very difficult to locate. Shown is a low ice cream shaped bowl in green with gold.

Beaded Stars and Swag

This pattern is from the Fenton Glass Company and found in opalescent as well as carnival glass, crystal, and even custard glass. Production dates to 1907 and there is a similar pattern from the same maker called Beaded Moon and Stars. Shapes are plates, bowls, rose bowls, and the banana bowl shape shown.

Beaded Swag

Bead Swag can be found in crystal, milk glass, ruby stain, custard, and emerald green. Shapes include a table set, water set, footed cake stand (shown), mug, rose bowl, cup and saucer, wine, syrup, and toothpick holder. Beaded Swag is from Heisey but most items are not marked (#1295 line, made in 1899 – 1904).

Beaded Swirl and Ball

This pattern is also known as Westmoreland's Puritan and was originally made by Leerdam of Holland. Westmoreland's mug, made in the 1905 – 1910 era, can be found in crystal, emerald green, cobalt blue, amethyst, and dark brown, all with gold trim. Other shapes in this pattern are a wine glass and an egg cup. The mug is found in both four ounce and eight ounce sizes.

Beaded Swirl and Lens

This very attractive pattern can be distinguished by its "lens." A table set, water set, berry set, and possibly other shapes can be found. This is not the same pattern as Beaded Swirl and Disc by U.S. Glass.

Beaded Tulip

Beaded Tulip was shown in McKee & Brothers' 1894 catalog in clear, blue, emerald green, and amber. Shapes include an oval 9½" bowl, table set, cake stand, champagne, covered or open compotes, cordial, oblong ice cream dish, goblet, jam jar, pickle dish, milk pitcher, water set, bread or dinner plates, relish, sauce (flat or footed), water tray, wine tray, and wine glass.

Beads and Bars

This pattern was named by Marion Hartung when it was first found in a carnival glass rose bowl shape. The maker is unknown to my knowledge. Shapes are a creamer, sugar, and rose bowl. It is also found in crystal.

Beautiful Lady

Beautiful Lady was from Bryce, Higbee and Company in 1905. It can be found in an extended table service including water sets, table sets, berry sets, plate, wine, and toy cake stand in crystal or ruby stain.

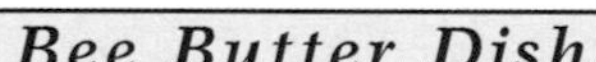

Bee Butter Dish

While this Bryce Brothers' pattern is known as a bee pattern and a butter dish, it is advertised in a U.S. Glass catalog (Bryce was the factory B of U.S. Glass) as a "Fly pickle dish." It can be found in clear, vaseline, amber, or blue.

Begging Dog

Credited to the Iowa City Glass Works from about 1881, this mug closely resembles its Dog mug. Colors are clear, amethyst, and possibly cobalt blue. The mug is 2⅜" tall and has a diameter of 2".

Belladonna

Belladonna was made by the Northwood Glass Company as the #31 pattern and was shown in a 1906 catalog. It is found in crystal, green, and ruby stained. Shapes include a table set, berry set, water set, and toothpick holder (shown). The design is very plain except for the ring of beading with notching on each side.

Bellaire

This pattern was made by the Bellaire Goblet Co., circa 1891 as its #91 line. It is often confused with Findlay's "Giant Bullseye" pattern, which has no toothpick holder. A small tableware line was made as well as the toothpick holder (shown), a castor set, and cologne set. It can be found in crystal.

Bellflower

First attributed to Boston & Sandwich Company in the 1840s and then Bryce, McKee Glass Company, this flint glass pattern is found in variations that include Single Vine with Fine Rib, Double Vine with Fine Rib, both Single and Double Vine with Course Rib, and Cut Bellflowers. Colors are clear, amber, vaseline, blue, green, milk glass, opaque blue, sapphire blue, and opalescent (all colors considered quite rare). The many shapes include bowls, table set, cake stands, celery vase, castor set, open or covered compotes, wines, cordials, goblets, celery vase, plates, water set, mug, pickle dish, lamps, decanter, syrup, milk pitcher, and a covered sweetmeat. Many shapes have wide variations in design and sizes. Shown is a vintage goblet and the very well done "reproduction" pitcher by Imperial Glass for the Metropolitan Museum of Art which clearly shows the "single vine-fine rib" design. With exception of the reproductions, prepare to pay dearly for pieces in this pattern.

Belmont #100

This pattern was also called Belmont's Daisy and Button and was made in 1886, with a daisy and button as part of the design. Shapes include a table set, celery (on the cover of the second edition), 12½" plate, and cheese dish, but other shapes probably were made. Some crystal pieces are engraved and all pieces are made in plain crystal, as well as the beautiful vaseline glass. The twisted design seen in the handle of the syrup is called an "air twist." This is seen on handled items from different companies, indicating that workers probably traveled from factory to factory seeking employment and applying their skills from previous jobs.

Belmont Diamond

This Belmont Glass Company pattern from 1897 resembles both Blockade (from Belmont) and King's Curtain. It can be found in round bowls, oval bowls, and the cruet shape. The cruet dates to 1885 and was thought the only shape in this pattern for many years.

Belted Icicle

This pattern, made by Fostoria as their #162 line in 1899, can be found in an extended table service as well as a wine. It is found in crystal only.

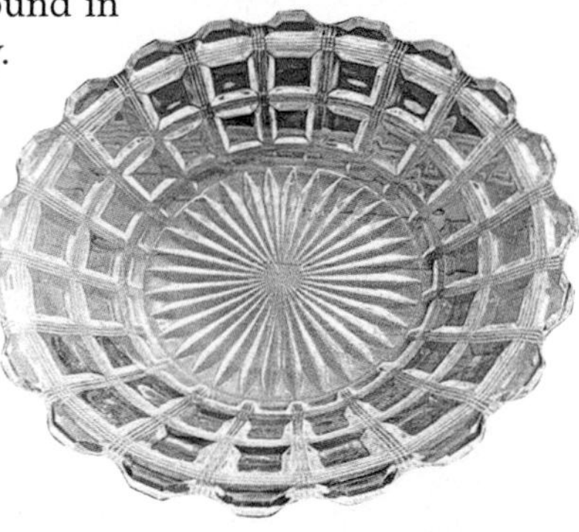

Berlin

Berlin was made by Adams and Company in 1874 and U.S. Glass in 1891, and is also called Reeded Waffle. Shapes include a table set, water set, cruet, wine, cracker jar, goblet, and the ice bowl shown. Berlin is found in crystal, ruby stain, or amber stain.

Berry

With the butter dish shown, this pattern was obviously made in a table set and I suspect there have to be other shapes such as a celery vase, goblets, or wines. In design it somewhat resembles the Fairfax Strawberry pattern but isn't the same.

Berry Boat

Recent information indicates this to be from MB Fains in France as their #720 pattern. This two-handled bowl or boat dates to the 1889. I believe this piece may have been made in crystal as well as the vaseline shown and likely other shapes were made as well.

Berry Cluster

Found in a table set (with open or covered sugar), celery vase, water set, goblet, and perhaps other shapes, this realistic pattern is easily identified by the curved twig ring and the clusters of berries and leaves that stand out greatly. I believe this pattern dates to the 1890s.

Berry Spray

This short-stemmed wine from the Indiana Tumbler and Goblet Company at Greentown seems to be found only in clear glass. Shards were found at the factory and only the one shape is reported. The design is a spray of well-stippled leaves and two clusters of fruit without tendrils. Production was in the 1890s.

Bethlehem Star

Bethlehem Star, from Indiana Glass Company in 1910, is found in a table set, water set, celery vase, covered compote (4½", 5", 8"), cruet, goblet, relish, sauce, wine, and jelly compote. Only clear has been reported.

Bevelled Buttons

Bevelled Buttons, from U.S. Glass, was originally Duncan #320 made in 1891. Shapes include a table set, pickle jar, sauce, bowls, celery vase, and open compotes made in three sizes (7", 8", and 9"). While only crystal pieces are known, some are gold decorated.

Bevelled Diamond and Star

The shapes in this pattern made by Tarentum Glass Company in 1898 in both clear and ruby stained glass include a table set, shakers, water set, syrup, cruet, and bread plate. The pattern is a strong one that covers only the lower portion of the piece, permitting the upper area to be engraved on some pieces.

Bicycle Girl

This very fine 1880s Dalzell, Gilmore and Leighton Glass pattern is known only in the tankard pitcher shape. The design shows a young girl in the dress of the late 1800s, riding a bicycle through a leafy bower. The mould work is excellent.

Big Basketweave

First made by Dugan (1910) and then by Diamond Glass (1913), this well-known vase pattern is mostly found in carnival glass, in vases, handled baskets (in two sizes), and bowl exteriors. I have seen vases in crystal and celeste or sapphire blue, while in baskets I have found crystal and a light amethyst.

Biliken Flute

The title seems to be generic, but this wine glass shown is always called Biliken Flute. Other shapes known include a table set, pickle dish with tab handle, and a goblet. I do not know the maker and suspect more than one factory in more than one timeframe made versions of this simple design.

Birch Leaf

The maker of this pattern is unknown. It was made in the 1870s in crystal, vaseline, and milk glass. Shapes include a leaf shaped berry set, table set, covered or open compotes, goblet, wine, egg cup, master salt dip, pickle dish, and celery vase. Shown is the berry set in vaseline.

Birch Leaf (Portland)

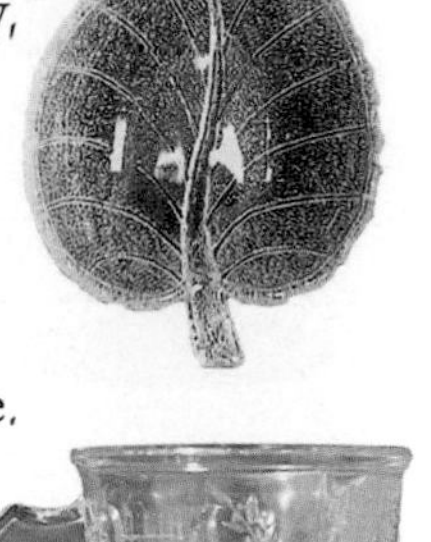

Metz credits this leaf-shaped berry dish (also made in a master berry size) to the Portland Company, 1880s. The pattern is very similar to the Hobbs Tree of Life design. Colors reported are crystal, ruby, canary, blue, or green.

Bird and Cherry

Bird and Cherry is shown in a McKee catalog reprint from the 1890s. This is normally referred to as a toothpick or salt, but is a mustard when found with a lid, which is likely its original intended use. It can be found in crystal, vaseline, green, blue, and amber. It has been reproduced.

Bird and Harp

This mug was made by McKee & Brothers Glass Company about 1880 and can be found in three sizes. It is found in clear and purple slag glass. The design is interesting with a harp on each side of the handle and a bird nesting on a bough.

Bird and Strawberry

This well known Indiana Glass Company pattern from the 1910 – 1920 era can be found in clear or with blue-green-red staining. It was made in a table set, water set, berry set, various odd bowls (5", 9", 10"), cake stand, celery tray, celery vase, hat (made from tumbler and very rare), cup, goblet, chop plate, sandwich plate, relish dish, and wine. The compote and relish dish have been reproduced.

Bird Basket

Credited to Bryce Brothers in 1886, this novelty toothpick or match holder is a real find. It is shown in amber but also came in clear or blue.

Bird in Nest with Flowers

This mug was made by Challinor & Taylor Ltd. in the 1880s. It is 3⅜" tall and has a top diameter of 3⅛". It was made in crystal and the purple slag shown. There is a variant with a starred bottom rather than the normal cat on the base.

Bird on a Branch

From a line of mug patterns first made by Bryce and then U.S. Glass, this has two robin-like birds on opposite sides and an owl opposite the handle. Between the birds are branches and leaves. The mug's handle is knobbed and the base notched and prismed.

Birds at Fountain

The maker of this pattern seems to be unknown, but it dates to the early 1880s and was made in clear or milk glass. Shapes are few and include a small bowl, flat sauce, goblet, miniature mug, cake stand, covered compote, and table set.

Birds in Swamp

Like so many novelty goblets, this one shows off a designer's imagination. It has a threaded background, tree branches, leaves, and two birds nesting. Perhaps the threading is meant to be the woven nest but it's hard to tell. I believe the goblet dates to the 1880s.

Blackberry (Hobbs)

Blackberry was made in 1870 by Hobbs, Brockunier in crystal or opal ware (Hobbs called this treatment porcelain) with the pattern #3829. Shapes are many and include celery, tall celery, champagne, high and low compotes, high and low covered compotes, egg cups (single or double), goblet, nappy, syrup, water set, table set, relish, salt dip, wine, and oil lamps (8½", 9½", 11½"). Shown is the covered sugar. The creamer, goblet, spooner, and sugar were reproduced.

Blazing Cornucopia

This U.S. Glass pattern, made in 1913, is also known as Paisley or Golden Jewel by some collectors. It is found in clear, painted (purple, pink, or olive green), and gold trimmed glass. Shapes include a table set, water set, berry set, cruet, goblet, wine, cup, pickle dish, jelly compote, nappy, olive dish, celery tray, and toothpick holder.

Bleeding Heart

Bleeding Heart was first made by King & Son in the 1870s and then by U.S. Glass in 1898 in crystal or opaque glass. It is an available pattern found in oval or round covered bowls (5", 7", 8", 9"), waste bowl, table set, cake stand in three sizes, oval or round compotes, covered compotes (7", 8", 9"), egg cup, goblet, jelly dish, honey dish, mug, pickle tray, water set, plate, oval platter, relish tray, and master and individual salts. Shards were found at Iowa City Flint Glass Company.

Blockade

This cousin of Red Block was made by U.S. Glass (Challinor #309) in 1891 and often called Diamond Block with Fan. Shapes include a table set, water set, finger bowl, celery vase, open compote in 4", 6", 7", 8" sizes, covered compote in three sizes, goblet, square dish in 7", 8", 9" sizes, and nappy in two sizes.

Block and Bar

This flint glass pattern is from Boston and Sandwich circa 1840 - 1850, and although it preceded the dates for this book I feel it should be shown nonetheless. I know of only the creamer shown, a water pitcher, a sugar, and a goblet. Both crystal and vaseline examples exist.

Block and Circle

Block and Circle was originally named Mellor and produced by Gillinder in 1880. Shapes include a table set, celery vase, 6" covered sweetmeat, open compote in three sizes, berry set, water set, goblet, oval dish, miniature lamp, and beer mug.

Block and Fan

This was Richards and Hartley's #544 from 1888, then from U.S. Glass in 1891. It is also called Romeo and can be found in clear, ruby stained, and milk glass. Shapes include a table set, cake stand, biscuit jar, berry set, finger bowl, rose bowl, waste bowl, carafe, castor set, cake stand, celery tray, vase, open and covered compotes, decanter, goblet, ice bucket, lamp, water set, milk pitcher, plate, sugar shaker, and wine.

Block and Jewel

This is very similar to a pattern called Milton, but it has a round jewel in the square rather than a diamond prism design. The maker is unknown at this time but I suspect this pattern was made by Bellaire Goblet or Dalzell, Gilmore & Leighton at Finlay, Ohio. The only shape reported is the stemmed wine shown.

Block and Pillar

Although only found on salt and pepper shakers and this vase shape, I suspect this pattern may well be found on table sets, water sets, and other table pieces. The pattern is a simple one, adaptable to nearly any shape. This pattern is also referred to by some collectors as Panelled English Hobnail from Tarentum Glass, circa 1901. The vase shown is 8" tall and has traces of gold trim around the flared rim.

Block and Rosette

This pattern was made by Duncan and Miller in 1902 as their #50 line and can be found in plain crystal or gilded, but is also reported in some pieces in a rare ruby stain. Some of the shapes shown in old catalog ads are various bowls, a water set, table set, punch set, several stemmed pieces and salt shakers.

Block and Star

Don't confuse this with the U. S. Glass pattern Block & Star (Valencia Waffle) as they are two different patterns. This well done pattern has not been attributed to a maker that I'm aware of. Found in vaseline to date in a pitcher and tumbler shape.

Block and Triple Bars

I have very little information about this pattern except to say it was made in a table set as well as a goblet. Additional items probably exist. The goblet has a fan added at the top of the design.

Blocked Thumbprint Band

Besides the mug shape shown, this Duncan & Miller pattern is found in a cruet, toothpick holder, wine, and shot glass in both clear and ruby stained glass. The pattern was made in 1904 and continued for nearly a decade.

Block #331 (Duncan)

Sometimes called Late Block or #331 Block, this Geo. Duncan and Sons pattern originated in 1889 (made for U.S. Glass's "Factory D" in 1891), in crystal or ruby stained glass. There are many shapes, including a parlor lamp, syrup, celery boat, square bowl, tri-cornered bowl, punch set, mustard jar, square sauce, cruet, ice tub (shown), handled relish, jelly compote, lamp (rare) sugar shaker, salt shaker, rose bowl, and table set (a 4" rose bowl is reported in vaseline but I haven't seen it to date).

Blooms and Blossoms

This Northwood Company pattern can be found in carnival (rarely), opalescent, ruby stain, gilding, enameled, clear, vaseline, or emerald green glass. Shapes include a one-handled nappy, bowls, and plates. This pattern dates to 1905 and is also called Mikado, Flower and Bud, and Lightning Flower by some collectors.

Blueberry

This Fenton whimsey vase, made from the pitcher, was from their #1562 line, circa 1914. This is a well known carnival glass pattern, but the cobalt vase whimsey shown is the only non-iridized example reported to date.

Blue Heron

Blue Heron is also known as Heron or Stork, and is found with the Crystalography process from Dithridge & Company. Shown is a creamer.

Boar

The maker of this circa 1890s humidor has not been established to my knowledge. This very collectible item is found in a blue satin or camphor glass treatment and no other colors have been reported at this time.

Boot

This little boot, shown in a Butler Brothers catalog in 1907, was also iridized or ruby stained as shown and usually sold as a souvenir.

Bosc Pear

This was the #150 pattern from Indiana Glass in 1913. Its shapes include a berry set, four-piece table set, and a water set, as well as a scarce celery vase. It can be found in crystal, gilded crystal, and purple flashed fruit.

Boston Tree of Life

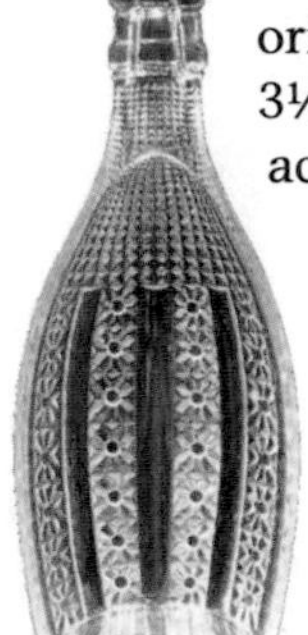

This Boston & Sandwich Glass Company pitcher with a "hook" for the mug had a stand originally. It was made in at least two sizes (the one shown has an 8¼" tall pitcher and a 3½" tall mug). Besides the crystal sets, the larger pitcher is known in amethyst, according to Mordock and Adams in their mug book.

Bottle Pickle Dish

This half bottle shaped pickle dish was made by the Central Glass Company from their #823 line. Colors are amber, vaseline, and blue.

Bouquet

This is Indiana Glass's #162 pattern from 1917. It can be found in crystal, gilded crystal, and stained glass. Shapes include water sets, table sets, berry sets, compotes, and other shapes.

Bow Tie

This was Thompson Glass's pattern #18 from 1889. Shapes include bowls in four sizes, a table set, butter pat, cake stand, celery vase, high or low compotes in several sizes, goblet, jam jar, orange bowl, milk pitcher in two sizes, water set with three sizes of pitchers, punch bowl, relish dish, flat and footed sauces, and both master and individual salt dips.

Boxed Star

Boxed Star was from Jenkins in 1908 as their #100 pattern and from Federal Glass in 1914 as their #100. Shapes include a berry set, table set, water set, and ice tea tumbler. Most shapes seem hard to find.

Box Pleat

This Adams & Company pattern from 1875 is sometimes called O'Hara's Crystal Wedding, and can be found in a table set, compote, water set, celery vase, and cake stand. Most pieces have feet.

Boy and Girl Face

Found with a matching saucer that is called Acorn, this cup was a product of the Columbia Glass Company of Findlay, Ohio, in the late 1880s and then U.S. Glass after 1891. The cup shows a boy on one side, a girl on the other, while the saucer has a vining of acorns. Both pieces were made in clear, blue, or amber.

Boy with Begging Dog

Collectors feel this mug was made in the 1890s and may be a companion piece to the Deer & Cow and Heron & Peacock mugs since the three mugs make a graduated size grouping and because of the similar shape. Colors are clear, blue, opaque blue, and milk glass. One side shows the boy and begging dog while the other shows a boy in a kneeling position with a food bowl.

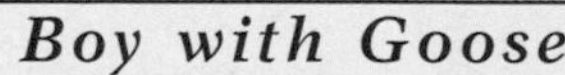

Boy with Goose

Although unconfirmed, this compote is reported to have been made by Portland Glass in the 1870s. The top section shows a circling of etched leaves and I've included a photo of the frosted stem and base showing the boy carrying a basket on his shoulders and the goose pecking at his leg.

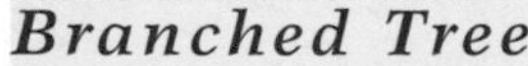

Branched Tree

Branched Tree was from Dalzell, Gilmore, and Leighton in the 1890s and found in crystal, amber, and blue glass. Shapes include a table set, water set, celery vase, covered compote, and goblet. The unimaginative design isn't easy to mistake.

Brass Nailhead

I've heard this mug is found in flint opalescent glass but the example here is not opalescent. In addition, this example is marked "France," so the pattern is probably not compatible with the lacy saucer that has been linked with it. The mug is 1¾" and is distinguished by the two spiked collars that span it.

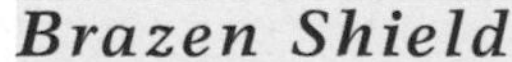

Brazen Shield

Brazen Shield was from Central Glass as its #98, then Cambridge Glass in 1905, and finally from Indiana Glass. Shapes include a table set, water set, berry set, pickle dish, salt shakers, goblet, wine, and the jelly compote shown.

Brazilian

Brazilian was advertised as Fostoria's #600 pattern in 1898, and is also known as Cane Shield. Shapes include a table set, toothpick holder, salt shaker, pickle jar, vase, sauce, handled olive, water set, finger bowl, compote, carafe, celery tray, celery vase, cracker jar in three sizes, berry set, cruet, sherbet, and rose bowl.

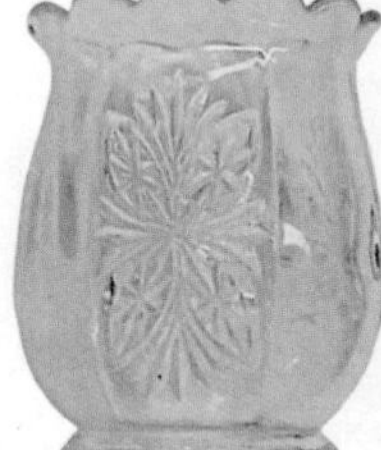

Brilliant

Riverside Glass Company's #436 pattern from circa 1895 is also known as Petaled Medallion or Miami. It was made in clear, ruby, or amber stained and is sometimes found with engraving. Shapes include a berry set, table set, celery vase, covered compote, goblet, water set, shakers, sauce, syrup, toothpick holder, and wine.

Bringing Home the Cows

This was made by the Dalzell, Gilmore, and Leighton Glass Company in 1890 in clear only. Shapes include a four-piece table set and the water pitcher shown. Neither matching tumblers have been reported nor the usual accompanying table items.

Britannia Lily

Shown is the creamer and I feel certain that other shapes were made. I am told by the owner that this pattern is of English origin.

Britannic

This well-balanced McKee Glass Company pattern from 1894 can be found in clear, amber stained, and ruby stained glass. Shapes include a fruit basket, banana stand, carafe, oval bowl (7", 8", 9"), round bowl, rose bowl, square bowl, table set, cake stand (large or small), castor set, celery tray, celery vase, covered compote, open compote (5", 6", 7", 8½", 10"), cruet, custard cup, olive dish, pickle dish, goblet, honey jar, cracker jar, lamp (two types and sizes), mug, shakers, sauce, syrup, toothpick holder, ice cream tray, vase, and wine.

Broken Arches

This well-done geometric pattern, made by Imperial Glass in 1914 in carnival glass and crystal, bears a catalog designation of Snap-14 and can be found on punch sets and an 8½" bowl. The bowl is ruffled and the punch bowl may be either ruffled or just round with serrated edges.

Broken Pillar and Reed

This was Model Flint's #909 pattern, also known as Kismet. It can be found in crystal, blue, amber, green, gold flash, Maiden's Blush, and opalescent colors. Pieces include a bonbon, 8" bowl, table set, cake stand, celery vase and celery tray, cologne, compote, custard cup, soap dish, jelly compote, pickle tray, squat pitcher, plate, shakers, syrup, tankard water set, tray, and toothpick holder.

Bryce Fashion

This pattern was made in the 1880s and can be found in crystal, amber, amethyst, blue, vaseline, ruby stained glass, and a rare blue example that is ruby stained. It is also known as Daisy & Button with Red Dots in stained glass. Shapes include the toothpick holder shown, a creamer formed from a cup shape, and a creamer formed from the toothpick holder mould.

Bryce Fashion Butter Dish

This very unusual U.S. Glass butter dish from factory B (Bryce Brothers) in 1891 seems to have no matching pieces and must have been one of the several single butter dish designs like Lorne. It is known in crystal and here I show the vaseline version, but likely blue and amber were made as well.

Bryce Hobnail

Bryce Hobnail, also called Panelled Hobnail, was first made by Bryce Brothers in the 1880s and then as part of U.S. Glass after 1891. Shapes include bowls, a table set, wine, mug, open or covered compotes, celery vase, pickle dish, and a goblet. Colors are clear, amber, canary, blue, or milk glass.

Bryce Panel

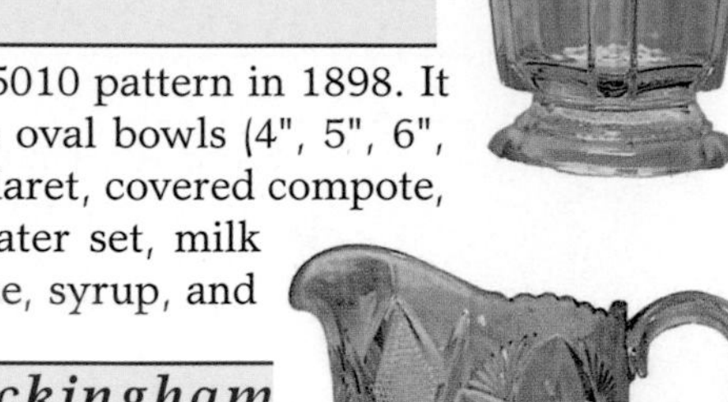

Bryce Panel was from U.S. Glass in the 1880s. Shapes include a syrup, table set, and the celery vase shown. The design is minimal and one wonders why a second pattern wasn't used. It is found in clear and clear with gold trim.

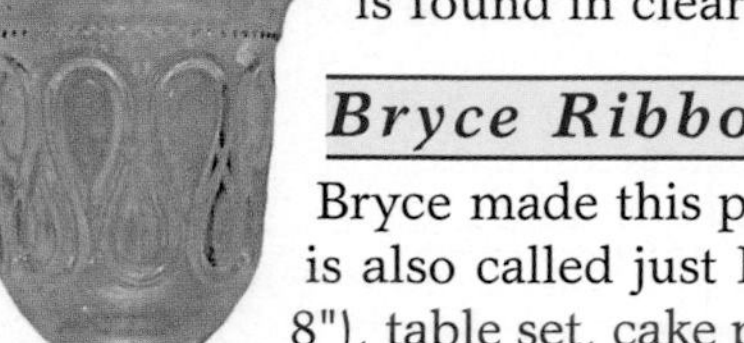

Bryce Ribbon Candy

Bryce made this pattern in 1885 and U.S. Glass made it as its #15010 pattern in 1898. It is also called just Ribbon Candy. Shapes include covered or open oval bowls (4", 5", 6", 8"), table set, cake plate, cake stand, child's table set, celery vase, claret, covered compote, cruet, cordial, cup and saucer, honey dish, lamp, pickle dish, water set, milk pitcher, 6", 7", 8", 9" 10" plates, bread plate, relish, shakers, sauce, syrup, and wine.

Buckingham

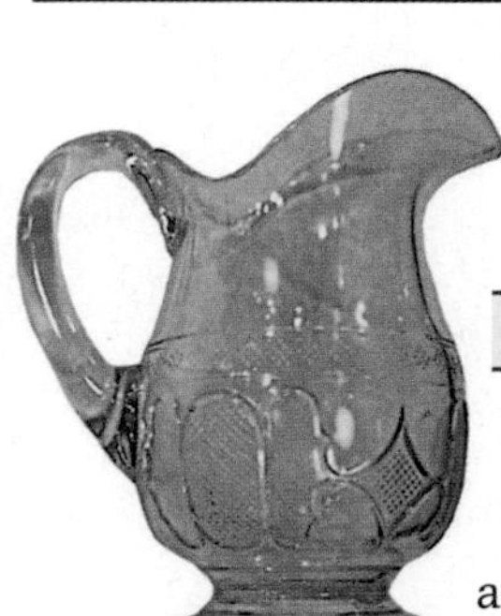

Buckingham was advertised as U.S. Glass design #15106 in 1907 and produced at the Glassport factory. Shapes include a table set, water set, berry set, and a sauce which can be found with advertising (shown elsewhere in this edition).

Buckle and Diamond

Buckle and Diamond was made by McKee and Brothers Glass in 1880. This unusual pattern's shapes include a table set, water set, bowls, and goblet. The design is one of a band of opposing forms that include ovals, diamonds, and scrolls, some clear and some with finecut file.

Buckle with English Hobnail

This very well-done pattern was from Westmoreland as their #122 from circa 1920. It can be found in a table set, berry set, shakers, pickle dish, and celery vase. Certainly other shapes may exist.

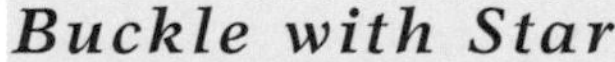

Buckle with Star

Buckle with Star was made in clear only in 1880 by Bryce, Walker and then by U.S. Glass in 1891 at the Bryce factory ("B"). Shapes include covered bowls in four sizes, table set, cake stand, celery vase, cologne bottle, covered and open compotes, goblet, honey dish, mug, mustard jar, water set, relish tray, master salt, flat or footed sauces, syrup, wine, and handled tumbler.

Bullet Emblem

Bullet Emblem was made by U.S. Glass Company in 1898 as a Spanish-American War commemorative and also called Shield. Pieces were originally decorated in red, white, and blue with the bullet finial in silver. Shapes are a table set consisting of covered butter dish, covered sugar bowl, creamer, and spooner.

Bulls-Eye and Daisy

This U.S. Glass pattern was made in Glassport in 1909 and originally called Newport. Besides clear, it can be found in emerald green as well as decorated bull's-eyes. Shapes are table sets, water sets, syrup, toothpick holder, shakers, and wine. Some pieces may also be found with ruby staining. The goblet and vase were reproduced.

Bulls-Eye and Diamond Point

This Dalzell, Gilmore & Leighton pattern (#49) was made in 1891 and is also known as Reverse Torpedo. It can also be found in an extended table service that includes a basket and wine as well as a banana dish in crystal and ruby stain.

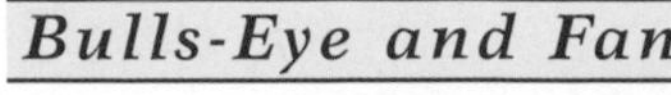

Bulls-Eye and Fan

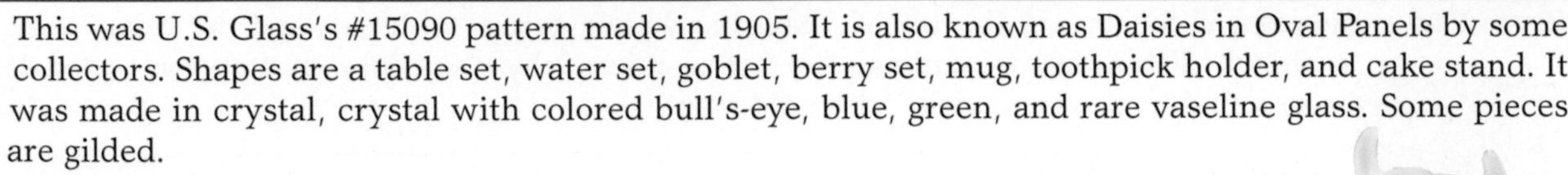

This was U.S. Glass's #15090 pattern made in 1905. It is also known as Daisies in Oval Panels by some collectors. Shapes are a table set, water set, goblet, berry set, mug, toothpick holder, and cake stand. It was made in crystal, crystal with colored bull's-eye, blue, green, and rare vaseline glass. Some pieces are gilded.

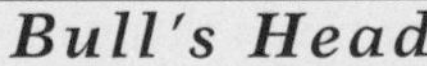

Bull's Head

From Atterbury, circa 1888, this novelty mustard container has a glass tongue (missing from the example shown) and can sometimes be found with a painted eye. Colors are blue and milk glass (Opal as referred to by some collectors).

Bushel Basket

This very popular Northwood item was first produced in carnival glass, circa 1910 and beyond, and was also made in the late teen's and early 20s in non-iridized examples. Non-iridized colors reported are black (ebony) and crystal.

Butterfly

This U.S. Glass pattern (#6406) is found in crystal in a table set, water set (scarce), celery vase, pickle dish, mustard jar, salt shakers, relish dish, and bowls. Handles on some pieces are frosted. It is known as Big Butterfly by some carnival glass collectors where only the tumbler can be found (rare).

Butterfly (Frosted)

This Aetna Glass pattern from 1883 is also known as Butterfly Handles. Shapes include a table set, covered compote, celery vase, shakers, and probably other shapes. The frosting occurs on both the lid and the bowl of the compote shown.

Butterfly (Plain)

Like the frosted compote shown above, this one is also from the Aetna Company from about 1883 and is also called Butterfly Handles by some. Shapes include a table set, covered compote, celery vase, shakers, and water set.

Butterfly and Berry

Besides the carnival glass pieces and the amberina vase whimsey (pulled from a tumbler) I showed in the last edition of this book, I am pleased to show pieces of the first reported berry set in this pattern in crystal. It was made by Fenton in 1911 and was one of the company's major patterns for two decades. It has been reproduced, mainly in carnival glass.

Butterfly and Thistle

This is almost certainly a Cambridge item, due especially to the spot-on match in shape and size to the Snow Flake pitcher. This pattern is found in an extended table service, oil bottle, and other shapes. Crystal is the only reported color.

Butterfly with Spray

Butterfly with Spray was made by Bryce, Higbee and Company in 1885 and is also known as Acme. Shapes include a mug in two sizes, table set, celery vase, covered compotes in high or low standard, and water set. Covered pieces have butterfly handles and finials. This pattern should not be confused with the Butterfly and Fan goblet that is part of the Japanese or Grace pattern.

Button Arches

This pattern is shown in factory catalog ads by George Duncan & Sons in Washington, Pennsylvania, as their #39 line. It can be found in crystal or ruby stained pieces that were used as souvenir glass, often with a frosted band. It can also be found in clambroth coloring. There are many shapes including a water set, toothpick holder, table set, compote, syrup, cruet, cup, shakers, and wine. It is also known as Red Top or Scalloped Daisy and was reproduced in various shapes.

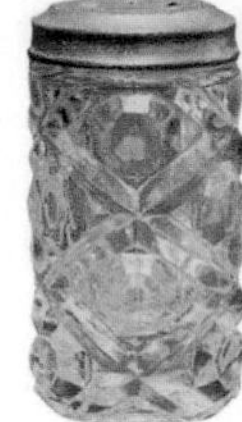

Button Block

The only shape reported to me in this pattern to date is the salt shaker shown, which is known in crystal or vaseline. Other shapes may certainly exist, but I haven't heard of them.

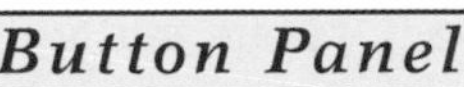

Button Panel

In the company's advertising, this was Duncan's #44 pattern, made in 1900. It can be found in crystal, ruby stained glass, and gold decorated glass in a toothpick holder, berry set, table set, cruet, toy (child's) table set, shakers, pickle dish, and celery vase.

Button Panel with Bars

Button Panel with Bars was possibly a McKee pattern from around 1905. It can be found in an extended table service in crystal and ruby stain. Shown is a punch bowl (minus the base). All pieces are a bit hard to find.

Buttressed Loop

This uncomplicated pattern was made by Adams and Company (#16) from 1874. It can be found in crystal, green, blue, amber, and canary glass. Shapes include a compote, covered bowl, and table set.

Buzz Saw

This pattern is a part of Cambridge Glass Company's #2699 pattern (AKA: Cane Pinwheel) which has several different design forms. Shapes of this variation include a table set, quart pitcher, squat quart pitcher, cruet, syrup, cologne bottle, celery tray, berry set, and odd bowls.

Buzz-Star

Buzz-Star is also known as Whirligig and was made by U.S. Glass as #15101 in 1907 at the Bryce factory. Shapes include a table set, water set, toy table set (called Whirligig by collectors), berry set, pickle dish, goblet, wine, toy punch set, and salt dip.

Cabbage Rose

This design, not to be confused with the famous Central Glass pattern of 1870, is from the goofus period. It can be found in vases in 5", 7", and 10" sizes. The roses, like the poppies in another goofus pattern I show, are puffed out and very artistic but appear too gaudy in the painted pieces. Still, these vases are collectible.

Cabbage Rose (Central)

Cabbage Rose was made by Central Glass as #140 in 1870 and is found in crystal. Mosser Glass reproduced the goblet and spooner in amber, clear, green, amethyst, and blue in 1963. Shapes include a bitters bottle, handled basket, oval or round bowls (covered or open in several sizes), a table set, cake plate, cake stand (six sizes), celery vase, champagne, covered compote (eight sizes and high or low shapes), open compotes (four sizes), cordial, egg cup, goblets, mug, pickle dish, milk pitcher, water set, sauce, relish dish, master salt, and a wine (shown).

Cable

This early Boston and Sandwich Glass pattern is flint glass and is mostly found in crystal (rare colors exist in amber stain, jade, opaque green, opalescent blue, or white). Shapes include bowls, table sets, cake stand (very rare), castor set, celery vase, champagne, high or low open compotes, decanter, egg cup, goblet, honey dish, three styles of oil lamps, mug, plate, water set, syrup, and wine. The goblet has been reproduced.

Cable and Thumbprint Match Holder

This match or toothpick holder has a hexagonal base and may well be from England or Europe. It is a product of the 1860s I believe.

Cactus

Far different from the Greentown pattern with the same name, this Millersburg design is on bowls only as an exterior intaglio pattern. It is found on both carnival glass and crystal and was made from 1909 to 1912 only when the factory was sold to Jefferson Glass. Millersburg crystal is clear, sparkling, and top quality in every instance. It is very collectible.

Cadmus

Cadmus was credited to first Beaumont Glass in 1903 and then Dugan Glass in 1915. Only a goblet, a wine, and the compote shown are reported at this time.

Cambridge #2351

This geometric pattern was made in crystal in a table set, berry set, water set, 7" vase, oil bottle, half-gallon jug, cologne bottle, orange bowl, punch set, spoon tray, whiskey set with tray, handled olive, sweet pea vase, shakers, toothpick holder, wine, footed jelly, sherbet, celery tray, celery vase, 7" large compote, and a small punch bowl that stands 9" tall and is also found in carnival glass in a few shapes. Production dates from 1906.

Cambridge #2511

This pattern was made first in 1910 or 1911 by the Cambridge Glass Company in a berry set, table set, and possibly a water set, and is not well known. The example shown is a ruffled bowl.

Cambridge #2658

This was a specialty pattern from Cambridge in 1910 and can be found on a creamer, mug, or tumbler shape. Colors are clear, ruby stained, enameled crystal, and carnival glass (mug or tumbler only). The design is much like others in the era of ruby stained souvenir items where the top portion is unpatterned for lettering.

Cambridge #2694

This pattern is from the Cambridge Nearcut Design #2694 line and can be found in an extended table service as well as a few other shapes in crystal.

Cambridge Buzz Saw

This was advertised by Cambridge as the #2699 Buzz Saw pattern. Shapes include a squat handled basket, cruet, olive nappy, sherbet, rose bowl, 5" and 7" nut bowls, 5", 6", 7", 8", 9" bowls, celery tray, water set, berry set, table set, milk pitcher in two sizes, celery vase, syrup, cologne, and salt shakers. It is also called Double Star.

Cambridge Heron

This was shown in old Cambridge ads, circa 1920, as their #1111 line in 9", 12", 16", and a massive 20" example. This figural flower holder is known in both clear crystal and a pale green glass that is the color of old Coca-Cola bottles. These pieces fit inside various sized bowls and held flowers. Imagine the size of bowl that held the larger herons!

Cambridge Near-Cut #2653

This pattern is shown in Cambridge Company catalogs and marked "Near-Cut." Shapes include a pickle tray, ice cream tray, celery tray, 5" individual square ice cream dish, water set, goblet, footed jelly compote, tall handled celery, double handled cracker jar with lid, squat quart pitcher, punch bowl with base, handled custard cup, and footed sherbet. It is also known as Cambridge's Nearcut Ribbon.

Cambridge Semitar #2647

This very fine Cambridge Glass Company pattern's shapes include a table set, water set (squat or tankard), water carafe, cruet, whiskey tumbler, jelly compote, footed bonbon, shakers, pickle tray, celery tray, spoon tray, 6", 7", 8" plates, various bowls, small punch set (sometimes with advertising), large punch set, and a 9" bowl advertised as a "special deep bowl."

Canadian

Canadian has been attributed to the Burlington Glass Works of Ontario in the 1870s. Shapes include covered or open bowls, table set, cake stand, covered and open compotes (high or low) in several sizes, goblet, jam jar, mug, milk pitcher, water set, bread plate, dinner plates in five sizes, sauce, and wine.

Cane

Cane was first a product of Gillinder & Sons and then McKee Glass Company in 1884. Colored crystal (amber, apple green, blue, and vaseline) and clear were made in this well-designed pattern. Shapes include a berry set, table set, water set, oval bowl, finger bowl, waste bowl, celery vase, compote, cordial, goblet, honey dish, match holder in a kettle shape, pickle dish, milk pitcher, small plate, relish, shakers, slipper tray, and wine.

Cane Horseshoe

Cane Horseshoe was made in clear and gold trimmed by U.S. Glass as #15118 in 1909. It was also called Paragon. Shapes include a cruet, salt shakers, cake stand, berry set, water set, table set, celery tray, and compote.

Cane Insert

This is a Tarentum Glass Company pattern made in 1898 in crystal or emerald green. It is sometimes called Arched Cane and Fan. Shapes include a table set, carafe (shown), cake stand, celery vase (rare), berry set, goblet, hair receiver, mug, and water set. Some pieces have gold trim.

Cannonball Pinwheel

This pattern was advertised as U.S. Glass pattern #15094 in 1906 and later made by Federal Glass in 1910. Other names for it are Caldonia or Pinwheel. Shapes include a 10" cherry tray, square olive, 7½" pickle dish, tall handled sugar, sherbet, nappy, shakers, milk pitcher, celery vase, water set, table set, berry set, cup, wine, goblet, jelly compote, 6" square plate, and 9" fruit plate.

Cannon on a Drum

This novelty container from Portieux in France, circa early 1930s, is slightly over the dates covered in this book but it is such a nice item I felt it worthy to show nonetheless. Colors are crystal and milk glass.

Canton House

The only reference I've found is Metz (a creamer) but here I show a very rare item from Green Valley Auctions: a covered cheese dish with a sailing ship scene.

Capitol

This pattern was made by Westmoreland in the early 1900s, and is called Estate by carnival glass collectors. In crystal it can be found with gold trim or color flashed. Shapes include a mug (shown), toothpick holder, puff box, creamer and sugar, and perfume bottle.

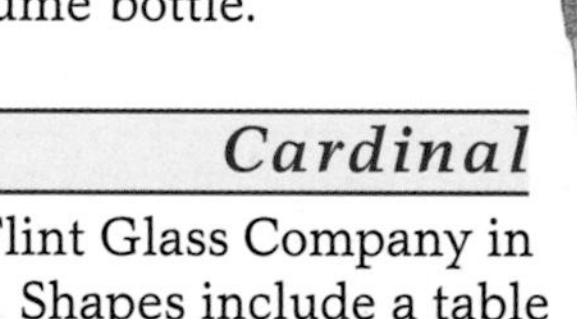

Cardinal

This pattern, also called Blue Jay or Cardinal Bird, is attributed to the Ohio Flint Glass Company in 1875 and I am told that it was also made in Canada. It is found only in clear. Shapes include a table set, cake stand, berry set, goblet, honey dish, water set, and flat or footed sauce in two sizes. The honey dish is found either open or with a cover. The goblet and creamer have been reproduced.

Carltec

This is one of the "tec" patterns from McKee and Brothers Glass. It was made in 1894 and re-issued in 1917. There are many shapes, including a table set (two shapes in creamers), water set, berry set, various bowls, handled basket, rose bowl, spoon tray, pickle dish, celery bowl, olive tray, bon-bon, handled compote, 11" plate, and two preserve dishes. Bowls can be square or round.

Carmen

Carmen was Fostoria's #575 pattern in 1898, and is also known as Panelled Diamonds and Finecut. Shapes are many and include a table set, berry set, 9" compote, and a cruet. It can be found in crystal or yellow flashed.

Carnation (Lancaster)

This crystal and decorated crystal pattern was made by the Lancaster Glass Company in 1911 and differs greatly from the New Martinsville Carnation design. Shapes include a table set, water set, berry set, goblet, pickle dish, and possibly a milk pitcher.

Carnation (New Martinsville)

This pattern was made by New Martinsville Glass in 1904 or 1905 and is far different from the Lancaster pattern with the same name. It is found in crystal mostly but can also be found in rare ruby stained pieces, often with gilding like the tumbler shown here. Shapes include a toothpick holder, a water set, wine, goblet, and a pickle dish but certainly other shapes may exist.

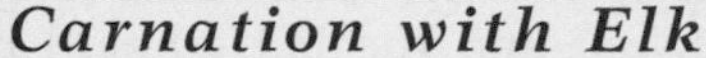

Carnation with Elk

This 11" plate (the carnation is also known on bowls and smaller plates with flower centers) is a rare item and is mostly found with a goofus treatment (this one was stripped). Carolyn McKinley in her goofus glass book calls this "Carnation cake plate with Elk" and lists a 13" size too. I suspect this pattern was created in the early 1900s.

Carriage

This novelty 9" long carriage bowl was made by McKee & Brothers, circa 1886 and can be found in crystal, amber, blue, and green.

Castor and Toothpick Set

Although this set has a slightly different design, I still feel it may be from McKee, because it has the same configuration of a base, three bottles, and a stemmed toothpick holder on top as McKee's Champion set. Some believe it to be a part of Belmont's #100 line.

Cathedral

This pattern, originally called Orion, was made by Bryce Brothers in 1885, and U.S. Glass after 1891. The creamer, which is somewhat of a variant in pattern design, is occasionally referred to as Waffle and Fine Cut. It can be found in amber, amethyst, blue, vaseline, clear, and clear with ruby stain. Shapes include 5", 6", 7", 8" bowls, table set, cake stand, celery vase, covered compote, open compote, cruet, goblet, lamp, mug, water set, relish tray, salt boat, and sauce, flat or footed.

Cat in a Tangle

This whimsical mug dates from the 1880s and can be found in both clear and amber colors. The design is of a cat caught in a tangle of flowers and vines that seem to have a life of their own. The mug is 2" tall and has a diameter of 1¾".

Cat on a Hamper – Low

This is Indiana Tumbler and Goblet Company's (referred to as Greentown glass) low version of the popular Cat on a Hamper. This low example is much harder to locate than the tall version. Colors are crystal, vaseline, and chocolate glass.

Cat on a Hamper – Tall

The novelty container shown here is the Indiana Tumbler and Goblet Company's (Greentown) tall version. It can be found in crystal, canary, green, chocolate, Nile Green, cobalt blue, teal, white opaque, red agate, or white agate. Shown are various colors in the tall version. This pattern has been reproduced.

Cat's Eye and Fan

This design, from George Duncan & Sons in 1878, is found in a table set, berry set, compote, sauce, and large footed bowl. Other shapes certainly may exist. It was originally called Roman.

Cat up a Tree with Dog

What a sense of humor glass designers had and the tall tankard pitcher shown typifies that humor. Here we have a cat clinging to the tree trunk while the dog is trying to bring the feline down. Even the abstract dog and cat are funny. I know of no other shapes in this pattern but they may certainly exist.

Celtic Cross

Celtic Cross was from George Duncan and Sons (#771) in 1883, and can be found in an extended table service including a table set, water set, relish, celery tray and a goblet. Pieces may be just crystal or engraved.

Centipede

Nortec, part of McKee's vast "tec" series of patterns produced from 1901 to 1930, was produced in 1903. It can be found in a berry set, table set, plates (8" - 10"), punch bowl with base, custard cup, tall compote, bonbon, nappy, celery tray, shakers, brush holder, card tray, horseradish with lid, 9" vase (shown), cruet, water set, and syrup. Several shapes, especially the vase, have been reproduced in colors not originally made. It is commonly called Centipede.

Chain

Chain was made circa 1870s. Only clear pieces have been found in a table set with stemmed pieces, covered compote, cordial, wine, and berry set. The design is somewhat similar to Chain with Star.

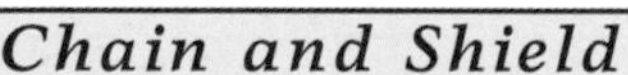

Chain and Shield

This very interesting pattern is attributed to Portland Glass Company and was made in the late 1870s. Shapes include a table set, water set, goblet, 7" and 11" plates, sauce, wine, celery vase, and oval platter.

Chain and Swag

This pattern is sometimes confused with Fostoria's Frisco #1229 pattern from 1903–1905, but Chain and Swag has the chain design and was made in ruby stain. Chain and Swag can be found in milk glass as well as crystal and ruby stain. Pieces known are a syrup, the cruet shown, and shakers, but certainly others may exist.

Chain with Star

Chain with Star was Bryce Brothers's pattern #79, and was made in 1882. Shapes include a table set, bowl, cake stand, covered or open compotes (both high and low), oval pickle dish, goblet, water set, plates, bread plate, relish dish, sauce, syrup, and wine.

Champion

Champion was from McKee (Greentown made a similar pattern, its #11). It is found in an extended table service that includes a goblet, carafe, decanter, tray, wine, plate, and the usual bowl.

Chandelier

Chandelier was from O'Hara Glass Company (1888) and then U.S. Glass (1891). Shapes are numerous and include high or low banana stands, bowls in 6", 7", and 8" sizes, finger bowl, stemmed fruit bowl, violet bowl, table set, cake stand, castor set, celery vase, covered and open compotes in high and low standards, goblet, ink well (marked "Davis Automatic – May 8, 1889"), pitchers in half-pint, pint, quart, and half-gallon sizes, shakers, master salt, sauce, sponge dish, water tray, tumbler, and rare wine.

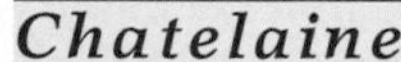

Chatelaine

Chatelaine is perhaps one of Imperial Glass Company's better water set patterns. It is well-known in purple carnival glass which brings a premium price. In crystal, the pieces are nearly as scarce and are always in demand. No other shapes are known.

Checkerboard

Checkerboard was originally Westmoreland's #500 pattern and is also known as Bridle Rosettes, Old Quilt, Block and Fan, or Square Block. The pattern is found in both crystal and carnival glass (scarce) and has been widely reproduced in various treatments. Shapes include a water set, table set, goblet, wine, covered compote, celery tray, pickle tray, celery vase, honey dish, open compote, and cake plate. Crystal pieces were sometimes ruby stained.

Cherry

This pattern was made by Bakewell, Pears & Company in about 1870 in crystal and opaque opalescent glass. Shapes include a rare plate, goblet, champagne, berry set, table set, stemmed wine, open or covered compotes, and novelty bowls in several shapes. The champagne and goblet were reproduced.

Cherry and Cable

This well-known Northwood pattern is also known as Panelled Cherry and mistakenly called Cherry Thumb-prints. It was made in crystal and carnival glass and is currently being reproduced in opalescent glass and decorated glass. Shapes include a table set, water set, berry set, sauce, syrup, and compotes with or without lids. The pattern was first made in the early 1900s.

Cherry and Fig

Cherry and Fig was made by Dalzell, Gilmore & Leighton. Shapes include a table set, water set, berry set, covered or open compotes, pickle dish, goblet, celery vase, and wine.

Cherry Chain

This Fenton pattern, from circa 1914, is well known in carnival glass but not so in non-iridized glass. This 6" cobalt blue bowl is the only shape and color reported to date in non-iridized glass.

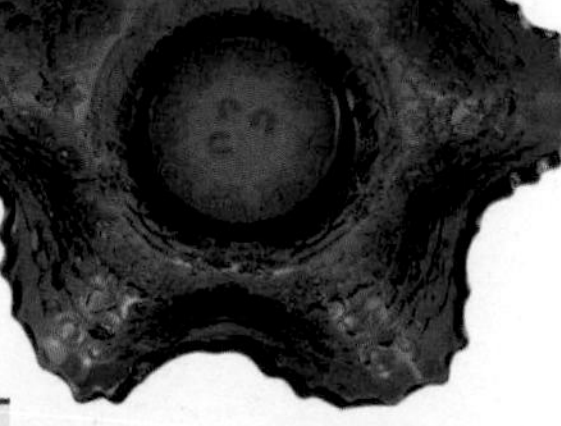

Cherry Lattice

This short-lived design from the Northwood Glass Company in 1907 is found only on decorated crystal. Reproduction pieces in carnival glass were made in the 1970s. Shapes made are a table set, berry set, water set, and compote. The butter dish was reproduced.

Cherry with Thumbprints

This very nice pattern, from Jenkins in the 1920s, can be found in a water set, berry set, sauce, stemmed wine, toothpick holder, syrup, lemonade tumbler, mug, covered bowls, and the covered bean pot shown. Besides plain crystal, this pattern can be found with decoration.

Chick and Pugs

Chick and Pugs was from Bryce Brothers in the 1880s and then from U.S. Glass after 1891. It was made in clear, amber, canary, blue, and amethyst glass and is small for a mug being 2" tall and having a diameter of 1⅞". It has the same shape as other mugs from Bryce including Feeding Deer and Dog, and Robin in Tree.

Chicken Foot Stem

What a superb piece of glass this is and so imaginative. The goblet has a chicken done in the crystalography technique while the stem is a chicken leg with the foot holding up the bowl!

Chrysanthemum (#408)

This was shown in old catalog ads from Riverside Glass and is occasionally referred to as Double Daisy. It was made in 1893 in crystal or ruby stain. Some of the shapes include a berry set, table set, water set, syrup, jelly compote, shakers, covered and open compotes, goblet, open salt, salver, celery vase, cruet, spoon tray, toothpick holder, and individual cake plates.

Chrysanthemum Leaf

Chrysanthemum Leaf was made by Boston and Sandwich Glass in the 1880s and later by National Glass after 1900. It can be found in a variety of shapes in crystal, often with gold trim, and chocolate. Be prepared to pay dearly for most chocolate pieces as they are highly sought after.

Chrysanthemum Sprig

This Northwood pattern is found in custard glass (ivory) and turquoise opaque, often with gilding and decorated enameling. Various shapes are available but beware, the toothpick has been reproduced. It is also known as Pagoda.

Church Windows

U. S. Glass's #15082 line from 1903 is also known as Tulip Petals or Columbia to some collectors. Various shapes are known in crystal and some can be found with gold trim.

Circle and Swag

This pattern, made by Ohio Flint Glass circa 1904, can be found in crystal in an extended table service and other shapes. Shown is the water pitcher.

Circular Saw

This pattern is also known as Rosetta and is credited to Beaumont Glass, but it was shown in 1905 National ads as being made at the Riverside Glass Works, so I question the Beaumont attribution. It can be found in crystal and rose stain, and the shapes include a table set, berry set, breakfast set (creamer and sugar), cruet, punch set, and water set.

Clam Shell

This novelty candy container was produced in the early 1890s and shows a good likeness to an actual clam shell. It is found only in crystal to date.

Classic

This well-known Gillinder & Sons' pattern from 1875 can be found either with a collar base or twig footed. Pieces are clear or with an acid finish, but rare milk glass is known. Shapes include covered or open bowls, table set, celery vase, covered or open compotes, goblet, jam jar, milk pitcher, water pitcher, five plates with different subjects, sauces, and sweetmeat jar.

Classic Intaglio

Recent evidence from Siegmar Geiselberger indicates these salt holders with intaglio (incised) designs are from the Czechoslovakian firm of Heinrich Hoffman in 1927. The round one has a Cupid and Psyche design and the 2½" long rectangular one shows Diana on a chariot.

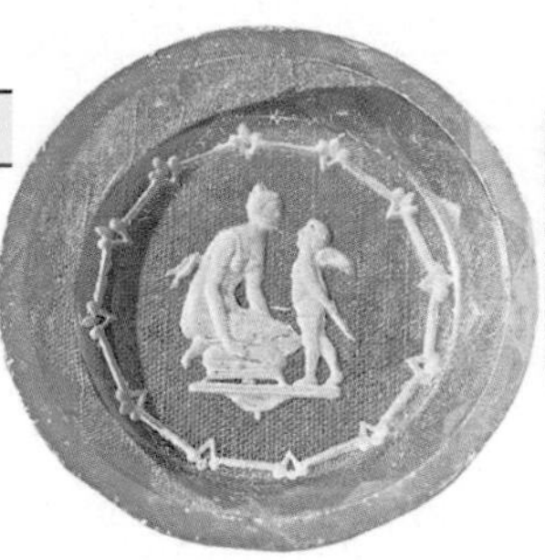

Classic Medallion

This pattern dates from the 1870s and 1880s. Some collectors call this pattern Cameo. Shapes include flat or footed bowls, table set, celery vase, covered or open compotes, goblet, water pitcher (if tumblers were made, I haven't been able to verify them), and sauce.

Clear Diagonal Band

Clear Diagonal Band was made in 1880 by Ripley and Company, Pittsburgh (they joined U.S. Glass in 1891 as Factory F) and was later made by a Canadian company. Shapes are a table set, water set, platter, goblet, salt shaker, berry set (flat or footed), celery vase, low or high compote, and marmalade jar. It is typical of early, less decorated patterns.

Clear Lion Head

Clear Lion Head was from Fostoria (#500) in 1895 and is also known as Atlanta, Square Lion, or Late Lion. Shapes include a table set, water set, compotes, celery vase, wine, toothpick holder, and others. Pieces are sometimes etched.

Clear Ribbon

Clear Ribbon was reportedly made by George Duncan and Sons in the 1880s (although this is suspect) in crystal or ruby stained crystal. Shapes include a table set, compote, celery vase, footed sauce, bread tray, pickle dish, goblet, and water set. The raised ribbons are separated by threaded sections, giving this pattern its name.

Clio

This Challinor, Taylor, Ltd. pattern, also known as Daisy Button and Almond Band, was first made in 1885 in clear crystal, green, canary, and blue glass. The company was a part of U.S. Glass. Shapes cataloged are a table set, water set, covered compote, goblet, celery vase, and plates in both 7" and 10" sizes. The plate has no panels or thumbprints. The butter dish has been reproduced.

Clover (Richards & Hartley)

Clover was first made by Richards & Hartley Glass in the 1880s and then by U.S. Glass in 1891. Shapes include a table set, berry set, sauce, 6" bowl, 11" bowl, and various compotes. It can be found in crystal, emerald green, and stained glass in amber or ruby. It is often confused with another U.S. Glass pattern called Panelled Daisy and Button.

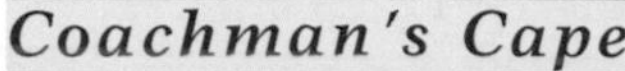

Coachman's Cape

This was made by the Bellaire Goblet Company (1880s) and U.S. Glass (1891) in clear crystal. The only shapes reported are a goblet and the stemmed wine. Since a number of patterns were also made in cordials, this one may show up in that shape also.

Coal Bucket

This little coal bucket, made by Westmoreland and shown in a 1914 Butler Brothers ad, is found as shown in ruby stain or occasionally in carnival glass.

Coarse Cut and Block

This pattern, credited to Model Flint in 1890 by some, can be found in a table set, pitcher, pickle dish, celery dish, goblet, and probably other shapes. Shown is a milk pitcher that is 5½" tall.

Coarse Zig Zag

From Bryce, Higbee and Company in 1905, this pattern is often found in malls and shops, especially in small pieces like a creamer. It was made in a table set, water set, wine, plate, salt shakers, and berry set in clear crystal only.

Coin and Dew Drop

I've looked for other shapes in this attractive pattern and surely there must be some, but to date I can only substantiate the goblet shown. On a stippled background, the rings or circles seem to float like bubbles in champagne. I'd be happy to hear about other shapes in this pattern.

Coin Spot

This Dugan/Diamond compote is primarily known in iridized glass as well as the occasional opalescent example and is shown throughout several years in Butler Brothers catalogs. Shown here is an amethyst compote which is the first example reported outside the two previously mentioned treatments.

Colonial Lady

This is a line of silver or gold decorated items from Westmoreland designated the #1700 line. It was made in 1912 in many pieces including a table set, 6" and 9" vases, cruet, and salt shakers. The metallic designs may vary from shape to shape and indeed, other glassmakers like Dugan/Diamond made this filigree work also.

Colonial Stairsteps

This pattern is reported in opalescent glass with a Northwood trademark. It is found in only a few shapes including a table set and the toothpick holder shown. Pieces are known in both crystal and blue opalescent.

Colonis

Colonis, U.S. Glass pattern #15145 from 1913, is found in a berry set, table set, pickle dish, water set, milk pitcher, cake stand, cordial, celery vase, syrup, egg cup, oval dish, and tray. This pattern can be found decorated in gold, blue, or rose.

Colorado

Colorado, made by U.S. Glass as one of the States series, dates from 1897 and was made in clear crystal, ruby or amethyst stain, green, or cobalt blue, all with or without decoration. Rare pieces are also known in clambroth. The variety of shapes includes tri-cornered bowls, table set, water set, footed cheese dish, cup, 12" vase, toothpick holder (also found with souvenir lettering), sauce, shakers, and a smaller open individual sugar with handles.

Columbia

Several patterns are called by this name but this is Imperial's design, well-known to carnival glass collectors. It was made in 1909 and can be found in a compote, rose bowl, footed plate, and vase shapes, all from the same mould.

Columbia

This unusual bread tray, from an 1891 U.S. Glass (Ripley, Factory F) catalog, is a treasure. Shaped like a shield, it is similar in design to a U.S. Glass butter dish called Banner, shown elsewhere in this edition, and the two pieces make a fine display. The tray, shown here in vaseline, is a rare item in any color. It is also known as National.

Columbia #100

This pattern was made by Beaumont Glass circa 1898–1900 and is sometimes called Beaumont's Columbia. It is found in clear, ruby stain, amber stain, or vaseline (some of which can also be engraved). Shapes are many and include a table set, water set, toothpick holder, and celery vase (shown). Note that there is also gilding around the middle of the piece and this is typical.

Columbian Coin

Columbian Coin was made by U.S. Glass in 1891 after the government stopped the use of U.S. coins for design. It is found in clear, frosted, and bronze or ruby stained glass and has been widely reproduced. The many shapes include a table set, berry set, cake stand, covered and open compotes, goblet, toothpick holder, pickle jar (shown), ale glass, covered or open bowls, celery tray or vase, champagne, claret, cruet, epergne, beer mug, milk pitcher, water pitcher, shakers, syrup, waste bowl, water tray, and wine. The goblet, tumbler, and toothpick holder have been reproduced.

Column Block

This was an O'Hara Glass Company pattern first made in the 1880s that was also called Panel & Star. It is found in both crystal and vaseline glass and shapes include a table set, salt shaker, toothpick holder, pitcher, celery vase, pickle dish, and a jelly compote.

Columned Thumbprints

Columned Thumbprints was made by Westmoreland in 1905 (their #185) and can be found in at least 25 shapes including table sets, shakers, toothpick holder, berry set, water set, and celery vase.

Comet in the Stars

This pattern made by U.S. Glass as #15150 in 1914 can be found in table sets, bowls of all sorts, water set, handled relish, celery vase, and a celery tray. The design shows differently from piece to piece and may be a bit hard to recognize, but basically contains a large whirling star, smaller hobstars, and sections of fan. No colors have been reported, but examples with gold trim are known.

Connie

This well-known Northwood pattern is normally found in carnival glass, but here we sec a non-iridized enameled example in a clear frosted glass pitcher. A tumbler is also known in this same treatment with a matching enameled design.

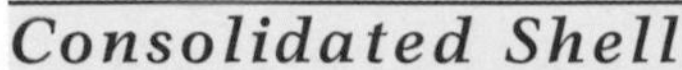

Consolidated Shell

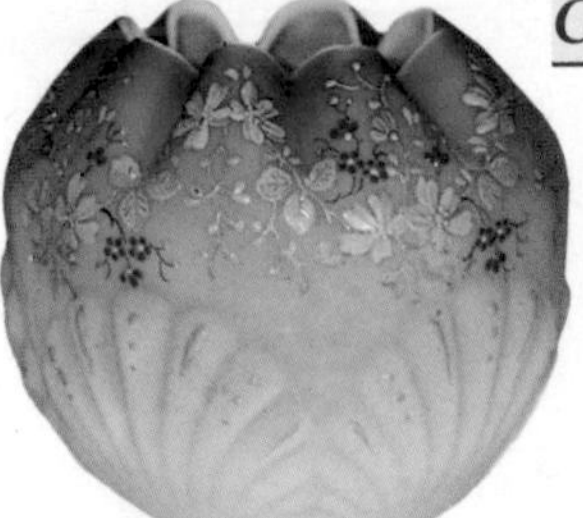

I showed this Consolidated Lamp & Shade Company pattern in the fourth opalescent glass book in Rubina Verde, but here is an example in a beautiful decorated satin glass with blue and gold. This wonderful piece stands 5" tall and has a center width of 5½".

Co-op's Columbia

This was a pattern from Cooperative Flint Glass Company in the early 1900s that can be found in clear, decorated, and gold trimmed. Shapes include a table set, shakers, goblet, pickle dish, relish tray, bowls, and wine.

Co-op's Royal

Co-op's Royal, made by the Co-operative Flint Glass Company in 1890s, can be found in crystal and ruby stained glass. Shapes include a table set, goblet, celery vase, pickle dish, bowls, shakers, water set, toothpick holder (shown), and a wine.

Coral Gables

This pattern can be found in crystal only in a goblet, wine, cruet, and table set, but certainly other shapes may exist.

Cord Drapery

Cord Drapery was first made at Greentown, Indiana, by National in 1899, and later at the Indiana Glass Company after 1907. It is found in clear, amber, blue, green, opal, cobalt, and chocolate glass. Shapes include, but are not limited to, oval, round, and rectangular bowls; table set; cake stand; covered and open compote; cruet; mug; pickle dish; pitcher; tumbler; shakers; syrup; toothpick holder; water tray; wine; and sauces.

Cornell

This Tarentum Glass Co. pattern, circa 1898, can be found in an extended table service, jam jar, plates, and a variety of other shapes. Colors are crystal and emerald green with gold.

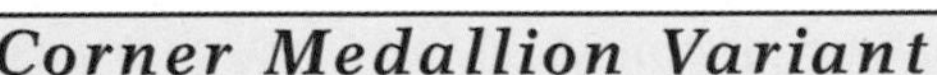

Corner Medallion Variant

This Central Glass (its #720) covered honey dish (there is a matching covered butter) is part of a small pattern group that has a Daisy and Button pattern. Other shapes include a salt shaker, square-footed match box, and a cake stand. Colors are crystal, blue, amber, or vaseline.

Cornflower

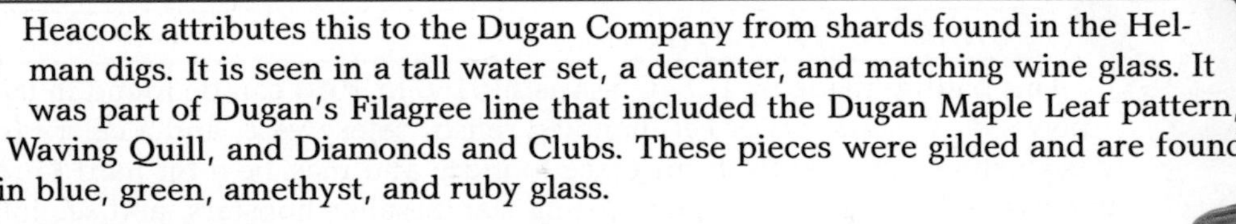

Heacock attributes this to the Dugan Company from shards found in the Helman digs. It is seen in a tall water set, a decanter, and matching wine glass. It was part of Dugan's Filagree line that included the Dugan Maple Leaf pattern, Waving Quill, and Diamonds and Clubs. These pieces were gilded and are found in blue, green, amethyst, and ruby glass.

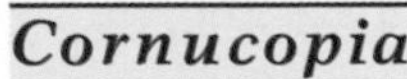

Cornucopia

Cornucopia was made by Dalzell, Gilmore & Leighton Company in 1885. The pitcher has a fruit-filled cornucopia on one side and may have either cherries and figs, blackberries and grapes, or strawberries and currants on the other. Shapes include a table set, water set, cake stand, celery vase, covered compote, goblet, mug, berry set, wine, cordial, and small lamps that may have come along at a later date. Some shapes, such as the goblet, have been reproduced.

Cornucopia Creamer

This pattern consists of four diamonds within a square, a paneled top, and a cluster of fruit just above the base. I decided to show this interesting piece although the maker is unknown at this time.

Cosmos

Cosmos, also called Seamless Daisy, was made by Consolidated Lamp and Glass in 1898 in clear, opaque, and cased colors. Shapes include a table set, condiment set, water set, lemonade set, shakers, syrup, perfume, various trays, pickle castor, and several sizes of lamps. Some clear pieces as well as opaque ones have enameling.

Cosmos (Northwood)

Another of Northwood's Verre D'or patterns is shown here on the large and small bowls of a berry set, which can either have a standard collar base or a ground base. Cosmos dates from 1907 and was part of the sizeable "glass of gold" line. Shapes include bowls, plates, compotes, and nappies in patterns that include Ice Poppy, Grape Friese, Ribbon Star and Bows, Ribbons, and Overlapping Squares. Colors can be green, amethyst, or blue glass.

Cosmos and Cane

Cosmos and Cane was primarily a carnival glass pattern but can also be found in crystal in some shapes. The pattern is from U.S. Glass and after its run in this country, some of the moulds ended up in Europe. Shown is a shallow square bowl (a two handled basket was shown in previous editions). Other shapes may include a water set, jelly compote, or a tall-stemmed compote since these shapes are known in carnival glass.

Cosmos Variant

This pattern was made by the Diamond Glass Company and is primarily found in carnival glass. I am happy to show it in rare uniridized glass in a superb emerald green. I suspect a clear example was made also and since both bowls and plates exist in carnival glass, surely both shapes were made in clear or green uniridized glass.

Cottage

Cottage was made by Adams in 1874, then U.S. Glass in 1891, and finally Bellaire Goblet Company in 1889, in clear, amber, blue, emerald green, and ruby stain. It was made in an extended table service including a mug, goblet, shakers, and a syrup. All colors are considered very scarce. The goblet and wine were reproduced.

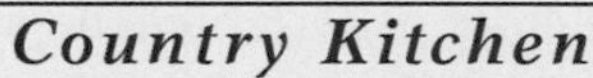

Country Kitchen

This Millersburg Glass pattern is best known in carnival glass. Shapes include a berry set; ice cream set; plates in 5", 7", 9", and 11"; and a table set. Some bowls and plates have advertising on them. There is a variant in flint opalescent glass (rare) and a sister pattern called Potpourri that is known in compotes, salvers, and a scarce milk pitcher. Crystal is the only color found, but some rare bowls are known with alternating lemon and ruby stained stars.

Covered Frog

This 5½" covered novelty frog dish was made by the Co-operative Flint Glass Co. This item can be found on occasion with an "H" superimposed over a "I." Although primarily found in pastel carnival colors, this item has been reported in the non-iridized colors of crystal and crystal frosted.

Cradle

This novelty cradle has a well done design of bellflowers, leaves, and vines. Vaseline is the only color reported to me at this time and the maker is unknown.

Cradled Prisms

This very interesting Challinor, Taylor Glass Company pattern from the 1880s can be found in a basic table set of covered butter, covered sugar, creamer, spooner, and goblet shape. Just why so few shapes seem to have been made is a mystery, and I'd be very interested in hearing of any others.

Cranesbill

I believe this pattern to be from circa 1890. Shapes include a table set, berry set, and water set. Shown is the pedestal water pitcher. The top rim is distinctive with its file edge.

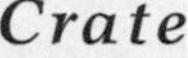

Crate

I am told this novelty paperweight, often referred to as a trunk or box, was a product of Vallerysthal Glass in 1908. Take notice of the detailed work on the wood that even includes individual nails.

Crested Hobnail

This very nice child's mug is shown here with a twist handle in blue but can also be found with a square handle in crystal (both have nine rows of hobs). It is credited to Columbia Glass by one reference and to Bellaire Glass by another. Research shows Columbia made a similar mug with a plain handle while Bellaire is the maker of the rope or twist handled version. The mug is found in clear, amber, or blue and stands 3" tall.

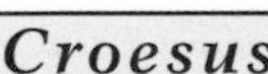

Croesus

Croesus was first made by Riverside Glass in 1897 and then McKee and Brothers in 1901, in clear, green, or amethyst with gold trim (occasionally found without gold trim). Shapes are many and include covered flat or footed bowls, open bowls, table set, cake stand, celery vase, covered or open compotes, condiment set, pickle dish, cruet, water set, toothpick holder, and condiment tray. The butter, creamer, spooner, sugar, tumbler, and toothpick holder have been reproduced.

Cross Bands

The few shapes reported in this pattern include a creamer, covered sugar, a spooner, and a covered butter dish. The date of production seems to be in the late 1870s. The design is similar to Two Band but has the cross pattern breaking up the diamond banding.

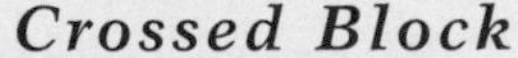

Crossed Block

Crossed Block is also known as Roman Cross. Shapes include a table set, goblet, oval bowl, and pickle dish. The pattern was first advertised in 1890. Only clear crystal seems to be found.

Crossed Discs

This pattern is believed to be from circa 1890. I've seen it only in crystal in a water set, table set, egg cup, celery vase, and a pickle dish, but certainly other shapes may well exist.

Crossed Shield

This was Fostoria's #1303, made in the 1890s. Shapes include a table set, water set, berry set, four sizes of compotes including a jelly compote, goblet, wine, cordial, celery vase, and pickle dish.

Crown Salt

This heavy salt dip was shown in old ads under this name and was made by Bakewell, Pears in 1872. The design is simple but distinctive and could be used with many table pieces. Clear crystal is the only treatment I am aware of.

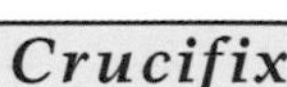

Crucifix

This very collectible candlestick was made by both Imperial and Cambridge in slightly different configurations. It was also made in carnival glass by the Imperial Company, and these are rare and expensive. The example shown is from Imperial and is very well done. It is 9½" tall and of very heavy crystal.

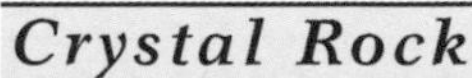

Crystal Rock

This U.S. Glass pattern from about 1905 is found in clear and decorated glass. Shapes include a table set, water set, and berry set, all shown in a 1905 U.S. Glass ad.

Crystal Star

These very pretty vaseline auto vases are nearly identical to a set shown in old McKee catalog ads and I believe this set came from McKee as well. They were made in the 1920s, are about 7¾" long, and have an engraved pattern of star-like flowers, stems, and leaves below a series of notching and ball bordering. As auto vases go, these are better than most and deserve attention.

Crystal Wedding

This prolific pattern, also called Crystal Anniversary, was made by Adams Glass in the early 1880s and was a part of U.S. Glass. There are many shapes including a water set, table set, vase, shaker, salt dip, pickle dish, cruet, open compote, covered compote (high and low in three sizes), banana stand, shakers, claret, celery vase, cake stand, goblet, and other shapes. Westmoreland later reproduced this pattern, especially in the compote shapes, so look for glass clarity when buying. It has also been reproduced in a candle holder, goblet, and lamp. It can be found in crystal, crystal frosted, and ruby stained.

Crystolite

This Cambridge pattern is from their #1503 line. Various shapes were made but here we see the popular spittoon shape. Various colors are known with an iridized carnival treatment but crystal is the only non-iridized color reported.

Cupid and Venus

This Richards & Hartley Glass pattern from 1875 was reissued by U.S. Glass in 1891. It was made in clear, amber (limited), and vaseline (limited) in a berry set, table set, cake stand, celery vase, covered or open compotes, cordial, cruet, goblet, jam jar, three sizes of mugs, pickle castor, pitcher, bread plate, relish, and wine glass. It is also known as Guardian Angel.

Cupid Compote

This marvelous 8½" tall compote with a frosted cupid stem may be from France (it hasn't shown up in books on American glass to date). The top is oval and measures 7¼" x 9½" with an intaglio design of leaf fans.

Cupid Riding Lion

This was the name given to me for this nice bread plate (which was a late addition I couldn't resist showing). I have little information to offer other than the crystallography process in the design indicates it may be a product of either Dithridge or possibly Iowa City glass; both of which are unconfirmed at this time. The scene depicts cupid riding on the lion's back and each tab handle shows what some call the demonic Mephistopheles, although they appear to be more of a mythical Old Man Winter of sorts. This is the only shape reported to me and crystal is the only color.

Cupids (Northwood)

This Northwood Company goofus piece shows its familiar Poppy Scroll type pattern with an added center design of Cupids.

Cupids Hunt

This beautiful piece is animated around the entire bowl with figures. This is attributed to Dithridge and Co. in the 1880s. Some of the shapes known are bowls, compotes of various sizes, bread plate, relish, sherbet, and others. It is also known as Cupids.

Curled Leaf

This mug can be found in clear, cobalt blue, canary, or light amethyst. A water pitcher is also known and other shapes certainly exist. The makers were King Glass Company in the 1880s and then U.S. Glass after 1891. The mug can also be found (rarely) with a mustard lid, indicating it was a promotional item. It is also known as King's #198 or Vine Band.

Currant

Currant was made by Campbell, Jones & Company in 1871 (attributed to Boston and Sandwich Co. by glass shards from the factory's location in Sandwich, MA). Shapes include oval bowls, table set, cake stand (three sizes), celery vase, covered high and low compotes, open compote, cordial, egg cup, goblet, honey dish, jam jar, water set, milk pitcher, plates, relish dish, salt, sauces, and wine.

Currier & Ives

Currier & Ives, from the Bellaire Goblet Company in Findlay, Ohio, in 1889 (Co-operative Flint Glass Company is also a reported maker), can be found in clear and rarely in amber, blue, cobalt blue, and vaseline. Shapes include a table set, canoe-shaped bowl, covered or open compote, cordial, cup and saucer, decanter, goblets, oil lamp, mug, pickle dish, milk pitcher, water set, bread plate, dinner plate, relishes, shakers, salt dip, sauce, syrup, wine, and the water tray ("Balky Mule") made in 9½" and 12¼" sizes.

Curtain

Also known as Sultan, this Bryce Brothers pattern dates from 1875 to 1885. It is found in crystal, amber, and blue and shapes include a celery vase, table set, berry set, water set, waste bowl, and square plate.

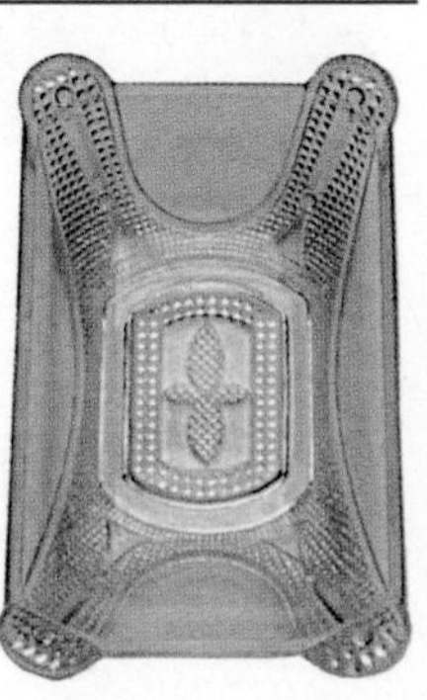

Curtain Tie-back

Shapes include square bowls, table set, celery vase, celery tray, covered compote, goblet, plate, pickle dish, water set, relish, shakers, sauce, water tray, and wine.

Curtain Tie-back Ornament

These decorative items with pewter rod fasteners are found in many designs from several glassmakers. They were used to hold back heavy over-curtains at windows and were very fashionable after the Civil War. Shown are two examples in vaseline, an elongated floral design and a round flower patterned example (Boston & Sandwich Company, circa 1860s). Colors found are crystal, amber opaque, canary/vaseline, pink, blue, green, and on occasion ebony. Many shapes and sizes can be found and various ones were reproduced.

Curved Star

This pattern is a puzzle since evidence points to several glass companies. First we find it in carnival glass where it accompanies the U.S. Glass version of the Headdress pattern. It is also shown in catalogs of Brockwitz of Germany. Finally, catalogs from Iittala-Karhula in Finland and Eda of Sweden show versions of this design. Apparently moulds traveled freely in Europe with this pattern. Various shapes are known and colors are mostly crystal, but some pieces can be found in red. The pattern is also known as Cathedral by some collectors.

Cut Block

Cut Block is A.H. Heisey's #1200 pattern. It can be found in clear and ruby stained glass. Shapes include a table set, cruet, individual sugar and creamer, pickle dish, celery vase, and a syrup. The pattern dates to 1896.

Cut Log

Greensburg Glass's Cut Log was originally called Ethol but is now also known as Cat's Eye and Block. Shapes found are a table set, water set, berry sets, large and small cake stand, celery vase, 6" and 8" covered compote, open compote on low and high stems in 7", 8", and 10" sizes, goblet, mug, nappy, 16½" vase, and stemmed wine. Cut Log was made in 1885. The compote was reproduced.

Dagger

This novelty candy container in a dagger shape is quite detailed. Although Dalzell made a similar dagger candy container I cannot attribute this particular example to that concern at this time. Crystal is the only reported color.

Dahlia

Dahlia was made by Bryce Brothers in 1885. Colors include apple green, blue, vaseline, and clear. Shapes include oval bowls, table set, cake stands, covered or open compotes, cordial, egg cup (double or single), mugs, goblet, pickle dish, water set, milk pitcher, bread plate, dinner plate, platter with either fan or grape handles, jam jar, relish, salt dips, syrup, sauce, and wine.

Dahlia (Goofus Pattern)

Known by this name to goofus glass collectors, it is actually the #131 pattern from Indiana Glass. (Canton Glass also made a Dahlia pattern in the 1880s.) Shapes I've seen are the 11" plate, and 4", 9", and 10" bowls. These pieces were designated by factory ads as decorated ware. The design is well done and the glass clear and sparkling under the goofus.

Daisy and Bluebell

Daisy and Bluebell was from the Mosaic Glass Company and was originally called "The Mosaic" pattern (#51) in 1891. Shapes are many and include a table set, water set, bowls, celery vase, pickle dish, goblet, wine, and cake stand.

D

Daisy and Button (Hobbs)

While many companies had a try at this pattern, the Hobbs, Brockunier Company's #101 was the best known. It can be found in crystal, Old Gold, sapphire, marine green, canary, ruby, and amberina. There were many shapes, including a bar bottle, finger bowl, round or square bowls, star-shaped bowls, table set (three shapes), castor set, basket, canoe, hanging canoe, flared celery dish, shoe celery dish, cheese dish, cologne, ice bowl with drainer, match safe, molasses cans, pickle yacht, pickle jar, plates, shades, water set (three sizes), ice cream tray, toothpick holder, and whiskey tumbler. Be aware that Daisy and Button patterns from various makers have been widely reproduced in multiple shapes and colors.

Daisy and Button Slipper

This Geo. Duncan & Sons slipper dates from 1886 and was patented by John E. Miller. It is very similar to a D & B slipper produced by Bryce Brothers but with a higher heel. I show a crystal one in the Commemorative and Advertising section. Beware of reproductions.

Daisy and Button Variant

This butter dish believed is to be a U.S. Glass pattern (Bryce Brother's factory B) and I feel certain there are other shapes that were made. It has been reported only in crystal to date.

Daisy and Button Wheelbarrow

Almost everyone had a try at a Daisy and Button pattern so I can't identify the maker of this unusual novelty piece, but I can ascertain that it is old. Like the Seitz Bath piece or the slippers, hats, canoes, or boats in this pattern, this one could be used on the table or just admired. It is on vaseline glass and has a brass wheel and pinnings.

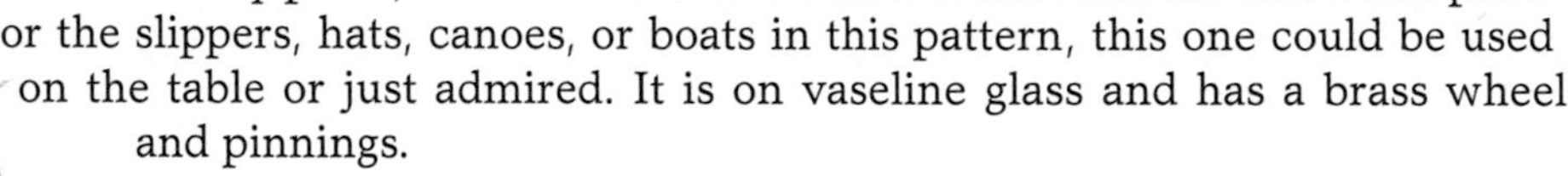

Daisy and Button with Crossbars

This was originally a Richards & Hartley pattern (#99) called Mikado that was reissued by U.S. Glass in 1891. It is found in clear, dark amber, canary, and blue. Shapes include a catsup bottle, finger bowl, oval bowls (6", 8", 9"), waste bowl, table set, celery vase, high or low compotes (open or covered), cordial, cruet, goblet, pickle jar, oil lamp, mug (two sizes), pickle dish, water set, milk pitcher, plate, shakers, sauce, syrup, toothpick holder, water tray, and wine.

Daisy and Button with Narcissus

This pattern, also known as Clear Lily, was made by the Indiana Glass Company of Dunkirk, Indiana, in 1910. Shapes found are a table set, water set, decanter, goblet, compote, shakers, celery tray, water tray, wine, celery vase, sauce, and bowl. This is a quality pattern that is very collectible. Oval bowls, vases, and the wine were reproduced.

Daisy and Button with Shells

This is an interesting little item with a shell used for a tab type handle. It stands 4½" tall and I would certainly like to see other shapes in this nice pattern.

Daisy and Button with Thumbprint Panel

This pattern was made first by Adams and Company in 1885 and then by U.S. Glass in the 1890s. It is found in table sets, water sets, berry sets, square bowls, covered or open compotes, cake stand, celery vase, goblet, and wine. Besides the crystal pieces, blue or amber items are known.

Daisy and Button with V Ornament

This well-known pattern was originally Beatty's #555 and #558 and is also known as Daisy with V Ornament. It is available in clear, amber, blue, and vaseline. The pattern was later reissued by both Federal and U.S. Glass. Shapes include an octagonal bowl, berry set, finger bowl, table set, celery vase, goblet, match holder, mug in four sizes, pickle castor, pickle jar, water set, milk pitcher, plate in four sizes, gas shade, sherbet, toothpick holder, sauce, water tray, and wine.

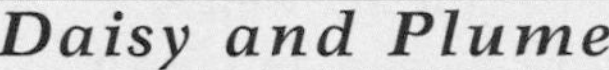

Daisy and Plume

This well-known Northwood pattern (later made by Dugan/Diamond) can be found in crystal, carnival glass, and opalescent glass. Shapes are a stemmed rose bowl, footed rose bowl, compote, and stemmed compote. The footed pieces have three square feet. It is also called Daisy and Palm.

Daisy and Plume (Dugan)

Here is the Dugan version of this pattern that was also made by Northwood. All Dugan pieces are found with three square legs and may be shaped into rose bowls, open bowls, or flared into a compote shape. The example shown is opened into a bowl shape with three-in-one edging, a typical Dugan edge treatment. Daisy and Plume is found in opalescent, carnival, goofus, and crystal glass.

Daisy and Scroll

Daisy and Scroll was made by U.S. Glass as pattern #15104 in 1907, and is also known to collectors as Buzz Saw in Parentheses or U.S. Victoria. Some of the shapes known are a table set, berry set, water set, shakers, and syrup. It can be found plain or decorated with gold.

Daisy and Tree Limb

This very fine pattern is a bit of a mystery. It is believed to be an Atterbury pattern by some dating from 1881. Belknap refers to it in milk glass. The tray shown is in a beautiful amber glass and is 14" long and 9½" wide. The handles and rim have branches, with daisies on the handles and additional flora in the inner scrolling.

Daisy Band

Daisy Band was made by Columbia Glass in the 1880s and U.S. Glass after 1891, and is found in clear, amber, and blue glass. Shapes are the handled cup and matching saucer. Two sizes of cups are known, one with two bands and the other with three bands (which is of course taller).

Daisy Banded Crystal Wedding

Like the standard Crystal Wedding pattern shown elsewhere, this one was made by Adams & Company and then by U.S. Glass in 1891. Original production included clear, acid finish, and ruby stained pieces (some amber stain is known as are blue and vaseline). Here we have a mould change that added a band of daisy-like flowers around the lid, compote bowl, and the stem.

Daisy-in-Square

Daisy-in-Square was from U.S. Glass (Duncan's #330) in 1891, and is found in an extended table service including a table set, water set, and the tall oil bottle shown. Some pieces, like the piece shown, have wheel-etched designs added.

Daisy Medallion

This pattern, also known as Sunburst Medallion, can be found in table sets, water sets, berry sets, compote, goblet, and cake stand. The design is soft and delicate.

Daisy Pleat

Some call this pattern Daisy Pleat, but it may well have another name. I've seen only the mug shape which has a diagonal banding with a flower in a square, a section of pleating, and a spray of stem and leaves.

Dakota

Dakota is also known as Baby Thumbprint or Thumbprint Band. It was first made by Ripley & Company in 1885 and then as a U.S. Glass State pattern in 1898 in clear, ruby stained, or cobalt glass. Shapes include a cake basket (flat or footed), cologne bottle, sauce bottle, berry set, waste bowl, table set, cake stand in several sizes, celery tray, celery vase, open and covered compotes in five sizes, cruet, cruet set, goblet, honey dish, mug, water set, milk pitcher (pitchers are tankard or bulbous), plates, sauces, water tray, and wine tray. The tankard pitcher has been reproduced.

Dalton

Dalton has been attributed to Tarentum Glass from 1904. Shapes include a table set, water set, cup, goblet, 10½" plate, miniature rose bowl, toothpick holder, and two-piece breakfast set consisting of a creamer and open sugar.

Dalzell's Columbia

This pattern was shown in an 1893 advertisement from Dalzell, Gilmore & Leighton and may be plain or etched. The mechanical crimping of the tops was a first, patented by Harry Northwood according to Kamm.

Dalzell Squirrel

Although shaped exactly like the Dalzell Swan pitcher shown elsewhere, this piece is a puzzle since Dalzell, Gilmore & Leighton made another Squirrel pitcher with a dome base like the Fox and Crow, Deer and Oak Tree, and Branched Tree pitchers. Also shown is a plate with the same large leaf configuration as the pitcher.

Dalzell Swan

I've heard this piece called Swimming Swan or Floating Swan, but since I am convinced it was made by Dalzell, Gilmore & Leighton (the shape is like others from that company), I am giving it their name. The stance of the bird resembles Millersburg's Nesting Swan bowls also, with the arched neck and wings raised in a strong pose.

Dandelion

This is Fostoria's #1819, made in 1911. Shapes include a berry set, toothpick holder, and stemmed sherbet. Certainly other shapes were made. Some traces of gold trim can be found on a few pieces.

Darwin

This toothpick or match holder is also called Monkey Head. It was made by Richards and Hartley Glass in the 1880s and was named after the death of Charles Darwin in 1882. It is found in clear, amber, or blue.

Davidson Tulip Vase

This stemmed vase is of English origin and resembles several patterns from the George Davidson Company of Gateshead, England. I believe it was made in crystal as well as the vaseline shown.

Deep Cut

This was reported to be from the Westmoreland Specialty line and that "Deep Cut" was one of their marks, and that it was late in their tableware line. Shapes I can confirm are bowls and plates but certainly others may exist.

Deer Alert

More realistic than many of the "deer" patterns, this one has fine foliage and a realistic deer with wide rack, looking alertly over its shoulder. The pitcher seems to be the only shape reported, and it is a tankard on a short pedestal base. All deer pieces are very collectible and this one is no exception According to its shape, this pitcher is typical of those made by Dalzell.

Deer and Cow

Shaped like the Boy with Begging Dog mug shown elsewhere in this edition, this 1880s mug is 2" tall and has a diameter of 1⅞". It is found in clear, blue, blue opaque, or milk glass. It shows a deer on one side and the head of a cow or steer on the other. The mould work is outstanding.

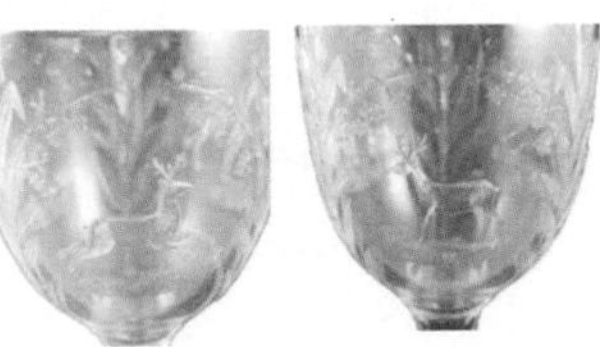

Deer and Doe with Lily of the Valley

This very nicely done goblet shows three scenes: a doe and fawn, a standing buck, and a running buck. Crystal is the only known color.

Deer and Dog

Deer and Dog was from Gillinder & Sons circa 1870s (shards were also found in Canada's Burlington Glass Works). Pieces are clear or acid finished. Shapes include a table set, celery vase, champagne, cheese dish, covered compote (high or low) in two sizes, cordial, goblet, marmalade jar, mug, water pitcher, flat or footed sauces, and wine. Some collectors feel LaBelle Glass first made this pattern.

Deer and Oak Tree

This superior deer pattern was from Dalzell, Gilmore, and Leighton and then Indiana Tumbler and Goblet (Greentown) in the 1880s, It is known in crystal or chocolate glass in the water pitcher shape and a mug shape. All pieces are very collectible.

Deer and Pine Tree

Deer and Pine Tree has been credited to both McKee & Brothers and Belmont Glass and is also called McKee's Band Diamond or Deer and Doe. The bread plate shown can be seen in a McKee factory catalog reprint from the 1890s and is listed as Band Bread Plate. The mug shown in the last edition is shown in the same catalog in three sizes: 2½ ounce, 5 ounce, and 6 ounce. It was made in a waste bowl, table set, cake stand, celery vase, covered or open compotes (7", 8", 9"), jam jar, goblet, pickle dish, milk pitcher, water pitcher, sauce, oblong dishes (7", 8", 9"), and a water tray. Colors include clear, amber, apple green, blue, or canary. Colored pieces may be found with or without gilt. The goblet has been reproduced.

Delaware

Delaware is U.S. Glass's pattern #15065, made in 1899. It is similar to the Bohemian pattern and is also known as New Century or Four Petal Flower. Treatments include crystal, emerald green, custard, ruby stain, and milk glass. Shapes include a berry set, table set, water set, cruet, celery vase, shakers, custard cup, breakfast creamer and sugar, toothpick holder, banana bowl, basket in silver holder, finger bowl, pin tray, compote, pomade box, puff box, gas or electric shade, and a stemmed claret. The butter dish, creamer, and sugar were reproduced.

Delos

Delos was from Dalzell, Gilmore & Leighton (as National) in 1901, and is found only in clear or engraved glass. It was made in an extended table service. Shown is a 7¼" open compote with an evenly scalloped rim.

Derby

This 1897 pattern can be found in crystal, vaseline, or gilded vaseline. Shapes include a table set, individual creamer and sugar, toothpick holder, water set, jelly compote, goblet, berry set, square berry bowls (small), 8" octagon bowl, cruet, covered compote (5", 6", 7"), open compote (7½", 8½"), breakfast set (creamer and sugar), and probably a pickle dish as well as a wine goblet.

Dew and Raindrop

Dew and Raindrop was made by Kokomo Glass in 1905 in crystal or ruby flashed. Shapes include a table set, berry set, goblet, mug, water set, shakers, sherbet, and wine. Some pieces are reported to have also been made by Federal Glass in 1914. Also, the cordial, custard cup, goblet, and wine are reported to have been reproduced.

Dewberry

This circa 1910 pattern by Cooperative Glass Co. was their #375 line and is found only in crystal. Shown is the water pitcher.

Dewdrop

This Columbia Glass pattern, also known as Hobnail, was later reissued by U.S. Glass in 1891. It was advertised in the same set as Double-Eye Hobnail. Shapes include a table set, shakers, handled cake tray that is shown, sugar shaker, castor set, wine, and syrup.

Dewdrop (Riverside)

This was Riverside's #90 line, circa 1881. It can be found in an extended table service. Shown here is a pitcher with the press moulded handle, but it can also be found with an applied handle. It is known in crystal as well as opalescent glass.

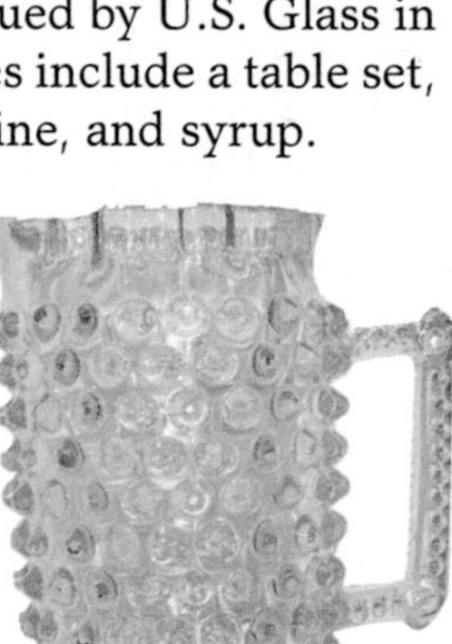

Dewdrop in Points

Shapes in this 1880 Greensburg Glass Company pattern include a table set, covered or open compote, pickle dish, goblet, water set, plate, sauce, and bread plate.

Dewdrops and Flowers

Dewdrop and Flowers is also known as Quantico, Stippled Violet, and Starflower. It may be of Canadian origin, where it is called Nova Scotia Starflower. It is found in a water set and table set as well as the stemmed cake plate shown.

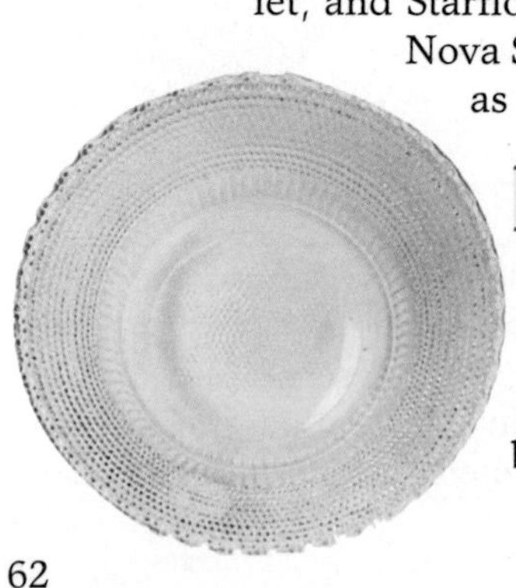

Dewdrop with Star

This simple pattern from Campbell, Jones and Company, Pittsburgh, was first made in 1877 and extended over several years. Shapes are a table set, cake stand, cheese dish, compotes on both high or low standards, pickle dish, water set, plates (several sizes from 4" to 11"), and sauce (flat or footed). The basket, plate, master salt, and sauce were reproduced in both crystal and colors.

Dewey

Dewey is also known as Flower Flange and was made by Indiana Tumbler & Goblet Company in 1898 in clear, canary, amber, blue, emerald green, and chocolate glass. It is scarce in opaque white and Nile green. Shapes include a berry set, table set (butter and creamer in two sizes), cruet, mug, parfait glass, water set, plate, shakers, sauce, trays in two sizes, and breakfast set. It was made by U.S. Glass until 1904 after the Greentown plant closed. The butter dish was reproduced by Imperial.

Diagonal Band

This is McKee's Jewel pattern found in crystal or apple green glass. Shapes are a table set, water set, goblet, covered compote, bread plate, relish, flat sauce, and wine.

Diagonal Band with Fan

This U. S. Glass Co. 1880s (Ripley, 1891) pattern is found in crystal in an extended table service as well as several additional stemmed pieces. Shown is the celery.

Diamond

Diamond is reported to be from the Ohio Flint Glass Company in 1897 and was shown in the company's ads. Shapes include the vase shown, table set, water set, berry set, compote, pickle dish, goblet, pickle jar, toothpick holder, and wine. Some collectors have confused this pattern with Buckingham, a U.S. Glass pattern, but close examination will show the differences.

Diamond and Fan (Millersburg)

The only shape reported is the bowl with the exterior pattern. In carnival glass it is found with the famous Nesting Swan interior. Here we have one of three crystal bowls known with a plain interior. The bowl has an 8¼" diameter.

Diamond and Sunburst (Imperial)

This Imperial Glass Co. pattern (primarily found in carnival glass) is often confused with the U. S. Glass pattern of the same name, but upon examination it is easy to see they are not the same. Shapes are a decanter, wine (shown), and a goblet, all in crystal.

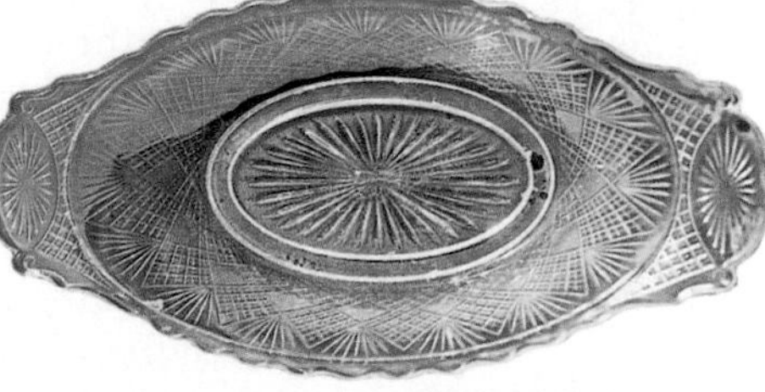
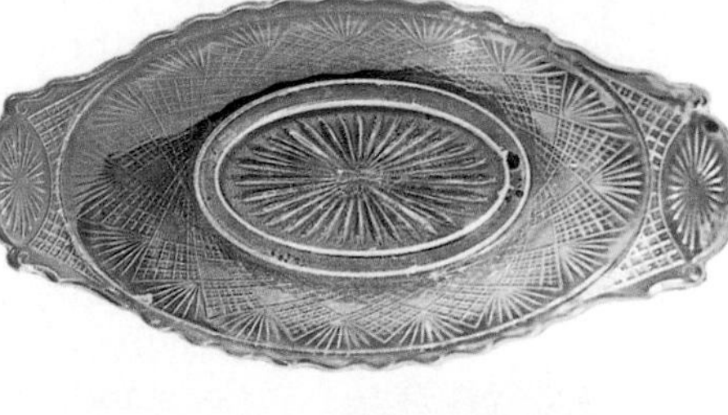

Diamond and Sunburst (Portland)

This Portland Glass pattern from 1865 is much like others with a similar name. It can be found in a table set, wine, pickle dish, celery dish, and perhaps other shapes.

Diamond and Sunburst (U.S. Glass)

This U.S. Glass pattern was their #15018 made in 1893. It is sometimes called Diamond and Sunburst Zippers. It is found on table sets, a square bowl, water set, pickle dish, shakers, wine, goblet, and a celery vase. It was made in crystal and ruby stained glass.

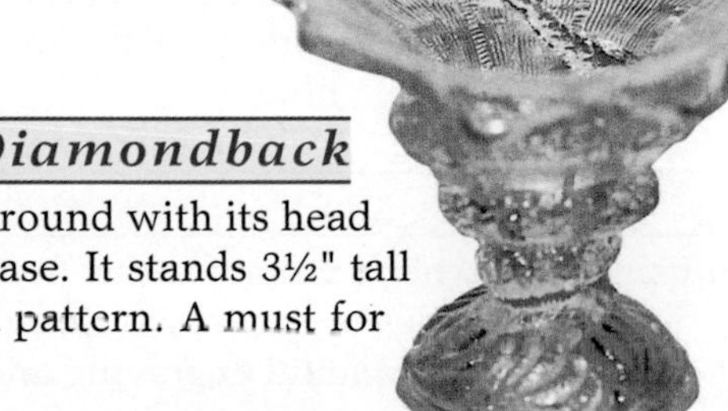

Diamondback

This unusual compote is named for the diamondback rattlesnake that wraps around with its head on the back of the JIP piece and its tail (complete with rattles) on the dome base. It stands 3½" tall and measures the same across the top. The glass is very thin on a two-mould pattern. A must for animal pattern collectors.

Diamond Band

Indiana Glass's #169 pattern from 1915 can be found in berry sets, table sets, and water sets. The water pitchers are all squat as shown, but were made in three sizes. It can be found in crystal or gilded crystal.

Diamond Bridges

Diamond Bridges was made by U.S. Glass Company in 1897 as the #15040 pattern in crystal or emerald green glass. Shapes include a table set, water set, berry set, compotes, pickle dish, goblet, wine, and pickle jar.

Diamond Cut with Leaf

This pattern is credited to the Windsor Glass Company from around 1890. It can be found in a table set, goblet, cordial, wine, shakers, a plate, and the very scarce mug shown. Colors are clear, amber, canary, blue, and green. I suspect even more shapes were made and wouldn't be surprised to see a water set. The goblet and wine were reproduced.

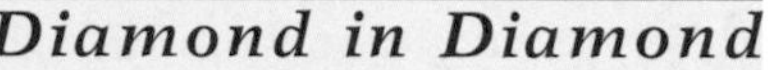

Diamond in Diamond

What an appropriate name for this pattern that is found in a table set, compotes, water set, bowls, toothpick holder, pickle dish, goblet, and wine. Certainly other pieces may exist.

Diamond Lace

This well known Imperial pattern is mostly found in carnival glass but can also be found in crystal in two sizes of bowls, a pitcher, and tumbler. Here we see a non-iridized tumbler in rare amethyst.

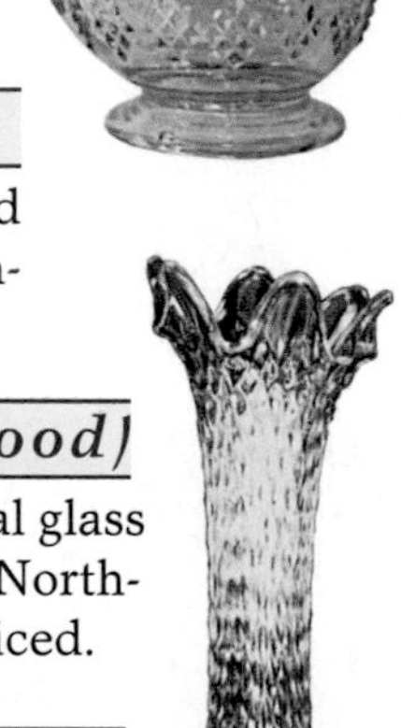

Diamond Point (Northwood)

This well-known vase was made by the Northwood Company. It is found mostly in carnival glass and opalescent glass but was obviously made in crystal (shown). It usually bears the Northwood trademark. Sizes range from 7" to 12" with the short size being the highest priced.

Diamond Point Columns

This pattern was made by the Fenton Art Glass Company in 1911, mainly in carnival glass and opalescent glass. The example shown is almost crystal (there are tiny bits of iridization on the flames at the top of the vase). It is 7" tall but these were also swung to taller sizes and some were pulled into bowl shapes too.

Diamond Point Disc

Diamond Point Disc was made first by J.B. Higbee in 1905 and then at New Martinsville Glass as #601. Shapes include a berry set, table set, shakers, cake stand, compote, celery vase, and individual salt dips.

Diamond Point Loop

The maker of this beautiful pattern still seems to be a mystery (at least to me). I'd like anyone with information to contact me. It dates from the 1890s. Shapes known include a berry set, table set, goblet, celery dish, pickle dish, celery vase, the square plate shown. It is known in crystal, vaseline, apple green, amber, or blue.

Diamond Point with Cannonballs

I am using the owner's name for this fine tankard pitcher since I have found no other name to date. The only design is a series of spheres in three rows with a convex diamond separating each of them. The rest of the pitcher has a fanciful engraving and the handle is applied.

Diamond Points

Credited to the Northwood Glass Company, this rare basket shape (a very rare footed rose bowl is also known) is found in carnival glass as well as crystal. All pieces are rare and the carnival pieces bring huge prices. If you will compare this piece to the Diamond Points Variant rose bowl shown below, you will see the differences. The variant piece is probably the York pattern from Fostoria.

Diamond Points Variant

This is the name given to the rare carnival rose bowl, but I am rather sure this pattern is really Fostoria's York pattern. In crystal, shapes reported are a table set, berry set, the rose bowl, 5½" banana bowl, custard cup, cruet, two styles of shakers, and syrup. Some items are gold trimmed, like the rose bowl shown.

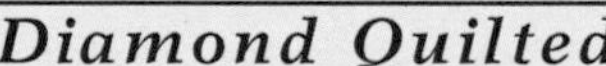

Diamond Quilted

This pattern, which dates from 1880 from an unknown maker, is found in crystal, amethyst, amber, blue, and vaseline. Shapes include an open oval bowl, a round bowl (6", 7"), champagne, high or low open or covered compotes, cordial, goblet, mug, table set, water set, sauce, salt (master or individual), water tray (round or clover shaped), 9" vase, and a wine. Shown is a seldom found milk pitcher. The goblet and wine were reproduced.

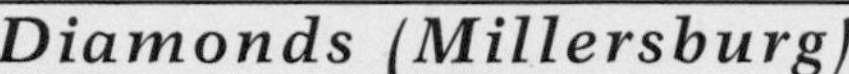

Diamonds (Millersburg)

Shown is a rare Millersburg Diamonds tumbler in amethyst glass. This pattern has been seen on a crystal punch bowl base, a pitcher, and a tumbler, but anything other than a carnival piece is very rare.

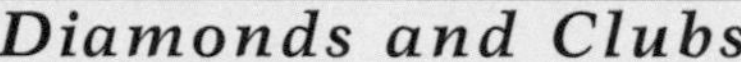

Diamonds and Clubs

This is one of the better designs for vessels made by the Dugan/Diamond factory in Indiana, Pennsylvania, beginning in 1907. It can be found in opalescent glass, crystal, green, ruby, and blue glass, and with the colors decorated. Shapes include a water set with tankard pitcher and wine decanter and matching wine glasses. In addition some of the water sets are known as Swastika because of an opalescent overlaid swastika pattern.

Diamond Spearhead

This was Northwood's #22 design when it was part of National Glass. It ca be found in many shapes in opalescent glass as well as clear crystal and occasionally green. Shapes include a table set, water set, goblet, berry set, toothpick holder, relish tray, syrup, celery vase, shakers, mug, jelly compote, tankard creamer, tall compote, sugar shaker, water bottle, and rose bowl.

Diamond Strawberry

This is Fostoria's #402 design made in 1900. It is also called Strawberry and Fan Variant. Shown is the tumbler shape, but it was also made in a squat pitcher and probably other shapes as well.

Diamond Sunburst

Made by Bryce, Walker Company in 1894, this well-known pattern can be found in many shapes, including a table set, oval bread plate, master salt, pickle dish, sauce, cake stand, and celery vase. There are several variations, possibly made by other glass companies, but close examination will reveal the differences. Some have notched diamonds while others have differences in the crosshatching.

Diamond Swirl

This U.S. Glass pattern dates 1895 and is found in clear or ruby stained glass. Shapes include a table set, salt shakers, water set, syrup, and toothpick holder, as well as an individual sugar and creamer. It is also known as Zippered Swirl and Diamond.

Diamonds with Double Fans

This Indiana Glass Co. pattern, circa 1907, can be found in an extended table service and additional goblet shape. It was produced in crystal and ruby stained.

Diamond with Circle

Do not confuse this with the Diamond In Circle pattern. This 1880s design seems to be a companion to the Upright Rabbit and Wolf patterns since they both have the bent twig handle. Colors reported are clear, amber, blue, and apple green.

Diamond with Fan

This is the Imperial Glass Company's #538 pattern made in 1909. Shapes known are a water set, berry set, pickle dish (oval), and table set. The glass is quite thick. Some pieces may be decorated with gilding.

Diamond with Peg

Diamond with Peg was first made by the McKee Glass Company in 1894 and then by the Jefferson Glass Company after 1913. It can occasionally be found with Jefferson's "Kry-stol" mark. It is found in clear or ruby stained glass that can often be decorated. Shapes include a table set, water set, berry set, toothpick holder, pickle dish, shakers, a goblet, wine, and celery vase. A sister pattern called Banded Diamond with Peg is shown elsewhere in this book. The pitcher and tumbler were reproduced.

Dirigo Pear

This Portland Glass pattern is found only in three styles of relish dish. The example shown measures 4" wide and 5" long. These were made in the late 1860s and dirigo means "I lead."

Divided Hearts

Divided Hearts was made by the Boston & Sandwich Company in the 1860s. It is found on a table set, lamp, open compote, egg cup, footed salt, and goblet. The pedestal water pitcher is shown.

Dog Cart

Dog Cart is also known as Boys in Cart and was part of a series (Frolic, Boys in a Cart, and Boys Falling Over Log) by Gillinder and Sons in the 1880s. The plates measure 10¾".

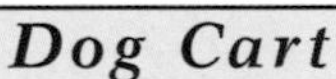

Dog Cart with Ape Lid

This rare holder has the same ape design as the novelty toothpick shown elsewhere. A Tiffin Glass ad from 1886 shows three designs: Pony Cart, Goat Cart, and the Dog Cart. All were available with the Ape lids.

Dog Chasing Cat

This is George Davidson's #5812 pattern from 1886 found in crystal or opaque white. It can be found on a cream jug and sugar basin that can be open or covered as shown.

Dog Chasing Deer

Dog Chasing Deer was a Bryce Brothers pattern from the 1880s and then a U.S. Glass after 1891. Colors reported are clear, frosted, amber, blue, and milk glass. The shape and handle are like those on Pointing Dog, Swan, and Bird on a Branch. This mug measures 3¾" tall and has a diameter of 3¼".

Dog Hunting

This humorous pattern is attributed to Dalzell by some collectors and Greentown by others. It seems to be found only on the tankard water pitcher shown. The mould work is quite good and the shape of the pitcher is like that of some Deer Alert pitchers.

Dog Plate

Dog Plate was made by the Columbia Glass Company of Findlay, Ohio, in the late 1880s and is sometimes called Findlay Dog. It is really one-half of a set that included a Cat Plate. Both are 6" in diameter and considered rare finds for collectors.

Dog Vase

This rare pattern is attributed to the Columbia Glass Company in the 1880s. It is shown in all three known colors. The very idea of a dog standing on its hind legs holding a daisy and button cornucopia vase calls for a special sort of humor that is as rare today as are these vases.

Dog with Collar

This 1880s Iowa City Glass Company mug is found in clear as well as amethyst and is a retooled version of the Dog without Collar pattern. After the first moulds were used in 1881, someone decided to add the collar. The mug is 3⅜" tall.

Dog with Pail

This novelty, made by Belmont Glass in 1885, is either a toothpick holder or a match holder. It is scarce and desirable and would be a treasure for any collector of novelty glass items. This pattern was reproduced in several different types of glass and is also known as Dog with Hat.

Dog with Rabbit in Hole

This nicely done pattern (maker unknown) shows a dog that has just chased a rabbit into its den. Animal patterns are a favorite among collectors and this pitcher should be no exception. It is reported in crystal to date.

Dolphin

This 1880 pattern is credited to Hobbs, Brockunier. It is found either clear or with a frosted base. Shapes include a celery vase (shown), covered or open compotes in two sizes, covered oval bowls in two sizes, a covered pickle jar, pitcher (jug), a table set, and a master salt.

Dolphin (Gillinder and Sons)

The one-piece compote with a dolphin base on a scalloped platform can be found in crystal, vaseline, blue, and amber. The top has piercing and a flower and leaf medallion. The base of the dolphin is domed and has an interwoven scroll effect. Shown here is the amber compote and the hard to find bowl in vaseline. Other colors are certainly a possibility in that shape. This pattern is from circa 1880s – 1890s and reported to be from Gillinder and Sons. It is also known as Grape Leaf by some collectors.

Dolphin and Herons

This very fine item was called simply Dolphin by Model Flint Glass. It is usually found in small stemmed pieces called card trays in blue, white, and canary opalescent. Here I show the very rare vase shape in crystal. The stem of this piece is a dolphin holding the bowl in its mouth while herons are around the bowl of the vase.

Dolphin Candlestick

Dolphin Candlesticks were first made in a square flat base and then in a step base by Sandwich Glass and Mt. Washington Glass, and later by Bakewell, Pears. Early examples date from the 1850s. Later copies were made with hexagon bases by Westmoreland and in Europe. The candlesticks shown are flint glass and found in crystal, vaseline, and possibly blue. This shape was reproduced by the Metropolitan Museum of Art in the 1970s, and embossed with "MMA" on the base. Original candlesticks will have a hollow head.

Dolphin Match Holder

This 4½" Dolphin match holder is credited to Bryce Brothers by some (due to its similar shape to the Peek-A-Boo match holder) and Bellaire Glass Company by others. It can be found in crystal, amber, blue, or canary glass. Besides the dolphins around the stem, the design appears to have a striking resemblance to the Stars and Bars pattern that is definitely a Bellaire pattern.

Dolphin Mustard

This mustard is one of the best known novelties from the Indiana Tumbler and Goblet Company of Greentown, Indiana. This animal piece (also known as Greentown Dolphin) is mostly known in chocolate glass but can also be found in Nile green, amber, cobalt blue, clear, emerald green, and the rare Golden Agate treatment. The dolphin's mouth may be sawtoothed, beaded, or smooth. It has been widely reproduced.

Dot

This confusing pattern is credited to U.S. Glass in 1891. It is also wrongly called Raindrop, a pattern that does not have the banded top that cuts through the first row of dots. Shapes reported in the Dot pattern are table set, relish, and square berry set. Some pieces have gold trim.

Double Beetle Band

This pattern was made by the Columbia Glass Company in the 1880s in crystal, amber, blue, and yellow glass. Shapes include a table set, water set, goblet, flat or footed sauce, pickle dish, celery vase, and wine.

Double Crossroads

This pattern (maker unknown) can be found in crystal, amber, and vaseline (not all shapes have been reported in all colors). Other colors are certainly possible since the shakers have been found in carnival glass in amethyst. It is found in an extended table service as well as a few other shapes.

Double Pinwheel

Although originally called Juno by Indiana Glass in 1915, most collectors call this pattern Double Pinwheel. Shapes include a table set, berry creamer and sugar, water set, covered compote, open compotes (two sizes), condiment tray, toothpick holder, syrup, heart-shaped nappy (no handles), and a wine. The pattern has also been called Star Whorl by some collectors.

Double Relish

This double relish, made by Campbell, Jones and Company of Pittsburgh (became Jones, Cavitt and Company in 1883) may likely have another name but I am not currently aware of it. The date attributed to the production of this piece is 1879.

Double Ribbon

This pattern was first made by King Glass in 1870 and later became a part of the U.S. Glass line in 1891. It can be found in either clear or frosted in a bread plate, footed sauce, compote, pickle dish, egg cup, shakers, a table set, water set, and covered compote.

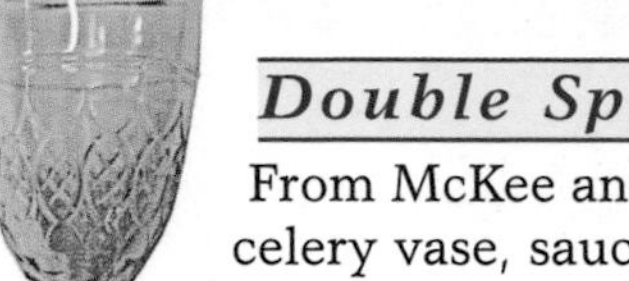

Double Spear

From McKee and Brothers in the 1880s, this pattern's shapes include a table set, compote, celery vase, sauce, goblet, pickle dish and relish, and water set.

Double Vine

Virtually nothing seems to be known about this plate, with both maker and date of production a mystery. It is shown in Lee's *Early American Pressed Glass* (Plate 187) with text on page 645. The edging is identical to Columbia Glass's Dog Plate and Cat Plate, but I have no connecting proof.

Douglass

This Cooperative Flint Glass pattern can be found in crystal, ruby stained, or etched glass in water sets, berry sets, table sets (two styles of butter dish), toothpick holder, shakers, and punch set. Shown is one of the plain individual berry bowls but these are also known with etched fleur-de-lis designs.

Dove

This 6" vase, made by the Canton Glass Company of Marion, Indiana, in 1919 (reproduced by Guernsey Glass in 1949 in azure blue), has a companion piece called Peacock (a card stand). Original colors seem to have been crystal, blue, and possibly amber. Canton Glass began in Canton, Ohio, in 1883, then moved to Beaver Falls, Pennsylvania, in 1890, and then to Marion in 1891. It was located in Hartford City, Indiana, after 1958.

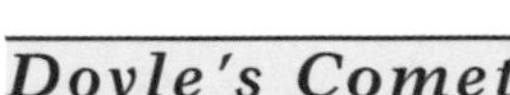

Doyle's Comet

This pattern was made by Doyle & Company in the 1880s and then by U.S. Glass after 1891. It is found in clear, amber, or vaseline. Shapes include a table set, water set, bowls, celery vase, goblet, wine, and a pickle dish. It is also known as U.S. Comet.

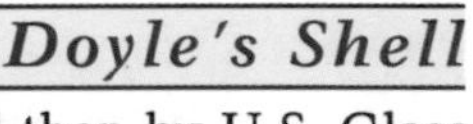

Doyle's Shell

This pattern was first made by Doyle & Company in the 1880s, and then by U.S. Glass after 1891. It is also known as Knight, Cube and Fan, or U.S. Shell. It is found in clear, amber, ruby stain, and blue. Shapes include a table set, waste bowl, water tray, wine (shown), celery vase, and pickle dish. In addition there is a mug that varies slightly in design.

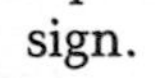

Dragon

This strange creature is a real find, especially on the plate shape shown, where it can be viewed to the best advantage. Other shapes include a table set, small compote, open sugar, and goblet. All pieces are considered rare, but the goblet is most often found.

Dragon and Lotus

Pattern #1656 from the Fenton Art Glass Company was made for several years primarily in carnival glass in bowls and plates. Here we have a scarce uniridized ruffled bowl in crystal glass that was probably just overlooked by the sprayer. It is also found in red and cobalt blue non-iridized.

Drape

This mug was produced in the late 1880s or early 1890s I believe. It measures 3⅛" tall, has a diameter of 2¼" and is often found with gilding on the top banding.

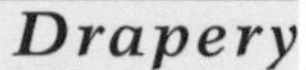

Drapery

Draypery, also called Doyle's #30 or Lace, was made by Doyle & Company in 1870 and then U.S. Glass in 1891. Shapes include a covered compote, table set, egg cup, oval dish, water set, goblet, plate, and a sauce.

Drapery Variant (Northwood)

Normally found only in carnival glass, this uniridized vase in emerald green came as quite a surprise. It may have also been made in crystal but I've heard of no examples. The vase is about 10" and is marked with the Northwood trademark.

Drum

Drum was made by Bryce, Higbee & Company in the mid-1880s as a toy or child's table set in crystal or blue. The Drum set is considered rare. Before the set was made, a covered mustard was advertised, and a child's mug in three sizes is also known. The finials on the butter and the sugar are shaped like tiny cannons.

Drum and Eagle

This very attractive child's mug, although similar to the Drum pattern from Higbee, is now recognized as a Westmoreland pattern. It is found in clear, ruby stained, or with gilt. It stands 2¼" tall and is also called Eagle drum by some collectors. Date of production is circa 1909.

Duchess

This seldom discussed pattern is shown in a U.S. Glass ad in a half-gallon pitcher, matching tumblers, water tray, and spill bowl, all numbered with a #137 engraving. Strangely, the engraving differs from the one shown on the pitcher you see here.

Dugan's Honeycomb

Although it was made by the Dugan Glass Company of Indiana, Pennsylvania, primarily as a carnival glass pattern, this honeycombed item can also be found in opalescent glass and the "Japanese" treatment shown with silver glass graining. Shapes from the same mould are bowls, nut bowls, or the rose bowl. Colors in the Japanese treatment were blue, green, or amethyst glass.

Duncan #13

This mug shape is one of a line of simple, paneled utility pieces made by George Duncan and Sons around 1900. It is a bit harder to find than the tumblers in the same pattern. Also made were goblets, wine glass, and stemmed sherbet.

Duncan #98

This was shown in Geo. Duncan and Sons ads as their #98 pattern. It was first made in 1887 and discontinued by 1890. Shapes known are a creamer, open sugar, and jelly set (covered bowl with an underplate shown) that has a silver finial. Colors are crystal, amber, canary, or blue.

Duncan #904

Seldom discussed, Duncan #904 is similar to a host of other designs from George Duncan and Sons Glass Company. Shapes include a table set, water set, cup, goblet, and various bowl shapes. The base spears are always the same length and are seamed in the center of each one.

Duncan Hobnail Slipper

This is actually the same slipper as the advertising one I show and call Daisy and Button. The original name was Hobnail and duplicate patents were issued to Duncan and Bryce in 1886. Duncan's version has a taller heel and is found in crystal, advertising crystal, blue, amber, and the canary shown.

Duncan Homestead

Made as Duncan #63, this pattern is found in many shapes. The key to the design is the seashell in the center of the hobstar. Shapes include a table set, punch set, toothpick holder, celery vase, syrup, cruet, two styles of shakers, finger bowl, individual salt dip, compotes, vases, berry set, individual creamer and sugar, and odd bowls in several sizes.

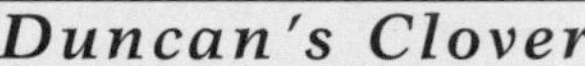

Duncan's Clover

This pattern was made by Duncan and Miller circa 1905. It was made in crystal in an extended table service that includes a water set, table set, berry set, toothpick holder, wine, and finger bowl. It can be found with gilding as in the example shown.

Dutch Mill

Here is another mug from the 1880s which can be found in clear, as shown, and in blue or amethyst glass. It measures 2⅞" tall and has a 2¾" diameter. I do not know the maker of this mug, but a variation called Dutch Mill Variant is credited to George Davidson & Company.

Early Panelled Grape Band

Information about this pattern is sketchy but some attribute it to Sandwich in the 1870s. Shapes include a table set, water set, berry set, compotes, pickle dish, open salt, goblet, wine, bread tray, egg cup, and celery vase. Some shapes seem to have more threaded banding than others.

Edgewood

This well-known Fostoria pattern dates from 1899 and can be found in a table set, salt shakers, toothpick holder, water carafe, syrup, cup, and sherbet. Originally known as #675, Edgewood may be decorated or gilded.

Egg in Sand

Also known as Bean, this 1880s pattern, maker unknown, can be found in crystal, amber, or blue glass. Shapes include a table set, cake stand, covered jelly compote, swan center dish, goblet, jam jar, water set, milk pitcher, rectangular platter, relish, shakers, sauce, bread tray, water tray, and wine.

Egyptian

Egyptian, also called Parthenon, was made by Adams and Company circa 1884. Shapes include bowls, table set, rare pyramid-shaped butter mould, celery vase, covered high or low compotes, open compote, goblet, honey dish, pickle dish, water pitcher, closed handle plate in three sizes, plate with pyramid handles, relish tray, flat or footed sauces, the Cleopatra platter, and a Salt Lake Temple platter. The bread tray was reproduced.

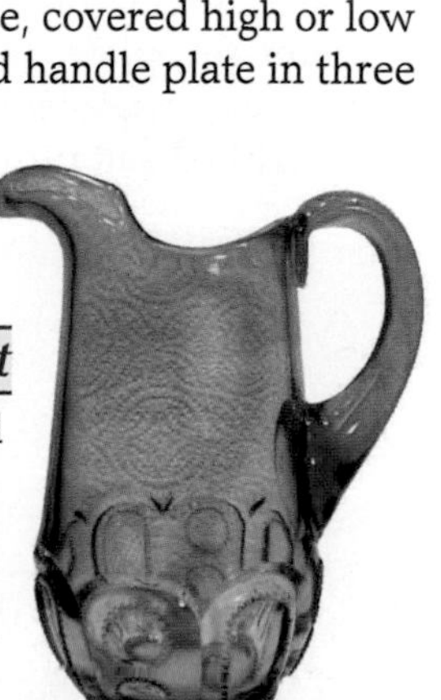

Eight-O-Eight

Eight-O-Eight is also known as Indiana and was made by Model Flint Glass (Albany) and continued by National Glass. The pattern normally shows the design as having a likeness to the numbers "808," with the exception of certain pieces such as salvers, compote lids, and some larger pieces which will simply have "000" on them. This pattern is found in an extended table service including a wine, rose bowl, and open compotes, but a staggering number of other shapes exist, with varieties found in most all shapes. Colors are crystal, amber, green, and extremely rare cobalt blue.

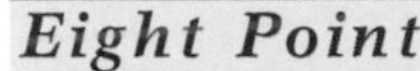

E

Eight Point

This pattern is reported to be U.S. Glass #1000, but that is unconfirmed. The goblet shown has a frosted top and the eight-point star appears to be cut.

Eldorado

I am using the original name for this pattern but it is also known as Mitered Frieze or Banded Diamond Point by some collectors. Similar to so many other allover diamond patterns, this one has a serrated edge, and the design is ringed at the bottom and banded at the top. Shapes reported are a table set, berry set, and the goblet shown. Other shapes may certainly exist. The maker was Columbia in 1889 and then U.S. Glass in 1891.

Electric

Electric, #15038 from U.S. Glass in 1891, was made in crystal, emerald green, and ruby stained. Shapes include a table set, salt shakers, cracker jar, sauce, bread plate, pickle dish, relish dish, and toothpick holder.

Elephant (King)

Made by the King Glass Company in 1890, this rare wall pocket novelty match holder is an outstanding piece of glass, measuring 5" tall and 4½" across. It shows a circus elephant with a tasseled head cover and has to be the prize of any novelty collection. This has been reproduced in colors.

Elephant Head

This super toothpick holder novelty was made by the Findlay Flint Glass Company of Findlay, Ohio, in 1890, but has been reproduced. It can be found in crystal, dark amber, blue, and opal (milk glass). The mould detail is outstanding and the features very realistic.

Ellipses

Ellipses from Beaumont Glass (its #106 design) can be found in an extended table service in crystal or cranberry washed glass. Both wines and goblets are known.

Elson Dewdrop #90

This pattern made in 1887 by Elson Glass has long been mistakenly attributed to the Northwood Company. It is found in crystal or flint opalescent glass in a table set, water set, berry set, mug, celery vase, and two-piece breakfast set (creamer and sugar).

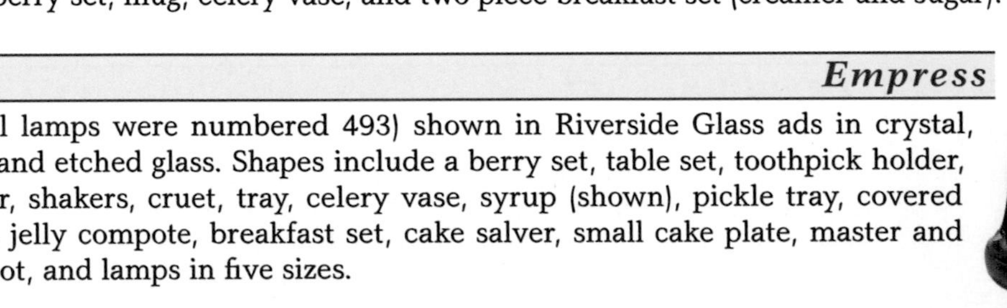

Empress

This was the #492 pattern (oil lamps were numbered 493) shown in Riverside Glass ads in crystal, gilded, green, blue, amethyst, and etched glass. Shapes include a berry set, table set, toothpick holder, water set, plate, footed pitcher, shakers, cruet, tray, celery vase, syrup (shown), pickle tray, covered or open compotes (four sizes), jelly compote, breakfast set, cake salver, small cake plate, master and individual salt dips, mustard pot, and lamps in five sizes.

Enchantment

I have little about this very well done compote except that it has an 8" diameter with a cupped-in top, two sprays of Enchantment lilies, and a woman's features with flowing hair.

English Colonial

This Mckee pattern, made as #75 in 1915, is found in nearly 50 shapes! These include a table set, water set, berry set, cruet, syrup, toothpick holder, salt shakers, punch set, compote, wine, cordial, claret, sauce, decanter, plate, jelly compote, and relish.

English Daisy and Button

The only shape reported is this 9" dome-based bowl, but surely other shapes exist. Notice the Daisy and Button work is separated by fans with Daisy and Button centers. It bears the English identification Rd #95625 (circa 1888).

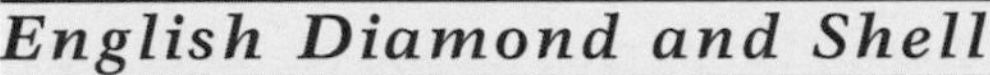

English Diamond and Shell

I believe this beautiful compote with a design of shells and clusters of diamonds is English, possibly Greener or Sowerby but have no confirmation of such. The coloring is pink slag.

English Oval Candlesticks

These English flint candlesticks stand 8½" tall and have been found in crystal as well as the canary examples shown. The name is derived from the ovals that appear both on the base in a flower petal form and on the stem.

Essex

This was made by Fostoria Glass in 1905. Shapes include a table set, water set (two shapes in the pitchers), claret, toothpick holder, champagne, sauce, wine, berry set, cup, sugar shaker, syrup, celery vase, and sundae dish.

Esther

This is a product of Riverside Glass from 1896 and is known as Tooth and Claw by some collectors. It is found in berry sets, table sets, tall compotes, jelly compote, cruet, goblet, relish, shakers, syrup (rare), toothpick holder, jam jar, lamp, and a castor set. Colors are crystal, green, ruby, or amber stained glass.

Etched Mustard Pot

I am informed that this quality mustard pot, from the 1890s, with metal lid and a beautiful etching of leaves, is a Mt. Washington product but I haven't located it in reference material from that concern to date. The glass is a good quality and the etching outstanding.

Etta

Etta was made by Paden City Glass in 1915 (#203 pattern), and illustrated in company catalogs. It is found in crystal or gilded crystal. Shapes include a berry set, table set, water set, cruet, plate, handled nappy, custard cup, wine, shakers, and a tankard pitcher.

Eureka

Eureka was made by the National Glass Company in 1901 in crystal or ruby stain. It can be found in an extended table service that includes a berry set, water set, table set, and other pieces. Shown is a salt shaker in ruby stain.

Evelyn

I've also heard this pattern called Thumballa. It was made by the Fostoria Glass Company, according to their former director of design, Marvin G. Yutzey. I've seen this pattern in both carnival and emerald green glass in the bowl or plate shapes but suspect it may have also been produced in crystal. Production seems to have been in the 1930s, and all pieces known have a ground base.

Everglades

Also called Carnellian, this Northwood pattern was made in 1903, primarily in opalescent colors, but also custard, purple slag, and the rare clambroth glass shown. Most pieces had decoration like the gilded creamer and shapes include a berry set (oval), table set, water set, cruet, jelly compote, and salt shakers.

Excelsior

Early Excelsior was first made by Boston and Sandwich in the late 1850s, then by Ihmsen and Company and McKee Brothers in 1860. It is also called Giant Excelsior, Barrel Excelsior, or Flare Top Excelsior. Shapes include an ale glass, bar and bitters bottles, a water bottle, bowls, table set, candlesticks, champagne, claret, covered or open compote, cordial, decanter (quart or pint), egg cup (double or single), jelly, goblet, lamp, mug, pickle jar, milk pitcher, water set, master salt, spill holder, syrup, whiskey tumbler, vase, and a wine. Only crystal is known.

Eyewinker

Also known as Cannon Ball or Winking Eye, this Dalzell, Gilmore & Leighton pattern dates from 1889. It is found only in clear crystal. Shapes include a banana dish, berry set, covered bowl, table set, cake stand in three sizes, celery vase, covered compote in nine sizes, open compote in nine sizes, cruet, honey dish, oil lamp, water set, milk pitcher, square plate in five sizes, round or square sauce, salt shakers, and syrup. It has been reproduced widely by L.G. Wright in various shapes and colors.

Faceted Flower Swirl

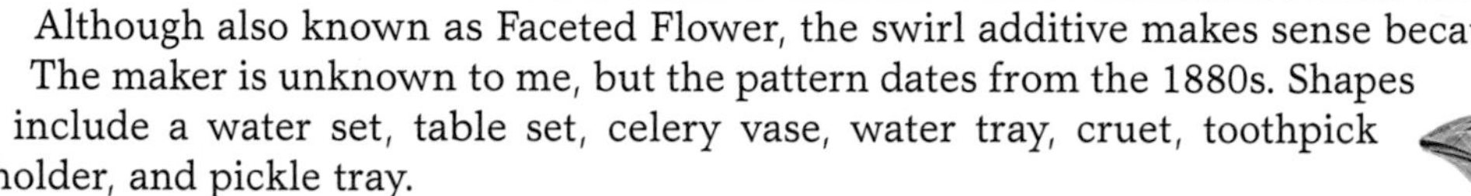

Although also known as Faceted Flower, the swirl additive makes sense because the glass swirls. The maker is unknown to me, but the pattern dates from the 1880s. Shapes include a water set, table set, celery vase, water tray, cruet, toothpick holder, and pickle tray.

Fairfax Strawberry

This Bryce, Walker & Company pattern (shards were also found at the Boston & Sandwich site) dates from 1870. It is also known as simply Strawberry and was originally made in clear and milk glass. Shapes include an oval bowl, table set, celery vase, covered high or low compote, egg cup, goblet, honey dish, pickle tray, water set, relish, master salt, sauce, syrup, and wine.

Famous

Famous, also known as Panelled Thumbprint or Thumbprint Panel, was made by Cooperative Flint Glass Company in 1899. It can be found in an extended table service that includes a table set, toothpick holder, salt shaker, syrup (scarce), oil lamp, and the goblet shown. Other shapes probably exist and a water set is quite possible as well as a berry set.

Fan

Fan was made by Dugan Glass (later Diamond Glass) in 1906. It can be found in opalescent glass, carnival glass, clear, colored glass, and custard glass. Shapes are the usual table set, water set, or berry set pieces.

Fan Band

This design, also called Bryce Yale or Scalloped Flower Band, was made by Bryce, Higbee and then U.S. Glass from 1885. Pieces may be engraved and shapes include a table set, water set, compote, tray, finger bowl, and wine.

Fancy Husk Corn Vase

This vase was made by the Dugan Glass Company, primarily in opalescent glass, from 1905 to 1912. The example shown is a much harder to find green, the rarest piece is a single marigold carnival and crystal is also known. L.G. Wright reproduced this vase with a flatter top and closed husks in both opalescent glass and a host of other treatments.

Fancy Arch

This National Glass Co. pattern from 1901 – 1906 is found in an extended table service with some additional pieces. The colors reported are crystal and ruby stained. Shown is the covered butter in crystal.

Fancy Cut

This Cooperative Flint Glass pattern, made in 1905, is well known by toy set collectors. It is also called Rex and the tiny water pitcher is found in carnival glass. Shapes include toy punch sets, water sets, berry sets, and table sets. The example shown is a vase whimsey and is previously unlisted. It has some variation from the smaller pieces in that the top is serrated and the design has fans above the diamonds.

Fancy Loop

A. H. Heisey's #1205 was made in 1897. Shapes include a table set, water set, spoon tray, punch set, shakers, toothpick holder, jelly compote, cracker jars, wine, goblet, celery vase, bonbon, champagne, claret, cruet, jelly dish, master or individual salt dips, sherry, bar tumbler, and vase. It can be found in crystal (gilded or plain) and some pieces in colors.

Fandango

Fandango was made by the A. H. Heisey Company as #1201 in 1896 and is also known as Diamond Swag. Shapes include a table set, pickle tray, celery vase, nappy, cracker jar, tall cookie jar, rose bowls, cheese plate, tankard creamer, jelly compote, salver, banana stand, compotes in several sizes, toothpick holder, wine, assorted bowls, individual and hotel table pieces, berry set, water set, carafe, finger bowl, custard cup, mustard pot, bar bottle, syrups, cruets, butter pat, salt dip, horseradish jar, sugar shaker, salt shakers, and ice bowl with underplate.

Fan with Diamond

Sometimes called Shell, this McKee and Brothers pattern was first made in 1880. It is available on a water set, wine, table set, 9" x 6½" oval dish, egg cup, goblet, pickle dish, syrup, and high and low covered compotes. The design is typical of early non-flint glass patterns that were not too busy.

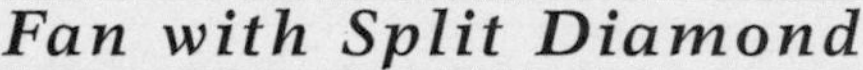

Fan with Split Diamond

Fan with Split Daimond was made by Westmoreland in 1890. Shapes include a table set, water set, berry set, and mustard pot. The pieces are often found with gold trim. A covered piece called a mustard sugar was advertised in the 1890s and sold with mustard inside when Westmoreland's own mustard was packaged at the company.

Fan with Star

Fan and Star was made by Challinor, Taylor in 1880 as the #304 pattern and the next year by U.S. Glass. It can be found in berry sets, table sets, celery vase, open 8" compote, goblet, water set, and 7" plate. It was made in slag glass, amber, blue, canary, as well as crystal.

Fashion

From the Imperial Glass Company catalog of 1909, I know when this pattern was first made in crystal. It was one of the company's leaders in carnival glass, also. Shapes are a berry set, water set, table set, small covered butter, covered jelly compote, toothpick holder, sherbet, custard cup, 4", 5½", 6½", 8½", and 10" compotes, punch set, orange bowl with standard, 9", 10", and 12" bowls, 7" rose bowl, nappy, 11" plate, 8" salver, and 12" salver. It has been reproduced.

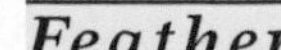

Feather

Here is a pattern with more names than any ought to have. It is also known as Indiana Swirl, Prince's Feather, Doric, Fine Cut and Feather, Swirl, and Feather Swirl. It was made by McKee and Brothers in 1896 in a wine, table set, water set, cake stand, 8" bowl, celery vase, cordial, goblet, 10" plate, and compote. The goblet was reproduced.

Feather and Heart

Feather and Heart made by Millersburg in 1910. It is and found only in a water pitcher and matching tumbler. This pattern is best known in carnival glass, but crystal pieces do exist (the pitchers are somewhat scare and the tumblers rare). The design is often confused by beginning collectors with the Inverted Feather pattern made by Cambridge.

Feather Band

This U.S. Glass Company pattern from 1919 was advertised in an export catalog on that date, indicating it was shipped for sale to both Mexico and South America. Shapes known are a table set, water set, and berry set, but I suspect other shapes were made, especially pickle dish, celery vase, or set of shakers.

Feather Duster

Feather Duster is also known as Huckle or Rosette Medallion and #15043 from U.S. Glass, in clear or emerald green. Shapes include 5", 6", 7", 8" covered or open bowls, table set, cake stand (four sizes), high or low covered compotes (four sizes), open compotes (four sizes), saucer (four sizes), egg cup, mug, pickle dish, milk pitcher, water set, plates, platter, shakers, relish tray, sauces, water tray, and wine.

Feathered Arrow

This unusual pattern is found in carnival glass (marigold), crystal, olive green glass, and rose glass. It is seen in bowls, a nut bowl, rose bowl, and a bowl with a retourné (or rolled) rim. The pattern is all exterior and because of the color selection, I feel this pattern was a product of the 1920s.

Feathered Medallion

Snow Star was made by Bryce, Higbee in 1905, and then Higbee in 1909, and was often advertised with Palm Leaf Fan and Atlanta designs. Shapes include a table set, cruet, pitcher, assorted bowls, and various other shapes. This pattern was well advertised in Butler Brothers from 1906 to 1909.

Feathered Ovals

This pattern has been seen in both table sets and water sets (water pitcher shown), all with the same pedestal-type bases, but handle types differ from one piece to the next as do pouring spouts. It was from Cambridge (#2579) and later Federal.

Feathers

This is a vase shape made by the Northwood Glass Company in 1905. It is found in crystal, opalescent, carnival, and colored glass. The vase may stand as short as 9" or be pulled to 14". Many pieces are marked with the Northwood trademark.

Federal #1605

This pattern was made by Federal Glass in 1914 and is found in a table set, wine, and possibly other shapes.

Federal #1910

This geometric Federal Glass design from 1910 was offered in more than 30 shapes including vases in three shapes, cup, wine, mayonnaise set, goblet, water set, table set, berry set, celery vase, shakers, jelly compote, milk pitcher, celery tray, salad bowls, master compote, toothpick holder, and pin tray.

Feeding Dog and Deer

This well-done mug was made by Bryce Brothers in the 1880s and then by U.S. Glass after 1891. It is found in crystal, amber, blue, canary, and a lavender or pale amethyst. On one side is a dog, the other an elk. Shown is the Deer, or elk side. This pattern is sometimes referred to as Feeding Deer and Dog or Dog Chasing Deer.

Fentec

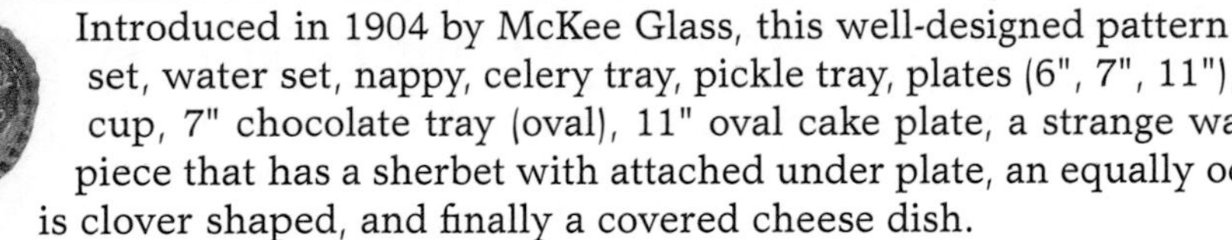

Introduced in 1904 by McKee Glass, this well-designed pattern is found in a punch set, table set, water set, nappy, celery tray, pickle tray, plates (6", 7", 11"), footed jelly, footed cup, 7" chocolate tray (oval), 11" oval cake plate, a strange wafer and ice cream piece that has a sherbet with attached under plate, an equally odd fancy plate that is clover shaped, and finally a covered cheese dish.

Fenton's Flute

This Fenton Art Glass Company pattern is found only in the vase shape usually in iridized examples. Here we see a very hard to find vase in non-iridized sapphire blue.

Fern Band and Wreath

Some collectors believe this is a U.S. Glass lamp pattern, similar to its Fern Band lamp design, however, no documentation has surfaced of such. This is one of the better patterns in miniature lamps. It is found in crystal or blue as shown.

Fern Burst

This was made by Westmoreland and shown in a 1906 Butler Brothers catalog beside another Westmoreland pattern called Atlanta. Shapes reported are bowls, table set, compotes, goblet, and sauce. The design is a very good one, made on quality glass.

Fernette

Advertised under this name in a January 1, 1906, ad from the Evansville Glass Company of Evansville, Indiana, this seldom discussed pattern is a very good one, not easily forgotten. Shapes include a table set, berry set, water set, and toothpick holder.

Fern Garland

This pattern is from McKee Glass in the 1890s and is sometimes called Colonial with Garland. Shapes include the goblet shown, a table set, celery vase, water set, celery tray, violet vase, wine, shakers, and cup. Pieces may be ruby stained and all old pieces are marked "Prescut." The plain version found without the garland design is called Old Colony.

Ferris Wheel

Ferris Wheel was made by Indiana Glass in 1910 and later in Germany. It is called Lucile by carnival glass collectors and the factory called it Prosperity. Shapes include a table set, water set, berry set, compotes, and a wine.

Festoon

Festoon was first advertised in Montgomery Ward's catalog in 1894 as Frosted Glass Water Set.The maker is unknown. Shapes include a finger or waste bowl, round or rectangular bowls, table set, cake stand in two sizes, covered or open compotes, mug, pickle castor, pickle dish, pickle jar, water set, relish tray, water tray, and plates in four sizes.

Fiddle Bottle

This very interesting bottle is a very well done representation of a fiddle or violin, if you prefer. The body is made of amber glass, the fretboard is of wood, and it actually has twine strings as well as tuners, making for an original piece. The label on the bottom reads; "Hilmar Ehrmann & Co. SW. Cor. Floyd & Market St." - "Distillers & Importers. Family Wines & Liquors A Specialty."

Field Thistle

This U.S. Glass pattern from 1912 is found in crystal as well as carnival glass. Shapes include a berry set, table set, water set, nappy (shown), 9" plate, open compote, 6" plate, chop plate (11"), olive dish, and a castor set. Some pieces may have gilding.

Fighting Wyverns

This covered bowl features a pair of mythical dragon-like figures in a face off against each other. This design is repeated about the bottom as well as the lid. The maker is unknown. The only reported color at this time is vaseline.

File

File was made by Imperial in 1909 as #256. It is found in both crystal and carnival glass. Crystal shapes include a water set, table set, shakers, 7" vase (shown), berry set, oil bottle, grape plate, 8½" shallow bowl, 5½" and 7" rose bowls, 8" banana bowl, 4", 6", 8", and 10" plates, and pickle dish. It is also credited to Columbia Glass.

Finecut

Finecut is credited first to Bryce Brothers in the 1870s and then U.S. Glass after 1891. This well-designed pattern's shapes include a table set, finger bowl, sauce, tray, toothpick holder, compote, pickle dish, celery vase, celery dish, pickle jar, plates, and the relish boat shown. Colors are crystal, amber, blue, vaseline, and canary.

Finecut and Block

Finecut and Block is also known as King's #25 and attributed to King, Son & Company, Portland Glass, and the Model Flint Glass Company (1890 - 1891). It is known in clear, clear with amber, blue, pink stained blocks, and all amber, blue, or canary. There are many shapes, including cologne and perfume bottles, many types of bowls, table set, cake stand (five sizes), celery tray, champagne, claret, compotes, cordial, custard and egg cups, goblets, lamp, mug, water set, milk pitcher, plates, soap dish, and wine. It has been reproduced in many forms by Fenton Art Glass.

Finecut and Panel

Finecut and Panel was made by Bryce Brothers, Richards & Hartley (1889), and then U.S. Glass as #260 in 1891. Colors are crystal, amber, blue, or canary. Shapes include a berry set, waste bowl, cake stand, table set, covered or open compotes, cordial, cup, goblet, pickle dish, dishes (7", 8", 9"), milk pitcher, water set, plates, oval platter, relish tray, bread tray, water tray, and a wine.

Finecut Heart

Finecut Heart is found primarily as an exterior pattern on Millersburg's Primrose bowl in carnival glass. This very attractive crystal version is a rare find. It measures about 10" across the top and can be straight sided or ruffled. Millersburg has few equals with geometric patterns or glass quality.

Finecut Ovals

This Millersburg exterior bowl pattern is usually found in carnival glass paired with a Whirling Leaves interior pattern, but here I show one of the very few examples reported of a crystal bowl.

Finecut Shield and Inverted Thumbprint

The maker of this fine covered compote is unknown, so this name has been given to it. It has a twin thumbprint finial; thumbprints around the top of the cover, the bottom of the bowl, and on the base; and shields of finecut on both pieces and engraving.

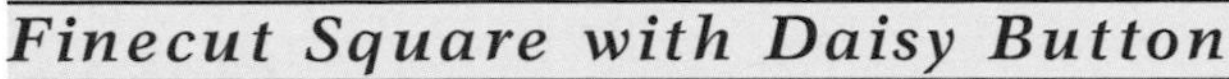

Finecut Square with Daisy Button

This pattern is a part of the Jumbo line from Canton Glass from 1884 (and probably Aetna Glass also). The design matches the square-based covered butter dish. It is also seen in crystal and amber glass.

Finecut Star and Fan

This was made by Bryce, Higbee in 1903 and continued by J. B. Higbee in 1910. Shapes include a children's table set, large and small banana bowls, wine, covered sugar, and a berry set. Other shapes probably exist.

Finecut Umbrella

This very nice novelty piece may have been designed as a pickle dish but I can't be sure. It measures 9½" in length and has a very nice handle. The design fills veined areas that resemble the spars of an umbrella. The maker is unknown.

Fine Prisms and Diamonds

This vase appears in old Butler Brothers catalogs along with another pattern from U. S. Glass, so we now know the maker. It can be found in carnival glass as well as crystal. It ranges in height from 11" to 15", has a ruffled top, and a simple pattern of three rows of rope-like banding.

Fine Rib

This vase shape by the Fenton Art Glass Company dates from 1909 in carnival glass. It is shown in non-iridized colors in Butler Brothers catalogs around 1921 and can be found in crystal, opalescent, light blue, lime green, and a color from the mid-20s Fenton called "Flame Orange." The vases range in size from 8" to 12" tall.

Fish and Seaweed

This rare pattern is also called Fish-in-Pond, Fish, Midwestern Pamona. It can be found in a table set, berry set, water set, cruet, celery vase, syrup, and water bottle (plain or frosted). The maker is often listed as Model Flint, but this is pure speculation. The glass has a satin finish and gold, blue, orange, black, or green decorations. Pieces are blown and quite rare with prices reflecting this.

Fish and Swans

This very unusual, previously unlisted pattern is shown on a creamer, the only reported shape so far. It shows swans floating on waves while fish swim below.

Fish Figural Butter

This 8" novelty is attributed to Atterbury & Company of Pittsburgh in the 1870s. It is known in crystal, blue, or canary. Although these are referenced as butter dishes I am also told they were used to serve relish or candies and were quite popular from 1870 to 1900.

Fishscale

Fishscale was first made by Bryce and then reissued by U.S. Glass in 1891. Shapes include an ashtray (daisy and button slipper on fishscale tray), covered bowls, open bowls, table set, cake stand in four sizes, celery vase, both covered and open compotes in six sizes, goblet, finger lamp, mug, pickle scoop dish, water set, milk pitcher, square plate in four sizes, relish, shakers, flat or footed sauce, syrup, condiment tray, and round water tray.

Flamingo

This well-done pattern, maker unknown, is found in table sets, pickle jar, and goblet. It should not be confused with Frosted Stork. All pieces have the rings for finials or stems, and the goblet has a many-ringed stem. Shown is the covered pickle jar.

Flattened Diamond and Sunburst

This 1870s Model Flint Glass pattern is also known as Sunburst or Peerless. It can be found in clear and amber glass, and shapes include a table set, sauce, celery vase, toy table set, cordial, water set, egg cup, goblet, pickle dish, double relish, cake stand, bread plate (motto), and 6", 7", 11" plates.

Flattened Hobnail

Flattened Hobnail is like many hobnail patterns, except it has no points on any hob. Shapes include a table set, salt shakers, celery vase, goblet, toothpick holder, and possibly wine. It has been reproduced in the tumbler shape.

Fleur-de-Lis (Greentown)

Fleur-de-Lis was made in chocolate glass and is credited to the Indiana Tumbler and Goblet Company. It is known in a water set and table set.

Fleur-de-Lis and Drape

This U.S. Glass pattern from 1891 is also called Fleur-de-Lis and Tassel. It was made in a mustard pot, tray, shakers, cruet, bowl, compote, finger bowl, tray, cordial, wine, water set, claret, and sauces in either flat or footed types. Besides clear, this pattern can be found in emerald green or milk glass.

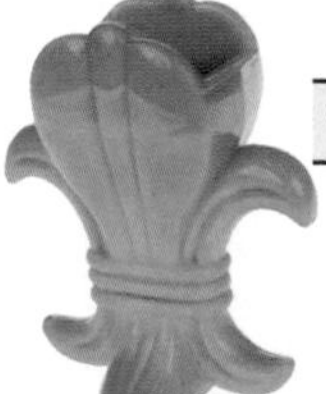

Fleur-de-Lis Toothpick

Like the crystal example I showed in a previous book, this very rare Nile Green toothpick was made by U.S. Glass (1906) I believe. This is the first one I've heard of. It is very much like Fenton's or Greentown's Nile Green. The toothpick is also known as "Royal Lily" by some collectors.

Flora

This 1898 Beaumont Glass pattern is most often found in opalescent glass, but it is also known in crystal (shown) and emerald green. Shapes include a berry set, table set, water set, cruet, syrup, toothpick holder, a celery vase, a compote, and several novelty bowl shapes.

Floradora

Floradora is also called Bohemian and was made by the U.S. Glass Company as their #15063 pattern in 1899. It can be found in crystal, emerald green, rose-flashed, and frosted, often with decoration. Shapes include a table set, water set, berry set, tall straw jar, celery vase, pickle dish, goblet, wine, and a toothpick holder.

Floral Colonial

This etched line was made in 1911 by Westmoreland in crystal or vaseline. It is shown in ads in a table set, compote, tumbler, cruet, goblet, and the footed, handled bowl shown, as well as a larger collar based bowl.

Floralore

This is one of Northwood's bowls from a Mosaic assortment of glass dating from 1903. It is often called purple slag by collectors. This glass was also made by Sowerby and others in England before Harry Northwood produced it in the United States. The bowl is 7⅝" in diameter and has a candy ribbon ruffling.

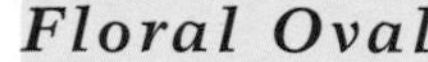

Floral Oval

Floral Oval was made by Higbee and New Martinsville Glass in 1910 in a table set, water set, square plate, bowl, jelly compote, and wine. Some pieces have been reproduced including the plate and relish.

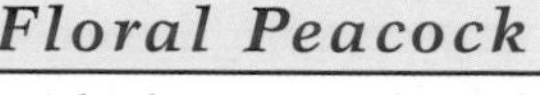

Floral Peacock

This quality piece of glass is 10" wide and 5" deep with the peacock and flower sprays intaglio into the bowl's marie. The rest of the design is also intaglio around the bowl and consists of fans in a sunrise. Other shapes are certainly a possibility.

Florene

Florene was from New Martinsville Glass (their #720) and is found in an extended table service in crystal, gilded crystal, or ruby stain. The pattern dates from 1912 or 1913.

Florentine (Riverside)

This 1906 Riverside Glass pattern is also known as Single Rose or Wild Rose. It can be found in crystal, green, milk glass, gilded, decorated, or carnival glass. It is found in an extended table service, berry set, water set, relish, and probably other shapes as well.

Florentine Candlestick

Several glassmakers had similar candlesticks, including Northwood and Dugan/Diamond, but the one shown was from Fenton's #449 line. It can be found in both 8" and 10" sizes in colors that include crystal, vaseline, blue, and green; carnival colors of marigold, red, blue, green, and white; and opaque colors of black, yellow, or blue.

Florida

Florida was made by U.S. Glass as #15056 in clear or emerald green and is also known as Green Herringbone or Panelled Herringbone. Shapes include a table set, covered or open compote and bowls, celery vase, mustard pot, pickle dish, water set, plates, relish trays, shakers, sauces, syrup, and wine.

Flower and Panel (#23)

Flower and Panel is also known as Stylized Flower. It was made by Challinor, Taylor & Company in 1885 and later by U.S. Glass in 1891. It is found in crystal, opalescent, amber, and mosaic (slag). Shapes include a covered butter dish (shown), creamer, sugar, spooner, as well as a pitcher. The goblet and plate have been reproduced.

Flower and Pleat

Credited to Crystal Glass in the early 1890s, this pattern is also known as Midwestern Pomona by some collectors. It is found in crystal, frosted crystal, ruby stained (rare), and color-washed glass. Shapes include a table set, toothpick holder, shakers, pickle dish, and probably others.

Flower Band

Flower Band is also called Bird Finial or Frosted Flower Band. Production is believed to be from circa 1870. Both clear and clear with frosted bands are known. Shapes include a table set, celery boat, water set, custard cup, milk pitcher, flat or footed sauces, and covered compotes that can be either round or oval. The bird finial is outstanding. Several pieces in this pattern have been reproduced by Fenton Art Glass.

Flower Fan

Called Snowflower by some collectors, this U.S. Glass pattern was its #35135 made in 1912 (Bryce). Shapes include a table set, water set, cruet, shakers, compote, cake stand, pickle dish, and vase. Some pieces are gold trimmed.

Flowering Vine

I believe this pattern may well be English. The feet are reeded just like the handle and the creamer's top is ruffled in a typical English manner. I suspect Davidson may be the maker. Colors reported to date are crystal, blue, and vaseline. It is also known as Daisy Swag.

Flower Medallion

This pattern was made by Indiana Glass Company in 1919. Shapes include a table set, a water set, a berry set, a sauce dish, and a toothpick holder. Many pieces are found with gold trim and some are seen with ruby, green, or blue staining as well. This pattern has been reproduced by Indiana in the 1980s and 1990s. A few rare old tumblers in marigold carnival are known.

Flower Oval

This 8" oval bowl from Central Glass Company's #764 line has what appears to be a circling of sunflowers below the scalloped rim. The oval bowl in the only shape shown in old catalog reprints and colors are clear and vaseline.

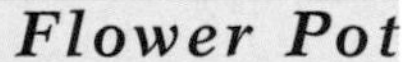

Flower Pot

This pattern appears to be from Bryce, Higbee. It is also called Potted Plant and can be found in clear, amber glass, and rare vaseline. Shapes include a table set, cake stand, covered or open compotes, goblet, milk pitcher, water set, shakers, flat or footed sauce, and "In God We Trust" bread tray.

Flower with Cane

This is U.S. Glass's #15141 which dates from 1895. It is also known to collectors as Diamond Gold. Shapes include a table set, water set, toothpick holder with fancy base, berry set, and custard cup. Pieces may be clear, gold trimmed, or ruby stained.

Flute

Virtually every company had a try at a flute or wide panel pattern. In carnival glass they were often secondary patterns used on the exterior to complement the primary interior pattern. Here is a typical example. Most shapes can be found, including table sets, water sets, berry sets, compotes, toothpick holders, goblets, shakers, punch sets, and vases.

Flute (Northwood)

Northwood primarily made this pattern in a variety of shapes in iridized glass as well as crystal pieces, but here is the first reported example of a colored piece in a non-iridized shape. Shown is what is referred to as the individual nut cup (actually a salt dip) in a rich sapphire blue. The piece measures 1⅜" tall and 3" across the top. Shapes known in crystal are a water set, berry set, butter dish, celery vase, and sherbet, all pieces scarce.

F

Flute and Cane

This Imperial pattern, sometimes called Huckabee, is better known in carnival glass. The crystal pieces, listed as #666, date from 1919. They can be found in a water set, berry set, 6" plate, table set, celery vase, compote, champagne, cordial, goblet, cup and saucer, milk pitcher, and handled bowl in either 5" or 7" sizes.

Flying Swan

Although there is another pattern called Flying Swan, which is credited to the Westmoreland Specialty Glass Company, the piece shown is not the same pattern but is also called Flying Swan. The Westmoreland swan is found on opaque glass although it was made in other types of glass. This Flying Swan pattern was made in crystal only and its maker is unknown at this time.

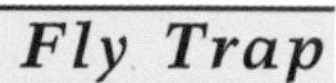

Fly Trap

Fly Tray was shown in an assortment of glass in a Co-operative Flint Glass catalog fom 1893. It is marked "Fly Trap. Pat." on the underside of the lid. Thanks to James Wilkins for sharing it.

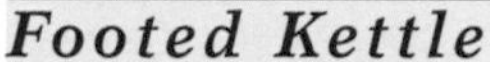

Footed Kettle

These souvenir pieces, shown in a 1914 Butler Brothers catalog, are believed to have been Westmoreland products. I welcome any information from readers about these kettles.

Forget-Me-Not in Scroll

The maker of this 1870s pattern seems to be unknown, but the design is found on an extended table service including a goblet and the beautiful plate shown.

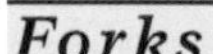

Forks

Shown in Cambridge ads as the #2696 line, the covered cracker jar shows up in Imperial's 1909 line as the #410. Just how Imperial got the mould is a mystery, but the factory catalog is hard to dispute, and I know patterns moved from one maker to another with some consistency.

Four Pillars

Four Pillars was first made by the Northwood Glass Company at the Indiana, Pennsylvania, plant and later by Dugan/Diamond Glass at the same location. It is known in carnival glass, opalescent glass, crystal and black amethyst (shown). Some Northwood pieces have advertising on the base, and a few Dugan/Diamond pieces have their trademark.

474

The pattern is from Imperial Glass and is found in crystal as well as carnival glass. Shapes include a berry set, table set, water set (two sizes of pitchers), punch set, milk pitcher, compote, vases (three sizes), sherbet, wine, goblet, a cordial, several condiment containers, and a seldom-seen mug shape.

474 Variant

Comparison with the standard Imperial Four-Seventy-Four pattern will reveal both designs were made from the same mould with the variant coming after the mould had been retooled. Shapes in this variant include a table set and a water set. The mould change covered only the floral portion of the design. It is difficult to imagine why such a change was made.

Fox and Crow

While one writer credits this pattern to the Indiana Tumbler and Goblet Glass Company of Greentown, Indiana, most of us label this pattern as maker unknown because Greentown information does not indicate it came from that factory. Only the water pitcher is known to me and production seems to have been in the 1890s.

Framed Jewel

Framed Jewel was from the Canton Glass Company as their #140 pattern, made in 1893. It is found in crystal and ruby stained crystal. Shapes include a table set, water set, goblet, toothpick holder, and wine. The design of overlapping optic and thumbprint with beaded edge is a bit difficult to see on most pieces.

Fringed Drape

Fringed Drape was made by McKee Glass Company in 1901 and is frequently called Crescent by collectors. Shapes include a table set, jelly compote, celery vase, celery tray, 6" deep bowl, 5" – 11" oval bowls, round bowl in four sizes, cordial, cruet, cup, pickle jar, pickle tray, sauce, shakers, syrup, handle for salad fork (rare and unique), 10" and 14" flat vase, 6", 8", and 9" footed vase.

Frisco

This was Fostoria's #1229 line from 1903 – 1905. It comes in an extended table service and a few other shapes. Pieces made before 1930 are found only in crystal.

Frog and Leaf

This Co-operative Flint Glass Company match or toothpick holder was made in 1911. It shows a realistic frog holding a tulip-like flower that is the receptacle. It all sits on a dome base that is ribbed and is very well done indeed.

Frog and Shell

This novelty toothpick holder, from the Ohio Flint Glass Co. circa 1897, is found in crystal and colors. Vintage pieces measure 3¾" and 1½" at the top section. It was reproduced by L. G. Wright in amber, blue, green, amethyst, and milk glass.

Frolicking Bears

This whimsical pattern was made by U.S. Glass Company in the early 1900s. It is known mostly to carnival glass collectors in rare olive green pitchers and tumblers that bring astronomical prices. In crystal it is found in clear pitchers and tumblers, but here I show a very rare item, a crystal piece with a sterling silver overlay. It is the only one reported in this technique so far.

Frost Crystal

Frost Crystal, from Tarentum Glass in 1906, was made in clear, gold trimmed, and ruby stained glass. Shapes include a table set, water set, celery boat, custard cup, shakers, bowls, plate, and the huge stemmed fruit bowl shown. The glass on this piece is very thick and heavy.

Frosted Chicken

This pattern was made by Riverside Glass in 1883. It can be found in plain or engraved examples, and shapes include a table set, covered bowl on a low standard, celery vase, covered compote, goblet, jam jar, shakers, and sauce. Finials are chicks emerging from shells, but open pieces are determined by clear concave panels, separated by clear vertical convex panels.

Frosted Circle

Sometimes called Horn of Plenty, this is U.S. Glass pattern #15007 from Bryce Brothers in 1876. Shapes are a table set, covered or open bowls in two sizes, cake stand in three sizes, water set, celery vase, covered compote, and pickle jar. The sugar bowl was reproduced.

Frosted Eagle

This early 1880s pattern is attributed to Crystal Glass by some, and found in both clear and frosted. Shapes are in an extended table service and all covered pieces have the eagle finial. Shown are a covered cheese dish and a covered sugar.

Frosted Fleur-de-Lis

Frosted Fleur-de-Lis was first made by King, Son & Company in 1885 and then U.S. Glass in 1891. Shapes include a table set, water set, pickle dish, celery vase, goblet, wine, and small or large cake stand. It is also known as Stippled Fleur-de-lis and can be found in crystal, amber, blue, green, milk glass, and possibly ruby stain.

Frosted Fruit

This very attractive and well-executed pattern was made by the Beatty-Brady Glass Company of Dunkirk, Indiana, in 1896, as a part of the National combine. It can be found in water sets, table sets, and berry sets. The design of basketweave and a series of fruits, including grapes, cherries, peaches, and apples, along with natural vines is very appealing. Pieces can be found either with a frosted finish or plain crystal. If you'll hunt very closely you can find the very tiny hidden squirrel sitting on one of the branches. The factory designation for this pattern was #1/105.

Frosted Heron

Althought difficult to see since the pattern is entirely engraved, this Heron design is distinguished by the elongated pitcher spout, the squared handle that has a banding, and blossom design. The heron is posed with its head looking back over its body. No other pieces are reported to me to date.

Frosted Leaf

Frosted Leaf is attributed to Boston and Sandwich Glass (1860) and then Portland Glass (1873 – 1874) in clear glass with machine ground frosted leaves. Some shapes were reproduced by Imperial in 1978 for the Smithsonian and are marked "S.I." Shapes in old glass include a celery vase, table set, champagne, open or covered compote, cordial, decanter (pint or quart), egg cup, goblet (lady's or gent's), oil lamp, water set, salt dips, sauce, and a wine. The goblet has been reproduced.

Frosted Ring

Apparently this is another pattern from Boston Silver Company, dating from the 1870s, and then made later by someone else. It seems to be a variant of the Beaded Mirror pattern, sometimes called Beaded Medallion. The finial of a well-done acorn is the same. The lid has rings of frosting, hence the name, and certainly other shapes exist.

Frosted Stork

Frosted Stork was reported to have been made by Crystal Glass of Bridgeport, Ohio, in 1879, but shards have also been found at Burlington of Canada. It is also called Flamingo or Frosted Crane. Shapes include berry set, finger bowls, ice bowl, oval bowl, table set, goblet, jam jar, pickle jar, pitcher, handled plate, oval platter (One-O-One border or Scenic border), relish tray, sauce, and a water tray. Shown is a stemmed celery vase. In addition, recent evidence suggests this pattern may have been also made at the Iowa City Flint Glass Works, especially items with the oval-and-bar border.

Frosted Stork Platter

Like the companion ABC plate shown elsewhere in this edition, this platter was made in two sizes. This one measures 12" x 8¼" and a larger water tray measures 15½" x 11". The design shows three storks amid tropical vegetation and varies from one size to the next. All pieces have a frosted center. It was from the Iowa City Flint Glass Company.

Fuchsia

This pattern comes in clear glass only, as far as I know. Shapes include a table set, celery vase, cake stand, goblet, open compote, tumbler, 8" and 10" plates, and the mug shape shown.

Gaelic

Gaelic was made by Indiana Glass in 1908. It can be found in an extended service that includes a table set, water set, berry set, punch set, wine, and the footed nut bowl shown.

Galloway

Galloway was from U.S. Glass (#15086) and is also known as Virginia, U.S. Mirror, Woodrow, or Jefferson's #15601 (Jefferson also made this pattern in Canada). It can be found in crystal, ruby stain, or rose blush. Shapes are many in an extended table service. The punch bowl, punch cup, underplate, and toothpick have been reproduced.

Garden of Eden

This pattern was made in the 1870s or early 1880s by an unknown firm (maybe Portland Glass) and is also known as Fish, Lotus, or Turtle. Shapes include a table set, cake stand, compote, egg cup, goblet (plain stem or the very scarce serpent stem), honey dish, mug, pickle dish, water set, plate (Give Us This Day), round plate, relish (with or without handles), and sauce.

Garden Path Variant

This Dugan Glass pattern from circa 1911 is found primarily in iridized carnival glass, but here we see the large bowl in a non-iridized lime green. Two of these lime examples have been reported in non-iridized glass but so far no other colors have been found.

Garden Pink

Garden Pink was made at Indiana Glass in 1913 as the #167 pattern. Shapes include 4½", 5½", 7½" footed bowls, 9½" footed oval bowl, handled nappy, goblet, wine, jelly compote, water set, pickle dish, covered 8½" compote, cake stand (salver), and heart-shaped dish.

Garfield Drape

This reported Adams and Company pattern is also suspected to be Canadian. It is also called Canadian Drape. The date of production may be 1881, following Garfield's death. Shapes include a berry set, table set, water set, milk pitcher, cake stand, covered compote (high and low), open compote, goblet in two sizes, honey dish, oil lamp, pickle dish, memorial bread plate, mourning plate, star center plate, and relish.

Gatling Gun Toothpick

This novelty toothpick holder is actually a trench mortar. It was made by Bryce Higbee, circa 1885, and was shown in early 1890s Butler Brothers catalog ads. Colors are crystal and blue. It can be found with match striker grooves on the base or without the grooves.

Gem Star

Gem Star, made by the West Virginia Glass Company in 1894, can be found in an extended table service including a table set, water set, celery vase, berry set, and the cruet shown. The design is quite conservative as patterns go, and only the eight-pointed star with rays make up the design.

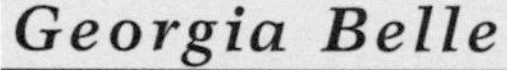

Georgia Belle

Georgia Belle was made by U.S. Glass (#15097) in 1906 ans also known as Western Star. It can be found in an extended table service that includes a goblet, wine, and several odd bowls like a banana bowl.

German Clock

I'm told by the owner, who gave this pattern name to me, that this clock is a product from Germany. The case is square and complete with works that are functioning. It has been reported only in vaseline to date.

Giant Bulls-Eye

This pattern was originally made by the Bellaire Goblet Co. as their #151 line, circa 1889, then Model Flint Glass, circa 1891, and finally by the U. S. Glass Co. (their #157 line) circa 1891. It is also known as Excelsior, Bulls Eye and Spearhead, or Bulls Eye Variant, The wide selection of shapes in this pattern are found in crystal only.

Gibson Cameo Plate

This very nice plate was originally offered in a goofus treatment. It measures 8½" in diameter and has the design on the exterior, showing the profile of the famous Gibson Girl while the rim is filled with scroll work.

Gibson Girl

This was originally called Medallion and made by the National Glass Company in 1903. It is considered a rare pattern in all shapes, which include a table set, water set, bowl, relish dish, 4" flat sauce, and 10" plate. No goblets or wines have been reported.

Giraffe

This is one of many etched novelty goblet patterns (maker is unknown). This one is very popular with collectors and was part of a series dealing with African animals.

Girl with a Fan

This novelty goblet is one of several from the Bellaire Goblet Company of Findlay, Ohio. Production was around 1890 for this piece, and fragments have been unearthed at the factory site. The only color is clear. The goblet has been reproduced.

Girl with Laden Apron

This fine pattern is attributed to Crystal Glass Company in 1880, but recent evidence points to Iowa City Flint Glass as the maker. The border of the plate has the same "one-hundred-one" sort of design as the Frosted Pheasant oval covered dish, so the maker must be the same.

Globe and Star

Probably from the 1890s, this pattern's shapes include a table set, covered compote, open compote (shown), cake stand, jelly compote, sauce, pickle dish, celery vase, goblet, and wine. It is found in crystal as well as amber, blue, and possibly other colors like canary.

Goat's Head

This rare pattern is attributed to Hobbs, Brockunier Glass Company in 1878 and found with frosting or completely clear. The only pieces I can confirm are a covered butter dish, creamer, spooner, half-gallon pitcher, oval bowl, covered compote, and sugar that can be either covered or open. The goat is found on the footed base extension as shown.

Goddess of Hunt

This fine platter is actually part of the Psyche and Cupid line from Riverside Glass Works (1880). The treatment is called crystalography, first used by Washington Beck at Dithridge & Company. The piece is a handled rectangular tray with griffins and scroll on the sides and a center motif of the huntress with bow and arrows. It is also called Virginia Dare.

Goliath

Since I have never seen an official name for these huge Fenton vases I'm taken the liberty to assign one to it. I own three of these mammoth vases; cobalt, red, and black glass. And I can say that at 18" - 20" tall and some having a top span of 8" or more, they are really a sight to behold. The exterior is plain and the interior has panels. I've seen other colors in iridized glass but only red, cobalt, and black in non-iridized versions.

Gonterman Swirl

This pattern, called Adonis Swirl by its maker, Aetna Glass Company in 1888, and its companion patterns (Adonis Hobnail and Adonis Pineapple) are found in opalescent glass as well as the non-opal treatment shown with a frosted base. Tops are found in blue or amber and shapes include a berry set, table set, water set, cruet, celery vase, lamp shade, cologne bottle, finger bowl, toothpick holder (shown), and a shaker is suspected.

Goofus Grape

This pattern has doubled the vines, stems, leaves, and clusters of grapes so that they virtually cover every area of the bowl, with tendrils twining everywhere. I am confident that plates as well as the bowls are known and probably in more than one size. It is somewhat like the Dugan/Diamond Grape Intaglio pattern.

Gooseberry

With shards found at Boston & Sandwich and at Burlington in Canada, the maker of this pattern is cloudy. It is found in crystal or milk glass in a berry set, table set, water set, covered compote (three sizes), mug, goblet, syrup, and a handled lemonade glass. The goblet, mug, and wine have been reproduced.

Gooseberry Variant

This 1880s small mug (1⅞" tall and 1⅞" diameter) is very much in design like some of the Fenton berry patterns and may well have been the inspiration for them years later. It can be found in clear, blue, milk glass, opaque blue, or opaque teal glass.

Goose Boy

This pattern, also called Boy with Goose (there is a similar compote showing a girl with goose), is believed to be made by Portland Glass Company (1864 - 1873) of Portland, Maine. The stems and bases are frosted on the piece shown, but both boy and girl compotes are also found in clear.

Gordon

This well-done covered compote, from the Burlington Glass Company of Canada (1875 - 1909), is known by this name to Canadian collectors. Other shapes probably exist. The design is mostly a series of bull's-eyes that ride on beading and the beading even extends in rows down the stem.

Gothic

This circa 1904 McKee Brothers pattern, also known as Spearpoint Band, can be found in crystal or ruby stained in an extended table service including a champagne, cordial, wine, and other shapes. Not all pieces found in ruby stained.

Gothic Grape

Besides a very fine dresser set, this pattern is found on a massive 9" vase shape as well. It was made in Europe in the early 1920s I believe. I show a mini lamp made from the perfume shown in previous editions. The leaves on all pieces are frosted while the grapes are clear.

Gothic Windows

Gothic Windows was made by Indiana Glass Company as #166 in the 1920s in clear and gold-trimmed glass. Shapes include a table set, water set, pickle dish, berry set, and both open and covered compotes.

Grand

Grand is credited to both Bryce, Higbee and Diamond Glass, Limited, of Canada in 1885. It can be found in clear or ruby stain and colors may exist. Shapes include a covered bowl (flat or footed), open footed bowls, table set, cake stand in two sizes, celery vase, covered or open compotes (high or low) in three sizes, cordial, decanter, goblet, mug, water set, plates, relish, and shakers.

Grape

While similar to another mug by King, Son & Company called Grapevine, this mug has a different handle and has no vines or leaves, only sparse clusters of grapes. Found only in clear glass, the Grape mug measures 2¾" tall and has a base diameter of 2".

Grape and Cable

Northwood's Grape and Cable, while primarily a carnival glass pattern, can also be found in crystal, opalescent glass, custard, and the white satin with gilding and yellow paint shown. The many shapes include a covered sweetmeat, cologne bottle (shown), footed orange bowl, plate, and a handled bonbon.

Grape and Cable (Fenton)

Fenton's version of the Grape and Cable pattern is nearly identical to Northwood's. It is found in carnival glass as well as crystal, lime green, and an odd "coke bottle" green on a few pieces. Non-iridized shapes reported to date are the large footed orange bowl, candlesticks, and a rare punch set (bowl and cups) with scroll feet. There is also a variant to the large fruit bowl with leaves circling the collar base.

Grape and Cable with Thumbprints

Usually lumped with Northwood's regular Grape and Cable, this variation with the added thumbprints on the base should be considered on its own. Shapes are found mostly in carnival glass and include a table set, water set (standard or tankard pitchers), covered cracker jar, berry set, whiskey set, tobacco jar, and whimsey hat shape. Recently a berry set in crystal surfaced and is the only one reported at this time. This pattern has been reproduced.

Grape and Festoon

This pattern was first made by Boston & Sandwich Glass, then Doyle & Company, and finally U.S. Glass in 1891. It is found with four variations: clear leaf, stippled leaf, veined leaf, or stippled grapes. Shapes include a 6" bowl, table set, celery vase, high or low covered compote, egg cup, goblet, 7½" lamp, pickle tray, milk pitcher, water pitcher, plate, relish tray, sauce, wine, and master salt.

Grape Arbor

This Northwood pattern, circa 1911, is mostly known in carnival glass but can also be found in custard glass with nutmeg stain, as shown here in a hat shaped whimsey made from the tumbler. The pitcher and tumbler are also known is custard glass with staining of various shades.

Grape Band

Grape Band was made by Bryce, Walker and Company around 1870 in clear crystal only. Shapes include a table set, compote, wine, egg cup, celery vase, cordial, goblet, 6" plate, master footed salt dip, pickle dish, high or low covered compotes, as well as a water set. The goblet was reproduced.

Grape Bunch

I understand this pattern was made in the 1870s, either by Sandwich Glass or by Doyle and Company. Verified shapes are a wine, goblet, table set, water set, celery vase, and pickle dish. It has been reported in crystal and vaseline.

Grape Frieze

Grape Freize is another of Northwood's patterns designed for its Verre D'or line of gold decoration. Here is an unusual custard glass 10½" footed plate with nutmeg staining.

Grape on Crackle

Along with its companion vases showing roses or poppies on a crackle background, these 9" vases originally had a goofus treatment of gold, red, and green colors. They are advertised in Butler Brothers catalogs over many years, from 1906 to 1924, and were only part of the huge goofus invasion of the glass world during that time.

Grapes and Roses on Basketweave

As is typical of many goofus glass vase patterns, this one is hourglass shaped. It has a cluster of grapes on the lower lattice and a rose above. This vase is 10" tall with an acid finish.

Grapes with Overlapping Foliage

This pattern was made by Hobbs, Brockunier primarily in opal (the company's porcelain treatment) but possibly in crystal, around 1870. Shapes include a celery vase, 4" nappy, 8" nappy, a four-piece table set, and the pedestal-based water pitcher shown. Hobbs opal glass was a very dense milk glass that has a pinkish glow under ultraviolet light.

Grapevine and Cherry Sprig

Grapevine and Cherry Sprig was made by the Northwood Company in the early 1900s and can be found in a water set, square-footed bowl, and table set. Some pieces are etched and some have a goofus treatment. The design is very realistic and the quality of glass very fine. Pieces are scarce and desirable.

Grapevine Basket

This nice basket with a metal handle measures 8¾" long, 6¼" wide, and is 4¼" tall. It has a basketweave design with grapes, leaves, and grapevines on each side.

Grapevine Lattice

This Dugan pattern, circa 1910 – 1920, is primarily known in carnival glass, but here we see a hat shaped Jack-in-the-Pulpit whimsey made from the tumbler in a deep amethyst. No other colors are reported in non-iridized glass.

Grape without Vine

This was Federal Glass pattern #507, also known as Federal Grape. It can be found in a water set, table set, berry set, four sizes of covered compotes, four sizes of open compotes, four sizes of covered bowls, and four sizes of open utility bowls.

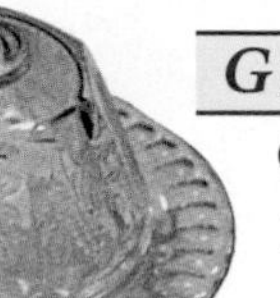

Grape with Thumbprint

Grape with Thumbprint has been attributed to the Jenkins Glass Company after 1900. Shapes include a table set, water set, toothpick holder, salt shaker, cup, covered compote, and bowls. It was made in crystal, milk glass, and possibly colored glass.

Grape with Vine

This pattern, found in clear, carnival, and goofus glass, is similar to the Jefferson Vintage bowl that is found in opalescent glass. Shapes include a table set, covered compote, a plate, large and small bowls, sauce, honey dish, and a water set. The pattern dates from about 1900.

Grasshopper

This pattern was made by Riverside in 1883 in clear, amber, blue, or vaseline glass. There are three variations: with insect, without insect, and with long spear. The example shown is with insect. Shapes include a covered bowl, open footed bowl (deep or shallow), table set, celery vase, covered compotes, jam jar, pickle dish, pitcher, footed 8", 9", and 10½" plates, salt dip, shakers, and flat or footed sauces. It is also known as Locust or Long Spear.

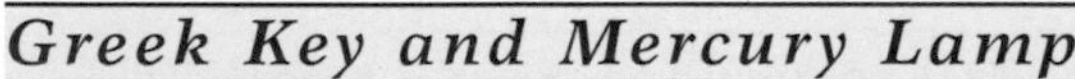

Grated Diamond and Sunburst

This George Duncan and Sons, #20 pattern, circa 1894, can be found in a table set, salt shakers, punch set, toothpick holder, salt dip, water carafe, and several sizes of bowls. The pattern is often found with gold trim.

Greek Key and Mercury Lamp

I have not seen a lamp with this odd combination of a vaseline glass font and a mercury glass base and stem, although I feel other examples are likely. The maker in unknown.

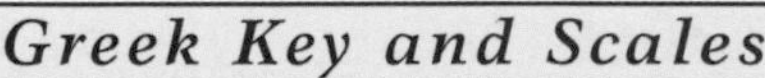

Greek Key and Scales

This 1906 Northwood Company bowl pattern with a dome base was first made in opalescent glass, but is best known in carnival glass. This crystal treatment was made as part of the extensive Northwood goofus line and probably predates the carnival treatment. There is a companion pattern called Greek Key and Ribs that can also be found in all three treatments.

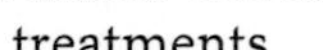

Greensburg's Florida

Greenburg's Florida from 1893 is also known as Sunken Primrose. It can be found in crystal or ruby stain in an extended table service. Shown is a stemmed banana bowl.

Greentown Squirrel

I realize this pattern is usually just called Squirrel, but two other patterns are known by this name so I've made the addition. It was made by the Indiana Tumbler and Goblet Company (Greentown), only in a pitcher (can be flat or scalloped on the top), in crystal or chocolate glass.

Grenade

Although similar to the Austrian pattern, I have no proof that they were made by the same company. It is found in crystal or ruby stain and shapes reported are a table set and a berry set (10" bowl shown).

Grogan

I've mainly heard of crystal examples in a table set, goblet, wine, and celery vase (other shapes probably exist). I have seen the goblet shape in amber. I can't confirm its age and the maker is unknown.

Groove and Slash

This Heisey pattern (#1250) is from 1897. Shapes include a table set, water set, shakers, bonbon, spoon tray, cruet, bowls, pickle jar, sauce, cracker jar, compotes, plates in two sizes, berry set, and the whimsey vase shown.

Grumpy Woman and Man

This toy mug (2" tall and 1⅞" in diameter), also known as Captain Hook, can be found in clear, frosted, or opaque blue and is reported in opalescent glass. Production dates from the 1880s. Shown is the "old man" side.

Hamilton

Hamilton was made by Cape Cod Glass in the 1860s and shards have been found at Boston & Sandwich too. It can be found primarily in crystal or deep blue in a table set, castor set, covered or open compotes, goblet, egg cup, hat whimsey (very rare), decanter, salt dip, water set, sauce, syrup, whiskey tumbler, and a wine. Shown is the egg cup.

Hand

Hand was from the O'Hara Glass Company (pattern #90) in 1880. The finials on covered pieces are a clinched hand holding a bar, while the primary designs are clear and diamond point panels. Shapes include bowls, table set, cake stand, celery vase, covered and open compotes, cordial, goblet, honey dish, jam jar, mug, pickle tray, water set, platter, syrup, water tray, and wine.

Hand and Torch

This open compote, attributed to Bakewell, Pears and Company of Pittsburgh, has the distinguishing hand and torch stem for which it was named. The bowl has been frosted and then engraved in a flower and leaf pattern, but it can also be found without engraving.

Hand Vase

These vases, also called Cornucopia Vase, were shown in both the 1886 and 1890 company catalogs of George Duncan and Sons Glass. They were made in two sizes (at least), 7⅞" tall and 6" tall, and Fenton copied the larger size in the 1930s. Colors known are crystal, amber, canary, or blue, and some were made with etching on the hand.

Hand with Fan

The date of production of this match holder is circa 1889 – 1890. It is similar in concept to another pattern called Hand with Flower but I do not believe they are the same. Clear and milk glass have been reported but other colors likely exist.

Hanging Basket Variant

The shape shown is a handled celery vase that is 7¼" tall with a 5" base. The design is outstanding with very detailed handles. No other shapes or colors are reported to me to date.

Hanover

Hanover, also called Block with Stars, was first a Richards and Hartley design in 1888 and then from U.S. Glass in 1891. Shapes include bowls, table set, cake stand, celery vase, cheese dish with cover, covered high or low compotes, cruet, goblet, mug in two sizes, water set, milk pitcher, plates, platter, sauce, and wine. It is found in clear, amber, vaseline, or blue glass.

Hare and Chicken

This shaker, circa 1900, is likely made by the Eagle Manufacturing Co. since similar shakers are known to be from that concern. One side shows a sitting hen and the other a running rabbit. It is found in milk glass with a reddish brown goofus treatment.

Harp Double Relish

This is not the same pattern as the well-known Harp pattern by Bryce Brothers. This one has a very fancy scroll design with a center rolled handle of acanthus leaves. This beautiful double relish tray probably dates from the 1880s.

Hartford

Hartford, from Fostoria in the early 1900s, is found in an extensive table service including table sets, berry sets, and the plate shown. It can be found in clear, amber, or ruby stain.

Hartley

This pattern, from Richards & Hartley and then U.S. Glass in 1891, is also known as Paneled Diamond Cut or Daisy and Button with oval panels. It can be found in crystal, vaseline, amber, blue, or etched crystal. Shapes include bowls (four sizes), table set, water set, milk pitcher, bread or cake plates, covered or open compotes, goblet, wine, relish tray, and celery vase.

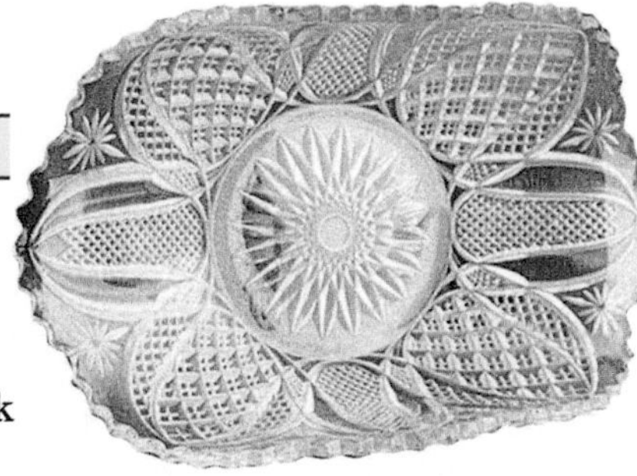

Harvard Yard

Harvard Yard was made by Tarentum in 1896 and is also called Tarentum's Harvard. It can be found in crystal, emerald green, ruby stain, or gilded glass. Shapes include bowls, a table set, cake stand, condiment set, cordial, egg cup, goblet, syrup jug, water set, 10" plate, salt dip, shakers, sauce, oval tray, toothpick holder, water set, wine, and the pickle dish shown.

Hattie

Imperial Glass Company's #496 line is normally found on carnival glass examples in various colors, but here we see a very hard to find crystal 8" bowl. No other shapes are reported at this time.

H

Hawaiian Lei

This 1913 Bryce, Higbee pattern (#44629) was called Gala by the company. Shapes are many and include round or square plates, a table set, handled basket, sauce, cake stand, compote, one-handled nappy, rose bowl, twin relish dish, sherbet, tall jelly compote, oval pickle dish, vase, stemmed ice cream, wine, salver, claret, nut bowl, salad bowl, honey dish, goblet, celery tray, child's table set, water set (three sizes in pitchers), mayonnaise bowl, water stand, swing vase, and a handled toothpi(holder.

Heart and Sand

Heart and Sand is also known as Vincent's Valentine and was made by New Martinsville Glass as the #724 pattern. It can be found in clear, gold decorated, enameled, or ruby stained glass. Shapes include a table set, water set, berry set with 8", 7", and 4½" bowls, and toothpick holder.

Heart Band

Heart Band, from McKee Glass in 1897, can be found in crystal, ruby stained, green, and rarely carnival glass. Some pieces are gilded. Shapes include a table set, toothpick holder, shakers, celery vase, tumbler, and a mug. Often the ruby stained items were lettered as souvenir items.

Heart Plume

Also known as Marlboro, this was U.S. Glass pattern #15105 from 1907. It was made in clear, rose flashed, and gold-trimmed glass. Shapes include a table set, shakers, relish tray, water set, compote, pickle dish, syrup, and wine.

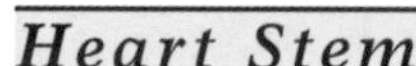

Heart Stem

I feel certain this pattern design dates from the late 1880s or early 1890s. Shapes include a table set, celery with two handles, covered compote, goblet, salt shaker (rare), and handled sauce. Occasionally pieces of Heart Stem turn up with engraved designs.

Heart with Thumbprint

This Tarentum Glass Company pattern, sometimes called Tarentum's Hartford or Columbian, was made in 1898 in clear, ruby stain, emerald green, Nile green, cobalt blue, and custard. Many pieces were gold trimmed. Shapes include a banana boat in two sizes, barber bottle, cologne, berry set, table set, cake stand, carafe, card tray, celery vase, compote in two sizes, cruet, goblet, hair receiver, ice bucket, oil lamp, mustard jar, water set, plates, powder jar, punch set, rose bowls, syrups, condiment tray, vases, and wine.

Heavy Finecut

This pattern was made by Geo. Duncan & Sons in 1883 and is found in crystal, canary, amber, and blue. Shapes include a molasses can, celery vase, celery boat, cheese plate and cover, cologne (five sizes), decanter, finger bowls (four variations), lamp, mustard, oil, bottle, pickle boat, pickle jar, water set, butter pat, plate (three sizes), salt, salver (three sizes), champagne, claret, cordial, goblet, wine, tray, and water bottle. It is also known as Diamond Block and Little Jewel.

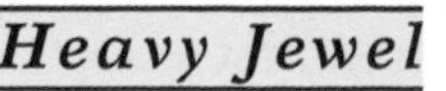

Heavy Jewel

Fostoria Glass made this pattern in 1900 in crystal only. Shapes reported are a table set, water set, and toothpick holder (rare). The sugar bowl may be open or with a lid. Other shapes may certainly exist.

Heavy Leaf

The owner of this 9" bowl tells me this is the name of the pattern, but I have no knowledge of its maker or date of production. Other shapes may exist but haven't been reported to me at this time.

Helmet Butter Dish

Attributed to King, Son & Company of Pittsburgh, this novelty butter dish is a real collector's find and is considered a rarity. It was made in clear, amber, or blue glass and I know of no matching pieces. Even damaged examples bring sizable prices, and perfect examples are very rare.

Henrietta

Henrietta was made by the Columbia Glass Company (#14) in 1889 and U.S. Glass in 1892 in clear, engraved, ruby stained, or emerald green. Shapes include a rectangular bowl, rose bowl, round bowls, table set, cake stand, castor set, celery vase or tray, compote, cracker jar, cruet, cup, bone dish, olive dish, confection jar, lamp, mustard jar, pickle jar, bulbous or tankard water set, bread plate, breakfast creamer and sugar, salt dips, sauce, shades, syrup, and 5", 7", and 9" vases.

Hercules

This Hercules compote is similar to the Atlas compote. It matches the Atterbury lamp base with the same design, so this is also from Atterbury. It is also found on a pure white opaque glass.

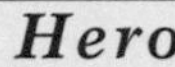

Hero

Hero is sometimes called Ruby Rosette and was made by the West Virginia Glass Company as #700 in 1894. Shapes include a table set, shakers, cruet, berry set, mustard pot, celery vase, cake stand, goblet, oil lamp, hand lamp, and pickle jar.

Heron

Heron is believed to have been made in the 1880s (not from the Greentown line). The design has the crystalography look about it, but I can't be sure. No other colors or shapes are reported at this time.

Heron (Greentown)

This circa 1890 Indiana Tumbler and Goblet Co. pitcher is known in crystal (shown) as well as chocolate glass.

Heron and Peacock

The Heron and Peacock mug is from the late 1800s and is similar to several other mugs. It is found in clear, blue, milk glass, opaque blue, and opalescent glass. It has been widely reproduced, first by Degenhart and then by others.

Herringbone

Herringbone is from the 1880s. Shapes reported are a table set, stemmed celery vase, goblet, water set, flat sauce, wine, and open compote. The sugar bowl may be either open or with a lid. The design is a bit like one by the Cambridge Company called Inverted Feather.

Herringbone Buttress

This circa 1898 Indiana Tumbler and Goblet Co. pattern (#140 line) is found in a host of shapes including, but not limited to an extended table service. Colors are crystal, amber, and green (shown here in a wine).

Hexagonul Block

Also called Hexagon Block, this was a product of Hobbs Glass (its #335) and then U.S. Glass. It is found in an extended table service in crystal, ruby stain, gold stain, and etched glass.

Hexagonal Block Band

Production of this pattern dates from circa 1890. Shapes include a table set, water set, berry set, goblet, celery vase, pickle dish, and wine.

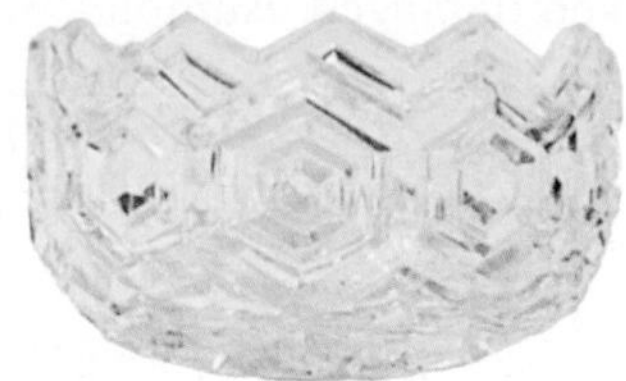

Hexagonal Bulls-Eye

This distinctive 1890 Dalzell, Gilmore, and Leighton pattern is also known as Creased Hexagon Block or Double Red Block (when ruby stained). Shapes include a table set, celery vase, goblet, water set, sauce, and wine.

Hickman

Hickman, made by McKee and Brothers in 1897, can be found in bowls, jelly compote, three styles of salt shakers, sauce, toothpick holder, banana stand, pepper bottle, table set, celery, champagne, cologne, condiment set, cruet, covered and open compotes, punch set, toothpick holder, and many other shapes. It was made in clear, green, and two shades of amber. The vase has been reproduced.

Hidalgo

This was first an Adams & Company pattern and then reissued in 1891 by U.S. Glass in clear, clear etched, clear with amber panels, or ruby stain. Shapes include a berry set, finger bowl, waste bowl, table set, high or low compotes in four sizes (covered), open compotes, cruet, cup, saucer, goblet, pickle dish, water set, milk pitcher, bread plate, master and individual salt dips, syrup, and water tray. It is also called Adams #5 or Frosted Waffle.

High Hob

This is Westmoreland's #550 pattern from 1915. It is found in crystal as well as ruby stain, in 32 shapes. Tumblers have been reproduced in opalescent glass in recent years.

Hinoto

This Boston & Sandwich flint pattern was made in the late 1850s and into the 1860s, in clear and then in vaseline. It is also known as Diamond Point with Panels and Banded Diamond Point. Shapes include a celery vase, champagne, egg cup, goblet, master open salt, sweetmeat with cover, table set, tumbler (flat), whiskey tumbler (footed) that I show here, and a wine.

Hobbs #94

This clear, stemmed molasses was shown in a Hobbs, Brockunier 1885 catalog. It has an original lid that is marked "Pat't-July '72." Thanks to James Wilkins for the photo.

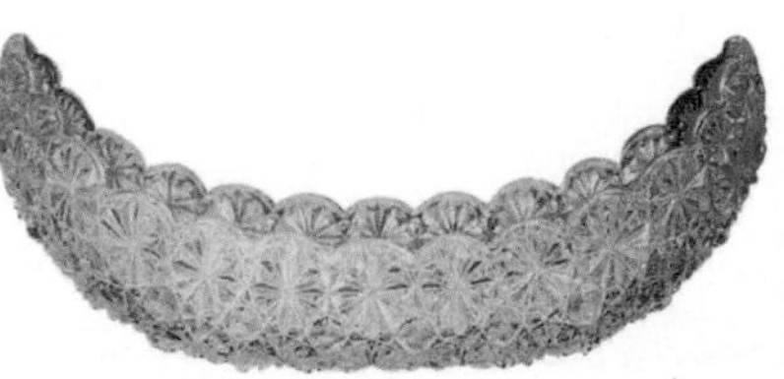

Hobbs Canoe

This is part of Hobbs #101 Daisy & Button line. It is found in two types (the one shown that sits and a hanging canoe) in Old Gold (amber), canary, clear, amberina, ruby, sapphire, or Marine green. Production dates from 1884.

Hobbs Hobnail

This was first made by Hobbs as the 323 pattern and by U.S. Glass after 1891 I understand. It is found in crystal, Old Gold (amber), sapphire, green, canary, ruby rubina, ruby amber, ruby sapphire, ruby verde, canary opalescent, and many other opal treatments. Shapes include a bitters bottle, bowls (round or square) in three sizes, celery vase, pitchers (five sizes), syrup, cruet, pickle jar, table set, water tray, tumbler, water bottle, vase (two shapes), toy tumbler, and shakers. This pattern is also called Dewdrop. The barber bottle, butter, compote, creamer, cruet pitcher, shaker and tumbler have been reproduced.

Hobbs Polka Dot

Hobbs Polka Dot was made in 1884 in crystal, Old Gold, sapphire, green, canary, cranberry, rubina, rubina verde, ruby amber, ruby sapphire, and opalescent colors. Shapes include pitchers (five sizes), covered cheese dish (shown), footed 8" bowl, cruet, water bottle, tumbler, sauce, deep sauce, oil bottle, celery vase, covered sugar (handled or without handles), champagne glass, a buttermilk tumbler, bar bottles, lemonade mug, shakers, custard cup, and a mustard pot.

Hobnail

This was made by many companies over many years in virtually every shape imaginable, but I do not intend to show all the variations here. The stemmed shakers shown are unique because of the ruby staining and the original tops. Some pieces are made in opalescent glass, some in carnival glass, some in colors, gold trimmed, or stained. Shapes include water sets, berry sets, lamps, table set, toothpick holders, goblets, trays, bone dishes, vases, and perfumes.

Hobnail Band

This very recognizable pattern dates from the early 1880s (maker is unknown at this time). It can be found in a table set, water set, sauce, plate, cup and saucer, coaster, celery tray, champagne, candlesticks, wine, goblet, custard cup, and syrup (shown).

Hobnail-in-Square

Made by the Aetna Glass and Mfg. Company in 1887, Hobnail-in-Square is best remembered for the opalescent pieces, but it was also made in crystal and colored glass. Crystal shapes reported are a water set, table set, celery vase, cake stand, and salt shakers. In recent years, this pattern has been reproduced by the Fenton Company in several treatments and is known as their Vesta pattern.

Hobnail Mug

Hobnail patterns were made by various companies in a wide array of colors and shapes, and this mug is no different. It can be found with a square handle, a round plain handle, and a round rope style handle. Central Glass Company is a possibility as maker. Colors are, but not limited to, crystal, amber, vaseline, blue, and green.

Hobnail with Bars

Hobnail with Bars was made by U.S. Glass in 1891 and is also known as Hobnail in Big Diamond (Challinor #307). It can be found in an extended table service. Shown is the spooner.

Hobnail with Fan Top

There is a bit of uncertainty concerning this pattern. Some feel it is from Adams (#150), then U.S. Glass in 1891, while others believe Dalzell to be the maker. Nonetheless, it is reported in a table set, water set, goblet, dish, salt, tray, and wine. Shown is the bowl in mosaic glass (purple slag).

Hobstar (Imperial's #282)

Hobstar was surely one of Imperial's most prominent patterns. It dates from 1909 in both crystal and carnival glass. The shapes include a 13" salver, rose bowls in 5½", 7", 9", plate in 5", 10½", fruit bowl, orange bowl, punch set, compotes in 10", 10½", 11", jelly compote, sherbet, sundae, wine, goblet, water set, water tray, syrup, milk jar with lid, celery vase, table set, cookie jar with lid, and large and small berry bowls that are round, crimped, or shallow. It has been reproduced.

Hobstar and Feather

Hobstar and Feather was made by Millersburg in 1910 and can be found in carnival glass, crystal, and ruby stain or lemon and red stain. It can be found in a large number of shapes, including both bowls shown, the rare ruby stained bowl, and the very rare bowl with a protruding rim above the sawtooth edge, which has a metal band applied to it. This pattern was later made in Canada by Jefferson Glass.

Hobstar and Tassel

This scarce pattern from the Imperial Glass Company is mostly seen in crystal, but a few rare items in carnival glass are known. It dates from 1909. In crystal shapes include 7½" plate, 5" rose bowl, 5½" berry bowl, 7" crimped bowl, 7½" grape (ruffled) plate, 6½" ice cream bowl, 4" lily bowl, and 4" rose bowl. All items are from the same mould, and some crystal pieces have gilding.

Hobstar Band

This pattern's maker is undecided but many feel it may be U.S. Glass. It can be found in both crystal and carnival glass. Shapes known are a flat-based pitcher, a pedestal-based pitcher (sometimes with advertising), a tumbler that can be flared or straight, large bowls of various shapes, and a scarce handled celery vase.

Hobstar Flower

Illustrated in a 1909 Imperial catalog as #404C, this 5½" compote is known to carnival glass collectors as Hobstar Flower. In crystal, besides the compote, there is a 10" shallow berry bowl, 11" orange bowl, 9" berry bowl, 10½" nut bowl, 13" fruit bowl, punch set, 9½" compote, 12" fruit bowl on a stand, and 9½" stemmed fruit bowl.

Holland

This pattern was from McKee Glass in 1894 and is also known as Oat Spray. Shapes include a table set, water set, berry set, open or covered compotes, pickle dish, toothpick holder, goblet, and stemmed wine.

Hollis

This early 1900s pattern is found in a water set as well as the celery vase shown. The design is one of repeated diamonds and is similar to a pattern called Diamond Bar and Block. Probably other shapes exist, especially table pieces.

Holly

Shards of this pattern were found at Boston & Sandwich Glass Company and date of production is from the late 1860s and early 1870s. Shapes include covered bowls either flat or footed, table set, celery vase, cake stand, high or low covered compote, egg cup, goblet, pickle dish, water set, salt dip, sauce, syrup, and wine. Tumblers are either flat or footed.

Holly (Fenton)

This has to be one of Fenton's most popular and longest running patterns. It was first made circa 1911 and the mould is still in use today. It is found in abundance in a wide variety of carnival colors and shapes. Here we see the small compote in a very rich cobalt blue.

Holly Amber

This famous pattern, created by the Indiana Tumbler and Goblet Company (Greentown), was made in clear (Holly Clear) and Golden Agate (shown), referred to by some as Chocolate. An extremely rare spooner is known in Rose Agate and an equally rare footed toothpick is known in White Agate. Shapes include bowls, a table set, covered compotes, mugs, nappies, pickle tray, a water set, plates, shakers, syrup, and toothpick holders (shown). The pattern has been reproduced in several types of glass including carnival in the 1970s.

Honeycomb

Many companies, including Bakewell, Pears made the Honeycomb pattern, but it is uncertain who produced this particular one. Some feel it is English in origin. Many shapes are known including table sets, bowls, compotes, celery vases, decanter, egg cup, vase, and pickle dish. The particular piece shown is in rare vaseline.

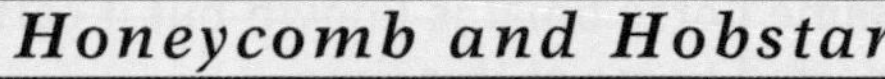

Honeycomb and Hobstar

This was first made by Ohio Flint Glass in 1907 and called Gloria. It is found in crystal and ruby stained glass (some with gilding). When Ohio Flint closed, the moulds went to Jefferson Glass with the vase mould finding its way to Millersburg in 1909 where it was made in carnival glass. Shapes include a berry set, water set, table set, vase, water bottle, compote (two sizes), cruet, and several whimsied shapes.

Honeycomb with Star

Honeycomb with Star was made by Fostoria Glass in 1905. Shapes include a table set, water set, cake stand, sauce, compote, cruet, celery vase, pickle dish, and vase shape. The stars that are centered in some of the honeycomb sections are hard to see.

Hops Band

This circa 1871 King Glass Co. pattern is found in an extended table service only in crystal. A wine is also known to complement the extended table service.

Horn of Plenty

Horn of Plenty, also known as Comet or Peacock Tail, was made by McKee and Company in the 1860s. Shards have been reported from Boston and Sandwich also. Colors are crystal, canary, blue, amber, amethyst, or milk glass. Shapes include bottles, bowls, cake stand, celery vase, champagne, claret, covered or open compotes (nine sizes in the latter), table set, egg cup, goblet, lamp, mug, plate, water set, salt, and wine. An extremely rare honey casket and underplate are known and will bring astronomical prices. The goblet, hat, lamp, pitcher, and tumbler were reproduced.

Horse

Apparently part of a series of early etched pieces, Horse is found on the tumbler shown (on one side only) as well as on a goblet shape that is identical to that of Dog with Rabbit in its Mouth, Fern Circles, Dot Band with Cord and Tassel, and Forsythia Leaf. I believe these pieces all date from the 1870s.

Horse and Cart

This is another of those novelty pieces meant for either matches or toothpicks. It is credited to the Central Glass Company in the 1890s. This one has a horse and cart pulling a gigantic barrel with a tiny driver standing on one of the barrel staves. It is also known as #865, Horse Pulling Barrel.

Icicle with Star

This pattern is Imperial Glass Company's #76 line, circa 1902. A pitcher and tumble are shown in a 1909 catalog reprint and a lemonade set sitting on a #231 tray. The tumblers do not have the star in the pattern. Crystal is the only color reported.

I-H-C

IHC, from the McKee Glass Company in 1894, has been reported in crystal and green with gilding. Shapes include a table set, berry set, water set, compotes, sauce, pickle dish, celery vase, and the 7" bud vase shown. This vase is advertised in a 1900 Butler Brothers catalog ad which says; "Green and Gold, or Crystal and Gold, Tiffany Vase, 82 cents per dozen."

Illinois

The U.S. Glass design #15052 was made in 1898 in clear, emerald green, and with ruby stain. It is also called Clarissa or Star of the East. Shapes include a handled basket, bonbon, cruet, berry sets in round or square, finger bowl, table set, cake stand, candlesticks, celery tray and vase, cheese dish, jelly compote, olive dish, water jug, banquet lamp and shade, jam jar, pickle jar, water set (tankard or standard), plate, puff box, and straw holder. A butter dish and celery were reproduced.

Imperial Grape

Although primarily a carnival glass pattern, this Imperial pattern is also found in milk glass, slag, crystal, red, amberina and teal. Non-carnival shapes include a handled sandwich plate, decanter, stemmed cordial, goblet, berry set, and a rose bowl.

Imperial Nu-Cut #91/500

Much like other whirling star patterns, this one from Imperial comes in a jelly compote, nappy, 6", 8", and 10¼" bowls, a 6½" vase, breakfast set (sugar and creamer), mayonnaise bowl, and plate (oval). It is sometimes gold trimmed.

Imperial Nu-Cut #91/607

Made in 1909 and shown in the catalog, this Imperial Glass pattern can be found in bowls of various sizes and the two-handled pickle dish shown. The design is mostly hobstars separated by diamonds of file pattern.

Imperial Nu-Cut #212

This pattern was made by Imperial Glass in 1913 and is marked Nu-Cut. It can be found in both a creamer and open sugar (there may well be other shapes).

Imperial's #262

Shown in Imperial's 1909 catalog, this seems to be the only shape shown. It is a 5" nappy the company calls an "olive nappy." It is a shallow, diamond-shaped piece with one knobby handle. Any additional information on this pattern would be appreciated.

Imperial's #300

This pattern was made by the Imperial Glass Company of Bellaire, Ohio, from 1905 to 1909. Shown is the 9" pitcher that, along with taller tumblers, was part of a lemonade set.

Imperial's #347

This pattern, shown in the Imperial 1909 company catalog, is quite distinctive and very strong. It can be found on berry sets that are ruffled or flared as well as on ice cream sets. The glass is clear and sparkling and ranks among Imperial's best.

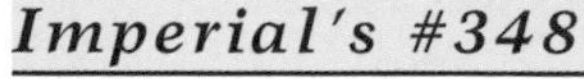

Imperial's #348

Shown in a 1909 Imperial company catalog, this pitcher seems to be the only shape in this pattern. Its distinct shape makes it easily recognized.

Imperial's #403½

This water set pattern, which was found in the 1909 Imperial catalog, has never been named (as far as I know). It is a very nice design with an applied rope handle and large icicles that seem to extend over a field of diamond cut. No other shapes are reported in either crystal, ruby stain, or with gild.

Imperial's #404

This outstanding geometric design was shown in the 1909 Imperial company catalog in a large variety of shapes. The glass is very thick, measuring almost ½", and weighing a hefty seven pounds. I have heard this pattern called Thunderbolt. It has been reproduced in the large compote and possibly other shapes.

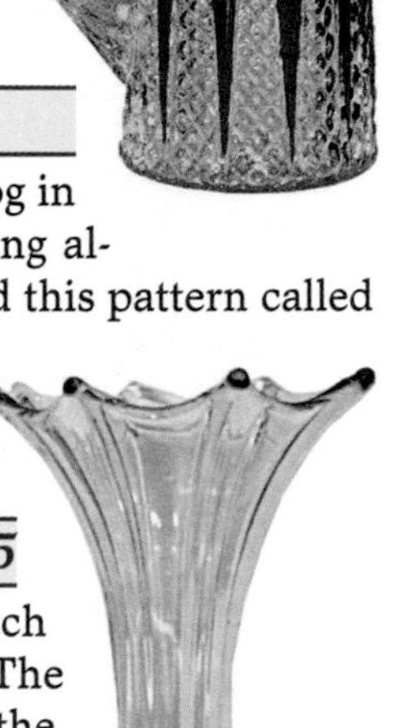

Imperial's #405

Imperial made a series of vases in 1909 that were pretty much alike except for size and a few details in the base makeup. The example shown has a "star and thistle" design on the inside of the base. These vases came in 9" - 13" sizes and many were also used in carnival glass production.

Imperial's #427

This is the only shape that was available in the 1909 Imperial catalog. Although I don't like numbered patterns, I'll stick with the factory number unless an established name is revealed.

Imperial's #438

This pattern was made by the Imperial Glass Company (1910 - 1914) and reissued in the 1950s in carnival glass (the original bowls were made in crystal only).

Imperial's #453

This pattern is singed NUCUT, so we know it's from that particular Imperial line. The nappy is the only shape reported to date and only found in crystal.

Imperial's #483

This is one of a line of specialty bowls from the Imperial Glass Company in 1911 or 1912. This one measures 7½" across and is signed "Nucut."

Imperial's #678

The "Part-Cut" line was produced in crystal, green, or rose glass in water sets, table sets, berry sets, compote, covered candy jar, vase, celery tray, pickle tray, one-handled nappy, and the two-handled nappy shown. This pattern was the company's D'Angelo pattern. The date of production was 1925.

Imperial's #2122

Imperial's #2122 was part of Imperial's Nu-Cut line in 1904. Shapes include a 6" bowl (shown), handled pickle dish, two-handled nappy, oval spoon tray, 5" nappy, 5" compote, berry bowl, creamer and open sugar, and a 6" vase.

Imperial's #3888

This pattern shown in a 1909 factory catalog can be found on a 7½" rose bowl (called a nut bowl in the catalog), 10" master bowl, 9" crimped berry bowl, and 4½" individual berry bowl. The primary design seems to resemble a maltese-like cross, separated by a hobstar in an oval.

Imperial's Bellaire (#0464)

Bellaire is shown in the July 1914 Butler Brothers catalog in a banquet size punch set which is accompanied by 12 cups (the bowl and base weigh 21 lbs!) and an 8½" deep salad bowl. The punch set is 15" tall and the bowl top measures 15" across. All pieces including the cups are marked "Nu-Cut." When I bought this set years ago it was the first time I had seen this pattern in person and believe me, the design is a masterpiece of Imperial craftsmanship.

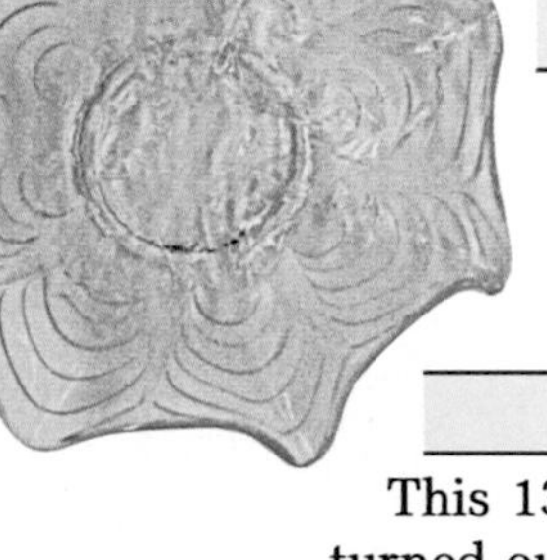

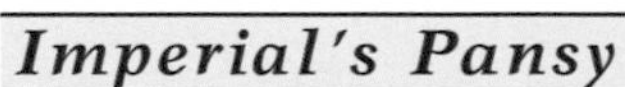

Imperial's Pansy

This realistic 1908 Imperial Glass pattern is widely known in carnival glass. It shows the Scroll Embossed exterior pattern. Crystal pieces are a bit scarce but still bring less than their iridized counterparts.

Imperial's Thunderbolt

This 13" bouquet vase is a fine example of the geometric pedestal vases being turned out by the company in Bellaire, Ohio. This pattern was advertised as Imperial's #4047 in 1909.

Imperial's Wicker Basket (#428½)

This was shown in a 1909 Imperial Glass Company catalog as their #428½ pattern. Only the handled basket that held matching salt and pepper shakers seems to have been made. Finding the complete set is difficult but even the basket alone is worth owning.

Indiana

Indiana was produced as U.S. Glass pattern #15029, in 1897. It can be found in clear and rare ruby stained glass. Shapes include a perfume, carafe, catsup bottle, finger bowl, table set, celery tray, bowls in five sizes, celery vase, cruet, compote, oval bowls in three sizes, nappy, jelly dish, water set, shakers, sauce, syrup, oblong tray, and ice tub.

Indiana's #115

This often-seen pattern was made by the Indiana Glass Company of Dunkirk, Indiana, about 1915. It can be found in the basic pieces: a table set, berry set, and water set. The most identifiable portion of the design would be the two plain almond ovals at each side of the whirling star circle.

Indiana's #123

This 1890s pattern by the Indiana Glass Company very closely resembles an Imperial pattern known as Octagon. Shapes of #123 include a table set, celery vase, cruet, covered compotes, 12" plate, celery tray, jelly compote, cake stands, goblet, wine, pitchers, tumbler, berry set, punch sets, covered compotes, toy table sets, water sets, and punch sets. Some collectors call this pattern Panelled Daisies and Finecut.

Indiana's #161

Indiana's #161 from 1915 was made in crystal, gilded, or ruby stained. Shapes include a water set, table set, footed berry set, cake stand, covered compote, and various footed bowl shapes.

Indiana's #165

This was made by the Indiana Glass Company of Dunkirk, Indiana, in the early 1900s. Shapes include a table set, breakfast set, water set (three pitcher sizes), salts (two sizes), celery, olive, pickle dish, berry set (two sizes), vase, footed jelly, footed sauce, handled compote, open compote (three sizes), syrup, berry creamer and sugar, water bottle, and several sizes in utility creamers and sugars.

Indiana Silver

This was made by the Indiana Glass Company in Dunkirk, Indiana, in about 1918. It is their silver overlay pattern #151. Shapes include a table set, berry set, goblet, sherbet, and footed rose bowl. The design has a modern look that fit into the Art Deco design of the time.

Indian Sunset

Dating from 1905, this geometric pattern is quite similar to several others. Shapes include a table set, water set, berry set, celery tray, bonbon, salt shakers, and pickle dish. Some examples may be gold trimmed.

Innovation #407

This was another part of the McKee Innovation line (there were numbers 407, 408, 410, 411, 414, 415, 417, and others) that featured pressed patterns with wheel-cut flowers. Here is a 10" cylinder vase with a star band, but this same design came in a compote, bonbon, footed rose bowl, creamer and open sugar, nappy, celery tray, 8" bowl, fernery, basket, and a lamp with matching shade.

Innovation #420

This was one of the many patterns in a line McKee called Innovation that was made in 1917. Shapes include a creamer and open sugar, an 8" bowl, a stemmed trumpet vase, a 12" corset vase (shown), a 10" three-footed salad bowl, celery tray, 10" oval salad bowl, and a large stemmed compote with separate footed stand. All items are pressed with a wheel-cut flower in the design.

Innovation #1024

This was made late in McKee's Innovation line (1917). It can be found in a berry set, table set, and table pieces, some of which are footed.

Inside Ribbing

This Beaumont Glass pattern from 1900 is also called Pressed Optic. It can be found in opalescent glass as well as clear, vaseline, emerald green, and blue glass. Pieces may be plain or decorated with enameling as shown. Shapes include a table set, berry set, celery vase, syrup, cruet, pickle dish, and a toothpick holder. This was Beaumont's #101 pattern.

Intaglio (Northwood)

This Northwood pattern was first made in 1898. It is best known in opalescent glass, but can also be found in gilded glass and decorated custard. Shapes are stemmed and include a berry set, table set, water set, shakers, cruet, a jelly compote, and novelties (bowls).

Intaglio Butterflies

Intaglio Butterflies was made by the Dugan/Diamond Company beginning in 1905, using the goofus process. It had many bowls, compotes, and sauces showing fruits, flowers, and butterflies. The patterns are exterior intaglio ones and only the designs were painted, unlike most goofus treatments.

Intaglio Morning Glory

This well-designed Dugan Intaglio line pattern has morning glories around the bowl and one in the center of the piece. Please note the bowl's edges are nipped like other Dugan designs and part of the goofus treatment remains.

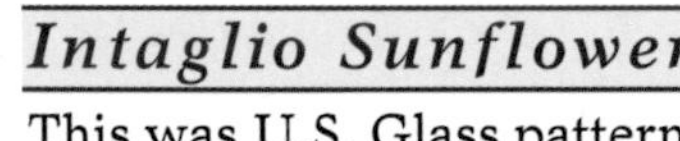

Intaglio Sunflower

This was U.S. Glass pattern #15125, made in 1911 in clear and decorated crystal. Shapes include a table set, water set, toothpick holder, and tall straw holder with a lid.

Inverted Fan and Feather

This pattern was made by Northwood (1890s) in crystal, green, and custard, and then by Dugan in opalescent glass. Shapes are a berry set, table set, water set, toothpick holder, jelly compote, shakers, and a punch set. The shaker, sugar, toothpick and tumbler have been reproduced.

Inverted Feather

Cambridge's #2651 can be found in carnival glass as well as crystal. Crystal pieces are known in punch sets, tall wine decanter, goblets, whiskey tumbler, covered cracker jar, footed sherbet, tall footed sherbet, and oil bottle. This pattern is quite popular with collectors.

Inverted Fern

This well-known design was possibly made by Boston and Sandwich Glass (no proof is known) in the 1860s. Shapes include a table set, egg cup, sauces, champagne, open compote, goblet, honey dish, 6" plate, water set, master salt dip, and a wine. The goblet was reproduced.

Inverted Fish

Cambridge's Inverted Fish is a companion pattern to the Inverted Peacock water set. This one is harder to find. It was made in the tankard pitcher shown and matching tumblers. The pattern is also known as Inverted Trout. The handle on the pitcher is shaped like a fish. In a 1915 Butler Brother catalog ad this set is shown with the tray with a honeycomb pattern. It will be hard to spot since it has nothing in the design that matches the pitcher or tumblers.

Inverted Peacock

Inverted Peacock was made by Cambridge in 1914 (its #2837). It can be found only in the beautiful tankard pitcher and tumblers. This was a companion set to the Inverted Fish water set shown elsewhere. The tumbler (shown) is quite difficult to come by. The same tray with a honeycomb design that goes with the Inverted Fish pitcher is shown with this set as well. I have yet to see one in person.

Inverted Strawberry

Inverted Strawberry was from Cambridge Glass in 1908 and can be found in carnival glass, clear, colors (rare), and decorated glass (very scarce). Shapes include a table set, toy table set, candlesticks, compote, footed creamer and sugar, footed bonbon, jelly compote, oil bottle, water set, wine, goblet, celery vase, berry set, custard cup, squat basket, stemmed sweet pea vase, rose bowl, covered powder jar, and footed fruit bowl. It has been reproduced in various shapes by Fenton Art Glass.

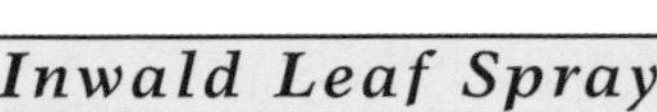

Inverted Thumbprint and Star

This goblet can be found in clear, canary, amber, blue, and apple green. There is a star between each of the inverted thumbprints.

Inwald Leaf Spray

This nicely done pattern has been traced to a 1914 catalog from the Czechoslovakian firm of Josef Inwald. It is found in bowls, a water set, plates, and the goblet shown. Some pieces have gilding and some are stained. Inwald was a very large firm, making many patterns in crystal and then carnival glass.

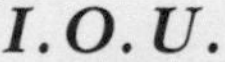

I.O.U.

This scarce and very desirable West Virginia Glass Company pattern (#219) and dates from 1898. It was made in a complete table service that includes a table set, water set, berry set, celery vase, syrup, and pickle dish in vaseline, crystal, amber, and emerald green.

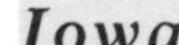

Iowa

Iowa was made by U.S. Glass (#15069) as part of their States series. It is found in crystal, rose flashed, and gilded. Shapes include a table set, water set, berry set, celery vase, pickle dish, goblet, cake stand, compote, and the wine shown which has gilding on the ribs.

Iowa City Elephant

This is not the same as the Jumbo line from Canton Glass. This piece was apparently a lone item from Iowa City Glass, according to Miriam Righter in her book about that company. The goblet has Iowa City's Oval and Bar border that pretty much seals the matter.

Iris

Iris, from Bryce, Higbee (1917) and Paden City (1918), their #206 line, is commonly called Pineapple. Shapes include a table set, water set, salvers, bowls, compotes, plates, and a lily vase. It was made in crystal, with some pieces found in colors. Some pieces are reported to have been made by Kemple. A pitcher in amber and the rose bowl in crystal are shown.

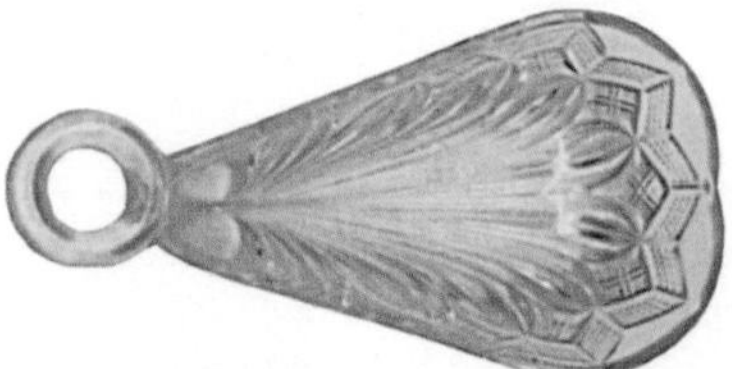

Ivanhoe

This pattern, from Dalzell, Gilmore, and Leighton in 1897, is often confused with Amboy. Shapes include a table set, cake salver, celery vase, cracker jar, creamer, cup, jelly compote, nappy, 10" plate, relish, sauce, syrup, toothpick holder, spoon tray (shown), and a water set.

Iverna

This pattern is credited to Ripley in 1911 as #303, to Paden City, and Imperial Glass after 1915, and since pieces are known with the "Krys-tol" mark some pieces had to be made by either Ohio Flint Glass or Jefferson Glass! Shapes include a berry set, table set, water set, compote, footed fruit bowl, punch set, biscuit jar, vase, handled sherbet, pickle dish, celery tray, spoon tray, and handled jelly.

Jacob's Ladder

Jacob's Ladder was from Bryce, McKee & Company, then U.S. Glass in 1891, then Diamond Glass of Canada (U.S. Glass #4778) and was then reproduced by Imperial. It was made in clear, amber, blue, canary, green, pink, and rarely in carnival glass. Shapes include a cologne bottle, castor set, covered or open bowls, celery vase, covered or open compotes, cruet, goblet, honey dish, jam jar, mug, water set, 6" plate, platter, relish dish, master salt, sauces, syrup, wine, and rose bowl. Pieces with the Maltese Cross finial will demand greater prices.

Japanese

Japanese was made by George Duncan & Sons in 1880 and is known by several other names, including Butterfly and Fan and Japanese Fan. Shapes include a bowl, table set, celery vase, covered or open compotes, goblet, pickle jar with lid, plate, water pitcher, and flat or footed sauce. Finials on Japanese pieces are square with a half-sphere on the top.

Jefferson Wheel

Jefferson Glass's #260 design was made in 1905. It is found primarily in opalescent glass, but as you can see, it was also made in crystal, and has been reported in carnival glass for years without a single example known to date.

Jenkin's #286

This was made by the Jenkins Glass Company, a concern well-known for combinations of geometric and engraved pieces. It was their #286 line but with a different cutting than the Dahlia cut. This one is found in a table set, water set, compote, vase, and various other shapes.

Jenkins's Swan

Several companies had a try at these open Swan pieces. This one was from the Jenkins Glass Company in 1915. It was the #460 and advertised as a 12 ounce Swan dish. Many of these swan pieces were used to hold salt, relish, jelly, or even sugar, but the intended use of this one isn't known.

Jenny Lind

Numerous articles have been made to honor this singer, and the compote shown is one. It was made by Challinor and Taylor and is shown in the opal glass treatment with enameled flowers on the base. Others were made in crystal, frosted crystal, and in colors by various makers. Most date from the late 1880s to the 1890s.

Jersey Lily

This pattern was once attributed to LaBelle Glass, but has now been found to be from Riverside Glass Works. It was made in 1883. It was named after Lillie Langtry, and is also known as Center Medallion. Shapes include a pitcher, covered stemmed pieces in all sizes, a table set, and other table pieces.

Jersey Swirl

This Windsor Glass pattern from 1887 also is known as Windsor Swirl, Swirl and Diamonds, and Windsor. Shapes include bowls, table set, cake stand, candlesticks, cruet, covered and open compotes, goblet, mini spittoon (toothpick), and a water set. It was made in crystal, amber, canary, and blue. Several shapes of this pattern were reproduced in the 1960s and 1970s by L. G. Wright.

Jeweled Butterflies

This was the Mikado pattern from Indiana Glass of Dunkirk, Indiana. It is also known as Late Butterfly. Shapes include a table set, berry sugar and creamer, water set, handled nappy, cruet, shakers, and 5", 6", 7", and 8" bowls. I believe this pattern dates to 1907 or shortly after.

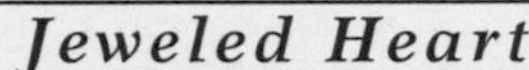

Jeweled Heart

Dugan/Diamond produced this pattern for many years in carnival glass, opalescent glass, and crystal where the shapes are bowls, 9" rose bowl, salt shakers, berry set, cruet set (cruet, shakers, tray, and toothpick holder), water set, table set, syrup, and plate. Jewelled Heart is found in aqua glass, goofus, and gold decorated, and can even be found with enamel work. It has been reproduced by L. G. Wright in various shapes.

Jeweled Loop

This Imperial pattern was made in 1909 as #261. It can be found in a table set, celery vase, water set, goblet, jelly compote (low), 8" compote, berry set, pickle dish, and 11" celery tray. Some pieces have gold trim.

Jewel with Dewdrop

This was made by Cooperative Flint Glass and then reissued by U.S. Glass in 1907 as a States pattern called Kansas. Jewel with Dewdrop can be found in a berry set, table set, toothpick holder, wine, cake stand, celery vase, bread plate, open or covered compote, goblet, covered jelly jar, nappy, shakers, syrup, and preserve dish (oval). In addition, U.S. Glass added a small mug, and some of their production was color stained glass.

Jockey Cap

Jockey Cap is similar in design to the Helmet butter dish and is believed to also be from King Glass. It is known in blue, crystal, amber, and vaseline, with only a handful reported in each color.

Johnson Child's Mug

This pattern is also called Dart and Ball, and I believe it may be a product of the King Glass Company. It is found in toy pieces that include a table set, mug, and goblet. Colors are clear (rare), cobalt, opal, and milk glass.

Jubilee

Jubilee was from McKee in 1894 and is also known as Iris or Radiant Daisy and Button. Shapes include a table set, celery tray, compotes, goblet, pickle dish, plate, wine, and water set.

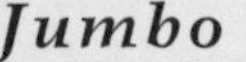

Jumbo

Jumbo is attributed to Aetna as well as Canton Glass (1884). It can be found in clear, acid finished, amber, blue, or canary (all colors are quite rare). Shapes include a table set, covered compotes, a water pitcher, and the famous spoon rack shown.

Jumbo Castor Set

This beautiful, three-piece castor set was part of the elephant craze in glassware in the late 1800s. It is found in crystal, amber, blue, and canary.

Kaleidoscope

Kaleidoscope is found in carnival glass on bowls only, but can be found in crystal on bowls, rose bowls, table sets, and water sets. The overall design is really a series of rings of pattern, none of which is all that distinctive, but taken together are pleasant enough. The only information I can supply to date is that this is shown in Butler Brothers catalog ads starting in 1915.

Kanawha

Kanawha was made by Riverside Glass in 1906. The moulds were sold to McKee in 1915 where the line was expanded as the #75 Colonial pattern. Examples from Riverside are known in crystal, ruby stain, rose stain, gilded, and marigold carnival. It can be found in a table set, water set, punch set, berry set, cruet, 5" candlesticks, and a lamp.

Kayak

This unusual pattern is from Imperial Glass. It is known in water sets, compotes, berry set, cake stand, and tray. The primary design is a divided oval that is then sectioned with diamonds of file and hobstar between the groups of oval.

Keg

This imaginative design is shaped like a keg or barrel. This interesting lamp was made by Central Glass Company, circa 1880, as their #725 pattern. It was shown in factory catalogs as being available in five sizes.

Kentucky

Kentucky was from U.S. Glass (#15051) in 1897. It is found in clear or emerald green glass. The clear can be amber stained or ruby stained, and in rare instances, cobalt blue stained. Kentucky was retooled from the Millard pattern. Shapes include bowls, table set, cake stand (two sizes), celery tray (two sizes), celery vase, covered compotes (four sizes), open compote (four sizes), goblet, olive dish, water set, cruet, plates, shakers, sauces, syrup, toothpick holder, and wine.

Keyhole

This Dugan/Diamond pattern is more familiar to carnival glass collectors, but can also be found in opalescent glass, goofus, and crystal, like the bowl shown. The only shapes are large dome-based bowls that may be round, ruffled, or shaped like a banana bowl. Keyhole is an exterior pattern and in carnival glass has an interior design called Raindrops.

Keystone

Keystone was from McKee and Brothers in 1901 and is found in an extended table service. Shown is the squared cruet or ketchup (stopper missing). It can be crystal, etched, or ruby stained.

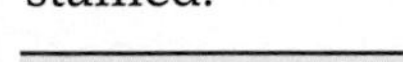

King Arthur

King Arthur was made by Duncan and Miller in 1908 as its #65 pattern in an extended table service that even included a punch bowl (shown) and cups as well as salt shakers.

King's Block

King's block was originally King's Glass pattern #312. It continued as a U.S. Glass design in 1891, in crystal or vaseline glass. Shapes include a table set, cruet, oval bowls, pickle tray, goblet, and wine.

King's Crown

This very familiar pattern is also called Excelsior or Ruby Thumbprint, and came from U.S. Glass (Adams factory) in 1891. Many shapes are known, including a table set, pickle castor, fruit basket, footed orange bowl, toothpick holder, square honey dish, cup and saucer, mustard jar, lamps (very rare parlor lamp), and individual salt dip. King's Crown is found in plain crystal, amber stained crystal, or ruby stained crystal. It has been reproduced.

King's Curtain

I believe this pattern dates to the 1880s. Shapes include a table set, water set, goblet, 7" plate, shakers, sauce, wine, cake stand, and bowl.

Kitten on a Pillow

This was made by Richards & Hartley Glass in the 1880s. Richards & Hartley became factory E of U.S. Glass and then Tarentum Glass in 1894. The novelty piece is known in crystal and colors and features a cat lying on its back on a cushion while holding a button and daisy holder for toothpicks. This pattern has been reproduced.

Klear-Kut #705

This was introduced as Klear-Kut by the New Martinsville Glass Company in 1906. This design is found on a water set as well as a table set. Some pieces were given a gold-trimmed treatment.

Klondike

Klondike was made by Dalzell, Gilmore & Leighton in 1898. This pattern has many names including Amberette, English Hobnail Cross, and Dalzell #75. It can be found in clear, clear with acid finish, and amber stain. Shapes include square bowls, table set, cake stand, champagne, oblong celery tray, condiment set, cruet, cup, goblet, water set (round or square pitcher), relish tray, shakers, syrup, toothpick holder, tray, wine, and vases in four sizes. The sugar bowl has been reproduced.

Knife Rest

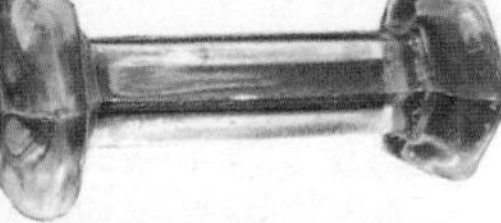

Knife Rest can be found in many sizes and a large variety of designs. Most are plain patterned or geometric designs. Most are crystal but various colors are known as well. Shown is a rather plain vaseline example with six panels.

Knobby Bulls-Eye

This was a U.S. Glass pattern advertised as their #15155, made in 1915. It was available in an extended table service including a table set, toothpick holder, berry set, two types of salt shaker, celery tray, wine, decanter, and stemmed compote. Both plain crystal and decorated crystal are known as well a rare tumbler and a sugar with lid (shown) in vaseline. This pattern was also known as Cromwell.

Knotted Beads

Knotted Beads was made by Fenton Glass in 1911. It was primarily a carnival glass vase pattern, although it is sometimes found in crystal. Here I show an extremely rare red example with amberina edges and base. Red carnival pieces are also known. These vases range in size from 9" to 14" tall.

Kokomo

This ordinary pattern, made by Jenkins Glass as the #400 line in the 1920s, is like many others relying on allover diamonds. Shapes reported in a Jenkins ad are a table set, water set, berry set, covered casserole, jam jar, jelly compote, nappy, covered compote, and pickle dish.

Krys-tol Colonial

This was first made by Ohio Flint Glass in 1906 as part of their Krys-tol line (Kenneth, Gloria, and Chippendale). When the company closed in 1907, the moulds went to Jefferson and then in 1909 some were purchased by John Fenton for the Millersburg plant. The punch bowl shown became the exterior for Millersburg's famous Big Thistle punch bowl in carnival glass. In addition, Ohio Flint made other Colonial lines, including their famous 1776 Colonial.

La Belle Rose

Primarily a goofus pattern from 1910, this is a sister pattern of the Carnation design. It can be found on large plates, large bowls, and smaller bowls as well as a smaller saucer-size plate.

Lacy Daisy

Lacy Daisy was made in 1912 by Westmoreland as their #909 pattern and can be seen in old catalog ads from that factory. Shapes include a table set, jam jar, jelly compote, cruet, rose bowl, cake plate, puff box, service plates, three-legged bowls, individual salt, and toy table set. Rare staining of ruby or amber is reported.

Lacy Dewdrop

This is a Cooperative Flint Glass Company pattern dating from 1890 that is found in crystal, milk glass, and scarce iridized items. Shapes include a table set, berry set, mug, water set, sauce, covered berry set, and open or covered compotes. Original pieces were only made in crystal. This pattern has been widely reproduced.

Lacy Medallion

Lacy Medallion has no feet and is lettered. It was produced by U.S. Glass in 1905 according to McCain. It is also known as Jewel and is very similar to the Colorado pattern. It is found in crystal, cobalt blue, ruby stain, green, clambroth, and a vaseline child's mug shown. Shapes include a mug, salt shaker, toothpick holder, wine, and a toy table set. The toothpick holder, creamer and wine have been reproduced.

Lacy Spiral

Lacy Spiral, also known as Colossus, was made in the 1880s in an extended table service including table sets, water sets, berry sets, covered compote, and goblet. It was possibly a Canadian pattern from Burlington Glass Works.

Ladders (Tarentum's #292)

This was Tarentum Glass Company's #292 pattern made in 1901. Shapes include a table set, water set, vase, celery vase, berry set, cup, and cruet. Pieces are often gold trimmed.

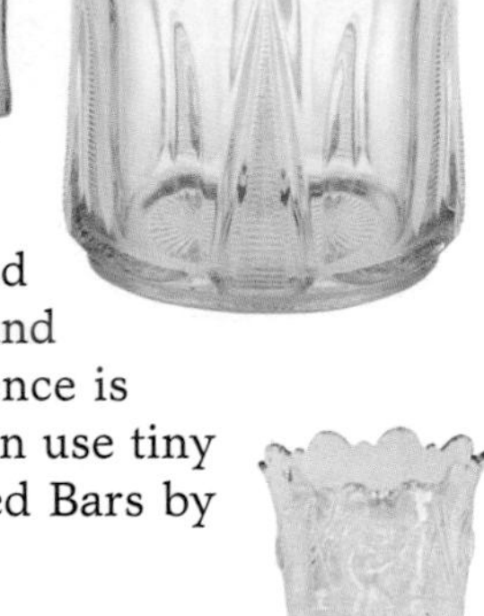

Ladder with Diamonds

This was Duncan and Miller's #52 pattern, and the Tarentum Glass Company's, both circa 1903. Shapes include a table set, water set, celery vase, berry set, cruet, cup, goblet, 9¼" plate, toothpick holder, shakers, and vase. Some pieces are gold trimmed like the creamer shown. According to William Heacock on pages 90 and 91 of his book *Old Pattern Glass* (1981), the easiest way to tell the difference is Tarentum used tiny buttons within their diamond pattern whereas Duncan use tiny diamonds inside their diamond pattern. This is called Fine Cut and Ribbed Bars by some collectors.

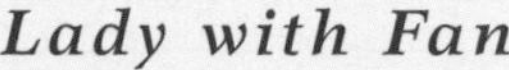

Lady with Fan

Shown is a stemmed celery that was advertised with this name. It may be a part of a pattern known as Girl with a Fan made by the Bellaire Glass Company in 1886 in a goblet, but I can't be sure.

Lamb

This shape matches mugs from the Iowa City Flint Glass Works and was made about 1881. It is found in clear, blue, turquoise, and the amethyst shown. It stands 3" tall and has a 2¾" diameter. A variant is known without beading on the handle and with more stylized and less detailed grass in front and beneath the lamb.

Lantern

This candy holder is found in at least two sizes and was a favorite of children. Like many other pieces designed to hold candy, some pieces have been reproduced. Major manufacturers of the original pieces include Westmoreland, Victory Glass, J.H. Millstein, L.E. Smith, J.C. Crosetti, Eagle Glass, and Play Toy. Even Cambridge had a try at a few pieces. Lantern pieces are all thought to be old.

The Last Supper Plate

Based on Leonardo da Vinci's famous painting, this popular plate with grape borders was first made by Model Flint Glass Co. and then by the Indiana Glass Company where it was in production until 1960, a production period of nearly 50 years. It is 11" long x 7" wide. It has of course been reproduced. Old examples are easy to spot because of their clarity and the quality of the glass.

Late Block with Thumbprint

This pattern is found in a berry set, a table set, water set, pickle dish, celery dish, and possibly other shapes. The simple design of circles in squares is not a pattern that gets collectors too excited. Nonetheless, it has its place here.

Late Honeycomb

This pattern can be seen in water sets and berry sets. From the shape of the water pitcher, it is certain this pattern came along after 1915.

L

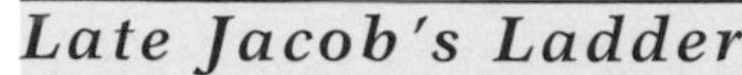

Late Jacob's Ladder

This U.S. Glass pattern is called Jacob's Ladder Variant by carnival glass collectors. It can be found in a table set, bowls, a rose bowl, and even a dresser set (perfume, powder box, pin tray). It is similar to the original design but without the fine file pattern inside the diamonds. The creamer and sugar were reproduced.

Lattice

Lattice is also called Diamond Bar and was made by King and Son in 1880 and then U.S. Glass in 1891. It is found in a table set, plate, platter, cake stand, celery vase, egg cup, water set, sauce, wine, cordial, salt shaker, and covered compote.

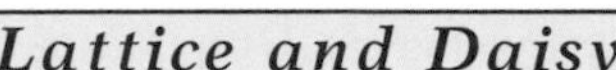

Lattice and Daisy

Lattace and Daisy was from the Dugan Glass Company in opalescent glass and then by the Diamond Glass Company (Dugan's successor) in carnival colors. Here I show a previously unreported crystal tumbler.

Lattice and Notches

This pattern, also known as Lattice and Lens, can be found in a table set, berry set, and goblet. The pattern dates to 1880 and the maker isn't known. Both plain crystal and gilded glass are known.

Lattice-Edge

Lattice-Edge was made by U.S. Glass in crystal, opaque, or mosaic (slag), and can be found in several sizes. Date of production was early 1900s, and opal colors included white and turquoise, according to ads.

Lattice Medallion with Buds

This variant of the regular Northwood pattern is found on opalescent pieces. This crystal treatment (often with goofus) has added buds on the lattice work and omits the starburst design inside the medallions. Production must date from the 1908 – 1909 period.

Laverne

This Bryce Brothers pattern, also known as Star in Honeycomb, dates from the late 1880s. Shapes include oval or round bowls, table set, cake stand, celery vase, both covered or open compotes, goblet, pickle tray, water set, relish dish, flat or footed sauce, and wine.

Leaf and Beads

Leaf and Beads was made by Northwood in 1911, primarily in carnival glass and opalescent glass. Here is the flared, footed bowl in a treatment Northwood called "Rosita" (1924).

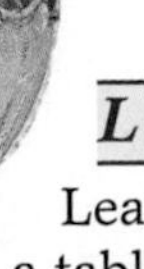

Leaf and Dart

Leaf and Dart is credited to Richards and Hartley in 1875 and U.S. Glass in the 1890s. Shapes include a table set, footed bowl, celery vase, covered or open compotes, egg cup, goblet, honey dish, finger lamp, milk pitcher, water set, relish tray, master salt, sauce, syrup, and a wine.

Leaf and Rib

The maker of this nice pattern is Central Glass. Pieces are found in clear, amber, blue, and canary. Shapes include a berry set, table set, water set, shakers, celery vase, and a pickle dish.

Leaf and Star

This pattern is New Martinsville Glass #711. It is also known as Tobin. It dates from 1910 and is found in clear, ruby stained, and has been listed in carnival glass (I'm skeptical). Shapes include a banana boat, berry set, fruit bowl, nut bowl, celery vase and tray, jelly compote, cruet, dresser jar, goblet, hair receiver, humidor, plate, water set, toothpick holder, vase, and wine.

Leaf Bracket

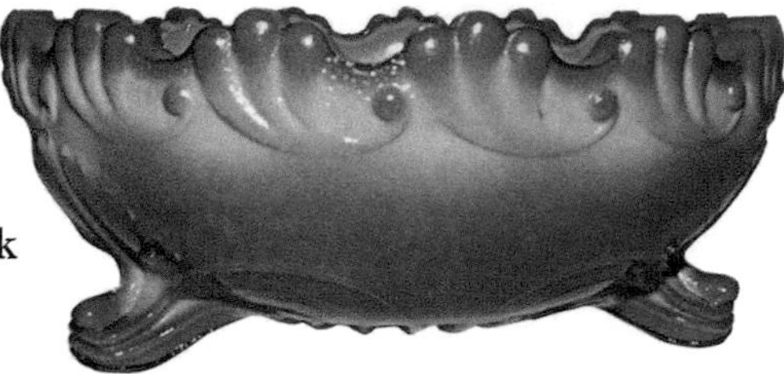

Leaf Bracket was made by the Indiana Tumbler and Goblet Company (Greentown) in 1900 in crystal, opalescent, Nile green, or chocolate glass. Shapes include a table set, cruet, berry set, celery tray, shakers, toothpick holder, water set, and tri-cornered bowl.

Leaf Flanged

This nice butter dish has an almost total covering of leaf design on the base and lid, with a twig finial. Vaseline is the only color reported at this time and the butter is the only shape reported to me. Bryce is reported to be the maker.

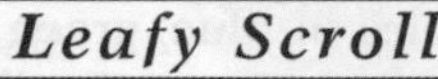

Leafy Scroll

This was U.S. Glass's #15034 pattern. Shapes include a table set, berry set, water set, goblet, wine, and toothpick holder. The company ad says "One of Our 1896 Patterns," so I know this is the date of original production.

Lenox

Lenox was made by McKee Glass in 1898. It apparently can be found in opal as well as crystal (the tankard pitcher shown has a touch of opal on the handle and a fine silver lip). Shapes include a table set, water set, berry set, toothpick holder, breakfast set, mug, cruet, jelly compote, and individual salt dip. It is also reported to have been made by Cambridge as their #2581 pattern.

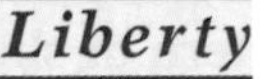

Liberty

This pattern, which is also known as Cornucopia by some collectors, was made by McKee & Brothers in 1892 and then by Cambridge Glass in 1903. Shapes include a berry set, table set, water set, water tray, goblet, wine, champagne, and cordial. Some pieces are gilded.

Lighthouse and Sailboat

Lighthouse and Sailboat can be found in three sizes (2½" tall, 3⅛" tall, and 3⅝" tall) in clear, amber, or blue. It has the same handle formation and shape as the Dutch Mill mug, but there are other differences. A lighthouse on one side and a sailboat on the other are ringed by a floral wreath.

Lightning

Lightning was first made by Tiffin, then U.S. Glass in 1893 It is also known as Chain Lightning. It is found in an extended table service that includes both wines and cordials.

Multiple Scroll

This well-done pattern was from the Canton Glass Company in the early 1890s. It is found in various shapes including a table set, bowls, celery vase, pickle dish, wine, mug, and a square plate. Colors reported are clear, amber, and blue. This was Canton's #130 pattern.

Multiple Scroll with Swirl Center

This piece is also from Canton Glass. It is like the other square plate but has a different marie (base) design that is called a swirl center.

Mutt Jug

The Mutt Jug was produced by New Martinsville Glass Company as #46 (there was also a Jeff mug #36). As you can probably guess, the Mutt was a tall jug and the Jeff a squat one. No other shapes are found in this pattern.

Nail

Nail was made by U.S. Glass in 1892 as #15002, in clear, engraved, and ruby stained. It is sometimes called Recessed Pillar-Thumbprint Band. Shapes include a berry set, table set, cake stand, celery vase, covered or open compotes, cordial, goblet, water set, bread plate, dinner plate, sauce, wine, and oil lamp.

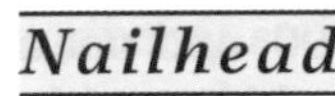

Nailhead

Bryce, Higbee and Company made Nailhead in the 1880s in clear, decorated glass, and aquamarine. Shapes include a goblet, berry set, table set, cake stand, celery vase, covered or open compotes, cordial, water set, bread tray, bread and dinner plates, sauce, and wine.

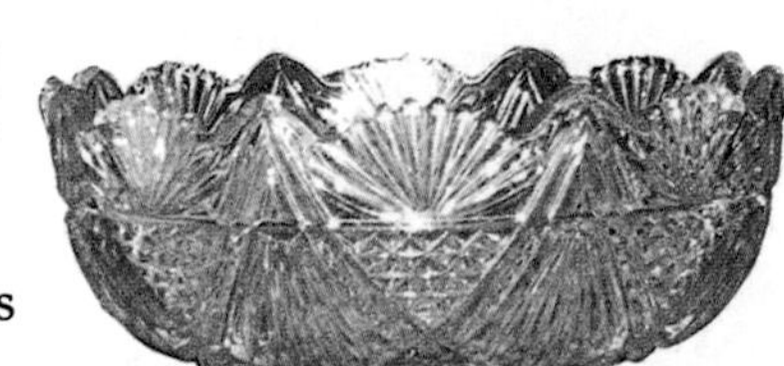

Napoleon

Napoleon was made by McKee Brothers in 1896. It can be found in a table set, water set, bowls (round or oval), a goblet, and probably other shapes. The design somewhat resembles the same company's Champion pattern.

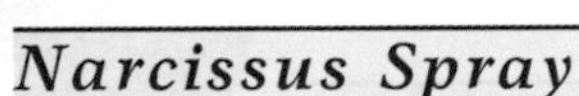

Narcissus Spray

Narcissus Spray was an Indiana Glass pattern made in 1915 and several years after. Besides clear glass, decorated pieces are known. Shapes include a berry set, table set, water set, decanter, jelly compote, plate, celery, wine, and round or oval bowls.

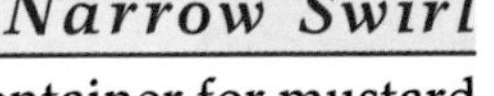

Narrow Swirl

This tall narrow creamer was reportedly used as a container for mustard, honey, relish, and horseradish and had a metal lid. It is hard to imagine how such a lid fit, but I will accept the premise until I hear otherwise.

National Star

National Star was made by the Riverside Glass Works (#508) in 1900, in clear, gilded, ruby stain, ruby stain over vaseline (rare), and vaseline glass. Shapes include a table set, a water set, a berry set, and a jelly compote.

Navarre

This pattern is from McKee and Brothers Glass in 1900 and is found in crystal and ruby stained. Only a table set, toothpick holder, and handled nappy are known.

Nearcut #2636

This Nearcut pattern was made by Cambridge Glass in 1906. It can be found in a table set, bowls, water set, cruet, handled basket, wine, celery vase, salt shaker, berry set, and massive 8" vase.

Nearcut #2697

Nearcut #2697 was from Cambridge in 1909 and is similar to its Buzz Saw (shown elsewhere). This pattern is found on a basic toy set or water set, table set, and berry set.

Nearcut Daisy

This well-done pattern was made by the Cambridge Glass Company in 1910. It is found in bowls, a table set, water set, cruet, oil lamp, and a rose bowl. This was Cambridge's #2760 pattern, but in the 1930s, the bowl shapes were made in Finland's Iittala-Karhula plant, and examples so marked are found in carnival glass. It is also known as Red Sunflower.

Near Cut Wreath

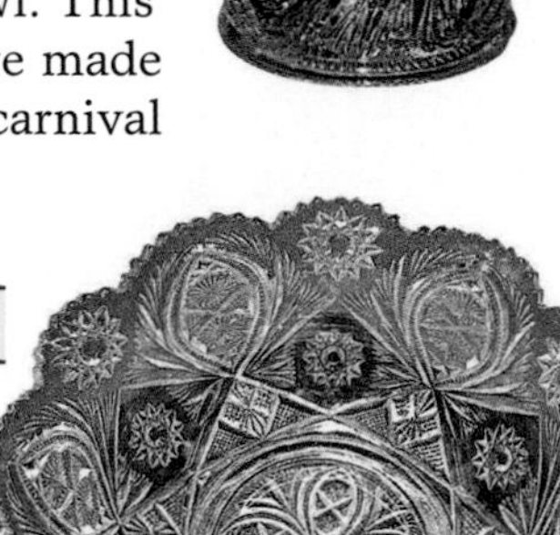

This Millersburg Glass Company design was mostly used on the exterior of Holly Whirl and Holly Sprig bowls in carnival glass. It is very rare in crystal, found only in bowls (four or five), one plate, and a rose bowl shape advertised in 1910.

Nelly

Nelly was made by McKee Glass in 1894 in an extended table service in crystal only. Shapes include a table set, celery vase, cake stand, shakers, and compote. It is also known as Sylvan or Florence by some collectors.

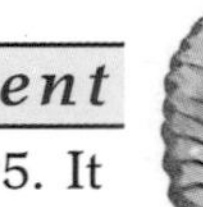

New Crescent

New Crescent was from Bryce, Higbee in 1900 – 1905. It can be found only in crystal in a berry set, table set, 7½" compote, grape boat (5" x 8"), and a square bowl.

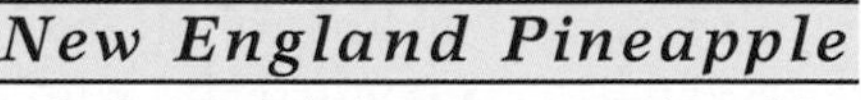

New England Centennial

This pattern is found on the hand lamp shown as well as a goblet (both are very scarce). I believe these items date from 1876 but have no proof. The lamp has this date in the design, but the goblet reads "1776."

New England Pineapple

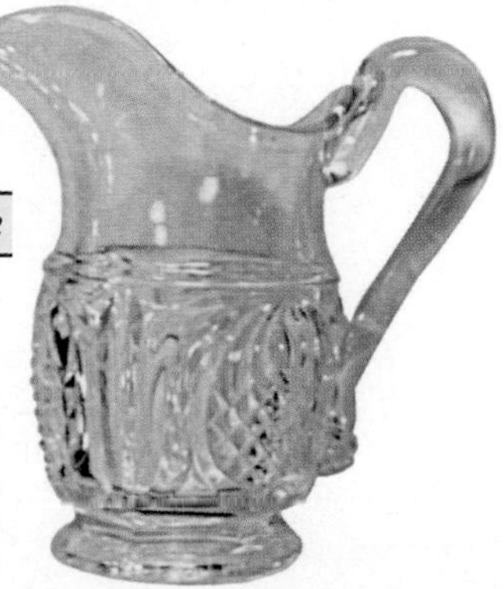

This pattern is from either New England Glass or Boston & Sandwich (1850 – 1870) and is also known as Loop and Jewel, Pineapple, or Sawtooth. Shapes include a castor bottle, oil bottle, berry set, fruit bowl, table set, castor set, champagne, covered compotes, open compotes, cordial, cruet, decanter (pint or quart), egg cup, goblets, honey dish, mug, pickle dish, milk pitcher, water set, 6" plate, salts, flat or footed sauce, spill holder, sweetmeat, bar tumbler, whiskey tumbler, and wine. The compote, goblet, sherbet, and wine were reproduced.

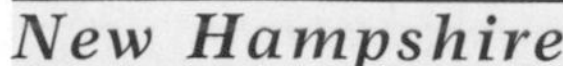

New Hampshire

New Hampshire was from U.S. Glass in 1903 as one of the States series patterns, #15084, in crystal, ruby stained, or gold trimmed glass. Shapes include a biscuit jar, carafe, square or round bowls, table set, cake stand, celery vase, covered or open compotes, breakfast set, cruet, custard cup, pickle dish, water set (bulbous or tankard), 8" plate, relish tray, shakers (three sizes), syrup, vase, toothpick holder, and wine.

New Jersey

New Jersey was another of the States patterns from U.S. Glass (#15070) in 1900 and is also known as Loops and Drops. Shapes include a water carafe, bowls, cake stand, celery tray, celery vase, covered and open compotes, cruet, fruit bowl on stand, goblet, olive dish, pickle tray, water set (two types of pitchers), plates, salt shakers, gas shade, two shapes of syrups, toothpick holder, and wines. It can be found in crystal, ruby stained, and some pieces with gilding.

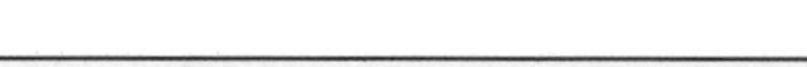

New Martinsville #169

Many glass companies had a try at similar candlesticks, but this 7" tall pair came from New Martinsville. These were marketed shortly before the factory was destroyed in a fire caused by the Ohio River flooding and causing stored lime to heat and burn. The factory reopened nine months later.

Niagara

This pattern should be called U.S. Niagara to distinguish it from the Fostoria pattern with the same name. U.S. Glass made this design as its #15162 in 1919. Shapes include a table set, berry set, syrup, cruet, cracker jar, plate, compote, cup, mustard jar, and handled jelly. Some pieces were gold trimmed.

Nickel Plate's Richmond

This pattern was made by Nickel Plate Glass (its #76 pattern) in 1889 and then U.S. Glass after 1891. It is also known as Akron Block, Bars and Buttons, Bar and Block, or Block and Double Bar. Shapes include a water set, table set, goblet, celery vase, wine, and water bottle. The pattern may run horizontal or vertical depending on the piece and treatments include crystal or ruby stain. Water pitchers are known in three sizes and shapes.

Nogi

This frequently found Indiana Glass pattern from 1906 is also called Pendant or Amulet. Its shapes include a table set, water set, goblet, pickle dish, plate, shakers, a 6" berry bowl, a vase, and a 6" compote. Nogi can be found in clear glass as well as ruby stain and gilded items. Production extended for several years.

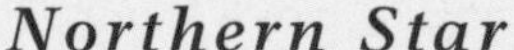

Northern Star

This Fenton Art Glass pattern is found in carnival glass in small bowls, in opalescent glass in bowls and plates (three sizes), and in crystal in both bowls and plates. The design of a six-pointed star with file inside is an easy one to remember.

North Star

This pattern is shown in Butler Brothers catalogs from 1910 to 1915 and is credited to Lancaster Glass. Shapes reported are a 9" bowl, the punch bowl shown, berry set, table set, and a water set.

Northwood Near-Cut #12

This 1906 Northwood pattern was made in crystal in a water set, table set, berry set, nappy (sometimes with advertising), compote, goblet, wine, salt shakers, celery vase, pickle dish, punch set, toothpick holder, and others (34 shapes are known). It can be rarely found in carnival glass in limited shapes.

Notched Bar

Notched Bar was made by McKee (its #492) in 1894. It is also known as Ball. It can be found in an extended table service including shakers, cruet, and oil set with tray. In 1889, Belmont Glass continued and expanded the line.

Notched Panel

Notched Panel can be found in a table set, toothpick holder, shakers, berry set, relish, and square bowls. It was made by Tarentum Glass in 1902, in clear or ruby stained glass,

Nu-Cut #537

As part of Imperial Glass Company's 1914 Nu-Cut line, this 4½" tall compote was apparently made in very limited amounts, especially in carnival glass where it is found only in marigold. Shapes in #537 also include bowls, but only in crystal.

Nu-Cut Pinwheel (Imperial)

This bowl pattern was made by the Imperial Glass Company from 1910 to 1914 and seldom gets much attention from collectors. It was Imperial's #504 pattern from the Nu-Cut line and was part of an assortment of bowls, a single vase, and a salad bowl (shown).

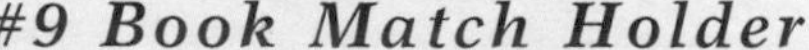

#9 Book Match Holder

This book-shaped match holder is credited to Adams and Company who joined U.S. Glass in 1891 as factory A. It is listed as the #9 pattern. It can be found in crystal, amber, blue, and vaseline.

Nursery Rhyme Bowl

This is different in design than the other plates with this motif. This one shows an outer ring of grapes, characters from children's stories, and an inner design of more grapes.

Oak Leaf

This pattern was from the Model Flint Glass Co. of Albany, Indiana, 1893 - 1902, in crystal only. It is limited to small and large oblong footed bowls and a decanter.

Octagon

Imperial's Octogon (its #501 pattern) can be found in carnival glass and crystal. Shapes include a berry set, table set, water set, stemmed vase, toothpick holder, decanter, wine, cordial, goblet, nappy, milk pitcher, plate, sherbet, punch set, and a compote in two sizes. Shown is a pitcher with rich ruby staining.

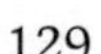

O'Hara's Crystal Wedding

This pattern, also known as Box Pleat, was made by Adams & Company in 1875. Shapes include a table set, water set, cake stand, and celery vase. All pieces have three rolled feet and handles are applied.

O'Hara's Diamond

This pattern was from O'Hara Glass in 1885 and then as the #15001 pattern from U.S. Glass after 1891. It was made in crystal and ruby stained glass. Shapes include a table set, banana stand, shakers, plain tray, cup and saucer, finger bowl, bowls, sauce, toothpick holder, pickle dish, and a water set. Some pieces were souvenir decorated items.

Ohio Star

Ohio Star was made by Millersburg Glass in 1909 and later at Jefferson's Canadian factory. This pattern is best known in carnival glass, but a wide assortment of shapes were made in crystal. These include a table set, water set, berry set, assorted bowl shapes and sizes, water pitchers (three sizes), tumblers (three sizes), compotes (tall and standard), cruet, syrup, toothpick holder, shakers, punch set, plates (four sizes), pickle dishes (three sizes), water bottle, and a vase. The glass is heavy and clear and the quality superior. In addition, the compote is found in a rare sapphire blue (two reported) and the vase has been found in amethyst (one known) and a rare blue (one known).

Old Colony

This pattern, advertised as #97 under the name Old Colony, is found in clear or with gold trim as shown. Shapes include a table set, water set, and berry set. This pattern dates from the 1910 – 1912 era and is simple but very dynamic.

Old Glory

Old Glory, also called Mirror Star, was made by New Martinsville Glass Company in 1910. This pattern is known in a table set and water set in both clear and gold trimmed. The original pattern number was 719.

Old Sandwich

This Heisey pattern (#1404) is found in crystal, amber, blue, pink, and green. Shapes include an ashtray, basket, mug (four sizes), oval or round bowls, candlesticks, catsup bottle, claret, champagne, 6" open compote, creamer (open or round, three sizes), cup and saucer, decanter, finger bowl, goblet, pitcher, ice pitcher, juice glass, cruet, parfait, pilsner, plate (three sizes), shakers, sherbet, sugar (round or oval), sundae, tumbler, and wine.

Omnibus

Omnibus was from U.S. Glass (#15124) as part of its export line. It is also known as Pathfinder or Keystone. It can be found in an extended table service that includes the usual berry set, table set, water set, pickle dish, and celery tray.

Oneata

Oneata, also known as Chimo, was made by Riverside in 1907. It was made in an extended table service that includes a table set, wine, child's table set, water set, cruet, individual cake plate, and others.

One-O-One

Duncan & Sons' One-O-One, from 1885, is also known as Beaded One-O-One. Shards are also known from Canada's Burlington Company. This pattern was made in an extended table service that includes an oil lamp, compotes, a celery vase, a vase, and a wine. Here I show a beautiful opaque green piece that is sometimes called Nile Green. The goblet has been reproduced.

Open Plaid

This is attributed to Central Glass in 1885 as their #861 pattern and U.S. Glass in 1891. Shapes include a table set, berry set, cordial, plate, salt shakers, water set, juice tumbler, champagne, wine, and syrup. It is also called Open Basketweave.

Open Rose (Imperial)

This was one of Imperial Glass Company's most popular patterns (#489). It can be found in carnival glass, clear crystal, and some rare colored crystal like the large rose bowl shown (this one has the old Imperial Iron-Cross trademark). Shapes include a plate, berry sets, and the rose bowl in two sizes. A sister pattern called Lustre Rose has the same catalog number and was made in many additional shapes.

Open Rose (Moss Rose)

The maker of this is unknown despite shards found at Boston and Sandwich. Shapes include round or oval bowls, a table set, cake stand, celery vase, covered compote (6", 7", 8", 9"), open low compote (6", 7", 7½", 8", 9"), cordial, egg cup, goblet (gents' or ladies'), pickle dish, milk pitcher, relish tray, water set, salt dip, and a sauce. It is also called Moss Rose which is a better name.

Opposing Pyramids

Opposing Pyramids, also known as Truncated Cube or Flora, was found in clear or etched glass from Bryce, Higbee Glass in 1890. Shapes include a table set, water set, cake slaver, celery vase, compote, goblet, shakers, a vase, and a wine. The pattern seems to be a bit hard to find. There are two pitcher sizes (a quart pitcher and one gallon tankard), but only the tankard has been found to date.

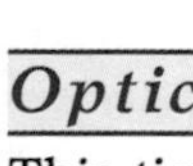

Optic

This tiny salt dip has more angles than anything else. Because it is virtually covered in gold trim, it would be a standout in a salt dip collection. It dates from the early 1900s.

Orange Peel

This Westmoreland design, although primarily known in carnival glass, is also found in decorated crystal or clear. Shapes are a punch set, custard cups (flared tops), and stemmed sherbets. All were made in the 1915 – 1920 era.

Orange Tree

Fenton's Orange tree is best known in carnival glass, but was also made in a wide range of shapes in other types of glass. Colors are crystal, lime green, pink (mug and bowl only), custard glass, and red. The exterior pattern on the bowls is called Bearded Berry.

Oregon

U.S. Glass pattern #15073 was made for many years beginning in 1901. Shapes include a water carafe, table set, bowls (open or covered), cake stands, celery vase, covered compotes, cruet, goblet, honey dish, covered horseradish, mug, olive dish, pickle dish, water set, bread plate, relish, salt dips (master and individual), sauce, syrup, vase, toothpick holder, and wine. The sugar bowl has been reproduced.

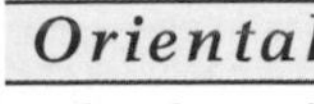

Oriental

The date of production for this pattern is believed to be around 1885. Shapes include a table set, celery vase, covered compote, pickle jar (shown), tray, water set, goblet, wine, and various bowls.

Oriental Poppy

This famous pattern was made by the Northwood Company in the early 1900s, primarily in carnival glass, where the pitcher was a tankard shape. Here in the seldom seen sapphire tumbler. Pitchers can be found in a squat or standard shape. Some pieces are found with gilding.

Orinda

National's #1492 pattern can be found in a table set, pickle dish, toothpick holder, shakers, berry set, syrup, pitchers, and the covered compote shown.

Orion Thumbprint

This Canton Glass Company pattern from 1894 can be found in crystal, milk glass, colored crystal, and black glass. Shapes include a water set, table set, goblet, celery vase, compote (open or covered), oval platter (Daisy and Button center), and sauce.

Ornate Star

This Tarentum Glass pattern from 1907 is also called Hobstar Fancy, Divided Star, and Ladders and Diamonds with Star. It was once believed to be a Millersburg pattern. Shapes include a berry set, water set, table set, celery vase, pickle tray, goblet, wine, cordial, and a stemmed dessert.

Our Girl/Little Bo-Peep

Made by McKee & Brothers about 1887, this mug is a companion to the Our Boy/Jester on a Pig mug by the same company. It stands 3⅜" tall and can be found in clear, amber, blue, canary, and apple green. A girl with a lamb is shown on one side while the reverse side is lettered "Our Girl."

Oval Basket

Adams & Company's #4 toothpick or match holder is shown in catalog reprints. It is three footed with a bent handle and can be found in crystal, amber, vaseline, blue, and reportedly in blue slag.

Oval Diamond Panel

This pattern, also known as Oval Panel, is known in the goblet shown, in crystal and vaseline. The design is simple but effective with pointed ovals that are filled with diamond crosshatching.

Oval Loop

This U.S. Glass pattern was made in 1891 and is also called Question Mark. It is found in clear, frosted, and gold-trimmed glass. Shapes include oval and round bowls, table set, candlesticks, celery vase, open and covered compotes, goblet, pickle jar, water set, milk pitcher in standard or tankard sizes, shakers, sauce, sugar shaker, bread tray, and wine.

Oval Medallion

This is a U.S. Glass pattern from 1891 that is also called Argyle or Beaded Oval Window. It is found in clear, canary, amber, blue, and a rare amethyst. Shapes include a table set, bowls, pickle dish, toy table set, toy water set, toy berry set, compotes, a goblet, and a wine. Footed and oval pieces have a Maltese cross in relief on the bottom and covered pieces have a finial that is a large flat double ellipse on each side of what appears to be a raised relief of a Maltese cross.

Oval Miter

Oval Miter was made by McKee in 1864 and is known in a table set, goblet, sauce, covered compotes, and celery vase. Shown is a stemmed spooner.

Oval Panel

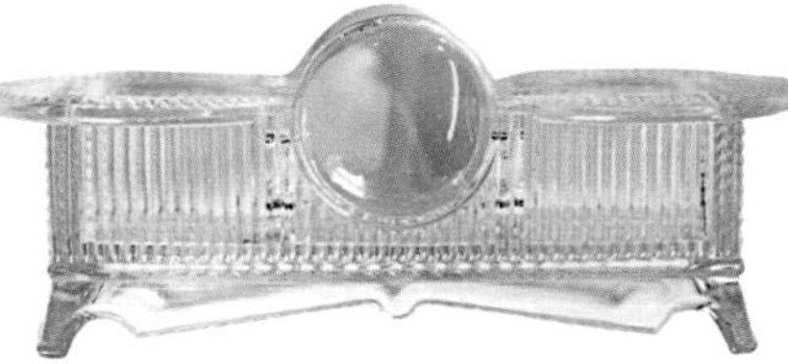

Oval Panel was made by Challinor, and then U.S. Glass in 1892. It is also called Oval Sett and can be found in crystal, purple slag, or opaque white. Shapes include a berry set, table set, water set, wine, and the three-section relish dish shown.

Oval Window Lamp

This lamp was from Dalzell, Gilmore & Leighton. It is also called the Eyewinker Thumbprint lamp and can be found in clear and green as shown. Please note this lamp is not the same as the Eyewinker pattern that had its own lamp shape.

Overall Lattice

This crystal and vaseline glass pattern was from the Indiana Tumbler and Goblet Company of Greentown, Indiana. Shapes include a table set, wine, plate, ruffled bowl, goblet, and compote.

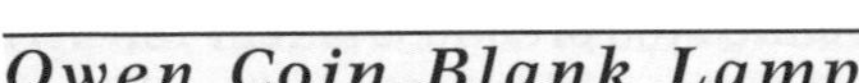

Owen Coin Blank Lamp

This was a product of U.S. Glass in 1893 and was made until 1909. Besides the vaseline shown, I feel confident this lamp was also made in crystal and possibly other colors.

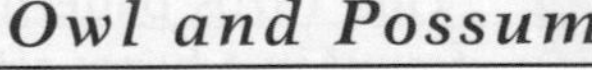

Owl and Possum

This very imaginative goblet is the only shape I've seen in this pattern to date and I believe it was made in the 1880s. On one side is the owl in the tree and on the other a possum in the same tree. The goblet's stem is a tree trunk pattern, and the whole piece has a rich, whimsical look. This has been reproduced.

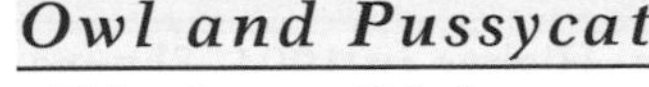

Owl and Pussycat

This cheese dish has exceptional mould work and its theme seems to have been a bit humorously designed. The owl holds the cat by the tail around the top while standing on a brick wall. The scene is again displayed on the inside of the base.

Owl on a Branch

This large 3¾" tall mug has an unusual shape and a pedestal base. Only clear has been reported. It is credited to Dithridge and Company partly because of the crystalography treatment. The date of production is about 1879, and the design is a simple one, owls sitting on branches on both sides of the mug.

Peacock at the Fountain

This is one of Northwood's best-known carnival glass patterns and is sometimes called Peacock and Palm. Very rare pieces in emerald green glass with gold trim are known. Shown is a water pitcher, and tumblers and pieces of the berry set are reported. (The small bowls do not have a peacock.) This pattern dates from 1912, when it was patented.

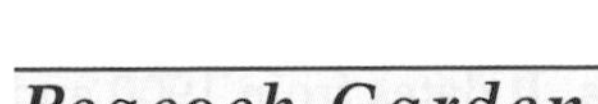

Peacock Feather

This U.S. Glass pattern (#15076), also called Georgia or Peacock Eye, was made in crystal or blue. Shapes include a table set, berry set, water set, mug, cruet, cake stand, shakers, jelly compote, syrup, large compote, 7" and 9" lamps, plate, sauce, relish, toy table set, celery tray, high or low covered compotes, pickle dish, decanter, and condiment set on a stand.

Peacock Garden

Peacock Garden was first made by Northwood, circa 1915, in carnival glass. (It has been seen with Northwood's trademark and one example with a paper label.) This well-done pattern shows a peacock on a limb with flowers, branches, and leaves circling the vase. It is not certain how the mold arrived at the Fenton factory, but nonetheless it has been widely produced by Fenton from 1924 – 1926 to the present year. With the exception of the rare 8" emerald green vase made circa 1940, Fenton suspended production of the early vases around 1935. They wouldn't be produced again until 1971. Fenton also made the earlier 4", 6", and 10" vases in addition to the original 8" vase. According to the late Frank M. Fenton the 4" and 6" molds were sold for scrap during World War II. There are well over 100 colors and shapes in all the years of production of this vase. Pre-1930 colors in non-iridized glass are flame orange, venetian red, and the brown slag shown. Dates on some colors are uncertain due to early attempts to perfect the mandarin red color, which resulted in a variety of odd colors including the three colors listed. Fenton currently makes the 8" and 10" sizes. All are marked with a small ½" oval logo located on the side of each vase about 2" left of the end of the peacock's tail near the bottom of the vase.

Peanut Lamp

This U.S. Glass (#9939) lamp was made in five sizes. It has a matching shade and can be found in crystal as well as colors.

Peas and Pods

This is #5602 made by U.S. Glass (Bryce Factory) in 1891. It is found in crystal and ruby stain. The only shapes documented are a wine set consisting of a decanter, stemmed wine, and tray. The decanter is known both with and without a handle.

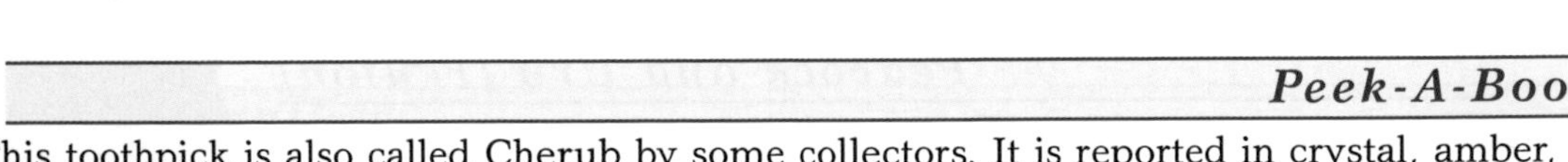

Peek-A-Boo

This toothpick is also called Cherub by some collectors. It is reported in crystal, amber, blue, and vaseline (also documented in carnival glass). This novelty item is shown in an old catalog reprint by McKee from the 1890s. This piece has been reproduced and the later version is slightly shorter.

Peek-A-Boo Perfume

Some feel that this perfume is possibly from the same line as the toothpick holder with the same name. Personally I can find no proof of such. This piece has a similar cherub peeking out from around the spiraled base and the stopper has a diamond-like design. It can be found in crystal.

Peerless

This pattern is a Model Flint Glass product circa 1896. Colors are clear, amber, blue, green, canary, and canary opalescent, but not all shapes are found in all colors. Shapes include an extended table set, vases, two sizes of decanter sets, and many other shapes.

Penelope

This unusual pattern is also known as Leaf in Oval and it can be found in clear, ruby stained, and gold trimmed. Shapes include a table set, pickle dish, punch set, water set, berry set, and the pickle tray shown.

Pennsylvania

U.S. Glass #15048 was made in 1898 in clear, emerald green, or ruby stained glass. It is also known as Balder or Kamoni. Shapes include a table set, water set, berry set, toy table set, water carafe, covered cheese dish, round or square sauce, toothpick holder made from a toy spooner, oil bottle, goblet, celery tray, cruet, and several other shapes. The spooner has been reproduced.

Pentagon

This pattern, also called Five-footed Oval, has a very distinctive design. Shapes include a table set, milk pitcher, celery vase, pickle dish, goblet, and a wine. The piece shown is 5¾" tall.

Pequot

The maker of this pattern seems to be in question, but shards have been found at the Burlington Glass Works of Canada. It is found in clear, blue, and amber. Shapes include a table set, celery vase, champagne, covered or open compotes, goblet, jam jar, water set, castor set, wine, and sauce.

Perkins

This pattern, first made as Fortuna by Higbee, was later released as New Martinsville's #100F and called Perkins. It can be found in a table set, water set, celery vase, 12" handled cake plate, rose bowl, and cruet. Pieces may be clear or gold trimmed.

Persian

Persian, also known as Block and Pleat, was made by Bryce, Higbee and Company in 1885 and then U.S. Glass. Shapes include a table set, shakers, syrup, cruet, toothpick holder, claret, sauce, berry set, salt dip, cheese dish, water set, jelly compote, carafe, celery vase, celery dish, cup, finger bowl, and the goblet shown.

Persian Medallion

This Fenton product, circa 1911, was their #1044 line. It was made in abundance in carnival glass but is considered very scarce in non-iridized glass. Shown is the two handled bonbon in crystal. This is the only shape and color reported to date.

Peter Rabbit

This is another very collectible candy container, with outstanding detail and very good glass quality. I've seen this piece with black enameled eyes.

Petticoat

Petticoat was made by Riverside Glass in 1899, in crystal, gilded crystal, and vaseline. It is also known as Riverside's National. Shapes include a berry set, table set, water set, cruet, toothpick holder, shakers, spoon tray, mug, syrup, covered mustard, match holder, covered and open compotes, jelly compote, salver, celery vase, and breakfast creamer and sugar. Some pieces are also gilded as shown.

Pheasant (Frosted)

This pattern is Central Glass's #758 line. It measures 8" x 8½" in diameter. The bird may be clear or frosted and I've seen an example with a ring of design below the pheasant.

Picket Band

This pattern was made by Doyle and Company in 1876 in both crystal and blue glass. It is also called Staves with Scalloped Band or Pen. Shapes include a table set, toothpick holder, pickle dish, celery vase, goblet, open compote, covered compote (shown), shakers, and a wine.

Pickle Vine

This well-done covered pickle jar with matching lid is credited by some to U. S. Glass. The design is very realistic with a leafed vine trailing around the center of the jar with pickles suspended.

Pigs in Corn

I believe the date of production of this goblet to be in the 1875 – 1885 period. The goblet is a very collectible item, much sought. The corn decoration can be found bent either to the left or to the right.

Pilgrim

This 1901 McKee Glass pattern is found in an extended table service in crystal as well as ruby stained.

Pilgrim Bottle

Pilgrim Bottle was made by Central Glass (#731) in 1885 in clear, amber, blue, and canary. Shapes include a table set, cruet, shakers, syrup, celery dish, and a pickle dish.

Pillar

Pillar was made by Findlay Flint Glass in 1890 as its #45 pattern. Shapes are a berry set, table set, water set, goblet, and celery vase. Shown is a tankard pitcher (the pitcher came in two sizes).

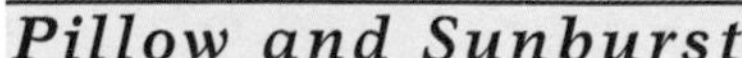

Pillow and Sunburst

Pillow and Sunburst was originally named Elite by Westmoreland Glass in 1904. It can be found in crystal, carnival glass, and a pale amethyst the company called Wisteria. Over 100 shapes are known including berry sets, table sets, water sets, hotel sets, individual creamer and sugar, and many more.

Pillow Encircled

This was Model Flint's #857 pattern made in the 1890s, in crystal, frosted, etched, decorated, and ruby stained glass. It is also called Midway. Shapes include bowls (4", 7", and 8"), nut bowl, table set, cake salver, celery vase, covered compote (5", 6", 7", 8"), shakers, half-gallon pitcher, quart pitcher, tumbler, and a toothpick holder. Cambridge may have continued this pattern in 1903.

Pimlico

This pattern, which was also called Lotus Leaf by Kamm, is reported to be from New Martinsville Glass in the 1900 – 1910 era. Shown is a handled cake plate but it is also known in a celery vase, pickle dish, open salt, goblet, and a table set. This pattern has a ring of leaves on a stippled background with a net of cross-lines that have flower centers. The center has a six-pointed star of raised prisms with a hex-button center.

Pineapple

This Sowerby (England) pattern is better known to carnival glass collectors but it can also be found in crystal or the azure blue shown. Shapes include a creamer, covered butter dish, open sugar that can be stemmed or flat, a rose bowl, or the bowl shape shown on a separate base. The butter dish has the pattern on the inside of the lid, and bowls range from 6" to 8". It is also known as Pineapple and Bows.

Pineapple and Fan (Heisey)

Like other Heisey patterns, this one is found in many shapes including a table set, toothpick holder, custard cup, salt dip, shakers in two styles, oil bottle, molasses can, nut bowls, mug, hotel creamer and sugar, berry set, odd bowls, celery vase, nappy, pickle tray, celery tray, banana bowl, cheese plate, cake stand, salver, pickle jar, cracker jar in three sizes, compotes, and water set with five sizes of pitchers.

Pineapple and Fan (U. S. Glass)

This U.S. Glass pattern, made in 1895, was its #15041. It was first made by Adams & Company and is sometimes known as Holbrook or Cube with Fan. Shapes include a table set, berry set, cake stand, celery vase, custard cup, goblet, mug, relish, water set, cruet, decanter, plate, rose bowl, and punch set. It can be found in clear, emerald green, ruby stained, and rarely in carnival glass.

Pine Cone (Fenton)

Pine Cone was made by Fenton in 1911 (its #1064) and is also called Pine Cone Wreath. This bowl and plate (6" and 7½") pattern is mostly found in carnival. Shown is a quite rare opaque red bowl (strangely red carnival pieces are unknown) that may have been a sample piece.

Pinwheel and Fan

Pinwheel and Fan was produced as Heisey's #350 pattern (there is a variant handled basket identified as #460). Shapes include a creamer, sugar, puff box, water set (with a three-pint pitcher), punch set, and 4", 5", and 8" bowls (called nappies by the maker). Colors are clear crystal and vaseline.

Pioneer #15

Pioneer #15 is credited to Pioneer Glass as well as to Westmoreland. This pattern can be found in the puff box shown as well as oil bottles.

Pipe Match Holder

This match holder is from the Eagle Glass & Manufacturing Company in the mid/late 1890s. It is found in plain milk glass and can be gilded or decorated.

Pistol

Here is another of the popular collectible candy containers that were made for children. Cambridge made a similar 5½" pistol container, a revolver, and this small pistol, the #2842. Sometimes these containers were enameled or gilt trimmed.

Pittsburgh Fan

Pittsburgh Fan can be found in a table set, goblet, cake stand, pickle dish, and the plate. Other shapes probably exist. The pattern dates from the late 1880s. Shown is a gilded pickle boat in emerald green, a rare color for this pattern.

Plaid

This pattern, circa 1880s, is found in an extended table service. Colors in this pattern are crystal and vaseline, although others are certainly possible. The maker is unknown.

Pleat and Panel

Pleat and Panel was from Bryce, Walker and Company in the late 1870s and then U.S. Glass in 1891. It can be found in clear, amethyst, canary, and blue. Shapes include a table set, compote, covered bowl, cake stand, square plate, water tray, lamp, candy jar with lid, relish dish, bread tray, shakers, and footed sauce. The goblet and plate were reproduced.

Pleated Bands

This interesting Dalzell pattern, circa 1899, was made in a tankard pitcher and matching tumblers as well as a goblet. I suspect it was also made in the usual table pieces including a table set, pickle tray, and perhaps other stemmed pieces but haven't seen them to date. It is alson known as Reeding Bands.

Pleated Medallion

Pleated Medallion was produced in 1908 as New Martinsville #713. Shapes include a table set, cruet, plate, toothpick holder, pickle dish, and cake stand. Some pieces may be gold trimmed or even ruby stained with gold trim.

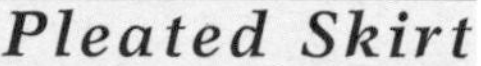

Pleated Skirt

This alabaster souvenir mug says "Middle La Have N. S.," likely Nova Scotia. Colors are crystal, cobalt, green, the alabaster shown, and custard glass. When found in alabaster with souvenir lettering, this mug will, for the most part, have enameled decoration, as shown on the example here.

Plume (Adams)

Plume was made by Adams and Company in 1874 and U.S. Glass in 1891. Shapes include bowls, cake stand, sauce, celery vase, footed bowls, lamp, goblet, table set, and various footed and non-footed pieces. It can be found in clear or ruby-stained glass. The design can be either horizontal or vertical.

Plume and Block

Plume and Block, also known as Feather and Block, was made by Richards & Hartley (#189) and U.S. Glass in 1891. The pattern was made in an extended table service in crystal or ruby stain. Shown is a celery vase.

Plums and Cherries

Northwood's Plums and Cherrys can be found in rare carnival items and decorated crystal. Shapes include a water set, table set, and covered bowl. Pieces may be stained or gilded or both.

Plutec

Plutec was part of McKee Glass Company's "tec" series in 1900. Shapes include a table set, water set, berry set, celery vase, compote, decanter, goblet, pickle dish, 11" plate, syrup, water tray, cake stand, wine, and nut bowl. Pieces are marked "Pres-Cut."

Plytec

Plytec was part of McKee's "tec" series. It can be found in crystal or ruby stain. Besides the usual table set, berry set, and water set pieces, there are salt shakers, syrups, cruets, vases, compotes, pickle dishes, and celery dishes.

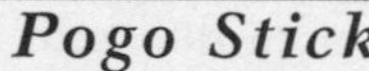

Pogo Stick

This pattern is attributed to Lancaster Glass in 1910 and found in an extended table service including the stemmed cake stand shown. The pattern is also called Crown.

Pointed Jewel

Pointed Jewel was made by Columbia Glass and then U.S. Glass as the #15006 pattern. The child's table service is called Long Diamond in this pattern. Shapes include a table set, cup, toy table set, celery vase, pickle dish, bowls, shakers, syrup, compote (shown), goblet, and a wine. It seems to be found only in crystal. The creamer was reproduced.

Pointing Dog

This pattern was first made by Bryce in the 1880s and then by U.S. Glass after 1891, in clear, frosted, amber, blue, and milk glass. The mug is 2⅝" tall and has a diameter of 2⅜". The design shows a dog on both sides of the mug.

Polar Bear

This pattern is now attributed to the Crystal Glass Company of Pittsburgh, Pennsylvania (some items are marked "C.G.C"). It was made in clear or machine ground. Shapes include an ice bowl, waste bowl, goblet, pickle dish, water pitcher, bread tray, sauce, and oval or round tray. It was originally advertised as the Arctic pattern in June 1880. It is also called Alaska, Ice Berg, North Pole, or Polar Bear and Seal. The goblet was reproduced.

Polka Dot

This pattern, also known as Inverted Thumbprint, is found in crystal, blue, and vaseline (shown in a pitcher). It is also known in a blue open compote, and I'm certain other shapes were made as well.

Polka Dot

This pattern is also called Inverted Coin Dot by many collectors, and is found in crystal, sapphire, marine green, cranberry, rubina, rubina verde, and amber as well as opalescent colors. Examples were made by Hobbs, Brockunier as well as Fenton, Northwood, and Dugan. Shapes include table sets, berry sets, water set (several shapes and sizes), bar bottles, cruets, decanters, carafes, mugs, custard cups, celery vase, footed bowls, mustard jar with lid, and both salt and sugar shakers. Hobbs pieces date to 1884 and the rest to the early 1900s.

Polka Dot (Geo. Duncan and Sons)

Polka Dot was made by Geo. Duncan and Sons (Factory D of USGC) in blown glass in 1884 – 1890 and in pressed glass in 1891. It can be found in clear, canary, amber, and blue. Shapes include finger bowls, cruet, shakers, tankard pitcher, toothpick holder, syrup, champagne glass, tumbler, water bottles (four shapes and sizes), footed bowls, covered compote, celery vase, covered cheese dish, sauces, wine, cordial, claret, goblet, and a pedestal-based pitcher. Note the "air twist" design in the handle of this syrup pitcher.

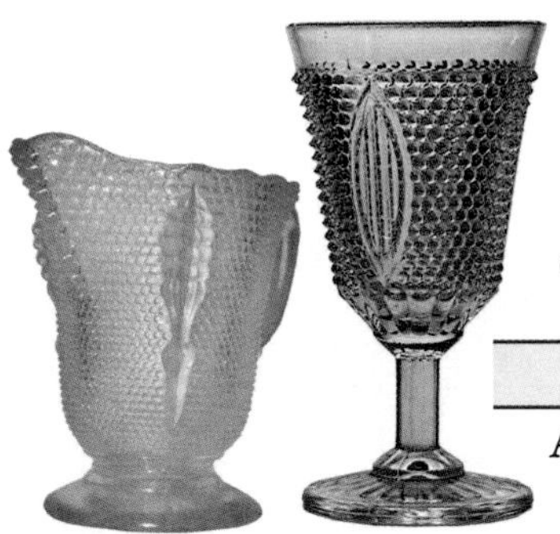

Popcorn

Popcorn was made by Boston & Sandwich Glass in the late 1860s. It can be found with a raised ear of corn or a flat ear of corn. Shapes include a table set, cake stands (8" or 11"), cordial, goblet (with ear or with lined ear), sauce, water pitcher, or wine. Shown is a creamer with raised husk and a wine.

Poppy Variant (Northwood)

Although this pattern is different than Northwood's regular poppy pattern, it has been given this name by carnival glass collectors where it is most often seen. It is also found in crystal (often with the goofus treatment shown here). Only bowls are reported and they bear the Northwood trademark.

Portrait

This fine goblet is shown in Metz, who says it is found in three versions (one with a man, the second with a woman, and the third with a boy).

Post Script

This 1905 Tarentum Glass Company pattern is quite well balanced and was made in a table set, shakers, berry set, individual creamer and sugar, cruet, goblet, handled olive, salt shakers, and wine.

Potpourri

This Millersburg Company crystal or carnival glass pattern is much like the Country Kitchen design from the same maker, except Potpourri has an added daisy wheel. It can be found on rare milk pitchers and 7" tall compotes in deep, flared, or salver shapes. Carnival glass compotes have the Poppy pattern on the interior while crystal ones do not. A rare compote is known in sapphire blue.

Powder and Shot

Powder and Shot is attributed to Boston and Sandwich, Portland Glass, and others from the 1870s. Shapes include a table set, castor bottle, celery vase, egg cup, goblet, water pitcher, sauce, tumbler, covered compote, and master salt.

Pressed Diamond

Pressed Diamond, also called Block and Diamond or Zephyr, was made by the Central Glass Company (#775) in 1885 and then by U.S. Glass in 1891. Colors found are clear, amber, blue, and canary. Shapes include berry sets, a table set, finger bowl, cake stand, celery vase, open or covered compotes, cruet, custard cup, goblet, water set, 11" plate, salt dip, shakers, and a wine.

Pressed Leaf

This simple pattern, also called New Pressed Leaf, was first made by McKee Brothers in 1868 and later by Central Glass in 1881. It can be found in a table set, compote, wine, cake stand, oval dish, cordial, egg cup, lamp, berry set, syrup, water set, and goblet. The compotes are found in open and covered as well as low or high stems.

Pretty Maiden

This very well designed toothpick, or match holder as called by some, is only found to date in crystal and the maker remains unknown at the present time.

Pride

This pattern, also known as Bevelled Star, came from the Model Flint Glass Company in 1900. It was made in crystal, emerald green, cobalt blue, vaseline, and amber glass. Shapes are table sets, berry sets, water sets, celery tray (5" x 10½"), salt shakers, cruet, and a tall standard covered compote. It was sold through Sears in 1900. All colors bring higher prices than crystal.

Primrose

Primrose, from Canton Glass (#10), was first made in 1885. The pattern is also known as Stippled Primrose. It can be found in crystal, amber, blue, canary, apple green, milk glass, slag, and black opaque glass. Shapes include a berry set, waste bowl (shown), cake stand, high or low compotes, cordial, creamer, egg cup, goblet, finger lamp, pickle dish, water set, milk pitcher, oval platter, relish tray, sauce, water tray, wine, and plates in five sizes.

Prince of Wales Plumes

This was A. H. Heisey Company's #335 made in 1900. Gilded, decorated, and rare ruby stained pieces are known. Shapes are a table set, water set, shakers, berry set, and toothpick holder.

Priscilla

This was a Dalzell, Gilmore & Leighton product from 1888 and later Cambridge's #2769 "Alexis" pattern. Shapes include a banana stand, biscuit jar, covered bowls, square bowl, rose bowl, table set, cake stands, celery vase, compote, covered jelly compote, condiment set, cracker jar, cruet, cup, donut stand, goblet, mug, pickle dish, water set (bulbous or tankard), plate, relish, shakers, syrup, toothpick holder, and wine. It is also known as Alexis or Sun and Star.

Priscilla (Fostoria)

Priscilla was made as Fostoria's #676 in clear or emerald green (with or without gilding) in 1898. Shapes include a water bottle, bowl, table set, cake stand, celery vase, covered or open compote, cruet, sherbet, egg cup, goblet, oil lamp, jam jar, pickle dish, water set, shakers in two sizes, salt dip in two styles, syrup, toothpick holder, and vase. It has been reproduced in a wide variety of shapes.

Prism Bars

This 1890s prism design (maker unknown) with the double banded top can be found in a table set, celery vase, goblet, water set, berry set, relish, and pickle tray.

Prism with Ball and Button

Shown is a 6" creamer which is the only shape reported in this pattern. It is found only in crystal to date.

The Prize

The Prize, from the National Glass Company (McKee) in 1901, can be found in clear, emerald green, and ruby stained glass. Shapes include a table set, water set, toothpick holder, shakers, syrup, goblet, pickle dish, and cruet. Please note the ornate metal crown on the pitcher shown.

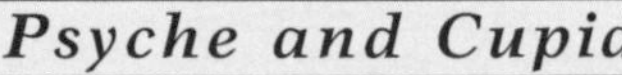

Psyche and Cupid

This 1870s pattern (maker unknown) can be found in a table set, celery vase, covered compote (high or low), goblet, wine, milk pitcher, water pitcher, and jam jar.

Pulled Loop

Although better known in both carnival glass and opalescent glass, this Dugan/Diamond vase pattern was also made in crystal in limited amounts. Sizes range from 9" to 15" tall, depending on the amount of swinging or slinging done.

Punty and Diamond Point

Punty and Diamond Point was made by Heisey as #305 from 1899 to 1913. Shapes include a berry set, punch set, cruet, shakers, vase, water set, water carafe, decanter, sugar shaker, platter, toothpick holder, bitters bottle, sauce, and the celery dish shown.

Punty Band

Punty Band was made by Heisey (#1220) in 1896, in crystal, ruby stain, or custard glass. The many shapes include a table set, water set, berry set, mug, basket, wine, toothpick holder, cake stand, syrup, and salt dip.

Puritan (McKee's)

Several companies had Puritan patterns, but this one was made by McKee Glass in 1910. It was made in crystal, as well as ruby stained glass. Shapes include a water set, table set, bowls, and a toothpick holder. Shown is the 8" bowl with gilding.

Quadruped

This pattern was made by Indiana Glass in 1908 and is found in clear as well as ruby stain. Shapes include a table set, berry set, jelly compote, vase, sundae dish, shakers, tumbler, short stemmed compote, pickle dish, relish dish, hotel creamer and sugar, and a mid-size bowl. It is also known as Chippendale.

Quartered Block

Shown in *Oil Lamps of the Kerosene Era in North American* by Thuro, this very sturdy oil lamp dates from the 1880s (no maker established to date) and was produced for two decades. It can be found in at least four sizes including a flat handled lamp, stemmed handled lamp, and two sizes of stemmed parlor lamps. There are reports of this being made by Duncan & Miller in 1905 as their #52 pattern. However, Duncan #52 is clearly shown in old catalog ads in Heacock's *Old Pattern Glass*, page 90 and 91, as well as Monograph #48 from *The West Virginia Museum of American Glass, Ltd.*, page 55; listed as the "Ladder With Diamonds" pattern, which is shown and discussed earlier in this edition.

Quatrefoil

This pattern was made in the 1880s and can be found in either clear or apple green. Shapes include bowls, a table set, water set (tumblers are rather rare), a rare goblet, salt shakers, open compotes, and covered compotes (as shown).

R

Queen

Queen, by McKee and Brothers Company in 1894, is also known as Pointed Panel, Panelled Daisy and Button, or Sunk. Shapes are a table set (three styles), cake stand, claret, covered compote, open compote, oval dish, goblet, water set, wine, cruet, relish dish, celery vase, and sauce. It has been reproduced in crystal, blue, cobalt, and vaseline.

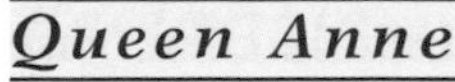

Queen Anne

Queen Anne is credited to LaBelle Glass Company in 1880 as #12006. It was made in clear, copper engraved, and amber. Shapes show variations but include covered bowls, table set, 7" or 8" casserole, celery vase, high or low covered compotes, egg cup, pitcher, milk pitcher, plate, shakers, sauce, and syrup.

Queen's Necklace

This was a Bellaire Glass pattern first (1891) and then a U.S. Glass pattern (after 1891). Shapes include a 10" bowl, table set, cake salver, celery vase, cologne bottle, open 10" compote, cruet, goblet, lamp, oil bottle, rose bowl, shakers, syrup, vases (8", 9", and 10"), water set, and wine. One rare stemmed vase is known in iridized glass. It is also called Queen's Jewel(s).

Quilted Fan Top

This circa 1895 – 1905 pattern, also called Shepherd's Plaid, is found in an extended table service that includes a water set, goblet, wine, plate, shakers, and a table set.

Quintec

Quentec was made by McKee Glass in the early 1900s and marked "Pres-Cut." Shapes include a berry set, table set, water set, handled punch bowl and cups, syrup, salt shakers, cake stand, plates, compote, a 6" cracker bowl, swung vase, cruet, jelly compote, whiskey decanter, bonbon, handled bowl (shown), jelly jar, pickle tray, celery tray, biscuit jar, cracker jar, and small vases. Some shapes were reproduced by Kemple.

Rabbit Sitting

Rabbit Sitting was first from the Central Glass Company in the 1880s and then U.S. Glass after 1891. It is found on clear, vaseline, and amber glass. This mug is 3⅜" tall and has a 3⅛" diameter and features rabbits sitting on one side and running on the other.

Rabbit Upright

Like many other mugs, this was made in the 1880s. It is found in clear, amber, blue, apple green, and probably canary glass. The mould is identical to one called Wolf and has a rabbit standing on its hind legs on both sides. Upon close inspection, some feel that this gives the appearance of a kangaroo or perhaps a jack rabbit.

Racing Deer & Doe

This pattern, which is sometimes called Deer Racing, was made by the Indiana Tumbler and Goblet Company (Greentown) in the late 1890s in both clear and chocolate glass. This pitcher can be found with either a flat top or with scallops.

Rib Band

This rather simple pattern is reported to have been made by Dalzell circa 1890. It has little going for it except quality. The handle is applied and there is a short pedestal base. Only table sets and water sets have been reported. Similar pieces are known in milk glass.

Ribbed Ellipse

Ribbed Ellipse, also called Admiral, was from J. B. Higbee Glass Company in 1905. Shapes include a table set, cake plate, mug, plate, compote, berry set, water set, and the vase shape shown.

Ribbed Forget-Me-Not

This pattern from Bryce Brothers in the 1880s and then U.S. Glass in 1891 is also called Pert Set. Colors are clear, amber, blue, canary and amethyst (all colors are scarce). Shapes include a table set, bowls, cake stands (9", 10", 11"), celery vase, covered or open compotes, goblet, water set, plates, master salt, sauce, cup and saucer, toothpick holder, water tray (Herons, Aquatic, or Storks), wine, toy table set, handled mustard cup (shown), and an individual creamer.

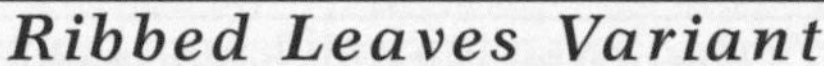

Ribbed Leaves Variant

Ribbed Leaves Variant was made by the Federal Glass Company and shown in the Federal Glass Company's Packer's Catalogue in 1914. It was made only in clear and is 2⅝" tall. There is another Ribbed Leaves mug that stands 3⅜" tall that may also be a Federal product.

Ribbed Palm

Ribbed Palm from McKee Brothers' design #1748 from the 1860s. Shapes include a table set, celery vase, champagne, covered compote, open compote, egg cup, goblet, lamp, water set, 6" plate, master salt dip, sauce, and wine. The goblet has been reproduced in clear by Imperial Glass.

Ribbon

This clear or frosted pattern was made by Bakewell, Pears & Company in 1870 and Geo. Duncan in 1878. It is also known as Rebecca at the Well or Frosted Ribbon. Shapes include a cologne bottle, berry set, waste bowl, table set, cake stand, celery vase, champagne, covered cheese dish, covered or open compotes, the famous Dolphin compote in round or oval (shown), goblet, pickle jar, water set, milk pitcher, plate, platter, shakers, sauce, water tray, or wine. The bowl, candlestick, compote, and goblet were reproduced.

Ribbons and Overlapping Squares

This was part of Northwood's 1906 Verre D'or line and is found in small compotes, small and large bowls, and a handled nappy. Colors are amethyst, blue, and green.

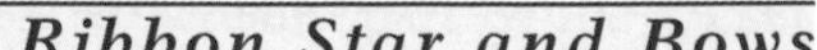

Ribbon Star and Bows

This is another pattern in Northwood's 1906 Verre D'or line. It can be found in the usual colors of amethyst, cobalt blue, and emerald green, in bowls, compotes, and possibly a handled nappy. Shown is a tri-cornered bowl in amethyst.

Rib Over Drape

Rib Over Drape was from D.C. Jenkins and is found in a water set, nappy, 8" bowl (shown), table set, vase, ice tea glass, and the ice bucket.

Rindskopf Gooseberry

This tumbler was made by the Josef Rindskopf Glass Works of Teplice, Czechoslovakia, in 1920 – 1927. It has a companion tumbler that features strawberries. Both are found in crystal and gilded crystal and the strawberry one can be found with staining.

Ring and Beads

This pattern was first from Ohio Flint Glass and then Jefferson Glass. It is found on the creamer shown, an open sugar that resembles a toothpick holder, and a vase. The pattern dates from 1905 to 1915.

Ringed Crane

This vase 7" tall, is also called a stork by some collectors. The design is flanked by palm trees and has two rings above and below.

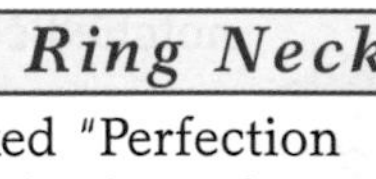

Ring Neck

This water bottle was made by the Perfection Glass Company. It is marked "Perfection Bottle Company – Wilkes Barre – March 30 – 97." The "N" in Perfection is backwards. It has a metal ring which unscrews and allows the top and bottom section to be separated. The company called this the Imperial #251 style. The Perfection factory was actually located in Washington, Pennsylvania, with a bottle factory in Wilkes-Barre. An oil bottle with the same type metal screw off band is also known.

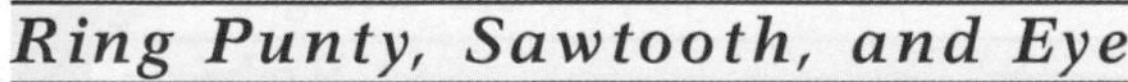

Ring Punty, Sawtooth, and Eye

This fine oil lamp was made in the 1860s and may be a product of the New England Glass Company.

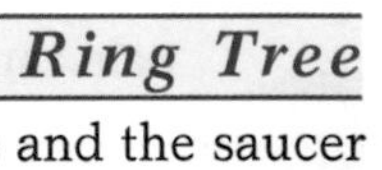

Ring Tree

Ring trees were meant to hold jewelry overnight. "Limbs" held rings and the saucer or bowl held other jewelry. They were made by various companies from the late 1800s to the 1920s and beyond. Shown is Heisey's example of the very rare Winged Scroll design in green.

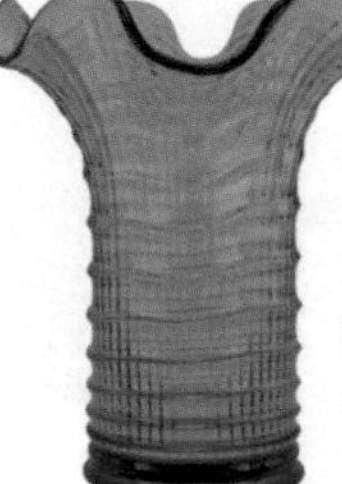

Ripple

Ripple was made in several sizes in carnival glass and rarely in opalescent glass. The vase from Imperial Glass was also made in crystal, cobalt blue, amber, and sapphire blue in three base diameters and several heights. Not all colors can be found in all sizes. The pattern is very much like one called Ribbed Spiral made by Model Flint Glass of Albany, Indiana, in 1902, in opalescent glass.

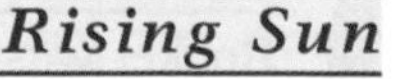

Rising Sun

This well-known pattern from U.S. Glass was #15110 made in 1908. Shapes include a water set (two pitcher shapes), cruet, cup, table set (two shapes known in the sugar), wine, toothpick holder, compote, large water tray, and a host of other shapes. Rising Sun is well known in carnival glass and can be found in crystal with ruby or green stain with gilding.

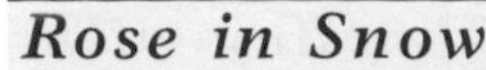

Rose in Snow

The square form of Rose in Snow was from Bryce Brothers in the 1880s; the round form was from Ohio Glass and then from U.S. Glass in 1891. Colors are amber, blue, or canary, and the crystal. Shapes include a bitters bottle, open or covered compotes, cake stand, oval dish, table set, goblet, jam jar, mug, pickle dish, water set, plates (four sizes), oval platter, relish dish, covered sweetmeat, toddy jar, and sauces (flat or footed). The bottle, goblet, mug, pickle dish, plate, and sugar bowl have been reproduced.

Rose Point Band

Rose Point Band was from Indiana Glass Company in 1913. It is also called Waterlily or Clematis. Shapes include a table set, sauce, compote, celery vase, footed bowl, berry set, water set, and goblet.

Roses in the Snow

In a previous edition of this book I showed an 11" plate in this often "goofus" treated pattern. Here is the beautiful 10" lamp and there is also a 9" bowl known.

Rose Sprig

This pattern from Campbell, Jones, and Company in 1886 can be found in crystal, amber, blue, and canary. Shapes include a biscuit jar, seitz shape bowl, cake stand, celery vase, covered compotes (7", 8"), open compotes (high or low in 7", 8"), goblet, mug, square nappy, pickle dish, plate (6", 6½", 8", 10"), footed punch bowl, relish tray, salt (sleigh shape), sauce (flat or footed), water tray, water set, and a wine. The goblet and salt dip were reproduced.

Rosette

Rosette, also known as Magic, was made by U.S. Glass in 1891. Shapes include a table set, plate, tray, shakers, water set, jelly compote, covered bowl, tall celery vase, fish relish, and handled plate.

Rosette and Palms

Rosette and Palms was made by the J. B. Higbee Glass Company in 1910. Shapes include a table set, water set, goblet, wine, salt shakers, relish tray or dish, 9" plate, celery vase, banana stand, cake stand, and sauce.

Rosette with Pinwheels

Rosette and Pinwheels was made by Indiana Glass in 1905 (#171 pattern) in a table set, water set, berry set, covered compote, celery vase, and honey dish.

Rotec

Rotec was made by McKee in 1904 in crystal or ruby stained glass. Shapes include a table set, water set, berry set, lamp, and a punch set that includes a large punch tray. Like most of the "tec" lines, this one was produced in quantity over several years, so a lot of it exists today.

Royal

Royal, also known as Royal Lady or Belmont's Royal, is found on an extended table service. It was made by the Belmont Glass Works in 1881.

Royal Crystal

Royal Crystal, also called Tarentum's Atlanta, Diamond and Teardrop, or Shining Diamonds, was made by Tarentum Glass in 1894. Colors include clear or clear with ruby stain. Shapes include flared or straight bowls (5", 6", 7", 8"), rectangular bowls, square bowls, cologne bottle, water bottle, table set, cake stands, celery vase, compotes (6", 7"), cracker jar, cruet (two sizes), goblet, candy jar, milk pitcher, water set (bulbous or tankard), plate (oval or round), shakers, sauce (flat or footed), syrup, toothpick holder, and a wine.

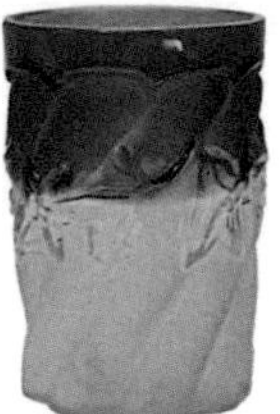

Royal Ivy

This 1890 Northwood product is found in clear or frosted glass that fades to pink and in amber crackle glass. Shapes include berry sets, table sets, water sets, shakers, syrup, toothpick holder, pickle castor, cruet, jam jar, and even a lamp.

Royal Jubilee

Royal Jubilee, found primarily in blue or canary opalescent glass, was made by Greener & Company of Sunderland, England. This footed novelty basket is a real find without the opal treatment. The design dates to the 1890s when James A. Jobling controlled the factory.

Royal King

Royal King is reported, although unconfirmed, to have been made by King Glass of Pittsburgh which became Factory K of U.S. Glass Combine in 1891. The piece shown is a shot glass that is ruby stained and lettered "Eugene, Oregon."

Ruby

Ruby was made by La Belle Glass in 1878 in a crystal extended table service. The design is a bit plain but interesting.

Ruby Diamond

The design, like many patterns chosen to be given a ruby stain treatment, is little more than a geometric band at the bottom of the piece. Ruby Diamond is also found in crystal and was made in 1893. Shapes include a table set, water set, goblet, wine, toothpick holder, and sauce.

Ruffled Eye

This strange product of the Indiana Tumbler and Goblet Company (Greentown) was advertised in a company ad in 1900 but was made earlier. Colors are crystal, canary, amber, emerald green, and chocolate glass. The design is one of vining flora and strange sun-and-ray spots. The pitcher sits on three feet, making the whole design a bit awkward.

Saddle

This novelty toothpick hold was made circa the 1890s. The maker is unknown, and while I show it in amber, it was also made in crystal. It features a saddle over a barrel.

S

St. Alexis Clock Set

In past editions two different versions of this 20s – 30s era Fostoria clock and candlestick set were shown together under one pattern name. I've decided to break up that listing and put each under their proper name. A cousin to the St. Clair set, this variation has a more rounded, streamlined look to it. It has bracket style feet and the dial isn't marked. Vaseline is also the only color reported to date.

Saint Bernard

Saint Bernard was made by Fostoria in 1894 as the #450 pattern in clear or copper wheel engraved glass. Shapes include a berry set, table set, cake stand, celery vase, covered high and low compotes, open low compotes, cruet, goblet, jam jar, sauce, pickle dish, water set, and salt shakers. It is also known in green and blue glass.

St. Clair Clock Set

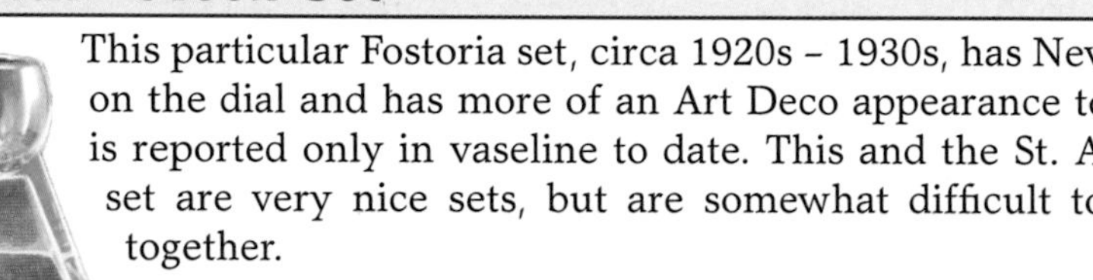

This particular Fostoria set, circa 1920s – 1930s, has New Haven on the dial and has more of an Art Deco appearance to it. It is reported only in vaseline to date. This and the St. Alexis set are very nice sets, but are somewhat difficult to put together.

Salamander

No information has come to light on this pattern to date. Besides the crystal I previously showed, here is green, and I have reports of blue and amber examples. Iridized examples also exist.

Sandwich Scroll Salt Dip

This beautifully designed open salt dip was typical of the high style during the 1850 – 1870 period of flint glass. It is found in crystal, amber, vaseline, and blue glass and had many similar "cousins."

Sandwich Star

As the name suggests, this was a pattern from Boston & Sandwich Glass, first made in the 1850s and continued into the 1860s in flint glass. It is found in clear, amethyst, and canary (all colors are rare). Shapes include a dolphin-based compote, cordial, decanter, goblet (very rare), champagne, wine, table set, and a stemmed spill holder.

Sawtooth

Sawtooth was made over a long time by several companies including Bryce, Richards, McKee, and U.S. Glass in clear, amber, amethyst, opal, sapphire blue, and milk glass. It had several other names, such as Diamond Point and Pineapple Mitre. Shapes include the usual table pieces, child's table set, decanter, pomade jar, oil lamps, and cordial. It has been reproduced in various shapes.

Sawtooth Bottom

Sawtooth Bottom was made by King & Son in 1888 as its #27 pattern in crystal or ruby stain. The pattern is also called Noonday Sun and is found in many table pieces including a goblet, wine, open compote, waste bowl, table set, and water set.

Sawtoothed Honeycomb

This pattern was first made by Steimer Glass in 1906, and two years later the moulds were sold to Union Stopper Company. Shapes include a punch set, table set, bonbon, goblet, nappy (with advertising), sauce (flat or footed), syrup, toothpick holder, celery vase, compote, water set, and shakers. It is also known as Serrated Block and Loop or Union's Radiant.

Scalloped Flange

This tumbler was made by the Perfection Glass Company of Washington, Pennsylvania, in 1903. It comes in five styles (I show three, #34, #50, and #40). Inside the tumbler are teeth in a row that were designed to keep ice away from the mouth, "avoiding an embarrassing sipping noise." Do not confuse it with Greentown's Scalloped Flange pattern in chocolate glass.

Scalloped Six-Point

George Duncan and Sons' #30 line, circa 1895, can be found in round or square bowls, table set, butter pat, cake stand (round or square), celery vase and tray, claret, cocktail, high or low compotes, cordial, cracker jar, cruet, custard cup, sherbet cup, egg cup, goblet, mustard pot, nappy, pickle dish, tankard or bulbous water set, ice cream plate, rose bowl, and vases.

Scalloped Skirt

This pattern was made by Jefferson Glass in 1904 in table sets, berry sets, a jelly compote, toothpick holder, pickle dish, a vase, and various bowls. It was made in crystal, blue, green, and amethyst, and can often be found with enameled work and gilding.

Scalloped Swirl

Scalloped Swirl was first a Ripley and Company pattern and then U.S. Glass pattern #15026 in 1892. It is found in crystal, ruby stained, and green (scarce). Shapes include a berry bowl, table set, cake plate, celery vase, goblet (shown), toothpick holder, a water set, and compotes.

Scallop Shell

This simple pattern with shells at the base is reported in water sets, table sets, table dishes, and specialty shapes, including the celery vase shown. Pieces may be plain or etched.

Scheherezade

I believe the Dugan/Diamond factory made this pattern, mostly in opalescent glass. The design closely resembles their Reflecting Diamonds pattern also found on opalescent bowls. Scheherezade combines file triangles, fine cut triangles, and hobstars in a rather unique way on this rare bowl.

Scroll with Cane Band

This very recognizable and well designed pattern was made by West Virginia Glass Company in 1897. Shapes include a table set, celery vase, toothpick holder, salt shakers, compotes, cruet, and water set. Some pieces have gold trim.

Scroll with Flowers

Scroll with Flowers was made by McKee Glass in the Modern line. It is found in clear, amber, green, and blue. Shapes include a table set, cake plate with handles, cordial, egg cup, goblet, water set, covered mustard, salt dip with handle, wine, plate, and relish. The plate and sauce are double handled.

Sectional Block

The only information I have on this pattern is that it comes in a goblet and the stemmed dessert or compote shown. Other shapes are certainly a possibility.

Sedan

Sedan is also called Panelled Star & Button. The maker is unknown and the date of production seems to be in dispute (1870s by one writer, 1900 by another). Shapes include a berry set, table set, water set, celery tray, celery vase, covered or open compotes, goblet, mug, pickle tray with double handles, relish tray, salt shaker, and the wine shown.

Seitz Bath

This circa 1880s – 1890s novelty Daisy and Button piece is a rare item found in crystal, amber, blue, green, and canary. The maker is unknown.

Sengbusch Ink Well

This product was patented as #1-1507 by the Sengbusch Self-Closing Inkstand Co., 2222 W. Clybourn St., Milwaukee, Wisconsin. It is called a "self-closing inkwell" and has a novel insert top that springs closed when the pen is removed. The glass portion is heavy and of fine quality.

Sequoia

Sequola, also known as Heavy Panelled Finecut and Panelled Diamond Cross, was made by U.S. Glass (Duncan's #800) in 1891 in clear, blue, amber, and canary. Shapes include a table set, various bowls, tray, plate, berry set, butter pat, decanter, pickle jar, canoe-shaped bowl, relish, salt dip, covered or open compotes, celery vase or boat, wine, goblet, water set, nappy, cheese plate, shakers, cruet, and syrup.

Serpent with Diamond Band

This bud vase is 6" tall and has a diamond banding at the top and a scaled serpent winding around the body. The snake is stained, giving it a finished look.

Sextec

This superior pattern was made by McKee Glass Company in 1894 as one of the "tec" series. Shapes include a table set, berry set, berry creamer, punch set, syrup, cruet, shakers, pickle jar, orange bowl, plate, nut bowl with handle, goblet, wine relish, and celery tray.

Shasta Daisy

Shasta Daisy, from Northwood's 1906 Verre D'or line, is found in amethyst, blue, green, and custard glass (rarely iridized). Shapes are large and small bowls, a 7" compote, and possibly a handled nappy.

Sheaf and Block

This 1893 Co-operative Flint Glass design is sometimes called Fickle Block. Shapes include a table set, celery vase, pickle dish, goblet, shakers, berry set, water set, and wine.

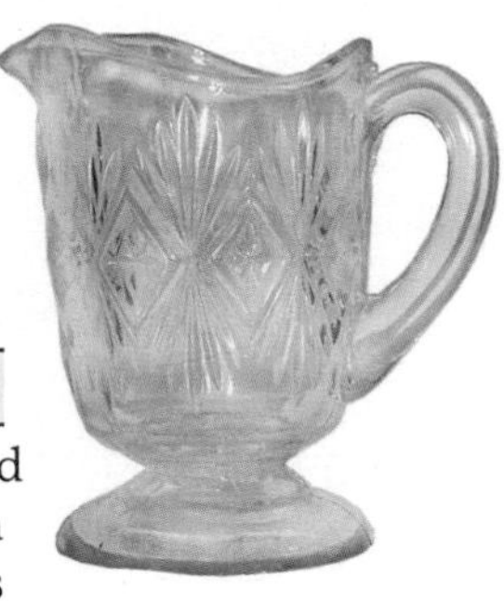

Sheaf and Diamond

Sheaf and Diamond was made by Bryce, Higbee in 1905. It can be found in bowls, a cake plate, pickle dish, table set, and celery plate.

Shell and Jewel

Shell and Jewel was originally known as Victor by Westmoreland in 1893, and then as the #618 line by Fostoria in 1898. It was also attributed to Sydenham Glass of Canada in 1895 as the Nugget pattern and finally to Jefferson Glass of Canada in 1920. Shapes include a table set, cake stand, compote, water set, shakers, bowls, banana dish, and water tray. The goblet was reproduced.

Shell and Tassel

This very desirable pattern was made by George A. Duncan & Sons (#555) in 1880. It is available in clear (occasionally etched) and very rarly in amber, blue, or canary glass. Shards have also been found at Canada's Burlington Glass Works. The pattern is found on either square or round shapes including covered bowls, berry set, table set, cake stands, celery vase, covered compotes, rectangular dishes, goblet, pickle jar, water set, plates, platters, salt dip, shakers, ice cream tray, vase, sauces (flat or footed), and various shapes and styles. Some covered pieces can be found with the Frosted Dog finials. Shown is a very rare vaseline 7½" "octagon shaped" (according to catalog photos) bowl.

Sheraton

This is a Bryce, Higbee pattern from the 1880s which is also called Ida. It was made in crystal, amber, blue, vaseline and green. Shapes include a berry set, table set, goblet, water set, milk pitcher, bread plate, platter, relish tray, sauce, wine, and round or eight-sided bowls.

Shield

Westmoreland's #160 line from 1899 is sometimes confused with a similar design by U.S. Glass. Shield shapes include a water set, 5" sauce (note the notching on the sides of the bowl), celery vase, flower vase (14", 15", and 16"), a knife rest, table set, and a goblet.

Shimmering Star

Shimmering Star is credited to the Kokomo Glass Company of Kokomo, Indiana (Jenkins), in 1905. Shapes include a table set, berry set, water set, shakers, and a pickle dish. This very well-done pattern is also known as Beaded Star.

Shoe Bootie

This novelty shoe consists of a fine cut diamond upper section and heal and a "gilled" front with a bow on top. The colors are crystal and vaseline reported to date.

Shoshone

This 1896 U.S. Glass pattern is also known as Victor or Floral Diamond. It is found in clear, green, amber stain, and ruby stained pieces. Shapes include a berry set, table set, water set, cruet, claret, goblet, wine, mustard jar, ice tub, punch set, pickle dish, celery dish and others. Shown is the bowl in green.

Shrine

This was first an 1880 Beatty-Brady design. Then it was an Indiana Glass pattern from the 1890s. Shapes are a berry set, table set, goblet, water set, toothpick holder (scarce), pickle tray, compote, and others. Shrine, also known as Jewelled Moon and Star, is found in either clear or frosted crystal.

Shuttle

This well-known factory #29 pattern was originally from the Indiana Tumbler and Goblet factory at Greentown in 1896, and then from Indiana Glass in 1898. It was made in clear and limited pieces of chocolate glass. Shapes include a berry set, table set, celery vase, cordial, cruet, custard cup, goblet, mug, water set, shakers, sauce, and wine. It is also called Hearts of Loch Laven.

Side Wheeler

This circa 1880s pattern comes in an extended table service in crystal. The maker is unknown at this time.

Singing Birds

This well-known pattern was first made in 1903 by the Northwood Company. It is found in carnival glass, opalescent glass (mug only), custard, and clear, canary, amber, and blue glass. Shapes include a table set, water set, mug, berry set, sherbet, stemmed claret, goblet, and the rare cup shown. Not all shapes are found in all treatments. Tumblers have been reproduced in carnival and opalescent glass.

Six Panel Finecut

Six Panel Finecut is credited to Dalzell, Gilmore, and Leighton in 1890. It is found in clear or stained glass (amber or ruby). Shapes include a table set, water set, compote, sugar shaker, syrup, cruet, goblet, and various bowl shapes.

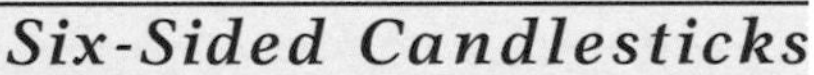

Six-Sided Candlesticks

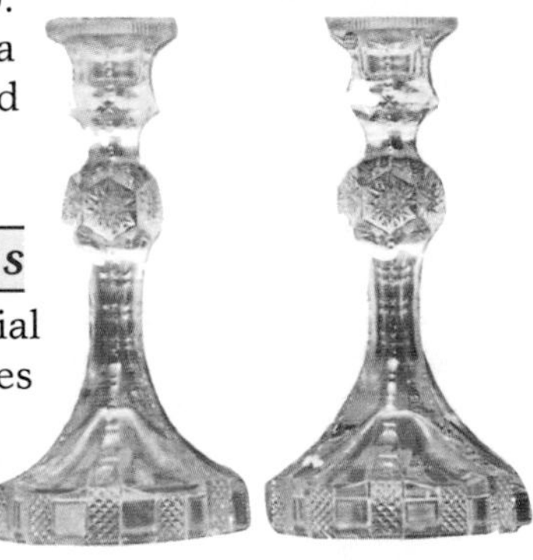

These easily recognizable 7½" tall candlesticks are from the Imperial Glass Company and found mostly in carnival glass. The crystal examples have been reproduced in the 1960s but are marked with the "IG" mark.

Skilton

Skilton was made by Richards and Hartley in 1890 and then U.S. Glass in 1891 in crystal or ruby stained glass. Shapes include bowls (4", 5", 6", 7", 8", 9"), a table set cake stand, celery vase, covered compotes (7", 8"), open compotes (7", 8"), goblet, olive dish, pickle dish, milk pitcher, water set, shakers, water tray, and a wine. This pattern is also called Early.

Slashed Swirl

Slashed Swirl was made by American Glass in 1890 and Riverside (#348) in 1891. It is also known as America, Swirl and Sawtooth, Diamond with Ovals, or Swirl and Diamond. It can be found in an extended table service.

Slewed Horseshoe

Slewed Horsehoe was made by U.S. Glass (#15111) in 1908 and is also known as Radiant Daisy or U.S. Peacock. Shapes include a berry set, table set, water set, punch set (with tray), goblet, and stemmed vase. It has been widely reproduced in the U.S. and Europe.

Snail

George Duncan and Sons introduced the Snail line #360 in 1890 (some pieces were still being made by U.S. Glass in 1904) in crystal, engraved crystal, and ruby stained glass (blue reported). Shapes include a table set, open and covered compotes, berry set, covered bowls, celery vase, fruit stand, cake stand, rose bowl, syrup, cruet, goblet, shakers, tankard table set, tankard water set, squat water set, finger bowl, pickle dish, custard cup, and a sugar shaker.

Snake Drape

Apparently the goblet shown is the only reported shape in this 1880s pattern. The design is interesting and unusual with stippled draping above a section of criss-cross threading.

Snow Flake

This is Cambridge Glass Company's #2635. It was made in several shapes including a water set, table set, toothpick holder, nappy (four sizes), compote (three sizes), bread plate, pickle tray, celery tray, celery vase, oil bottle, salt shakers, condiment set on a tray, and vases in 6" and 8½" sizes. This pattern is also known as Snowflake and Sunburst and as Fernland.

Solar

Solar was made by U.S. Glass (#15150) in 1908 and is also known as Feather Swirl. Shapes are a water set, bowls, wine, stemmed pieces, cruet, trays, goblet, compotes, and other shapes.

Southern Gardens

This 1906 Northwood Verre D'or design is a bit harder to find than some. Shown is a 10½" bowl in amethyst, but compotes and small bowls are reported.

Southern Ivy

This early Northwood pattern is found in basic table pieces including a table set, berry set, water set, plus an egg cup. The tumbler is shown.

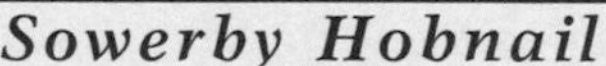

Sowerby Hobnail

This basket's shape is a giveaway as to its maker since others shaped like this are found in a Sowerby catalog dated 1885. These baskets are found in crystal as well as vaseline and in Queen's Ware and Malachite. The strange placement of the handle down on the bowl with the edge above pulled in is typical.

Spanish Moss

I showed this attractive hatpin holder in the carnival book in iridized marigold with gold trim. Here it is in crystal and as you can see, the gold is nearly perfect. The piece stands 7" tall and looks like the base of a tree around the bottom with leaves and moss at the top. The maker is unknown at this time. It is known in 7" and 10" sizes.

Specialty

This pattern was made by the Specialty Glass Company in 1891 – 1892 as the #100 pattern. It was obviously made in crystal and ruby stained glass. Shapes I can confirm are a table set, goblet, and the toothpick holder shown. Surely other shapes were made.

Spills

Spills were small vase-like vessels that held slivers of wood or paper rolled into small wands. These were used to light oil lamps before matches existed in great numbers. Many flint spills like these shown here were made in crystal, vaseline, amber, and blue glass and existed from the 1850s to the 1870s.

Spiral Diamond Point

This vase, shown in crystal, is known primarily as a carnival glass pattern. The design is spiral or plain with diamond spiraling with band fans edging the top. There is a ledge inside the top, possibly to hold a flower frog (flower disk), but I've also been told this was a container for pickles. Whatever its use, it is a very nicely patterned vase.

Spiralex

This Dugan Glass Co. circa 1907 – 1910 pattern is commonly found in carnival glass and opalescent glass, but here we find an example in a beautiful sapphire blue. These vases can twist either to the right (as shown) or to the left. When twisted to the left they are sometimes called Twisted Ribs. These have eight ribs, same as the variant below but they have a distinctive sharp edge running the length of the ribs. This vase has a 32 rayed base. Sizes range from 10" to 14".

Spiralex Variant

Compared side by side, this variant has an obviously smaller base diameter with 20 rays. The eight ribs on this vase are smooth, compared to the sharper raised ribs on the regular vase listed above. Colors to date are the amethyst and crystal. Sizes are 5" – 8".

Spiralled Ivy

This interesting pattern dates from the mid-1880s (maker unknown) and is found in a water set, a four-piece table set, and a sauce bowl. No goblets or the usual table set pieces are reported but some were likely made. I've heard of only clear crystal items.

Spirea Band

This Bryce, Higbee pattern was originally called Earl by the company in 1885. It is now also known as Nailhead Variant, Squared Dot, or Spirea. Shapes include a table set, cake stand, water set, open and covered compotes, goblet, oval platter, shakers, wine, celery vase, and honey dish. Spirea Band was made in clear, amber, apple green, vaseline, and blue.

Spittoon

This miniature spittoon shape is primarily used as a toothpick holder. It is known in clear, canary, and blue, and it stands 1½" tall and measures 3" across the middle. The maker is unknown.

Split Waffle

Split Waffle is credited to O'Hara (U.S. Glass in 1891). It can be found in an individual creamer and sugar, a syrup, and the bowl shown, in crystal, blue, amethyst, and amber.

Sprig

This Bryce, Higbee pattern from the 1880s is also known as Royal. It can be found in berry sets, table sets, celery vase, open or covered compotes, honey dish, mustard, pitcher, oval platter, goblet, and wine. The pieces known as Royal are simply from the same mould without the sprigs of flowers added.

Squat Pineapple

Squat Pineapple was made by McKee in 1898 and is also known as Gem or Lone Star. It can be found in a table set, water set, berry set, vase, pickle dish, plate, and stemmed compote.

Squirrel

Squirrel was first made by Adams and Company in the 1880s and then by U.S. Glass after 1891. It is reported in a mug and the pitcher shown. Colors reported are clear, a rare blue, and a rarer opaque blue glass.

Squirrel and Stump

Here is a novelty toothpick holder that shows imagination. I suspect it dates from the 1890s like most of the other similar items, and it has been reproduced.

Squirrel in Bower

Squirrel in Bower, originally called Squirrel, was made by Portland Glass. Several squirrel patterns are known, but this one has the squirrel within a protective bower of branches. Shapes include a bowl, table set, water pitcher, a very rare goblet, an oil lamp, and a sauce.

Squirrel with Nut

Only the pitcher shown is reported, but the quality of the design certainly would have been perfect for a table set. The large squirrel is standing on hind legs on a tree branch with a nut held to its mouth.

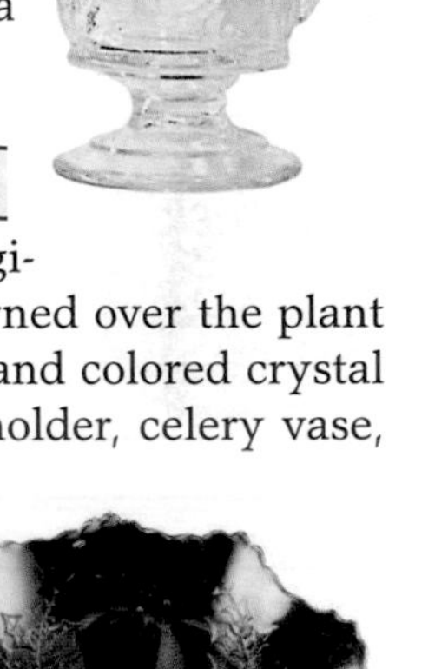

S-Repeat

This pattern is a Dugan/Diamond product made in Indiana, Pennsylvania. It was originally called National and first produced in early 1904 when Northwood had turned over the plant to Dugan. It can be found in limited carnival pieces, opalescent glass, crystal, and colored crystal (sometimes decorated). Shapes include a table set, shakers, cruet, toothpick holder, celery vase, water set, compotes, decanter, wine, tray, and punch set. Shown is the decanter and wine in blue with gold decoration. It has been reproduced in a variety of colors and shapes.

Stag and Holly

Stag and Holly was from the Fenton Art Glass Co. circa 1912. This is a very common pattern in carnival glass but not quite so in non-iridized glass. The non-iridized examples are mostly found on the flat collar based bowls and rarely on the ball footed example as shown in a nice amber. Colors are crystal, amber, cobalt blue, pink, lime green, and red.

Star

While neither the owner nor anyone I've contacted has any idea who made this unusual covered butter dish, I suspect U.S. Glass as a possible maker. It can be found in amber, vaseline, and crystal.

Star and Crescent

Star and Crescent was the U.S. Glass #15108 pattern in 1908. Shapes that include a table set, water set, berry set, cruet, pickle dish, and salt shakers. The pattern is distinctive, well done, and quite collectible.

Stars and Bars

This pattern is from the Bellaire Goblet Co. and U. S. Glass circa 1890. It is found in a table set, water set, salt shakers, jam jar, lamp, tray, and a child's table set. Colors are crystal, amber, and blue. It is also known as Daisy and Cube and Evangeline. Shown is a compote in crystal.

Stars and Bars with Leaf

This pattern for the most part is identical to the regular Stars and Bars pattern with the exception of the added leaf and vine patterned section. I suspect the maker is the same but this is uncertain at this time. It can be found in a table set and toy table set in crystal and vaseline.

Stars and Stripes

Stars and Stripes was made by Jenkins Glass Company in 1899 and originally called Brilliant. This pattern is found in clear glass as well as milk glass. Shapes include a berry set, table set, water set, shakers, sauce, cup, vase, goblet, square candy tray, a mug, and a hat shape (from the tumbler). The bowl, cordial, mug, and wine were reproduced.

The States

The States, also called Cane and Star Medallion, was made by U.S. Glass in crystal, green, and gilded crystal. Shapes include a table set, water set, compote, goblet, plate, punch set, and shakers.

Stellar

This U.S. Glass pattern (#15103) was made in 1907. Shapes include a berry set, table set, water set, pickle dish, celery dish, and a compote. It is also known as Squared Sunburst.

Sterling

This pattern was made by Westmoreland Glass in 1891 and again in 1917. It is also known as Pinwheels or Blazing Star. Shapes include a table set, toy table set, water set, punch set, bowls, goblet, wine, and compote. Some pieces are gilded, as with the bowl shown.

Stippled Bar

Stippled Bar was from U.S. Glass Company's #15044, made in 1895. Shapes include a table set, water set, various bowls, and the plate shown. Some variations in the pattern appear from shape to shape. The design isn't always easy to recognize, but the main design shown on the plate is the wider panel with serrated edges that is stippled except for the cross bar.

Stippled Chain

Stippled Chain was made by Gillinder and Sons in 1880 in clear only. Shapes include a berry set, table set, cake stand, celery vase, oval dish, egg cup, goblet, pickle tray, water set, relish dish, and master salt dip.

Stippled Cherry

The maker of this 1880s pattern is unknown. Shapes include a berry set, table set, water set, 6" plate, 9" bread plate, mug, celery vase, and relish dish. The design is realistic and the mould work well done.

Stippled Daisy

Despite its name, this pattern can be found either plain or stippled. It was made in the 1880s. Shapes are a table set, water set, open compote, oblong dish, flat sauce, goblet, wine, and relish. It is found only in crystal.

Stippled Dart and Balls

This circa 1890 pattern can be found in a crystal extended table service including a wine.

Stippled Fans

This pattern was from Lancaster Glass in 1910 (misnamed in a previous edition), and is very close to North Star (shown elsewhere). It is found in a berry set, water set, and table set. Some pieces have gilding.

Stippled Forget-Me-Not

Stippled Forget-Me-Not was from Findlay (1890) and Model Flint (1891) in clear, amber, blue, white, and milk glass. Shapes include a shell shaped bowl, bitters bottle, waste bowl, table set, cake stands in 9", 10", and 12", celery vase, toy table set, toy mug, large mug, covered compotes in three sizes, open compotes in three sizes, cordial, cup, goblet, water set, milk pitcher, plates (baby face, star, or kitten centers), oval relish master salt, syrup, toothpick holder, water tray (with Wildlife scene), and wine.

Stippled Forget-Me-Not with Kitten

Although made by Findlay in 1891, this plate with the unusual center is not generally mentioned as part of this pattern. A similar 7" plate called Baby Face is known with the Stippled Forget-Me-Not edging. The piece shown has a cat in the center of pussy willow branches. Shards were also found at the Model Flint factory from 1891.

Stippled Leaf, Flower, and Moth

This circa 1870s pattern (maker unknown) consists of large leaves, daisy like flowers, and moth or butterfly. The pattern is reversed on opposite sides. It is found in a table set and water set in crystal.

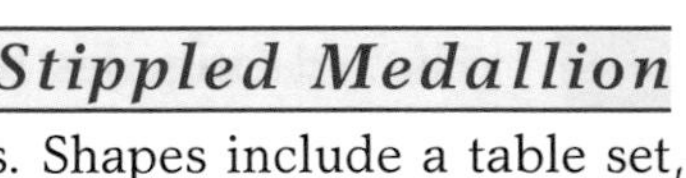

Stippled Medallion

Stippled Medallion was made by the Union Glass Company in the late 1860s. Shapes include a table set, egg cup, plate, cake plate, sauce, goblet, and low compote.

Stippled Peppers

Stippled Peppers was made in crystal only by Boston & Sandwich Glass in the 1870s. Shapes include a table set, water pitcher, footed tumbler, egg cup, footed salt, and sauce. Shown is the footed tumbler.

Stippled Sandbur

This nice pattern with the unusual name was made by Beatty-Brady Glass Company in 1903. It can be found in a berry set, table set, water set, celery vase, covered compote, goblet, toothpick holder, pickle jar, and wine.

T

Teardrop and Tassel

Teardrop and Tassel was made by the Indiana Tumbler and Goblet Company (Greentown) around 1900. There are two variations of this pattern; the tumbler shown being the less elaborate version. Amber, teal blue, cobalt blue, canary, several shades of green, Nile green, white opaque, and chocolate glass are all known besides the clear pieces. Shapes include a table set, water set, goblet, wine, and shakers.

Teardrop Flower

This interesting 1905 Northwood pattern is found in a table set, berry set, water set, shakers, and cruet. Colors are decorated amethyst, blue, green, and crystal.

Teasel

A bit of uncertainty lingers over this pattern. It is reported by some to be from Bryce Brothers Glass circa 1870s as their #57 line, but some think not. Teasel is found in clear, green, amber, milk glass, Nile green, chocolate, and blue. Shapes include a table set, celery vase, compote, cruet, sauce, plate, shakers, cake stand, wine, bowl, cracker jar, toothpick holder (scarce), covered honey dish, and goblet.

Ten-Pointed Star

This 1907 J B. Higbee pattern can be found in an extended table service that includes a vase, cruet, milk pitcher, salvers, and a shape called a "compotier."

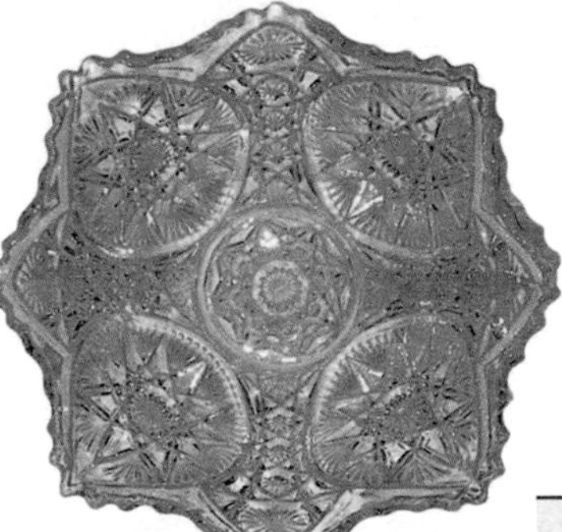

Ten-Pointed Star Variant

Just why Bryce, Higbee made a variant at the same time as its Ten-Pointed Star pattern is a mystery, but here it is. Shapes include the plate shown and a milk pitcher.

Tepee

This is also known as Wigwam or Nemesis. It was made by Geo. Duncan and Sons (#28 line) in Washington, Pennsylvania, circa 1896. Shapes include a table set, wine, berry set, syrup, handled jelly, jelly compote, shakers, rare covered fish dish, water set, plate, and toothpick holder, especially rare in green.

Teutonic

This 1894 – 1898 McKee pattern is found in an extended table service in crystal and occasionally vaseline (shown here).

Texas

Texas, also known as Loop with Stippled Panels, was made by U.S. Glass as #15067 in 1900. It can be found in clear, rose stained, ruby stained, and gold trimmed. Shapes include a carafe, open and covered bowls, cake stands, bread tray, compotes, cruet, goblet, covered horseradish, olive dish, pickle tray, water set, plate, shakers, hotel salt, master salt, sauce, syrup, toothpick holder, wine, and vases. The individual creamer and sugar as well as the wine were reproduced.

Texas Start

Texas Start, also known as Snowflake Base, was made by Steimer Glass in 1891. Shapes make up an extended table service that includes oval bowls and a plate.

Thin Rib (Northwood)

This was a standard vase design from the factory found in many glass treatments including carnival glass, opalescent glass, opaque glass, clear crystal, colored crystal, and custard glass. It was made in at least three base sizes and can be found in examples as short as 9" or as tall as 17". The piece shown is black amethyst glass with enameled floral sprays and dates to 1918.

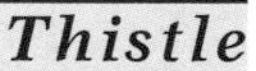

Thistle

Thistle was made by Bryce, McKee & Company in 1872 in clear only. It is also called Early Thistle or Scotch Thistle. Shapes include a berry set, table set, cake stand, covered compote, open compotes (6", 8"), cordial, oval dish, egg cup, goblet, pickle dish, milk pitcher, water set, large plate, relish tray, master salt, syrup, and a wine. The goblet was reproduced.

Thistleblow

Jenkins's well-known #514 pattern was made from 1905 to 1909, and is also called Panelled Iris. Shapes include a berry set, table set, stemmed jelly, pickle dish, celery dish, water set, wine glass, punch cup, berry, creamer and sugar, 6" vase, nappy, and a stemmed sundae dish.

Thonged Star

Thronged Star was made by Imperial (#91, #212, #2122) around 1909. Shapes include an individual sugar and creamer, berry bowl, nappy, spoon tray, pickle dish, compote, and vase.

Thousand Eye

Thousand Eye was made by many companies, including Adams & Company (1874), Richards & Hartley (1880), and U.S. Glass (1891) in crystal, amber, blue, vaseline, green, and opalescent colors. Shapes include an ABC plate, cologne bottle, bowls, table set, cake stand, celery vase (two variations), open compotes (6", 7", 8", 9", 10"), cordial, cruet (shown), square dish, honey bowl, inkwell, jelly jar, lamp (12", 15"), mug (two sizes), pickle dish, milk pitcher, water set, square plate (6", 8", 10"), platters, salt dips, sauce (flat or footed), string holder, syrup, toothpick holder (three variations), water tray (round or oval), and a wine. This pattern was widely reproduced in a host of shapes and colors.

Thousand Eye with Fan

The owner of this stemmed compote suspects it to be from England or Europe. I'd certainly like to hear from anyone with additional information about it. In this country Thousand Eye was made by a host of glass companies so tracking each one is difficult.

Threading

Threading from Duncan and Sons is also called English Thread. Shapes include a berry set, table set, nappy, goblet, covered compote, wine, celery vase, and water set.

T

Three Birds

This strange pattern from Dalzell, Gilmore & Leighton Glass Company in the 1880s seems to be known only on the water pitcher shown. On one side are the three birds sitting in tree branches and on the other a wicker basket filled with fruit sitting on what appears to be a brick wall.

Three Face

Three Face was made by Geo. Duncan and Sons in 1878 and U.S. Glass in 1891 and has been highly reproduced over the years. Shapes include a very rare biscuit jar, a table set, cake stand, celery vase, champagne, covered or open compotes (very rare with beaded rim), goblet, cordial, jam jar, pitcher, milk pitcher, and several sizes of oil lamps. Pieces can also be found decorated with a design called Frosted Sunflower Band. It has been reproduced in a variety of shapes.

Three Fruits

This Northwood pattern is usually found in carnival glass bowls or plates (a variant stemmed bonbon is also known). The crystal pieces are quite scarce. Here is the plate shape that measures about 9" in diameter. The fruits are cherries, pears, and apples.

Three-In-One

Three-In-One was originally Imperial's #1 pattern. It is known to some collectors as Fancy Diamonds. This well-known pattern was shown in a 1909 factory catalog in a 13" salver, 9" and 10" cake stands, 8" salver, handled olive, 4", 4½", 5", 7", 8", 9", 9½" bowls, 6", 8", 9", 10" covered or open compotes, stemmed jelly compote in 4½" and 5", wine, goblet, water set, whiskey decanter and tumblers, wine decanter, carafe, catsup cruet, oil cruet, syrup, candlesticks, covered mustard, 6", 8", 10" pedestal vases, table set, and covered biscuit jar. It is known in some shapes in carnival.

Three Panel

Three Panel was first Richards & Hartley's pattern #25 in the 1880s and then it was reissued by U.S. Glass in 1891 in clear, amber, blue, and vaseline. Shapes include bowls in three sizes, table set, celery vase, open compotes, cruet, goblet, large or small mug, water set, milk pitcher, and sauce.

Thumbprint Windows

This circa 1890s pattern is found in an extended table service in crystal only.

Tidal

This 1889 Bryce, Higbee pattern is also known as Florida Palm to some collectors. In 1903 it appeared in a Ward catalog as the Perfection pattern. Shapes include a berry set, table set, water set (two pitcher styles), wine, goblet, 9½" plate, oval bowl, celery vase, pickle dish, and the castor set shown.

Tidy

Tidy was made by McKee and Brothers in 1880. Shapes include a table set, water set, compote, goblet, wine, and celery vase. In addition, there are two variations of this pattern, one with a short shield and one with a long shield. Other names for this pattern are Stayman or Drapery Variant.

Tile

Tile is also known as Optical Cube (a better name) and was from the Thompson Glass Company (#19) in 1890. It was made in 75 shapes including a table set, water set, open or covered compote, goblet, cruet, shakers, pickle dish, cake stand, toothpick holder, wine, and cordial.

Togo

Togo was made by Indiana Glass of Dunkirk, Indiana, about 1913. Shapes include a table set, individual creamer and sugar, relish tray, cruet, jelly compote, 5" square plate, leaf-shaped olive dish, berry set, 7" footed bowl, and water set with pedestal based pitcher.

Tokyo

Tokyo was made by the Jefferson Glass Company as their #212 pattern in 1904. It is primarily found in opalescent glass, but crystal, blue, canary, and green exist. Shapes include a table set, water set, berry set, shakers, vase, jelly compote, syrup, plate, and a toothpick holder. Non-opalescent pieces were often gilded. It has been reproduced in some shapes.

Toltec

This is one of McKee's "Tec" series patterns from circa 1894. Toltec can be found in a wide variety of shapes in crystal and ruby stained. Shown is the tall celery in crystal.

Torpedo

This is a Thompson Glass pattern made in 1889. Shapes include a banana stand, covered or open bowls, table set, cake stand, celery vase, covered and open compotes, cruet, cup and saucer, decanter, finger bowl, lamps, goblet, jam jar, pickle castor, water set, milk pitcher, salt dips, syrup, trays, and wine. It is also known as Pigmy or Fish Eye.

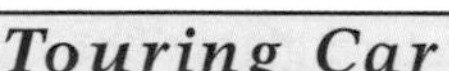

Touring Car

This very collectible 2½ oz. candy container is from the Cambridge Glass Company. It was listed in ads as #2845 Automobile, but most collectors know it as Touring Car. It is clear with a black enameled roof and great detail.

Tree

This pattern was made by Paden City Glass in 1918. There seems to be slight variations from one shape to another. Minnie Watson Kamm describes this pattern as a "stiff formal evergreen or column of graduated herringbone with long oval thumbprints around the body." Shapes include a table set, water set, toothpick holder, and celery vase. Some pieces are ruby stained, green stained, or gold trimmed. This was Paden City's #202 pattern.

Tree Bark

Tree Bark can be found in a table set, water set, berry set, and probably other shapes. It is known in crystal and amber glass. While the design is a bit on the weak side, the quality is good and the shapes are interesting. The maker is unknown at this time.

Whisk Broom

This novelty pickle dish, made by Campbell & Jones as well as Geo. Duncan & Sons (1886), comes in two sizes and can be found in crystal, canary, blue, and amber. It is marked "Pat appd for." I can't explain why Campbell & Jones received the patent and then let Duncan make it.

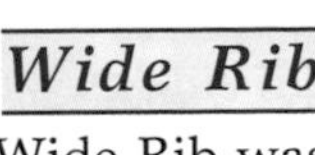

Wicker Work

This two handled small basket has been attributed to Bryce Brothers. A basket is the only reported shape. Colors are crystal, amber, and vaseline to date.

Wide Rib

Wide Rib was made by the Northwood Glass Company in 1907 in carnival glass, opalescent glass, clear, and colored crystal. There are several variations of this simple pattern, and almost all are covered in my writings in carnival glass. Wide Rib vases measure 7" to 13" tall usually, but taller examples are sometimes found.

Wildflower

This well-known pattern was first made by Adams in 1874 and then U.S. Glass in 1891. It can be found in amber, apple green, blue, vaseline, etched, and clear. Shapes include an oval cake basket, round and square bowls, table set, cake stand, celery vase, champagne, covered compotes, goblet, water set, cake plate, oval bread plate, platter, relish, shakers, salt dip, syrup, water tray, and wine. It has been reproduced in a host of shapes and colors.

Wildflower (Northwood)

Wildflower is primarily known in carnival glass where it sometimes has an interior pattern called Blossomtime. This 6" compote with the screw-type stem can also be found in crystal or emerald green glass as shown. Pieces are often found with the Northwood trademark. Some of the crystal or green pieces show traces of goofus paint or gilding.

Wild Rose Lady's Medallion Lamp

This lamp was made by Riverside Glass before 1907 and then retooled after 1909 by Millersburg Glass and made in a rare carnival glass version. Shown is the goofus treatment. All treatments are considered very collectible, and the Millersburg versions of this lamp are all rare. It is also called Riverside Lady or Lucille.

Wild Rose Lamp

This pattern was first made by Riverside Glass as part of the Lucille line of oil lamps and later by the Millersburg Glass Company (1910) in carnival glass. It can be found in fours sizes (here I show the first reported handled hand lamp). These lamps are companions to the Riverside Ladies (Ladies Medallion) lamp as well as the Riverside Colonial lamp.

Wild Rose with Bow Knot

This was made by McKee and Sons (National Glass 1901) in crystal, frosted crystal, colors, and goofus decorated. Shapes include a table set, water set, toothpick holder, shakers, sauce, berry set, smoke set on a tray, and rectangular tray (shown). It has been reproduced in various shapes and colors.

Wild Rose Wreath

This U.S. Glass pattern is also known as Miniature Intaglio to some carnival glass collectors. It was advertised as a "stemmed almond" so I know it was a nut cup. In carnival glass, it can be found in marigold or white and in crystal most examples have a gold or goofus treatment. The nut bowl stands 2½" tall and is about 3" across the bowl.

Willow Oak

Willow Oak was a Bryce pattern in 1890 and a U.S. Glass pattern in 1891. This pattern is also known as Oak Leaf, Stippled Star, Acorn, Thistle, and Wreath. Shapes are a tray, plate, mug, shakers, water set, sauce, celery vase, waste bowl, cake stand, compotes, bowls, and berry set.

Wiltec

Wiltec, made by McKee Glass about 1905, was one of the well-advertised "tec" patterns. Pieces are usually marked with McKee's "Prescut" mark. Shapes include a berry set, table set, water set, bonbon, cigar jar, custard cup, a scarce flower pot, punch sets, and plates in 6", 8", 10", and 12" sizes. The water pitchers can be squat or tankard and are very massive.

Wilted Flowers

This Dugan/Diamond pattern was part of the Intaglio line from 1906 to 1911. It was made in clear, goofus, opalescent, and carnival glass where it is known as Single Flower by some. Shapes are mostly bowls or rare plates, but handles have also been applied to some pieces to form baskets.

Windflower

Although found primarily in carnival glass, this Dugan/Diamond pattern was also made in crystal, pink, ebony, and opalescent glass. Shapes are mostly bowls, but plates and the handled nappy occasionally found.

Windmill Server

This item was shown in a 1928 Butler Brothers catalog and listed as a Windmill Spigot Decanter. It has little pattern other than panels with diagonal ribs within. According to *Yellow-Green Vaseline* authors Jay Glickman and Terry Fedosky, it is nickel plated and the windmill actually turns.

Windsor Anvil

This novelty paperweight is in the shape of a blacksmith's anvil. It is attributed to the Windsor Glass Company of Pittsburgh in 1887 – 1889. It is found in clear, amber, or blue glass.

Winged Scroll

Winged Scroll was made by the A.H. Heisey Company in about 1888 and can be found in clear, milk glass, custard (Ivorina verde), and this emerald green. Shapes include a syrup, table set, smoker's set, cruet, berry set, bonbon (no handles), pickle dish, cup and saucer, cake stand, cologne, trinket box, humidor, celery vase, olive dish, toothpick holder, and a high standard compote.

Country Kitchen Advertising Pieces

Both plates and bowls are advertising items. The one shown is a shallow bowl shape known as an ice cream bowl. It says "Compliments of S.I. Frank Furniture & Stoves - Credit To All - 709-711 W. North Ave." All Millersburg advertising items are rare, whether in crystal or carnival glass. They can also be found with "Compliments - Louis Mankowitz." Others may exist as well.

Daisy & Button Advertising Slipper

Patented by the Geo. Duncan & Sons Company in 1886, this Daisy & Button patterned slipper is very similar to one by Bryce (the patents for both were issued the same day). Duncan called this the "Hob Nail Slipper," and made it in crystal, amber, blue, canary, and ruby glass. The Duncan slipper says, "Patd...Oct...19/86," and the heel is higher than that on the Bryce version.

Dewey

This is credited to Beatty-Brady from the late 1890s. It is similar to the Spanish-American set shown elsewhere, but is much more detailed, has a better glass quality, and is scarcer. The pitcher shows shells standing on end, a laurel-wreathed portrait of Admiral Dewey, and a scroll, flags, sunbursts, and a column with a globe on top. Both tumblers (rare) and the pitcher (very scarce) are known, and both are very desirable. It has been reproduced from new moulds.

Dewey Bust (AKA: Gridley)

Among the many items honoring Admiral George Dewey is this 5½" tall satinized bust or statuette. It is on clear glass with an acid finish. It says: "Dewey...Manila...1898." Dewey was a hero of the Spanish-American War, defeating the Spanish fleet at Manila Bay on May 1, 1898. It was reproduced in colors.

Dice

This is 3⅛" tall and has a removable lid. It is marked "BRANDLE & SMITH CO., PHILA., USA, PAT PENDING."

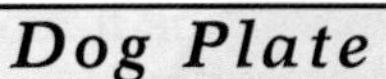

Dog Plate

This ABC plate with a dog in the center was made by Bryce, Higbee in 1893 and shown in one of its catalogs, and was later made by New Martinsville Glass in 1919. Original colors include clear, blue, and amber. It was originally called Rovers in the company ads and measures 6½" in diameter. New Martinsville examples may be marked with "S.I." between the letters of T and U, indicating reproductions issued for the Smithsonian Institute.

Easter Greetings Chick

These little plates are found with various edge treatments, several seasonal themes, and in many types of glass. They were made by several companies over a long span of time. The example shown is on crystal with goofus treatment, dating it from about 1905.

Flower Bouquet ABC Plate

This is one of the better ABC plates. It has a very well-done center design of floral spray with the alphabet around the outer rim on a stippled background. I believe this piece dates from the 1880s. It is credited to Gillinder & Sons of Philadelphia, which in 1891 was a member of U.S. Glass (Factory G).

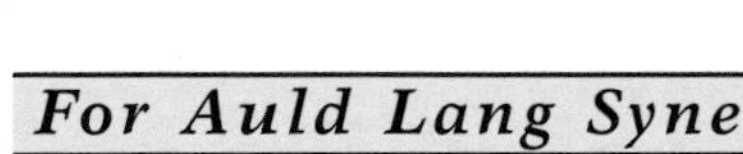

For Auld Lang Syne

This piece seems to have the same border treatment as another called the Rule Brittania Plate, so both are probably British in origin. This plate is from circa 1900.

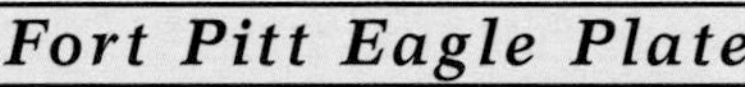

Fort Pitt Eagle Plate

This milk glass plate has a 24-star design and gilded eagles. It is certainly a nice addition to any collection.

Frische

The name on this interesting butter dish means "fresh" in German. The maker and date are currently unknown and this is the only shape I'm aware of at this time.

Frosted Stork ABC Plate

The plate shown here is part of a set of known flat glass items (see the oval platter shown elsewhere in this edition). The design shows the stork, fern branches, a palm tree, and tropical plants. It was made by Iowa City Flint Glass Company. It is very different from the iridized Stork ABC plate made by Belmont in Depression glass.

F.R. Rice Mercantile Cigar Company

What a neat piece of advertising this cigar container is. It says "Mercantine - Air-Tight - Registered Nov. 13th, 94 - Patented, Dec 31, 94 - Patented Jan 15, 85 - Cigars - Saint Louis, Mo." And on the lid, the lettering says "F.R. Rice Mercantile Cigar Co. - Manufacturers, St. Louis." On the base is the lettering: "Factory No. 305 - 1st Dist. - of Mo. - 50 Cigars."

Garden of Eden "Our Daily Bread"

Shown is the oval bread plate or tray with the "Give Us This Day Our Daily Bread" slogan that was part of the Garden of Eden pattern made in the 1870s or early 1880s. The rest of the piece duplicates the design in this unusual pattern. Pieces are found with or without a serpent in many shapes that are discussed elsewhere.

GAR Encampment Goblet (Milwaukee)

These items were issued to honor the Grand Army of the Republic, organized in 1866, and composed of men who enlisted in the army of the Union 1861 - 1865. The goblet is 6¾" tall. This says "23rd National Encampment...Milwaukee...Aug. 27th to 30th...1889." (the St. Louis Encampment was in 1887). There are others known (GAR St. Louis, 1887).

Garfield Alphabet Plate

This memorial plate is by Campbell, Jones and Company in 1881. It is not part of the Garfield Drape pattern. It measures about 7" in diameter, with a portrait and the letters of the alphabet. Garfield's death brought on a wave of these commemorative items.

Garfield and Lincoln Mug

This mug was made by Adams & Company in 1881 to commemorate the deaths of the two assassinated presidents with a bust of Garfield on one side and Lincoln on the other. The bottom of the mug says, "Our Country's Martyrs," and there are the names, birthdates, and dates of the deaths of the two presidents.

Garfield Drape Mourning Plate

This mourning plate was a part of the Lee & Adams Garfield Drape line produced after President Garfield's death in 1881. It bears a picture of the president, the familiar drape pattern, and the wording "We Mourn Our Nation's Loss." A second plate with a star center was also made in this pattern.

Garfield Memorial

Like the Garfield Alphabet plate shown above, this one is from Campbell, Jones and Company in 1881. It simply says, "Memorial" and has a portrait and a wreath of laurel leaves.

Garfield Plate with 101 Border

Evidence seems to indicate that this plate, like others with this 101 border, are products of Iowa City Glass despite being previously attributed to Crystal. This very nice piece dates to 1881 and has a frosted bust of Garfield.

Garfield Star Plate

Credited to the Crystal Glass Company in 1880 – 1881, this 6" plate has a bust of Garfield, a starred border with thirteen stars, and a flag shield. Garfield's name is inscribed below his portrait which may be clear or frosted as shown.

George VI Coronation

This beautifully done basket is a real find and would make a nice addition to any collection. It is from England and honoring the coronation of George VI.

Give Us Our Daily Bread

This Hobbs, Brockunier & Company plate has a well-known theme. The example shown is also referred to as the Sheaf of Wheat plate. It was reproduced by the Imperial Glass Co. and the reproductions are embossed "OSV" Old Sturbridge Village, Sturbridge, Massachusetts.

Glassport Brave

What an exciting piece of advertising crystal! It is 5½" tall and 4¼" wide and reads "1903 – Buy Glassport Lots." It was obviously made by U.S. Glass at their Glassport factory. This piece has also been seen in cobalt and amber glass, and both are rare finds today.

Go Further and Fare Worse

No maker and date has been established on this interesting little plate that I'm aware of. The lettering on this center leaf designed plate reads "You Can Go Further and Fare Worse."

Golden Rule Plate

With a center design like a feather fan and a row of ribbing, followed by the lettering: "DO UNTO OTHERS AS YOU WOULD HAVE THEM DO UNTO YOU," this nicely lettered piece would enhance any glass collection. The plate measures 9" in diameter and has a rolling beaded edge.

A Good Boy

The maker of this mug and its companion, A Good Girl, is McKee and Brothers. It is 3½" tall, has a 3" diameter, and dates from 1882. It can be found in crystal, amber, and blue.

Good Luck

This interesting relish dish is not part of the Good Luck or Prayer Rug design but has a strong interlocking six-pointed star and band design of its own. It does have a horseshoe in the center and the words "good luck."

Grand Army of The Republic (GAR) Tray

What a glorious piece of glass this is! The tray measures 7⅝" x 11⅛". The center is a copy of a war medal and is inscribed Grand Army of the Republic as is the outer borders along with American shields in the corners.

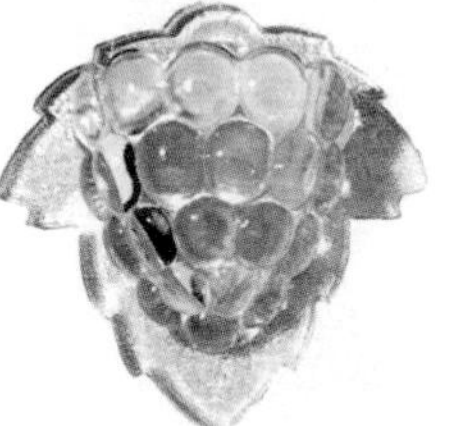

Grape Match Holder

Shown is a very attractive match safe. The crystal was made by Adams & Co. and the blue opaque was made by Challinor, Taylor & Company.

Harshaw's Ashtray

Although rather plain in design, this is a nice advertising piece. Vaseline is the only color reported to me at this time. The lettering reads "ASHES Will Not Worry You If You INSURE With HARSHAW"S Established 1898, 150 Broad St., Grove City, Pa."

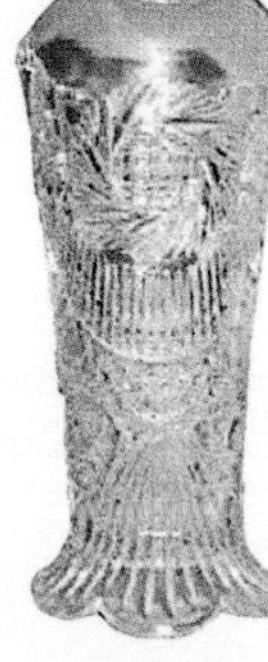

Hartman Pitcher

The advertising on this Aztec Sunburst (McKee's Sunburst) tankard pitcher says "Let Hartman Feather Your Nest." This pattern dates from 1910 and was reproduced in colors, but the advertising pieces are obviously old. It was reproduced by Fenton in iridized glass.

Hatchet

This small hatchet (7¾" long) has a ruby stained handle and a gilded blade. Various advertising mottos are found on these. The one shown has "Souvenir of Fredricksburg, VA" on it. These were listed as 97 cent items in early 1900s ads in Butler Brothers catalogs.

Heart Plume Advertising

Here is an advertising pitcher that says "Compliments of the Illinois Furniture Co. - 3609 - 11 So. Halstead St." It was from U.S. Glass (Bryce) and is also known as Marlboro.

Heroes of Bunker Hill

This oval bread tray was made by Gillinder and Company for the Philadelphia Exposition in 1876. Handles are flag shields and the lettering says "Prescott - Stark - Warren - Putnam - 1776 - 1876 The Heroes of Bunker Hill - The Spirit of Seventy-Six." In the center are the monument, the town, and "Birthplace of Liberty."

Hey Diddle Diddle

This is another in the series of nursery rhyme plates for children. The series consists of this plate, a Little Bo Peep plate, and a This Little Pig Went to Market plate.

Higbee Advertising Mug

What a treat to read this mug. It says "Higbee hot or cold sanitary vacuum bottle...for home & domestic use...keeps hot 48 hours...keeps cold 48 hours. Compliments John B. Higbee Glass Co...Bridgeville, PA...Higbee Sanitary Bottle" (photo of a bottle). The lettering says it all on this clear mug, and the bottle it advertises is quite rare.

Hobstar Band

Hobstar Band is better known in carnival glass. It is suspected to be an Imperial Glass pattern. Few examples are found in crystal but here is the pedestal-base water pitcher with the lettering "Bernheimer Brothers - Anniversary 1913."

Horseshoe Paperweight

This paperweight measures 7" tall and has an oval base that is about 3" x 5". The piece is frosted and inscribed "JUSTICE TO ALL." It was also made in milk glass.

Humpty Dumpty Mug

This mug says "Humpty Dumpty" on one side and "Tom, Tom, the Piper's Son" on the other, with illustrations of both characters. It dates from the 1880s and can be found in clear and amber. Pink, blue, and green are believed to exist also.

I.H.S.

This unusual oval plate or tray has the beaded cross in the center and the IHS banner, which is a miscopy of the IHE OTE monogram for Jesus, Savior of Men.

Illinois Advertising Toothpick Holder

This somewhat square U. S. Glass toothpick holder has lettering on the bottom that reads "Fort Wayne Outfitters Co." One has to assume from the name that this item was made for a company located in Indiana. Crystal is the only reported color to date.

Imperial's Cube Cut

Just what this covered jar is advertising and by who is uncertain, although the possibility of the product being chewing tobacco exists. The base is lettered "Imperial - Cube Cut."

Independence Hall Mug

This mug says, "Independence Hall," with a picture of the building. In addition, the example shown is engraved "Alice...1876," indicating it was indeed produced for the Philadelphia Centennial Exhibition. It was made by Boston & Sandwich Glass and with the same moulding as the Plain Dodecagon mug.

"In Remembrance"

This well-known memorial platter was issued following the Garfield assassination in 1881. The platter shows Garfield, Washington, and Lincoln and can be found totally clear or with frosted portraits. Some examples have been reported with gilding also.

It Is God's Way – His Will Be Done

This small plate or oval platter is another of those memorial items created to honor the fallen McKinley in 1901. It has a full-length portrait of him in the center with a laurel wreath edge. It says, "It Is God's Way – His Will Be Done." It also lists McKinley's date of birth and death.

Jefferson's Diamond with Peg

The piece shown is signed "Krys-tol" so I can be sure it was made after McKee relinquished the pattern to Jefferson in 1900. It then became part of Jefferson's Starline and dates between 1913 and 1915. The Gettysburg souvenir marking indicates it was sold at that place (note the date).

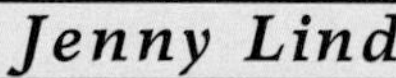

Jenny Lind

Recently gleaned information places this match safe as a product of the Enterprise Mfg., Co., of Akron, Ohio. These are marked "Pat'd. June 13, 1876." They are 4½" tall and are found in a clear or frosted finish with both shown here.

John Bull Eye Cup

This nice example of an eye cup says on the base "Pat. Aug 14, 1917 - 23659 - Trade Mark - USA - John Bull - Reg. U.S. Pat. Off." Eye cups were used in the early part of the century by both doctors and people at home, and the old ones are quite collectible (many reproductions exist however).

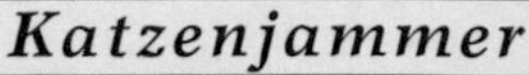

Katzenjammer

In a previous edition I showed this German mug in crystal, so here is a rich amber example. I've learned this mug was made from 1908 to 1916 in Germany and was an import item to this country. It has three panels of cats with lettering and stands 5" tall.

Knights of Labor Goblet

Just like the stein or mug shown below, this goblet was made by the Central Glass Company as an honor to the Knights of Labor organization and shows a worker and a union knight shaking hands. It says "Knights of Labor." There is also a matching crystal platter that measures 11¾" in length with the same center design and a border that shows railroads, a ship, a horse, a farm worker, and "United We Stand...Divided We Fall."

Knights of Labor Mug

This mug credited to the Central Glass Company by many collectors (they made the Knights of Labor goblet above). It can be found in clear either 4¾" tall or 6½" tall. The mug or stein reads "Knights of Labor" and shows a laborer shaking hands with the union's knight. This union was established in 1869.

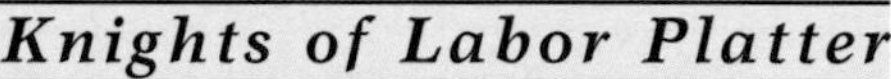

Knights of Labor Platter

This platter is about 12" long and is found in crystal, amber, vaseline, green, and blue.

Lansburgh & Bros. Advertising Nappy

This U.S. Glass advertising piece has the #15110 "Rising Sun" pattern from 1908 as its background. The advertising says "Lansburgh & Bros – Dry Goods Only – Washington, DC." The piece has three handles and is called a sweetmeat in the company ads. One book calls it a three handled jelly.

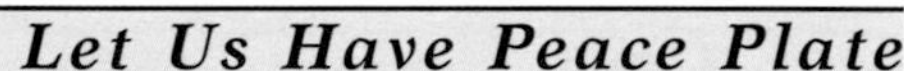

Let Us Have Peace Plate

This 10½" plate was actually part of the Maple Leaf pattern made by Gillinder and Sons in 1885. It notes the passing of U.S. Grant and can be found in clear, amber, blue, canary, and frosted glass. It has never been reproduced.

Liberty Bell

This well-known commemorative pattern was made by Adams and Company circa 1876 and also called Centennial. Old pieces are found in crystal and rare milk glass in a berry set, table set, celery vase, compote, goblet, toy table set, mug, pickle dish, plate, platter (shown), salt dish, shakers, water set, and a footed or flat sauce. The platter and goblet were reproduced (some pieces are dated 1776 – 1976).

Liberty Bell Bank

This 4⅛" bank was made for small coins. It can be found in clear and amber glass. The bottom is a threaded metal base that is lettered "Robinson & Loeble...723 Wharton St...Phila. PA." The bell itself says "Liberty 1776" and "Patented Sept., 22, 1885."

Lincoln Logs

These rare 6¾" x 8" plaques are very hard to find. They are found in opaque white, ebony, and amber glass and are said to be campaign items by Bessie Lindsey in *American Historical Glass*.

Lion and Cable Bread Plate

As part of the regular Lion and Cable line from Richards & Hartley Glass Company, this lettered bread plate is a very attractive piece of glass. In the center is the "proud lion" design while the lettering around the outer rim says "Give Us This Day...Our Daily Bread." The outer rim is bound with a cable effect, and there are two handles that match those on the covered butter dish. (The original plate measures 12¼", while the reproduction plate only measures 10½".)

Little Bo Peep

This is one of several designs that are part of a nursery rhyme set that features Hey Diddle Diddle and This Little Pig Went To Market. All are the same size with the same figural borders.

Little Bo-Peep (Dithridge)

This 1879 Dithridge & Company mug was an advertisement for the crystalography surface treatment used. It says "Little Bo-Peep" on one side and "Has Lost Her Sheep" on the other. One side shows several sheep with a fence in the background, while the others shows the girl and a dog.

Little Buttercup

This mug says "Little Buttercup" on one side with a picture of girls and a ship's crew standing on the deck and "H.M.S. Pinafore" on the other side with a ship. The surface is the crystalography treatment. The mug is the same mould shape as the Little Bo-Peep mug. It is also from Dithridge & Company in 1879.

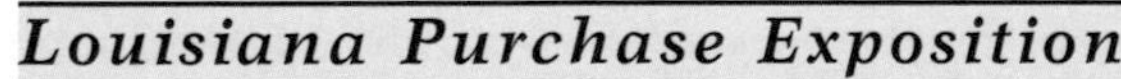

Louisiana Purchase Exposition

This very fine 5" tall ice tea tumbler was a St. Louis World's Fair item to celebrate the Louisiana Purchase. Although it is usually found in crystal or milk glass, here is a very rare "army" green example. A 7½" plate also exists.

"Loves Request Is Pickles"

The center design of this Adams and Company platter (or tray as some call it) is a figure of a girl that was thought to be one of the Actress line.

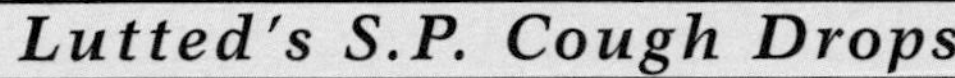

Lutted's S.P. Cough Drops

This was made by Central Glass (the #748 bowl and lid) as part of the Log Cabin pattern. This 7" covered piece is lettered on the lid: "Lutted's S.P. Cough Drops" and in the bottom of the base: "Jas. Lutted-Buffalo, N.Y. - U.S.A." Old pieces are found in crystal and the blue shown (canary and amber are also known). This piece has been reproduced without the bottom lettering and is planked.

Manhattan Advertising Tray

This well-done platter in the U.S. Glass Manhattan pattern shows center advertising, which can vary. This one says "Bailey Co. – Cleveland, Ohio." It is also found with "Denver Furniture & Carpet Co."

Meis' Store

Shown is a toothpick holder in the Minnesota pattern from U.S. Glass. On the base is the advertising "Meis' Store."

Memphis Advertising Pieces

Here is one of the advertising pieces found on Northwood's Memphis pattern. This one is a handled nappy. The lettering reads "Cash ROTHERT'S FURNITURE CARPETS Altoona, Pa. Credit." Other advertising common to this nappy is "Pickering Furniture and Carpets – 10 & Penn – NufCed." Then there is a rare 10" bowl which says "The Hub... Furniture...Carpets...7th & D Sts...NW...Washington, D.C." Originally the lettering was gilded, but most pieces have lost this long ago. Only crystal is reported.

Millner's Ashtray

J.R. Millner Company is a Lynchburg, Virginia, concern that must have believed in advertising because the famous Millner tumbler in carnival glass is well known. It has the Cosmos and Cane design by U.S. Glass. Here we see a very plain, modern 4" long crystal ashtray with cigarette dips on opposing corners. The lettering is on the bottom.

Minnesota Advertising Toothpick Holder

I can't say that this piece is advertising the same company as the Hartman pitcher in the Aztec Sunburst pattern but it may well be. This three handled toothpick has lettering on the bottom that reads "Hartman Furniture & Carpet Co."

Moerleins

This beer pilsner or ale goblet is 6" tall and bears the inscription "Moerleins – National Lager Beer – Good Luck – Cincinnati." It was obviously an advertising give-away item from a Cincinnati company. It was made by the Bellaire Goblet Company that in 1888 moved to Findlay, Ohio, from Bellaire, Ohio.

Nellie Bly

What an interesting item this is! The platter is 6¾" x 12¾" and has a full portrait of the famous traveler Nellie Bly. In addition the lettering tells the information of her trip around the world with the time it took, the places she visited, the dates of each stop, and the date the trip ended.

Northwood's Near-Cut #12 Advertising

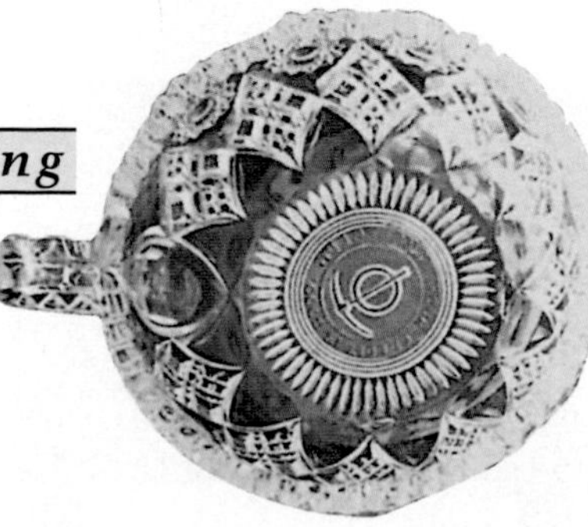

This very nice nappy, found on Northwood's #12 or Near-Cut pattern, had the pattern and advertising on the exterior. The pattern was introduced in 1906 in a water set, table set, berry set, nappy, two-handled mayonnaise dish, cake plate, oval pickle dish, and shakers. The advertising piece is rare and says "Your Credit Is Good – Nuf Ced." along with an anchor.

Northwood's Good Luck

This 1909 pattern is found in bowls or plates from the same mould, usually in carnival glass. Rare examples are known in crystal and scarce bowls are found in custard glass (shown here with a nutmeg stain). The mould was advanced from an advertising pattern called Jockey Club and may have either a basketweave or a fine rib exterior.

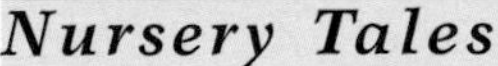

Nursery Tales

Apparently a child's set, this pattern features such stories as Little Red Riding Hood, Jack and the Candlestick, and See-Saw. The set consists of the creamer, sugar, compote, punch set, pitcher, cups, butter-chip saucers, and tumblers. The maker is believed to be U.S. Glass after 1900, according to Kamm.

Oklahoma Vinegar Company

This very nice advertising piece is 5½" tall and has a 2¼" top diameter. The base is hollow for more than 1½". The advertising reads "Oklahoma Vinegar Co. - Fort Smith, Ark." All vinegar advertising items are highly collectible.

Old State House

This fine 1876 Co-operative Flint Glass round plate or platter bears a picture of the building and says, "Old State House - Philadelphia." The border design contains Daisy and Button with ovals of fine file, and the roping on the edge.

Panama Advertising Pieces

This U. S. Glass rose bowl says "Michaelson's 1508-1514 Larimer St." It is also found reading "Erlanger's," There is also a rare spittoon shape with "Joe Kuhn and Co. Clothier's - Champaign's."

The Patriot Soldier

The design of this plate is a good one with a well-done portrait in satin and satinized lettering that reads "The Patriot and Soldier - Gen. Ulysses S. Grant."

Peabody

Peabody was from Greener (Wear Flint Glass) & Company in England with a registry mark (shown) of July 31, 1869. Pieces known are a mug, saucer, creamer, and open sugar (shown). George Peabody was a philanthropist in England and America. Pieces are known in crystal, blue, and amethyst.

Philadelphia 1876 Centennial

This circa 1875 Adams and Co. pattern is reported only in a goblet according to some references, but in various shapes in other references. It is only found in crystal.

P

Pope Leo XIII Plate

This rare plate was made by Bryce, Higbee in 1903 to commemorate the death of the Pope in that year. It shows a side-view bust of the Pope and various Roman Catholic religious symbols around the rim between sections of raised beading. It seems to have been made only in crystal.

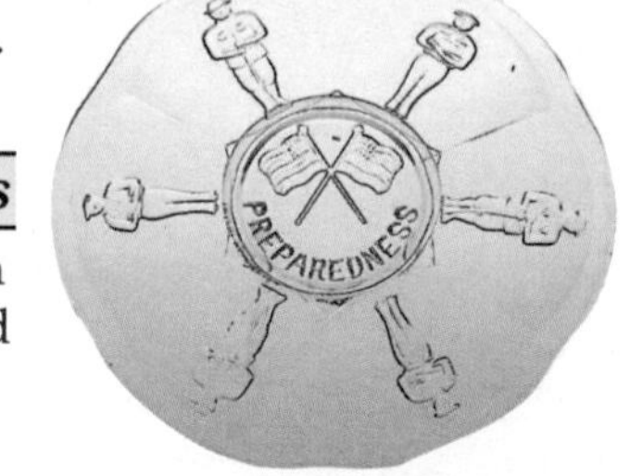

Preparedness

This is an attractive 10¾" plate that honors the soldiers of WWI in a simple but effective design of six figures and a center of crossed flags and the "PREPAREDNESS."

Present for a Friend

This toothpick or match holder says "A Present For A Friend." Although Adams & Company made a similar novelty item this one cannot be placed at that concern to date. Colors reported are crystal and vaseline.

President McKinley Assassination Water Set

William McKinley was the twenty-fifth president of the United States and was assassinated by an anarchist in 1901. This scarce water set was made in commemoration of his death and says "Our Martyr'd President." It bears a portrait of McKinley, his signature, and the dates of his birth and death.

Protection and Plenty

This mid-size plate was made by McKee Brothers and Company for the election of 1896. It shows presidential candidate McKinley's bust on a shield with "Protection and Plenty." There is also a mug in this pattern shown elsewhere in this edition.

Protection and Plenty Mug

This mug (the cover is missing) was also made by McKee Brothers and Company for the 1896 presidential campaign of McKinley. The front of the mug has a McKinley bust with his name, "Maj. Wm. McKinley" beneath it, and above it "Protection and Plenty." The opponent, William Jennings Bryan, had a similar covered mug.

Pure Pack Mug

Made from the Necco Sweets mug mold, the Pure Pack mug is an equal mystery since I have no knowledge of who made either. Both are 2⅛" tall and have a 1⅝" diameter, with a banded top and 12 panels around it. Both have been seen only in clear glass.

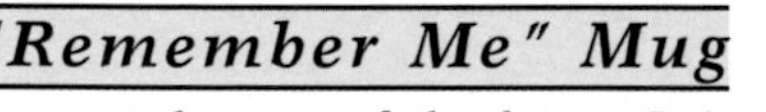

"Remember Me" Mug

Mugs for children have a charm all their own, and this one has to be near the top of the heap. It is faced with an irregular shield that says "Remember Me." Below the shield are crossed leaves with leaves and scroll above it. I have a strong feeling this may be from U.S. Glass since it is shaped like so many mugs from that company. Although it is found mostly on amber, here is a scarce clear example.

Richard Wallace Compote

Richard Wallace was the natural son of the Marquis of Hertford; he inherited much of the Marquis's estate. He served as Commissioner of the Paris Exhibition in 1878, was made a Knight Commander of the Bath, and a trustee of the National Gallery. When he died, he left the estate as a house museum to the English nation. This compote was made by the Greener Glass Company and bears the 1877 Lion and Star trademark. It is a superb piece of glass with outstanding design.

Rooster ABC Plate

This alphabet plate shows a large rooster and smaller chickens with a brick wall in the background. The design is good but not outstanding. No collection of alphabet pieces would be complete without it. It is credited to the King Glass Company of Pittsburgh which became U.S. Glass Factory K in 1891.

Salt Lake Temple Platter

The Salt lake Temple platter was part of the Egyptian (Parthenon) line by Boston & Sandwich Glass in 1870. It is one of the most sought and desirable pieces. It shows the great temple of Salt Lake City in a satinized portrait, is lettered "Salt Lake Temple," and measures 8½" x 13".

St. Louis Encampment

This unusual goblet is lettered "21 Encampment – September 27, '87 – St. Louis, Mo." On the reverse side there is an American flag and shield, topped by an eagle, with a military emblem below them all.

St. Louis World's Fair Hatchet

There are really two versions of this hatchet. The one shown here has a portrait of George Washington and "The Father of His Country" on one side, and the other has on the handle "St. Louis World's Fair 1904." The hatchet measures 8" long. The second version is shown under Washington Hatchet in this chapter.

Sawtoothed Honeycomb

This puzzling pattern was originally called either Radiant or Serrated Block and Loop. It was first made by Steiner Glass of West Virginia and then Union Stopper in 1908. Shapes known are a table set, punch set, berry set, goblet, syrup, toothpick holder (clear or ruby stained), flat or footed sauce, and the nappies (two variations) shown which advertise Bernheimer Brothers.

Schrafft's Chocolates

Advertising items have an appeal all their own, and this one certainly fills that bill. It is a square plate with a nice geometric design and a small centered rectangle that says "Schrafft's Chocolates."

Sheaf of Wheat

This has a very stylish sheaf of wheat with the motto bracketed with wheat stems on each end. It was made by McKee circa 1890s and shown in old factory catalog reprints from that period. It is similar to the "Give Us This Day" plate shown elsewhere.

Spanish-American

This pitcher and matching tumbler and water set called Dewey were made, Indiana, by Beatty-Brady Glass as a commemoration of Admiral Dewey's part in the Spanish-American War, in the 1890s. The Dewey pitcher and tumblers are very hard to find. They have bullets rather than the cannon balls in the design, as well as other pattern changes.

Star in Bull's-Eye Advertising

This one is advertises "Lansburg & Bros. – Dry Goods Only – Washington, D.C." It was made in 1905 by U.S. Glass with an exterior pattern called Star-in-Bull's-Eye (#15092). The pattern was later made by New Martinsville Glass (1918) but without the advertising.

Swan with Ring Handle Advertising

This mustard is the first advertising piece in this pattern I've seen to date. This crystal piece has the lettering "G. P. Gerber & Co., German Mustard, Baltimore, Md." This piece is missing its lid, which had a ring handle finial matching the side handles.

Terrestrial Globe

The continents of the world are well shown with the wide banding being the equator. The lid has a man's (boy's?) head. This rare piece is from the O'Hara Glass Co., circa 1876.

Texas Centennial

Shown are four Texas Centennial pieces that include a pitcher, a 9" x 11½" platter, a covered sugar, and a creamer (no butter dish has been reported at this time). In addition there are tumblers, plates, and coasters known but all the pieces are quite scarce. The finial on the sugar is a "lone star" and the streamers say "Alamo – 1836 – 1936."

Theodore Roosevelt Platter

This platter honoring the nation's twenty-sixth president is a beauty. It has a portrait of Teddy Roosevelt in the center (can be either frosted or clear) and a rim of symbols including teddy bears, golf, tennis, hunting, music, dancing (all things associated with Roosevelt), an eagle, shield, and crossed clubs. The border reads "A Square Deal," Roosevelt's slogan. The platter measures 7¾" x 10¼".

This Little Pig Went to Market

Here is the third in the series of nursery rhyme plates that have the same border. The other pieces, Little Bo Peep and Hey Diddle Diddle, complete the set.

Three Graces

This 11½" handled plate shows the Three Graces: Faith, Hope, and Charity. It says "Three Graces – Pat'd Nov. 23. 1875" and was made for the Centennial Exposition in Philadelphia by Atterbury.

Three Presidents Goblet

This fine goblet honors Washington, Lincoln, and Garfield, with Washington in the center and an eagle above flags. It is well worth owning for the collector of commemorative items.

U. S. Glass Cross

This ashtray from the U. S. Glass Company says "Boston 1895, PITTSBURG 1898, U S Glass Co." It is found in crystal only to date.

U.S. Grant – Patriot and Soldier

This beautiful 11" square plate can be found in crystal and rarely in amber. It shows a portrait of Grant in military uniform and says "The Patriot and Soldier. . . Gen. Ulysses S. Grant." Corners of the plate are mitered and the edge has a bead moulding, while the interior has a stylized daisy design. It was made in 1885 by Bryce, Higbee.

U.S. Lady

This interesting paperweight is marked "U.S. Glass Co...Pittsburgh, PA." The bust of a lady is in the center and is satinized, while around her is a beaded oval. There is another with identical lettering but the bust of the lady is different. Often glass companies made advertising items to promote their own business and this one, like the Glassport Brave, is an example of this practice.

Volunteer Plate

Recent information places this plate as a design from McKee and Brothers in 1898, so it would be a commemorative of the Spanish-American War. It is said to have been made in crystal, green, amber, canary, and blue.

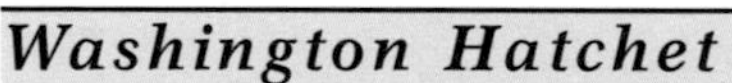

Washington Hatchet

Here is the second version of this hatchet, and like the first, it has a portrait of George Washington on the blade and "The Father of His Country." On the handle are the words "Libbey Glass Co. Toledo, Ohio." On the reverse side of the blade is "World's Fair...1893." Both of these hatchets were made by Libbey Glass, I believe, for they are identical in form and measure 8" long.

Wedding Day and After

This eight sided lettered plate reads "Three Weeks After The Wedding Day" and shows a smiling couple when held in one position and a frowning couple when turned in the opposite direction. The color is a rich amber.

Wm. J. Bryan Tumbler

William Jennings Bryan was a Democratic presidential candidate in 1896 and in 1900 (losing both times to McKinley) and a third time in 1908 (losing to Theodore Roosevelt) and later Wilson's Secretary of State. The tumbler says "The people's choice...1896 - 1900...Wm. J. Bryan." The decoration is like that of the Dewey tumbler shown elsewhere in this edition.

Yutec Hub

Here is a McKee pattern called Yutec that has the Hub advertising. It is similar to the Hub advertising bowl shown in the Northwood Memphis pattern.

Bibliography

Bredehoft, Neila and Tom. Hobbs. *Brockunier & Company Glass.* Paducah, Kentucky: Collector Books, 1997.

Bredehoft, Neila M., Geo. A. Fogg, and Francis C. Maloney. *Early Duncan Glassware.* Self published, 1987.

Davis, Sue C. *Picture Book of Vaseline Glass.* Atglen, Pennsylvania: Schiffer Books, 1999.

Edwards, Bill. *Millersburg Crystal Glassware.* Paducah, Kentucky: Collector Books, 1982.

_________. *Standard Encyclopedia of Opalescent Glass.* Paducah, Kentucky: Collector Books, 1997.

Edwards, Bill and Mike Carwile. *The Standard Encyclopedia of Carnival Glass,* 6th ed. Paducah, Kentucky: Collector Books, 1998.

Glickman, Jay L., and Terry Fedosky. *Yellow-Green Vaseline.* Marietta, Ohio: Glass Press, 1998.

Hallock, Marilyn R. *Central Glass Co.* Atglen, Pennsylvania: Schiffer Publishing Ltd., 2002.

Heacock, William. *Fenton Glass – The First Twenty-Five Years.* Marietta, Ohio: O-Val Advertising Corp, 1978.

_________. *Old Pattern Glass.* Marietta, Ohio: Antiques Publications, 1981.

Heacock, William and Fred Bickenheuser. *Encyclopedia of Victorian and Colored Glass*, Book 5. Marietta, Ohio: Antiques Publications, 1978.

Heacock, William, James Measell, and Berry Wiggins. *Harry Northwood – The Early Years.* Marietta, Ohio: Antiques Publications, 1991.

_________. *Harry Northwood – The Wheeling Years 1901 – 1925.* Marietta, Ohio: Antiques Publications, 1993.

_________. *Dugan/Diamond.* Marietta, Ohio: Antiques Publications, 1993.

Jenks, William and Jerry Luna. *Early American Pattern Glass, 1850 – 1910.* Radnor, Pennsylvania: Wallace-Homestead Book Company, 1990.

Lang Rottenberg, Barbara with Judith Tomlin. *Glass Manufacturing In Canada: A Survey of Pressed Glass Patterns.* History Division, National Museum of Man; Ottawa, Canada. 1982

Lecher, Doris Anderson. *Toy Glass.* Marietta, Ohio: Antiques Publications, 1989.

Lindsey, Bessie M. *American Historical Glass.* Rutland, Vermont & Tokyo, Japan: Charles E. Tubble Company, Inc. 1967-1980.

Loomis, Jean Chapman. *Krys-tol! Krys-tol! Krys-tol!* Self published, 2001.

McCain, Mollie Helen. *Collector's Encyclopedia of Pattern Glass.* Paducah, Kentucky: Collector Books, 1994.

McGee, Marie. *Millersburg Glass.* Marietta, Ohio: The Glass Press, 1995.

Measell, James. *Greentown Glass.* Grand Rapids, Michigan: Grand Rapids Museum Association, 1979.

Measell, James and W. C. "Red" Roetteis. *The L. G. Wright Glass Company.* Marietta, Ohio: The Glass Press, Inc. 1997.

Metz, Alice Hulett. *Early American Pattern Glass.* Paducah, Kentucky: Collector Books, 1977 – 1978.

Miles, Dori and Robert W. Miller. *Price Guide to Pattern Glass.* Radnor, Pennsylvania: Wallace-Homestead, 1986.

Mordock, John B. and Walter L. Adams. *Pattern Glass Mugs.* Marietta, Ohio: Antiques Publications, 1995.

Peterson, David A. *Vaseline Glass Rarities.* Self Published. Layout by blurb.com, 2007.

Reilly, Darryl and Bill Jenks. *Early American Pattern Glass,* 2nd Edition. Lola, Wisconsin: Krause Publications, 2002.

Righter, Miriam. *Iowa City Glass*, price guide compiled by Dr. J. W. Carlberry. Des Moines, Iowa: Wallace-Homestead, 1981.

Rottenberg, Barbara Lang and Judith Tomlin. *Glass Manufacturing in Canada: A Survey of Pressed Glass Patterns.* Ottawa, Canada; History Division Paper No. 33, National Museum of Man. 1982.

Sanford, Jo and Bob. *Victorian Glass Novelties.* Atglen, Pennsylvania: Schiffer Publishing Co., 2003.

Schroy, Ellen Tischbein. *Warman's Pattern Glass.* Radnor, Pennsylvania: Wallace-Homestead Book Company, 1993.

Spillman, Jane Shadel. *Knopf Collector's Guide to American Antiques – Glass, Tableware, Bowls, and Vases.* New York, New York: Chanticleer Press, Inc., 1982.

Stevens, Gerald. *Canadian Glass, 1825 – 1925.* Toronto, Canada: Coles Publishing Company Limited, 1979.

Sutton-Smith, Peter and Barbara. *Canadian Handbook of Pressed Glass Tableware.* Markham, Ontario: Fitzhenry and Whiteside Limited, 2000.

Teal, Ron Sr. *Albany Glass.* Marietta, Ohio: Antiques Publications, 1997.

Thuro, Catherine M. V. *Oil Lamps – The Kerosene Era in North America.* Paducah, Kentucky: Collector Books, 1976. Updated values, 2001.

Vogel, Clarence W. *Heisey's Art and Colored Glass, 1922 – 1942, Heisey's Colonial Years, 1906 – 1922, Heisey's First Ten Years, 1896 – 1905, Heisey's Early and Late Years, 1896 – 1958,* books I, II, III, and IV. Plymouth, Ohio: Heisey Publications, 1970.

Weatherman, Hazel Marie. *Colored Glass of the Depression Era II.* Ozark, Missouri: Weatherman Glass Books, 1974.

Webb Lee, Ruth. *Early American Pressed Glass.* Massachusetts: Lee Publications, 1931 – 1960.

Webb Lee, Ruth. *Victorian Glass.* Massachusetts: Lee Publications, 1944.

Welker, John and Elizabeth. *Pressed Glass in America.* Antique Acres Press, Ivyland, Pennsylvania: 1985.

Welker, Mary, Lyle and Lynn. *The Cambridge Glass Company, A Reprint of Old Company Catalogs*, books I and II. Self Published, 1970 and 1974.

Whitmyer, Margaret and Kenn. *Fenton Art Glass.* Paducah, Kentucky: Collector Books, 1996.

Wilson, Charles West. *Westmoreland Glass.* Paducah, Kentucky: Collector Books, 1996.

Price Guide

All prices are for crystal, unless otherwise noted.

ABC CLOCK
- Plate 50

ACORN
- Butter 75
- Celery Vase 30
- Compote 60
- Compote, open 40
- Creamer or Spooner 25
- Egg Cup 25
- Goblet 40
- Pitcher 95
- Sugar 35

ACORN (FENTON)
- Bowl, ruffled, 7" - 8", rare 100

ACORN BAND
- Bowl 30
- Bowl, covered 55
- Celery Vase 20
- Compote, covered 65
- Compote, open 25
- Creamer or Spooner 25
- Dessert, stemmed 15
- Egg Cup 20
- Goblet 40
- Pitcher 85
- Sauce, flat or ftd. 10
- Sugar 30
- Tumbler 25
- Wine 15

ACTRESS
- Bowl, covered, 6" - 9½" .... 90 - 140
- Bowl, open, 6" - 9½" .... 40 - 80
- Butter 225
- Cake Stand, 9" - 10" 150
- Candlesticks, ea. 110
- Celery Vase, actress head 145
- Celery Vase, HMS Pinafore 200
- Cheese Dish 300
- Compote, covered, 8" - 10" .... 135 - 200
- Compote, open, high, 10" - 12" .... 100 - 300
- Creamer or Spooner 70
- Dresser Tray 90
- Goblet 130
- Jam Jar 135
- Jelly Compote, 5" - 7" 60
- Milk Pitcher 400
- Mug 100
- Pickle Dish 50
- Platter, HMS Pinafore 125
- Platter, Miss Neilson 100
- Pitcher 500
- Relish, 3 sizes .... 45 - 70
- Shakers, ea. 100
- Sauce, 4" - 5", flat or ftd. .... 20 - 25
- Sugar 125
- Tumbler 85

ADA
*Condensed list.
- Berry Bowl, lg. 45
- Berry Bowl, sm. 15
- Butter 75
- Celery Dish 20
- Compotes, various .... 25 - 55
- Creamer or Spooner 25
- Cruet 45
- Pickle Dish 15
- Pitcher 95
- Shakers, ea. 20
- Sugar 30
- Tumbler 25

ADAM'S APOLLO
- Lamp 75
  - amber 110
  - vaseline 175
  - green/blue 150

ADAM'S PLUME
- Bowls, flat .... 10 - 30
  - ruby stain .... 15 - 40
- Bowls, ftd. .... 15 - 35
  - ruby stain .... 20 - 50
- Butter 50
  - ruby stain 75
- Cake Stand 45
  - ruby stain 50
- Celery Vase 25
  - ruby stain 30
- Creamer or Spooner 25
  - ruby stain 30
- Goblet 30
  - ruby stain 55
- Lamp 65
  - ruby stain 100
- Sauce 10
  - ruby stain 20
- Sugar 30
  - ruby stain 50

ADMIRAL DEWEY PLATE
- Plate, 7" 90

ADMIRAL DEWEY TUMBLER
- Tumbler 65

ADONIS
- Berry Bowl, sm. 10
  - vaseline 20
  - green/blue 25
- Berry Bowl, lg. 30
  - vaseline 65
  - green/blue 55
- Butter 60
  - vaseline 140
  - green/blue 125
- Cake Stand 100
  - vaseline 275
  - green/blue 300
- Celery Vase 40
  - vaseline 275
  - green/blue 310
- Compote, covered 60
  - vaseline 100
  - green/blue 135
- Creamer or Spooner 40
  - vaseline 60
  - green/blue 65
- Jelly Compote 25
  - vaseline 45
  - green/blue 35
- Milk Pitcher 55
  - vaseline 85
  - green/blue 95
- Plate, 10" - 11" .... 25 - 30
  - vaseline .... 40 - 65
  - green/blue .... 45 - 75
- Pitcher 65
  - vaseline 140
  - green/blue 145
- Relish Tray 20
  - vaseline 40
  - green/blue 35
- Shakers, ea. 45
  - vaseline 65
  - green/blue 75
- Sugar 45
  - vaseline 80
  - green/blue 95
- Syrup 110
  - vaseline 300
  - green/blue 325
- Tray, 11" 40
  - vaseline 65
  - green/blue 75
- Tumbler 35
  - vaseline 60
  - green/blue 70

AFRICAN SHIELD
- Vase, 2⅞" 20

ALABAMA
- Bowl, 8", rectangular or round .... 45 - 100
- Butter 110
  - ruby stain 225
- Cake Stand 200
- Castor set, complete; 4 bottles & stand 235
- Celery Vase 75
  - ruby stain 135
- Compote, covered 95
- Creamer or Spooner 60
  - ruby stain 85
- Honey Dish w/lid, rare 375
- Jelly Compote 55
- Nappy 50
- Mustard w/Lid 100
- Pitcher 125
- Relish Dish, 3 sizes .... 25 - 50
  - ruby stain .... 40 - 80
- Sugar 90
- Syrup 200
  - ruby stain 250
- Toothpick 80
  - ruby stain 150
- Tray, 11" 95
- Tumbler 80

ALASKA
- Berry Bowl, lg. 40
  - green/blue 65
  - cobalt 325
- Berry Bowl, sm. 25
  - green/blue 35
- Butter Dish 75
  - green/blue 150
- Creamer, spooner or sugar 35
  - green/blue 55
- Cruet 185
  - green/blue 265
- Jewel Tray 40
  - green/blue 50
- Pitcher 125
  - green/blue 225
- Rose Bowl 45
  - green/blue 70
- Tumbler 30
  - green/blue 50

ALDINE (BEADED ELLIPSE)
- Bowl, oval, covered 45
  - chocolate 1500
- Butter 60
  - chocolate 500
- Celery Dish 25
- Creamer or Spooner 30
  - chocolate 125
- Pickle Dish 25
- Pitcher 95
- Sugar 40
  - chocolate 165
- Tumbler 20
- Wine 30

ALEXIS (FOSTORIA)
- Bowls, various .... 10 - 45
- Butter 60
- Celery Tray 25
- Celery Vase 30
- Champagne 20
- Claret 25
- Cocktail 20
- Cordial 25
- Creamer or Spooner 30
- Cruet, 3 sizes .... 35 - 70
- Custard 15

Decanter...65
Egg Cup...20
Finger Bowl...20
Goblet...35
Ice Bowl w/Underplate...65
Ice Tea Set w/Plates...80
Ketchup...45
Mayonnaise Plate/Bowl...40
Nasturtium Vase...40
Nut Bowl...25
Olive Tray...20
Pickle Tray...15
Pitcher, 3 sizes...75 - 145
Relish Jar...20
Salt, 2 sizes...15 - 25
Shakers, ea...25
Sherbet...15
Sugar...45
Sugar Sifter...55
Sweet Pea Vase...25
Syrup...65
Toothpick...50
Tumbler, 3 sizes...20 - 35
Tumbler, whiskey...30
Water bottle...45
Wine...15

ALLIGATOR
Novelty Toothpick Holder...175
amber...225
green/blue...300
milk glass...225

ALL-OVER-DIAMOND
Berry Bowl, sm...20
ruby stain...35
Berry Bowl, lg...35
ruby stain...60
Butter...55
ruby stain...80
Creamer...30
ruby stain...40
Egg Cup...25
ruby stain...50
Pitcher...75
ruby stain...100
Spooner...25
ruby stain...35
Sugar...35
ruby stain...50
Tumbler...15
ruby stain...25
Wine...20
ruby stain...30

ALMOND
Stemmed Wine...25
Wine Decanter...65
Wine Tray...30

ALMOND THUMBPRINT
Butter...50
Celery Vase...25
Champagne...30
Creamer or Spooner...35
Cologne Bottle w/Stopper...90
Compote, high covered, 5", 7" & 10"...40 - 85
Compote, low covered, 5", 7" & 10"...35 - 80
Cordial...20
Cruet...60
Decanter...70
Goblet...35
Pitcher...95
Punch Bowl...135
Punch Cup...20
Salt Dips, 2 sizes...15 - 30
Sugar...40
Sweetmeat, covered...65
Tumbler...40
Wine...20

ALPHABET & CHILDREN
Mug...40

ALPHABET PLATE
Plate...70

AMARYLLIS
Bowl, 8"...45

AMAZON
Banana Stand...80
Bowl, oval, covered...70
Bowl, rnd., w/lid, 5" - 7"...40 - 50
Bowl, rnd., w/lid, 8" - 9"...60 - 90
Butter...75
Celery Vase, ftd. or flat...40
Champagne...50
Child's Table Set, 4 pieces...250
Claret...50
Compote, covered, 4" - 6"...40 - 50
Compote, covered, 7" - 8"...60 - 90
Compote, open, 4" - 6"...25 - 45
Compote, open, 7" - 8"...30 - 60
Cordial...40
Creamer or Spooner...35
Cruet...60
Egg Cup...30
Goblet...40
Pitcher...80
Sauce...10
Salt Dip, ind....15
Salt Dip, master...30
Sugar...60
Syrup...85
Tumbler...30
Vase, 2 styles...50 - 70
Wine...30

AMBERETTE
Bowl, covered, 7" - 8"...185 - 210
Bowl, open, 7" - 8"...85 - 100
Bowls, various shapes and sizes...70 - 125
Butter...185
Butter Pat...70
Cake Stand...375
Celery Tray...70
Celery Vase...85
Creamer or Spooner...75
Cruet...290
Finger Bowl...50
Gas Shade...125
Milk Pitcher...300
Olive Dish...60
Pickle Dish...70
Pitcher...400
Plate, 7" - 11"...60 - 125
Sauce, collared, 4" - 4½"...35
Sauce, flat, 4" - 4½"...30
Shakers, ea...125
Sugar...130
Tumbler...75

*All pieces in crystal are crystal with amber stain.
*Add 100% for pieces found in vaseline.
*Add 25% for pieces found in ruby stained.

AMBOY
Berry Bowl, sm...15
Berry Bowl, lg...40
Butter...65
Celery Dish...15
Creamer or Spooner...20
Goblet...35
Pickle Dish...15
Spoon Dish...15
Sugar...25

AMERICAN BEAUTY
Berry Bowl, lg...35
Berry Bowl, sm...10
Butter...55
Creamer or Spooner...20
Jelly Compote...30
Pitcher...75
Sugar...25
Tumbler...20

ANGEL'S CROWN
Jelly Tumbler...60

ANGELUS
Butter...60
Celery Vase...20
Creamer or Spooner...25
Pickle Dish...20
Pitcher...80
Sugar...30
Tumbler...20
Waste Bowl...25
Wine...30

ANGULAR
Butter...65
Compote, covered...45
Creamer or Spooner...20
Pitcher...85
Sugar...30
Tumbler...25

ANTHEMION
Butter...75
Creamer...35
Goblet...40
Pickle Dish...25
Spooner...30
Sugar...40
Wine...25

APE WITH BASKET
Toothpick Holder, very rare...275

APPLE BLOSSOM (DUGAN)
Bowl, 7", very scarce
black...75

APPLE TREE (FENTON)
Giant Spittoon, from pitcher, rare...300
black...400

APPLIED FILIGREE
Footed Pitcher
amber...350

APPOMATTOX
Hand Mirror (glass hndl.)...75

AQUARIUM
Pitcher, very scarce...300

AQUARIUS LAMP
Table Lamp, 6 sizes...95
amber...185
vaseline...250
green/blue...225
Footed Finger Lamp, 2 sizes...80
amber...165
vaseline...225
green/blue...200

AQUATIC
Pitcher...200
Tumbler...40

ARCADIA LACE
Berry Bowl, lg...40
Berry Bowl, sm...15
Butter...55
Candy Dish, covered...35
Celery Vase...25
Compote, covered...45
Creamer or Spooner...25
Jelly Compote...25
Nappy...30
Pickle Dish...20
Pitcher...70
Plate, 11"...30
Plate, 6"...25
Rose Bowl...30
Sugar...25
Tumbler...20
Vase, 6" & 10", 2 styles...30 - 35
Wine...20

ARCH & FORGET-ME-NOT BANDS
Berry Bowl, sm...15
Berry Bowl, lg...35
Butter...45
Creamer or Spooner...25
Jam Jar...30

Sauce 10
Sugar 30

ARCHED FLEUR-DE-LIS
Banana Stand 35
ruby stain 125
Butter 65
ruby stain 100
Cake Stand 40
Creamer or Spooner 25
ruby stain 65
Dish, 7" 15
Jelly Compote 30
Mug 40
ruby stain 50
Olive, hndl 20
Pitcher 100
ruby stain 300
Plate, 7", sq 20
ruby stain 50
Relish 15
Sauce 10
ruby stain 25
Shakers, ea 20
ruby stain 65
Sugar .... 20 - 35
ruby stain .... 70 - 100
Toothpick Holder 65
ruby stain 100
Tumbler 30
ruby stain 55
Vase 30
ruby stain 75
Wine 20
ruby stain 55

ARCHED GRAPE
Butter 70
Celery Vase 60
Champagne 75
Compote, covered 100
Creamer or Spooner 40
Goblet 55
Pitcher 300
Sauce, flat or ftd 15
Sugar 60
Tumbler 55
Wine 40

ARCHED OVALS
Berry Bowl, sm. 20
green/blue 30
Berry Bowl, lg 45
green/blue 55
Butter 60
green/blue 85
ruby stain 100
Cake Stand 40
Celery Vase 25
green/blue 35
Compote, covered 45
Compote, open 35
Creamer or Spooner 25
green/blue 35
ruby stain 40
Cruet 45
green/blue 75
Goblet 30
green/blue 40
ruby stain 50
Mug 25
green/blue 30
ruby stain 35
Pitcher 65
green/blue 100
Plate 30
green/blue 35
Relish 25
Sauce 15
Shakers, ea 25
green/blue 60
Sugar 25
green/blue 65
Syrup 55
Toothpick Holder 30
green/blue 35
ruby stain 40
Tumbler 20
Wine 15
green/blue 25
ruby stain 35

ARGENT
Bread Plate, 9"x13" 45
Butter 65
Cake Stand 45
Celery Vase 30
Compote, covered 60
Creamer or Spooner 25
Goblet 35
Plate, 7" 25
Platter 35
Sugar, open 25
Tumbler 20
Wine 15

ARGUS (THUMBPRINT)
Ale Glass 100
Berry Bowl, sm. 50
Berry Bowl, lg 95
Bitters bottle 80
Butter 90
Celery Vase 120
Champagne 90
Compote, covered, various .... 90 - 200
Compote, open, 10½" 235
Cordial 85
Creamer 125
Decanter 100
Egg Cup, with or without handle .. 30 - 90
Honey Dish 25
Jelly Glass 60
Mug 100
Oil Lamp 175
Paper Weight 325
Pickle Jar 200
Punch Bowl, 2 sizes .... 600 - 1,000
Pitcher 700
Salt Dip, master 35
Salt Dip, ind. 15
Sauce Bowl 15
Spooner 55
Sugar 90
Tumbler 80
Whiskey, hndl., scarce 100
Wine 50

ARGYLE
Goblet 45
Pitcher 90
Tumbler 25

ARMY HAT
Novelty, 3½" x 1" 100

ARROWHEAD
Butter 55
vaseline 110
Celery Dish 20
vaseline 35
Compote 35
vaseline 125
Creamer or Spooner 25
vaseline 45
Pickle Dish 20
vaseline 35
Sugar 30
vaseline 65

ARROWHEAD-IN-OVAL
Basket 50
Berry Bowl, sm. 20
Berry Bowl, lg 45
Butter 80
Cake Stand 35
Celery 20
Creamer or Spooner 25
Pitcher 90
Plate, 7" 20
Punch Bowl 125
Punch Cup 10
Rose Bowl, stemmed 35
Sherbet 15
Sugar 30
Toy Table Set 100
Tumbler 20

ART
Banana Stand 125
ruby stain 375
Berry Bowl, sm. 55
Berry Bowl, lg 100
Biscuit Jar 275
ruby stain 725
Butter 80
ruby stain 165
Cake Stand .... 80 - 110
Celery Vase 45
ruby stain 95
Compote, open .... 50 - 75
Compote, covered, 7" - 10" .... 90 - 150
ruby stain .... 100 - 200
Creamer .... 65 - 125
ruby stain .... 90 - 125
Cracker Jar 85
Cruet 100
ruby stain 325
Fruit Basket, 10" 85
Goblet 70
ruby stain 200
Milk Pitcher 100
ruby stain 200
Mug 90
ruby stain 175
Pitcher, various .... 175 - 200
ruby stain .... 275 - 425
Relish 25
ruby stain 60
Sauce, flat 20
Spooner 45
ruby stain 95
Sugar 70
ruby stain 125
Tumbler 70
ruby stain 100
Wine 30

ARTICHOKE
Bobeche 40
Bowl, 7" - 10" .... 175 - 250
Butter 235
Cake Stand 325
Celery Vase 145
Compote, covered, 6" - 8" .... 300 - 425
Compote, open, 10" 365
Creamer or Spooner 135
Cruet 335
Finger Bowl 125
Finger Lamp, 2 styles .... 250 - 425
Miniature Lamp, w/shade 375
Oil Lamp, 7½" - 9½" .... 400 - 550
Pitcher, bulbous 400
Pitcher, tankard 300
Sauce, flat or ftd. 70
Shakers, ea 200
Sugar 200
Syrup 300
Tumbler 100
Water Tray 225
Vase, 2 sizes .... 95 - 150

ASHBURTON
Ale Glass 100
Bitters bottle 80
Bowl 100
Butter 135
Cake Stand 100
Candlesticks, ea. 80
Celery Vase 145

Champagne 90
Claret 100
Compote, open 135
Cordial 125
Creamer 195
Decanter 95
Egg Cup, single & double .... 30 - 100
Goblet 60
Lamp 350
Mug 100
Pitcher 875
Sauce 10
Spooner 70
Sugar 135
Tumbler, various sizes and styles .... 75 - 125
Tumble-up, complete 2 pieces 300
Wine 40

*Add 50% for any colored pieces.

ASHMAN
Bowl 25
Bread Tray 30
Butter 60
Cake Stand 35
Compote covered 45
Compote, open 30
Creamer or Spooner 20
Goblet 40
Pickle Jar 35
Pitcher 75
Relish 15
Sugar 25
Tumbler 20
Water Tray 25
Wine 15

ATLANTA
Berry Bowl, lg. 35
Berry Bowl, sm. 15
Butter 45
Celery Vase 30
Compote, jelly 35
Creamer, spooner or sugar 25
Goblet 30
Lamp Shade, gas or ele. 50
Shakers, ea. 20
Syrup 45
Toothpick Holder 30
Wine 25

ATLANTIS
Tray (Master Salt) 55

ATLAS (ATTERBURY)
Compote
milk glass 250

ATLAS (BRYCE - U.S. GLASS)
Bowl, covered, 4 sizes .... 50 - 90
ruby stain .... 65 - 120
Bowl, open, 4 sizes .... 30 - 65
ruby stain .... 50 - 90
Butter 65
ruby stain 110
Cake Stand, 3 sizes .... 70 - 125
ruby stain .... 150 - 250
Celery Vase 45
ruby stain 80
Compote, covered, 3 sizes .... 85 - 125
ruby stain .... 140 - 200
Compote, open, 3 sizes .... 35 - 70
ruby stain .... 50 - 90
Cordial 60
ruby stain 85
Creamer or Spooner, covered 50
ruby stain 90
Finger Bowl 50
ruby stain 70
Goblet 40
ruby stain 65
Hotel Butter 60
ruby stain 100
Hotel Creamer or Spooner 50
ruby stain 80
Hotel Sugar 60
ruby stain 80
Jam Jar 100
ruby stain 165
Mug 30
ruby stain 60
Milk Pitcher 60
ruby stain 95
Pitcher 95
ruby stain 165
Salt, lg. or sm. .... 15 - 25
ruby stain .... 20 - 30
Shakers, ea. 40
ruby stain 65
Sugar 60
ruby stain 90
Syrup 90
ruby stain 135
Toothpick Holder 25
ruby stain 50
Tumbler 35
ruby stain 70
Whiskey Tumbler 30
ruby stain 50
Wine 40
ruby stain 70

ATLAS (NORTHWOOD)
Butter 75
Creamer 35
Spooner 30
Sugar 40

*Add 15% for gilding or maiden blush.

AURORA
Box, open, rectangular shape 75
ruby stain 85
chocolate 375
Bread Plate, 10" 35
ruby stain 65
Butter 60
ruby stain 125
Compotes, covered .... 60 - 100
ruby stain .... 125 - 200
Compotes, open .... 40 - 55
ruby stain .... 100 - 145
Creamer or Spooner 40
ruby stain 90
Decanter 65
ruby stain 135
Goblet 60
ruby stain 100
Milk Pitcher 55
ruby stain 150
Pickle Dish 20
ruby stain 35
chocolate 100
Pitcher 85
ruby stain 200
Shakers, ea. 40
ruby stain 85
Sugar 45
ruby stain 125
Tray 50
ruby stain 75
Tumbler 30
ruby stain 70
Vase 40
ruby stain 90
Wine 25
ruby stain 70

AUSTRIAN
Banana Stand 200
amber 375
Berry Bowl, sm. 65
vaseline 150
Berry Bowl, lg. 70
vaseline 250
Bowl, rectangular 60
vaseline 135
Butter 225
vaseline 550
Child's Table Set 175
vaseline 1100
Child's Butter 75
vaseline 525
chocolate 2,000
Child's Creamer 25
vaseline 125
chocolate 300
Child's Spooner 45
vaseline 150
chocolate 300
Child's Sugar w/Lid 50
vaseline 300
chocolate 900
Compotes, open, high & low .... 60 - 110
vaseline .... 225 - 325
Cordial 80
amber 250
vaseline 200
green/blue 350
Creamer or Spooner 40
amber 175
vaseline 145
chocolate 85
Goblet 80
vaseline 265
Mug, Child's 80
vaseline 125
Nappy, covered 65
amber 250
vaseline 125
chocolate 250
Pitcher 200
amber 425
vaseline 425
Plate, sq. 100
vaseline 225
Punch Bowl 165
Punch Cup 35
amber 175
vaseline 125
amethyst 525
Rose Bowl, 3 sizes .... 75 - 125
vaseline .... 200 - 225
Shakers, ea. 75
vaseline 150
Sugar 55
vaseline 250
Tumbler 60
amber 250
vaseline 150
Vase, 6" - 10" .... 55 - 90
vaseline .... 200 - 350
Nile green 900
Wine 45
amber 500
vaseline 225
green/blue 300

AZMOOR
Butter 60
Bowl, Deep 25
Creamer or Spooner 25
Cruet 45
Nappy 20
Pitcher 85
Punch Bowl 130
Punch Cup 15
Relish, oval 25
Sugar 35
Tumbler 20

AZTEC
Berry Bowl, lg. 40
ruby stain 60
Berry Bowl, sm. 20
ruby stain 25
Butter 60
ruby stain 90
Celery Bowl 25

ruby stain 35
Champagne Glass 25
ruby stain 40
Claret 20
ruby stain 30
Cordial 30
ruby stain 45
Creamer or Spooner 30
ruby stain 55
Goblet 40
ruby stain 60
Lamp w/Matching Chimney 200
Pickle Dish 15
ruby stain 25
Pitcher 75
ruby stain 150
Punch Bowl 115
ruby stain 195
Punch Cup 10
ruby stain 20
Rose Bowl 25
ruby stain 50
Straw Holder w/Lid 200
Sugar 35
ruby stain 65
Water bottle 45
ruby stain 80
Whiskey Jug w/Stopper 100
Wine 20
ruby stain 30

AZTEC SUNBURST
Berry Bowl, sm. 15
Berry Bowl, lg. 40
Berry Creamer & Open Sugar 30
Butter 65
Cake Plate, tall 55
Celery Vase 30
Celery Tray 30
Compote, 7", 8" & 9" .... 25 - 45
Compote, tall 55
Compote, w/advertising; "Greater Harold Furniture Co." 70
Cracker Bowl 35
Creamer or Spooner 25
Handled Nappy 25
Pickle Dish 20
Pitcher w/advertising; "Let Hartman Feather Your Nest" 100
Rose Bowl 50
Rose Bowl, tall ftd. 60
Salver 60
Saucer, 8" 35
Shakers, ea. 30
Sugar 25
Vase 25
Vase, sweet pea 30

BABY ANIMALS
Mug 175

BABY FACE
Butter 300
Celery Vase 175
Champagne 600
Compote, covered, 5" - 8" .... 300 - 525
Compote, open, 7" - 8" .... 275 - 300
Cordial 100
Creamer or Spooner .... 175 - 200
Goblet 425
Pitcher 3,500
Salt Dip 100
Sugar 250
Wine 200

BABY MINE
Elephant Novelty, multi-use holder 80
amber 125

BAKEWELL WAFFLE
Butter, very rare 435
Compote, open, either base, very rare 400
Creamer, rare 285
Pitcher, snake hndl., very rare 1,500
Spooner, very rare 350
Sugar, very rare 375
Tumbler, very rare 180

BALKY MULE
Water Tray, 9½" - 12½" .... 75 - 130

BALL & BAR
Butter 60
Celery Dish 20
Creamer 25
Milk Pitcher 40
Pitcher 70
Spooner 25
Sugar 30
Tumbler 20

BALL & SWIRL
Butter 55
ruby stain 85
opaque white 75
Cake Stand 30
ruby stain 45
opaque white 40
Candlesticks, ea. 25
ruby stain 30
opaque white 25
Celery Vase 15
ruby stain 25
opaque white 20
Compote, covered 90
Compote, open 45
Cordial 15
ruby stain 25
opaque white 20
Creamer or Spooner 30
ruby stain 30
opaque white 25
Decanter 75
ruby stain 145
opaque white 120
Jelly 25
ruby stain 35
opaque white 30
Milk Pitcher 45
Mug, 3 sizes .... 20 - 40
ruby stain 35
opaque white 30
Plate 30
ruby stain 25
opaque white 25
Pitcher 65
ruby stain 120
opaque white 100
Shakers, ea. 40
ruby stain 30
opaque white 25
Sugar 45
ruby stain 45
opaque white 40
Syrup 65
ruby stain 85
opaque white 75
Tumbler 20
ruby stain 25
opaque white 25

BALL BROTHERS
Plate 100

BALTIMORE PEAR
Bowl, covered, 5" - 9" .... 85 - 100
Bowl, open, 5" - 9" .... 45 - 95
Bread Plate 100
Butter 145
Cake Stand 300
Celery Vase 90
Compote, covered, 5" - 8" .... 100 - 250
Compote, open, 5" - 8" .... 90 - 165
Creamer or Spooner 55
Goblet 90
Honey Dish 35
Milk Pitcher 200
Pickle Tray 75
Plate, 8" - 10" 70
Pitcher 160
Relish Tray 85
Sauce 30
Sugar 90
Water Tray 80

BAMBOO BEAUTY
Berry Bowl, sm. 25
Berry Bowl, lg. 55
Butter 90
Creamer or Spooner 35
Pitcher 110
Sugar 40
Tumbler 25

BAND & DIAMOND SWIRL
Vase, 6" 65

BANDED BASE
Tumbler (frosted add 10%) 20

BANDED BUCKLE
Bowl 60
Butter 90
Compote, open 50
Compote, covered 100
Cordial 30
Creamer 75
Egg Cup 30
Goblet 40
Pitcher 325
Salt Dip, ftd. 40
Spooner 40
Sugar 90
Tumbler 60

BANDED DIAMOND WITH PEG
Butter 45
Creamer, spooner or sugar 25
Pitcher 65
Shakers, ea. 25
Toothpick Holder 35
Tumbler 20

BANDED FINECUT
Bowl, 8" 35
Goblet 55
Nappy 25
Wine 20

BANDED FLEUR-DE-LIS
Butter 65
Celery Vase 20
Creamer or Spooner 20
Egg Cup 30
Jelly Compote 25
Milk Pitcher 60
Pitcher 85
Shakers, ea. 15
Sugar 30
Syrup 45
Tumbler 20

BANDED PORTLAND
Bowl, covered, various .... 50 - 70
ruby stain .... 70 - 90
Bowl, open, various .... 30 - 50
ruby stain .... 50 - 80
Butter 70
ruby stain 200
Cake Stand 90
ruby stain 225
Candlesticks, ea. 90
ruby stain 170
Carafe 85
ruby stain 230
Celery Tray 50
ruby stain 80
Celery Vase 45
ruby stain 80
Cologne Bottle 75
ruby stain 175
Compote, covered 3 sizes .... 60 - 100
ruby stain .... 80 - 135
Compote, open, various .... 30 - 60
ruby stain .... 50 - 90

Creamer 25
  ruby stain 65
Cruet 60
  ruby stain 195
Cup 20
  ruby stain 30
Decanter 80
  ruby stain 235
Dish, oval, 5 sizes ..... 30 - 60
  ruby stain .....50 - 110
Dresser Tray 45
  ruby stain 125
Goblet 40
  ruby stain 95
Marmalade w/Lid 70
  ruby stain 160
Nappy 25
  ruby stain 70
Pickle Dish 25
  ruby stain 40
Pin Tray 30
  ruby stain 50
Pitcher 130
  ruby stain 310
Pomade Jar w/Lid 40
  ruby stain 70
Puff Box w/Lid 40
  ruby stain 80
Punch Bowl, flat or ftd., rare 240
  ruby stain 600
Sardine Box w/Lid 135
  ruby stain 240
Sauce 15
  ruby stain 25
Spooner 40
  ruby stain 90
Sugar 50
  ruby stain 100
Sugar Shaker 70
  ruby stain 200
Syrup 90
  ruby stain 300
Toothpick Holder 35
  ruby stain 75
Tumbler 40
  ruby stain 75
Vase 40
  ruby stain 65
Wine 40
  ruby stain 110

*Add 25% to other colors or stained pieces.

BANDED RAINDROPS
Bowls, various ..... 15 - 40
  amber ..... 20 - 50
  milk glass ..... 15 - 45
Butter 60
  amber 85
  milk glass 75
Compote, covered, 7" 45
  amber 65
  milk glass 60
Creamer or Spooner 20
  amber 30
  milk glass 25
Cup & Saucer 45
  amber 55
  milk glass 50
Goblet 60
  amber 80
  milk glass 75
Pitcher 85
  amber 135
  milk glass 125
Plate, 7½" - 9" ..... 15 - 30
  amber ..... 20 - 55
  milk glass ..... 15 - 50
Relish, sq. 15
  amber 20
  milk glass 15
Sauce 10
  amber 15
  milk glass 10
Shakers, ea 20
  amber 45
  milk glass 40
Sugar 30
  amber 45
  milk glass 40
Tumbler 15
  amber 25
  milk glass 20
Wine 10
  amber 25
  milk glass 20

BANDED STAR
Butter 50
Celery Vase 15
Compote, covered, high 65
Compote, covered, low 55
Creamer or Spooner 25
Creamer, ind. 20
Pickle Dish 15
Pitcher 90
Sauces 10
Sugar 30
Sugar, ind. 25
Tumbler 20

B AND H SHOE
Tall shoe; 5½" bouquet holder 40
  amber 55
  vaseline 100
  green/blue 100
  milk glass 75

BANNER
Butter, scarce 70

BAR & BLOCK
(NICKEL PLATE'S RICHMOND)
Butter 80
Celery Vase 20
Creamer or Spooner 25
Finger Bowl 15
Mustard Jar 50
Pitcher 95
Shakers, ea 15
Sugar 35
Tumbler 25
Wine 15

BAR & DIAMOND
Butter 50
  ruby stain 90
Celery Vase 20
  ruby stain 30
Compotes, various ..... 15 - 40
  ruby stain ..... 25 - 55
Creamer or Spooner 30
  ruby stain 40
Cruet 55
  ruby stain 85
Decanter 45
  ruby stain 65
Lamp, hand size 65
  ruby stain 120
Shakers, ea 25
  ruby stain 35
Sugar 40
  ruby stain 55
Sugar Shaker 50
  ruby stain 70
Toy Table Set, complete 85
  ruby stain 145
Wine 15
  ruby stain 25

BARBERRY
Bowls, various, 5" - 9" ..... 30 - 60
Bowls, covered, 6" - 8" .....60 - 100
Butter, 2 styles .....80 - 145
Cake Stand 200
Compote, covered, 6" - 8" .....90 - 145
Compote, open, 7" - 8" ..... 60 - 80
Creamer 70
Cup Plate 40
Egg Cup 35
Goblet 50
Honey Dish 20
Pickle Tray 20
Pitcher 275
Plate 40
Salt 2 styles 45
Sauce 15
Spooner 40
Sugar 80
Syrup 200
Tumbler 90
Wine 45

BARLEY
Bowl, various ..... 40 - 50
Butter 65
Cake Stand, 4 sizes .....60 - 100
Celery Vase 50
Compotes, covered ..... 60 - 95
Compote, open 55
Cordial 35
Creamer, spooner or sugar ..... 30 - 40
Goblet 45
Jam Jar 90
Pickle Castor 125
Pickle Dish 25
Pitcher, pressed & applied hndl. .60 - 200
Plate, 6", scarce 45
Platter, oval, scarce 65
Relish 30
Sauce, ftd. 15
Tumbler 45
Wine 30

BARRED FORGET-ME-NOT
Bowls, various ..... 15 - 35
  amber ..... 20 - 45
  vaseline ..... 35 - 60
  green/blue ..... 25 - 40
Butter 60
  amber 75
  vaseline 95
  green/blue 80
Cake Stand 45
  amber 65
  vaseline 85
  green/blue 75
Compote 40
  amber 60
  vaseline 75
  green/blue 70
Cordial 20
  amber 25
  vaseline 45
  green/blue 30
Creamer 25
  amber 30
  vaseline 45
  green/blue 35
Goblet 35
  amber 40
  vaseline 50
  green/blue 45
Pickle Dish, w/sq. hndls. 25
  amber 30
  vaseline 45
  green/blue 35
Plate, 2 hndl. 25
  amber 30
  vaseline 45
  green/blue 35
Pitcher 70
  amber 80
  vaseline 100
  green/blue 90
Spooner 25
  amber 30

- vaseline ... 45
- green/blue ... 35
- Sugar ... 30
  - amber ... 35
  - vaseline ... 50
  - green/blue ... 40
- Tumbler ... 15
  - amber ... 20
  - vaseline ... 35
  - green/blue ... 30
- Wine ... 20
  - amber ... 25
  - vaseline ... 35
  - green/blue ... 40

BARRELED THUMBPRINT
- Bowl, 7" - 9" ... 30
- Butter ... 55
- Celery Vase ... 25
- Creamer, spooner or sugar ... 25
- Goblet ... 30
- Nappy, 4 sizes ... 25 - 40
- Pickle Dish ... 30
- Pitcher ... 80
- Shakers, ea ... 25
- Tumbler ... 15
- Water bottle ... 60
- Wine ... 25

BARRY
- Plate ... 35

BASKET EPERGNE
- 6 Basket Centerpiece ... 250

BASKETWEAVE
- Berry Bowl, sm. ... 10
  - amber ... 15
  - vaseline ... 20
  - green/blue ... 20
- Berry Bowl, lg ... 30
  - amber ... 35
  - vaseline ... 50
  - green/blue ... 45
- Butter ... 65
  - amber ... 85
  - vaseline ... 145
  - green/blue ... 130
- Cake Plate ... 40
  - amber ... 50
  - vaseline ... 70
  - green/blue ... 65
- Compote, open, high or low ... 25 - 40
  - amber ... 30 - 50
  - vaseline ... 40 - 60
  - green/blue ... 35 - 55
- Compote, covered, high or low ... 40 - 65
  - amber ... 45 - 70
  - vaseline ... 55 - 80
  - green/blue ... 50 - 75
- Cordial ... 20
  - amber ... 25
  - vaseline ... 35
  - green/blue ... 30
- Creamer or Spooner ... 25
  - amber ... 30
  - vaseline ... 40
  - green/blue ... 35
- Egg Cup, single & double ... 15 - 25
  - amber ... 20 - 35
  - vaseline ... 30 - 45
  - green/blue ... 25 - 40
- Finger Bowl ... 25
  - amber ... 30
  - vaseline ... 35
  - green/blue ... 30
- Goblet ... 45
  - amber ... 55
  - vaseline ... 60
  - green/blue ... 55
- Milk Pitcher ... 60
  - amber ... 75
  - vaseline ... 95
  - green/blue ... 90
- Mug ... 35
  - amber ... 40
  - vaseline ... 50
  - green/blue ... 45
- Pickle Dish ... 20
  - amber ... 25
  - vaseline ... 30
  - green/blue ... 30
- Pitcher ... 90
  - amber ... 115
  - vaseline ... 165
  - green/blue ... 125
- Salt Dip, flat or ftd. ... 20
  - amber ... 30
  - vaseline ... 40
  - green/blue ... 35
- Sauce ... 10
  - amber ... 15
  - vaseline ... 20
  - green/blue ... 20
- Saucer ... 15
  - amber ... 20
  - vaseline ... 25
  - green/blue ... 25
- Sugar ... 40
  - amber ... 50
  - vaseline ... 65
  - green/blue ... 60
- Syrup ... 70
  - amber ... 90
  - vaseline ... 125
  - green/blue ... 100
- Tumbler ... 15
  - amber ... 20
  - vaseline ... 30
  - green/blue ... 25
- Waste Bowl ... 20
  - amber ... 25
  - vaseline ... 30
  - green/blue ... 25
- Water Tray ... 40
  - amber ... 45
  - vaseline ... 65
  - green/blue ... 50
- Wine ... 20
  - amber ... 25
  - vaseline ... 30
  - green/blue ... 25

BASKETWEAVE AND MEDALLION
- Lamp, 2 sizes, scarce ... 300 - 350

BASSETTOWN
- Bowls, rnd. or sq. ... 15 - 40
- Butter ... 70
- Celery Tray ... 25
- Compote, open, 10 sizes ... 20 - 75
- Creamer or Spooner ... 25
- Creamer, ind. ... 15
- Finger Bowl ... 20
- Nappy ... 20
- Pitcher ... 75
- Pitcher w/Metal Top ... 135
- Pitcher, tankard ... 90
- Plate, 8" ... 25
- Punch Bowl ... 200
- Punch Cup ... 15
- Punch Tray ... 45
- Shade, Gas ... 35
- Shakers, ea ... 15
- Sugar ... 40
- Sugar, ind. ... 25
- Tumbler ... 30
- Vase, 6 sizes ... 15 - 45

BEACON #410 INNOVATION
- Basket, hndl ... 65
- Bowl, ftd., round ... 30
- Bowl, ftd., oval ... 40
- Cylinder Vase, etched, 12" ... 55
- Square Vase, 10" - 12" ... 45

BEAD & SCROLL
- Butter ... 55
- Creamer or Spooner ... 25
- Goblet ... 50
- Jelly Compote ... 35
- Pitcher ... 80
- Shakers, ea ... 30
- Sugar ... 35
- Toothpick Holder ... 30
- Toy Table Set, rare ... 125
- Tumbler ... 25

BEAD COLUMN
- Berry Bowl, sm. ... 10
- Berry Bowl, lg ... 35
- Butter ... 55
- Creamer or Spooner ... 20
- Pitcher ... 70
- Sugar ... 20
- Tumbler ... 15

BEADED ACORN MEDALLION
- Butter ... 95
- Champagne ... 80
- Compote, covered ... 145 - 165
- Creamer ... 65
- Egg Cup ... 50
- Fruit bowl ... 70
- Goblet ... 60
- Pitcher ... 350
- Relish Dish ... 35
- Salt ... 40
- Sauce ... 15
- Spooner ... 40
- Sugar ... 75
- Wine ... 35

BEADED ARCH PANELS
- Butter ... 60
- Creamer or Spooner ... 25
- Goblet ... 45
- Mug ... 30
- Sugar ... 35

BEADED BAND
- Butter ... 55
- Cake Stand ... 60 - 90
- Compote ... 70 - 100
- Creamer, Spooner or Sugar ... 35 - 45
- Sauce ... 10
- Syrup ... 100
- Wine ... 20

BEADED CABLE
- Candy Dish ... 40
- Rose Bowl ... 65

BEADED CHAIN
- Butter ... 70
- Celery Vase ... 25
- Creamer or Spooner ... 25
- Goblet ... 35
- Plate ... 30
- Sauce ... 15
- Sugar ... 30

BEADED COARSE BARS
- Butter ... 50
- Creamer or Spooner ... 20
- Goblet ... 40
- Mug ... 25
- Pickle Dish ... 25
- Shakers, ea ... 20
- Sugar ... 30
- Water Carafe ... 35

BEADED COMET BAND
- Berry Bowl, lg ... 35
- Berry Bowl, sm. ... 15
- Butter ... 50
- Creamer, Spooner or Sugar ... 25
- Cruet ... 45
- Pickle Dish ... 30
- Plate, 10" ... 40

BEADED DART BAND
- Bowl, 7", 8" & 9" ... 20 - 35

amber .... 30 - 45
vaseline .... 45 - 65
green/blue .... 35 - 50
Bread Plate 25
amber 35
vaseline 65
green/blue 35
Butter 45
amber 55
vaseline 95
green/blue 40
Creamer 20
amber 25
vaseline 40
green/blue 35
Goblet 30
amber 35
vaseline 60
green/blue 35
ruby stain 30
Pickle Castor 40
amber 50
vaseline 85
green/blue 50
Spooner 30
amber 35
vaseline 45
green/blue 35
Sugar 35
amber 40
vaseline 70
green/blue 40

BEADED DIAMOND
Berry Bowl, sm. 20
Berry Bowl, lg. 40
Butter 55
Creamer or Spooner 20
Pitcher 75
Sugar 25
Tumbler 20

BEADED ELLIPSE & FAN
Berry Bowl, lg. 30
Butter 55
Creamer 25
Pitcher 65
Plate 30
Spooner 25
Sugar 30
Tumbler 15

BEADED GRAPE (CALIFORNIA)
Bowl, covered, 3 sizes .... 60 - 90
green/blue .... 90 - 120
Bowl, open, 6 sizes .... 15 - 60
green/blue .... 20 - 85
Butter 100
green/blue 115
Cake Stand 200
green/blue 250
Celery Tray 35
green/blue 45
Celery Vase 40
green/blue 70
Compote, covered .... 50 - 100
green/blue .... 60 - 125
Compote, open .... 25 - 75
green/blue .... 35 - 100
Cordial 100
green/blue 165
Creamer or Spooner 45
green/blue 65
Milk Pitcher 90
green/blue 125
Pickle Dish 25
green/blue 35
Pitcher, rnd. or sq. 100
green/blue 125
Plate 45
green/blue 55
Sauce, various .... 15 - 25
green/blue .... 20 - 45
Shakers, ea 40
green/blue 55
Sugar 75
green/blue 80
Toothpick Holder 50
green/blue 75
Tumbler, rnd. or sq. 40
green/blue 50
Vase, 3 sizes .... 50 - 100
green/blue .... 75 - 125
Wine 50
green/blue 75

BEADED GRAPE MEDALLION
Bowl 60
Butter 100
Cake Stand 475
Castor Set, complete 250
Celery Vase 120
Champagne 90
Compote, covered .... 125 - 165
Compote, open .... 95 - 125
Creamer or Spooner 50
Dish, covered, various .... 125 - 165
Egg Cup 40
Goblet, various .... 23 - 70
Pickle Dish 35
Plate 60
Pitcher 250
Relish, covered and open .... 60 - 150
Salt, ind. 25
Salt, master 40
Sugar 90
Tumbler 60
Wine 65

BEADED MEDALLION
Butter 45
Celery Vase 25
Creamer or Spooner 25
Egg Cup 20
Jelly Compote 30
Open Salt 20
Pitcher 65
Sugar 25
Tumbler 15

BEADED OVAL MEDALLION
Pitcher
vaseline 300
Tumbler
vaseline 65

BEADED PANEL & SUNBURST
Butter 50
Creamer or Spooner 20
Sugar 25
Toothpick Holder 25

BEADED SHELL
Berry Bowl, lg. 30
green/blue 35
Berry Bowl, sm. 10
green/blue 15
Butter 45
green/blue 55
Compote 35
green/blue 40
Creamer or Spooner 30
green/blue 35
Cruet 55
green/blue 75
Cruet Set 95
green/blue 115
Mug 35
green/blue 40
Pitcher 80
green/blue 135
Shakers, ea 25
green/blue 35
Sugar 45
green/blue 50
Toothpick Holder 40
green/blue 45
Tumbler 15
green/blue 25

BEADED STARS & MUMS (VERRE D' OR)
Bowl
green/blue 80
amethyst 90
Compote
green/blue 95
amethyst 110
Nappy
green/blue 85
amethyst 95

BEADED STARS & SWAG
Banana Bowl 65
Bowls, various .... 15 - 35
Plates, various .... 20 - 50
Rose Bowls, various .... 25 - 60
Rose Bowl, advertising, "Lion Store, Hammond Louisiana," rare 100

BEADED SWAG
Cup & Saucer 45
green/blue 55
ruby stain 75
custard 60
Mug 35
green/blue 45
ruby stain 55
custard 50

BEADED SWIRL & BALL
Child's Mug 30

BEADED SWIRL & LENS
Butter 75
Cake Stand 35
Celery Vase 20
Compote, covered 50
Compote, open 40
Creamer or Spooner 20
Egg Cup 20
Goblet 60
Mug 30
Pitcher 95
Sauce, flat or ftd. 15
Sugar 30
Syrup 45
Tumbler 10
Wine 15

BEADED TULIP
Bowl 40
Bread Plate 30
Butter 100
green/blue 135
Cake Stand 135
Champagne 90
Compote, covered 90
Compote, open 40
Creamer 45
green/blue 85
Goblet 50
Ice Cream Dish 45
Jam Jar 90
Milk Pitcher 60
green/blue 80
Pickle Dish, oval 20
Plate 45
Pitcher 80
Sauce 10
Spooner 90
Sugar 110
green/blue 80
Water Tray 60
Wine 25
Wine Tray 50

BEADS AND BARS
Creamer 30
Rose Bowl 40
Sugar 35

BEAD SWAG
Butter...65
vaseline...130
green/blue...95
ruby stain...110
milk glass...125
Cake Stand...40
vaseline...80
green/blue...65
ruby stain...80
milk glass...90
Creamer...25
vaseline...45
green/blue...35
ruby stain...45
milk glass...55
Cup...15
vaseline...40
green/blue...30
ruby stain...40
milk glass...50
Mug...35
vaseline...60
green/blue...45
ruby stain...60
milk glass...70
Pitcher...75
vaseline...145
green/blue...90
ruby stain...100
milk glass...125
Rose Bowl...30
vaseline...55
green/blue...40
ruby stain...50
milk glass...60
Saucer...15
vaseline...35
green/blue...20
ruby stain...30
milk glass...40
Spooner...30
vaseline...50
green/blue...35
ruby stain...40
milk glass...55
Sugar...40
vaseline...65
green/blue...45
ruby stain...50
milk glass...65
Syrup...60
vaseline...120
green/blue...70
ruby stain...80
milk glass...95
Toothpick Holder...30
vaseline...65
green/blue...35
ruby stain...40
milk glass...50
Tumbler...20
vaseline...35
green/blue...25
ruby stain...30
milk glass...40
Wine...20
vaseline...30
green/blue...25
ruby stain...30
milk glass...40

BEAUTIFUL LADY
Banana Stand...65
Berry Bowl, sm....15
ruby stain...25
Berry Bowl, lg...30
ruby stain...40
Butter...80
ruby stain...90
Cake Stand...70
Creamer...50
ruby stain...35
Milk Pitcher...45
Pitcher...75
ruby stain...100
Plates, various...30 - 45
ruby stain...40
Spooner...50
ruby stain...35
Sugar...70
ruby stain...45
Toy Cake Plate...50
ruby stain...75
Tumbler...35
ruby stain...30
Vase...25
Wine...20
ruby stain...30

BEAVER BAND
Goblet, very rare...1,400

BEE
Butter w/Cover...125
amber...150
vaseline...425
green/blue...200

BEGGING DOG
Mug...50
amethyst...85

"BE INDUSTRIOUS"
Platter, oval, either lettering...80

BELLADONNA
Berry Bowl, lg...45
green/blue...55
ruby stain...65
Berry Bowl, sm....20
green/blue...25
ruby stain...30
Butter...60
green/blue...70
ruby stain...90
Creamer or Spooner...35
green/blue...40
ruby stain...45
Pitcher...85
green/blue...100
ruby stain...135
Sugar...45
green/blue...50
ruby stain...65
Toothpick Holder...40
green/blue...45
ruby stain...55
Tumbler...25
green/blue...30
ruby stain...40

BELLAIRE
Castor Set, complete...175
Cologne Set...185
Creamer or Spooner...35
Sugar...40
Toothpick Holder...45

BELLFLOWER
*Condensed list.
Bowls, various...100 - 600
Butter, various bases...150 - 375
Cake Stand, 2 sizes...3,500 - 5,000
Cake Stand, with diamond background...8,000
Castor Set...250
Celery Vase...300
Celery Vase, banded, no pattern...425
Champagne...225
Compote, various sizes, covered or open...325 - 650
Cordial...145
Creamer or Spooner...400
Decanter, with bar lip, 2 sizes...375
Decanter w/stopper, rare...950
Egg Cup...50
Goblets, various...75 - 300
Hat Shape, from tumbler, very rare..3,500
Honey Dish...200
Lamp...350 - 1,500
Milk Pitcher...1,500
Mug...1,000
Pickle Dish...80
Pitcher...425
Plate...150
Relish Dish...75
Master Covered Salt...125
Open Salt...75
Sauce...25
Sugar...150
Octagonal Sugar w/mushroom finial...2,000
Syrup, applied handle...550
Syrup, 10 sided...3,000
Sweetmeat...350
Tumbler...200
Whiskey Tumbler...325
Wine...175

*Some pieces may be found in amber, cobalt blue, green, fiery opal, milk glass, opaque blue, sapphire blue, or vaseline. These are very rare and may add an additional 25 - 50% or higher to the value, depending on the piece.
*Reproduction prices are not included.

BELMONT #100 (DAISY & BUTTON)
Butter...85
vaseline...250
green/blue...300
Bowl w/Underplate...45
vaseline...250 - 350
Cheese Dish, covered...95
vaseline...275
Compote, covered...95
vaseline...250
Celery Vase, scarce...80
vaseline...300
Creamer or Spooner...35
vaseline...125
Plate, 12½"...40
vaseline...90
Sauce, flat or ftd....15 - 20
vaseline...45 - 65
Sugar...50
vaseline...175

BELMONT DIAMOND
Bowl, oval...35
Bowl, rnd...30
Cruet...50

BELTED ICICLE
Bowls, various...20 - 40
Butter...55
Celery Vase...30
Creamer or Spooner...30
Milk Pitcher...50
Plate...30
Pitcher...75
Relish...30
Salt Shaker, ea...30
Sugar...40
Syrup...65
Tumbler...25

BERLIN
Bowl, 7"...30
ruby stain...35
amber stain...35
Butter...90
ruby stain...100
amber stain...100
Compote, covered...85
ruby stain...110
amber stain...110
Compote, open...60
ruby stain...70
amber stain...70

Creamer or Spooner 40
ruby stain 50
amber stain 50
Dish, oval 25
ruby stain 35
amber stain 35
Egg Cup 25
ruby stain 35
amber stain 35
Honey Dish 30
ruby stain 40
amber stain 40
Milk Pitcher 100
ruby stain 125
amber stain 130
Pickle Dish 30
ruby stain 40
amber stain 40
Pitcher 150
ruby stain 165
amber stain 170
Plate, 7" 30
ruby stain 40
amber stain 40
Sauce 15
ruby stain 20
amber stain 20
Shakers, ea 45
ruby stain 55
amber stain 60
Sugar 50
ruby stain 60
amber stain 60
Tumbler 30
ruby stain 40
amber stain 40

BERNHEIMER
Creamer with advertising, rare 175

BERRY
Butter 65
Creamer or Spooner 30
Sugar 45

BERRY BOAT
Handled Boat Shape Bowl 70
vaseline 125

BERRY CLUSTER
Butter 55
Celery Vase 20
Creamer or Spooner 20
Goblet 30
Pitcher 75
Sugar 30
Tumbler 20

BERRY SPRAY
Egg Cup 30

BETHLEHEM STAR ....
Bowl, 8½" 50
Butter 90
Celery Dish 30
Celery Vase 80
Compote, covered, 4½" - 8" .... 55 - 100
Creamer or Spooner 40
Cruet 65
Goblet 55
Milk Pitcher 70
Pitcher 100
Relish 20
Sauce 15
Sugar 70
Syrup 100
Tumbler 40
Wine 65

BE TRUE ....
Plate 125

BEVELLED BUTTONS
Bowls .... 15 - 30
Butter 45
Celery Vase 20
Compote 30
Creamer or Spooner 20
Pickle Jar 30
Sauce 10
Sugar 25

BEVELLED DIAGONAL BLOCK
Butter 65
Cake Stand 35
Celery Vase 20
Cordial 20
Creamer or Spooner 20
Goblet 45
Jam Jar 40
Pitcher 85
Plate 20
Shakers, ea 20
Sugar 30
Tumbler 20
Wine 15

BEVELLED DIAMOND & STAR
Bowl, 7" - 8" 20
ruby stain 40
Butter 55
ruby stain 100
Cake Stand, 2 sizes .... 60 - 80
ruby stain .... 200 - 250
Celery Vase 30
ruby stain 90
Compote, 5" - 7", covered .... 45 - 70
ruby stain .... 200 - 250
Compote, 5" - 8", open .... 40 - 60
ruby stain .... 125 - 200
Cracker Jar w/Lid 90
ruby stain 250
Creamer or Spooner .... 35 - 50
ruby stain .... 45 - 90
Cruet 60
ruby stain 200
Decanter w/Stopper 75
ruby stain 165
Goblet 90
ruby stain 275
Milk Pitcher 60
ruby stain 275
Pickle Dish 20
ruby stain 40
Pitcher 80
ruby stain 250
Plate 20
ruby stain 35
Shaker 60
ruby stain 150
Sugar 50
ruby stain 100
Syrup 80
ruby stain 250
Toothpick 25
ruby stain 80
Tray 40
ruby stain 80
Tumbler 20
ruby stain 55
Wine 20
ruby stain 50

BEVELLED STAR
Bowl, 9" 35
Berry Bowl, lg 40
Berry Bowl, sm 15
Butter 55
Celery Tray 35
Compote, covered 50
Creamer, spooner or sugar 25
Cruet 45
Pitcher 70
Syrup 65
Tumbler 20

BIBLE BREAD TRAY
Tray 90

BICYCLE GIRL
Pitcher, rare 475

BIG BASKETWEAVE ....
Basket w/Handle 35
light amethyst 75
Vase 30
sapphire 175

BIG FISH
Bowl, very rare 1,000
Plate, very rare 1,700

BILIKEN FLUTE
Butter 55
Creamer or Spooner 20
Goblet 30
Pickle Dish 20
Sugar 30
Wine 15

BIRCH LEAF
Berry Bowl, sm. leaf shaped 30
vaseline 55
Berry Bowl, lg. leaf shaped 55
vaseline 75
Butter 80
vaseline 135
Celery Vase 20
vaseline 45
Compote, covered 65
vaseline 95
Compote, open 45
vaseline 55
Creamer or Spooner 30
vaseline 40
Egg Cup 25
vaseline 45
Goblet 45
vaseline 65
Pickle Dish 20
vaseline 40
Salt Dip, master 20
vaseline 45
Sugar 40
vaseline 60
Wine 15
vaseline 25

BIRCH LEAF (PORTLAND)
Leaf Shaped Master 70
vaseline 110
green/blue 80
ruby stain 90
Leaf Shaped Sauce 40
vaseline 70
green/blue 60
ruby stain 65

BIRD & CHERRY
Mustard Jar Holder 100
amber 165
vaseline 225
green/blue 165

*Add 25% for cover.

BIRD & HARP
Mug 55
purple slag 80

BIRD & STRAWBERRY
Berry Bowl, lg 165
Berry Bowl, sm 60
Bowls, ftd. .... 60 - 75
Butter 135
Cake Stand 75
Celery Tray 95
Celery Vase 110
Chop Plate 175
Compote, covered, 4" - 6" .... 150 - 235
Compote, open, 4½" - 7½" .... 125 - 200
Creamer or Spooner 90
Cup 35
Goblet, rare 500
Hat, from Tumbler, rare 1,200
Pitcher 345
Relish 85
Rose Bowl, ftd., lg 175
Sandwich Plate 175

Sugar 125
Tumbler 80
Wine 70
*Add 100% for stained pieces.

BIRD BASKET
Match holder. 85

BIRD IN NEST WITH FLOWERS
Mug 65
purple slag 100

BIRD ON A BRANCH
Child's Mug 160

BIRDS & CHERRIES (FENTON)
Bonbon, very scarce
cobalt 150

BIRDS AT FOUNTAIN
Bowl, sm. 25
Butter 175
Compote, covered 135
Creamer or Spooner 70
Goblet 85
Mug, miniature 65
Sauce 25
Sugar 90

BIRDS IN SWAMP
Goblet 75

BLACKBERRY (HOBBS)
Butter 135
milk glass 175
Celery Vase, 2 sizes .... 70 - 100
milk glass .... 90 - 110
Compote, covered, 2 sizes .... 100 - 135
milk glass .... 140 - 170
Creamer or Spooner 50
milk glass 65
Egg Cup, single 35
milk glass 40
Egg Cup, double 45
milk glass 55
Goblet 60
milk glass 75
Honey Dish 15
milk glass 25
Lamp, 3 sizes .... 125 - 225
Pitcher 725
milk glass 2,175
Relish 20
milk glass 35
Salt Dip, master 50
milk glass 50
Sauce 15
Milk glass 20
Sugar 75
milk glass 95
Syrup 275
milk glass 550
Tumbler 90
milk glass 225

BLAZING CORNUCOPIA
Berry Bowl, sm. 20
Berry Bowl, lg. 45
Butter 100
Celery Tray 25
Creamer or Spooner 30
Cruet 65
Cup 20
Goblet 65
Jelly Compote 35
Nappy 30
Olive Dish 20
Pickle Dish 25
Pitcher 165
Sugar 40
Toothpick Holder 35
Tumbler 25
Wine 15

BLEEDING HEART
Bowl, covered, 2 sizes .... 95 - 200
Bowl, open, various shapes
and sizes .... 25 - 80
Butter 110
Cake Stand, 9" - 11" .... 100 - 200
Compote w/Lid, 7" - 9" .... 150 - 275
Compote, oval or rnd. .... 100 - 225
Creamer .... 60 - 90
Egg Cup 50
Egg Serving Dish, very rare 1,650
Goblets, various shapes .... 35 - 80
Honey Dish 20
Jelly 40
Milk Pitcher 250
Mug 50
Pickle Tray 30
Pitcher 300
Plate 90
Platter, oval 125
Relish Tray 25
Relish Tray, sectional 175
Salt, open 135
Salt, covered 225
Sauce 20
Spooner 100
Sugar 135
Tumbler 150
Waste Bowl 95
Wine 145

BLOCKADE
Butter 65
Celery Vase 20
Compote, covered, 6" - 8" .... 35 - 65
Compote, open, 4" - 8" .... 20 - 45
Creamer or Spooner 20
Dish, sq., 7" - 9" .... 15 - 30
Finger Bowl 20
Goblet 45
Nappy, 4½" - 6" 30
Pitcher 85
Sugar 25
Tumbler 20

BLOCK & BAR
Creamer 40
vaseline 60
Goblet 65
vaseline 80
Pitcher 95
vaseline 175
Sugar 50
vaseline 70

BLOCK & CIRCLE
Berry Bowl, sm. 10
Berry Bowl, lg. 35
Butter 55
Celery Vase 20
Compote, covered 45
Compote, open, 7" - 9" 30
Creamer or Spooner 20
Dish, oval, 7" - 9" .... 15 - 30
Goblet 40
Lamp, mini 85
Mug 35
Pitcher 85
Sugar 30
Tumbler 20

BLOCK & FAN
Berry Bowl, sm. .... 20 - 40
ruby stain .... 55 - 80
Berry Bowl, lg. .... 55 - 75
ruby stain .... 70 - 90
Biscuit Jar 90
ruby stain 200
Bowl, rectangular 40
ruby stain 70
Butter 85
ruby stain 165
Cake Stand, 2 sizes .... 90 - 120
ruby stain .... 275 - 325
Carafe 65
ruby stain 130
Castor Set w/Tray 65
ruby stain 90
Celery Tray 35
ruby stain 70
Celery Vase 50
ruby stain 100
Compote, covered, 7" - 8" .... 100 - 130
ruby stain .... 250 - 300
Compote, open, 4" - 8" .... 50 - 60
ruby stain .... 90 - 115
Creamer, 2 sizes .... 30 - 50
ruby stain .... 50 - 100
Cruet 60
ruby stain 200
Decanter 90
ruby stain 250
Goblet 70
ruby stain 200
Ice Bucket 80
ruby stain 165
Ice Cream Dish, oblong 45
ruby stain 80
Lamp 145
Milk Pitcher 60
ruby stain 150
Pickle Dish 20
ruby stain 40
Plate, 6" - 10" .... 30 - 40
ruby stain .... 50 - 70
Pitcher 85
ruby stain 200
Relish Tray 30
ruby stain 60
Rose Bowl 60
ruby stain 95
Sauce, flat or ftd. 10
ruby stain 35
Shakers, ea. 30
ruby stain 80
Spooner 40
ruby stain 80
Sugar 70
ruby stain 120
Sugar Shaker 90
ruby stain 200
Syrup 165
ruby stain 300
Tumbler 50
ruby stain 80
Waste Bowl 45
ruby stain 90
Wine 80
ruby stain 150

BLOCK & JEWEL
Wine 30

BLOCK & PANEL
Butter 45
Celery Vase 25
Creamer or Spooner 25
Shakers, ea. 20
Sugar 30

BLOCK & PILLAR
Shakers, ea. 20
Vase 30

BLOCK & ROSETTE
Berry Bowl, lg. 50
Berry Bowl, sm. 20
Bowls, various .... 20 - 65
Butter 70
Champagne 35
Claret 30
Creamer or Spooner 25
Cruet 70
Finger Bowl 25
Goblet, straight top or cupped top 60
Pitcher 85
Punch Bowl w/Base 150
Punch Cup 15
Rose Bowl 30
Toothpick Holder 45

Tumbler....20
Shakers, ea....30
Sugar....40
Wine....30
*Add 10% for gold decorated.
*Add 75% for ruby stained pieces. All are rare.
BLOCK & STAR
Pitcher
vaseline....285
Tumbler....
vaseline....65
BLOCK & TRIPLE BARS
Butter....45
Creamer or Spooner....20
Goblet....35
Sugar....25
BLOCKED THUMBPRINT BAND
Cruet....50
ruby stain....75
Mug....35
ruby stain....45
Shot Glass....30
ruby stain....40
Toothpick Holder....45
ruby stain....60
Wine....15
ruby stain....25
BLOCK #331 (DUNCAN)
Bowl, sq....40
ruby stain....50
Bowl, tri-cornered....45
ruby stain....55
Butter....75
ruby stain....95
Celery Boat....35
ruby stain....40
Creamer....30
ruby stain....40
Cruet....60
ruby stain....85
Ice Tub....50
ruby stain....90
Jelly Compote....35
ruby stain....45
Ketchup bottle....55
ruby stain....70
Mustard Jar....45
ruby stain....60
Nappy, handled,
various shapes & sizes....25 - 45
ruby stain....30 - 60
Parlor Lamp....150
ruby stain....200
Punch Bowl....125
ruby stain....170
Punch Cup....20
ruby stain....25
Relish, hndl....30
ruby stain....35
Rose Bowl, 5 sizes, 3" - 7"....45
vaseline (4" size)....150
ruby stain....55
Sauce, sq....25
ruby stain....30
Salt Shaker....30
ruby stain....50
Spooner....35
Sugar....35
ruby stain....45
Sugar Shaker....45
ruby stain....60
Syrup....60
ruby stain....85
BLOOMS & BLOSSOMS (AKA: MIKADO)
Bowls, various....15 - 60
vaseline....20 - 75
green/blue....20 - 50
Butter....150
vaseline....185
green/blue....130
Compote....65
vaseline....80
green/blue....60
Creamer or Spooner....45
vaseline....65
green/blue....40
Cruet....165
vaseline....195
green/blue....130
Nappy....35
vaseline....65
green/blue....35
Plate....40
vaseline....75
green/blue....40
Pitcher....225
vaseline....265
green/blue....175
Tumbler....35
vaseline....75
green/blue....35
Sugar....55
vaseline....75
green/blue....55
*All prices in crystal are for decorated pieces.
BLUEBERRY
Vase Whimsey
cobalt....300
BLUE HERON
Butter....250
Creamer....85
Pitcher....400
Spooner....90
Sugar....100
Tumbler....90
BOAR
Humidor
green/blue....375
BOAT RELISH
One Shape....75
BOOT
Novelty Shape....25
ruby stain....35
BOSC PEAR
Berry Bowl, lg....30
purple flash....50
Berry Bowl, sm....10
purple flash....20
Butter....50
purple flash....90
Celery Vase....25
purple flash....30
Creamer or Spooner....30
purple flash....35
Pitcher....75
purple flash....110
Sugar....35
purple flash....50
Tumbler....20
purple flash....30
BOSTON TREE OF LIFE
Mug, 2 sizes, rare....100
Pitcher, w/hook for mug,
rare....800
amethyst....900
Matching Stand, rare....300
BOTTLE PICKLE DISH
Novelty Pickle Dish
amber....80
vaseline....110
green/blue....90
BOUQUET (INDIANA'S #162)
Berry Bowl, sm....15
ruby stain....25
Berry Bowl, lg....30
ruby stain....45
Butter....55
ruby stain....70
Compote....35
ruby stain....50
Creamer....25
ruby stain....35
Novelty Bowls....15 - 35
ruby stain....20 - 50
Pitcher....65
ruby stain....90
Spooner....25
ruby stain....35
Sugar....30
ruby stain....45
Tumbler....15
ruby stain....25
BOW TIE
Bowls, 7" - 11"....40 - 90
Butter....135
Butter Pat....50
Cake Stand....250
Celery Vase....95
Compote, high,
7" - 11"....75 - 200
Compote, low,
7" - 11"....60 - 90
Creamer or Spooner....65
Goblet....100
Jam Jar....95
Milk Pitcher, 2 sizes....150 - 165
Orange Bowl....185
Pitcher, 3 sizes....200 - 250
Punch Bowl....150
Relish....40
Salt, master....80
Salt, ind....45
Sauce, flat or ftd....25
Sugar....120
Tumbler....90
BOXED STAR
Berry Bowl, sm....15
Berry Bowl, lg....30
Butter....65
Carafe, water....45
Creamer or Spooner....25
Goblet....45
Pitcher....70
Tumbler (ice tea)....20
Sugar....35
Wine....20
BOX PLEAT
Butter....45
Cake Stand....40
Celery Vase....20
Compote....30
Creamer or Spooner....20
Pitcher....65
Sugar....25
Tumbler....10
BOY & GIRL FACE
Cup w/Saucer....65
amber....110
green/blue....85
BOY WITH BEGGING DOG
Mug....60
green/blue....90
milk glass....95
BOY WITH GOOSE
Compote....250
BRANCHED TREE
Butter....145
Celery Vase....35
Compote, covered....90
Creamer or Spooner....40
Goblet....65
Pitcher....170
Sugar....60
Tumbler....35
BRASS NAILHEAD (FRANCE)
Mug....50
opal....70

BRAZEN SHIELD
Berry Bowl, sm. 15
Berry Bowl, lg. 45
Butter 75
Creamer or Spooner 25
Goblet 45
Jelly Compote 35
Pickle Dish 20
Pitcher 95
cobalt 275
Shakers, ea. 20
Sugar 30
green/blue 250
Tumbler 20
green/blue 60
cobalt 45
Wine 20

BRAZILIAN
Berry Bowl, sm. 20
Berry Bowl, lg. 45
Butter 65
Carafe 40
Celery Tray (shown) 25
Celery Vase 30
Compote 35
Cracker Jar, 7" - 9" 25 - 40
Creamer or Spooner 25
Cruet 60
Finger Bowl 20
Pitcher 80
Tumbler 25
Olive, hndl. 25
Pickle Jar 30
Rose Bowl 35
Salt Shaker 20
Sauce 15
Sherbet 20
Sugar 30
Toothpick Holder 30
Vase 35

BRAZILIAN ADVERTISING PIECES
Advertising Pieces, 8" x 4¼" 50

BRILLIANT
Berry Bowl, sm. 35
ruby stain 55
Berry Bowl, lg. 60
ruby stain 120
Butter 80
ruby stain 165
Celery Vase 100
ruby stain 145
Compote, covered 90 - 140
ruby stain 200 - 300
Compote, open 70 - 125
ruby stain 125 - 250
Creamer or Spooner 50
ruby stain 85
Goblet 70
ruby stain 125
Pitcher 100
ruby stain 235
Sauce 10
ruby stain 35
Shakers, ea. 45
ruby stain 80
Sugar, 2 sizes 40 - 70
ruby stain 70 - 115
Syrup 135
ruby stain 300
Toothpick Holder 35
ruby stain 100
Tumbler 35
ruby stain 70
Wine 45
ruby stain 75

*Amber stained 10% more than ruby stained.

BRINGING HOME THE COWS
Butter 325
Creamer or Spooner 200
Pitcher, tankard 650
Sugar 250

BRITANNIA LILY
Creamer 50
vaseline 145

BRITISH LION
Paperweight 250

BRITTANIC
Banana Stand 125
ruby stain 200
Bowl, oval, 7" - 9" 35 - 45
ruby stain 50 - 70
Bowl, rnd., 8" 50
ruby stain 65
Bowl, sq. 35
ruby stain 55
Butter 80
ruby stain 145
Cake Stand, lg. or sm. 90 - 120
ruby stain 300 - 350
Carafe 60
ruby stain 135
Castor Set 200
ruby stain 475
Celery Tray 35
ruby stain 70
Celery Vase 50
ruby stain 95
Compote, open, 5" - 8" 20 - 60
ruby stain 40 - 95
Compote, open, 7½" - 10" 40 - 70
ruby stain 85 - 120
Cracker Jar 65
ruby stain 90
Creamer or Spooner 45
ruby stain 95
Cruet 65
ruby stain 200
Custard Cup 20
ruby stain 40
Fruit Basket 70
ruby stain 200
Goblet 40
ruby stain 90
Honey Jar 250
ruby stain 400
Ice Cream Tray 50
ruby stain 100
Lamp, two types, two sizes 100 - 150
Mug 30
ruby stain 50
Olive Dish 35
ruby stain 55
Pitcher 90
ruby stain 180
Rose Bowl 40
ruby stain 80
Sauce, rnd. or sq. 15
ruby stain 35
Shakers, ea. 30
ruby stain 75
Sugar 60
ruby stain 125
Syrup 100
ruby stain 300
Toothpick Holder 30
ruby stain 90
Tumbler 40
ruby stain 60
Vase 35
ruby stain 75
Wine 20
ruby stain 55

*Amber stained 10% more than ruby stained.

BROKEN ARCHES
Bowl, 8½" 25
Punch Bowl 75
vaseline 400
Punch Cup 10
vaseline 30

BROKEN COLUMN
Banana Dish, flat. 90
Banana Stand 275
ruby stain 950
Basket, hndl. 100
Biscuit Jar 75
ruby stain 175
Bowls, various sizes and styles 50 - 125
ruby stain 100 - 200
Bowl, covered, 5" - 8" 90 - 150
ruby stain 300 - 625
Butter 165
ruby stain 500
Cake Stand 125 - 200
ruby stain 650 - 775
Celery Tray 50
ruby stain 125
Celery Vase 100
ruby stain 225
Champagne 200
ruby stain 750
Claret 165
ruby stain 625
Compote, covered, 5" - 8" 100 - 200
ruby stain 375 - 850
Compote, open, 5" - 8" 65 - 125
ruby stain 200 - 350
Creamer or Spooner 70
ruby stain 200
Cruet 165
ruby stain 600
Custard Cup 30
ruby stain 165
Decanter w/Stopper 165
ruby stain 900
Finger Bowl 65
ruby stain 95
Goblet 95
ruby stain 425
Pickle Castor 150
ruby stain 625
Plate, 4" - 8" 40 - 90
ruby stain 80 - 160
Pitcher 165
ruby stain 600
Sauce 30
ruby stain 65
Shakers, ea. 100
ruby stain 250
Sugar 125
ruby stain 425
Syrup 300
ruby stain 675
Tumbler 80
ruby stain 135
Water Carafe 250
ruby stain 750

BROKEN PILLAR & REED
Bonbon 15
amber 20
green/blue 30
Bowl, 8" 20
amber 25
green/blue 40
Butter 45
amber 55
green/blue 75
Cake Stand 35
amber 40
green/blue 50
Celery Tray 20
amber 25
green/blue 35
Celery Vase 25
amber 30
green/blue 40
Cologne 40
amber 45

green/blue ... 55
Compote ... 35
amber ... 40
green/blue ... 45
Creamer or Spooner ... 30
amber ... 35
green/blue ... 40
Custard Cup ... 15
amber ... 20
green/blue ... 25
Jelly Compote ... 25
amber ... 30
green/blue ... 35
Pickle Tray ... 20
amber ... 25
green/blue ... 30
Pitcher, 2 sizes ... 55 - 70
amber ... 65 - 80
green/blue ... 75 - 100
Plate ... 20
amber ... 25
green/blue ... 30
Shakers, ea ... 20
amber ... 25
green/blue ... 30
Soap Dish ... 20
amber ... 25
green/blue ... 30
Sugar ... 35
amber ... 40
green/blue ... 50
Syrup ... 60
amber ... 75
green/blue ... 90
Toothpick Holder ... 40
amber ... 50
green/blue ... 55
Tray ... 30
amber ... 35
green/blue ... 40
Tumbler, 2 sizes ... 15 - 25
amber ... 20 - 30
green/blue ... 25 - 35
*Add 15% for stained pieces.

BRYAN, WM. J.
Tumbler ... 95

BRYCE FASHION
Creamer, from cup ... 30
amber ... 35
vaseline ... 50
green/blue ... 45
ruby stain ... 40
amethyst ... 45
Creamer, from toothpick ... 35
amber ... 45
vaseline ... 60
green/blue ... 55
ruby stain ... 45
amethyst ... 50
Cup ... 20
amber ... 25
vaseline ... 35
green/blue ... 30
ruby stain ... 25
amethyst ... 35
Toothpick Holder ... 25
amber ... 30
vaseline ... 45
green/blue ... 45
ruby stain ... 30
amethyst ... 40

BRYCE FASHION BUTTER DISH
Specialty Butter Dish w/Lid ... 175
vaseline ... 375

BRYCE HOBNAIL
Bowls, various ... 15 - 30
vaseline ... 45 - 90
green/blue ... 30 - 70
ruby stain ... 25 - 60
Butter ... 85
vaseline ... 195
green/blue ... 125
ruby stain ... 110
Celery Vase ... 25
vaseline ... 50
green/blue ... 40
ruby stain ... 35
Compote, covered ... 60
vaseline ... 175
green/blue ... 145
ruby stain ... 80
Compote, open ... 35
vaseline ... 95
green/blue ... 80
ruby stain ... 40
Creamer or Spooner ... 30
vaseline ... 65
green/blue ... 55
ruby stain ... 40
Goblet ... 40
vaseline ... 70
green/blue ... 60
ruby stain ... 55
Mug ... 35
amber ... 70
vaseline ... 75
green/blue ... 60
ruby stain ... 50
Pickle Dish ... 20
vaseline ... 35
green/blue ... 30
ruby stain ... 25
Sugar ... 40
vaseline ... 50
green/blue ... 40
ruby stain ... 60
Wine ... 20
vaseline ... 35
green/blue ... 25
ruby stain ... 30
*Add 10% to crystal price for milk glass pieces.

BRYCE PANEL
Butter ... 50
Celery Vase ... 20
Creamer or Spooner ... 20
Sugar ... 25
Syrup ... 45

BRYCE RIBBON CANDY
Bowl, oval, w/lid, 4" & 5" ... 45
Bowl, oval, w/lid, 6" & 8" ... 65
Bowl, oval, open, 4" & 5" ... 35
Bowl, oval, open, 6" & 8" ... 50
Bread Plate ... 25
Butter ... 60
Cake Plate ... 35
Cake Stand ... 50
Celery Vase ... 25
Child's Table Set ... 100
Claret ... 20
Compote w/lid, high or low, 5" & 6" .. 30 - 50
7" & 8" ... 35 - 60
Compote, open, high or low, 5", 6" & 7" . 20 - 40
8" & 10" ... 30 - 50
Cordial ... 20
Creamer or Spooner ... 20
Cruet ... 50
Cup & Saucer ... 30
Goblet ... 35
Honey Dish ... 25
Lamp ... 70
Milk Pitcher ... 55
Pickle Dish ... 20
Plate, 6" & 7" ... 20
Pitcher ... 75
Plate, 8" - 10" ... 30
Relish ... 20
Sauce, flat or ftd. ... 15
Shakers, ea ... 25
Sugar ... 25
Syrup ... 60
Tumbler ... 20
Wine ... 15

BUCKINGHAM
Basket ... 45
Bowl, adv., tri-corner ... 60
Butter ... 60
Celery Vase ... 25
Compote, covered ... 45
Compote, open ... 35
Creamer or Spooner ... 25
Goblet ... 40
Pitcher ... 85
Sugar ... 30
Toothpick Holder, 3 hndls. ... 30
Tumbler ... 20

BUCKLE & DIAMOND
Bowls ... 10 - 35
Butter ... 65
Creamer or Spooner ... 20
Goblet ... 45
Pitcher ... 80
Sugar ... 30
Tumbler ... 20

BUCKLE WITH ENGLISH HOBNAIL
Berry Bowl, sm. ... 15
Berry Bowl, lg. ... 40
Butter ... 70
Celery Vase ... 30
Creamer or Spooner ... 25
Pickle Dish ... 25
Shakers, ea. ... 25
Sugar ... 25

BUCKLE WITH STAR
Bowls, covered, 7" - 10" ... 35 - 75
Butter ... 75
Cake Stand ... 35
Celery Vase ... 25
Cologne Bottle ... 50
Compote, covered, 7" ... 90
Compote, open, 9½" ... 60
Creamer or Spooner ... 25
Goblet ... 55
Honey Dish ... 20
Mug ... 60
Mustard Jar ... 70
Pitcher ... 200
Relish Tray ... 50
Salt, master ... 30
Sauce, flat or ftd. ... 15
Sugar ... 60
Syrup ... 165
Tumbler ... 60
Tumbler, hndl. ... 90
Wine ... 25

BULLET EMBLEM
Butter ... 475
Creamer or Spooner ... 225
Sugar ... 350
*Add 25% for painted pieces.

BULLS-EYE & DAISY
Bowl ... 25
ruby stain ... 70
Butter ... 50
ruby stain ... 100
Creamer or Spooner ... 35
ruby stain ... 55
Cruet ... 60
ruby stain ... 100
Decanter ... 90
ruby stain ... 125
Goblet ... 30
ruby stain ... 50
Pitcher ... 70
ruby stain ... 125
Shakers, ea. ... 35
ruby stain ... 55
Sugar ... 50

ruby stain 70
Syrup....85
ruby stain 150
Toothpick Holder....55
ruby stain 90
Tumbler....30
ruby stain 45
Wine 20
ruby stain 40
*Green stained pieces add 10% to ruby stained.

BULLS-EYE & DIAMOND POINT
Basket....150
Biscuit Jar....175
Bowl, various.... 40 - 80
Butter....90
Cake Stand 75
Celery Vase....50
Compote, covered, various sizes. 70 - 150
Compote, open, various sizes .... 40 - 80
Creamer 40
Goblet 90
Honey Dish, covered 150
Jam Jar, covered....95
Lamp, various sizes.... 150 - 225
Milk Pitcher 100
Pitcher....165
Plate....40
Relish 25
Salt Shaker....50
Sauce....20
Spooner 75
Sugar w/Lid 90
Syrup....200
Tray....100
Tumbler....50

BULLS-EYE & FAN
Berry Bowl, lg....35
green/blue 60
Berry Bowl, sm....45
green/blue 75
Biscuit Jar w/Lid....125
green/blue 300
Butter....70
green/blue 125
Cake Stand 70
green/blue 135
Celery Tray....30
green/blue 50
Celery Vase....40
green/blue 70
Champagne 50
green/blue 80
Compote, open 40
green/blue 90
Creamer or Spooner....35
vaseline 250
green/blue 80
Goblet 35
green/blue 75
Mug....40
green/blue 85
Pitcher, 2 sizes.... 50 - 75
green/blue ....90 - 140
Sauce....10
green/blue 25
Sherbet....50
green/blue 80
Sugar....55
vaseline 325
green/blue 90
Toothpick Holder....30
green/blue 45
Tumbler....25
green/blue 60
Wine 20
green/blue 45
Vase, scarce 50
green/blue 70
*Add 10% for stained pieces.

BULL'S HEAD
Novelty Mustard Container
green/blue 450
milk glass 200

BUSHEL BASKET
Handled Basket....265
black 95

BUTTERFLY
(Frosted or Plain, same shapes)
Bowls, various .... 20 - 50
Butter....95
Celery Vase....40
Compote, covered....65
Creamer or Spooner....35
Mustard Jar 60
Pickle Dish 30
Pitcher....250
Relish Dish....25
Shakers, ea....35
Sugar....50
Tumbler....35
*Add 10% for frosted pieces.

BUTTERFLY (U.S. GLASS) AKA: BIG BUTTERFLY
Bowls, various .... 15 - 35
Butter....85
Celery Vase....35
Creamer 35
Mustard Jar 45
Pickle dish....35
Pitcher....145
Relish dish....30
Salt Shakers, ea. 45
Spooner 40
Sugar....55
Tumbler....35

BUTTERFLY & BERRY (FENTON)
Master Bowl, very scarce....135
Small Bowl, very scarce....30
Vase, scarce 40
red 125

BUTTERFLY & THISTLE
Bowl, 9", scarce....50
Butter....75
Celery Tray....25
Celery Vase....40
Compote, sm. 35
Compote, med, 2 sizes .... 45 - 65
Compote, lg, 2 sizes .... 55 - 75
Creamer or Spooner....35
Nappy 35
Oil Bottle....65
Pickle Dish 35
Pitcher....100
Shakers, ea....30
Sugar....45
Toothpick Holder....40
Tumbler....20
Vase, 6" - 8¼"....30

BUTTERFLY WITH SPRAY
Butter....75
Celery....20
Compote, covered, high or low....50
Creamer or Spooner....20
Mug....25
Mug, child's....40
Pitcher....90
Tumbler....20

BUTTON & PANEL
Berry Bowl, sm....15
ruby stain 25
Berry Bowl, lg....30
ruby stain 45
Butter....55
ruby stain 75
Creamer 25
ruby stain 35
Pitcher....65
ruby stain 80
Punch Bowl....80
ruby stain 100
Punch Cup 10
ruby stain 20
Spooner....25
ruby stain 35
Sugar....30
ruby stain 40
Tumbler....15
ruby stain 25

BUTTON ARCHES
Bowl....30
ruby stain 80
Butter....70
ruby stain 135
Cake Stand 100
ruby stain 225
Celery Vase....40
ruby stain 90
Compote, jelly 30
ruby stain 55
Creamer or Spooner....40
ruby stain 70
Cruet....70
ruby stain 200
Milk Pitcher 65
ruby stain 100
Mustard Jar 80
ruby stain 145
Pitcher....100
ruby stain 145
Salt Shaker, ea....30
ruby stain 45
Sauce....15
ruby stain 25
Syrup....70
ruby stain 200
Toothpick Holder....25
ruby stain 45
Toy Mug....30
ruby stain 75
amethyst 100
Tumbler....20
ruby stain 40
Wine 20
ruby stain 35

BUTTON BLOCK
Salt Shaker 25
vaseline 60

BUTTON CENTER ABC
Plate....75

BUTTON PANEL
Berry Bowl, sm....15
Berry Bowl, lg....35
Butter....60
Creamer or Spooner....25
Cruet....55
Pickle Dish 20
Sauce....15
Sugar....20
Toothpick Holder....35
Toy Table Set,
complete....85

BUTTON PANEL WITH BARS
Berry Bowl, lg....45
ruby stain 55
Berry Bowl, sm....20
ruby stain 25
Butter....95
ruby stain 110
Creamer 45
ruby stain 55
Punch Bowl with Base 125
ruby stain 165
Punch Cup 20
ruby stain 25
Spooner....35
ruby stain 45
Sugar....40
ruby stain 50

Price Guide

BUTTRESSED LOOP
- Bowl, covered....50
- Butter....55
- Compote....30
- Creamer or Spooner....20
- Sugar....25

BUZZ SAW
- Berry Bowl, sm....15
- Berry Bowl, lg....40
- Bowls, various.... 10 - 35
- Butter....70
- Celery Tray....20
- Cologne bottle....50
- Creamer or Spooner....25
- Cruet....50
- Pitcher, qt., 2 shapes.... 85 - 100
- Sugar....35
- Syrup....60

BUZZ-STAR
- Berry Bowl, sm....20
- Berry Bowl, lg....45
- Bridge Set Pickle Dish, any shape: club, diamond, heart, or spade....25
- Butter....65
- Creamer or Spooner....25
- Goblet....45
- Pickle Dish....20
- Pitcher....85
- Salt Dip....15
- Sugar....30
- Toy Punch Set....145
- Toy Table Set (WHIRLIGIG)....125
- Tumbler....20
- Wine....15

BY-JINGO
- Mug....60

CABBAGE ROSE
- Basket, hndl....75
- Bitters Bottle....100
- Bowl, oval or rnd., 6" - 8".... 50 - 90
- Butter....100
- Cake Stand, 9" - 12½".... 80 - 125
- Celery Vase....95
- Champagne....75
- Compote, covered, 6" - 11".... 70 - 135
- Cordial....40
- Creamer or Spooner....65
- Egg Cup, no handle and handled. 75 - 150
- Goblet....70
- Milk Pitcher....175
- Mug....70
- Pickle Dish....25
- Pitcher....250
- Relish Dish....30
- Salt Dip, master....50
- Sugar....125
- Tumbler....70
- Wine....80

CABBAGE ROSE CENTRAL
- Basket....55
- Bitters Bottle....80
- Bottle....65
- Bowl, oval....30
- Bowl, round....25
- Butter....75
- Cake Plate, 6 sizes.... 30 - 75
- Celery Vase....25
- Champagne....25
- Compote, covered, 8 sizes.... 60 - 110
- Compote, open, 4 sizes.... 45 - 90
- Cordial....20
- Creamer or Spooner....25
- Egg Cup....25
- Goblet....30
- Mug....35
- Pickle Dish....20
- Pitcher....100
- Relish Dish....20
- Salt, master....25
- Sauce....15
- Sugar....40
- Tumbler....25
- Wine....20

CABLE
- Bowls, various.... 75 - 125
- Butter....250
- Cake Stand, 9", very rare....4,000
- Castor Set, complete....325
- Celery Vase....100
- Champagne....275
- Compote, open, high....450
- Compote, open, low, 7" - 11".... 80 - 150
- Creamer....275
- Decanter, w/original stopper, rare....500
- Decanter, w/lip, scarce....200
- Egg Cup....75
- Goblet, 2 sizes.... 100 - 225
- Honey Dish....55
- Jelly Compote....95
- Milk Pitcher....1,500
- Mug....650
- Oil Lamp, 3 styles.... 200 - 265
- Pitcher....1,300
- Plate....95
- Salt, 2 sizes.... 50 - 80
- Spooner....65
- Sugar....165
- Syrup....550
- Tumbler, 3 styles.... 125 - 325
- Wine....235

*Add 50% for stained or colored pieces.

CABLE & THUMBPRINT
- Match Holder....30
  - vaseline....80

CACTUS
- Bowl, 8" - 9½", rare....300

CADMUS
- Compote....50
- Wine....25

CAMBRIDGE #2351
- Berry Bowl, sm....10
- Berry Bowl, lg....35
- Butter....75
- Celery, tall....25
- Cologne bottle....45
- Compote, lg....60
- Creamer or Spooner....25
- Custard Cup....10
- Jelly Compote....30
- Jug, squat....55
- Oil Bottle....40
- Olive, hndl....25
- Orange Bowl, ftd....55
- Pitcher....90
- Punch Bowl....125
- Punch Cup....10
- Shakers, ea....25
- Sherbet....15
- Spoon Tray....20
- Sugar....30
- Tumbler....20
- Vase, 7"....25
- Vase, Pedestal....30
- Whiskey Set w/Tray....100

CAMBRIDGE #2511
- Berry Bowl, sm....20
- Berry Bowl, lg....40
- Butter....80
- Creamer or Spooner....35
- Pitcher....100
- Sugar....45
- Tumbler....20

CAMBRIDGE #2658
- Creamer....30
  - ruby stain....45
- Mug....50
  - ruby stain....60

CAMBRIDGE #2694
- Butter....70
- Celery....25
- Compote, 2 sizes.... 35 - 50
- Creamer or Spooner....25
- Nappy, 3 sizes.... 20 - 30
- Pickle Dish....25
- Pitcher, tankard, 2 sizes.... 65 - 80
- Plate, 2 sizes.... 20 - 30
- Rose Bowl, 2 sizes.... 25 - 35
- Shakers, ea....30
- Sugar....35
- Tumbler....20
- Vase....35

CAMBRIDGE BUZZ SAW
- Basket, squat hndl....50
- Berry Bowl, sm....15
- Berry Bowl, lg....40
- Bowl, 5" - 7"....20
- Bowl, 8" - 9"....45
- Butter....65
- Celery Tray....30
- Celery Vase....25
- Cologne....70
- Creamer or Spooner....25
- Cruet....75
- Milk Pitcher, 2 sizes.... 45 - 60
- Nut Bowl, 5" - 7"....25
- Olive Nappy....20
- Pitcher....95
- Rose Bowl....35
- Shakers, ea....25
- Sherbet....25
- Sugar....30
- Syrup....65
- Tumbler....25

CAMBRIDGE HERON
- Figure Flower Holder, 9" - 20".. 65 - 165

CAMBRIDGE NEAR-CUT #2653
- Celery Vase....35
- Cracker Jar w/Lid....80
- Goblet....45
- Ice Cream Bowl, sm., rect....20
- Ice Cream Bowl, lg., rect....45
- Jelly Compote....35
- Pickle Tray....20
- Pitcher....125
- Pitcher, 1 qt., squat....80
- Punch Bowl w/Base....175
- Punch Cup....15
- Sherbet....20
- Tumbler....25

CAMBRIDGE SEMITAR #2647
- Bonbon, ftd....25
- Bowls, 4½" - 9".... 15 - 45
- Bowl, special deep, 9"....50
- Butter....70
- Celery Tray....30
- Creamer or Spooner....30
- Cruet....70
- Custard Cup....15
- Jelly Compote....25
- Nappy....20
- Pickle Tray....25
- Pitcher, 2 sizes.... 70 - 95
- Plate , 6" - 8"....35
- Punch Bowl, 2 sizes.... 125 - 160
- Punch Bowl, advertising....300
- Shakers, ea....25
- Spoon Tray....30
- Sugar....50
- Tumbler....25
- Water Bottle....60
- Whiskey Tumbler....30

CANADIAN
- Bowl, covered....175
- Bowl, open....75
- Butter....190
- Cake Stand....125

Compote w/Lid, high, 6" - 10". 100 - 180
Compote w/Lid, low, 6" - 8"...... 95 - 165
Compote, open, high or low....... 60 - 85
Creamer or Spooner.......70
Goblet.......70
Jam Jar.......265
Milk Pitcher.......150
Mug.......70
Pitcher.......145
Plate, 6" - 12"....... 50 - 100
Sauce.......30
Sugar.......165
Tumbler.......70
Wine.......45

CANE
Berry Bowl, sm.......10
amber.......15
vaseline.......25
green/blue.......20
Berry Bowl, lg.......25
amber.......30
vaseline.......35
green/blue.......35
Bowl, oval.......30
amber.......50
vaseline.......65
green/blue.......70
Butter.......45
amber.......60
vaseline.......95
green/blue.......75
Celery Vase.......20
amber.......25
vaseline.......30
green/blue.......25
Compote.......25
amber.......40
vaseline.......55
green/blue.......45
Cordial.......15
amber.......20
vaseline.......30
green/blue.......40
Creamer or Spooner.......20
amber.......30
vaseline.......45
green/blue.......45
Finger Bowl.......15
amber.......20
vaseline.......30
green/blue.......25
Goblet.......20
amber.......30
vaseline.......45
green/blue.......40
Honey Dish.......15
amber.......20
vaseline.......30
green/blue.......25
Match Holder, kettle shape.......35
amber.......50
vaseline.......75
green/blue.......90
Milk Pitcher.......40
amber.......65
vaseline.......100
green/blue.......100
Pickle Dish.......15
amber.......20
vaseline.......30
green/blue.......25
Pitcher.......70
amber.......95
vaseline.......145
green/blue.......165
Plate, 4½".......15
amber.......20
vaseline.......35
green/blue.......25
Relish.......15
amber.......20
vaseline.......35
green/blue.......45
Sauce, flat or ftd.......15
amber.......20
vaseline.......25
green/blue.......25
Shakers, ea.......25
amber.......40
vaseline.......65
green/blue.......60
Slipper.......25
amber.......30
vaseline.......60
green/blue.......45
Sugar.......25
amber.......40
vaseline.......65
green/blue.......70
Tray.......25
amber.......30
vaseline.......70
green/blue.......45
Tumbler.......20
amber.......25
vaseline.......40
green/blue.......30
Wine.......20
amber.......25
vaseline.......40
green/blue.......40
Waste Bowl.......15
amber.......20
vaseline.......30
green/blue.......30

CANE HORSESHOE
Berry Bowl, sm.......20
Berry Bowl, lg.......45
Butter.......60
Cake Stand.......40
Celery Tray.......25
Compote.......35
Creamer or Spooner.......25
Cruet.......50
Pitcher.......60
Shaker.......35
Sugar.......25
Tumbler.......15

CANE INSERT
Berry Bowl, sm.......15
Berry Bowl, lg.......35
Butter.......45
Cake Stand.......30
Carafe.......40
Celery Vase, rare.......75
Compote.......35
Creamer or Spooner.......20
Goblet.......35
Hair Receiver.......40
Mug.......30
Pitcher.......70
Sugar.......30
Tumbler.......20

CANNONBALL PINWHEEL
Berry Bowl, sm.......15
Berry Bowl, lg.......35
Butter.......70
Celery Vase.......25
Cherry Tray, 10".......30
Creamer or Spooner.......20
Cup.......15
Fruit Plate, 9".......25
Goblet.......35
Jelly Compote.......25
Milk Pitcher.......55
Nappy.......25
Olive Dish, sq.......25
Pickle Dish.......20
Pitcher.......75
Plate, 6", sq.......20
Shakers, ea.......20
Sherbet.......15
Sugar.......25
Tall Sugar, hndl.......30
Tumbler.......15
Wine.......20

CANNON ON A DRUM
Novelty Container.......90
milk glass.......125

CANTON HOUSE
Cheese Dish, covered, rare.......375
Compote, covered, rare.......350
Creamer, rare.......250
Pitcher, rare.......550

CAPITOL
Creamer.......25
Mug.......40
Perfume.......45
Puff Box.......50
Sugar.......30
Toothpick Holder.......35

CARDINAL
Berry Bowl, sm.......90
Berry Bowl, lg.......165
Butter.......150
Cake Stand, rare.......1,400
Creamer or Spooner.......60
Goblet.......70
Honey Dish, covered or open..... 35 - 60
Pitcher.......2,125
Sauce, flat or ftd.......45
Sugar.......125
Tumbler.......90

CARLTEC
Basket.......45
Berry Bowl, lg.......40
Berry Bowl, sm.......15
Bonbon.......20
Bowls, various....... 20 - 35
Butter.......65
Celery Bowl.......20
Compote, hndl.......45
Creamer or Spooner.......30
Olive Tray.......25
Pickle Dish.......20
Plate.......30
Pitcher.......85
Preserve Dishes, various....... 20 - 30
Rose Bowl.......30
Spoon Tray.......35
Sugar.......40
Tumbler.......20

CARMEN (FOSTORIA)
Berry Bowl, sm.......20
Berry Bowl, lg.......40
Butter.......70
Compote, 9".......50
Creamer or Spooner.......30
Cruet.......80
Sugar.......35
*Yellow Flashed add 25%.

CARNATION (LANCASTER)
Berry Bowl, sm.......15
Berry Bowl, lg.......40
Butter.......60
Creamer or Spooner.......20
Goblet.......40
Milk Pitcher.......65
Pickle Dish.......15
Pitcher.......80
Sugar.......25
Tumbler.......20

CARNATION (NEW MARTINSVILLE)
Goblet.......35
ruby stain.......45
Pickle Dish.......20
ruby stain.......25

Pitcher.....60
ruby stain.....80
Toothpick Holder.....35
ruby stain.....45
Tumbler.....15
ruby stain.....25
Wine.....20
ruby stain.....25
CARNATION WITH ELK
Plate, 9" - 13"..... 35 - 60
CARRIAGE
Novelty Coach or Carriage.....85
amber.....135
green/blue.....150
CARSON FURNITURE
Advertising Pickle Tray.....45
CASTOR & TOOTHPICK SET
Complete Set, very scarce..... 150
CATHEDRAL (U.S. GLASS - BRYCE)
Bowl, 5" - 6".....20
amber.....30
vaseline.....30
green/blue.....40
amethyst.....65
Bowl, 7" - 8".....45
amber.....35
vaseline.....50
green/blue.....45
amethyst.....85
Butter.....65
amber.....80
vaseline.....125
green/blue.....80
amethyst.....125
Cake Stand.....35
amber.....45
vaseline.....125
green/blue.....55
amethyst..... 85
Celery Vase.....25
amber.....30
vaseline.....55
green/blue.....40
amethyst.....55
Compote, covered.....55
amber.....65
vaseline.....150
green/blue.....75
amethyst.....100
Compote, open.....40
amber.....45
vaseline.....95
green/blue.....50
amethyst.....80
Creamer or Spooner.....20
amber.....25
vaseline.....55
green/blue.....35
amethyst.....50
Cruet.....60
amber.....85
vaseline.....150
green/blue.....90
amethyst.....125
Goblet.....45
amber.....60
vaseline.....70
green/blue.....75
amethyst.....100
Lamp.....75
green/blue.....210
Mug.....30
amber.....40
vaseline.....55
green/blue.....45
amethyst.....65
Pitcher.....100
amber.....185
vaseline.....250

Relish Tray.....15
amber.....25
vaseline.....55
green/blue.....30
amethyst.....40
Salt Boat.....20
amber.....30
vaseline.....40
green/blue.....40
amethyst.....50
Sauce.....15
amber.....20
vaseline.....20
green/blue.....30
amethyst.....40
Sugar.....30
amber.....40
vaseline.....65
green/blue.....50
amethyst.....70
Tumbler.....20
amber.....30
vaseline.....50
green/blue.....40
amethyst.....55
CAT IN A TANGLE
Mug.....70
amber.....90
CAT ON A HAMPER - LOW
Novelty with Lid, rare.....400
vaseline.....750
chocolate.....675
CAT ON A HAMPER - TALL
Novelty with lid, rare.....250
amber.....575
vaseline..... 1,500
green/blue.....700
chocolate.....425
CAT'S EYE & FAN
Berry Bowl, sm......20
Berry Bowl, lg......45
Bowl, lg., ftd......40
Butter.....55
Compote.....35
Creamer or Spooner.....25
Sauce.....15
Sugar.....30
CATTAILS & WATERLILY (NORTHWOOD)
Pitcher.....95
green/blue.....175
Tumbler.....20
green/blue.....45
sapphire.....100
CAT UP A TREE WITH DOG
Pitcher, tall, rare.....450
CELTIC CROSS
Butter.....65
Celery Tray.....25
Creamer.....25
Goblet.....40
Pitcher.....80
Relish.....25
Spooner.....25
Sugar.....35
Tumbler.....20
CENTENNIAL DRAPE
Bread Plate.....35
Butter.....65
Creamer or Spooner.....30
Goblet.....50
Pickle Dish.....25
Sugar.....45
CENTENNIAL EXHIBITION SHOE
Slipper.....200
CENTIPEDE
Butter.....45
Creamer or Spooner.....20
Pickle Dish.....15
Relish.....20

Shakers, ea.....25
Sugar.....25
CHAIN
Berry Bowl, lg......30
Berry Bowl, sm......10
Butter.....55
Compote, covered.....35
Cordial.....15
Creamer or Spooner.....20
Milk Pitcher.....60
Pitcher.....90
Sugar.....25
Tumbler.....15
Wine.....15
CHAIN & SHIELD
Butter.....65
Celery Vase.....20
Creamer or Spooner.....20
Goblet.....55
Pitcher.....90
Plate, 7" - 11"..... 20 - 40
Platter, oval.....35
Sauce.....10
Sugar.....30
Tumbler.....20
Wine.....15
CHAIN & SWAG
Cruet.....65
ruby stain.....85
milk glass.....95
Shakers, ea.....45
ruby stain.....60
milk glass.....80
Syrup.....70
ruby stain.....90
milk glass.....100
CHAIN WITH STAR
Berry Bowl, sm......20
Berry Bowl, lg......40
Bread Plate.....25
Butter.....65
Cake Stand.....30
Compote, covered..... 70 - 90
Compote, open..... 40 - 60
Creamer or Spooner.....25
Goblet.....25
Pickle Dish.....20
Pitcher.....135
Plate.....25
Relish.....20
Sauce.....15
Shakers, ea.....20
Sugar.....60
Syrup.....125
Wine.....20
CHAMPION
Berry Bowl, sm......15
Berry Bowl, lg......30
Butter.....60
Carafe.....40
Creamer or Spooner.....25
Decanter.....60
Goblet.....30
Plate.....25
Pitcher.....70
Sugar.....30
Tray.....25
Tumbler.....10
Wine.....10
CHANDELIER
Banana Stand.....125
Bowl..... 40 - 75
Butter.....100
Cake Stand.....125
Castor Set, complete.....200
Celery Vase.....45
Compote, covered..... 95 - 125
Compote, open, 8" - 9½"..... 80 - 100
Creamer or Spooner.....60

Finger Bowl....40
Goblet....85
Inkwell, lettered & dated....135
Pitcher, 4 sizes....75 - 150
Salt, master....65
Sauce....35
Shakers, ea....65
Sugar....90
Sugar Shaker....120
Tumbler....50
Violet Bowl....40
Water Tray....90

CHATELAINE
Pitcher....175
Tumbler....40

CHECKERBOARD
Butter....60
ruby stain....80
Cake Plate....35
ruby stain....45
Celery Tray....25
ruby stain....35
Celery Vase....25
ruby stain....35
Compote, covered....45
ruby stain....60
Compote, open....30
ruby stain....40
Creamer....25
ruby stain....30
Goblet....35
ruby stain....45
Honey Dish....30
ruby stain....40
Pickle Dish....20
ruby stain....30
Pitcher....95
ruby stain....140
Spooner....25
ruby stain....35
Sugar....40
ruby stain....50
Tumbler....25
ruby stain....35
Wine....20
ruby stain....30

CHERRY
Berry Bowl, lg....55
Berry Bowl, sm....20
Bowls, novelty....20 - 45
Butter....70
Champagne....25
Compote, covered....60
Compote, open....35
Creamer or Spooner....25
Goblet....30
Plate....35
Sugar....40
Wine....25

CHERRY
Child's Mug....30

CHERRY (MILLERSBURG)
Jardiniere Whimsey, very rare
green/blue....2,200
Pitcher, very rare....1,300

CHERRY & CABLE
Berry Bowl, sm....25
Berry Bowl, lg....55
Butter....80
Compote....55
Creamer or Spooner....30
Pitcher....125
Punch Bowl, rare....300
Punch Cup, scarce....25
Sugar....35
Syrup....80
Tumbler....25

CHERRY & FIG
Berry Bowl, sm....15
Berry Bowl, lg....55
Butter....85
Celery Vase....20
Compote, covered....55
Compote, open....30
Creamer or Spooner....25
Goblet....60
Pickle Dish....20
Pitcher....110
Sugar....35
Tumbler....25
Wine....20

CHERRY CHAIN
Bowl, 6"
cobalt....85

CHERRY LATTICE
Berry Bowl, sm....25
Berry Bowl, lg....55
Butter....70
Compote....50
Creamer or Spooner....25
Pitcher....90
Sugar....30
Tumbler....20

CHERRY WITH THUMBPRINTS
Bean Pot, covered....45
Berry Bowl, sm....15
Berry Bowl, lg....35
Covered Bowls,
several sizes....20 - 50
Lemonade Tumbler....25
Mug....20
Pitcher....65
Sauce....15
Syrup....50
Toothpick Holder....30
Tumbler....15
Wine....20

CHICK & PUGS
Mug....55
amber....65
vaseline....75
green/blue....85

CHICKEN FOOT STEM
Goblet, rare....300

CHIPPENDALE
Butter....75
Creamer or Spooner....25
Goblet....50
Pickle Tray....25
Pitcher....95
Relish Dish....20
Shakers, ea....30
Sugar....35
Toothpick Holder....40
Tumbler....20

CHRYSANTHEMUM (#408)
Berry bowl, master....75
ruby stain....8
Berry bowl, individual....30
ruby stain....40
Butter....100
ruby stain....135
Cake Salver....85
ruby stain....115
Compote, open, 3 sizes....75 - 100
ruby stain....90 - 135
Compote, covered, 3 sizes....90 - 125
ruby stain....100 - 150
Cracker Jar....70
ruby stain....95
Creamer or Spooner....30
ruby stain....45
Goblet....45
ruby stain....60
Jelly compote....35
ruby stain....45
Pitcher....145
ruby stain....165
Salt dip, open....30
ruby stain....40
Shakers, ea....30
ruby stain....45
Sugar....40
ruby stain....65
Tumbler, stemmed....40
ruby stain....55

CHRYSANTHEMUM LEAF
Berry Bowl, sm....35
chocolate....75
Berry Bowl, lg....70
chocolate....300
Bowl, 7"....80
chocolate....350
Butter....90
chocolate....700
Carafe....70
chocolate....2,400
Celery....75
chocolate....1,300
Compote, 4½", open....60
chocolate....300
Cracker Jar....80
chocolate....3,700
Creamer or Spooner....75
chocolate....425
Cruet....90
chocolate....800
Pitcher....225
chocolate....4,200
Sauce....30
chocolate....125
Shakers, ea....65
chocolate....450
Sugar....75
chocolate....850
Syrup....125
chocolate....1,600
Toothpick Holder....100
chocolate....900
Tumbler....55
chocolate....375
Vase, 6"....65
chocolate....400

*Add 10% for crystal with gold trim.

CHRYSANTHEMUM SPRIG (PAGODA)
Berry Bowl, lg.
custard....195
Berry Bowl, sm.
custard....75
Butter
custard....250
Celery Vase
custard....165
Compote
custard....100
Condiment Set
custard....325
Creamer or Spooner
custard....125
Cruet
custard....225
Pitcher
custard....450
Sugar
custard....165
Toothpick Holder
custard....125
Tumbler
custard....95

CHURCH WINDOWS
Bowl....20
Butter....65
Cake Stand....40
Celery Vase....25
Creamer or Spooner....20
Goblet....35
Jelly Compote, covered....45

Pitcher...70
Sardine Dish...25
Sugar...25
*Add 10% for crystal with gold trim.

CIRCLE & SWAG
Bowls, various... 20 - 40
Butter...60
Celery...30
Creamer or Spooner...30
Milk Pitcher...45
Pickle Dish...25
Pitcher...70
Plate...30
Sugar...35
Syrup...50
Tumbler...20

CIRCULAR SAW
Berry Bowl, sm....15
Berry Bowl, lg....40
Breakfast Set...45
Butter...55
Creamer or Spooner...25
Cracker Jar...30
Pitcher...65
Punch Bowl...85
Punch Cup...15
Sauce...15
Shakers, ea....20
Sugar...30
Tumbler...20

CIVIL WAR TUMBLER
Tumbler, 4¾", scarce...75

CLAM SHELL
Candy Container Novelty...90

CLARK'S TEABERRY GUM
Advertising Tray...65
vaseline...115
Advertising Tray w/Cover, very scarce
vaseline...240

CLASSIC
Bowl, covered, 7"...150
Butter...275
Celery Vase, 2 styles...125
Compote w/Lid, 6½" - 12½"... 150 - 250
Compote, open, 7¾"...125
Creamer or Spooner,
2 styles... 125 - 150
Goblet...300
Marmalade Jar w/Lid...350
Milk Pitcher, ftd....350
Pitcher, 2 styles... 300 - 500
Plate, "Blaine"...400
Plate, "Cleveland"...400
Plate, "Hendricks"...325
Plate, "Logan"...350
Plate, "Warrior"...175
Sauce, flat or ftd....45
Sugar, 2 styles... 175 - 225
Sweetmeat...200

CLASSIC INTAGLIO
Salt Holders (either)
green/blue...150

CLASSIC MEDALLION
Bowls, flat or ftd., 6½"...45
Butter...95
Celery Vase...75
Compote, covered...175
Compote, open...80
Creamer or Spooner...40
Goblet...80
Pitcher...285
Sauce...15
Sugar...70

CLEAR DIAGONAL BAND
Berry Bowl, lg....35
Berry Bowl, sm....15
Butter...55
Celery Vase...30
Compote, high standard...70
Compote, low...50
Creamer, Spooner or Sugar...30
Goblet...30
Marmalade Jar...85
Pitcher...75
Platter...50
Shakers, ea....30
Tumbler...30
Wine...20

CLEAR LION HEAD
Berry Bowl, sm....30
Berry Bowl, lg....55
Butter...75
Cake Stand...45
Creamer or Spooner...35
Jam Jar...45
Pickle Dish...35
Sauce...25
Shakers, ea....35
Sugar...35
Toothpick Holder...50
Toy Table Set...150

CLEAR RIBBON
Bread Tray...45
Butter...75
Celery Vase...30
Compote...50
Creamer or Spooner...25
Goblet...40
Pickle Dish...20
Pitcher...100
Sauce...15
Sugar...40
Tumbler...25

CLEOPATRA (EGYPTIAN)
Tray, rectangular...95

CLEVELAND
Tumbler, very scarce...95

CLIO
Bowl, sauce, 2 sizes...20
Bowl, lg. fan corners...40
Bowl, sm. fan corners...25
Bowl, 7" & 8" ftd. w/cover... 65 - 75
Butter, 2 sizes... 50 - 70
vaseline... 115 - 145
Celery...35
Compote, 4½", open...30
Compote, 7" & 8", flat...50
Creamer,
spooner or sugar...25
Pitcher...90
vaseline...170
Plate, 7" & 10"...35
vaseline... 65 - 95

CLOVER (RICHARDS & HARTEY)
Berry Bowl, sm....15
Berry Bowl, lg....35
Butter...45
Creamer or Spooner...20
Pitcher...65
Sauce...10
Shakers, ea....20
Sugar...25
Tumbler...10

COACHMAN'S CAPE
Goblet...40
Wine...25

COAL BUCKET
Novelty Shape...40
ruby stain...65

COARSE CUT & BLOCK
Butter...50
Celery Dish...20
Creamer...25
Goble...25
Milk Pitcher...45
Pickle Dish...20
Pitcher...70
Spooner...25
Sugar...30

COARSE ZIG ZAG
Berry Bowl, sm....20
Berry Bowl, lg....45
Butter...65
Creamer or Spooner...25
Pitcher...70
Plate...30
Shakers, ea....25
Sugar...30
Tumbler...20
Wine...20

COIN & DEW DROP
Goblet...50

COIN SPOT
Compote
amethyst...90

COLONIAL LADY - #1700
Creamer or Sugar...35
Vase, 6" & 9"...45

COLONIAL STAIRSTEPS
Butter...55
Creamer or Spooner...20
Sugar...30
Toothpick Holder...25

COLONIS
Berry Bowl, sm....15
Berry Bowl, lg....35
Butter...65
Cake Stand...40
Celery Vase...30
Cordial...25
Creamer or Spooner...25
Egg Cup...20
Milk Pitcher...50
Oval Dish...20
Pickle Dish, 7"...20
Pitcher...80
Sugar...25
Syrup...70
Tray...30
Tumbler...20

COLORADO
Banana Dish...20
green/blue...50
Bowls, various sizes and shapes. 20 - 40
green/blue... 30 - 80
Butter...70
green/blue...175
Cheese Dish, ftd....35
green/blue...60
Compote, open, various... 25 - 60
green/blue...50 - 130
Creamer or Spooner...35
green/blue...75
Cup, engraved...25
green/blue...45
Milk Pitcher...100
green/blue...250
Perfume, rare...100
green/blue...165
Pitcher...100
green/blue...225 - 500
Shakers, pr. ftd....85
green/blue...175
Sugar...55
green/blue...80
Toothpick Holder...45
green/blue...65
Toy Table Set, complete...135
green/blue...225
Tumbler, flat...45
green/blue...60 - 100
Vase...45
green/blue...115
Violet Bowl...35
green/blue...55
Wine...20
green/blue...65

COLUMBIA
Compote....30
Plate, ftd....50
Vases, various shapes....25
COLUMBIA (AKA: NATIONAL)
Tray, Shield Shaped, very scare/rare....85
vaseline....165
COLUMBIA #100
Berry Bowl, sm....10
vaseline....15
ruby stain....15
Berry Bowl, lg....25
vaseline....35
ruby stain....45
Butter....60
vaseline....115
ruby stain....90
Celery Tray....20
vaseline....25
ruby stain....30
Celery Vase....25
vaseline....30
ruby stain....30
Compote....30
vaseline....40
ruby stain....45
Creamer or Spooner....30
vaseline....35
ruby stain....40
Cruet....60
vaseline....85
ruby stain....85
Jelly Compote....25
vaseline....35
ruby stain....45
Pitcher....80
vaseline....130
ruby stain....145
Plates, various....15 - 25
vaseline....20 - 40
ruby stain....25 - 50
Salt Dip....20
vaseline....25
ruby stain....30
Sugar....35
vaseline....45
ruby stain....50
Syrup....70
vaseline....95
ruby stain....100
Toothpick Holder....35
vaseline....65
ruby stain....55
Tumbler....15
vaseline....40
ruby stain....35
Vase....30
vaseline....50
ruby stain....45
*Amber stain priced same as ruby stain.
COLUMBIAN COIN (U.S. COIN)
Ale Glass....100
Bowl, covered, 3 sizes....200 - 325
Bowl, open, 3 sizes, 2 style rims....150 - 225
Butter....225
Cake Stand, rare....375
Celery Vase....165
Champagne....200
Compote, covered, 6" - 8"....225 - 300
Compote, open, 7" - 8"....175 - 275
Claret....125
Creamer or Spooner....80
Cruet....250
Epergne....650
Goblet....165
Lamp, many sizes and styles....250 - 400
Milk Pitcher....300
Mug, beer size....200
Pickle Dish....85
Pickle Jar w/Lid....95
Pitcher....285
Shakers, ea....85
Sugar....165
Syrup....500
Toothpick Holder....85
Water Tray....225
Waste Bowl....100
Wine....135
COLUMBIAN EXPOSITION TUMBLER
Tumbler, very rare....275
COLUMBIAN EXPOSITION WITH RING STEM
Goblet, very scarce....135
COLUMBUS
Mug, very scarce....125
Saucer, very scarce....125
COLUMBUS LANDING
Mug....65
COLUMN BLOCK (#500)
Butter....65
vaseline....110
Celery Vase....30
vaseline....60
Creamer or Spooner....35
vaseline....55
Jelly Compote....40
vaseline....60
Pickle Dish....30
vaseline....45
Pitcher....100
vaseline....165
Salt Shaker....45
vaseline....60
Sugar....45
vaseline....60
Toothpick Holder....50
vaseline....65
COLUMNED THUMBPRINTS
Berry Bowl, sm....10
Berry Bowl, lg....35
Butter....50
Celery Vase....20
Creamer or Spooner....20
Cruet....45
Cup....10
Pitcher....65
Shakers, ea....15
Sugar....25
Syrup....60
Toothpick Holder....20
Tumbler....10
COMET IN THE STARS
Berry Bowl, lg....35
Berry Bowl, sm....15
Bowl, oval....20
Bowl, sauce....15
Butter....45
Creamer, Spooner or Sugar....25
Pickle Dish....30
Pitcher....65
Relish, hndl....25
Tumbler....15
COMPLIMENTS - ST. LOUIS COFFIN CO.
Punch Bowl & Base, very scarce....225
CONNECTICUT
Basket, hndl....35
Biscuit Jar....30
Bowls, 5" - 8"....10 - 35
Butter....55
Celery Tray....15
Celery Vase....20
Compotes, covered....25 - 45
Compotes, open....20 - 35
Creamer or Spooner....15
Cruet....60
Dish, oblong or rnd....20
Goblet....30
Jam Jar....25
Lemonade Mug....20
Oil Lamp....75
Pitcher, 2 styles & sizes....65 - 85
Plate....20
Relish Tray....15
Sauce, flat or belled base....15
Shakers, 3 shapes, ea....20
Sherbet Cup....10
Sugar....25
Sugar Shaker....35
Toothpick Holder....20
Tumbler....20
Vase....20
Water Bottle....35
Wine....10
CONNIE
Pitcher, enameled....125
Tumbler, enameled....40
CONSOLIDATED SHELL
Rose Bowl
blue satin....90
CONSTITUTION PLATTER
Platter or Bread Plate....65
CONTINENTAL PLATTER ("GIVE US THIS DAY")
Platter, oval, 1776 - 1876....90
CO-OP COLUMBIA
Bowl, various....15 - 35
Butter....50
Creamer or Spooner....20
Goblet....40
Pickle Dish....15
Relish Tray....20
Shakers, ea....20
Sugar....25
Wine....15
CO-OP REX
Berry Bowl, sm....10
Berry Bowl, lg....35
Butter....55
Creamer or Spooner....15
Goblet....30
Pickle Dish....10
Pitcher....65
Sugar....20
Tumbler....10
CO-OP'S ROYAL
Bowls, various....15 - 35
ruby stain....25 - 55
Butter....55
ruby stain....70
Celery Vase....25
ruby stain....30
Creamer or Spooner....30
ruby stain....35
Goblet....40
ruby stain....50
Pickle Dish....20
ruby stain....30
Pitcher....80
ruby stain....115
Shakers, ea....25
ruby stain....30
Sugar....40
ruby stain....55
Toothpick Holder....45
ruby stain....60
Tumbler....20
ruby stain....25
Wine....20
ruby stain....30
CORAL GABLES
Butter....125
Cruet....75
Goblet....60
Wine....40
CORD DRAPERY
Bowls, oval or rnd....30 - 55
amber....50 - 150
green/blue....150 - 200
cobalt....150 - 250

Price Guide

Butter ... 70
  amber ... 150
  green/blue ... 250
  cobalt ... 400
Cake Stand ... 60
  amber ... 125
  green/blue ... 225
  cobalt ... 250
Celery, tall ... 150
Compote, covered, 3 sizes ... 25 - 55
  amber ... 35 - 90
  green/blue ... 250
  cobalt ... 350
Compote, open, 8½" ... 95
  amber ... 325
  green/blue ... 225
  cobalt ... 300
Compote, 10" ... 150
  vaseline ... 550
  cobalt ... 675
Creamer or Spooner ... 55
  amber ... 65
  green/blue ... 200
  cobalt ... 175
Cruet ... 165
  amber ... 275
  green/blue ... 600
  cobalt ... 725
Goblet ... 125
  amber ... 60
  green/blue ... 300
  cobalt ... 350
Mug ... 70
  amber ... 85
  green/blue ... 200
  cobalt ... 235
Pickle Dish ... 40
  amber ... 125
  green/blue ... 150
  cobalt ... 300
Pitcher ... 100
  amber ... 300
  green/blue ... 775
  cobalt ... 350
Sauce, flat or ftd ... 60
  amber ... 300
  vaseline ... 350
  green/blue ... 125
  cobalt ... 150
Shakers, ea ... 80
  amber ... 400
  green/blue ... 200
  cobalt ... 235
Sugar ... 90
  amber ... 135
  green/blue ... 225
  cobalt ... 250
Syrup ... 150
  amber ... 300
  green/blue ... 425
  cobalt ... 500
Toothpick Holder ... 135
  amber ... 450
  green/blue ... 500
  cobalt ... 450
Tumbler ... 85
  amber ... 200
  green/blue ... 200
  cobalt ... 200
Water Tray ... 65
  amber ... 100
  green/blue ... 125
Wine ... 95
  amber ... 300
  vaseline ... 400
  green/blue ... 250
  cobalt ... 300

*All listing in green/blue are for emerald green pieces.

CORNELL (TARENTUM GLASS CO.)
Butter ... 45
  green/blue ... 65
Cake Salver ... 30
  green/blue ... 45
Celery ... 25
  green/blue ... 35
Cordial ... 20
  green/blue ... 30
Creamer or Spooner ... 25
  green/blue ... 35
Cruet ... 40
  green/blue ... 55
Goblet ... 25
  green/blue ... 30
Jam Jar ... 30
  green/blue ... 35
Perfume ... 45
  green/blue ... 60
Pickle Castor ... 40
  green/blue ... 55
Pitcher ... 65
  green/blue ... 80
Plate, 2 sizes ... 20 - 30
  green/blue ... 30 - 40
Punch Bowl w/Base ... 95
  green/blue ... 150
Punch Cup ... 10
  green/blue ... 20
Rose Bowl ... 25
  green/blue ... 30
Shakers, ea ... 25
  green/blue ... 35
Sugar ... 35
  green/blue ... 45
Syrup ... 50
  green/blue ... 70
Tumbler ... 20
  green/blue ... 30
Whiskey ... 15
  green/blue ... 20
Wine ... 15
  green/blue ... 20

CORNER MEDALLION VARIANT
Butter ... 65
  amber ... 75
  vaseline ... 110
  green/blue ... 70
Cake Stand ... 50
  amber ... 60
  vaseline ... 80
  green/blue ... 55
Honey Dish, covered ... 55
  amber ... 65
  vaseline ... 90
  green/blue ... 60
Match Box, sq. ftd ... 40
  amber ... 50
  vaseline ... 75
  green/blue ... 45
Shaker ... 35
  amber ... 45
  vaseline ... 60
  green/blue ... 40

CORNFLOWER
Decanter ... 50
  green/blue ... 80
  ruby ... 85
Tankard Pitcher ... 95
  green/blue ... 130
  ruby ... 140
Tumbler ... 20
  green/blue ... 30
  ruby ... 50
Wine ... 15
  green/blue ... 25
  ruby ... 40

CORNUCOPIA (DALZELL, GILMORE & LEIGHTON)
Berry Bowl, sm. ... 20
Berry Bowl, lg. ... 50
Butter ... 75
Cake Stand ... 35
Celery Vase ... 20
Compote, covered ... 45
Cordial ... 20
Creamer or Spooner ... 25
Goblet ... 60
Lamps, various ... 55 - 90
Mug ... 30
Pitcher ... 85
Sugar ... 30
Tumbler ... 20
Wine ... 15

CORNUCOPIA CREAMER
Creamer ... 45

COSMOS
Butter ... 70
Condiment Set ... 95
Creamer or Spooner ... 20
Lamps, lg. or mini ... 65 - 100
Lemonade Set ... 125
Perfume ... 45
Pickle Castor ... 35
Pitcher ... 90
Shakers, ea ... 20
Sugar ... 30
Syrup ... 65
Trays ... 20 - 45
Tumbler ... 15

COSMOS (NORTHWOOD)
Bowl
  green/blue ... 55
  amethyst ... 65
Compote
  green/blue ... 90
  amethyst ... 110
Nappy
  green/blue ... 45
  amethyst ... 65
Plate
  green/blue ... 60
  amethyst ... 75

COSMOS & CANE
Basket, 2 hndl., rare ... 150
Berry Bowl, 4" ... 15
Bowl, square ... 55
Bowl, tricorner ... 65
Butter ... 125
Relish/Pickle Dish ... 30
Spooner ... 30
Sugar, w/lid ... 50

COSMOS VARIANT
Bowl ... 40
Plate, scarce ... 65

COTTAGE
Banana Stand ... 250
Berry Bowl, sm. ... 35
Berry Bowl, lg. ... 70
Bowl, oval, 2 styles ... 35 - 65
Butter, 2 styles, ftd. ... 65 - 85
Butter, w/dinner bell lid ... 275
Cake Stand, 9" & 10" ... 80
  cobalt ... 200
Celery Vase ... 50
Champagne ... 80
  ruby stain ... 85
Claret ... 70
Compote, w/lid, 6" - 8" ... 90 - 140
Compote, open, 4" - 7" ... 25 - 60
Compote, open, 8" - 10" ... 65 - 110
Creamer or Spooner ... 35
  ruby stain ... 55
Cruet ... 135
Cup ... 25
Finger Bowl ... 30
Fruit Bowl ... 70
Goblet ... 40
Milk Pitcher ... 60

Mug....35
Pickle Dish....25
Plate, 6" - 8".... 25 - 60
ruby stain....40
Plate, 9" - 10".... 65 - 85
Pitcher....90
Relish Tray....25
Sauce, flat or ftd....15
Salt, 2 styles.... 60 - 70
Sugar....65
Syrup....125
Tumbler....80
Waste Bowl....40
Water Tray....60
Wine....30

COUNTRY KITCHEN
Bowl, 5½"....20
Bowl, 6", flared....40
Bowl, 7", ice cream shape....85
Bowl, 8" - 9"....65
Bowl, 9" - 10", ftd., very scarce....225
Bowl, sq., rare....150
Bowl, pinched in whimsey, rare....275
Bowl, w/adv....300
Butter....175
Creamer or Spooner....75
Plate, 5"....75
Plate, 7"....95
Plate, 10"....90
Plate, 12"....100
Plate, w/adv....425
Rose Bowl, sm....150
Rose Bowl, med....200
Rose Bowl, lg....275
Rose Bowl, "S.I. Frank" adv....900
Sugar....150
*All pieces, scarce.
*Double price for pieces with lemon & ruby stained stars.

COUNTRY KITCHEN ADVERTISING PIECES
Bowl, very scarce....350
Plate, rare....425
*Various advertisings found

COUNTRY KITCHEN VARIANT
Bowl, rare....250

COVERED FROG
Novelty Frog dish....115
*Frosted, 10% less.

CRADLE
Novelty cradle
vaseline....150

CRADLED PRISMS
Butter....55
Creamer or Spooner....20
Goblet....35
Sugar....30

CRANESBILL
Berry Bowl, sm....20
Berry Bowl, lg....45
Butter....60
Creamer or Spooner....20
Pitcher....80
Sugar....30
Tumbler....20

CRATE
Paperweight....175

CRESTED HOBNAIL (WITH TWISTED HANDLE)
Mug....65

CROESUS
Bowl, covered, 7"....225
green/blue....275
amethyst....400
Bowl, open, 7" - 9".... 100 - 145
green/blue....100 - 160
amethyst....60 - 100
Butter....135
green/blue....180
amethyst....285
Cake Plate, 10"....150
green/blue....165
amethyst....275
Cake Stand....275
green/blue....350
amethyst....575
Celery Vase....200
green/blue....275
amethyst....375
Compote, covered, 5" - 7".... 100 - 180
green/blue....225 - 400
amethyst.... 425 - 600
Compote, open, 4" - 7".... 150 - 225
green/blue....225 - 425
amethyst....400 - 625
Condiment Tray....80
green/blue....95
amethyst....125
Creamer or Spooner....120
green/blue....165
amethyst....250
Creamer, ind....100
green/blue....135
amethyst....225
Cruet....200
green/blue....265
amethyst....425
Pitcher....275
green/blue....300
amethyst....450
Plate, ftd., 8"....90
green/blue....115
amethyst....180
Relish, boat shape....60
green/blue....75
amethyst....150
Sauce, flat or ftd....45
green/blue....50
amethyst....80
Shakers, ea....60
green/blue....85
amethyst....110
Sugar....135
green/blue....145
amethyst....175
Sugar, ind....165
green/blue....180
amethyst....225
Toothpick Holder....80
green/blue....95
amethyst....170
Tumbler....60
green/blue....80
amethyst....170

CROSS BANDS
Butter....55
Creamer or Spooner....20
Sugar....25

CROSS BAR & CANE
Butter....45
Creamer or Spooner....20
Shakers, ea....15
Sugar....25

CROSSED BLOCK
Bowl, oval....30
Butter....55
Creamer or Spooner....20
Goblet....35
Pickle Dish....20
Sugar....30

CROSSED DISCS
Butter....60
Celery Vase....25
Creamer....25
Egg Cup....30
Pickle Dish....20
Pitcher....75
Spooner....25
Sugar....35
Tumbler....20

CROSSED SHIELD
Berry Bowl, sm....10
Berry Bowl, lg....35
Butter....65
Compotes, 4 sizes.... 20 - 55
Cordial....15
Creamer or Spooner....20
Goblet....45
Pickle Dish....20
Pitcher....85
Sugar....25
Tumbler....15
Wine....10

CROSS IN DIAMONDS
Bowls, various.... 10 - 35
Butter....55
Compote....30
Creamer or Spooner....20
Pitcher....75
Sugar....30
Tray....25
Tumbler....15

CROWN SALT
Individual Salt Dip....20

CRUCIFIX
Candlesticks, ea....60

CRYSTAL QUEEN (NORTHWOOD)
*Condensed list.
Basket, hndl....55
Berry Bowl, sm....20
Berry Bowl, lg....55
Butter....100
Celery Vase....40
Compotes, 2 sizes.... 45 - 70
Creamer or Spooner....30
Milk Pitcher....80
Pickle Dish....30
Pitcher....150
Sugar....40
Tumbler....35
Vase....30

CRYSTAL ROCK
Berry Bowl, sm....20
Berry Bowl, lg....45
Butter....55
Creamer or Spooner....20
Pitcher....65
Sugar....25
Tumbler....10

CRYSTAL STAR
Auto Vase, ea.
vaseline....50

CRYSTAL WEDDING
Banana Stand....175
ruby stain....450
Berry Bowl, 8" sq....100
ruby stain....175
Berry Bowl, 4½" sq....75
ruby stain....115
Berry Bowl, covered, 6" - 7"....165
ruby stain....225
Bowl, Sauce 4"....35
ruby stain....45
Butter....185
ruby stain....300
Cake Plate, flat or ftd.... 175 - 300
ruby stain....250 - 425
Celery....95
ruby stain....145
Claret....300
ruby stain....425
Compote, ftd., 3 sizes, covered. 135 - 225
ruby stain....200 - 300
Compote, flat, 3 sizes, open.... 90 - 140
ruby stain....100 - 165
Creamer or Spooner....80
ruby stain....140
Cruet, rare....255
ruby stain....775

Goblet 80
ruby stain 155
Oil Lamp various sizes .... 400 - 550
Milk Pitcher, 2 styles .... 185 - 230
ruby stain .... 350 - 425
Pitcher, 2 styles .... 300 - 350
ruby stain .... 475 - 525
Pickle Dish 50
ruby stain 60
Salt Dip, 2 sizes .... 60 - 90
ruby stain .... 95 - 135
Shaker, sq., ea. 100
ruby stain 200
Sugar w/lid 95
ruby stain 160
Syrup 400
ruby stain 1,225
Tumbler 70
ruby stain 125
Vase, 2 styles .... 225 - 300
Wine 165
ruby stain 275
*Add 10% for frosted pieces.

CRYSTOLITE
Spittoon 55

CUPID & VENUS
Bowls, 6" - 8" .... 90 - 125
Bread Plate 45
amber 125
vaseline 225
Butter 200
Cake Stand 135
Celery Vase 65
Compote, covered, low or high ... 125 - 200
Compote, open, low or high .... 90 - 120
amber 175
Cordial 95
Creamer or Spooner 65
Cruet 1,500
Goblet 100
Jam Jar 120
Milk Pitcher 80
amber 190
Mug, 3 sizes .... 50 - 70
Pickle Castor 175
Pitcher 100
amber 265
Relish 200
Sauce, flat or ftd. 30
Sugar 125
Wine 95

CUPID COMPOTE
Compote, 8½" 400

CUPID RIDING LION
Bread Plate 150

CUPIDS (NORTHWOOD)
Bowl 30
Plate 40
*Add 25% for goofus treatment.

CUPIDS HUNT (AKA: CUPIDS)
Bowl, scarce 150
Bread Plate 85
Compote, various .... 65 - 140
Relish 45
Sherbet 35

CURLED LEAF
Mug 40
vaseline 65
amethyst 65
Pitcher 80
vaseline 140
amethyst 145

CURRANT
Bowl, 2 sizes .... 40 - 50
Butter 100
Cake Stand, 3 sizes .... 100 - 165
Celery Vase 95
Compote, high, 8" - 12" .... 125 - 400
Compote, low 8" 100
Cordial 65
Creamer or Spooner 80
Egg Cup 50
Goblet 50
Jam Jar w/Lid 110
Milk Pitcher 200
Pitcher 225
Plate, oval, 2 sizes .... 40 - 50
Relish Dish 25
Salt, ftd. 45
Sauce, various .... 15 - 30
Sugar 95
Tumbler, ftd. 60
Wine 50

CURRIER & IVES
Bowl, oval, 10" 50
Butter 135
Cake Stand 140
Compote, covered, 7½" 165
Compote, open, 7½" 75
Creamer or Spooner 60
Cup & Saucer 60
Decanter 70
Dish, oval, 8" 40
Goblet 40
Lamp, various sizes .... 90 - 165
Milk Pitcher 80
Pitcher 65
vaseline 325
Plate, 10" 35
Relish 30
Salt, open 30
Sauce 60
Shakers, ea 55
Sugar 90
Syrup 135
Tray, Balky Mule 65
vaseline 140
Tumbler 65
Water Bottle 80
Wine 20
*Add 75% for any colors.

CURTAIN (AKA: SULTAN)
Bowls, covered .... 45 - 90
Bowls, open .... 30 - 50
Butter 70
Cake Stand .... 70 - 110
Castor Set, complete 200
Celery Vase 35
Compote,
covered 4 sizes .... 70 - 130
Compote, open 4 sizes .... 40 - 80
Creamer 50
Cruet 75
Milk Pitcher 95
Plate, sq. 35
Pitcher 125
Spooner 35
Sugar 60
Tumbler 35
Waste Bowl 30

CURTAIN TIE-BACK
Bowls, sq. .... 20 - 35
Butter 70
Celery Tray 30
Celery Vase 50
Compote, covered 100
Creamer or Spooner 45
Goblet, 2 styles .... 40 - 45
Pickle Dish 20
Plate 20
Pitcher 70
Relish 15
Sauce, flat or ftd. 10
Shakers, ea 40
Sugar 50
Tumbler 40
Water Tray 90
Wine 25

CURTAIN TIE-BACK ORNAMENT
Curtain Tie-back, each 45
amber 65
vaseline 125
green/blue 80
ebony 75

CURVED STAR
Bowls, various .... 10 - 35
Butter 50
Cake Stand 35
Celery Vase 25
red 75
Compote, sm. 30
Epergne, 3 part 100
Rose Bowl 30
Vase 25

CUT BLOCK (HEISEY)
Breakfast Set, 2 pcs. 85
ruby stain 115
Butter 70
ruby stain 95
Celery Vase 30
ruby stain 40
Creamer or Spooner 35
ruby stain 50
Cruet 90
ruby stain 125
Pickle Dish 30
ruby stain 40
Sugar 45
ruby stain 60
Syrup 75
ruby stain 90

CUT LOG
Banana Stand, very rare 450
Biscuit Jar 100
Bowl, 7" - 10" .... 35 - 60
Butter 125
Cake Stand, 2 sizes .... 150 - 200
Celery Tray 40
Celery Vase 70
Compote, 5½" & 7½", w/lid .... 100 - 165
Compote, 7", 8" &10", open .... 50 - 95
Creamer or Spooner 65
Goblet 80
Honey Dish 375
Jam Jar 200
Mug 40
Mustard Jar 130
Nappy 30
Olive Dish 30
Pitcher, 2 styles .... 110 - 140
Relish Dish 25
Salt Dip, lg. 120
Sauce, flat or ftd. .... 35 - 45
Shakers, ea 75
Sugar, 2 sizes .... 80 - 110
Tumbler 75
Vase, various .... 90 - 130
Wine 30
Novelty Candy Container 125

DAGGER
Compote, covered, 2 sizes .... 100 - 140
amber .... 120 - 145
vaseline .... 195 - 230
green/blue .... 165 - 210
Compote, open 60
amber 65
vaseline 80
green/blue 80
Cordial 70
amber 90
vaseline 120
green/blue 100
Creamer or Spooner 40
amber 45
vaseline 45
green/blue 40
Egg Cup, double 90

amber 100
vaseline 160
green/blue 130
Egg Cup, single 35
amber 40
vaseline 60
green/blue 50
Goblet 60
amber 65
vaseline 100
green/blue 90
Jam Jar 200
amber 225
vaseline 320
green/blue 280
Milk Pitcher 60
amber 70
vaseline 100
green/blue 110
Mug, 2 sizes .... 30 - 60
amber .... 60 - 70
vaseline .... 70 - 80
green/blue .... 50 - 65
Pickle Dish 20
amber 30
vaseline 40
green/blue 35
Pitcher, 2 styles .... 70 - 130
amber .... 80 - 140
vaseline .... 130 - 225
green/blue .... 125 - 175
Plate, dinner 25
amber 35
vaseline 50
green/blue 45
Platter, 2 styles hndls. 40
amber 50
vaseline 55
green/blue 45
Relish 15
amber 25
vaseline 30
green/blue 25
Salt Dip, ind. 30
amber 40
vaseline 50
green/blue 40
Sauce, flat or ftd. 10
amber 20
vaseline 25
green/blue 20
Sugar 60
amber 60
vaseline 100
green/blue 80
Syrup 85
amber 110
vaseline 165
green/blue 125
Wine 30
amber 45
vaseline 75
green/blue 55

DAHLIA (BRYCE)
Bowl, oval 25
amber 40
vaseline 40
green/blue 35
Bread Plate 20
amber 60
vaseline 60
green/blue 50
Butter 50
amber 100
vaseline 165
green/blue 110
Cake Stands .... 70 - 90
amber .... 80 - 100
vaseline .... 125 - 180
green/blue .... 110 - 140

DAHLIA (GOOFUS PATTERN)
Bowls,
various sizes .... 25 - 45
Plate, 11" 50

DAISY & BLUEBELL
Bowls, various .... 50 - 75
Butter 95
Cake Stand 70
Celery Vase 40
Creamer 35
Goblet 50
Pickle Dish 40
Pitcher 140
Spooner 40
Sugar 55
Tumbler 30
Wine 25

DAISY & BUTTON (HOBBS)
Bride's Basket 50
vaseline 115
Bowl 30
amber 40
vaseline 45
green/blue 45
Bread Plate 25
amber 40
vaseline 50
green/blue 50
Butter, 2 styles .... 55 - 110
amber .... 75 - 130
vaseline .... 95 - 165
green/blue .... 80 - 135
Butter Pat 30
amber 40
vaseline 45
green/blue 45
Canoe, 4" - 14" .... 10 - 35
amber .... 25 - 75
vaseline .... 45 - 110
green/blue .... 35 - 95
Castor Set, 4 bottle 75
amber 90
vaseline 135
green/blue 95
Castor Set, 5 bottle 110
amber 125
vaseline 180
green/blue 125
Celery, shoe shape 30
amber 50
vaseline 80
green/blue 65
Compote, covered 35
amber 50
vaseline 145
green/blue 110
Compote, open 55
amber 80
vaseline 100
green/blue 90
Creamer or Spooner 30
amber 40
vaseline 45
green/blue 40
Cruet 55
amber 125
vaseline 135
green/blue 125
Egg Cup 20
amber 25
vaseline 30
green/blue 25
Finger Bowl 25
amber 30
vaseline 35
green/blue 30
Goblet 35
amber 45
vaseline 60
green/blue 45
Hat 20
amber 30
vaseline 35
green/blue 30
Ice Cream Tray 40
amber 80
vaseline 90
green/blue 85
Ice Tub 40
vaseline 85
green/blue 80
Inkwell 30
amber 40
vaseline 45
green/blue 40
Parfait 20
amber 25
vaseline 30
green/blue 25
Pickle Castor 65
amber 130
vaseline 165
green/blue 150
Pitcher, 2 styles .... 60 - 85
amber .... 70 - 130
vaseline .... 100 - 195
green/blue .... 85 - 145
Plate, leaf shape 20
amber 35
vaseline 75
green/blue 55
Plate, rnd. or sq. 15
amber 20
vaseline 25
green/blue 20
Punch Bowl w/Base 115
amber 175
vaseline 325
green/blue 225
Sauce 10
amber 15
vaseline 20
green/blue 15
Shakers, ea. 25
amber 30
vaseline 50
green/blue 35
Shoe, 2 sizes .... 35 - 50
amber .... 40 - 55
vaseline .... 45 - 60
green/blue .... 40 - 50
Sugar 45
amber 55
vaseline 60
green/blue 55
Syrup 40
amber 70
vaseline 110
green/blue 60
Toothpick, 2 styles .... 20 - 50
amber .... 25 - 60
vaseline .... 45 - 80
green/blue .... 30 - 65
Tray 30
amber 75
vaseline 95
green/blue 80
Tumbler 20
amber 25
vaseline 45
green/blue 30
Vase (wall pocket) 125
amber 145
Wine 15
amber 25
vaseline 40
green/blue 30

Price Guide

DAISY & BUTTON ADVERTISING SHOE
- Slipper ... 90

DAISY & BUTTON SLIPPER (GEO. DUNCAN)
- Slipper ... 90
  - vaseline ... 125

DAISY & BUTTON TRIANGLE
- Butter ... 45
- Creamer or Spooner ... 20
- Goblet ... 35
- Salt Dip ... 25
- Sauce ... 15
- Sugar ... 25

DAISY & BUTTON VARIANT
- Butter ... 200

DAISY & BUTTON WHEELBARROW
- Novelty ... 185
  - vaseline ... 265

DAISY & BUTTON W/CROSSBARS
- Bowl, 7" - 9" ... 30
  - amber ... 40
  - vaseline ... 45
  - green/blue ... 40
- Bowl, oval, 6" - 9" ... 30
  - amber ... 35
  - vaseline ... 45
  - green/blue ... 40
- Butter, flat ... 60
  - amber ... 60
  - vaseline ... 90
  - green/blue ... 80
- Butter, pedestal ftd. ... 70
  - amber ... 70
  - vaseline ... 100
  - green/blue ... 90
- Celery Vase ... 40
  - amber ... 50
  - vaseline ... 70
  - green/blue ... 60
- Compote, covered, high or low ... 70 - 90
  - amber ... 70 - 105
  - vaseline ... 100 - 135
  - green/blue ... 90 - 120
- Compote, open, high or low ... 40 - 55
  - amber ... 45 - 60
  - vaseline ... 6 0 - 75
  - green/blue ... 50 - 60
- Cordial ... 25
  - amber ... 35
  - vaseline ... 55
  - green/blue ... 45
- Creamer or Spooner ... 35
  - amber ... 40
  - vaseline ... 50
  - green/blue ... 45
- Cruet ... 60
  - amber ... 70
  - vaseline ... 140
  - green/blue ... 120
- Finger Bowl ... 30
  - amber ... 35
  - vaseline ... 50
  - green/blue ... 45
- Goblet ... 35
  - amber ... 40
  - vaseline ... 65
  - green/blue ... 55
- Ketchup Bottle ... 70
  - amber ... 80
  - vaseline ... 135
  - green/blue ... 120
- Milk Pitcher ... 45
  - amber ... 60
  - vaseline ... 85
  - green/blue ... 70
- Mug, 2 sizes ... 35 - 35
  - amber ... 25 - 35
  - vaseline ... 30 - 50
  - green/blue ... 30 - 40
- Oil Lamp, 4 sizes ... 150 - 250
  - amber ... 150 - 225
  - vaseline ... 165 - 265
  - green/blue ... 155 - 250
- Pickle Dish ... 15
  - amber ... 20
  - vaseline ... 25
  - green/blue ... 30
- Pickle Jar ... 85
  - amber ... 100
  - vaseline ... 165
  - green/blue ... 140
- Pitcher ... 60
  - amber ... 65
  - vaseline ... 100
  - green/blue ... 85
- Plate ... 30
  - amber ... 35
  - vaseline ... 50
  - green/blue ... 45
- Sauce, flat or ftd. ... 15
  - amber ... 20
  - vaseline ... 20
  - green/blue ... 25
- Shakers, ea. ... 30
  - amber ... 35
  - vaseline ... 45
  - green/blue ... 40
- Sugar ... 35
  - amber ... 40
  - vaseline ... 55
  - green/blue ... 45
- Syrup ... 100
  - amber ... 135
  - vaseline ... 180
  - green/blue ... 160
- Toothpick Holder ... 25
  - amber ... 50
  - vaseline ... 65
  - green/blue ... 70
- Tumbler ... 25
  - amber ... 30
  - vaseline ... 45
  - green/blue ... 40
- Waste Bowl ... 25
  - amber ... 35
  - vaseline ... 40
  - green/blue ... 35
- Water Tray ... 45
  - amber ... 50
  - vaseline ... 65
  - green/blue ... 55
- Wine ... 20
  - amber ... 25
  - vaseline ... 40
  - green/blue ... 30

DAISY & BUTTON W/NARCISSUS
- Bowl, oval ... 50
- Butter ... 70
- Celery Vase ... 30
- Compote ... 45
- Creamer or Spooner ... 35
- Decanter ... 80
  - ruby stain ... 75
- Fruit Bowl, ftd. ... 45
- Goblet ... 40
- Milk Pitcher ... 70
- Pitcher ... 85
  - ruby stain ... 110
- Shaker, ea. ... 25
- Sugar ... 50
  - ruby stain ... 50
- Tray ... 30
  - ruby stain ... 45
- Tumbler ... 20
- Wine ... 15
  - ruby stain ... 25

DAISY & BUTTON W/SHELLS
- Sauce, 5" ... 25

DAISY & BUTTON W/THUMBPRINT PANEL
- Bowl, heart shaped, 7" ... 25
  - amber ... 35
  - vaseline ... 50
  - green/blue ... 40
  - ruby stain ... 30
- Bowl, sq., covered ... 60 - 80
  - amber ... 70 - 90
  - vaseline ... 100 - 130
  - green/blue ... 80 - 100
  - ruby stain ... 100 - 165
- Bowl, sq., open ... 30 - 50
  - amber ... 35 - 55
  - vaseline ... 50 - 75
  - green/blue ... 40 - 65
  - ruby stain ... 60 - 85
- Butter ... 60
  - amber ... 70
  - vaseline ... 85
  - green/blue ... 70
  - ruby stain ... 120
- Cake Stand ... 80
  - amber ... 90
  - vaseline ... 140
  - green/blue ... 100
  - ruby stain ... 200
- Celery Vase ... 40
  - amber ... 40
  - vaseline ... 60
  - green/blue ... 50
  - ruby stain ... 90
- Compote, open, 6" - 8" ... 80 - 100
  - amber ... 100 - 120
  - vaseline ... 110 - 180
  - green/blue ... 100 - 140
  - ruby stain ... 145 - 200
- Creamer or Spooner ... 35
  - amber ... 40
  - vaseline ... 50
  - green/blue ... 45
  - ruby stain ... 65
- Cruet ... 60
  - amber ... 75
  - vaseline ... 125
  - green/blue ... 90
  - ruby stain ... 200
- Goblet ... 35
  - amber ... 40
  - vaseline ... 50
  - green/blue ... 45
  - ruby stain ... 80
- Lamp ... 100
  - amber ... 135
  - vaseline ... 175
  - green/blue ... 160
  - ruby stain ... 275
- Mug ... 25
  - amber ... 30
  - vaseline ... 40
  - green/blue ... 40
  - ruby stain ... 60
- Pitcher ... 90
  - amber ... 100
  - vaseline ... 125
  - green/blue ... 115
  - ruby stain ... 235
- Sauce, ftd. ... 10
  - amber ... 15
  - vaseline ... 20
  - green/blue ... 20
  - ruby stain ... 45
- Sugar ... 40
  - amber ... 50
  - vaseline ... 60
  - green/blue ... 55
  - ruby stain ... 65
- Syrup ... 90
  - amber ... 100
  - vaseline ... 165

green/blue 145
ruby stain 325
Tumbler 25
amber 25
vaseline 40
green/blue 35
ruby stain 70
Wine 15
amber 20
vaseline 35
green/blue 25
ruby stain 60

DAISY & BUTTON W/ V ORNAMENT
Bowls, various sizes and shapes . 25 - 60
amber .... 30 - 70
vaseline .... 45 - 100
green/blue .... 40 - 85
Butter 65
amber 65
vaseline 125
green/blue 85
Celery Vase 25
amber 40
vaseline 60
green/blue 45
Creamer or Spooner 20
amber 30
vaseline 50
green/blue 40
Finger Bowl 20
amber 35
vaseline 60
green/blue 45
Goblet 30
amber 45
vaseline 65
green/blue 55
Match Holder 35
amber 35
vaseline 45
green/blue 40
Milk Pitcher 45
amber 65
vaseline 90
green/blue 70
Mug, 4 sizes .... 25 - 35
amber .... 30 - 35
vaseline .... 35 - 50
green/blue .... 35 - 45
Pickle Jar 80
amber 90
vaseline 135
green/blue 120
Pitcher 60
amber 70
vaseline 125
green/blue 100
Plate, 4 sizes .... 10 - 35
amber .... 15 - 45
vaseline .... 25 - 50
green/blue .... 20 - 50
Sauce 15
amber 25
vaseline 25
green/blue 30
Shade, gas 50
amber 60
vaseline 125
green/blue 90
Sherbet 20
amber 35
vaseline 40
green/blue 30
Sugar 45
amber 50
vaseline 60
green/blue 55
Toothpick Holder 25
amber 35
vaseline 60
green/blue 40
Tumbler 30
amber 30
vaseline 60
green/blue 50
Water Tray 60
amber 70
vaseline 120
green/blue 75

DAISY & PLUME (DUGAN)
Bowl, various shapes 30
Rose Bowl 40

DAISY & PLUME (NORTHWOOD)
Bowl, ftd., scarce 55
Compote, stemmed, rare 65
Rose Bowl, stemmed, rare 75
Rose Bowl, ftd., scarce 60

DAISY & SCROLL
Berry Bowl, sm. 15
Berry Bowl, lg. 35
Butter 60
Creamer or Spooner 25
Pitcher 65
Shakers, ea. 25
Sugar 30
Syrup 55
Tumbler 20

DAISY & TREE LIMB
Bowl, sm. sauce
amber 45
Tray, 14" - 9½"
amber 95
milk glass 80

DAISY & X-BAND
Berry Bowl, lg. 40
Berry Bowl, sm. 20
Butter 50
Celery, hndl. 35
Compote, low w/lid 55
Creamer, Spooner, or Sugar 30
Goblet 30
Jelly, hndl. 30
Pitcher 75
Rose Bowl, 8" 40
Sherbet 20
Sweetmeat 45
Tumbler 20
Vase, 10", 12" & 14" .... 25 - 50

DAISY BAND
Cup & Saucer 55
amber 80
green/blue 90

DAISY BANDED CRYSTAL WEDDING
Compote, covered, scarce 150
Compote, open, scarce 65

DAISY-IN-SQUARE
Berry Bowl, sm. 10
Berry Bowl, lg. 35
Butter 45
Celery Vase 15
Creamer or Spooner 15
Milk Pitcher 45
Oil Bottle 60
Pickle Tray 15
Pitcher 65
Sauce 10
Shakers, ea. 15
Sugar 20
Syrup 40
Tumbler 10
Vase 20
*Etched pieces add 25%.

DAISY MEDALLION
Berry Bowl, sm. 20
Berry Bowl, lg. 45
Butter 60
Cake Stand 40
Compote 35
Creamer or Spooner 25
Goblet 40
Pitcher 80
Sugar 30
Tumbler 20

DAISY PLEAT
Mug 45

DAKOTA ....
Berry Bowl, lg. 90
ruby stain 250
Bottle, Cologne, rare 90
ruby stain 275
Bottle, pepper sauce, rare 125
Butter, 2 sizes .... 40 - 50
ruby stain .... 135 - 170
Cake Basket, w/metal hndl., rare 250
Cake Stand, tall dome, 8" - 10", rare . 500 - 800
Cake Stand, tall dome, 15",
very rare 900
Cake Stand, reg., 8" - 10½" .... 90 - 165
ruby stain .... 275 - 325
Celery Vase .... 30 - 45
ruby stain 85
Compote, covered, 5" - 9" .... 80 - 100
ruby stain .... 200 - 300
Compote, open, 5" - 9" .... 40 - 55
ruby stain 125
Creamer or Spooner, 2 sizes 65
ruby stain 200
Cruet 135
ruby stain 325
Cruet Undertray 125
Goblet 30
ruby stain 70
Honey Dish 20
ruby stain 40
Milk Pitcher, 2 styles .... 90 - 130
ruby stain .... 150 - 325
Mug 200
Pitcher, 2 styles 90
ruby stain 165
Sauce, flat or ftd. 30
ruby stain 45
Shakers, ea. 100
Sugar 80
ruby stain 130
Tray, 3 sizes .... 100 - 225
Tumbler 30
ruby stain 60
Waste Bowl 40
ruby stain 100
Wine 40
ruby stain 45
*Add 25% for etched pieces.

DALTON
Breakfast Set,
2 pcs. 65
Butter 70
Creamer or Spooner 30
Cup 10
Goblet 35
Pitcher 70
Plate, 10½" 25
Rose Bowl, miniature 30
Sugar 35
Toothpick Holder 30
Tumbler 15

DALZELL'S COLUMBIA
Butter 95
Compote, covered 70
Compote, open 50
Creamer 30
Spooner 35
Sugar 45

DALZELL SQUIRREL
Pitcher, rare 950
Plate, rare 350

DALZELL SWAN
Pitcher, very rare 1,650

DANDELION (FOSTORIA)
- Berry Bowl, sm. ... 15
- Berry Bowl, lg. ... 40
- Toothpick Holder ... 25

DART & BALL
- Bowl ... 30

DARWIN
- Match Holder ... 145
  - amber ... 200

DAVIDSON TULIP VASE
- Stemmed Vase ... 50
  - vaseline ... 85

DEEP CUT
- Bowl ... 35
- Plate ... 45

DEER ALERT
- Pitcher ... 375
- Tumbler ... 100

DEER & COW
- Mug ... 65
  - green/blue ... 65
  - milk glass ... 55

DEER & DOE WITH LILY OF THE VALLEY
- Goblet ... 150

DEER & DOG
- Butter ... 200
- Celery Vase, signed and unsigned. 100 - 160
- Champagne ... 200
- Compote, covered, high, 7" - 8" . 250 - 325
- Compote, covered, low, 7" - 8" . 400 - 425
- Cordial ... 265
- Creamer or Spooner ... 100
- Goblet, 2 styles ... 100 - 120
- Marmalade Jar ... 475
- Pitcher ... 345
- Plate, dog center ... 85
- Sauce, flat or ftd. ... 40
- Sugar ... 150
- Wine ... 125

DEER & OAK TREE
- Butter ... 145
  - vaseline ... 175
- Creamer or Spooner ... 90
  - vaseline ... 100 - 125
- Pickle Dish ... 25
  - vaseline ... 40
- Plate, Bread ... 60
  - vaseline ... 95
- Platter, oblong ... 85
  - vaseline ... 150
- Mug ... 70
  - vaseline ... 100
  - chocolate ... 2,500
- Pitcher ... 425
  - chocolate ... 800
- Sugar ... 85
  - vaseline ... 125

DEER & PINE TREE
- Bowl, waste ... 100
- Butter ... 250
  - amber ... 325
  - green/blue ... 375
- Cake Stand ... 200
- Celery Vase ... 165
- Compote, covered, 7" - 9" ... 200 - 300
- Creamer or Spooner ... 100
  - amber ... 165
  - green/blue ... 150
- Dish, oblong, 3 sizes ... 60 - 90
- Goblet ... 100
- Marmalade Jar ... 300
- Milk Pitcher ... 200
- Mug, 2 sizes ... 50 - 70
  - amber ... 60 - 85
  - green/blue ... 80 - 100
- Pickle Dish ... 40
  - green/blue ... 75
- Plate, bread size, oblong ... 55
  - amber ... 275
  - green/blue ... 350
- Pitcher ... 185
- Sauce ... 30 - 40
- Sugar ... 135
- Tray ... 300
  - amber ... 135
  - green/blue ... 140

DELAWARE
- Banana Bowl ... 40
  - green/blue ... 70
  - ruby stain ... 90
- Basket, silver hldr., 2 sizes ... 60 - 90
  - green/blue ... 80 - 120
  - ruby stain ... 130 - 165
- Berry Bowl, sm. ... 25
  - green/blue ... 45
  - ruby stain ... 50
- Berry Bowl, lg. ... 35
  - green/blue ... 60
  - ruby stain ... 80
- Butter ... 65
  - green/blue ... 90
  - ruby stain ... 115
- Celery Vase ... 40
  - green/blue ... 75
  - ruby stain ... 90
- Claret Jug ... 40
  - green/blue ... 125
  - ruby stain ... 185
- Creamer or Spooner ... 30
  - green/blue ... 50
  - ruby stain ... 70
- Cruet ... 90
  - green/blue ... 225
  - ruby stain ... 350
- Cup ... 15
  - green/blue ... 30
  - ruby stain ... 50
- Finger Bowl ... 20
  - green/blue ... 40
  - ruby stain ... 50
- Pin Tray ... 40
  - green/blue ... 60
  - ruby stain ... 80
- Pitcher, squat ... 65
  - green/blue ... 120
  - ruby stain ... 135
- Pitcher, tankard ... 110
  - green/blue ... 175
  - ruby stain ... 200
- Pomade Box ... 155
  - green/blue ... 250
  - ruby stain ... 400
- Puff Box ... 150
  - green/blue ... 250
  - ruby stain ... 400
- Sauce, oval or rnd. ... 20
  - green/blue ... 30
  - ruby stain ... 40
- Shade, electric ... 60
  - green/blue ... 75
  - ruby stain ... 90
- Shade, gas ... 60
  - green/blue ... 75
  - ruby stain ... 90
- Shakers, ea., rare ... 160
  - green/blue ... 245
  - ruby stain ... 350
- Toothpick Holder ... 40
  - green/blue ... 100
  - ruby stain ... 150
- Tumbler ... 40
  - green/blue ... 50
  - ruby stain ... 60
- Vase, 6" - 9½" ... 35
  - green/blue ... 65
  - ruby stain ... 95

*Prices in ruby stained are for rose stained.
*All other colors, rare to v. rare, add 100%.

DELOS
- Butter ... 125
- Cake Plate ... 75
- Compote ... 65
- Creamer ... 45
- Goblet ... 60
- Pickle Dish ... 35
- Spooner ... 50
- Sugar ... 65

DELTA
- Pitcher ... 90
- Syrup ... 70
- Tumbler ... 20

DENVER FURNITURE & CARPET CO.
- Tray, oval ... 70

DERBY
- Berry Bowl, lg. ... 35
  - vaseline ... 60
- Berry Bowl, sm. ... 10
  - vaseline ... 30
- Bowls, sq. or octagon ... 25
  - vaseline ... 40
- Breakfast Set ... 45
  - vaseline ... 65
- Butter ... 75
  - vaseline ... 165
- Compote, covered, 3 sizes ... 40 - 80
  - vaseline ... 90 - 165
- Compote, open, 2 sizes ... 30 - 65
  - vaseline ... 65 - 120
- Creamer or Spooner ... 25
  - vaseline ... 45
- Cruet ... 80
  - vaseline ... 120
- Individual Creamer or Sugar, ea. ... 30
  - vaseline ... 50
- Jelly Compote ... 35
  - vaseline ... 60
- Pickle Dish ... 15
  - vaseline ... 30
- Pitcher ... 115
  - vaseline ... 185
- Sugar ... 35
  - vaseline ... 60
- Tumbler ... 15
  - vaseline ... 30
- Water Goblet ... 40
  - vaseline ... 65
- Wine Goblet ... 30
  - vaseline ... 40

DEW & RAINDROP
- Berry Bowl, sm. ... 15
- Berry Bowl, lg. ... 40
- Butter ... 75
- Creamer or Spooner ... 35
- Goblet ... 50
- Mug ... 20
- Pitcher ... 90
- Sauce ... 20
- Shakers, ea ... 40
- Sherbet ... 20
- Sugar ... 55
- Tumbler ... 40
- Wine ... 20

DEWBERRY
- Pitcher ... 85

DEWDROP
- Butter ... 50
- Cake Tray, hndl. ... 35
- Castor Set ... 75
- Creamer or Spooner ... 20
- Goblet ... 20
  - vaseline ... 45
- Shakers, ea ... 20
- Sherbet ... 15
- Sugar ... 25
- Sugar Shaker ... 35
- Tumbler ... 20
  - vaseline ... 40

Wine ...15
DEWDROP (RIVERSIDE)
Berry Bowl, sm. ...30
Berry Bowl, lg ...65
Butter ...125
Cake Salver ...75
Celery Vase ...50
Compote, open, 3 sizes ... 50 – 85
Compote, covered, 3 sizes ... 65 – 110
Creamer or Spooner ...45
Cruet ...90
Finger Bowl ...40
Goblet ...60
Plate, large ...70
Pitcher, 2 style handles ...165
Shakers, ea ...55
Sugar ...55
Syrup ...100
Water Tray ...70
DEWDROP IN POINTS
Bread Plate ...25
Butter ...65
Compote, covered ...70
Compote, open ...45
Creamer or Spooner ...20
Goblet ...40
Pickle Dish ...15
Pitcher ...120
Plate ...20
Sauce ...10
Sugar ...50
Wine ...25
DEWDROPS & FLOWERS
Butter ...70
Cake Stand ...45
Creamer ...35
Pitcher ...95
Spooner ...40
Sugar ...45
Tumbler ...20
DEWDROP WITH STAR
Butter ...50
Cake Stand ...60
Cheese Dish ...35
Compote w/Lid, high, 2 sizes ...65
Compote w/Lid, low, 2 sizes ...55
Creamer, Spooner or Sugar ...30
Lamp ...115
Pickle Dish ...30
Pitcher ...135
Plates, from 4½" – 11" ... 20 – 40
Sauce ...15
Sugar ...50
DEWEY (BEATTY-BRADY)
Berry Bowl, lg ...70
amber ... 60
vaseline ... 135
green/blue ...65
chocolate ... 225
Berry Bowl, sm. ...30
amber ... 35
vaseline ... 35
green/blue ...30
chocolate ... 65
Breakfast Set, 2 pcs. ...85
amber ... 80
vaseline ... 150
green/blue ...125
Butter, 4" ...60
amber ... 125
vaseline ... 165
green/blue ...135
chocolate ... 250
Butter, 5" ...80
amber ... 135
vaseline ... 150
green/blue ...165
chocolate ... 900
Creamer (4") or Spooner ...45
amber ... 75
vaseline ... 65
green/blue ...80
chocolate ... 150
Creamer, 5" ...60
amber ... 75
vaseline ... 125
green/blue ...100
chocolate ... 500
Cruet ...200
amber ... 225
vaseline ... 300
green/blue ...500
Nile green ... 950
Mug ...50
amber ... 60
vaseline ... 95
green/blue ...75
Nile green ... 200
Parfait Glass ...100
amber ... 40
vaseline ... 80
green/blue ...60
chocolate ... 165
Pitcher, very scarce ...100
amber ... 130
vaseline ... 165
green/blue ...175
Plate ...30
amber ... 45
vaseline ... 70
green/blue ...60
Sauce ...20
amber ... 25
vaseline ... 30
green/blue ...25
chocolate ... 75
Shakers, ea ...75
amber ... 95
vaseline ... 120
green/blue ...85
chocolate ... 900
Sugar ...45
amber ... 70
vaseline ... 80
green/blue ...90
chocolate ... 125
Tray, serpentine, 2 sizes ... 30 – 55
amber ... 35 – 60
vaseline ... 70 – 95
green/blue ... 60 – 80
chocolate ... 850 – 2,000
Tumbler ...50
amber ... 70
vaseline ... 100
green/blue ...80
emerald green ... 55
DEWEY BUST (AKA: GRIDLEY)
Paperweight ...250
DIAGONAL BAND
Bowl ...35
amber ...40
green/blue ...50
Bread Plate ...30
amber ...35
green/blue ...40
Butter ...55
amber ...70
green/blue ...95
Cake Stand ...80
amber ...110
green/blue ...150
Compotes, various ... 40 – 65
amber ... 50 – 80
green/blue ...60 – 120
Creamer or Spooner ...40
amber ...35
green/blue ...45
Goblet ...35
amber ...40
green/blue ...50
Milk Pitcher ...60
amber ... 80
green/blue ...100
Pitcher ...50
amber ...70
green/blue ...95
Plate ...30
amber ...35
green/blue ...50
Relish ...20
amber ...20
green/blue ...30
Sauce ...10
amber ...20
green/blue ...25
Sugar ...40
amber ...45
green/blue ...60
DIAGONAL BAND WITH FAN
Bowls, various ... 20 – 50
Butter ...75
Cake Salver ...55
Celery Vase ...35
Champagne ...25
Compote ...65
Cordial ...30
Creamer or Spooner ...30
Cruet ...60
Finger Bowl ...30
Goblet ...40
Plate ...40
Pitcher ...80
Shakers, ea ...30
Sugar ...25
Syrup ...70
Wine ...25
DIAMOND
Berry Bowl, sm. ...10
Berry Bowl, lg ...35
Butter ...70
Compote ...35
Creamer or Spooner ...20
Goblet ...45
Pickle Dish ...15
Pitcher ...80
Sugar ...30
Tumbler ...15
Vase ...25
Wine ...15
DIAMOND & FAN (MILLERSBURG)
Bowl, rare ...300
DIAMOND & SUNBURST (IMPERIAL)
Decanter w/Stopper ...65
Goblet ...40
Wine ...15
DIAMOND & SUNBURST (PORTLAND)
Butter ...50
Celery Vase ...25
Creamer or Spooner ...25
Pickle Dish ...15
Sugar ...40
Wine ...20
DIAMOND & SUNBURST
(U.S. GLASS)
Bowl, sq. ...25
Butter ...55
Celery Vase ...25
Creamer or Spooner ...30
Goblet ...35
Pickle Dish ...20
Pitcher ...80
Shakers, ea ...25
Sugar ...45
Tumbler ...15
Wine ...15
DIAMONDBACK
Vase, rare ...200

DIAMOND BAND
- Bowl, shallow ... 20
- Butter ... 50
- Celery Vase ... 35
- Compote, ftd., sm. ... 40
- Creamer, Spooner or Sugar ... 25
- Goblet ... 30
- Pitcher ... 70
- Tumbler ... 20
- Wine ... 30

*Gilded pieces add 10%.

DIAMOND BAND (INDIANA'S #169)
- Berry Bowl, sm. ... 15
- Berry Bowl, lg. ... 25
- Butter ... 50
- Creamer ... 25
- Pitcher ... 65
- Spooner ... 25
- Sugar ... 30
- Tumbler ... 15

DIAMOND BLOCK
- Candlestick, ea. ... 35
- Compote ... 45
- Cylinder Vase ... 35
- Juice Tumbler ... 20
- Milk Pitcher ... 60
- Pedestal Vase ... 40
- Rose Bowl ... 35

DIAMOND BRIDGES
- Berry Bowl, sm. ... 20
- Berry Bowl, lg. ... 50
- Butter ... 80
- Compotes ... 30 - 55
- Goblet ... 40
- Pickle Dish ... 15
- Pickle Jar ... 35
- Pitcher ... 90
- Sugar ... 30
- Tumbler ... 20
- Wine ... 15

DIAMOND CUT WITH LEAF
- Bowl, 8½" ... 40
  - amber ... 50
  - vaseline ... 80
  - green/blue ... 75
- Butter ... 60
  - amber ... 80
  - vaseline ... 100
  - green/blue ... 90
- Creamer or Spooner ... 40
  - amber ... 50
  - vaseline ... 70
  - green/blue ... 60
- Egg Cup ... 20
  - amber ... 30
  - vaseline ... 60
  - green/blue ... 45
- Goblet ... 35
  - amber ... 50
  - vaseline ... 75
  - green/blue ... 60
- Milk Pitcher ... 80
  - amber ... 90
  - vaseline ... 135
  - green/blue ... 120
- Mug ... 90
  - amber ... 100
  - vaseline ... 145
  - green/blue ... 130
- Pitcher ... 100
  - amber ... 120
  - vaseline ... 165
  - green/blue ... 140
- Platter ... 25
  - amber ... 30
  - vaseline ... 40
  - green/blue ... 35
- Shakers, ea. ... 60
  - amber ... 80
  - vaseline ... 100
  - green/blue ... 90
- Sugar ... 50
  - amber ... 60
  - vaseline ... 85
  - green/blue ... 75
- Tumbler ... 30
  - amber ... 40
  - vaseline ... 70
  - green/blue ... 60
- Wine ... 20
  - amber ... 25
  - vaseline ... 35
  - green/blue ... 30

DIAMOND IN DIAMOND
- Bowls ... 10 - 40
- Butter ... 65
- Compotes ... 20 - 55
- Creamer or Spooner ... 20
- Goblet ... 35
- Pickle Dish ... 15
- Pitcher ... 75
- Sugar ... 25
- Toothpick Holder ... 20
- Tumbler ... 15
- Wine ... 10

DIAMOND LACE
- Berry Bowl, sm. ... 15
- Berry Bowl, lg. ... 25
- Pitcher ... 125
- Tumbler ... 35
  - amethyst ... 100

DIAMOND POINT (NORTHWOOD)
- Vase, 7" - 12" ... 25 - 55

DIAMOND POINT COLUMNS
- Bowl ... 20
- Vase ... 35

DIAMOND POINT DISC
- Berry Bowl, sm. ... 15
- Berry Bowl, lg. ... 45
- Butter ... 80
- Cake Stand ... 45
- Compote ... 35
- Creamer or Spooner ... 25
- Salt, ind. ... 20
- Shakers, ea. ... 30
- Sugar ... 40

DIAMOND POINT LOOP
- Berry Bowl ... 25
  - amber ... 30
  - vaseline ... 40
  - green/blue ... 35
- Butter ... 55
  - amber ... 60
  - vaseline ... 85
  - green/blue ... 80
- Celery Dish ... 20
  - amber ... 25
  - vaseline ... 30
  - green/blue ... 30
- Celery Vase ... 25
  - amber ... 30
  - vaseline ... 35
  - green/blue ... 35
- Creamer or Spooner ... 25
  - amber ... 30
  - vaseline ... 40
  - green/blue ... 40
- Goblet ... 30
  - amber ... 35
  - vaseline ... 50
  - green/blue ... 45
- Pickle Dish ... 20
  - amber ... 25
  - vaseline ... 30
  - green/blue ... 30
- Plate, sq. ... 25
  - amber ... 30
  - vaseline ... 35
  - green/blue ... 35
- Sugar ... 35
  - amber ... 40
  - vaseline ... 60
  - green/blue ... 55

DIAMOND POINT WITH CANNONBALLS
- Butter ... 85
- Creamer or Spooner ... 30
- Pitcher ... 95
- Sugar ... 35
- Tumbler ... 20

DIAMOND POINTS
- Banana Bowl, rare ... 300
- Basket, 2 hndl., scarce ... 250
- Bowl, lg., round, scarce ... 150
- Rose Bowl, very scarce ... 375

DIAMOND POINTS VARIANT (YORK)
- Rose Bowl, scarce ... 85

DIAMOND QUILTED
- Bowls, oval or rnd. ... 10 - 40
  - amber ... 15 - 45
  - vaseline ... 20 - 55
  - green/blue ... 25 - 60
- Butter ... 50
  - amber ... 90
  - vaseline ... 165
  - green/blue ... 115
- Celery Vase ... 20
  - amber ... 70
  - vaseline ... 90
  - green/blue ... 65
- Champagne ... 15
  - amber ... 40
  - vaseline ... 70
  - green/blue ... 35
- Compote, covered, high or low... 50 - 60
  - amber ... 100 - 165
  - vaseline ... 250 - 325
  - green/blue ... 130 - 180
- Cordial ... 15
  - amber ... 30
  - vaseline ... 50
  - green/blue ... 40
- Creamer or Spooner ... 35
  - amber ... 60
  - vaseline ... 85
  - green/blue ... 65
- Goblet ... 30
  - amber ... 45
  - vaseline ... 60
  - green/blue ... 45
- Mug ... 25
  - amber ... 35
  - vaseline ... 50
  - green/blue ... 40
- Pitcher ... 60
  - amber ... 90
  - vaseline ... 200
  - green/blue ... 145
- Salt Dip, ind. & master ... 20 - 25
  - amber ... 25 - 30
  - vaseline ... 30 - 35
  - green/blue ... 35 - 40
- Sauce, flat or ftd. ... 15
  - amber ... 20
  - vaseline ... 25
  - green/blue ... 30
- Strawberry Plate, 10½" ... 65
  - amber ... 70
  - vaseline ... 100
  - green/blue ... 110
- Sugar ... 45
  - amber ... 50
  - vaseline ... 65
  - green/blue ... 75
- Tumbler ... 20
  - amber ... 40
  - vaseline ... 50

green/blue 35
Vase, 9" 30
amber 35
vaseline 45
green/blue 50
Water Tray, 2 shapes .... 25 - 35
amber .... 60 - 70
vaseline .... 80 - 90
green/blue .... 50 - 65
Wine 20
amber 25
vaseline 40
green/blue 35
*For other colors add 50% to amber prices.

DIAMONDS (MILLERSBURG)
Hat, from tumbler, very rare
green/blue 750
Punch Bowl, rare 600
Punch Base, rare 225
Tumbler 100
amethyst 425

DIAMONDS & CLUBS
Pitcher 135
Tumbler 25
Wine 15
Wine Decanter 85

DIAMOND SPEARHEAD
Berry Bowl, sm. 10
Berry Bowl, lg. 35
Butter 65
Celery Vase 20
Compote, tall 45
Creamer, 2 sizes .... 15 - 25
Goblet 40
Jelly Compote 30
Mug 25
Pitcher 85
Relish Tray 30
green/blue 135
Rose Bowl 25
Shakers, ea. 15
Spooner 25
Sugar 40
Sugar Shaker 50
Syrup 55
Toothpick Holder 35
Tumbler 20
Water bottle 45

DIAMOND STRAWBERRY (FOSTORIA #402)
Pitcher 95
Tumbler 25

DIAMOND SUNBURST
Bowl 40
Butter 55
Cake Stand 50
Celery Vase 35
Compote w/Lid 75
Decanter 65
Egg Cup 25
Lamp 75
Oval Platter 40
Pickle Dish 30
Pitcher 65
Sauce 15
Tumbler 20
Wine 15

DIAMOND SWAG
Banana Compote 45
Cracker Jar 40
Creamer or Spooner 20
Cruet 65
Jelly Compote 30
Jelly, tri-cornered 35
Pitcher 80
Relish 20
Spoon Tray 25
Sugar 25
Sugar Shaker 45
Syrup 75
Tumbler 20
Wine 20
Vase 30

DIAMOND SWIRL
Butter 45
Creamer or Spooner 20
Pitcher 75
Shakers, ea. 20
Sugar 25
Syrup 50
Toothpick Holder 20
Tumbler 15

DIAMOND THUMBPRINT
Ale Glass 90
Bitters Bottle 450
Butter 200
Celery Vase 185
Champagne 250
Compote, covered 250
Cordial 300
Decanter 175
Egg Cup 85
Finger Bowl 120
Goblet 300
Honey Dish 35
Milk Pitcher 450
Mug 200
Pitcher 500
Sauce 10
Sugar 25
Sweetmeat Jar,
covered 95
Tray, 7" x 11" 30
Tumbler 125
Whiskey Tumbler 125
Wine 250

DIAMONDS WITH DOUBLE FANS
Bowls, various .... 20 - 40
ruby stain .... 35 - 60
Butter 65
ruby stain 100
Cake Salver 40
ruby stain 75
Celery Vase 30
ruby stain 55
Compote 45
ruby stain 60
Creamer or Spooner 30
ruby stain 40
Cruet 60
ruby stain 85
Finger Bowl 25
ruby stain 35
Goblet 40
ruby stain 65
Pitcher 65
ruby stain 140
Plate 35
ruby stain 50
Shakers, ea. 25
ruby stain 60
Sugar 35
ruby stain 70
Syrup 50
ruby stain 125

DIAMOND WITH CIRCLE
Mug 30
amber 45
green/blue 55

DIAMOND WITH DIAMOND POINT
Butter 55
Celery Vase 20
Compote 35
Creamer or Spooner 20
Cup 15
Nappy 20
Pitcher 70
Shakers, ea. 20
Sugar 25
Tumbler 20

DIAMOND WITH FAN
Berry Bowl, lg. 40
Berry Bowl, sm. 15
Pitcher 65
Tumbler 20

DIAMOND WITH PEG
Berry Bowl, sm. 15
Berry Bowl, lg. 40
Butter 65
Celery Vase 20
Creamer or Spooner 20
Pickle Dish 15
Pitcher 90
Shakers, ea. 15
Sugar 30
Toothpick Holder 25
Tumbler 20

DICE
Paperweight 150

DIRIGO PEAR
Relish Dish, 2 sizes .... 75 - 100

DIVIDED HEARTS
Butter 65
Compote 40
Creamer or Spooner 25
Egg Cup 25
Goblet 30
Lamp 95
Pitcher 80
Salt 20
Sugar 30
Tumbler 15

DOG
Plate, 6" 50
amber 60
green/blue 70

DOG CART
Plate, scarce 85

DOG CART WITH APE LID
Toothpick Holder, very rare 325

DOG CHASING CAT (DAVIDSON)
Creamer 40
opaque white 65
Sugar 60
opaque white 85

DOG CHASING DEER
Mug 50
amber 70
green/blue 90
milk glass 60

DOG HUNTING
Pitcher, very scarce 325

DOG PLATE
Plate, rare 125

DOG'S HEAD ABC
Plate 150

DOG VASE (DAISY & BUTTON)
One Shape, rare 150

DOG WITH COLLAR
Mug 45
amethyst 65
Mug, without collar 60
amethyst 75

DOG WITH PAIL
Match Holder 70

DOG WITH RABBIT IN HOLE
Pitcher 225

DOLPHIN (HOBBS BROCKUNIER)
Bowls, covered, 7" & 8" .... 350 - 400
Butter 395
Celery Vase 125
Compote, open, 8" & 9" .... 175 - 200
Compote, covered, 8" & 9" .... 245 - 260
Creamer or Spooner 150
Pickle Jar w/Lid 350
Pitcher 550
Salt, master 65
Sugar 375

Price Guide

DOLPHIN (GILLINDER & SONS)
- Bowl
  - vaseline ... 175
- Compote, 1 piece ... 95
  - amber ... 250
  - vaseline ... 350
  - green/blue ... 190

DOLPHIN & HERONS
- Vase, very rare ... 550

DOLPHIN CANDLESTICKS
- Candlesticks, ea. ... 85
  - vaseline ... 150

DOLPHIN MATCH HOLDER
- Match Holder ... 30
  - amber ... 45
  - vaseline ... 75
  - green/blue ... 50

DOLPHIN MUSTARD
- Novelty w/lid, beaded or smooth rim ... 200
  - amber ... 600
  - green/blue ... 450
  - chocolate ... 400

DOT
- Berry Bowl, sq., sm. ... 10
- Berry Bowl, sq., lg. ... 30
- Butter ... 40
- Creamer or Spooner ... 20
- Relish ... 20
- Sugar ... 25

DOUBLE BEETLE BAND
- Butter ... 90
- Celery Vase ... 20
- Creamer or Spooner ... 25
- Goblet ... 60
- Pickle Dish ... 20
- Pitcher ... 125
- Sauce, flat or ftd. ... 10
- Sugar ... 35
- Tumbler ... 20
- Wine ... 15

DOUBLE CROSSROADS
- Bowls, various ... 20 - 40
- Butter ... 65
- Cake Salver ... 40
- Celery Vase ... 30
- Compote ... 45
- Creamer or Spooner ... 30
- Cruet ... 60
- Finger Bowl ... 25
- Goblet ... 40
- Plate ... 35
- Pitcher ... 65
- Shakers, ea ... 25
- Sugar ... 35
- Syrup ... 50

*For vaseline add 50%.
*For all other colors add 25%.

DOUBLE PINWHEEL
- Berry Bowl, sm. ... 15
- Berry Bowl, lg. ... 40
- Bowl, 7" ... 25
- Butter ... 60
- Compote ... 35
- Compote, covered ... 95
- Creamer or Spooner ... 25
- Pickle Dish ... 20
- Pitcher ... 75
- Shakers, ea ... 20
- Sugar ... 25
- Tumbler ... 20

DOUBLE RELISH (CAMPBELL, JONES)
- Double Relish ... 70

DOUBLE RIBBON
- Bread Plate ... 20
- Butter ... 65
- Compote, covered ... 50
- Compote, open ... 40
- Creamer or Spooner ... 25
- Egg Cup ... 20
- Pickle Dish ... 25
- Pitcher ... 80
- Sauce, ftd. ... 25
- Shakers, ea ... 25
- Sugar ... 30
- Tumbler ... 25

DOUBLE SPEAR
- Butter ... 45
- Celery Vase ... 20
- Compote ... 35
- Creamer or Spooner ... 20
- Goblet ... 40
- Pickle Dish ... 20
- Relish ... 20
- Sauce ... 10
- Sugar ... 30

DOUBLE VINE
- Plate ... 45

DOUGLASS
- Berry Bowl, sm. ... 20
  - ruby stain ... 30
- Berry Bowl, lg. ... 45
  - ruby stain ... 55
- Butter, 2 styles ... 60 - 75
  - ruby stain ... 75 - 100
- Creamer or Spooner ... 25
  - ruby stain ... 35
- Finger Bowl, sq. ... 30
  - ruby stain ... 45
- Pitcher ... 85
  - ruby stain ... 145
- Punch Bowl ... 110
  - ruby stain ... 225
- Punch Cup ... 15
  - ruby stain ... 25
- Shakers, ea ... 25
  - ruby stain ... 40
- Sugar ... 30
  - ruby stain ... 70
- Toothpick Holder ... 35
  - ruby stain ... 45
- Tumbler ... 25
  - ruby stain ... 35

DOVE (CANTON)
- Card Stand ... 80
  - amber ... 95
  - green/blue ... 135
- Vase ... 65
  - amber ... 75
  - green/blue ... 125

DOYLE'S COMET
- Bowls, various ... 15 - 35
  - amber ... 25 - 45
  - vaseline ... 50 - 70
- Butter ... 70
  - amber ... 90
  - vaseline ... 145
- Celery Vase ... 25
  - amber ... 35
  - vaseline ... 50
- Creamer or Spooner ... 25
  - amber ... 35
  - vaseline ... 50
- Goblet ... 45
  - amber ... 55
  - vaseline ... 70
- Pickle Dish ... 15
  - amber ... 25
  - vaseline ... 50
- Pitcher ... 85
  - amber ... 100
  - vaseline ... 165
- Sugar ... 35
  - amber ... 45
  - vaseline ... 65
- Tumbler ... 20
  - amber ... 30
  - vaseline ... 45
- Wine ... 15
  - amber ... 25
  - vaseline ... 40

DOYLE'S SHELL
- Butter ... 45
  - amber ... 55
  - green/blue ... 65
  - ruby stain ... 60
- Celery Vase ... 20
  - amber ... 35
  - green/blue ... 45
  - ruby stain ... 40
- Creamer or Spooner ... 25
  - amber ... 35
  - green/blue ... 45
  - ruby stain ... 40
- Mug ... 30
  - amber ... 40
  - green/blue ... 55
  - ruby stain ... 50
- Pickle Dish ... 20
  - amber ... 25
  - green/blue ... 35
  - ruby stain ... 30
- Sugar ... 30
  - amber ... 35
  - green/blue ... 45
  - ruby stain ... 40
- Water Tray ... 40
  - amber ... 45
  - green/blue ... 55
  - ruby stain ... 50
- Waste Bowl ... 30
  - amber ... 35
  - green/blue ... 40
  - ruby stain ... 35
- Wine ... 25
  - amber ... 30
  - green/blue ... 35
  - ruby stain ... 30

DRAGON
- Butter ... 300
- Compote, sm. ... 85
- Creamer or Spooner ... 65
- Goblet ... 100
- Plate ... 60
- Sugar, open ... 55

*All pieces rare.

DRAGON & LOTUS
- Bowl, rare ... 300
  - red ... 400
- Plate, rare
  - red ... 550

DRAPE
- Mug ... 40

DRAPERY
- Butter ... 70
- Compote, covered ... 90
- Creamer ... 50
- Egg Cup ... 30
- Goblet ... 40
- Oval Dish ... 30
- Pitcher ... 180
- Plate ... 35
- Sauce ... 15
- Spooner ... 40
- Sugar ... 60
- Tumbler ... 40

DRAPERY VARIANT (NORTHWOOD)
- Vase, rare
  - green/blue ... 100

DRUM
- Child's Table Set ... 85
  - green/blue ... 145
- Mug, 3 sizes ... 20 - 40
  - green/blue ... 30 - 60

DRUM & EAGLE
- Child's Mug ... 35

DUCHESS
- Pitcher ... 125

Tumbler 35
DUGAN'S HONEYCOMB
Bowl
green/blue 40
amethyst 55
Nut Bowl
green/blue 50
amethyst 65
Rose Bowl
green/blue 65
amethyst 75
DUNCAN #13
Mug 40
Tumbler's .... 10 - 30
DUNCAN #98
Berry Bowl, lg 30
amber 35
vaseline 55
green/blue 40
Berry Bowl, sm. 15
amber 20
vaseline 25
green/blue 20
Bowl w/Underplate 55
amber 65
vaseline 75
green/blue 60
Jelly Set 40
amber 50
vaseline 70
green/blue 60
Creamer 20
amber 25
vaseline 40
green/blue 35
Sugar 30
amber 40
vaseline 55
green/blue 40
DUNCAN #904
Bowls, various .... 10 - 35
Butter 70
Creamer or Spooner 20
Cup 10
Goblet 45
Pitcher 85
Sugar 30
Tumbler 20
DUNCAN HOBNAIL SLIPPER
Slipper, one shape 25
amber 35
vaseline 45
green/blue 35
DUNCAN HOMESTEAD (#63)
Berry Bowl, sm. 10
Berry Bowl, lg. 35
Bowls, various .... 10 - 50
Butter 65
Celery Vase 20
Compotes .... 25 - 50
Creamer or Spooner 20
Creamer, ind. 15
Cruet 50
Finger Bowl 20
Punch Bowl 125
Punch Cup 10
Salt, ind. 15
Shakers, ea., 2 styles .... 35 - 45
Sugar 35
Sugar, ind. 20
Syrup 55
Toothpick Holder 30
Vases, various sizes .... 15 - 40
DUNCAN'S CLOVER (#58)
Butter 40
Creamer, Spooner or Sugar 20
Finger Bowl 25
Pitcher 70
Toothpick Holder 35

Tumbler 20
Wine 20
DUTCH MILL
Mug 35
green/blue 55
amethyst 65
EARLY PANELLED GRAPE BAND
Butter 70
Celery Vase 20
Creamer or Spooner 25
Egg Cup 20
Goblet 50
Pickle Dish 20
Relish 20
Salt, open 15
Sugar 30
EASTER GREETINGS CHICK
Child's Plate 40
EDGEWOOD
Butter 50
Carafe 65
Creamer, Spooner or Sugar 30
Cup 20
Shakers, ea. 25
Sherbet 25
Syrup 60
Toothpick Holder 35
EGG IN SAND
Bread Tray 50
Butter 65
Cake Stand 95
Creamer or Spooner 40
Dish, swan center 55
Goblet 40
Jam Jar 80
Jelly Compote, covered 75
Milk Pitcher 60
Pitcher 75
Platter, rectangular 60
Relish 30
Sauce 10
Shakers, ea. 45
Sugar 60
Tumbler 40
Water Tray 55
Wine 30
EGYPTIAN
Bowl, covered and open .... 90 - 200
Bread Plate, Cleopatra 95
Bread Plate, temple 475
Butter 225
Celery Vase 100
Compote, covered, 2 sizes .... 300 - 340
Compote, open, 5" 95
Creamer or Spooner 60
Goblet, 2 styles .... 70 - 100
Honey Dish 30
Pickle Dish 30
Pitcher 325
Plate, 3 sizes .... 50 - 80
Plate, pyramid handles, 12" 275
Relish Dish 30
Sauce 20
Sugar 180
EIGHT-O-EIGHT
*Condensed list.
Berry Bowl, sm. 20
amber 25
green/blue 30
Berry Bowl, lg. 35
amber 40
green/blue 50
Butter 55
amber 65
green/blue 80
Celery 35
amber 40
green/blue 50
Compote, 3 sizes, various shapes .. 40 - 55

amber .... 45 - 60
green/blue .... 55 - 70
Creamer 35
amber 40
green/blue 50
Goblet 35
amber 40
green/blue 50
Jelly Compote 30
amber 35
green/blue 45
Milk Pitcher 45
amber 55
green/blue 60
Pitcher, 2 sizes .... 60 - 75
amber .... 65 - 80
green/blue .... 80 - 100
Rose Bowl 40
amber 60
green/blue 70
Shakers, ea. 25
amber 30
green/blue 35
Spooner 35
amber 40
green/blue 45
Sugar 40
amber 45
green/blue 50
Toothpick Holder 30
amber 35
green/blue 40
Tumbler 20
amber 30
green/blue 40
Water Bottle 45
amber 55
green/blue 65
Wine 20
amber 25
green/blue 30
Vases, various sizes .... 20 - 40
amber .... 25 - 45
green/blue .... 30 - 50
*For cobalt add 300% to highest prices listed.
EIGHT POINT
Goblet 45
ELDORADO
Berry Bowl, sm. 10
Berry Bowl, lg. 35
Butter 50
Creamer or Spooner 20
Goblet 35
Sugar 25
Sauce 10
Shakers, ea. 20
Sugar 25
Toothpick Holder 25
ELECTRIC
Bread Plate 30
green/blue 45
ruby stain 40
Butter 60
green/blue 85
ruby stain 75
Cracker Jar 45
green/blue 65
ruby stain 60
Creamer or Spooner 30
green/blue 45
ruby stain 40
Pickle Dish 25
green/blue 35
ruby stain 30
Relish 25
green/blue 30
ruby stain 25
Salt Shaker 40
green/blue 55

ruby stain 50
Sauce 20
green/blue 25
ruby stain 20
Sugar 35
green/blue 50
ruby stain 40
Toothpick 30
green/blue 45
ruby stain 30
*All pieces in green are emerald green.
ELEPHANT (KING)
Wall Pocket Vase, rare 350
amber 750
ELEPHANT HEAD
Toothpick Novelty 150
amber 185
green/blue 225
milk glass 200
ELLIPSES
Berry Bowl, sm. 15
cranberry 20
Berry Bowl, lg. 30
cranberry 35
Butter 55
cranberry 70
Creamer 25
cranberry 35
Goblet 35
cranberry 45
Pitcher 75
cranberry 95
Spooner 25
cranberry 35
Sugar 35
cranberry 45
Tumbler 20
cranberry 30
Wine 25
cranberry 35
ELSON DEWDROP #90
Berry Bowl, sm. 15
Berry Bowl, lg. 35
Breakfast Set, 2 pcs. 45
Butter 65
Celery Vase 30
Creamer or Spooner 20
Pitcher 80
Tumbler 20
Sugar 25
ELSON DEWDROP VARIANT
Creamer 25
Pitcher 90
Sugar 30
EMPRESS
Berry Bowl, lg. 70
green/blue 100
Berry Bowl, sm. 50
green/blue 75
Breakfast Set, 2 pcs. 140
green/blue 235
Butter 90
green/blue 145
Cake Stand 165
green/blue 295
Celery Vase 150
green/blue 275
Compote, covered, 3 sizes .... 175 - 250
green/blue .... 275 - 400
Compote, open, 4 sizes .... 150 - 235
green/blue .... 225 - 300
Creamer or Spooner 45
green/blue 80
Cruet 125
green/blue 235
Jelly Compote 65
green/blue 100
Lamps, 5 sizes .... 100 - 150
green/blue .... 200 - 265
Mustard Pot 160
green/blue 255
Pickle 40
green/blue 55
Pitcher 185
green/blue 265
Pitcher, ftd. 225
green/blue 285
Plate, 2 sizes .... 35 - 55
green/blue .... 50 - 80
Salts, master & ind. .... 70 - 90
green/blue .... 100 - 160
Shakers, ea. 45
green/blue 75
Sugar 70
green/blue 120
Sugar Shaker 60
green/blue 130
Syrup 200
green/blue 380
Toothpick Holder 100
green/blue 195
Tray 55
green/blue 85
Tumbler 35
green/blue 45
ENCHANTMENT
Compote, 8", rare 425
ENGLISH COLONIAL
*Condensed list
Berry Bowl, sm. 10
Berry Bowl, lg. 35
Butter 50
Claret 10
Compote 30
Cordial 20
Creamer or Spooner 20
Cruet 45
Decanter 50
Jelly Compote 25
Pitcher 65
Plate 20
Punch Bowl 75
Punch Cup 10
Relish 15
Sauce 10
Shakers, ea. 20
Sugar 25
Syrup 60
Toothpick Holder 25
Tumbler 15
ENGLISH DAISY & BUTTON
Bowl, Dome-based 80
ENGLISH DIAMOND & SHELL
Compote
pink slag 350
ENGLISH OVAL
Candlesticks, ea. 85
vaseline 200
ESSEX
Bowls, various .... 10 - 35
Butter 55
Celery Vase 25
Champagne 15
Claret 15
Creamer or Spooner 20
Cup 10
Sauce 15
Sugar 25
Sugar Shaker 35
Sundae Dish 20
Syrup 65
Toothpick Holder 25
Wine 15
ESTHER
Berry Bowl, sm. 65
green/blue 95
ruby stain 120
Berry Bowl, lg. 60
green/blue 90
ruby stain 100
Butter 90
green/blue 120
ruby stain 155
Cake Stand 95
green/blue 150
ruby stain 225
Castor Set 600
green/blue 825
ruby stain 1,000
Celery Vase 145
green/blue 225
ruby stain 265
Cheese Dish 155
green/blue 265
ruby stain 300
Compote, tall, covered,
various sizes .... 80 - 125
green/blue .... 125 - 200
ruby stain 125
Compote, open, various sizes .... 60 - 120
green/blue .... 90 - 165
ruby stain .... 100 - 250
Cracker Jar 155
green/blue 225
ruby stain 280
Creamer or Spooner 65
green/blue 95
ruby stain 115
Cruet 165
green/blue 250
ruby stain 275
Goblet 90
green/blue 140
ruby stain 165
Jam Jar 80
green/blue 100
ruby stain 165
Jelly Compote 60
green/blue 90
ruby stain 115
Lamp 135
green/blue 325
ruby stain 365
Pitcher 135
green/blue 375
ruby stain 325
Relish 50
green/blue 70
ruby stain 90
Shakers, ea. 50
green/blue 70
ruby stain 90
Sugar 90
green/blue 140
ruby stain 175
Syrup, rare 480
green/blue 650
ruby stain 1,350
Toothpick Holder 95
green/blue 150
ruby stain 200
Tumbler 40
green/blue 50
ruby stain 70
Vase 65
green/blue 100
ruby stain 135
Wine 50
green/blue 75
ruby stain 90
*Amber stained same as ruby stained prices.
ETCHED MUSTARD POT
Mustard Pot 50
vaseline 80
ETCHED VENICE
Pitcher
vaseline 150

green/blue ... 115
Tumbler
vaseline ... 40
green/blue ... 30
Tray
vaseline ... 70
green/blue ... 55

ETTA
Berry Bowl, sm. ... 20
Berry Bowl, lg. ... 40
Butter ... 65
Creamer ... 25
Cruet ... 55
Custard Cup ... 15
Nappy ... 20
Plate, 6" ... 25
Pitcher ... 60
Shakers, ea. ... 25
Spooner ... 25
Sugar ... 35
Tankard Pitcher ... 70
Tumbler ... 15
Wine ... 20

ETRUSCAN
Berry Bowl, sm. ... 15
Berry Bowl, lg. ... 40
Butter ... 70
Cake Stand ... 40
Compote ... 35
Creamer or Spooner ... 25
Egg Cup ... 20
Jelly Compote ... 30
Pitcher ... 85
Sauce ... 15
Sugar ... 30
Tumbler ... 20

EUREKA (NATIONAL)
Bottle w/Stopper ... 50
ruby stain ... 200
Bowl, 2 styles ... 35 - 50
ruby stain ... 60 - 90
Butter ... 70
ruby stain ... 155
Cake Stand ... 100
ruby stain ... 525
Celery Vase ... 40
ruby stain ... 95
Compote ... 45
ruby stain ... 65
Creamer or Spooner ... 40
ruby stain ... 95
Cruet ... 65
ruby stain ... 250
Jelly Compote ... 45
ruby stain ... 60
Pickle Dish ... 25
ruby stain ... 40
Pitcher ... 75
ruby stain ... 265
Shakers, ea. ... 35
ruby stain ... 75
Sugar ... 50
ruby stain ... 110
Syrup ... 90
ruby stain ... 365
Toothpick ... 30
ruby stain ... 45
Tumbler ... 30
ruby stain ... 65

EVANGELINE
Bowl, lg. ... 35
Bowl, sm ... 15
Bowl, high ftd. ... 60
Butter ... 50
Cake Plate, ftd. ... 45
Celery Tray ... 30
Compote, various shapes ... 55
Creamer or Sugar ... 30
Goblet ... 25
Pickle Dish ... 30
Pitcher ... 70
Tumbler ... 20
Wine ... 20

EVELYN (THUMBALLA)
Bowl, 7" - 8"
green/blue ... 75
Plate, 8½" - 9"
green/blue ... 100
Punch Bowl, large ... 250
Punch Cup ... 20
Water Tray, rectangle shape
green/blue ... 125

EVERGLADES (NORTHWOOD)
Berry Bowl, oval, sm.
custard ... 35
Berry Bowl, oval, lg.
custard ... 85
Butter
custard ... 165
Creamer
custard ... 65
Cruet
custard ... 145
Jelly Compote
custard ... 75
Pitcher
custard ... 250
Shakers, ea.
custard ... 75
Spooner
custard ... 70
Sugar
custard ... 85
Tumbler
custard ... 40

EXCELSIOR
Ale Glass ... 55
Bar Bottle ... 45
Bitters Bottle ... 60
Bowl, covered ... 135
Bowl, open ... 50
Butter ... 125
Candlesticks, ea. ... 130
Celery Vase ... 65
Champagne ... 55
Claret ... 50
Compote, covered ... 80
Compote, open ... 110
Cordial ... 80
Creamer or Spooner ... 65
Decanter, 2 sizes ... 80 - 100
Egg Cup, single ... 65
Egg Cup, double ... 85
Goblet, 2 styles ... 65
Jelly Glass ... 60
Lamp ... 110
Milk Pitcher ... 225
Mug ... 50
Pickle Jar w/Lid ... 50
Pitcher ... 325
Salt ... 40
Spill Holder ... 80
Sugar ... 95
Syrup ... 150
Tumbler, various ... 50 - 70
Vase ... 75
Water bottle ... 100
Wine ... 60

EYEWINKER
Banana Stand, 10", from compote ... 385
Banana Stand, 5" - 10" ... 95 - 195
Berry Bowl, lg. ... 135
Berry Bowl, sm. ... 65
Bowl, covered ... 250
Butter ... 145
Cake Stand, 8" - 10" ... 90 - 235
Celery Vase ... 160
Compote, covered, 4" - 6" ... 90 - 180
Compote, covered, 7" - 9" ... 250 - 500
Compote, open, 4" - 6" ... 70 - 100
Compote, open, 7" - 10½" ... 125 - 325
Creamer or Spooner ... 100
Cruet ... 245
Fruit Bowl, 2 sizes ... 325 - 400
Goblet ... 120
Honey Dish ... 35
Jam Jar w/Lid ... 390
Milk Pitcher ... 300
Oil Lamp ... 295
Pitcher ... 385
Plate, sq., 5" - 7" ... 50 - 65
Plate, sq., 8" - 10" ... 80 - 135
Sauce, round or sq. ... 30 - 40
Shakers, ea. ... 135
Sugar ... 155
Syrup ... 270
Tumbler ... 85

FACETED FLOWER SWIRL
Butter ... 45
Celery Vase ... 25
Creamer or Spooner ... 25
Cruet ... 65
Pickle Tray ... 20
Pitcher ... 90
Sugar ... 30
Toothpick Holder ... 25
Tumbler ... 20
Water Tray ... 30

FAIRFAX STRAWBERRY
Bowl, oval ... 50
milk glass ... 65
Butter ... 125
milk glass ... 195
Celery Vase ... 190
milk glass ... 395
Compote, covered, high or low .. 80 - 165
milk glass ... 100 - 200
Creamer or Spooner ... 75
milk glass ... 120
Egg Cup ... 45
milk glass ... 65
Goblet ... 50
milk glass ... 85
Honey Dish ... 15
milk glass ... 35
Milk Pitcher ... 395
milk glass ... 675
Pickle Tray ... 20
milk glass ... 30
Pitcher ... 240
milk glass ... 600
Relish ... 20
milk glass ... 30
Salt, master ... 40
milk glass ... 60
Sauce ... 10
milk glass ... 20
Sugar ... 95
milk glass ... 130
Syrup ... 200
milk glass ... 385
Tumbler ... 95
milk glass ... 225
Wine ... 185
milk glass ... 290

FAMOUS (AKA: PANELLED THUMBPRINT)
Berry Bowl, lg. ... 35
Berry Bowl, sm. ... 15
Butter ... 60
Celery Vase ... 25
Creamer, Spooner or Sugar ... 25
Oil Lamp ... 75
Pickle Dish ... 20
Pitcher ... 65
Shakers, ea. ... 20
Syrup ... 45
Toothpick Holder ... 30

Tumbler 15

FAN (DUGAN)
- Berry Bowl, lg. 40
- Berry Bowl, sm. 15
- Butter 70
- Creamer 25
- Pitcher 95
- Spooner 25
- Sugar 35
- Tumbler 15

FAN BAND
- Butter 30
- Compote 20
- Creamer or Spooner 15
- Finger Bowl 15
- Pitcher 65
- Sugar 25
- Tray 30
- Tumbler 15
- Wine 20

FANCY HUSK CORN VASE (DUGAN)
- Corn Vase, very scarce 95
  - green/blue 175

FANCY ARCH
- Bowls, various ..... 15 - 35
  - ruby stain ..... 25 - 65
- Butter 70
  - ruby stain 120
- Celery Vase 30
  - ruby stain 65
- Creamer 35
  - ruby stain 65
- Goblet 45
  - ruby stain 70
- Milk Pitcher 60
  - ruby stain 100
- Pitcher 95
  - ruby stain 165
- Plate 30
  - ruby stain 55
- Relish 25
  - ruby stain 40
- Sauce 15
  - ruby stain 25
- Shakers, ea 40
  - ruby stain 65
- Spooner 35
  - ruby stain 70
- Sugar 55
  - ruby stain 90
- Syrup 70
  - ruby stain 115
- Tumbler 30
  - ruby stain 55
- Wine 40
  - ruby stain 65

FANCY CUT (REX)
- Pitcher 95
- Punch Bowl 125
- Punch Cup 15
- Toy Table Set 85
- Tumbler 20
- Vase Whimsey 40

FANCY LOOP
- Bonbon 35
- Butter 80
- Celery Vase 20
- Champagne 15
- Claret 10
- Cracker Jars ..... 25 - 45
- Creamer or Spooner 25
- Cruet 60
- Goblet 50
- Jelly Compote 20
- Jelly Dish 15
- Pitcher 95
- Punch Bowl 125
- Punch Cup 15
- Salt Dip, ind. 10
- Salt, master 20
- Shakers, ea 15
- Sherry 15
- Spoon Tray 20
- Sugar 30
- Toothpick Holder 35
- Tumbler 25
- Tumbler, bar size 35
- Wine 10

*Add 50% for colors.

FANDANGO
- Banana Stand 45
- Bar Bottle 35
- Berry Bowl, lg. 40
- Berry Bowl, sm. 15
- Bowls, various ..... 10 - 50
- Butter 65
- Butter Pat 10
- Carafe 45
- Celery Tray, 7" - 9" ..... 15 - 25
- Celery Vase 20
- Cheese Plate 30
- Compote, 6" - 10" ..... 25 - 60
- Cookie Jar, tall 50
- Cracker Jar 35
- Creamer, 5 sizes ..... 10 - 50
- Cruet, 2 sizes ..... 45 - 60
- Custard Cup 10
- Finger Bowl 20
- Horseradish 35
- Ice Bowl w/Plate 50
- Jelly Compote 30
- Nappy 20
- Pickle Tray 15
- Pitcher, 2 sizes ..... 85 - 125
- Plate, sq. 20
- Rose Bowl, 2 sizes ..... 20 - 30
- Salt Dip 15
- Salt Shaker, 3 types ..... 30 - 55
- Salver 40
- Sugar Shaker 40
- Sugar, 3 sizes ..... 25 - 50
- Syrup, 3 sizes ..... 40 - 70
- Toothpick Holder 30
- Tray, 14" 25
- Tumbler 25
- Wine 10

FAN WITH DIAMOND
- Butter, 2 sizes ..... 40 - 60
- Compote, covered, high or low ..... 70 - 90
- Cordial 70
- Creamer or Spooner 40
- Egg Cup 30
- Goblet 40
- Relish, 9" x 5½" 40
- Pitcher 225
- Sauce 10
- Sugar 50
- Syrup 155
- Wine 25

FAN WITH SPLIT DIAMOND
- Berry Bowl, lg. 40
- Berry Bowl, sm. 15
- Butter 60
- Creamer or Spooner 20
- Mustard Pot 35
- Pitcher 80
- Sugar 35
- Tumbler 20

FAN WITH STAR
- Berry Bowl, lg. 35
- Berry Bowl, sm. 15
- Butter 45
- Celery Vase 25
- Compote 40
- Creamer, Spooner or Sugar 25
- Goblet 30
- Pitcher 65
- Plate, 7" 25
- Tumbler 15

FASHION
- Berry Bowl, sm. 10
- Berry Bowl, lg. 30
- Bowl, 9", 10" & 12" 30
- Butter, reg. 45
- Butter, sm. 40
- Compote, 4" - 6½" 35
- Compote, 5½", 8½" & 10" 45
- Creamer, Spooner or Sugar 25
- Custard Cup 10
- Jelly Compote w/Lid 35
- Nappy 25
- Orange Bowl w/Base 45
- Pitcher 85
- Plate, 11" 30
- Punch Bowl w/Base 110
- Punch Cup 15
- Rose Bowl, 7" 40
- Salver, 8" & 12" 50
- Sherbet 20
- Toothpick Holder 30
- Tumbler 20

FEATHER
- Banana Bowl, flat and ftd. ..... 100 - 400
  - green/blue 480
- Berry Bowl, lg. 50
  - green/blue 100
- Berry Bowl, sm. 25
  - green/blue 75
- Butter 70
  - green/blue 200
- Cake Stand 80
  - green/blue 210
- Celery Vase 40
  - green/blue 90
- Compote, covered , 6" - 8" ..... 100 - 225
  - green/blue ..... 450 - 800
- Compote, open, 4" - 8" ..... 80 - 140
  - green/blue ..... 200 - 300
- Cordial 100
  - green/blue 340
- Creamer or Spooner 40
  - green/blue 90
- Cruet 80
  - green/blue 275
- Goblet 70
  - green/blue 275
- Jelly Compote 50
  - green/blue 95
- Milk Pitcher 80
  - green/blue 325
  - chocolate 2,000
- Novelty Bowl 60
  - green/blue 125
- Pitcher 70
  - green/blue 200
- Plate, 10" 70
  - green/blue 140
- Plate, 7" - 8" ..... 90 - 160
- Relish 20
  - green/blue 60
- Shaker, ea. ..... 80 - 100
  - green/blue ..... 125 - 200
- Spooner 30
  - green/blue 100
- Square Sauce 50
- Syrup 225
  - green/blue 575
- Toothpick Holder 130
  - green/blue 335
- Tumbler 60
  - green/blue 95
- Wine 30
  - green/blue 120

*For amber stain add 35% to green prices.

FEATHER & HEART
- Pitcher, very scarce 200

Tumbler, scarce....45
*Add 10% for stained pieces.
FEATHER BAND
Bowl....30
Butter....45
Creamer or Spooner....25
Pitcher, 2 sizes....65
Sauce....15
Sugar, flat....25
Sugar, ftd.....30
Tumbler....20
FEATHER DUSTER
Berry Bowl, lg....50
green/blue....80
Berry Bowl, sm.....35
green/blue....60
Butter....50
green/blue....70
Cake Stand, 4 sizes.... 60 - 100
green/blue....80 - 130
Compote, covered 5" - 8".... 50 - 80
green/blue....80 - 100
Compote, open 5" - 10".... 30 - 55
green/blue.... 50 - 75
Covered Bowl, 9"....40
green/blue....60
Creamer or Spooner....25
green/blue....40
Egg Cup....30
green/blue....40
Milk Pitcher....40
green/blue....60
Pickle Dish....20
green/blue....25
Pitcher....50
green/blue....70
Plate....30
green/blue....50
Shakers, ea....30
green/blue....60
Sugar....25
green/blue....65
Tray....35
green/blue....65
Tumbler....25
green/blue....50
Wine....30
green/blue....50
FEATHERED ARROW
Bowl....50
green/blue....80
pink....60
Bowl, retourne rim, rare.... 80
Nut Dish....55
Rose Bowl, very scarce....75
pink....65
FEATHERED MEDALLION
Bowls, round, various.... 15 - 40
Bowl, square....45
Butter....65
Creamer or Spooner....20
Cruet....60
Fruit Bowl....45
Goblet....30
Relish....35
Pitcher....80
Sugar....30
Wine, either shape....25
FEATHERED OVALS
Butter....65
Creamer or Spooner....20
Pitcher....85
Sugar....25
Tumbler....15
FEATHERS
Vase....30
FEDERAL #1605
Butter....50
Creamer....25
Goblet....30
Spooner....25
Sugar....30
Wine....20
FEDERAL #1910
Berry Bowl, sm.....15
Berry Bowl, lg....35
Butter....65
Celery Vase....25
Creamer or Spooner....20
Cup....15
Goblet....40
Jelly Compote....30
Mayonnaise Set....45
Pitcher....80
Shakers, ea....20
Sugar....25
Tumbler....20
Vase, 3 sizes.... 20 - 40
Wine....15
FEEDING DOG & DEER
Mug....25
amber.... 35
vaseline....85
green/blue....70
lavender.... 65
FENTEC
Butter....45
Cake Plate, oval....40
Celery Tray....25
Cheese Dish, covered....50
Chocolate Tray....30
Creamer....20
Cup....15
Jelly Compote....20
Nappy....20
Olive Tray....20
Pickle Tray....20
Pitcher....60
Plates, 6" - 11".... 15 - 35
Plate, clover shaped....25
Punch Bowl w/Base....95
Punch Cup....10
Spooner....25
Sherbet w/Attached Plate....30
Sugar....30
Tumbler....15
FENTON'S FLUTE
Vase, 10" - 12", very scarce
sapphire....200
FERN BAND & WREATH
Miniature Lamp....75
green/blue....110
FERN BURST (PALM WREATH)
Bowl, 8" - 10"....55
Butter....75
Carafe....70
Creamer, Spooner or Sugar....40
Cruet....65
Tumbler, scarce....35
*All pieces scarce.
FERNETTE
Berry Bowl, sm.....10
Berry Bowl, lg....40
Butter....65
Creamer or Spooner....20
Pitcher....75
Sugar....30
Toothpick Holder....25
Tumbler....15
FERN GARLAND
Butter....65
Celery Tray....30
Celery Vase....25
Compote, low....35
Compote, tall....45
Creamer or Spooner....20
Cup....15
Goblet....50
Pitcher....95
Shakers, ea....25
Sugar....25
Tumbler....20
Violet Vase....30
Wine....15
FERRIS WHEEL (AKA: LUCILE)
Butter....65
Celery Vase....30
Creamer, Spooner or Sugar....25
Jelly Compote....35
Goblet....30
Pitcher....80
Shakers, ea....35
Tumbler....25
Wine....25
FESTOON
Bowls, various.... 30 - 50
Butter....85
Cake Stand.... 80 - 100
Compote, open....300
Creamer or Spooner....40
Finger Bowl....30
Marmalade Jar w/Lid....100
Mug....60
Pickle Castor....150
Pitcher....135
Plates, 4 sizes.... 25 - 70
Relish, oval....35
Sauce....20
Sugar....75
Tumbler....35
Waste Bowl....25
Water Tray....60
FIDDLE BOTTLE
Distillery Bottle
amber....300
FIELD THISTLE
Berry Bowl, lg....30
Berry Bowl, sm.....10
Butter....45
Castor Set....85
Chop Plate, 11"....40
Compote....30
Creamer or Spooner....20
Nappy....20
Olive Dish....15
Plate, 6" & 9".... 15 - 35
Pitcher....125
Sugar....30
Tumbler....40
FIGHTING WYVERNS
Covered Bowl
vaseline....225
FILE
Banana Dish, 8"....30
Berry Bowl, lg....30
Berry Bowl, sm.....10
Bowl, shallow, 8½"....25
Creamer or Spooner....20
Grape Plate....25
Oil Bottle....70
Pitcher....125
Plate, 4" - 6"....20
Plate, 8" - 10"....35
Rose Bowl, 5½" - 7"....35
Shakers, ea....25
Sugar....25
Tumbler....25
Vase, 7"....25
FINECUT
Bowl, 8¼"....35
amber....40
vaseline....55
green/blue....50
Butter....50
amber.... 55
vaseline.... 80
green/blue....60

Cake Stand 80
amber 90
vaseline 130
green/blue 100
Celery Tray 25
amber 30
vaseline 40
green/blue 35
Celery Vase 40
amber 50
vaseline 80
green/blue 70
Compote, covered 80
amber 90
vaseline 125
green/blue 100
Creamer or Spooner 30
amber 40
vaseline 50
green/blue 45
Goblet 30
amber 35
vaseline 50
green/blue 40
Pitcher 70
amber 90
vaseline 130
green/blue 120
Plate, 3 sizes .... 15 - 20
amber .... 20 - 25
vaseline .... 30 - 40
green/blue .... 25 - 35
Relish Tray 20
amber 20
vaseline 30
green/blue 25
Sauce 10
amber 15
vaseline 30
green/blue 20
Sugar 30
amber 40
vaseline 55
green/blue 45
Tray 40
amber 45
vaseline 70
green/blue 55
Tumbler 20
amber 25
vaseline 40
green/blue 30
Waste Bowl 20
amber 25
vaseline 40
green/blue 30
Wine 15
amber 20
vaseline 35
green/blue 25

FINECUT & BLOCK
Bowl, hndl. .... 20 - 45
Butter, 2 styles .... 50 - 80
Cake Stand, 5 sizes .... 60 - 125
Celery Tray 35
Compote, covered 95
Compote, open .... 70 - 90
Cordial .... 40 - 50
Creamer or Spooner 60
Custard Cup 20
Egg Cup 25
Finger Bowl 30
Goblet, 2 sizes .... 45 - 50
Milk Pitcher 70
Perfume Bottle 90
Pickle Jar w/Lid 80
Pitcher 85
Plate .... 15 - 25
Relish 20
Salt, ind. 15
Salt, master 30
Sauce, flat or ftd. 10
Soap Dish, 2 styles .... 50 - 90
Sugar 60
Tray, ice cream 70
Tray, water 75
Tumbler 40
Wine 30
*Add 125% for all solid colored pieces.
*Add 75% for color stained blocks pieces.

FINECUT & PANEL
Berry Bowl, lg. 20
amber 40
vaseline 60
green/blue 45
Berry Bowl, sm. 35
amber 35
vaseline 50
green/blue 40
Bread Tray 30
amber 35
vaseline 45
green/blue 50
Butter 50
amber 60
vaseline 85
green/blue 75
Cake Stand 80
amber 100
vaseline 145
green/blue 130
Compote, covered 70
amber 80
vaseline 140
green/blue 130
Compote, open 30
amber 40
vaseline 50
green/blue 45
Creamer or Spooner 25
amber 30
vaseline 40
green/blue 50
Cup 10
amber 15
vaseline 20
green/blue 25
Goblet 35
amber 40
vaseline 55
green/blue 45
Milk Pitcher 50
amber 55
vaseline 80
green/blue 70
Pickle Dish, 7" - 9" 20
amber 25
vaseline 30
green/blue 35
Pitcher 60
amber 70
vaseline 90
green/blue 80
Plate 20
amber 25
vaseline 30
green/blue 35
Platter, oval 25
amber 30
vaseline 35
green/blue 45
Relish Tray 15
amber 20
vaseline 25
green/blue 30
Sugar 35
amber 40
vaseline 55
green/blue 65
Tumbler 20
amber 25
vaseline 35
green/blue 30
Water Tray 50
amber 55
vaseline 70
green/blue 60

FINECUT HEART
Bowl, 8" - 9", very scarce 275

FINECUT OVALS
Bowl, 8" - 9", very scarce 275

FINECUT SHIELD & INVERTED THUMBPRINT
Compote, covered 80

FINECUT SQUARE WITH DAISY BUTTON
Butter 75
Creamer or Spooner 25
Sugar 35

FINECUT STAR & FAN
Berry Bowl, sm. 15
Berry Bowl, lg. 25
Banana Bowls, various .... 15 - 30
Children's Table Set 80
Sugar, covered 35
Wine 20

FINECUT UMBRELLA
One Shape 100

FINE PRISMS & DIAMONDS
Vase, 11" - 15" 45

FINE RIB (FENTON)
Vase 20
green/blue 35
flame orange 125

FISH & SEAWEED
Berry Bowl, sm. 100
Berry Bowl, lg. 175
Butter 400
Celery Vase 150
Creamer 100
Cruet 300
Pitcher 400
Spooner 100
Sugar 125
Syrup 300
Tumbler 90
Water bottle 275
*All pieces are considered quite rare.

FISH & SWANS
Butter 250
Creamer or Spooner 75
Sugar 95
*All pieces rare.

FISH FIGURAL BUTTER
Butter Dish, covered 165
vaseline 300
green/blue 235

FISHSCALE
Ashtray (Daisy & Button Slipper on Tray) 195
Bowl, covered, 6" - 9½" .... 50 - 90
Bowl, open, 5" - 10" .... 20 - 60
Butter 60
Cake Stand, 4 sizes .... 50 - 90
Celery Vase 40
Compote, covered, 5" - 10" .... 50 - 140
Compote, open, 4" - 10" .... 25 - 55
Condiment Tray 70
Creamer or Spooner 40
Finger Lamp 100
Goblet 40
Milk Pitcher 50
Mug 80
Pickle Scoop, tapered 20
Pitcher 70
Plate, 7" - 10" .... 30 - 50
Relish 20
Sauce, flat or ftd. 15
Shakers, ea. 95
Sugar 60

Syrup....260
Tumbler....100
Water Tray, rnd....40

FLAMINGO
Butter....125
Creamer or Spooner....40
Goblet....65
Pickle Jar....55
Sugar....50

FLATTENED DIAMOND & SUNBURST
Butter....45
Celery Vase....25
Cordial....15
Creamer or Spooner....20
Pickle Dish....20
Sauce....10
Sugar....25
Toy Table Set....75

FLATTENED HOBNAIL
Butter....65
Celery Vase....25
Creamer or Spooner....25
Goblet....40
Shakers, ea....25
Sugar....30
Toothpick Holder....25

FLEUR-DE-LIS (GREENTOWN)
Butter....250
chocolate....1,000
Celery....70
chocolate....200
Creamer....90
chocolate....275
Nappy....45
chocolate....90
Pitcher....350
chocolate....1,100
Spooner....85
chocolate....375
Sugar....100
chocolate....250
Tumbler....75
chocolate....200

FLEUR-DE-LIS & DRAPE
Bowl, various....15 - 25
green/blue....20 - 30
Butter....50 - 60
green/blue....70 - 80
Cake Stand....80 - 95
green/blue....100 - 130
Claret....50
green/blue....70
Compote, covered, high....50 - 90
green/blue....60 - 100
Compote, covered, low....40 - 70
green/blue....55 - 90
Compote, open, high....25 - 40
green/blue....40 - 60
Compote, open, low....25 - 35
green/blue....40 - 55
Cordial....20
green/blue....35
Creamer or Spooner....25
green/blue....45
Cruet....70
green/blue....95
Finger Bowl....20
green/blue....35
Milk Pitcher....50
green/blue....70
Mustard Jar....40
green/blue....55
Pitcher....60
green/blue....95
Plates, various sizes....20 - 35
green/blue....30 - 50
Sauces, flat or ftd....15
green/blue....25
Shakers, ea....30
green/blue....60
Sugar....50
green/blue....70
Tray....50
green/blue....65
Tumbler....30
green/blue....40
Water Bottle....70
green/blue....150
Wine....25
green/blue....40

FLEUR-DE-LIS
Toothpick Holder....65
Nile green opaque....250

FLOATING SWAN
Pitcher, rare....425

FLORA
Berry Bowl, lg....30
green/blue....40
Berry Bowl, sm....10
green/blue....25
Bowls, novelty....20 - 40
green/blue....35 - 65
Butter....60
green/blue....85
Celery Vase....15
green/blue....30
Compote....30
green/blue....45
Creamer or Spooner....20
green/blue....30
Cruet....80
green/blue....100
Pitcher....110
green/blue....135
Sugar....30
green/blue....40
Toothpick Holder....25
green/blue....35
Tumbler....15
green/blue....25

FLORADORA (BOHEMIAN)
Berry Bowl, lg....35
green/blue....45
Berry Bowl, sm....10
green/blue....15
Butter....55
green/blue....70
Celery Vase....25
green/blue....30
Creamer or Spooner....30
green/blue....35
Goblet....40
green/blue....50
Pickle Dish....15
green/blue....20
Pitcher....70
green/blue....85
chocolate....800
Straw Jar....75
green/blue....90
Sugar....50
green/blue....60
Toothpick Holder....35
green/blue....45
Tumbler....15
green/blue....20
Wine....20
green/blue....25

*Add 10% for rose flashed pieces.

FLORAL COLONIAL
Butter....55
Compote....30
Creamer....25
Cruet....50
Goblet....25
Handled Bowl, ftd....30
Spooner....25
Sugar....30
Tumbler....15

FLORALORE
Bowl, 7⅝"
purple slag....125

FLORAL OVAL
Bowl, rectangular....35
Butter....65
Creamer or Spooner....25
Honey Dish w/Lid....40
Jelly Compote....35
Pitcher....70
Plate, sq....25
Sugar....30
Tumbler....20
Wine....15

FLORAL PEACOCK
Deep Bowl, 10"....40

FLORENE
Butter....135
Creamer....45
Goblet....60
Pickle Dish....40
Spooner....50
Sugar....65
Wine....35

FLORENTINE (RIVERSIDE GLASS)
Berry Bowl, sm....25
green/blue....40
milk glass....45
Berry Bowl, lg....50
green/blue....60
milk glass....75
Butter....85
green/blue....110
milk glass....100
Creamer or Spooner....40
green/blue....60
milk glass....65
Pitcher....150
green/blue....175
milk glass....175
Relish Tray....30
green/blue....50
milk glass....55
Sugar....55
green/blue....65
milk glass....75
Syrup....85
green/blue....100
milk glass....110
Tumbler....25
green/blue....35
milk glass....45

FLORENTINE CANDLESTICK
Candlesticks, ea....20
vaseline....55
green/blue....45

FLORIDA
Bowl, covered, 8" - 9"....35
green/blue....60
Bowl, open, 8" - 9"....25
green/blue....35
Butter....50
green/blue....75
Cake Stand....85
green/blue....160
Celery Vase....40
green/blue....70
Compote, sq., covered or open....30 - 50
green/blue....40 - 70
Cordial....40
green/blue....90
Creamer or Spooner....20
green/blue....50
Cruet....70
green/blue....300
Goblet....45
green/blue....75
Mustard Pot....35

green/blue ... 65
Pickle Dish ... 20
green/blue ... 35
Pitcher ... 45
green/blue ... 70
Plate, sq., 7¼" - 9¼" ... 35
green/blue ... 55
Relish Tray, 2 shapes ... 15
green/blue ... 35
Sauce ... 15
green/blue ... 25
Shakers, ea ... 60
green/blue ... 85
Sugar ... 30
green/blue ... 55
Syrup ... 85
green/blue ... 325
Tumbler ... 20
green/blue ... 40
Wine ... 20
green/blue ... 70

FLOWER & PANEL (#23)
Butter ... 60
amber ... 80
slag ... 125
Creamer or Spooner ... 35
amber ... 45
slag ... 65
Pitcher ... 95
amber ... 135
slag ... 170
Sugar ... 40
amber ... 55
slag ... 80

FLOWER & PLEAT
Butter ... 55
ruby stain ... 70
Creamer or Spooner ... 30
ruby stain ... 40
Pickle Dish ... 20
ruby stain ... 25
Shakers, ea ... 20
ruby stain ... 30
Sugar ... 40
ruby stain ... 50
Toothpick Holder ... 35
ruby stain ... 45

FLOWER BAND
Butter ... 255
Celery Vase ... 150
Compote w/Lid,
2 shapes ... 235 - 350
Creamer or Spooner ... 120
Goblet ... 140
Milk Pitcher ... 265
Pitcher ... 285
Sauce, flat or ftd ... 40
Sugar ... 225

FLOWER BOUQUET
ABC Plate ... 150

FLOWER FAN
Bowl, lg. ... 15
Bowl, sm. ... 20
Butter ... 65
Cake Stand ... 35
Compote ... 35
Creamer or Spooner ... 20
Cruet ... 50
Pickle Dish ... 20
Pitcher ... 85
Shakers, ea ... 20
Sugar ... 25
Tumbler ... 15
Vase ... 30

FLOWERING VINE
Creamer ... 30
vaseline ... 70
Open Sugar ... 30
vaseline ... 65

FLOWER MEDALLION
Berry Bowl, lg ... 40
Berry Bowl, sm. ... 15
Butter ... 65
Creamer or Spooner ... 20
Pitcher ... 85
Sauce ... 10
Sugar ... 30
Toothpick Holder ... 25
Tumbler ... 20

FLOWER OVAL
Bowl, oval, 8" ... 50
vaseline ... 95

FLOWER POT
Bread Tray (In God We Trust) ... 80
Butter ... 75
vaseline ... 250
Cake Stand ... 65
Compote, covered ... 70
Compote, open ... 55
Creamer or Spooner ... 40
vaseline ... 125
Goblet ... 50
Milk Pitcher ... 75
Pitcher ... 110
Sauce, ftd. 2 handles ... 30
Shakers, ea ... 40
Sugar ... 55
vaseline ... 165
Tumbler ... 30

FLOWER WITH CANE
Berry Bowl, lg ... 30
Berry Bowl, sm. ... 15
Butter ... 45
Creamer or Spooner ... 20
Custard Cup ... 10
Pitcher ... 65
Sugar ... 25
Toothpick Holder, fancy base ... 30
Tumbler ... 15

FLUTE (All Other Companies)
*Condensed list.
Berry Bowl, lg ... 35
Berry Bowl, sm. ... 15
Butter ... 65
Compote ... 40
Compote, jelly size ... 30
Creamer or Spooner ... 20
Pickle Dish ... 20
Pitcher ... 85
Punch Bowl ... 100
Punch Cup ... 10
Shakers, ea ... 15
Sugar ... 25
Toothpick Holder ... 25
Tumbler ... 20
Vase ... 25

FLUTE (MILLERSBURG)
Bonbon, 2 shapes ... 175
Bowl, master ... 150
Bowl, Sauce ... 50
Butter, rare ... 250
Cake Plate, stemmed ... 400
Compote, 6" (Wildflower blank) ... 275
Compote, 9" (Peacock blank) ... 400
Compote, round whimsey ... 450
Creamer or Spooner ... 100
Milk Pitcher ... 150
Nappy (Holly Sprig blank) ... 200
Pitcher ... 250
Punch Bowl w/Base, rare ... 625
Punch Cup, scarce ... 45
Sugar, very scarce ... 175

FLUTE (NORTHWOOD)
Berry Bowl, sm. ... 20
Berry Bowl, lg ... 55
Butter ... 75
Celery Vase ... 45
Nut Cup ... 25
sapphire ... 85
Pitcher ... 100
Sherbet ... 35
Tumbler ... 25

FLUTE & CANE
Berry Bowl, lg ... 30
Berry Bowl, sm. ... 10
Bowl, hndl., 5" - 7" ... 15
Butter ... 50
Celery Vase ... 25
Champagne ... 15
Compote ... 30
Cordial ... 20
Creamer or Spooner ... 15
Cup ... 10
Goblet ... 15
Milk Pitcher ... 45
Pitcher ... 65
Plate, 6" ... 20
Saucer ... 10
Sugar ... 20
Tumbler ... 15
Vase ... 25

FLYING SWAN
Butter ... 275
Celery Vase ... 65
Creamer or Spooner ... 70
Jam Jar, open ... 80
Pitcher ... 325
Sugar ... 95
Toothpick Holder ... 65
Tumbler ... 50

FLY TRAP
Fly Catcher, rare ... 300
*Etched pieces add 15%.

FOOTED KETTLE
Novelty Piece ... 20
ruby stain ... 35
*Green stain add 50%.

FOR AULD LANG SYNE
Plate ... 55

FORGET-ME-NOT BANDS
Berry Bowl, lg ... 35
Berry Bowl, sm. ... 15
Butter ... 60
Celery Vase ... 30
Creamer, Spooner or Sugar ... 25
Jam Jar ... 25
Pitcher ... 80
Sauce ... 15
Tray ... 35
Tumbler ... 20

FORGET-ME-NOT IN SCROLL
Berry Bowl, sm. ... 10
Berry Bowl, lg ... 25
Butter ... 50
Goblet ... 25
Creamer or Spooner ... 25
Plate ... 25
Pitcher ... 65
Sugar ... 30
Tumbler ... 15

FORKS (CAMBRIDGE)
Berry Bowl, lg ... 40
Berry Bowl, sm. ... 15
Butter ... 70
Creamer or Spooner ... 20
Cruet ... 50
Milk Pitcher ... 65
Pitcher ... 80
Sugar ... 25
Tumbler ... 20

FORKS (IMPERIAL)
Cracker Jar ... 75

FORT PITT EAGLE
Plate, sm., very scarce ... 80
milk glass ... 150

FOUR PILLARS
Vase, scarce ... 40

black amethyst 90
474 (IMPERIAL)
Bowl, sq., 9", rare 65
Milk Pitcher 55
Pitcher....75
Punch Bowl w/Base 85
Punch Cup 20
Tumbler....25
Vase....45
Vase Whimsey, very rare....125
474 VARIANT
Bowls, various .... 10 - 30
Butter....40
Creamer or Spooner....20
Pitcher....55
Sugar....25
Tumbler....10
FOX & CROW
Pitcher, scarce 275
FRAMED JEWEL
Butter 50
ruby stain 70
Creamer or Spooner....25
ruby stain 35
Goblet 40
ruby stain 50
Pitcher....70
ruby stain 110
Sugar....35
ruby stain 50
Toothpick Holder....40
ruby stain 60
Tumbler....20
ruby stain 30
Wine 20
ruby stain 30
FRINGED DRAPE
Bowl, deep, 6" 20
Bowl, oval, 5" - 11".... 15 - 35
Bowl, rnd., 6" - 9" .... 20 - 40
Butter....65
Celery Tray....25
Celery Vase....20
Cordial 15
Creamer or Spooner....20
Cruet....55
Cup 10
Jelly Compote....30
Pickle Jar....35
Pickle Tray 25
Sauce....10
Salad Fork Handle, unique....55
Shakers, ea....20
Sugar 25
Syrup....55
Vase, flat, 10" - 14"....45
Vase, ftd., 8" - 9" 35
FRISCHE
Butter with Lid 125
FRISCO
Bowl, 7", open and covered.... 20 - 35
Butter 65
Candy w/Lid....45
Compote, 4 sizes .... 30 - 65
Creamer or Spooner....30
Cruet, oil....65
Fruit Bowl, 9"....45
Pitcher, 2 sizes .... 65 - 80
Shaker, ea. 35
Toothpick 45
Tumbler....30
Vase, 5 sizes; 3½" - 13".... 25 - 60
FROG & LEAF
Match Holder 80
FROG & SHELL
Novelty Toothpick holder
amber....125
green/blue....150
amethyst....150

FROLICKING BEARS
Pitcher, rare....3,900
Tumbler, rare....700
Tumbler, silver finish, very rare 1,500
FROST CRYSTAL
Berry Bowl, sm....15
ruby stain 20
Berry Bowl, lg....35
ruby stain 55
Butter....70
ruby stain 95
Celery Boat....30
ruby stain 30
Celery Vase....35
ruby stain 35
Creamer or Spooner....25
ruby stain 35
Custard Cup 15
ruby stain 20
Plate, 6"....20
ruby stain 30
Plate, 10"....50
ruby stain 40
Punch Bowl w/Base 85
ruby stain 250
Shakers, ea....30
ruby stain 45
Sugar....30
ruby stain 55
FROSTED CHICKEN
Bowl, 7" - 9".... 80 - 100
Butter....195
Celery Vase....80
Compote, covered, various .... 200 - 300
Creamer or Spooner....60
Egg Cup....80
Goblet 200
Horseradish, covered....360
Jam Jar, ftd. & flat, rare.... 325 - 425
Milk Pitcher 200
Pitcher....400
Sauce....30
Shakers, ea....80
Sugar....175
FROSTED CIRCLE
Bowl, covered, 5" - 9".... 50 - 80
Bowl, open, 5" - 9" .... 15 - 45
Butter....70
Cake Stand, 8" - 10" .... 70 - 120
Celery Vase....50
Champagne 80
Compote, covered, 4 sizes .... 70 - 100
Compote, open, 4 sizes.... 35 - 60
Creamer or Spooner....40
Pitcher....100
Sugar....85
Sugar Shaker....120
Tumbler....40
Wine 50
*Add 15% for frosted pieces.
FROSTED EAGLE
Bowl, covered, 6¼"....175
Butter 225
Celery Vase....75
Compote w/Lid, eagle finial....225
Creamer or Spooner....80
Jam Jar w/Lid 625
Pitcher....250
Salt, master....95
Salt, ind. 35
Sugar 160
FROSTED FLEUR-DE-LIS
Butter 45
amber 60
green/blue 70
milk glass 60
Cake Stand, lg. or sm. .... 35 - 55
amber .... 45 - 70
green/blue .... 55 - 85

milk glass .... 45 - 70
Celery Vase....25
amber 35
green/blue 50
milk glass 40
Creamer or Spooner....25
amber 35
green/blue 50
milk glass 40
Goblet 35
amber 45
green/blue 60
milk glass 50
Pickle Dish 20
amber 30
green/blue 40
milk glass 30
Pitcher....85
amber 100
green/blue 125
milk glass 85
Sugar....35
amber 40
green/blue 55
milk glass 40
Tumbler....15
amber 25
green/blue 35
milk glass 25
Wine 10
amber 20
green/blue 30
milk glass 20
FROSTED FRUIT
Berry Bowl, lg....55
Berry Bowl, sm....20
Butter....165
Celery Vase....45
Creamer or Spooner....50
Pitcher....275
Sugar....65
Tumbler....50
FROSTED HERON
Butter....165
Creamer or Spooner....65
Pitcher....225
Sugar....80
Tumbler....50
FROSTED LEAF
Butter....300
Celery Vase....225
Champagne 300
Compote, covered....400
Cordial 135
Creamer 375
Decanter, 2 styles.... 400 - 500
Egg Cup....100
Goblet, 2 sizes .... 225 - 250
Lamp, 2 types .... 300 - 400
Pitcher, very rare 2,800
Salt, ind. 55
Salt, master....100
Sauce....30
Spooner 150
Sugar....250
Tumbler, ftd. & flat .... 135 - 200
Wine 155
FROSTED RING (VT of BEADED MIRROR)
Compote, covered....75
FROSTED STORK
Bowl, various.... 60 - 80
Butter....165
Creamer or Spooner....70
Goblet 100
Jam Jar, covered....130
Pitcher....275
Plate, hndl., 9"....60
Platter, 8¼" - 12"....80
Relish Tray 50

Sauce....30
Sugar....135
Waste Bowl,....55
Water Tray, 11" - 15½"....110
*Add 15% for frosted pieces.

FROSTED STORK ABC
Plate, scarce....55

FROSTED STORK PLATTER
Platter....65

F.R. RICE MERCANTILE CIGAR COMPANY
Cigar Container....300

FUCHSIA
Bowls, open....30 - 50
Butter....100
Cake Stand....75
Celery Vase....200
Compote....65
Creamer or Spooner....80
Goblet....60
Mug....65
Pickle Tray....20
Pitcher....300
Sauce....20
Sugar....85
Tumbler....80

GAELIC (INDIANA GLASS)
Berry Bowl, sm....10
Berry Bowl, lg....25
Butter....45
Creamer....25
Nut Bowl....25
Pitcher....70
Punch Bowl w/Base....135
Punch Cup....10
Sugar....30
Spooner....30
Tumbler....10
Wine....15

GALLOWAY (VIRGINIA)
Basket, hndl....200
Bowls, round, 5 sizes, 2 shapes....30 - 70
Bowls, various other shapes....25 - 55
Butter, 3 sizes....70 - 90
Cake Stand, 3 sizes....100 - 140
Celery Vase....60
Compote, open, 7 sizes....40 - 115
Cracker Jar,
2 different lids....300 - 375
Creamer or Spooner, 2 sizes....40 - 80
Cruet....70
Custard Cup....20
Goblet....100
Ice Jug Pitcher....200
Jelly Compote....35
Milk Pitcher....80
Mug, 2 sizes....40
Olive Dish, hndl. or plain....30
Pickle castor....200
Pickle Dish....20
Pickle Jar....90
Pitcher, 3 sizes....90 - 140
Plate, 4 sizes....50 - 80
Punch Bowl....350
Punch Cup....25
Relish Tray....20
Ring Holder....75
Salt Dip, ind....20
Salt Dip, master....40
Shakers, 2 sizes, ea....40
Sherbet....25
Sugar....75
Syrup....100
Toothpick Holder....30
Tumbler....25
Underplate, for punch set....145
Vase, 4 types....50 - 100
Waste Bowl....50
Water Bottle....90
Water Tray, 2 sizes....110 - 135

*Table set pieces come in regular, individual, or hotel size.
*Add 125% for stained pieces.

GARDEN OF EDEN
Butter, 2 styles of stems....80 - 120
Cake Stand....120
Compote, open, 4 sizes....40 - 90
Creamer or Spooner....35
Egg Cup....40
Goblet, 2 styles....90 - 300
Honey Dish....20
Mug....50
Pickle Dish....30
Pitcher....120
Plate, rnd....35
Platter, "Our Daily Bread"....60
Relish, oval, 2 styles....20
Sauce....10
Sugar....90

GARDEN PATH & VARIANT
Bowl, ruffled, 9¼", rare
lime green....325

GARDEN PINK
Bowl, ftd., 4½" - 7½"....25 - 40
Bowl, oval, 9½"....35
Cake Stand....40
Compote, covered, 8½"....50
Dish, heart shape....25
Goblet....35
Jelly Compote....30
Nappy....25
Pickle Dish....25
Pitcher....75
Tumbler....15
Wine....15

GAR ENCAMPMENT
Goblet....165

GARFIELD ALPHABET
Plate, 7", ABC....75

GARFIELD & LINCOLN
Mug....65

GARFIELD DRAPE
Berry Bowl, sm....25
Berry Bowl, lg....45
Butter....100
Cake Stand....145
Celery Vase, 2 styles....80 - 100
Compote, covered, high or low....125 - 185
Compote, open....70
Creamer or Spooner....50 - 80
Goblet, 2 sizes....80 - 135
Honey Dish....25
Memorial Bread Plate....50
Mourning Plate....70
Milk Pitcher....130
Oil Lamp....250
Pickle Dish....25
Pitcher....200
Relish....20
Star Center Plate....50
Sugar....90
Tumbler....70

GARFIELD MEMORIAL
Plate....75

GARFIELD PLATE WITH 101 BORDER
Plate....80

GARFIELD STAR
Plate....150

GATLING GUN TOOTHPICK
Toothpick Holder, w/ or w/o striker....65
green/blue....95

GEM
Decanter....65
amber....80
green/blue....90
ruby stain....100
Goblet....35
amber....40
green/blue....50
ruby stain....55
Mug....40
amber....45
green/blue....55
ruby stain....45
Mustard Jar....55
amber....60
green/blue....75
ruby stain....85
Tray....35
amber....40
green/blue....50
ruby stain....45
Tumbler....25
amber....30
green/blue....40
ruby stain....35
Wine....20
amber....25
green/blue....35
ruby stain....30

GEM STAR
Berry Bowl, lg....30
Berry Bowl, sm....10
Butter....45
Celery Dish....20
Creamer, Spooner or Sugar....20
Cruet....45
Pickle Dish....25
Relish Dish....25

GEORGE VI CORONATION
Basket, scarce....125

GEORGIA BELLE
Banana Bowl....25
Berry Bowl, sm....10
Berry Bowl, lg....25
Butter....55
Creamer or Spooner....25
Goblet....30
Pitcher....70
Sugar....30
Tumbler....10
Wine....15

GERMAN CLOCK
Square Clock, complete with works
vaseline....125

GIANT BULLS-EYE
Bottle with Stopper, 3 sizes....40 - 65
Bowl, 8"....35
Butter....60
Cake Stand....90
Cheese Dish w/Lid....145
Compote, open....50
Compote, covered....90
Condiment Set, complete....190
Creamer or Spooner....35
Cruet....70
Decanter....120
Goblet....40
Lamp....325
Pitcher....70
Pitcher, tall tankard....90
Relish....20
Sugar....60
Syrup....100
Toothpick....55
Tray....50
Tumbler....40
Vase, 2 sizes....30 - 40
Wine....20

GIBSON CAMEO
Plate, 8½"....75

GIBSON GIRL
Bowl....125
Butter....300
Creamer or Spooner....100
Pitcher....525
Plate, 10"....175
Relish Dish....135

Sauce 80
Sugar 200
Tumbler 90

GIRAFFE
Goblet 95

GIRL WITH A FAN
Goblet 90

GIRL WITH LADEN APRON
Plate, rnd., scarce 125

GIVE US OUR DAILY BREAD
Plate w/Dew Drop Pattern 65

GLASSPORT BRAVE
Advertising Tray, very scarce 100
amber 125
green/blue 115

GLOBE & STAR
Butter 60
Cake Stand 35
Celery Vase 20
Compote, covered 50
Compote, open 30
Creamer or Spooner 25
Goblet 35
Jelly Compote 30
Pickle Dish 20
Sugar 45
Wine 20

GOAT'S HEAD
Butter 225
Creamer or Spooner 65
Sugar 100
*All pieces rare.

GODDESS OF HUNT
Tray, rectangular w/hndls. 110

GO FURTHER AND FARE WORSE
Plate, small 85

GOLIATH
Vase, 18" - 20"
green/blue 150
black (ebony) 225

GOLDEN RULE
Plate, rnd., scarce 65

GONTERMAN SWIRL
Berry Bowl, lg.
amber 55
green/blue 65
Berry Bowl, sm.
amber 25
green/blue 35
Butter
amber 120
green/blue 150
Celery Vase
amber 30
green/blue 40
Cologne Bottle
amber 85
green/blue 95
Creamer or Spooner
amber 35
green/blue 45
Cruet
amber 90
green/blue 110
Finger Bowl
amber 30
green/blue 45
Lamp Shade
amber 95
green/blue 115
Pitcher
amber 165
green/blue 190
Shaker
amber 45
green/blue 55
Sugar
amber 55
green/blue 75
Toothpick Holder
amber 45
green/blue 55
Tumbler
amber 25
green/blue 35

"A GOOD BOY"
Mug 45

GOOD LUCK
*Not Part of Prayer Rug line.
Relish Dish 35

GOOFUS GRAPE
Bowl 45
Plate 60

GOOSEBERRY
Berry Bowl, sm. 35
milk glass 50
Berry Bowl, lg. 60
milk glass 70
Butter 80
milk glass 95
Cake Stand 150
Compote, covered, 3 sizes .... 80 - 135
milk glass .... 95 - 160
Creamer 50
milk glass 60
Goblet 50
milk glass 60
Lemonade Glass, handled 90
Mug 40
milk glass 45
Pitcher 275
milk glass 495
Spooner 40
milk glass 45
Sugar 70
milk glass 85
Syrup 190
milk glass 280
Tumbler 45
milk glass 60
Wine 35
milk glass 50

GOOSEBERRY VARIANT
Mug 35
green/blue 40

GOOSE BOY
Compote, open 115

GORDON
Compote, covered 85

GOTHIC
Bowls, 2 sizes .... 80 - 100
ruby stain .... 100 - 135
Bowl, oval vegetable 60
ruby stain 90
Butter 55
ruby stain 125
Celery Vase 45
ruby stain 90
Creamer 35
ruby stain 60
Jelly Compote 30
ruby stain 60
Pitcher 85
ruby stain 165
Shakers, ea. 30
ruby stain 75
Spooner 35
ruby stain 70
Toothpick 25
ruby stain 90
Tumbler 30
ruby stain 60
Wine 25
ruby stain 50

GOTHIC GRAPE
Dresser Set w/Mirrored Tray 145
Lamp, from perfume 100
Vase, 9" 70

GOTHIC WINDOWS
Berry Bowl, sm. 15
Berry Bowl, lg. 40
Butter 65
Creamer or Spooner 20
Goblet 45
Pickle Dish 20
Pitcher 85
Sugar 30
Tumbler 20

GRAND
Bowl, covered, flat or ftd. .... 50 - 65
Bowl, open, ftd. .... 30 - 35
Butter 60
Cake Stand, 8" - 10" .... 60 - 90
Celery Vase 40
Compote, covered, high or low.. 60 - 100
Compote, open, high or low .... 30 - 55
Cordial 85
Creamer or Spooner 35
Decanter 170
Dish, oval, 7" - 9" .... 20 - 35
Goblet .... 30 - 35
Mug 50
Pitcher 75
Plate, 10" - 11" .... 30 - 35
Relish 20
Shakers, ea. 40
Sherbet 25
Sugar 50
Syrup 145
Waste Bowl 40
Water Tray 50
Wine 25

GRAND ARMY OF THE REPUBLIC (GAR)
Tray, rare 350

GRAPE (KING, SON & COMPANY)
Mug 100

GRAPE & CABLE (FENTON)
Candle holder
Coke bottle green 65
Fruit Bowl, large.,ftd.
lime green 150
Punch Bowl, very rare 500
Punch Cup, rare 40

GRAPE & CABLE (NORTHWOOD)
Banana Bowl 175
Orange Bowl 145
Sweetmeat, covered 175
Plate, very scarce 200
*All pieces scarce, rare.

GRAPE & CABLE W/THUMBPRINTS
Berry Bowl, sm. 35
Berry Bowl, lg. 100

GRAPE & FESTOON
Bowl 35
Butter 75
Celery Vase 30
Compote, covered, high 130
Compote, covered, low 75
Cordial 20
Creamer or Spooner 30
Egg Cup 25
Goblet 60
Lamp, 7½" 120
Milk Pitcher 190
Pickle Tray 20
Plate 30
Pitcher 165
Relish Tray 20
Salt, master 25
Sauce 10
Sugar 65
Wine 35

GRAPE ARBOR
Hat Shape, from tumbler
custard 75

Pitcher
custard 325
Tumbler
custard 55

GRAPE BAND
Butter 90
Celery Vase 35
Compote, covered, high or low.. 90 - 120
Compote, open 50
Cordial 35
Creamer or Spooner 60
Egg Cup 35
Goblet 40
Master Salt 35
Pickle Dish 20
Pitcher 175
Plate, 6" 25
Sugar 70
Tumbler 30
Wine 35

GRAPE BUNCH
Butter 55
vaseline 95
Celery Vase 20
vaseline 40
Cordial 20
vaseline 40
Creamer or Spooner 20
vaseline 45
Goblet 30
vaseline 50
Pickle Dish 20
vaseline 35
Pitcher 80
vaseline 150
Sugar 30
vaseline 55
Tumbler 15
vaseline 30
Wine 10
vaseline 25

GRAPE FRIEZE (VERRE D'OR)
Bowl
green/blue 70
amethyst 75
Compote
green/blue 60
amethyst 75
custard
green/blue 65
amethyst 75
Nappy
green/blue 75
amethyst 85
Plate
green/blue 90
amethyst 125

GRAPE MATCH HOLDER
Match Holder, very scarce 185
blue opaque 200

GRAPE ON CRACKLE
Vase, 9" 35

GRAPE & ROSES ON BASKETWEAVE
Vase, 10" 20

GRAPES WITH OVERLAPPING FOLIAGE
Butter 80
opal 135
Celery Vase 40
opal 70
Creamer or Spooner 50
opal 75
Nappy, 4"& 8" .... 25 - 40
opal .... 40 - 70
Pitcher 125
opal 325
Sugar 50
opal 80

GRAPEVINE & CHERRY SPRIG
Bowl, ftd. 125
Butter 145
Creamer or Spooner 45
Pitcher 275
Sugar 60
Tumbler 40

*Add 25% for gilded and/or stained pieces.

GRAPEVINE BASKET
Basket, metal handle 60
green/blue 80

GRAPEVINE LATTICE
Hat Whimsey JIP Shape, from tumbler
amethyst 85

GRAPE WITHOUT VINE
Berry Bowl, sm. 20
Berry Bowl, lg. 45
Bowls, 4 sizes .... 10 - 50
Bowls, covered, 4 sizes .... 15 - 60
Butter 65
Compote, covered, 4 sizes .... 35 - 85
Compote, open, 4 sizes .... 20 - 60
Creamer or Spooner 30
Pitcher 110
Sugar 30
Tumbler 20

GRAPE WITH THUMBPRINT
Bowl 30
Butter 70
Compote, covered 45
Creamer or Spooner 20
Cup 10
Pitcher 80
Shakers, ea. 20
Sugar 30
Toothpick Holder 25
Tumbler 20

GRAPE WITH VINE
Bowl, lg. 35
Bowl, sm. 15
Butter 45
Celery Vase 30
Compote 40
Creamer, Spooner or Sugar 25
Honey Dish 30
Salt Shaker, ea. 25

GRASSHOPPER
Bowl, covered 100
amber 165
vaseline 200
Bowl, open 80
Butter 200
amber 290
Celery Vase 175
amber 225
Compote, 7" - 8½" .... 200 - 245
Creamer or Spooner 100
amber 145
vaseline 190
Marmalade Jar 150
Pickle Dish 30
Pitcher 245
amber 360
Plate, 8½" - 10½" .... 50 - 70
amber .... 100 - 225
Salt Dip 70
Salt Shaker 90
Sauce, flat or ftd. 20
Sugar 155
amber 195

*Pieces without insect 30% less in price.

GRATED DIAMOND & SUNBURST
Bowl, various sizes .... 15 - 35
Butter 55
Carafe 40
Creamer or Spooner 25
Punch Bowl 95
Punch Cup 15
Salt Dip 25
Shakers, ea. 25
Sugar 30
Toothpick Holder 30

GRATED RIBBON
Bowls, various .... 15 - 35
Butter 55
Creamer or Spooner 20
Goblet 40
Pitcher 65
Sugar 25
Tumbler 15

GREEK KEY & MERCURY LAMP
Oil Lamp
vaseline 350

GREEK KEY & SCALES
Bowl, dome ftd. 45

GREENBURG'S FLORIDA
Banana Bowl, stemmed 35
ruby stain 45
Berry Bowl, sm. 20
ruby stain 30
Berry Bowl, lg. 45
ruby stain 60
Butter 65
ruby stain 80
Cake Stand 45
ruby stain 55
Creamer or Spooner 30
ruby stain 40
Pitcher 90
ruby stain 120
Sugar 40
ruby stain 50
Tumbler 20
ruby stain 30

GREENTOWN SQUIRREL
Pitcher, rare 450
chocolate 600

GRENADE
Berry Bowl, sm. 10
green/blue 20
Berry Bowl, lg. 30
green/blue 45
Butter 55
green/blue 70
Creamer or Spooner 25
green/blue 35
Sugar 30
green/blue 40

GROGAN
Butter 50
Celery Vase 15
Creamer or Spooner 20
Goblet 30
amber 50
Sugar 25
Wine 20

GROOVE AND SLASH
Berry Bowl, sm. 20
Berry Bowl, lg. 45
Bonbon 30
Butter 70
Celery Vase 30
Compote 55
Cracker Jar 50
Cruet 75
Pickle Jar 45
Pitcher 95
Plates, 5" & 6" 35
Shakers, ea. 25
Spoon Tray 35
Tumbler 20
Vase 40

GRUMPY WOMAN & MAN
Mug 60
opaque blue 90

HAMILTON (CAPE COD)
Butter 130
Castor Set, complete 225
Champagne 185
Compote, covered 165

Compote, open ... 130
Creamer, pressed and applied handles. . 60 – 185
Decanter ... 600
Egg Cup ... 470
Goblet ... 50
Hat whimsey, from tumbler,
very rare ... 1,900
Pitcher ... 1,500
Salt Dip ... 40
Sauce ... 20
Spooner ... 50
Sugar ... 130
Syrup ... 800
Tumbler ... 80
Whiskey Tumbler ... 100
Wine ... 95

*For deep blue add 15%.

HAND
Bowls, 7" - 10" ... 30 - 55
Butter ... 95
Cake Stand ... 35
Celery Vase ... 25
Compote, covered, 7" - 8" ... 45 - 65
Compote, open, 8" - 9" ... 30 - 50
Cordial ... 20
Creamer or Spooner ... 25
Dish, oval, 7" - 10" ... 20 - 35
Goblet ... 75
Honey Dish ... 35
Jam Jar ... 65
Mug ... 55
Pickle Tray ... 25
Pitcher ... 100
Platter ... 35
Sauce, flat or ftd ... 20
Sugar ... 40
Syrup ... 65
Tumbler ... 35
Water Tray ... 45
Wine ... 20

HAND & TORCH
Compote, open ... 90

HAND VASE
Vase, 5" & 6" ... 45
amber ... 65
vaseline ... 125
green/blue ... 100

HAND WITH FAN
Match Holder ... 70
milk glass ... 85

HANGING BASKET VARIANT
Celery Vase, handled ... 50

HANOVER
Bowl, 7" - 10" ... 20 - 40
amber ... 25 - 45
vaseline ... 35 - 55
green/blue ... 30 - 50
Butter ... 60
amber ... 60
vaseline ... 70
green/blue ... 65
Cake Stand ... 35
amber ... 70
vaseline ... 100
green/blue ... 90
Celery Vase ... 20
amber ... 45
vaseline ... 75
green/blue ... 65
Cheese Dish, covered ... 85
amber ... 100
vaseline ... 130
green/blue ... 120
Compote, covered, 7" - 8" ... 55
amber ... 90
vaseline ... 130
green/blue ... 115
Creamer or Spooner ... 25
amber ... 45
vaseline ... 60
green/blue ... 55
Cruet ... 45
amber ... 65
vaseline ... 90
green/blue ... 80
Goblet ... 45
amber ... 55
vaseline ... 75
green/blue ... 65
Milk Pitcher ... 65
amber ... 75
vaseline ... 95
green/blue ... 80
Mug, 2 sizes ... 25 - 30
amber ... 30 - 35
vaseline ... 45 - 55
green/blue ... 50 - 55
Pitcher ... 70
amber ... 80
vaseline ... 120
green/blue ... 90
Plate, 4" - 10" ... 20 - 30
amber ... 30 - 40
vaseline ... 40 - 60
green/blue ... 35 - 50
Platter ... 30
amber ... 40
vaseline ... 60
green/blue ... 50
Sauce ... 10
amber ... 15
vaseline ... 25
green/blue ... 20
Sugar ... 30
amber ... 45
vaseline ... 60
green/blue ... 50
Tumbler ... 20
amber ... 30
vaseline ... 50
green/blue ... 40
Wine ... 20
amber ... 30
vaseline ... 45
green/blue ... 35

HARE & CHICKEN
Shakers, each
milk glass ... 185

HARP
Double Relish, scarce ... 150

HARSHAW'S ASHTRAY
Ashtray, advertising
vaseline ... 85

HARTFORD (FOSTORIA) ...
Berry Bowl, sm. ... 15
amber ... 25
ruby stain ... 30
Berry Bowl, lg. ... 40
amber ... 50
ruby stain ... 60
Butter ... 70
amber ... 85
ruby stain ... 95
Creamer or Spooner ... 35
amber ... 45
ruby stain ... 50
Plate ... 35
amber ... 40
ruby stain ... 45
Pitcher ... 90
amber ... 110
ruby stain ... 130
Sugar ... 40
amber ... 50
ruby stain ... 65
Tumbler ... 20
amber ... 25
ruby stain ... 30

HARTLEY
Bowl, 6" - 9" ... 15 - 30
amber ... 20 - 35
vaseline ... 30 - 50
green/blue ... 25 - 40
Bread Plate ... 30
amber ... 35
vaseline ... 65
green/blue ... 40
Butter ... 50
amber ... 55
vaseline ... 90
green/blue ... 75
Cake Plate ... 70
amber ... 90
vaseline ... 130
green/blue ... 100
Celery Vase ... 25
amber ... 45
vaseline ... 70
green/blue ... 55
Compote, covered, 7" - 8" ... 60 - 70
amber ... 70 - 85
vaseline ... 80 - 140
green/blue ... 75 - 120
Compote, open, 7" - 8" ... 30 - 40
amber ... 35 - 45
vaseline ... 45 - 55
green/blue ... 40 - 50
Creamer or Spooner ... 20
amber ... 30
vaseline ... 55
green/blue ... 40
Goblet ... 35
amber ... 40
vaseline ... 50
green/blue ... 45
Milk Pitcher ... 75
amber ... 85
vaseline ... 120
green/blue ... 100
Pitcher ... 90
amber ... 100
vaseline ... 130
green/blue ... 120
Plate ... 25
amber ... 30
vaseline ... 60
green/blue ... 45
Relish Tray ... 15
amber ... 20
vaseline ... 25
green/blue ... 25
Sugar ... 40
amber ... 45
vaseline ... 65
green/blue ... 50
Tumbler ... 15
amber ... 20
vaseline ... 45
green/blue ... 30
Wine ... 15
amber ... 30
vaseline ... 55
green/blue ... 40

HARTMAN
Pitcher, scarce ... 165

HARVARD YARD
Bowls, various ... 20 - 40
green/blue ... 40 - 60
ruby stain ... 35 - 50
Butter ... 65
green/blue ... 80
ruby stain ... 85
Cake Stand ... 60
green/blue ... 90
ruby stain ... 75
Condiment Set, complete ... 85
green/blue ... 125

ruby stain 100
Cordial 25
green/blue 40
ruby stain 35
Creamer 25
green/blue 45
ruby stain 35
Egg Cup 20
green/blue 35
ruby stain 45
Goblet 25
green/blue 45
ruby stain 50
Oval Tray 25
green/blue 35
ruby stain 40
Pickle Dish 20
green/blue 25
ruby stain 30
Pitcher 75
green/blue 120
ruby stain 90
Plate, 10" 25
green/blue 45
ruby stain 35
Salt Dip 20
green/blue 40
ruby stain 30
Sauce 15
green/blue 35
ruby stain 25
Shakers, ea 40
green/blue 70
ruby stain 50
Spooner 25
green/blue 30
ruby stain 35
Sugar 35
green/blue 60
ruby stain 50
Syrup 60
green/blue 100
ruby stain 75
Toothpick Holder 35
green/blue 60
ruby stain 45
Tumbler 25
green/blue 45
ruby stain 35
Wine 20
green/blue 35
ruby stain 30

HATCHET
Novelty Piece 30
green/blue 50
ruby stain 65

HATTIE
Bowl, very scarce 75

HAWAIIAN LEI (AKA: GALA)
Basket 55
Butter 80
Cake Stand 50
Celery Tray 30
Child's Table Set, complete 95
Compote 40
Creamer or Spooner 30
Ice Cream, stemmed 35
Jelly Compote, tall 40
Mayonnaise Bowl 30
Nappy 25
Pickle Dish, oval 20
Pitcher, 3 sizes .... 65 - 110
Plates, various .... 20 - 50
Rose Bowl 30
Salver 45
Sauce 15
Sherbet 20
Sugar 40
Toothpick Holder 40
Tumbler 15
Twin Relish 30
Vase, 2 sizes .... 20 - 35
Wafer Stand 35

HEART & SAND
Bowl, 4½" - 9" .... 20 - 50
Butter 75
Creamer or Spooner 20
Pitcher 90
Sugar 30
Toothpick Holder 25
Tumbler 20

HEART BAND
Butter 55
ruby stain 80
Celery Vase 25
ruby stain 35
Creamer or Spooner 35
ruby stain 45
Mug 40
ruby stain 55
Shakers, ea 25
ruby stain 30
Sugar 55
ruby stain 65
Toothpick Holder 35
ruby stain 60
Tumbler 20
ruby stain 30

HEART PLUME
Butter 60
Compote 35
Creamer, "Illinois Furniture Co." 75
Creamer or Spooner 20
Goblet 25
Pickle Dish 20
Pitcher 75
Relish Tray 20
Shakers, ea 25
Sugar 30
Syrup 70
Tumbler 20
Wine 15

HEART STEM ....
Berry Bowl, lg 75
Berry Bowl, sm. 20
Cake Stand 115
Celery Vase 85
Compote 95
Creamer 65
Pitcher 175
Salt Shaker 40
Tray 85
Tumbler 35

HEART WITH THUMBPRINT
Banana Boat, 2 sizes .... 140 - 175
ruby stain .... 300 - 425
Barber Bottle 140
Berry Bowl, sm. 45
green/blue .... 150 - 200
ruby stain .... 130 - 175
Berry Bowl, lg 75
green/blue .... 160 - 225
ruby stain .... 175 - 375
Butter 165
green/blue 350
ruby stain 465
Cake Stand 550
ruby stain 1,500
Carafe 285
ruby stain 425
Card Tray 25
green/blue 60
ruby stain 90
Celery Vase 75
ruby stain 195
Compote, 2 sizes .... 350 - 450
green/blue 1,200
ruby stain .... 800 - 1,000
Condiment Tray 50
green/blue 75
ruby stain 55
Creamer, 2 sizes .... 25 - 90
green/blue .... 50 - 225
ruby stain .... 45 - 190
Cruet 135
Goblet 80
green/blue 295
ruby stain 450
Hair Receiver 95
green/blue 150
ruby stain 200
Ice Bucket 95
Mustard Pot 80
green/blue 125
Oil Lamp, table & finger styles. 100 - 300
green/blue .... 320 - 475
Pitcher, very rare 1,900
Plate, 6" - 10" .... 30 - 80
green/blue .... 50 - 100
ruby stain .... 60 - 120
Powder Jar 85
Punch Cup 30
green/blue 50
ruby stain 60
Rose Bowl, 2 sizes 85
ruby stain .... 125 - 160
Spooner 85
green/blue 150
ruby stain 200
Sugar, lg., covered 175
green/blue 250
ruby stain 300
Sugar, sm., open 30
green/blue 40
ruby stain 45
Syrup, 2 sizes .... 150 - 195
Tumbler 70
green/blue 90
ruby stain 120
Vase, 2 sizes .... 30 - 60
green/blue .... 90 - 130
ruby stain .... 125 - 155
Wine 60
green/blue 230
ruby stain 375

HEAVY FINECUT (#800)
Butter Pat 20
amber 30
vaseline 35
green/blue 30
Celery Boat 20
amber 30
vaseline 35
green/blue 30
Celery Vase 25
amber 35
vaseline 40
green/blue 35
Champagne 15
amber 25
vaseline 30
green/blue 25
Cheese Plate w/Cover 70
amber 85
vaseline 135
green/blue 95
Claret 20
amber 30
vaseline 40
green/blue 45
Cologne, 5 sizes .... 30 - 55
amber .... 40 - 65
vaseline .... 60 - 90
green/blue .... 70 - 95
Cordial 15
amber 25
vaseline 35

green/blue 40
Decanter 55
amber 65
vaseline 80
green/blue 70
Finger Bowl, 4 styles .... 20 - 40
amber .... 30 - 50
vaseline .... 40 - 60
green/blue .... 35 - 55
Goblet 30
amber 40
vaseline 50
green/blue 45
Lamp 75
amber 85
vaseline 165
green/blue 145
Molasses Can 40
amber 50
vaseline 65
green/blue 60
Mustard Jar 30
amber 40
vaseline 50
green/blue 40
Oil Bottle 50
amber 65
vaseline 85
green/blue 75
Pickle Boat 15
amber 20
vaseline 35
green/blue 30
Pickle Jar 25
amber 30
vaseline 40
green/blue 35
Pitcher 85
amber 95
vaseline 180
green/blue 145
Plate, 3 sizes .... 15 - 35
amber .... 20 - 40
vaseline .... 35 - 50
green/blue .... 30 - 45
Salt 15
amber 20
vaseline 30
green/blue 25
Salver, 3 sizes .... 25 - 60
amber .... 35 - 70
vaseline .... 60 - 100
green/blue .... 55 - 85
Tray 30
amber 40
vaseline 60
green/blue 50
Tumbler 20
amber 25
vaseline 35
green/blue 30
Water bottle 45
amber 55
vaseline 70
green/blue 65

HEAVY JEWEL
Bowl, lg. 40
Bowl, sm. 20
Butter 50
Celery Vase 35
Compote 40
Creamer, Spooner or Sugar 25
Tray Oval, 8"x14" 65

HEAVY LEAF
Bowl 40

HELMET
Butter/Novelty, rare 575
green/blue 1,200

HENRIETTA
Bone Dish 25
Bowl, rectangular 30
Bowl, rnd., 7" - 9" .... 20 - 35
Bread Plate 25
Butter 70
Cake Stand 90
Castor Set 100
Celery Tray 25
Celery Vase 20
Compote, open 25
Confection Jar w/Lid 95
Cracker Jar 85
Creamer or Spooner 30
Creamer, ind. 20
Cruet 60
Cup 15
Lamp 100
Mustard Jar 40
Olive Dish 20
Pickle Jar 90
Pitcher, 2 styles .... 75 - 125
Rose Bowl 30
Salt, ind. 10
Salt, master 25
Sauce 10
Shade, Electric 50
Shakers, ea., 2 styles .... 20 - 40
Sugar 50
Sugar, ind. 30
Syrup 90
Tumbler, 2 styles .... 20 - 35
Vase, 5" - 9" .... 20 - 30

HERCULES (ATTERBURY)
Compote
milk glass 125
Lamp
milk glass 300

HERO
Berry Bowl, sm. 15
Berry Bowl, lg. 40
Butter 70
Cake Stand 35
Celery Vase 25
Creamer or Spooner 20
Cruet 50
Goblet 35
Mustard Pot 25
Shakers, ea. 20
Sugar 30

HEROES OF BUNKER HILL
Bread Plate, oval 80

HERON
Pickle Castor 100

HERON (GREENTOWN)
Pitcher, very scarce 425
chocolate 650

HERON & PEACOCK
Mug 60
green/blue 85
milk glass 55

HERRINGBONE
Berry Bowl, lg. 35
Berry Bowl, sm. 10
Butter 50
Celery Vase 30
Compote w/lid 55
Creamer, Spooner or Sugar 30
Goblet 30
Pickle Dish 25
Pitcher 70
Relish 20
Tumbler 15

HERRINGBONE BUTTRESS
Bowls, various .... 30 - 65
amber .... 45 - 75
Butter 75
Butter, on pedestal 100
Cake Stand 65
Cordial, 2 sizes .... 35 - 40
amber 55
green/blue 65
Cracker Jar 65
Creamer or Spooner 40
Cruet 65
Goblet 55
Nappy 35
Pitcher 145
Punch Cup 25
Shakers, ea. 45
Sauce 30
Sugar w/Lid 50
Syrup 75
Tumbler, 2 styles 35
Vase, 3 sizes .... 25 - 45
Wine 30
amber 45
green/blue 65

HEXAGONAL BLOCK
Butter 65
Creamer 30
Goblet 40
Relish Dish 25
Spooner 35
Sugar 40
Wine 25

HEXAGONAL BLOCK BAND
Berry Bowl, sm. 15
Berry Bowl, lg. 45
Butter 65
Celery Vase 25
Creamer or Spooner 25
Goblet 50
Pickle Dish 20
Pitcher 110
Sugar 30
Tumbler 20
Wine 20

HEXAGONAL BULLS-EYE
Butter 55
Celery Vase 30
Creamer or Spooner 20
Goblet 35
Pitcher 75
Sauce 15
Sugar 25
Tumbler 20
Wine 15

HEY, DIDDLE DIDDLE
Nursery Rhyme Plate, one in a series 45

HICKMAN
Banana Stand 60
Bonbon, sq. 20
Bottle, Pepper 35
Bowls, 4" - 8" .... 15 - 40
green/blue .... 20 - 60
Butter 45
green/blue 75
Celery 20
green/blue 40
Champagne 20
Cologne bottle 40
Compote, covered, 7" 85
Compote, open, 8" 45
Cordial 25
Creamer 25
green/blue 40
Cruet 50
Custard Cup 15
Goblet 35
green/blue 50
Ice Bucket 55
Jelly Compote 35
green/blue 45
Lemonade 20
Mustard Jar w/Underplate 50
Nappy 15

Olive Dish 10
green/blue 15
Pickle Dish 15
green/blue 20
Pitcher 75
Plate 20
Punch Bowl 200
green/blue 425
Punch Cup 10
green/blue 20
Punch Cup, ftd. 40
Relish 15
green/blue 20
Rose Bowl 30
green/blue 40
Salt Dip, ind. 15
Sauce 10
green/blue 15
Shaker, 3 styles, ea. .... 20 - 35
green/blue .... 25 - 60
Sugar 45
green/blue 65
Toothpick Holder 40
green/blue 80
Toy Condiment Set 95
green/blue 150
Tumbler 30
Vase, 10" 15
green/blue 40
Wine 25
green/blue 30

HIDALGO
Berry Bowl, sm. 15
Berry Bowl, lg. 40
Bread Plate 30
Butter 65
Compote, covered, high or low... 40 - 55
Compote, open, 6" - 11" .... 25 - 45
Creamer or Spooner 20
Cruet 55
Cup & Saucer 35
Finger Bowl 15
Goblet 35
Milk Pitcher 60
Handled Nappy 20
Pickle Dish 20
Pitcher 75
Salt, ind. 10
Salt, master 25
Sugar 30
Syrup 90
Tumbler 20
Waste Bowl 15
Water Tray 35

HIGBEE MUG
Advertising Mug 70

HIGH HOB
Bowls, various .... 15 - 35
ruby stain .... 25 - 40
Butter 50
ruby stain 70
Compotes .... 25 - 45
ruby stain .... 35 - 50
Creamer 20
ruby stain 30
Goblet 35
ruby stain 45
Pitcher 70
ruby stain 85
Relish 20
ruby stain 30
Spooner 25
ruby stain 35
Sugar 35
ruby stain 45
Tumbler 20
ruby stain 30
Vase 25
ruby stain 35

Wine 20
ruby stain 30

HINTO
Butter 50
vaseline 110
Celery Vase 20
vaseline 35
Champagne 15
vaseline 25
Creamer or Spooner 20
vaseline 35
Egg Cup 25
vaseline 40
Goblet 40
vaseline 65
Master Salt, open 20
vaseline 30
Sugar 35
vaseline 45
Sweetmeat w/Cover 65
vaseline 100
Tumbler, flat 25
vaseline 40
Whiskey Tumbler 30
vaseline 50

HOBB'S #94
Molasses Can w/Metal Lid,
very scarce 150

HOBBS BLOCK
Bowl, oval, 7" - 10" .... 20 - 40
Butter 40
Celery Tray, boat shape 40
Creamer or Spooner 25
Cruet 55
Finger Bowl 20
Goblet 40
Pitcher 65
Sauce 15
Sugar 35
Syrup 50
Tumbler 20
Water bottle 40

*Add 10% for amber stain and
15% for frosted amber stained.

HOBBS CANOE - SEE DAISY & BUTTON (HOBBS)

HOBBS HOBNAIL (AKA: HOBBS DEWDROP)
Bitters Bottle 75
amber 95
vaseline 120
green/blue .... 100 - 130
Bowl, 3 sizes .... 45 - 60
amber .... 65 - 90
vaseline .... 80 - 110
green/blue .... 70 - 85
other .... 90 - 130
Bowl, oval, 3 sizes .... 55 - 80
amber .... 70 - 95
vaseline .... 75 - 115
green/blue .... 65 - 90
other .... 80 - 120
Butter 110
amber 135
vaseline 150
green/blue 140
other 140
Celery Vase 35
amber 50
vaseline 60
green/blue 55
other 70
Creamer or Spooner 30
amber 50
vaseline 60
green/blue 55
other 65
Cruet, Oil 60
amber 75
vaseline 85
green/blue 80

other 90
Finger Bowl 25
amber 40
vaseline 50
green/blue 45
other 60
Pickle Jar 45
amber 65
vaseline 75
green/blue 70
other 85
Pitcher 120
amber 155
vaseline 200
green/blue 165
other 265
Sauce 15
amber 30
vaseline 45
green/blue 40
other 50
Shaker 40
amber 60
vaseline 80
green/blue 75
other 85
Sugar 45
amber 65
vaseline 85
green/blue 80
other 95
Toy Pitcher 45
amber 55
vaseline 75
green/blue 60
other 80
Toy Tumbler 15
amber 45
vaseline 55
green/blue 50
other 65
Tray 30
amber 45
vaseline 65
green/blue 45
other 65
Tumbler 15
amber 35
vaseline 45
green/blue 40
other 50
Water bottle 50
amber 70
vaseline 90
green/blue 80
other 140
Vase 30
amber 50
vaseline 65
green/blue 60
other 80
Vase Whimsey, from pitcher 75
amber 90
vaseline 135
green/blue 85
other 125

HOBB'S POLKA DOT
Bar Bottle 65
amber 80
vaseline 90
green/blue 70
sapphire 110
Bowl, ftd. 55
amber 65
vaseline 75
green/blue 65
sapphire 90
Buttermilk Tumbler 30
amber 40

vaseline 65
green/blue 55
sapphire 80
Celery Vase 25
amber 35
vaseline 65
green/blue 55
sapphire 80
Champagne Glass 20
amber 40
vaseline 65
green/blue 50
sapphire 75
Cheese Dish, covered 50
amber 70
vaseline 100
green/blue 85
sapphire 145
Cruet 55
amber 65
vaseline 85
green/blue 70
sapphire 110
Custard Cup 20
amber 30
vaseline 55
green/blue 40
sapphire 75
Lemonade Mug 30
amber 40
vaseline 70
green/blue 60
sapphire 90
Mustard Pot 35
amber 45
vaseline 80
green/blue 70
sapphire 100
Oil Bottle 50
amber 60
vaseline 90
green/blue 75
sapphire 100
Pitcher, 5 sizes .... 75 - 115
amber .... 80 - 130
vaseline .... 125 - 250
green/blue .... 110 - 200
sapphire .... 145 - 300
Sauce 15
amber 25
vaseline 40
green/blue 30
sapphire 50
Shaker 40
amber 55
vaseline 70
green/blue 60
sapphire 75
Sugar, 2 styles 35
amber 50
vaseline 70
green/blue 55
sapphire 70
Tumbler 20
amber 30
vaseline 55
green/blue 40
sapphire 75
Water bottle 50
amber 65
vaseline 90
green/blue 70
sapphire 95

HOBNAIL
Bone Dish 15
Bowls, various .... 10 - 45
Butter 60
Celery Vase 30
Creamer or Spooner 25
Goblet 40
Mugs .... 15 - 50
Perfume 65
Pitcher 95
Shakers, ea. 25
Sugar 25
Toothpick Holder 40
Tray 35
Tumbler 20
Vase 30
Wine 25

HOBNAIL BAND
Butter 55
ruby stain 75
Candlesticks, ea. 20
ruby stain 30
Celery Tray 20
ruby stain 25
Champagne 15
ruby stain 30
Coaster 10
ruby stain 25
Creamer or Spooner 20
ruby stain 25
Cup & Saucer 35
ruby stain 40
Custard Cup 10
ruby stain 25
Goblet 40
ruby stain 60
Pitcher 65
ruby stain 95
Plate 20
ruby stain 45
Sauce 10
ruby stain 15
Sugar 30
ruby stain 45
Syrup 55
ruby stain 85
Tumbler 10
ruby stain 25
Wine 10
ruby stain 20

HOBNAIL-IN-SQUARE
Bowl, lg. 35
Bowl, sm. 15
Butter 45
Creamer, Spooner or Sugar 25
Cruet, rare 65
Pitcher 80
Shakers, ea. 20
Tumbler 20

HOBNAIL MUG
Mug, various sizes, either handle 40
amber 65
vaseline 85
green/blue 75

HOBNAIL WITH BARS
Berry Bowl, lg. 30
Berry Bowl, sm. 10
Butter 45
Cake Stand 45
Creamer, Spooner or Sugar 20
Cruet 45
Pitcher 75
Tumbler 20

HOBNAIL WITH FAN TOP
Bowl 35
amber 60
purple slag 125
Butter 45
amber 55
green/blue 60
Creamer or Spooner 20
amber 25
green/blue 30
Dish, oblong 20
amber 25
green/blue 30
Goblet 35
amber 45
green/blue 40
Pitcher 85
amber 100
green/blue 90
Salt Dip, ind. 15
amber 25
green/blue 20
Sauce 10
amber 20
green/blue 15
Sugar 25
amber 35
green/blue 30
Tray 30
amber 40
green/blue 35
Tumbler 15
amber 25
green/blue 20
Wine 10
amber 20
green/blue 15

HOBSTAR
Berry Bowl, sm. 10
Berry Bowl, lg. 30
Butter 55
Celery Vase 30
Compote, 10" - 11" 40
Cookie Jar w/Lid 40
Creamer or Spooner 20
Fruit Bowl, 10½" 35
Goblet 50
Jelly Compote 25
Nappy, 5" - 6" 20
Milk Jar w/Lid 60
Orange Bowl, 11" 35
Pitcher 75
Plate, 10½" 25
Plate, 5" 10
Punch Bowl 75
Punch Cup 15
Rose Bowl, 5½" 30
Rose Bowl, 7" - 9" 40
Salver, 13" 45
Sherbet 20
Sugar 25
Sundae 20
Syrup 55
Tumbler 15
Water Tray, 13" 25
Wine 20

HOBSTAR (U.S. #15124)
Butter 50
Candy Dish, covered 35
Celery Vase 20
Creamer or Spooner 20
Pickle Dish 15
Pitcher 70
Sugar 25
Tumbler 15

HOBSTAR & FEATHER
Apple Sauce Dish, 2 sizes .... 100 - 125
Banana Boat, 3 sizes .... 30 - 60
Banana Bowl, whimsey, from jelly 200
Basket, hndl., very scarce 300
Bowl, ice cream, lg. 60
Bowl, ice cream, sm. 25
maiden's blush 150
Bowl, lg. sq., scarce 200
Bowl, master berry 50
maiden's blush 900
Bowl, small berry 25
maiden's blush 350
Bowl, Tri-corner sauce, scarce 90
maiden's blush 150

Bowl, w/metal rim around edge, very rare ... 350
Bridge pcs., ea. ... 70
ruby stain ... 400
Bridge Set, complete ... 300
Butter ... 250
Card Tray ... 50
Card Tray Whimsey, from Spooner ... 325
Celery Boat, 10" - 5" ... 75
Compote Whimsey w/Metal Stem ... 250
Compote, giant whimsey ... 1,200
Cracker Jar ... 225
Creamer or Spooner ... 40
ruby stain ... 550
Jelly Compote, 6" ... 80
Master Boat, lg. ... 65
Master Boat, med ... 45
Master Boat, sm ... 25
Mint Bowl ... 150
ruby stain ... 600
Nut Bowl ... 150
Pickle Dish, lg. ... 55
Pickle Dish, med ... 40
sapphire ... 1,250
Pickle Dish, sm ... 25
Pitcher w/Metal Top, rare ... 700
Pitcher Whimsey, no spout, rare ... 750
Pitcher, mammoth, rare ... 800
Pitcher, standard ... 325
Plate, 11", 4 sides up, rare ... 275
Plate, 11" - 12", rare ... 200
Plate, 5" ... 75
Plate, 7" ... 95
Plate, 9" ... 100
Plate, diamond shape, rare ... 225
Plate, handgrip, rare ... 95
Platter, lg., rare ... 300
Platter, sm., rare ... 200
Punch Bowl w/Base ... 850
Punch Cup ... 20
Rose Bowl giant ICS whimsey ... 1,100
Rose Bowl, giant ... 900
Rose Bowl, lg., flat ... 125
Rose Bowl, sm., flat ... 95
Rose Bowl, stemmed ... 175
Sherbet, flared top ... 40
Sherbet, goblet shape ... 50
Sherbet, rose bowl shape ... 90
Spittoon Whimsey, very rare ... 1,500
Sugar w/Lid ... 50
ruby stain ... 800
Tumbler ... 60
*All pieces scarce, rare.
*Add 25% for frosted pieces.

HOBSTAR & TASSEL
Banana Bowl, 7" ... 50
Berry Bowl, 5" ... 30
Berry Bowl, 7" ... 35
Bowl, deep, 6" ... 30
Ice Cream, 6½" ... 30
Grape Plate, 7½" ... 45
Plate, 7½" ... 55
Nut Bowl, 5" ... 35
Rose Bowl, 3 sizes, rare ... 75

HOBSTAR BAND
Bowls, various ... 10 - 35
Pitcher, ftd. ... 75
Pitcher, ftd., adv, rare ... 200
Tumbler ... 35

HOBSTAR FLOWER
Compote ... 40
Cruet ... 60

HOLLAND (OAT SPRAY)
Berry Bowl, sm. ... 20
Berry Bowl, lg. ... 45
Butter ... 80
Compote, covered ... 60
Compote, open ... 40
Creamer or Spooner ... 25
Goblet ... 60
Pickle Dish ... 20
Pitcher ... 110
Sugar ... 30
Toothpick Holder ... 35
Tumbler ... 20
Wine ... 15

HOLLIS
Celery Vase ... 25
Pitcher ... 75
Tumbler ... 20

HOLLY
Bowl, covered, 2 styles ... 195 - 265
Butter ... 265
Cake Stand, 4 sizes ... 200 - 400
Celery Vase ... 200
Compote, covered, high ... 250 - 550
Compote, covered, low ... 225 - 425
Creamer or Spooner ... 195
Egg Cup ... 100
Goblet ... 120
Pickle Dish ... 100
Pitcher ... 250
Salt Dip ... 185
Sauce ... 40 - 50
Sugar ... 225
Syrup, rare ... 300
Tumbler, flat or ftd. ... 175 - 200
Wine ... 195

HOLLY (FENTON)
Bowl, very scarce
cobalt ... 225
Compote, very scarce
cobalt ... 90

HOLLY AMBER (GREENTOWN)
Bowl, 6" - 8½" ... 100 - 125
chocolate ... 600 - 800
Bowl, oval ... 125
chocolate ... 425
Bowl, oval, ftd. ... 200
chocolate ... 1,900
Bowl, rectangular ... 225
chocolate ... 1,000
Butter ... 325
chocolate ... 1,600
Butter, ftd. ... 900
chocolate ... 6,500
Cake Stand ... 350
chocolate ... 4,200
Compote, covered, 6½" - 8½" ... 300 - 425
chocolate ... 1,000 - 3,500
Creamer ... 175
chocolate ... 800
Cruet ... 400
chocolate ... 2,800
Jelly Compote ... 350
chocolate ... 1,100
Mug ... 165
chocolate ... 550
Mustard Pot ... 250
chocolate ... 1,500
Nappy ... 165
chocolate ... 625
Pickle Dish ... 90
chocolate ... 400
Pitcher ... 1,000
chocolate ... 2,200
Plate on Pedestal, square ... 2,000
chocolate ... 6,000
Plate, round & square ... 225
green/blue ... 2,500
chocolate ... 800
Shakers, ea ... 225
chocolate ... 800
Sauce ... 125
chocolate ... 325
Spooner ... 200
rose agate ... 25,000
Sugar, 2 styles ... 350
chocolate ... 1,000 - 3,000
Syrup ... 600
chocolate ... 2,000
Toothpick Holder ... 175
white agate ... 5,000
Toothpick Holder, ftd. ... 325
chocolate ... 3,000
Tumbler ... 250
chocolate ... 950
Tumbler w/Beaded Rim
chocolate ... 5,500
Tray ... 225
chocolate ... 1,350
Vase, 6" - 8" ... 250 - 350
chocolate ... 900 - 2,000
*Chocolate same as golden agate.
*Plate listed as green/blue is light blue.

HONEYCOMB
Bowl, covered, various ... 95 - 165
vaseline ... 325
Bowls, open, various ... 50 - 100
Butter ... 80
Cake Stand, 4 sizes ... 100 - 225
Celery Vase ... 50
Compote, covered, various sizes ... 90 - 170
Compote, open, various sizes ... 40 - 85
Creamer or Spooner ... 70
Decanter ... 85
Egg Cup ... 30
Jam Jar, covered ... 85
Milk Pitcher ... 135
Pickle w/Lid ... 185
Pitcher, various ... 100 - 165
Sugar ... 80
Tumbler ... 50

HONEYCOMB & HOBSTAR (GLORIA)
Bowl, 2 sizes ... 15 - 40
ruby stain ... 25 - 60
Butter ... 150
ruby stain ... 200
Carafe ... 135
ruby stain ... 165
Compote ... 70
ruby stain ... 90
Creamer or Spooner ... 65
ruby stain ... 80
Pitcher ... 250
ruby stain ... 300
Sugar ... 75
ruby stain ... 110
Tumbler ... 35
ruby stain ... 45
Vase ... 350
*All pieces scarce.

HONEYCOMB WITH STAR
Berry Bowl, sm. ... 10
Berry Bowl, lg. ... 35
Butter ... 60
Cake Stand ... 35
Celery Vase ... 20
Compote ... 30
Creamer or Spooner ... 20
Cruet ... 50
Pickle Dish ... 15
Pitcher ... 85
Sauce, flat ... 10
Sugar ... 25
Tumbler ... 15

HOPS BAND
Bowls, various ... 30 - 55
Butter ... 70
Compote ... 45
Celery ... 35
Creamer or Spooner ... 35
Cruet ... 65
Goblet ... 40
Pickle Dish ... 30
Pitcher ... 90

Shakers, ea 30
Sugar 45
Syrup 70
Tumbler 20
Wine 30

HORN OF PLENTY
Bottles 125 - 300
Bowls, various 100 - 165
Butter 200
Butter, acorn finial 265
Butter, Washington finial, rare 675
Cake Stand, rare 2,000
Celery Vase 250
Champagne 150
Claret, very rare 900
Compote, covered 380
Compote, covered, acorn finial 575
Compote, covered, Washington finial 2,350
Compote, open, high and low, various 100 - 500
Creamer, 2 sizes 275 - 325
Decanter, w/bar lip 100
Decanter, w/stopper, 3 sizes 200 - 625
Egg Cup 65
Goblet, 2 sizes 100 - 150
Honey, covered, *ext. rare 8,500
Honey Underplate, *ext. rare 6,500
Lamp 400
Milk Pitcher 1,200
Mug 625
Pitcher 775
Plate 80
Salt 85
Spooner 75
Sugar 200
Tumbler, water and whiskey 130 - 165
Wine 225

HORSE
Goblet 95
Tumbler 70

*All pieces are engraved.

HORSE & CART
Match Holder 100

HORSE & TURRET
Horseradish Jar 100
vaseline 245
green/blue 200

HORSE, CAT & RABBIT
Goblet, rare 265

HORSE HEAD MUSTARD
Horseradish or Mustard Jar 135

HORSE INKWELL
Double Inkwell, frosted 250
vaseline 375
green/blue 300

HORSEMINT
Banana Bowl, ftd. 45
ruby stain 60
Butter 60
ruby stain 90
Cabaret Bowl 30
ruby stain 45
Celery Tray 20
ruby stain 35
Compote 40
ruby stain 70
Creamer or Spooner 20
ruby stain 30
Goblet 45
ruby stain 40
Heart Shape Dish 20
ruby stain 35
Nappy 20
ruby stain 35
Nut Bowl 20
ruby stain 30
Pickle Dish 20
ruby stain 30
Pitcher 80
ruby stain 125
Plate, 12" 30
ruby stain 40
Salad Bowl, lg. 35
ruby stain 45
Salad Bowl, sm. 15
ruby stain 25
Sugar 25
ruby stain 35
Tumbler 20
ruby stain 25
Vase, pedestal ftd. 30
ruby stain 45
Wine 25
ruby stain 30

HORSESHOE (AKA: GOOD LUCK OR PRAYER RUG)
Bowl w/Cover, 3 sizes 100 - 175
Bowl, open, 3 sizes 40 - 55
Butter 135
Cake Stand, 3 sizes 150 - 245
Celery Vase 90
Cheese Dish, covered 285
Compote w/Lid 125 - 225
Creamer or Spooner 25
Jam Jar 25
Master Salt, rare 65
Plate, 8" - 10" 60 - 90
Relish 35
Sugar 100
Tray, 2 styles 40 - 125
Wine, rare 240

HORSESHOE DAISY (NEW MARTINSVILLE)
Bowls, various 15 - 35
ruby stain 25 - 70
Butter 70
ruby stain 110
Creamer or Spooner 25
ruby stain 45
Olive Dish 20
ruby stain 35
Pitcher 95
ruby stain 145
Sugar 35
ruby stain 60
Tumbler 15
ruby stain 25

HORSESHOE MEDALLION
Berry Bowl, sm. 20
ruby stain 25
Berry Bowl, lg. 40
ruby stain 50
Butter 60
ruby stain 80
Creamer or Spooner 25
ruby stain 35
Pitcher 80
ruby stain 100
Sugar 35
ruby stain 50
Tumbler 20
ruby stain 30

HORSESHOW PAPERWEIGHT
Paperweight, very scarce 150

HORSESHOE STEM
Butter 170
Cake Stand, 3 sizes 200 - 300
Celery Vase 125
Compotes, covered 300 - 350
Creamer 100
Goblet 125
Milk Pitcher 375
Pitcher 475
Sauce 30
Spooner 100
Sugar 165
Tumbler 80

HORSESHOE TUMBLER
Tumbler, with stippled horseshoe 30

HOURGLASS
Butter 60
Creamer or Spooner 25
Goblet 40
Pitcher 85
Sauce 10
Sugar 30
Tumbler 15

HOUSES MEDALLION
Mug, very scarce 50
amber 70
vaseline 95

HUBER (FALMOUTH)
Bitters bottle 75
Bowl, covered, various 70 - 90
Bowl, open, various 25 - 60
Celery Vase 60
Compote, covered, various 100 - 130
Compote, open, many sizes and styles 30 - 120
Creamer or Spooner 60
Decanter, with or without stopper 60 - 100
Egg Cup, hndl. 30
Mug 60
Pitcher, 2 sizes 225 - 300
Plate 30
Salt Dip 30
Sugar 60
Tumbler 50
Whiskey, hndl. 60
Wine 20

HUMMINGBIRD
Bowl, 5½" 70
amber 100
Butter 75
amber 90
vaseline 150
green/blue 130
Celery Vase 60
amber 90
vaseline 120
green/blue 100
Cheese Plate 45
amber 55
vaseline 70
green/blue 65
Compote 60
amber 80
vaseline 150
green/blue 120
Creamer or Spooner 40
amber 70
vaseline 85
green/blue 70
Goblet 75
amber 70
vaseline 140
green/blue 125
Milk Pitcher 60
amber 70
vaseline 120
green/blue 90
Pickle Dish 35
amber 40
vaseline 60
green/blue 50
Open Salt 25
amber 30
vaseline 40
green/blue 35
Pitcher 95
amber 100
vaseline 180
green/blue 150
Sauce 15
amber 25

vaseline ... 30
green/blue ... 25
Sugar ... 60
amber ... 80
vaseline ... 130
green/blue ... 100
Tumbler ... 50
amber ... 70
vaseline ... 95
green/blue ... 80
Wine ... 60
amber ... 70
vaseline ... 100
green/blue ... 90

HUMPTY DUMPTY
Mug ... 55

HUNDRED-LEAVED ROSE
Bowl ... 35
Butter ... 70
Creamer or Spooner ... 30
Pitcher ... 100
Sauce ... 15
Sugar, covered ... 50
Sugar, open ... 40
Tumbler ... 20

IBEX
Goblet, rare ... 225

ICELAND POPPY (VERRE D'OR)
Bowls
green/blue ... 80
amethyst ... 90
Compotes
green/blue ... 70
amethyst ... 85
Plates ...
green/blue ... 100
amethyst ... 120

ICELAND POPPY VARIANT (VERRE D'OR)
Bowls
green/blue ... 90
amethyst ... 100
Compotes
green/blue ... 85
amethyst ... 95

ICICLE
Bowls, flat oval ... 25 - 35
milk glass ... 40 - 55
Butter, 2 styles ... 60 - 80
milk glass ... 100 - 135
Butter, individual ... 50
milk glass ... 75
Celery ... 45
milk glass ... 55
Compote, covered or open ... 75 - 100
milk glass ... 100 - 200
Creamer, footed ... 75
milk glass ... 150
Goblet ... 50
milk glass ... 95
Honey dish ... 15
milk glass ... 25
Lamp, 9" ... 125
milk glass ... 200
Pitcher ... 250
milk glass ... 400
Salt, master ... 10
milk glass ... 15
Spooner ... 30
milk glass ... 70
Sugar ... 70
milk glass ... 135

*For other colors add 50% to milk glass prices.

ICICLE WITH STAR
Pitcher ... 75
Tumbler ... 20

I-H-C
Berry Bowl, sm. ... 15
Berry Bowl, lg. ... 45
Butter ... 70
Celery Vase ... 20
Compotes, various ... 20 - 50
Creamer or Spooner ... 20
Pickle Dish ... 20
Pitcher ... 95
Sauce ... 10
Sugar ... 30
Tumbler ... 20
Vase, 7" ... 35

*Add 25% for any green pieces.

I.H.S.
Oval Tray/Platter ... 45

ILLINOIS
Banquet Lamp & Shade, 2 sizes ... 1,200 - 2,000
Basket, hndl. ... 100
Berry Bowl, sm. ... 30
Berry Bowl, lg. ... 45
Bonbon, stemmed, 5" - 8" ... 60
Bowl, Ice Cream ... 40
Butter ... 80
Breakfast Set, 2 pcs. ... 70
Cake Stand ... 150
Candlesticks, ea. ... 300
Celery Tray ... 25
Celery Vase ... 50
Cheese Dish, covered ... 125
Compote, 9" ... 125
Creamer or Spooner ... 50
Cruet ... 80
Finger Bowl ... 60
Ice Cream Tray ... 20
Jam Jar ... 40
Jelly Compote ... 70
Olive Dish ... 20
Pickle Dish ... 25
green/blue ... 75
Pickle Jar ... 30
Pitcher, 2 sizes ... 90 - 125
green/blue ... 270
Plate, rnd. or sq. ... 35
Puff Box ... 75
Relish Tray ... 20
Salt, ind. ... 10
Salt, master ... 30
Sauce ... 10
Spoon Tray ... 25
Straw Holder w/Cover ... 365
green/blue ... 625
Sugar, various ... 30 - 70
Syrup ... 165
Toothpick Holder ... 30
Toothpick Holder, with advertising ... 60
Tumbler, 2 sizes ... 20 - 35
green/blue ... 45
Vase, 2 sizes ... 30 - 40
green/blue ... 100
Water Jug, squatty ... 75

IMPERIAL GRAPE
Bowls ... 15 - 25
Cordial ... 10
amberina ... 45
Goblet ... 20
Rose Bowl ... 25
amberina ... 75
Sandwich Platter, cntr. hndl. ... 25

IMPERIAL'S NU-CUT #91/500
Bowls, 3 sizes ... 15 - 35
Breakfast Creamer or Sugar ... 25
Jelly Compote ... 35
Nappy ... 25
Mayonnaise Bowl ... 25
Mayonnaise Plate, oval ... 25
Vase, 6½" ... 30

IMPERIAL NU-CUT #91/607
Bowls, various ... 15 - 40
Pickle Dish, hndl. ... 25

IMPERIAL'S NU-CUT #212
Creamer ... 20
Sugar, open ... 20

IMPERIAL SPITTOON
Novelty Spittoon, lg. ... 25

IMPERIAL'S #262
Olive Dish, hndl., 5" ... 35

IMPERIAL'S #300
Lemonade Set, complete ... 80
Pitcher ... 60
Tumbler ... 20

IMPERIAL'S #302
Berry Bowl, sm. ... 10
Berry Bowl, lg. ... 30
Bowl, 8½" - 9½" ... 25
Butter ... 45
Creamer or Spooner ... 20
Decanter ... 40
Goblet ... 30
Plate, 6" - 10" ... 20
Sugar ... 25
Sugar Shaker ... 45
Tumbler ... 15
Wine ... 10

IMPERIAL'S #303
Knife Rest ... 25

IMPERIAL'S #347
Berry Bowl, sm. ... 10
Berry Bowl, lg. ... 30
Ice Cream Bowl, sm. ... 15
Ice Cream Bowl, lg. ... 40

IMPERIAL'S #348
Pitcher ... 65

IMPERIAL'S #403½
Pitcher ... 65
Tumbler ... 15

IMPERIAL'S #404
Berry Bowl, sm. ... 15
Berry Bowl, lg. ... 25
Butter ... 40
Celery ... 20
Compote, 9½", various shapes ... 35
Cracker Jar ... 45
Creamer or Spooner ... 25
Cruet ... 45
Custard Cup ... 15
Finger Bowl ... 20
Goblet, 2 shapes ... 25
Jelly Compote ... 25
Orange Bowl, flat base, 11" ... 30
Pitcher ... 60
Punch Bowl and Base ... 85
Punch Cup ... 10
Rose Bowl, Banquet size, 10½" ... 60
Rose Bowl, 8", ground base ... 50
Rose Bowl, stemmed, 7" ... 30
Rose Bowl, 4", 2 shapes ... 25
Shakers, ea. ... 30
Spoon Tray ... 25
Sugar ... 40
Syrup ... 55
Tumbler ... 20
Vase, various sizes and shapes ... 35
Water bottle ... 40
Wine ... 15

IMPERIAL'S #405
Vase, 11" - 13" ... 30

IMPERIAL'S #427
Pitcher ... 75

IMPERIAL'S #438
Bowl ... 30

IMPERIAL'S #453
Nappy, handled ... 30

IMPERIAL'S #483
Bowl, 7½" ... 30

IMPERIAL'S #678
Berry Bowl, sm. ... 15
green/blue ... 25
Berry Bowl, lg. ... 30
green/blue ... 35
Butter ... 55

green/blue ... 65
Candy Jar, covered ... 40
green/blue ... 50
Celery Tray ... 20
green/blue ... 30
Compote ... 30
green/blue ... 40
Creamer ... 25
green/blue ... 35
Nappy, 1 or 2 handles ... 20
green/blue ... 30
Pickle Tray ... 25
green/blue ... 30
Pitcher ... 65
green/blue ... 75
Spooner ... 25
green/blue ... 30
Sugar ... 30
green/blue ... 35
Tumbler ... 15
green/blue ... 20
Vase ... 20
green/blue ... 25

IMPERIAL'S #2122
Berry Bowl ... 20
Bowl, 6" ... 15
Compote ... 35
Creamer ... 25
Nappy, 2 handled ... 25
Pickle Dish, handled ... 25
Spoon Tray, oval ... 35
Sugar, 6" ... 25
Vase ... 30

IMPERIAL'S #3888
Berry Bowl, 4" ... 20
Berry Bowl, 9" ... 35
Master Bowl, 10" ... 40
Rose Bowl, 7½" ... 30

IMPERIAL'S BELLAIRE
Bowl, 8½", scarce ... 65
Punch Bowl & Base, rare ... 475
Punch Cup, scarce ... 20

IMPERIAL'S CUBE CUT
Covered Jar, Advertising Piece ... 65

IMPERIAL'S NU-CUT PINWHEEL
Bowls ... 15 - 30
Salad Bowl ... 25
Vase ... 30

IMPERIAL'S PANSY
Bowl, 8" - 9" ... 40

IMPERIAL'S THUNDERBOLT
Bouquet Vase, 13" ... 35

IMPERIAL'S WICKER BASKET (#428½)
Castor Set, 3 pcs. ... 50

INDEPENDENCE HALL
Mug ... 50

INDIANA
Bowl, 5" - 9" ... 20
Bowl, oval, 7" - 9" ... 30
Butter ... 60
Carafe ... 35
Ketchup Bottle ... 40
Celery Tray ... 20
Celery Vase ... 25
Compote ... 30
Creamer or Spooner ... 20
Cruet ... 45
Finger Bowl ... 20
Ice Tub ... 45
Jelly Dish ... 20
Nappy, 5" & 6" ... 25
Perfume ... 35
Pitcher ... 85
Sauce ... 10
Shakers, ea ... 20
Sugar ... 25
Syrup ... 60
Tray, oblong ... 30
Tumbler ... 20

INDIANA'S #115
Berry Bowl, sm. ... 20
Berry Bowl, lg. ... 45
Butter ... 65
Creamer or Spooner ... 20
Pitcher ... 75
Sugar ... 25
Tumbler ... 15

INDIANA'S #123
Berry Bowl, sm. ... 10
Berry Bowl, lg. ... 45
Bowl, deep, 8½" ... 35
Butter ... 65
Cabarette Bowl, 11" ... 35
Cake Stand, 2 sizes ... 25 - 40
Celery Tray ... 20
Compote, covered, 4 sizes ... 30 - 70
Creamer or Spooner ... 25
Cruet ... 55
Custard Cup ... 10
Goblet ... 35
Jelly Compote ... 25
Orange Bowl, flat ... 50
Pitcher, 3 sizes ... 60 - 125
Plate, 12" ... 30
Punch Bowl, 4 shapes ... 145
Punch Cup ... 10
Sugar ... 40
Tumbler ... 25
Wine ... 15

INDIANA'S #161
Berry Bowl, lg. ... 25
ruby stain ... 30
Berry Bowl, sm. ... 10
ruby stain ... 15
Bowls, various ... 15 - 25
ruby stain ... 20 - 35
Butter ... 40
ruby stain ... 50
Cake Stand ... 30
ruby stain ... 40
Compote ... 25
ruby stain ... 35
Creamer or Spooner ... 20
ruby stain ... 25
Pitcher ... 65
ruby stain ... 75
Sugar ... 25
ruby stain ... 30
Tumbler ... 15
ruby stain ... 20

INDIANA'S #165
Berry Bowl, lg. ... 25
Berry Bowl, sm. ... 10
Berry Creamer ... 20
Berry Sugar ... 15
Celery ... 20
Compote, open, 3 sizes ... 25 - 50
Compote, handled ... 55
Creamer ... 25
Jelly ... 25
Olive Dish ... 25
Pickle Dish ... 20
Pitcher, 3 sizes ... 50 - 75
Salt, 2 sizes ... 20
Sauce, ftd. ... 10
Syrup ... 65
Vase ... 25
Water Bottle ... 35

INDIANA SILVER
Berry Bowl, sm. ... 15
Berry Bowl, lg. ... 45
Butter ... 75
Creamer or Spooner ... 25
Goblet ... 55
Rose Bowl, ftd. ... 35
Sherbet ... 20
Sugar ... 35

INDIAN SUNSET
Berry Bowl, sm. ... 10
Berry Bowl, lg. ... 40
Bonbon ... 25
Butter ... 70
Celery Tray ... 15
Creamer or Spooner ... 20
Pickle Dish ... 15
Pitcher ... 95
Shakers, ea. ... 20
Sugar ... 25
Tumbler ... 20

INNOVATION #407
Basket ... 40
Bonbon ... 20
Bowl, 8" ... 25
Celery Vase ... 20
Compote ... 40
Creamer ... 25
Fernery ... 45
Lamp & Matching Shade ... 115
Nappy ... 20
Rose Bowl, ftd. ... 30
Sugar, open ... 25
Vase, cylinder shape ... 30

INNOVATION #420
Bowl, 8" & 10" ... 20 - 35
Celery Tray ... 15
Compote, lg. on stand ... 55
Corset Vase, 12" ... 60
Creamer ... 20
Sugar ... 30
Trumpet Vase ... 40

INNOVATION #1024
Berry Bowl, sm. ... 15
Berry Bowl, lg. ... 35
Bowls, footed ... 15 - 35
Butter ... 60
Creamer or Spooner ... 30
Sugar ... 40
*Etched added 10%.

IN REMEMBRANCE
Platter, Washington, Lincoln, or Garfield ... 75

INSIDE RIBBING
Berry Bowl, sm. ... 10
vaseline ... 20
green/blue ... 20
Berry Bowl, lg. ... 30
vaseline ... 45
green/blue ... 40
Butter ... 50
vaseline ... 115
green/blue ... 70
Celery Vase ... 15
vaseline ... 25
green/blue ... 25
Creamer or Spooner ... 25
vaseline ... 35
green/blue ... 35
Cruet ... 55
vaseline ... 70
green/blue ... 65
Pickle Dish ... 10
vaseline ... 20
green/blue ... 20
Sugar ... 30
vaseline ... 45
green/blue ... 40
Syrup ... 60
vaseline ... 95
green/blue ... 70
Toothpick Holder ... 35
vaseline ... 55
green/blue ... 50

INTAGLIO (NORTHWOOD)
Berry Bowl, sm. ... 25
green/blue ... 40
custard ... 55

Berry Bowl, lg....40
green/blue....65
custard....85
Butter....65
green/blue....85
custard....125
Creamer....30
green/blue....45
custard....60
Cruet....65
green/blue....75
custard....110
Jelly Compote....35
green/blue....50
custard....70
Novelty Bowl....45
green/blue....55
custard....80
Pitcher....80
green/blue....95
custard....145
Shakers, ea....35
green/blue....55
custard....70
Spooner....30
green/blue 45....
custard....60
Sugar....45
green/blue....60
custard....80
Tumbler....20
green/blue....30
custard....45

INTAGLIO BUTTERFLIES
Bowl, 8½"....45
Compote, 7½"....55
Sauce, 5"....20

INTAGLIO DAISY
Berry Bowl, sm....15
Berry Bowl, lg....35
Butter....55
Cake Stand....30
Compote....35
Pitcher....80
Sugar....25
Tumbler....15

INTAGLIO MORNING GLORY
Bowl....30
Plate....45

INTAGLIO SUNFLOWER
Butter....50
Creamer or Spooner....20
Pitcher....75
Tumbler....15
Straw Holder w/Cover....65
Sugar....30
Toothpick Holder....25

INVERTED FAN & FEATHER
Berry Bowl, sm....20
green/blue....30
custard....40
Berry Bowl, lg....35
green/blue....50
custard....75
Butter....70
green/blue....85
custard....110
Creamer....30
green/blue....40
custard....60
Cruet....65
green/blue....75
custard....95
Jelly Compote....35
green/blue....40
custard....60
Pitcher....80
green/blue....100
custard....140
Punch Bowl....95
green/blue....140
custard....165
Punch Cup....15
green/blue....25
custard....40
Shakers, ea....30
green/blue....45
custard....60
Spooner....30
green/blue....45
custard....60
Sugar....40
green/blue....55
custard....70
Toothpick Holder....35
green/blue....45
custard....60
Tumbler....20
green/blue....30
custard....45

INVERTED FEATHER
Basket....50
Bonbon....35
Bowls,
various shapes & sizes....20 - 45
Bowl, berry, lg....40
Bowl, berry, sm....20
Butter....110
Cake Stand....45
Compote, lg....40
Compote, jelly....30
Celery Vase....25
Creamer, Spooner or Sugar....30
Cruet....80
Decanter....100
Pickle Tray....35
Pitcher....225
Plate....65
Punch Bowl w/Base....425
Punch Cup....20
Salt Shaker, ea....30
Sherbet....20
Toothpick Holder....75
Tray, rectangular....40
Tumbler....30
Water Bottle....80
Whiskey Jug....120
Wine....25
Vase....65

INVERTED FERN
Bowl, ftd....95
Butter....200
Champagne....185
Compote, open....100
Creamer....150
Egg Cup, 2 styles....40 - 60
Goblet, 2 styles....60 - 70
Honey Dish....25
Pitcher....750
Plate....110
Salt....40
Sauce....10
Spooner....90
Sugar....165
Tumbler....125
Wine....100

INVERTED FISH
Pitcher, scarce....325
Tumbler, v. scarce....100
Water Tray, rare....125

INVERTED PEACOCK
Pitcher, scarce....300
Tumbler, v. scarce....100
Water Tray, rare....125

INVERTED STRAWBERRY
Basket, squat w/handle....100
Berry Bowl, sm....40
Berry Bowl, lg....80
Bonbon, ftd....30
Butter....120
Candlesticks, ea....75
Celery Tray....60
Compote....70
Creamer, ftd....60
Custard Cup....30
Fruit Bowl, ftd....80
Goblet....100
Jelly Compote....30
Oil Bottle....100
Pitcher....200
Powder Jar w/Lid....100
Rose Bowl....80
Sugar, ftd....90
Sweet Pea Vase, stemmed....95
Tumbler....60
Wine....50
*Add 100% for colored or stained pieces.

INVERTED THUMBPRINT & STAR
Goblet....20
amber....25
vaseline....45
green/blue....40

INWALD LEAF SPRAY
Bowl....35
Goblet....40
Pitcher....80
Plate....35
Tumbler....25

I.O.U.
Berry Bowl, sm....10
amber....30
vaseline....20
green/blue....20
Berry Bowl, lg....30
amber....35
vaseline....45
green/blue....40
Butter....50
amber....60
vaseline....95
green/blue....65
Celery Vase....20
amber....35
vaseline....40
green/blue....30
Creamer or Spooner....25
amber....40
vaseline....45
green/blue....35
Pickle Dish....20
amber....50
vaseline....65
green/blue....25
Pitcher....80
amber....120
vaseline....150
green/blue....100
Sugar....30
amber....50
vaseline....55
green/blue....35
Syrup....40
amber....65
vaseline....90
green/blue....75
Tumbler....15
amber....25
vaseline....30
green/blue....20

IOWA
Berry Bowl, lg....40
Berry Bowl, sm....10
Butter....65
Cake Stand....50
Celery Vase....25
Compote....30
Creamer or Spooner....25

Goblet ... 30
Pickle Dish ... 15
Pitcher ... 80
Sugar ... 30
Tumbler ... 15
Wine ... 10
*Add 20% for rose flashed.
IOWA CITY ELEPHANT
Goblet, rare ... 350
IRIS (AKA: PINEAPPLE)
Berry Bowl, sm. ... 10
Berry Bowl, lg. ... 30
Butter ... 50
Creamer or Spooner ... 25
Jelly Compote ... 35
Lily Vase ... 30
Plate ... 25
Pitcher ... 75
amber ... 125
Rose Bowl ... 35
Salver ... 40
Sherbet ... 30
Sugar ... 30
Tumbler ... 15
amber ... 25
IT IS GOD'S WAY - HIS WILL BE DONE
Small Plate or Platter ... 85
IVANHOE
Butter ... 80
Cake Salver ... 45
Celery Vase ... 40
Cracker Jar ... 50
Creamer ... 30
Cup ... 15
Jelly Compote ... 25
Nappy ... 20
Plate, 10" ... 25
Pitcher ... 110
Relish ... 20
Sauce ... 15
Spoon Tray ... 45
Spooner ... 35
Sugar ... 45
Toothpick Holder ... 30
Tumbler ... 15
IVERNA
Berry Bowl, sm. ... 10
Berry Bowl, lg. ... 30
Berry, 6½" ... 15
Biscuit Jar ... 35
Butter ... 50
Celery Tray ... 25
Compote, 6½" ... 25
Creamer or Spooner ... 20
Fruit Bowl, 8½", ftd. ... 40
Jelly, hndl. ... 30
Pickle Dish ... 20
Pitcher ... 85
Punch Bowl ... 75
Punch Cup ... 10
Sherbet ... 20
Spoon Tray ... 20
Sugar ... 25
Tumbler ... 15
Vase ... 25
JACOB'S LADDER
Bowls, oblong ... 20 - 30
Bowl, 9" ftd., ornate ... 125
Butter ... 140
Cake Stand, 2 sizes ... 80 - 135
Castor Set, complete ... 175
Celery Vase ... 50
Cologne bottle ... 110
Compote, covered, 6" - 9½" ... 120 - 225
Compote, open, 7½" - 10" ... 40 - 65
Compote with Dolphin Stem, very rare ... 900
Creamer or Spooner ... 40
Cruet ... 165
Goblet ... 75
Honey Dish ... 25
Marmalade Jar ... 265
Mug, rare ... 300
Pitcher ... 350
Plate, 6¼" ... 35
Relish ... 30
Salt, master ... 25
Sugar ... 165
Syrup, 2 style finials ... 200 - 245
Tumbler ... 130
Wine ... 40
*Double prices for any colored pieces. Some pieces made in amber, vaseline & blue.
JAPANESE
Bowl ... 75
Butter ... 165
Celery Vase ... 150
Compotes, covered ... 250 - 300
Creamer or Spooner ... 65
Goblet ... 195
Pickle Jar w/Lid ... 70
Plate, Fan Shape ... 90
vaseline ... 225
Pitcher ... 625
Sauce, flat or ftd. ... 30
Sugar ... 130
JEFFERSON #271
Berry Bowl, sm. ... 10
green/blue ... 15
Berry Bowl, lg. ... 30
green/blue ... 35
Butter ... 65
green/blue ... 75
Celery Vase ... 25
green/blue ... 30
Compote ... 35
green/blue ... 40
Creamer or Spooner ... 30
green/blue ... 35
Pickle Dish ... 20
green/blue ... 25
Pitcher ... 70
green/blue ... 85
Sugar ... 40
green/blue ... 50
Toothpick Holder ... 45
green/blue ... 55
Tumbler ... 10
green/blue ... 15
Wine ... 20
green/blue ... 25
JEFFERSON'S DIAMOND WITH PEG (GETTYSBURG SOUVENIR)
Toothpick Holder, scarce custard ... 125
JEFFERSON WHEEL
Bowl ... 30
JENKIN'S #286
Berry Bowl, sm. ... 15
Berry Bowl, lg. ... 35
Butter ... 55
Candy compote ... 35
Compote ... 30
Creamer or Spooner ... 20
Jelly Compote ... 35
Mayonnaise ... 30
Nappy, handled ... 25
Pickle Dish ... 30
Pitcher ... 85
Plate, 11" ... 40
Sugar ... 25
Sundae, straight or flared ... 25
Saucer ... 25
Tumbler ... 15
Vase, 6" and 10" ... 25 - 35
JENKIN'S SWAN (#460)
Salt Dish ... 45
JENNY LIND
*Part of "Actress" line.
Compote ... 225
JENNY LIND MATCH SAFE
Match Safe ... 250
JERSEY LILY
Berry Bowl, sm. ... 65
Berry Bowl, lg. ... 95
Butter ... 200
Compote, covered, 3 sizes ... 200 - 250
Covered Dish, sq., 8¼"x 5¼" ... 165
Covered Dish, 9¼"x 7¼" ... 125
Creamer or Spooner ... 100
Lamp, 3 sizes ... 150 - 250
Pitcher ... 325
Shakers, ea. ... 75
Sugar ... 165
Syrup ... 375
Tray, 2 sizes ... 100 - 135
JERSEY SWIRL
Bowl ... 25
amber ... 55
vaseline ... 45
green/blue ... 55
Butter ... 55
amber ... 65
vaseline ... 95
green/blue ... 75
Cake Stand ... 35
amber ... 60
vaseline ... 95
green/blue ... 70
Candlesticks, ea. ... 30
amber ... 35
vaseline ... 50
green/blue ... 40
Compote, covered or open ... 75 - 125
amber ... 100 - 130
vaseline ... 125 - 200
green/blue ... 100 - 150
Creamer or Spooner ... 20
amber ... 45
vaseline ... 40
green/blue ... 45
Cruet ... 70
amber ... 70
vaseline ... 125
green/blue ... 85
Cup ... 10
amber ... 15
vaseline ... 30
green/blue ... 25
Dresser Tray ... 35
vaseline ... 60
Goblet ... 30
amber ... 40
vaseline ... 45
green/blue ... 45
Jam Jar ... 90
amber ... 110
vaseline ... 165
green/blue ... 150
Mini Spittoon, Toothpick Holder ... 65
amber ... 90
ruby stain ... 125
Pitcher ... 90
amber ... 100
vaseline ... 165
green/blue ... 145
Plate, 10" - 12" ... 30
amber ... 50
vaseline ... 40
green/blue ... 50
Plate, 6" - 8" ... 25
amber ... 40
vaseline ... 35
green/blue ... 40
Salt, ind. ... 10
amber ... 25

vaseline 25
green/blue 25
Salt, master 20
amber 30
vaseline 35
green/blue 35
Sauce 10
amber 20
vaseline 15
green/blue 20
Sugar 40
amber 45
vaseline 65
green/blue 55
Syrup 100
amber 125
vaseline 200
green/blue 165
Tumbler 25
amber 30
vaseline 55
green/blue 40
Wine 15
amber 35
vaseline 55
green/blue 40

JEWELED BUTTERFLIES
Bowls, various .... 15 - 35
Butter 55
Compote 35
Creamer, Spooner or Sugar 25
Milk Pitcher, scarce 90
Pitcher 165
Plate 30
Vase 30

JEWELED HEART
Berry Bowl, sm. 15
green/blue 25
Berry Bowl, lg. 35
green/blue 60
Bowl, 9" - 10" 30
green/blue 50
Butter 65
green/blue 125
Creamer or Spooner 30
green/blue 45
Cruet Set (Cruet, Shakers, Toothpick & Tray) 150
green/blue 225
Pitcher 85
green/blue 175
Plate 25
green/blue 55
Rose Bowl, 9" 35
green/blue 55
Shakers, ea. 25
green/blue 60
Sugar 30
green/blue 55
Syrup 75
green/blue 135
Toothpick Holder 50
green/blue 75
Tray 30
green/blue 65
Tumbler 20
green/blue 40

JEWELED LOOP
Berry Bowl,Sm. 20
Berry Bowl, lg. 45
Butter 65
Celery Tray, 11" 35
Celery Vase 30
Compote, 8" 45
Creamer or Spooner 30
Goblet 50
Jelly Compote, low 35
Pickle Dish, 7" 25
Pitcher 90
Sugar 30
Tumbler 25

JEWELED PALM LEAF
Bowl, 10" 45

JEWEL WITH DEWDROP
Banana Stand 95
Bowls, covered .... 75 - 100
Bowls, open .... 35 - 50
Bowl, Sauce 20
Cake Stand, various .... 80 - 165
Compote, covered, various .... 80 - 160
Compote, open, various .... 50 - 100
Compote, jelly 45
Cordial 55
Goblet, rare 145
Milk Pitcher 200
Pitcher 80
Plate, Bread Size 80
Relish 30
Shakers, ea. 60
Syrup 300
Toothpick Holder, very scarce 65
Tumbler 80
Wine 100

JOCKEY CAP
Butter, rare 200
amber 350
vaseline 750
green/blue 400

JOHN BULL
Eye Cup 50

JOHNSON'S CHILD'S MUG (KING GLASS #13)
Mug 25
Table Set, complete 75

JUBILEE
Butter 65
Celery Tray 20
Compote, high 55
Compote, low 45
Creamer or Spooner 20
Dish, oblong, 8" 20
Goblet 45
Pickle Dish 20
Plate, 9" 20
Pitcher 85
Tumbler 20
Sugar 30
Wine 15

JUMBO
Butter, oblong 650
Butter, rnd., Barnum head 500
Compote, covered, 3 sizes .... 700 - 1,500
Creamer 275
Pitcher 1,700
Sauce 100
Spoon Rack 425
Spooner, Barnum head 200
Sugar, Barnum head 500

JUMBO CASTOR SET
Castor Set, complete, rare 375
amber 425
vaseline 600
green/blue 450

KALEIDOSCOPE
Bowl 35
Butter 70
Creamer or Spooner 30
Pitcher 85
Rose Bowl 65
Sugar 35
Tumbler 20

KANAWHA
Berry Bowl, sm. 15
ruby stain 25
Berry Bowl, lg. 30
ruby stain 45
Butter 60
ruby stain 80
Candlesticks, ea., 5" 30
ruby stain 40
Creamer 25
ruby stain 30
Cruet 60
ruby stain 75
Lamp 85
ruby stain 100
Pitcher 70
ruby stain 85
Punch Bowl 100
ruby stain 125
Punch Cup 15
ruby stain 25
Spooner 25
ruby stain 30
Sugar 30
ruby stain 40

KATZENJAMMER
Mug, tall 185
amber 225

KAYAK
Berry Bowl, lg. 30
Berry Bowl, sm. 15
Cake Stand 40
Compote 35
Pitcher 65
Tumbler 20
Tray 25

KEG
Oil Lamp, scarce 245

KENTUCKY
Bowls .... 25 - 40
Butter 90
Cake Stand, 2 sizes .... 80 - 100
Celery Tray 35
Celery Vase 50
Compote, covered, 4 sizes .... 60 - 120
Compote, open, 4 sizes .... 25 - 45
Creamer or Spooner 50
Cruet 75
Cup 10
green/blue 35
Goblet 100
green/blue 135
Nappy 45
green/blue 65
Olive, hndl. 25
Pitcher 100
Plate, 3 sizes .... 40 - 50
Punch Cup 10
green/blue 30
Sauce 10
green/blue 30
Shakers, ea. 40
Sugar 70
Syrup Pitcher 125
Toothpick Holder 45
green/blue 120
Tumbler 40
green/blue 70
Wine 30
green/blue 60

KEYHOLE
Bowl, dome ftd. 45
Plate, dome ftd. 60

KEYSTONE
Square Cruet 80
ruby stain 110

KING ARTHUR
Berry Bowl, sm. 15
Berry Bowl, lg. 30
Butter 65
Creamer or Spooner 30
Pitcher 80
Punch Bowl 130
Punch Cup 15
Sugar 40
Tumbler 15

KING'S BLOCK
- Bowls, oval ... 15 - 40
- Butter ... 55
- Creamer or Spooner ... 20
- Cruet ... 50
- Goblet ... 35
- Pickle Tray ... 20
- Sugar ... 35
- Wine ... 15

KING'S CROWN
- Banana Stand ... 200
  - ruby stain ... 1,250
- Bowl, 2 sizes ... 35 - 45
  - ruby stain ... 75 - 90
- Butter ... 95
  - ruby stain ... 200
- Cake Stand ... 165
  - ruby stain ... 400
- Castor Set, complete ... 325
  - ruby stain ... 750
- Celery Vase ... 35
  - ruby stain ... 50
- Champagne ... 25
  - ruby stain ... 30
- Claret ... 30
  - ruby stain ... 45
- Compote w/Lid, 4 sizes ... 60 - 100
  - ruby stain ... 400 - 750
- Compote, open, 3 sizes ... 30 - 90
  - ruby stain ... 60 - 250
- Cordial ... 40
  - ruby stain ... 80
- Creamer or Spooner ... 20
  - ruby stain ... 60
- Cup & Saucer ... 50
  - ruby stain ... 75
- Custard Cup ... 15
  - ruby stain ... 25
- Finger Lamp ... 100
- Fruit Basket ... 45
  - ruby stain ... 80
- Goblet ... 25
  - ruby stain ... 50
- Honey Dish, sq. ... 195
  - ruby stain ... 1,650
- Jam Jar w/Lid ... 140
  - ruby stain ... 1,200
- Milk Pitcher ... 75
  - ruby stain ... 225
- Mustard Pot ... 90
  - ruby stain ... 265
- Oil Lamp, 7½" - 9½" ... 125 - 200
- Orange Bowl, ftd. ... 500
  - ruby stain ... 1,500
- Parlor Lamp (Vase), very rare ... 2,000
- Pickle Castor ... 200
  - ruby stain ... 850
- Pickle Jar w/Lid ... 165
  - ruby stain ... 1,000
- Pitcher, 2 styles ... 90 - 125
  - ruby stain ... 225 - 265
- Preserve Dish ... 35
  - ruby stain ... 65
- Salt, ind., sq. and rect. ... 30 - 50
  - ruby stain ... 75 - 100
- Salt, master, sq. and rect. ... 80 - 135
  - ruby stain ... 195 - 300
- Sauce, 4" ... 20
  - ruby stain ... 70
- Sugar, 2 sizes ... 30 - 60
  - ruby stain ... 60 - 185
- Toothpick Holder ... 30
  - ruby stain ... 45
- Tumbler ... 35
  - ruby stain ... 70
- Wine ... 15
  - ruby stain ... 40

KING'S CURTAIN ...
- Bowl ... 30
- Butter ... 55
- Cake Stand ... 30
- Creamer or Spooner ... 20
- Goblet ... 35
- Pitcher ... 70
- Plate, 7" ... 20
- Sauce ... 10
- Shakers, ea ... 20
- Sugar ... 25
- Tumbler ... 15
- Wine ... 15

KITTEN ON A PILLOW
- Novelty Piece ... 70
  - amber ... 125
  - vaseline ... 150
  - green/blue ... 100

KLEAR-CUT #705
- Pitcher ... 80
- Tumbler ... 20

KLONDIKE
- Bowl, sq., 7" - 11" ... 30 - 65
  - amber ... 125 - 200
- Butter ... 100
  - amber ... 165
- Cake Stand ... 125
  - amber ... 300
- Celery Tray, oblong ... 70
  - amber ... 120
- Champagne ... 225
  - amber ... 350
- Condiment Set, 4 pcs. ... 425
  - amber ... 575
- Creamer or Spooner ... 45
  - amber ... 80
- Cruet ... 150
  - amber ... 200
- Cup ... 30
  - amber ... 60
- Goblet ... 90
  - amber ... 225
- Pitcher, 2 styles ... 160 - 200
  - amber ... 275 - 325
- Relish Tray ... 45
  - amber ... 90
- Sauce, flat or ftd. ... 30
  - amber ... 60
- Shakers, tall or squat, ea. ... 65
  - amber ... 90
- Sugar ... 75
  - amber ... 120
- Syrup ... 135
  - amber ... 325
- Toothpick Holder ... 100
  - amber ... 185
- Tray ... 55
  - amber ... 95
- Tumbler, 2 styles ... 40 - 55
  - amber ... 65 - 80
- Vase, 7" - 10" ... 40 - 60
  - amber ... 90 - 145
- Wine ... 125
  - amber ... 200

*Amber prices are for amber stained.
*Add 75% for frosted amber stained.

KNIFE REST
- Knife Rest, various shapes and sizes ... 20
  - amber ... 35
  - vaseline ... 45
  - green/blue ... 40
  - ruby stain ... 35

KNIGHTS OF LABOR
- Goblet ... 175
- Mug ... 150
- Platter, 12" ... 225
  - vaseline ... 400
  - green/blue ... 300

KNOBBY BULLS-EYE
- Berry Bowl, lg. ... 30
  - green/blue ... 35
  - ruby stain ... 50
- Berry Bowl, sm. ... 15
  - green/blue ... 20
  - ruby stain ... 35
- Bowl, 10" ... 35
  - green/blue ... 40
  - ruby stain ... 55
- Bowl, deep oval, 7½" ... 30
  - green/blue ... 35
  - ruby stain ... 50
- Bowl, orange, 10½" ... 40
  - green/blue ... 45
  - ruby stain ... 55
- Butter ... 50
  - green/blue ... 60
  - ruby stain ... 85
- Celery Tray ... 20
  - green/blue ... 25
  - ruby stain ... 40
- Compote, open ... 40
  - green/blue ... 45
  - ruby stain ... 60
- Compote, covered ... 50
  - green/blue ... 60
  - ruby stain ... 90
- Creamer or Spooner ... 25
  - green/blue ... 40
  - ruby stain ... 45
- Decanter ... 55
  - green/blue ... 125
- Pitcher, 2 sizes ... 40 - 60
  - green/blue ... 65 - 90
  - ruby stain ... 100 - 175
- Plate, 5" & 8" ... 30
  - green/blue ... 35
  - ruby stain ... 55
- Punch Bowl ... 100
  - green/blue ... 125
  - ruby stain ... 165
- Punch Cup ... 10
  - green/blue ... 15
  - ruby stain ... 30
- Salt Shaker, 2 styles, ea. ... 20
  - green/blue ... 25
  - ruby stain ... 50
- Sugar, w/lid ... 30
  - vaseline ... 175
  - green/blue ... 55
  - ruby stain ... 40
- Toothpick Holder ... 30
  - green/blue ... 35
  - ruby stain ... 45
- Tumbler ... 20
  - vaseline ... 200
  - green/blue ... 25
  - ruby stain ... 40
- Underplate (for Punch Bowl) ... 50
  - green/blue ... 60
  - ruby stain ... 85
- Wine ... 25
  - green/blue ... 30
  - ruby stain ... 45

KNOTTED BEADS
- Vase ... 45
  - red ... 125

KOKOMO
- Berry Bowl, lg ... 30
- Berry Bowl, sm ... 15
- Butter ... 45
- Compote, covered ... 55
- Creamer or Spooner ... 25
- Jam Jar w/Lid ... 30
- Jelly Compote, low ... 20
- Nappy ... 20
- Pickle Dish ... 15
- Pitcher ... 60
- Sugar ... 30
- Tumbler ... 15

KRYS-TOL COLONIAL
- Bowl ... 35
- Compote, lg. ... 60
- Jelly Compote ... 45
- Plate ... 40
- Punch Bowl w/Base ... 120
- Punch Cup ... 15

LA BELLE ROSE
- Bowl, 5" - 9" ... 10 - 25
- Plate, 6" - 11" ... 20 - 40

LACY DAISY
- Bowls, 3 legged ... 10 - 50
- Butter ... 75
- Cake Plate ... 35
- Creamer or Spooner ... 25
- Cruet ... 50
- Jam Jar ... 35
- Jelly Compote ... 20
- Plates, various ... 15 - 35
- Puff Box ... 35
- Rose Bowl ... 25
- Salt, ind. ... 15
- Sugar ... 40
- Toy Table Set ... 95

LACY DEWDROP
- Berry Bowl, lg. ... 40
- Berry Bowl, sm. ... 20
- Bowl, covered, lg. ... 55
- Bowl, covered, sm. ... 30
- Butter ... 65
- Compote, covered or open ... 25 - 50
- Creamer or Spooner ... 20
- Goblet ... 35
- Mug ... 20
- Pitcher ... 85
- Sauce ... 10
- Sugar ... 25
- Tumbler ... 20

LACY MEDALLION
- Mug ... 40
  - vaseline ... 75
  - green/blue ... 50
  - ruby stain ... 60
- Shakers, ea ... 35
  - vaseline ... 50
  - green/blue ... 40
  - ruby stain ... 45
- Toothpick Holder ... 45
  - vaseline ... 60
  - green/blue ... 45
  - ruby stain ... 55
- Toy Table Set ... 115
  - vaseline ... 160
  - green/blue ... 135
  - ruby stain ... 145
- Wine ... 30
  - vaseline ... 45
  - green/blue ... 35
  - ruby stain ... 40

LACY SPIRAL (COLOSSUS)
- Berry Bowl, lg. ... 25
- Berry Bowl, sm. ... 10
- Butter ... 50
- Compote, covered ... 65
- Creamer or Spooner ... 25
- Goblet ... 30
- Pitcher ... 70
- Sugar ... 35
- Tumbler ... 15

LADDERS (TARENTUM'S #292)
- Berry Bowl, lg. ... 45
- Berry Bowl, sm. ... 15
- Butter ... 75
- Celery Vase ... 20
- Creamer or Spooner ... 20
- Cruet ... 45
- Cup ... 10
- Pitcher ... 85
- Sugar ... 30
- Tumbler ... 20
- Vase ... 25

LADDER WITH DIAMOND
- Butter ... 60
- Celery Vase ... 25
- Creamer or Spooner ... 25
- Cruet ... 70
- Cup ... 15
- Decanter ... 50
- Goblet ... 35
- Pitcher ... 80
- Plate, 9¼" ... 30
- Sugar ... 30
- Toothpick Holder ... 35
- Tumbler ... 20
- Vase ... 30

LADY BUST
- Paperweight ... 250

LADY WITH FAN
- Celery Vase ... 85

LAMB
- Child's Mug ... 75
  - green/blue ... 100
  - amethyst ... 125
- Child's Mug Variant ... 100
  - green/blue ... 125
  - amethyst ... 150

LANSBURG & BROS. ADVERTISING NAPPY
- Nappy, 3 handles ... 55

LANTERN
- Toy Candy Container ... 65

THE LAST SUPPER
- Plate ... 55

LATE BLOCK (DUNCAN'S #331)
- Berry Bowl, lg. ... 45
- Berry Bowl, sm. ... 20
- Bowls, sq. & rect., 4 sizes ... 15 - 50
- Butter ... 95
- Celery Boat ... 35
- Creamer or Spooner ... 30
- Cruet ... 65
- Horseradish Bottle ... 50
- Ice Tub ... 60
- Jelly Compote ... 35
- Lamp ... 95
- Mustard Pot ... 25
- Pickle Dish ... 20
- Pitcher ... 150
- Punch Bowl ... 250
- Punch Cup ... 20
- Relish, hndl. ... 25
- Rose Bowls, various ... 20 - 45
- Shakers, ea ... 25
- Sugar ... 35
- Sugar Shaker ... 45
- Syrup ... 70
- Tumbler ... 30
- Water Bottle ... 55

LATE BLOCK WITH THUMBPRINT
- Berry Bowl, lg. ... 45
- Berry Bowl, sm. ... 20
- Butter ... 65
- Celery Dish ... 25
- Creamer ... 25
- Pickle Dish ... 25
- Pitcher ... 60
- Spooner ... 30
- Sugar ... 35
- Tumbler ... 15

LATE HONEYCOMB
- Berry Bowl, lg. ... 35
- Berry Bowl, sm ... 20
- Pitcher ... 65
- Tumbler ... 20

LATE JACOB'S LADDER
- Bowl ... 30
- Butter ... 45
- Creamer ... 25
- Dresser Set, complete ... 95
- Rose Bowl ... 30
- Spooner ... 25
- Sugar ... 30

LATTICE
- Butter ... 65
- Cake Stand ... 35
- Celery Vase ... 25
- Cordial ... 20
- Creamer or Spooner ... 25
- Egg Cup ... 15
- Pitcher ... 75
- Plate ... 25
- Platter ... 35
- Sauce ... 10
- Shakers, ea ... 20
- Sugar ... 30
- Tumbler ... 15
- Wine ... 15

LATTICE & DAISY
- Tumbler, rare ... 70

LATTICE & NOTCHES
- Bowl ... 25
- Goblet ... 20
- Sauce ... 15

LATTICE EDGE
- Plates, various ... Slag 75 - 150

LATTICE EDGE (U.S. GLASS)
- Fruit Bowl, stemmed, 2 sizes ... 45 - 70

LATTICE MEDALLION WITH BUDS
- Bowl, ftd. ... 45

LATTICE MEDALLION VARIANT
- Bowl, ftd., various ... 15 - 45

LAVERNE
- Bowls, oval or rnd. ... 10 - 45
- Butter ... 60
- Cake Stand ... 40
- Celery Vase ... 20
- Compote, covered ... 70
- Compote, open ... 45
- Creamer or Spooner ... 20
- Goblet ... 50
- Pickle Tray ... 25
- Pitcher ... 90
- Relish Dish ... 15
- Sauce ... 10
- Sugar ... 30
- Tumbler ... 20
- Wine ... 15

LEAF & BEADS
- Candy Dish ... 25
  - pink - rosita ... 65
- Rose Bowl ... 35
  - pink - rosita ... 85

LEAF & DART
- Bowl, ftd. ... 40
- Butter ... 90
- Butter Pat ... 35
- Celery Vase ... 60
- Compote, covered ... 80 - 100
- Creamer or Spooner ... 45
- Cruet, rare ... 165
- Egg Cup ... 30
- Goblet ... 40
- Honey Dish ... 15
- Lamp ... 135
- Milk Pitcher ... 185
- Pitcher ... 145
- Relish Tray ... 20
- Salt, ftd., w/lid ... 90
- Sauce ... 10
- Sugar ... 70
- Syrup ... 200
- Tumbler ... 40
- Wine ... 25

LEAF & RIB
- Berry Bowl, lg. ... 30
  - amber ... 35
  - vaseline ... 45

green/blue 40
Berry Bowl, sm. 10
amber 20
vaseline 30
green/blue 25
Butter 65
amber 80
vaseline 110
green/blue 95
Celery Vase 25
amber 30
vaseline 40
green/blue 35
Creamer or Spooner 20
amber 25
vaseline 35
green/blue 30
Pickle Dish 15
amber 20
vaseline 30
green/blue 25
Pitcher 75
amber 80
vaseline 125
green/blue 100
Shakers, ea 25
amber 35
vaseline 45
green/blue 40
Sugar 30
amber 35
vaseline 50
green/blue 45
Vase 25
amber 30
vaseline 35
green/blue 30

LEAF & STAR
Banana Boat 40
Berry Bowl, lg. 40
Berry Bowl, sm. 25
Butter 55
Celery Tray 25
Celery Vase 35
Creamer or Spooner 25
Cruet 40
Custard Cup 10
Dresser Jar 35
Fruit Bowl 40
Goblet 30
Hair Receiver 35
Humidor 65
Ice Cream Dish 20
Jelly Compote 30
Nut Bowl 25
Pitcher, 2 styles ....45 - 70
Plate, 6" - 8" ....20 - 25
Relish Dish 20
Sauce, flat or ftd. 15
Toothpick Holder 25
Tumbler 20
Vase 30
Wine 15

LEAF BRACKET
Berry Bowl, lg. 40
chocolate 100
Berry Bowl, sm. 10
chocolate 35
Bowl, Tri-cornered 50
chocolate 120
Butter 125
chocolate 345
Celery Tray 60
chocolate 175
Creamer or Spooner 70
chocolate 200
Cruet 155
chocolate 250
Jam Jar 145
Nappy 50
chocolate 100
Pitcher 225
chocolate 500
Shakers, ea. 100
chocolate 150
Sauce 45
chocolate 60
Sugar 100
chocolate 175
Toothpick Holder 125
chocolate 300
Tumbler 90
chocolate 75

LEAF FLANGED
Butter ....
vaseline 225

LEAFY SCROLL (U.S. GLASS)
Berry Bowl, lg. 55
Berry Bowl, sm. 20
Butter 85
Creamer or Spooner 25
Goblet 55
Pitcher 90
Sugar 40
Toothpick Holder 30
Tumbler 25
Wine 20

LENOX
Berry Bowl, lg. 45
Berry Bowl, sm. 20
Breakfast Set 50
Butter 70
Creamer or Spooner 25
Cruet 65
Jelly Compote 35
Mug 25
Pitcher 85
Salt Dip, ind. 20
Sugar 30
Toothpick Holder 25
Tumbler 20

LET US HAVE PEACE
U.S. Grant Plate 75
vaseline 150

LEVERNE
(STAR IN HONEYCOMB)
Berry Bowl, lg. 50
Berry Bowl, sm. 20
Bowl, oval 35
Butter 70
Cake Stand 40
Celery Vase 25
Compote, covered or open ....35 - 60
Creamer or Spooner 25
Goblet 50
Pickle Tray 20
Pitcher 90
Relish 20
Sauce 15
Sugar 30
Tumbler 20
Wine 20

LIBERTY
Berry Bowl, lg. 40
Berry Bowl, sm. 15
Butter 65
Champagne 25
Cordial 20
Creamer or Spooner 25
Goblet 35
Pitcher 85
Sugar 35
Tumbler 15
Water Tray 25
Wine 20

LIBERTY BELL
Berry Bowl, lg. 110
Berry Bowl, sm 35
Butter 165
Celery Vase 45
Compote, 3 sizes ....65 - 110
Creamer or Spooner 100
Goblet 50
Mug, 2 styles ....225 - 400
Pickle Dish 50
Pitcher 900
Plate, 3 sizes ....70 - 85
Platter, 3 styles 75
Salt Dip 40
Sauce, flat or footed 35
Shakers, each 100
Sugar 125
Toy Table Set 550
Tumbler 100
*Milk glass, add 20%

LIBERTY BELL BANK
Bank 145

LIGHTHOUSE & SAILBOAT
Mug, 3 sizes 40
amber 55
green/blue 65

LIGHTNING
(CHAIN LIGHTNING)
Berry Bowl, lg. 25
Berry Bowl, sm. 10
Butter 45
Cordial 15
Creamer or Spooner 20
Pitcher 60
Sugar 25
Tumbler 10
Wine 10

LILY OF THE VALLEY
Berry Bowl, lg. 75
Berry Bowl, sm. 35
Butter 150
Cake Stand 285
Celery Vase 140
Champagne, very rare 350
Compote, covered 200
Creamer or Spooner 90
Cruet 475
Egg Cup 65
Goblet 120
Honey Dish 30
Milk Pitcher 225
Pickle Scoop 25
Pitcher 325
Salt, master, covered, 2 styles.. 185 - 290
Sauce, flat or ftd. 20
Sugar 160
Tumbler, 2 styles ....125 - 190
Wine, rare 200

LILY PAD
Novelty Compote, very scarce 225
amber 265
vaseline 300
green/blue 275

LINCOLN DRAPE
Butter 195
Celery Vase 95
Compote, covered, 8½" ....350 - 450
Compote, open, 6" - 7½" ....100 - 200
Creamer 225
Decanter w/Bar Lip 300
Egg Cup 60
Goblet, 2 sizes ....165 - 325
Honey Dish 30
Oil Lamp, various ....300 - 600
Pitcher, rare 4,250
Plate, 6" 100
Salt, master 75
Sauce 30
Spooner 80
Sugar 150
Syrup 295
Tumbler 300

Price Guide

LINCOLN LOGS
Wall Plaque
amber 250
ebony 300
LINED HEART
Vase 25
LION (GILLINDER & SONS)
Butter, scarce 200
Cheese Dish, covered, rare 675
Celery Vase, very scarce 100
Cologne w/Stopper, ext. rare 6,000
Compote, covered,
various sizes .... 165 - 475
Creamer 90
Egg Cup 110
Jam Jar 135
Goblet 120
Milk Pitcher, very scarce 1,800
Pitcher, scarce 625
Platter 125
Spooner 95
Sugar 165
Syrup, very scarce 450
Wine, rare 375
LION & BABOON
Butter 435
Celery Vase 265
Creamer or Spooner 150
Lamp, rare 475
Marmalade Jar w/Lid 250
Milk Pitcher 1100
Pitcher 850
Sugar 275
*All pieces rare.
LION & CABLE
Bread Plate 75
Butter 200
Celery Vase 65
Compote, covered, high, 7" - 9" 145
Compote, covered, low, 7" - 9" 95
Creamer or Spooner 45
Goblet 120
Jam Jar 70
Milk Pitcher 90
Pitcher 275
Sauce 30
Shakers, ea 45
Sugar 60
Tumbler 45
LION & HONEYCOMB
Compote, covered 250
LION HEAD
Butter 200
Compote, covered, 6" - 9" .... 125 - 235
Creamer or Spooner 50
Ink Well, very scarce 575
Jam Jar 100
Sauce, 4" - 5" 30
Sugar 75
Toy Table Set, butter, creamer, sugar,
spooner, cup, and saucer 600
LION LAMP
Lamp, rare 750
amber 825
green/blue 900
LITTLE BO PEEP
Nursery Rhyme Plate 45
LITTLE BO PEEP (DITHRIDGE)
Mug 55
LITTLE BUTTERCUP
Mug 45
LITTLE FISHES
Bowl, ftd., 5½", rare 100
Bowl, ftd., 9", rare 225
LITTLE GERMAN BAND CAP
Novelty Hat 65
amber 75
vaseline 125
green/blue 90

LITTLE OWL
Child's Pitcher 80
LITTLE SAMUEL
Candlesticks, ea. 45
Compote 70
Epergne 135
Lamp Stem 65
LOCKET ON A CHAIN
Berry Bowl, lg. 65
ruby stain 85
Berry Bowl, sm. 100
ruby stain 275
Butter 165
ruby stain 275
Cake Stand 135
Celery Vase 95
ruby stain 200
Compote, covered and open .... 300 - 650
ruby stain .... 450 - 750
Creamer or Spooner 100
ruby stain 185
Cruet, rare 300
ruby stain 1,450
Goblet, very scarce 165
ruby stain 500
Pickle Dish 50
ruby stain 85
Pitcher 110
ruby stain 135
Sugar 300
ruby stain 800
Syrup, rare 400
ruby stain 1,900
Toothpick Holder, very rare 350
ruby stain 950
Tumbler 100
ruby stain 200
Wine 75
ruby stain 150
*Colors considered rare.
*Add 100% to ruby stained.
LOGANBERRY & GRAPE
Butter 70
Celery Vase 20
Creamer or Spooner 35
Goblet, 2 types 50
Pitcher 95
Sugar 40
Tumbler 25
LOG CABIN
Bowl, covered 375
amber 900
vaseline 1,200
green/blue 1,500
Butter 500
amber 1,500
vaseline 1,800
green/blue 2,000
Compote, 6" - 8" .... 650 - 900
Creamer or Spooner 150
amber 375
vaseline 575
green/blue 750
Marmalade Jar w/Lid 500
amber 1,400
vaseline 2,200
green/blue 2,400
Pickle w/Lid 375
amber 650
vaseline 800
green/blue 900
Pitcher 800
amber 1,500
vaseline 3,000
green/blue 3,800
Sauce 100
amber 200
vaseline 235
green/blue 280

Sugar 300
amber 850
vaseline 1,100
green/blue 1,350
LOG CABIN (WESTMORELAND SPECIALTY CO.)
Mustard/bank
milk glass 350
LONE ELK
Creamer 80
Sugar, covered 125
THE LONE FISHERMAN
*Part of Actress Line
Cheese Dish, covered with
"Two Dromios" Base 400
LONG BUTTRESS
Butter 60
Celery Vase 20
Creamer or Spooner 25
Creamer, ind. 15
Pickle Jar 30
Pickle Dish 15
Pitcher 90
Salt Dip 10
Shakers, ea. 15
Sugar 30
Sugar, ind. 20
Syrup 45
Toothpick Holder 30
Tumbler 20
Vases, various sizes .... 15 - 35
LONG FAN WITH ACANTHUS LEAF
Berry Bowl, lg. 40
Berry Bowl, sm. 20
Butter 70
Creamer or Spooner 25
ruby stain 25
Berry Bowl, lg. 25
ruby stain 60
Butter 50
ruby stain 80
Compote 35
ruby stain 55
Creamer or Spooner 20
ruby stain 30
Goblet 35
ruby stain 50
Pitcher 85
ruby stain 120
Punch Bowl 135
ruby stain 225
Punch Cup 10
ruby stain 15
Sugar 30
ruby stain 40
Toy Table Set 85
ruby stain 135
Tumbler 15
ruby stain 25
Wine 10
ruby stain 25
Goblet 35
Pickle Dish 15
Pitcher 85
Shakers, ea. 15
Sugar 30
Tumbler 20
LONG MAPLE LEAF
Bowls, various .... 15 - 30
vaseline .... 25 - 55
Butter 60
vaseline 85
Celery Vase 25
vaseline 35
Compote 40
vaseline 55
Creamer or Spooner 25
vaseline 35
Pickle Dish 20
vaseline 30

Pitcher ... 85
vaseline ... 145
Sugar ... 30
vaseline ... 50
Tumbler ... 20
vaseline ... 35

LOOKING GLASS, THE
Platter ... 45

LOOP
Bitters Bottle ... 80
Bowl, covered ... 70
Butter ... 60
Cake Stand ... 40
Celery Vase ... 40
Compote, covered, 7" - 10" ... 35 - 70
Compote, open, 7" - 10" ... 25 - 45
Creamer or Spooner ... 25
Decanter, various ... 60 - 80
Egg Cup ... 25
Goblet, 2 styles ... 35 - 55
Milk Pitcher ... 100
Oil Lamp, 10" ... 150
Pitcher ... 125
Plate ... 30
Salt, master ... 20
Sugar ... 50
Syrup ... 100
Tumbler ... 25
Vase, 3 sizes ... 20 - 40
Wine ... 10

LOOP & BLOCK
Berry Bowl, lg. ... 35
ruby stain ... 45
Berry Bowl, sm. ... 10
ruby stain ... 20
Bowl ... 25
ruby stain ... 40
Butter ... 70
ruby stain ... 100
Celery Vase ... 30
ruby stain ... 40
Creamer or Spooner ... 35
ruby stain ... 45
Decanter ... 65
ruby stain ... 90
Goblet ... 45
ruby stain ... 60
Jelly Compote ... 35
ruby stain ... 40
Sauce ... 10
ruby stain ... 20
Sugar ... 50
ruby stain ... 65
Tray ... 40
ruby stain ... 45
Tumbler ... 30
ruby stain ... 45
Wine ... 20
ruby stain ... 30

LOOP & DART W/DIAMOND ORNAMENT
Bowl, oval ... 30
Butter ... 80
Celery Vase ... 60
Compote, covered, high or low ... 70 - 100
Compote, open, high or low ... 40 - 60
Creamer or Spooner ... 50
Egg Cup ... 40
Goblet ... 40
Pitcher ... 200
Plate, 6" ... 60
Relish Tray, oval ... 20
Salt, master ... 100
Sauce ... 10
Sugar ... 80
Tumbler ... 50
Wine ... 35

LOOP & JEWEL
Berry Sugar Bowl ... 35
milk glass ... 40
Bowls, 6" - 8" ... 15 - 30
milk glass ... 20 - 45
Butter ... 55
milk glass ... 65
Creamer or Spooner ... 25
milk glass ... 40
Dish, 5", sq. ... 20
milk glass ... 25
Goblet ... 35
milk glass ... 40
Pickle Dish ... 15
milk glass ... 25
Pitcher ... 85
milk glass ... 95
Plate, 5½", sq. ... 20
milk glass ... 25
Relish Tray ... 20
milk glass ... 25
Salt Dip ... 25
milk glass ... 35
Sauce, flat or ftd. ... 10
milk glass ... 20
Shakers, ea. ... 30
milk glass ... 40
Sugar ... 40
milk glass ... 55
Syrup ... 65
milk glass ... 80
Tumbler ... 15
milk glass ... 30
Vase ... 30
milk glass ... 30
Wine ... 15
milk glass ... 30

LOOP WITH DEWDROP
Bowls, various ... 20
Butter ... 60
Cake Stand ... 40
Celery Dish ... 20
Compote, covered, 8" ... 70
Condiment Set, complete ... 95
Creamer or Spooner ... 35
Cruet ... 65
Cup & Saucer ... 35
Goblet ... 35
Jelly Compote ... 35
Mug ... 35
Oval Dish ... 35
Pickle Jar ... 45
Pitcher ... 75
Shakers, ea. ... 25
Sugar ... 45
Syrup ... 100
Tray, hndl. ... 50
Tumbler ... 10
Wine ... 20

LOOP WITH FISH EYE
Berry Bowl, lg. ... 45
Berry Bowl, sm. ... 20
Goblet ... 55

LOOP WITH PRISM BAND
Butter ... 55
Creamer or Spooner ... 25
Goblet ... 35
Pitcher ... 65
Sugar ... 30
Tumbler ... 10

LORNE
Butter ... 75
vaseline ... 145

LOTUS & GRAPE VARIANT
Bonbon ... 65
Red ... 300
Bowl, ftd., with rolled rim, rare
black ... 150

LOUISIANA PURCHASE EXPOSITION
Plate, 7¼", very scarce ... 125
Tumbler, very scarce to rare ... 100
green/blue ... 250
milk glass ... 150

"LOVES REQUEST IS PICKLES"
Pickle Tray w/lettering ... 85
*Stained or gilded add 15%.

LOZENGES
Bowls, various ... 15 - 45
Butter ... 60
Compote ... 40
Creamer or Spooner ... 25
Sugar ... 30

LUCERE
Butter ... 70
Champagne ... 30
Compote, lg. ... 45
Creamer ... 30
Goblet ... 40
Pickle Dish ... 25
Spooner ... 35
Sugar ... 45
Wine ... 25

LUTTED'S S.P. COUGH DROPS
Covered Footed Butter (adv. piece from the Log Cabin pattern) ... 325
amber ... 350
vaseline ... 375
green/blue ... 350

MADEIRA
Butter ... 65
Creamer ... 25
Goblet ... 50
Relish ... 25
Spooner ... 30
Sugar ... 40
Wine ... 25

MAGNA
Berry Bowl, lg. ... 35
Berry Bowl, sm. ... 15
Butter ... 65
Celery Vase ... 20
Creamer or Spooner ... 20
Pickle Tray ... 15
Pitcher ... 85
Shakers, ea. ... 15
Sugar ... 25
Toothpick Holder ... 25
Tumbler ... 20

MAGNET & GRAPE
Butter ... 235
Celery Vase ... 300
Champagne ... 325
Compote, open and covered ... 150 - 400
Creamer or Spooner ... 200
Decanter, w/stopper,
2 sizes ... 350 - 450
Egg Cup ... 75
Goblet ... 100
Master Salt ... 100
Milk Pitcher ... 1,500
Mug, rare ... 750
Pitcher ... 1,200
Sauce ... 40
Sugar ... 235
Tumbler, 2 styles ... 150 - 275
Wine ... 165
Wine Jug, with and without inscription,
rare ... 3,200 - 4,000

MAIZE
Bowls, various ... 15 - 35
custard ... 35 - 65
Bowl, celery ... 25
custard ... 50
Bowl, finger ... 20
custard ... 40
Butter ... 65
custard ... 135
Carafe ... 35
custard ... 85
Condiment Set, complete ... 80
custard ... 175

- Creamer or Spooner ... 25
  - custard ... 50
- Decanter ... 40
  - custard ... 80
- Pitcher ... 95
  - custard ... 225
- Rose Bowl ... 35
  - custard ... 65
- Shakers, ea ... 25
  - custard ... 55
- Sugar ... 30
  - custard ... 60
- Sugar Shaker ... 45
  - custard ... 75
- Tumbler ... 15
  - custard ... 45

MALTESE

- Basket, 5" ... 45 - 55
  - amber ... 75
  - vaseline ... 85
  - green/blue ... 70
- Bowl, 8" ... 25
- Bread Plate ... 50 - 60
- Butter ... 90
- Celery, ftd. ... 55
- Celery Boat ... 25
- Compotes, covered ... 55 - 75
- Compotes, open ... 35 - 55
- Creamer or Spooner ... 50
- Custard ... 15
- Decanter (Brandy bottle) ... 55
- Finger Bowl ... 20
- Goblet ... 50
- Nappies ... 15 - 35
- Oil Bottle ... 55
- Orange Bowl, 7" & 9" ... 30 - 35
- Oval Bowls ... 25 - 35
- Pickle Boat ... 25
- Pickle Jar w/Lid ... 65
- Pitcher, 2 sizes ... 66 - 75
- Plates, 5" - 7" ... 25 - 35
- Sugar ... 65
- Tray, 9" x 15" ... 60
- Tumbler, 2 sizes ... 30 - 40
- Water Bottle ... 55
- Wine Tray ... 50

MALTESE & RIBBON

- Bowls, 3 sizes, oval and round ... 20 - 35
  - amber ... 30 - 45
  - vaseline ... 45 - 70
  - green/blue ... 40 - 60
- Bowl, sq., 7" & 8" ... 25 - 40
  - amber ... 35 - 50
  - vaseline ... 50 - 75
  - green/blue ... 40 - 65
- Finger Bowl ... 25
  - amber ... 40
  - vaseline ... 60
  - green/blue ... 55
- Lamp Shade, 2 sizes ... 50 - 70
  - amber ... 65 - 85
  - vaseline ... 80 - 120
  - green/blue ... 70 - 90
- Master Salt ... 25
  - amber ... 30
  - vaseline ... 45
  - green/blue ... 40
- Pickle Dish ... 20
  - amber ... 25
  - vaseline ... 35
  - green/blue ... 30
- Pitcher, 2 sizes ... 65 - 85
  - amber ... 80 - 115
  - vaseline ... 110 - 260
  - green/blue ... 90 - 185
- Tumbler ... 20
  - amber ... 25
  - vaseline ... 35
  - green/blue ... 30

*Sapphire 25% higher than amber prices.

MANHATTAN

- Basket ... 100
- Biscuit Jar ... 135
- Berry Bowls (6 sizes), from 7" - 12½" ... 25 - 75
- Butter or Cheese Dish ... 140
- Cake Stand, 3 sizes ... 100 - 135
- Celery Vase ... 50
- Compote, covered and open ... 90 - 200
- Cracker Jar ... 80
- Creamer or Spooner ... 35
- Cruet w/Stopper ... 90
- Custard Cup ... 15
- Goblet ... 60
- Milk Pitcher ... 130
- Pickle Castor, complete ... 200
- Pickle Dish ... 30
- Plate, 5" ... 20
- Plate, 9½" - 12" ... 20 - 50
- Punch Bowl, 2 styles ... 300 - 400
- Punch Cup ... 20
- Shakers, ea ... 50
- Straw Holder ... 475
- Sugar ... 60
- Syrup ... 100
- Toothpick Holder ... 40
- Tray, 2 sizes ... 50 - 70
- Tumbler, 2 sizes ... 25 - 30
- Water Bottle ... 80
- Wine ... 35

*Add 100% for maiden's blush pieces.

MANHATTAN ADVERTISING PIECES

- Tray, 6"x7½", various advertising, scarce ... 175

MAPLE LEAF

- Bowl, covered, 6" - 11" ... 35 - 55
  - amber ... 45 - 85
  - vaseline ... 85 - 150
  - green/blue ... 65 - 125
- Butter ... 60
  - amber ... 75
  - vaseline ... 180
  - green/blue ... 85
- Cake Stand ... 40
  - amber ... 65
  - vaseline ... 125
  - green/blue ... 85
- Celery Vase ... 25
  - amber ... 45
  - vaseline ... 70
  - green/blue ... 55
- Compote, covered, ftd. ... 50
  - amber ... 75
  - vaseline ... 150
  - green/blue ... 100
- Creamer or Spooner ... 30
  - amber ... 45
  - vaseline ... 65
  - green/blue ... 55
- Cup Plate ... 20
  - amber ... 25
  - vaseline ... 35
  - green/blue ... 30
- Dish, sq., 10" ... 30
  - amber ... 40
  - vaseline ... 75
  - green/blue ... 50
- Goblet ... 55
  - amber ... 85
  - vaseline ... 110
  - green/blue ... 95
- Maple (leaf border) ... 45
  - amber ... 60
  - vaseline ... 75
  - green/blue ... 70
- Milk Pitcher ... 75
  - amber ... 100
  - vaseline ... 195
  - green/blue ... 165
- Pitcher ... 90
  - amber ... 145
  - vaseline ... 250
  - green/blue ... 200
- Plate, 10½" (diamond center) ... 40
  - amber ... 60
  - vaseline ... 80
  - green/blue ... 70
- Platter, oval (diamond center) ... 50
  - amber ... 70
  - vaseline ... 90
  - green/blue ... 80
- Sauce, 3 ftd. ... 10
  - amber ... 25
  - vaseline ... 25
  - green/blue ... 30
- Sugar ... 30
  - amber ... 50
  - vaseline ... 95
  - green/blue ... 110
- Tray, oblong ... 80
  - amber ... 120
  - vaseline ... 165
  - green/blue ... 125
- Tray, oval, leaf trim ... 70
  - amber ... 100
  - vaseline ... 200
  - green/blue ... 130
- Tumbler ... 50
  - amber ... 60
  - vaseline ... 90
  - green/blue ... 70
- Twin Relish, leaf handles. ... 60
  - amber ... 70
  - vaseline ... 95
  - green/blue ... 80

MAPLE LEAF VARIANT

- Plate, 10" ... 45
  - vaseline ... 80
- Platter, 10½" ... 55
  - vaseline ... 100

MARDI GRAS

- Banana Bowl ... 60
  - ruby stain ... 200
- Bitters bottle ... 80
  - ruby stain ... 195
- Bonbon ... 45
  - ruby stain ... 75
- Bowls, various ... 30 - 55
  - ruby stain ... 60 - 90
- Butter ... 100
  - ruby stain ... 225
- Butter Pat ... 15
  - ruby stain ... 30
- Cake Stand, 3 sizes ... 90 - 130
  - ruby stain ... 225 - 35
- Celery Tray ... 40
  - ruby stain ... 70
- Champagne ... 30 - 40
  - ruby stain ... 70 - 80
- Claret ... 50
  - ruby stain ... 90
- Cocktail ... 25
  - ruby stain ... 60
- Compote, covered ... 80
  - ruby stain ... 175
- Compote, open, 4 sizes ... 40 - 60
  - ruby stain ... 70 - 90
- Cordial ... 70
  - ruby stain ... 145
- Cracker Jar w/Lid ... 85
  - ruby stain ... 190
- Creamer, 2 sizes ... 25 - 35
  - ruby stain ... 50 - 65
- Cruet ... 65
  - ruby stain ... 180
- Egg Cup ... 25
  - ruby stain ... 55

Epergne 235
Goblet 50
ruby stain 185
Lamp Shade 40
ruby stain 150
Milk Pitcher 120
ruby stain 265
Miniature Honey Jug 80
ruby stain 190
Miniature Table Set, complete 600
ruby stain 1,000
Mustard Jar 60
ruby stain 100
Nappy, 2 styles, 2 sizes .... 20 - 30
ruby stain .... 40 - 60
Olive Dish 20
ruby stain 40
Pickle Dish 15
ruby stain 35
Pickle Jar w/Lid 90
ruby stain 235
Pitcher, various styles, 2 sizes . 100 - 145
ruby stain .... 200 - 325
Plate, 5" - 8" .... 25 - 40
ruby stain .... 40 - 60
Pomade Jar 70
ruby stain 135
Puff Box 80
ruby stain 145
Punch Bowl 200
ruby stain 425
Punch Cup 20
ruby stain 40
Relish 10
ruby stain 25
Salt Shaker, various .... 40 - 50
ruby stain .... 60 - 75
Salt, ind. 10
ruby stain 30
Salt, master 25
ruby stain 70
Sauce, various .... 10 - 15
ruby stain 25
Saucer 10
ruby stain 20
Sherry 30
ruby stain 65
Spooner 50
ruby stain 75
Sugar 80
ruby stain 165
Syrup 100
ruby stain 325
Toothpick Holder 40
ruby stain 130
Tray 50
ruby stain 85
Tumbler, 4 sizes .... 30 - 45
ruby stain .... 60 - 80
Vase, various .... 25 - 35
ruby stain .... 60 - 90
Water Bottle 70
ruby stain 135
Wine 30
ruby stain 70
Wine Jug 70
ruby stain 125

MARILYN
Pitcher, rare 250
Tumbler, rare 65

MARJORIE (SWEETHEART)
Berry Bowl, lg. 45
Berry Bowl, sm. 15
Butter 80
Card Set 75
Carafe 60
Cookie Jar, hndl. 55
Cracker Jar, 2 sizes .... 55 - 70
Creamer or Spooner 25
Cruet 60
Knife Rest 25
Napkin Ring 25
Nappy, 2 hndl. 30
Olive Dish, hndl. 25
Pickle Tray 25
Pitcher, squat 75
Pitcher 150
Punch Bowl 250
Punch Cup 20
Rose Bowl 50
Salt Dip 25
Shakers, ea. 25
Spittoon Whimsey, rare 265
Sugar 35
Syrup 55
Toothpick Holder 40
Tray, clover leaf 35
Tumbler 25
Tumbler, tea 35

MARQUISETTE
Butter 55
Celery Vase 20
Champagne 25
Compote, covered 50
Compote, open 40
Cordial 20
Creamer or Spooner 20
Goblet 25
Pitcher 75
Sauce 10
Sugar, open 25
Tumbler 15
Wine 10

MARSH PINK
Bowl, 9" 25
Butter 60
Cake Stand 45
Compote, covered 60
Creamer or Spooner 35
Dish w/Lid, 5" 30
Honey Dish 65
Jelly Compote 35
Pickle Castor 115
Pitcher 90
Plate, 10" 40
Salt Shaker 25
Sauce, flat or ftd. 10
Sugar 40

MARTEC
Berry Bowl, lg. 30
Berry Bowl, sm. 10
Bowl, Deep, 4" & 8" 25
Breakfast Set 35
Butter 55
Celery Tray 15
Compote, high ftd. 35
Cruet 55
Creamer or Spooner 25
Jelly Compote 35
Jelly Dish, oval 20
Lemonade Set, (tankard) 95
Pickle Tray 25
Pitcher 60
Plates, 3 sizes .... 15 - 35
Punch Bowl 110
Punch Cup 10
Shakers, ea. 20
Stemmed Dessert 25
Sugar 35
Syrup 65
Water bottle 40

MARY ANN
Vase 50
Loving Cup, rare 140

MARYLAND
Banana Dish 65
ruby stain 150
Bowl, 6" - 9" .... 10 - 30
ruby stain .... 40 - 90
Bread Plate 40
ruby stain 95
Butter 70
ruby stain 190
Cake Stand, 8" - 10" .... 30 - 60
ruby stain .... 165 - 235
Celery Tray 30
ruby stain 60
Celery Vase 50
ruby stain 135
Compote, covered, 6" - 8" .... 50 - 100
ruby stain .... 180 - 290
Compote, open, 5" - 8" .... 30 - 65
ruby stain .... 90 - 140
Creamer or Spooner 35
ruby stain 85
Cup 20
ruby stain 40
Goblet 45
ruby stain 165
Honey dish 25
ruby stain 30
Jelly Dish 25
ruby stain 30
Milk Pitcher 50
ruby stain 200
Olive Dish 20
ruby stain 30
Pickle Dish 15
ruby stain 30
Pitcher 85
ruby stain 250
Plate, dinner 25
ruby stain 100
Relish 20
ruby stain 50
Shakers, ea. 50
ruby stain 130
Sugar 60
ruby stain 150
Toothpick Holder, very scarce 125
ruby stain 350
Tumbler 40
ruby stain 80
Wine 50
ruby stain 115

MASCOTTE
Banana Stand 200
Bowls, covered, various .... 50 - 140
Bowls, open, various .... 30 - 75
Butter, 2 styles .... 100 - 250
Cake Stand, 4 sizes .... 60 - 100
Celery 50
vaseline 300
Cheese Dish w/Cover 125
Compotes, covered,
various sizes .... 30 - 90
Compotes, open, various sizes ... 70 - 145
Cookie Stand 60
Creamer or Spooner 50
Cruet 85
Goblet 40
Jar, Egyptian 150
Jar, Fish Globe 300
Jar, Patent Globe 200
Jar, Pyramid w/lid and
underplate, 3 jars 500
Jar, Pyramid w/lid and
underplate, 4 jars 1,000
Jar, Pyramid w/lid and
underplate, 5 jars 2,000
Pickle 60
Pitcher 100
Relish 40
Sample Bottle w/Cover, 15" 500
Sugar 70
Syrup 125
Tray, water 90

Tumbler ... 45
Wine ... 30
*For vaseline add 125% unless prices is listed.
*For etched or stained pieces add 75%.

MASONIC
Bowls, 4" - 9" ... 15 - 50
Butter, 2 styles ... 50 - 65
Cake Stand, 9" - 10" ... 35 - 45
Celery Vase ... 20
Compote, covered ... 55
Compote, open ... 35
Creamer or Spooner ... 30
Cruet ... 45
Custard Cup ... 10
Goblet ... 35
Handle Salad Fork ... 25
Honey Dish w/Lid ... 45
Nappy ... 25
Pitcher ... 90
Relish Dish ... 15
Salt Dip, 2 styles ... 20
Sardine Box ... 35
Shakers ea., 2 styles ... 15 - 25
Sugar ... 50
Syrup ... 85
Toothpick Holder ... 35
Tumbler ... 20
Wine ... 20

MASSACHUSETTS
Banquet Lamp, rare ... 1475
Basket, 2 sizes ... 100 - 135
Bottles; brandy, cologne, liqueur, bar, tabasco, water, and wine ... 65 - 200
Bowls, open, various ... 30 - 55
Butter ... 75
Candy Dish ... 30
Champagne ... 60
Compote, open ... 60
Creamer or Spooner ... 40
Cruet, 2 sizes ... 50 - 70
Decanter w/Stopper ... 125
Goblet ... 70
Pitcher, 2 sizes ... 100 - 150
Plate, 8" ... 30 - 40
Rum Jug ... 80 - 120
Shakers, ea ... 40 - 60
Shot Glass ... 30
Sugar ... 60
Table Lamp ... 600
Toothpick Holder, rare ... 165
Tray, various ... 40 - 60
Tumbler, various ... 30 - 50
Vase, 7" - 10" ... 30 - 50

MAYFLOWER
Bowl, 8" - 9", very scarce ... 250

McKEE'S #2 PUFF JAR
Puff Jar, open ... 30

McKEE'S #1004
Vase, 8" (Globe Vase) ... 50

McKEE'S TAMBOUR ART CLOCK
Clock ... 95
amber ... 150
vaseline ... 235
green/blue ... 170
amethyst ... 200

MEDALLION
Butter ... 45
amber ... 55
vaseline ... 80
green/blue ... 70
Cake Stand ... 90
amber ... 100
vaseline ... 150
green/blue ... 125
Castor Bottles ... 45
amber ... 55
vaseline ... 90
green/blue ... 70
Celery Vase ... 35
amber ... 40
vaseline ... 70
green/blue ... 60
Compote, covered ... 70
amber ... 80
vaseline ... 135
green/blue ... 125
Egg Cup ... 30
amber ... 40
vaseline ... 60
green/blue ... 50
Goblet ... 35
amber ... 40
vaseline ... 50
green/blue ... 45
Pickle Dish ... 20
amber ... 25
vaseline ... 30
green/blue ... 30
Pitcher ... 65
amber ... 70
vaseline ... 125
green/blue ... 125
Relish Tray ... 20
amber ... 25
vaseline ... 30
green/blue ... 30
Sauce, flat or ftd ... 10
amber ... 15
vaseline ... 20
green/blue ... 25
Sugar ... 45
amber ... 50
vaseline ... 80
green/blue ... 70
Tumbler ... 20
amber ... 25
vaseline ... 50
green/blue ... 40
Waste Bowl ... 35
amber ... 40
vaseline ... 60
green/blue ... 50
Water bottle ... 45
amber ... 60
vaseline ... 80
green/blue ... 70
Wine ... 20
amber ... 25
vaseline ... 30
green/blue ... 35

MEDALLION SUNBURST
Banana Dish, flat or stemmed ... 35
Bowl, rnd. or sq. ... 25
Butter ... 65
Cake Stand, 9" - 10½" ... 40
Celery Tray ... 25
Celery Vase ... 20
Creamer or Spooner ... 20
Cruet ... 55
Custard Cup ... 10
Individual Creamer or Sugar ... 15
Jam Jar ... 25
Milk Pitcher ... 45
Mug ... 25
Mustard Jar ... 20
Olive Dish ... 15
Pitcher ... 85
Plate, rnd., 6" - 9" ... 15 - 30
Plate, sq., 7¼" ... 25
Relish Tray ... 20
Salt Dip, ind. ... 15
Shakers, ea ... 20
Sugar ... 25
Toothpick Holder ... 30
Tumbler ... 15
Vase, 9½" ... 25
Wine ... 10

MEIS' STORE
Toothpick Holder, with advertising ... 70

MELON WITH LEAF
Novelty Bowl, covered ... 55
amber ... 75
vaseline ... 120
green/blue ... 95
milk glass ... 55

MELROSE
Bowl, 2 styles ... 30 - 40
Butter ... 65
ruby stain ... 125
Cake Stand ... 80
ruby stain ... 125
Celery Vase ... 35
ruby stain ... 45
Compote, covered ... 65
ruby stain ... 85
Compote, open ... 45
ruby stain ... 60
Creamer or Spooner ... 35
ruby stain ... 55
Goblet ... 40
ruby stain ... 60
Jelly Compote ... 35
ruby stain ... 45
chocolate ... 125
Milk Pitcher ... 65
ruby stain ... 80
Nappy ... 30
ruby stain ... 45
chocolate ... 65
Pitcher, tankard ... 75
ruby stain ... 90
Plate ... 30
ruby stain ... 60
chocolate ... 800
Sugar ... 45
ruby stain ... 80
Tumbler ... 25
ruby stain ... 40
Water Tray ... 60
ruby stain ... 75
Wine ... 20
ruby stain ... 30

MELTON
Butter ... 55
Creamer or Spooner ... 20
Goblet ... 35
Sugar ... 25
Wine ... 10

MEMPHIS
Bowl, berry, lg. ... 55
Bowl, berry, sm. ... 25
Butter ... 100
vaseline ... 3000
Creamer, Spooner or Sugar ... 40
Decanter w/Stopper ... 175
Fruit Bowl, on metal base ... 100
Nappy ... 65
Nappy, adv., various lettering ... 75
Pitcher ... 275
Punch Bowl w/Base, master ... 700
Punch Bowl w/Base, reg. ... 375
Punch Cup ... 30
Shakers, ea. ... 50
green/blue ... 90
Stemmed Cuspidor, rare ... 400
Syrup ... 90
Toothpick Holder ... 95
Tumbler ... 35

MEMPHIS ADVERTISING PIECES
Bowl, 10" ... 100
Nappy, with handle ... 60

MENAGERIE
Toy Spooner, fish shape ... 90
amber ... 110
green/blue ... 130
opaque ... 165

MEPHISTOPHELES
Ale Glass ... 95
opaque white ... 110
Mug... 125
opaque white ... 140
Pitcher... 275
opaque white ... 300
MICHIGAN (AKA: DESPLAINES, LOOP & PILLAR, PANELED JEWEL)
Bowls, various shapes, 6" - 10" .. 10 - 55
ruby stain ... 35 - 85
Bride's Basket ... 85
ruby stain ... 165
Butter, 2 sizes ... 60 - 90
ruby stain ... 100 - 165
Celery Vase ... 60
ruby stain ... 100
Compotes, covered ... 60 - 85
ruby stain ... 100 - 140
Compotes, open ... 40 - 85
ruby stain ... 70 - 145
Creamer or Spooner ... 45
ruby stain ... 70
Cruet ... 100
ruby stain ... 325
Goblet ... 50
ruby stain ... 135
Lemonade, hndl. ... 40
ruby stain ... 85
lemon stain ... 80
Milk Pitcher ... 75
ruby stain ... 125
Pickle Dish ... 20
ruby stain ... 30
Pitcher, 2 styles ... 90
ruby stain ... 225
Plate ... 30
ruby stain ... 60
Salt Shaker, ea ... 35
ruby stain ... 100
Sauce ... 15
ruby stain ... 35
Sugar ... 75
ruby stain ... 135
Syrup ... 100
ruby stain ... 325
Toothpick Holder, rare ... 60
ruby stain ... 100
Miniatures, 8 pieces ... 20 - 150
ruby stain ... 25 - 600
Tumbler ... 40
ruby stain ... 70
Vase, 6" - 17" ... 30 - 95
ruby stain ... 50 - 135
Water Bottle ... 60
ruby stain ... 175
MILLARD
Bowl, 7" - 9" ... 25
ruby stain ... 35
Butter ... 50
ruby stain ... 75
Cake Stand ... 30
ruby stain ... 45
Celery Tray ... 20
ruby stain ... 25
Celery Vase ... 25
ruby stain ... 35
Compote ... 25
ruby stain ... 45
Creamer or Spooner ... 20
ruby stain ... 30
Cruet ... 60
ruby stain ... 80
Cup ... 10
ruby stain ... 25
Dish, oblong ... 20
ruby stain ... 30
Goblet ... 35
ruby stain ... 55
Pitcher ... 75
ruby stain ... 125
Plate ... 20
ruby stain ... 30
Sauce, flat or ftd. ... 10
ruby stain ... 25
Shakers, ea. ... 25
ruby stain ... 45
Sugar ... 25
ruby stain ... 45
Syrup ... 55
ruby stain ... 75
Toothpick Holder ... 30
ruby stain ... 65
Tumbler ... 15
ruby stain ... 35
Wine ... 15
ruby stain ... 25
MILLERSBURG CHERRY
Jardiniere Whimsey, very rare
green/blue ... 3,000
Milk Pitcher, rare ... 1,200
Pitcher, rare ... 1,400
MILLERSBURG TULIP
Compote, ruffled ... 500
Compote, goblet shaped ... 650
Compote, salver shaped ... 650
MILLNER'S
Advertising Ashtray ... 75
MINERVA
Bowls, open, various ... 30 - 50
Bread Plate, lettered, 2 styles ... 60 - 80
Butter ... 100
Champagne, rare ... 625
Compote, covered, 7" - 8" ... 125 - 165
Compote, open, 10½" ... 200 - 300
Creamer or Spooner ... 40
Goblet ... 125
Honey Dish ... 35
Jam Jar ... 250
Milk Pitcher ... 200
Pickle Dish ... 40
Pitcher ... 250
Plate, 8" - 9" ... 50 - 60
Platter, oval ... 95
Sauce, flat or ftd. ... 20
Sugar ... 100
Tumbler ... 45
MINNESOTA
Banana Stand ... 60
Basket ... 100
Biscuit Jar ... 85
ruby stain ... 165
Bonbon ... 35
Bowls, various ... 20 - 45
Butter ... 70
Carafe ... 60
Celery Tray ... 25
Compote, rnd. or sq. ... 40 - 80
Creamer or Spooner ... 30
Cruet ... 50
Cup ... 20
Fruit Bowl, various ... 50 - 85
Goblet ... 50
ruby stain ... 85
Hair Receiver ... 80
Humidor ... 175
Match Holder ... 45
Mug ... 40
Pitcher, 3 sizes ... 100 - 150
ruby stain ... 200 - 275
Plate ... 35
Pomade Jar ... 80
Shaker ... 40
Sugar ... 70
Syrup ... 125
Toothpick Holder ... 35
ruby stain ... 125
Toothpick Holder
with advertising ... 65
Tray, various ... 25 - 90
Tumbler ... 40
ruby stain ... 60
Vase ... 40
Wine ... 35
MISSOURI
Bowl, open, 6" - 8" ... 20 - 35
green/blue ... 40 - 70
Butter ... 65
green/blue ... 125
Cake Stand ... 35
green/blue ... 60 - 125
Celery Vase ... 50
green/blue ... 80
Compote, covered, 5" - 8" ... 45 - 70
green/blue ... 60 - 125
Compote, open, 5" - 10" ... 25 - 65
green/blue ... 30 - 60
Cordial ... 50
green/blue ... 135
Creamer or Spooner ... 30
green/blue ... 55
Cruet ... 70
green/blue ... 250
Dish w/Lid, 6" ... 75
green/blue ... 135
Doughnut Stand, 6" ... 50
green/blue ... 80
Goblet ... 65
green/blue ... 150
Milk Pitcher ... 50
green/blue ... 100
Mug ... 50
green/blue ... 75
Pickle Dish ... 15
green/blue ... 30
Pitcher ... 100
green/blue ... 150
Relish Dish ... 10
green/blue ... 30
Salt Shaker ... 45
green/blue ... 100
Sauce ... 10
green/blue ... 25
Sugar ... 60
green/blue ... 80
Syrup ... 95
green/blue ... 325
Tumbler ... 20
green/blue ... 65
Wine ... 50
green/blue ... 100
MITERED DIAMOND
Berry Bowl, lg. ... 30
amber ... 35
vaseline ... 45
green/blue ... 40
Berry Bowl, sm. ... 10
amber ... 15
vaseline ... 25
green/blue ... 20
Butter ... 45
amber ... 50
vaseline ... 95
green/blue ... 60
Compote ... 30
amber ... 35
vaseline ... 55
green/blue ... 45
Cordial ... 20
amber ... 25
vaseline ... 35
green/blue ... 30
Creamer or Spooner ... 25
amber ... 30
vaseline ... 40

green/blue 35
Platter 30
amber 35
vaseline 70
green/blue 40
Sauce 10
amber 15
vaseline 30
green/blue 20
Shakers, ea 25
amber 30
vaseline 50
green/blue 35
Sugar 35
amber 40
vaseline 60
green/blue 45
Wine 15
amber 20
vaseline 40
green/blue 30

MITTED HAND
Bowl, 6" 75

MODEL'S GEM
*See RED BLOCK

MOERLEINS
Pilsner, 6", advertising, 2 styles lettering 50

MONARCH
Bowl, 9" 35
Cruet 45
Punch Bowl 115
Punch Cup 10

MONKEY
Bowl, master 295
opal 525
Butter 600
opal 1,300
Celery Vase, rare 875
opal 1,400
Creamer 300
opal 450
Mug, 2 styles 100
opal 225
Pickle w/Lid 725
opal 1,350
Pitcher 4,800
opal 9,000
Sauce 100
opal 135
Spooner 165
opal 275
Sugar 50
opal 495
Tumbler 250
opal 400
Waste Bowl 300
opal 425
*All pieces scarce, rare.

MONKEY & VINES
Mug 60

MONKEY WITH DIAMOND BASE
Mug 175

MONKEY WITH FANCY HANDLE
Mug, rare 125
green/blue 250
amethyst 300

MOON & STAR
Bowl, covered, 6" - 10" ..... 80 - 300
ruby stain ..... 125 - 575
Bowl, open, 6" - 10" ..... 35 - 70
ruby stain ..... 90 - 145
Bowl, salad, 12" 400
ruby stain 700
Bowl, waste 55
ruby stain 65
Bread Tray ..... 50 - 100
ruby stain ..... 100 - 300
Butter 80
ruby stain 250
Cake Stand ..... 100 - 125
ruby stain ..... 285 - 300
Carafe 100
ruby stain 300
Celery Vase 60
ruby stain 100
Champagne 100
ruby stain 110
Cheese Plate 35
ruby stain 50
Claret 90
ruby stain 165
Compote, w/lid, 6" - 10", low ..... 90 - 300
ruby stain ..... 150 - 725
Compote, w/lid, 6½" - 10½", high ..... 100 - 60
ruby stain ..... 200 - 1,000
Compote, open, 6" - 10½", low ..... 40 - 80
ruby stain ..... 90 - 140
Compote, open, 5½" - 10½", high ..... 50 - 110
ruby stain ..... 100 - 1,250
Creamer or Spooner 90
ruby stain 165
Cruet 200
ruby stain 400
Egg Cup 70
ruby stain 135
Goblet 90
ruby stain 375
Oil Lamp 300
Pickle Tray 30
ruby stain 45
Pitcher 300
ruby stain 600
Relish Tray 15
ruby stain 35
Salt Dip 15
ruby stain 40
Sauce 10
ruby stain 20
Shakers, ea 50
ruby stain 120
Sugar 90
ruby stain 165
Syrup 185
ruby stain 625
Tumbler 80
ruby stain 60
Water Bottle 125
ruby stain 300
Wine 50
ruby stain 95

MORNING GLORY
Butter 850
Champagne 250
Creamer or Spooner 175
Dessert, stemmed 125
Egg Cup 95
Goblet 1,850
Pitcher 1,200
Salt Dip 100
Sugar 200
Tumbler, ftd. 95
Wine 115

MT. VERNON
Bowls, rectangular ..... 15 - 40
Butter 50
Creamer or Spooner 20
Goblet 35
Pickle Dish 15
Relish 15
Sugar 25

MULBERRY
Tray, 8" x 13¼", rare 350

MULTIPLE SCROLL
Bowls, various ..... 15 - 25
amber ..... 20 - 35
Butter 55
amber 60
green/blue 70
Celery Vase 20
amber 30
green/blue 40
Creamer or Spooner 25
amber 35
green/blue 45
Mug 40
amber 50
green/blue 60
Pickle Dish 15
amber 20
green/blue 25
Plate, sq. 20
amber 25
green/blue 30
Sugar 40
amber 55
green/blue 65
Wine 20
amber 25
green/blue 30

MULTIPLE SCROLL W/SWIRL CENTER
Plate 35

MUTT JUG #46
Pitcher, tankard 95

NAIL
Berry Bowl, lg. 50
ruby stain 100
Berry Bowl, sm. 30
ruby stain 70
Butter 80
ruby stain 200
Cake Stand 100
ruby stain 295
Celery Vase 50
ruby stain 120
Claret 30
ruby stain 75
Creamer or Spooner 40
ruby stain 90
Cruet 75
ruby stain 300
Finger Bowl 30
ruby stain 70
Goblet 50
ruby stain 120
Jelly Compote 40
ruby stain 80
Mustard Pot 65
ruby stain 135
Pitcher 135
ruby stain 265
Sauce, flat or ftd. 10
ruby stain 30
Shakers, ea. 40
ruby stain 90
Sugar 50
ruby stain 135
Sugar Shaker 75
ruby stain 200
Tumbler 30
ruby stain 80
Vase, 7" 25
Water Bottle 70
ruby stain 285
Water Tray 70
ruby stain 200
Wine 30
ruby stain 85

NAILHEAD
Berry Bowl, lg. 40
Berry Bowl, sm. 15
Butter 70
Cake Stand 35
Celery Vase 25
Compote, covered, 6" - 8" ..... 25 - 60
Compote, open, 6" - 8" ..... 20 - 45
Cordial 15

Creamer or Spooner 20
Goblet 50
Pitcher 90
Plate, bread 15
Plate, dinner 25
Sauce 10
Sugar 25
Tumbler 20
Wine 15

NAPOLEAN
Bowl, round or oval 50
Butter 95
Creamer 45
Goblet 60
Pitcher 125
Spooner 45
Sugar 55
Tumbler 30

NARCISSUS SPRAY
Berry Bowl, lg. 45
Berry Bowl, sm. 20
Bowl, ftd., 7½" 25
Bowl, rnd. or oval 30
Butter 60
Celery Tray 30
Celery Vase, ftd 20
Creamer or Spooner 20
Decanter 65
Jelly Compote 25
Pitcher 85
Plate 25
Sugar 25
Tumbler 20
Wine 15

NARROW SWIRL
Pitcher, small 65

NATIONAL STAR
Berry Bowl, sm. 10
vaseline 20
ruby stain 15
Berry Bowl, lg. 30
vaseline 50
ruby stain 45
Butter 65
vaseline 110
ruby stain 80
Creamer or Spooner 25
vaseline 40
ruby stain 35
Jelly Compote 30
vaseline 45
ruby stain 40
Pitcher 75
vaseline 160
ruby stain 125
Sugar 30
vaseline 65
ruby stain 45
Tumbler 15
vaseline 40
ruby stain 30

*Add 25% to vaseline pieces with ruby stain.

NAVARRE (McKEE & BROS, 1900)
Butter 85
ruby stain 120
Creamer or Spooner 35
ruby stain 45
Nappy 25
ruby stain 35
Sugar 45
ruby stain 60

NEARCUT #2636
Basket, hndl. 45
Berry Bowl, lg. 45
Berry Bowl, sm. 20
Bowl, various 20 - 35
Butter 65
Celery Vase 25
Creamer or Spooner 25
Cruet 65
Pitcher 90
Salt Shakers, ea. 20
Sugar 30
Tumbler 20
Vase 30
Wine 15

NEARCUT #2697
Toy Berry Set, complete 90
Toy Table Set, complete 110
Toy Water Set, complete 125

NEARCUT DAISY
Bowls, various 15 - 35
Butter 65
Creamer or Spooner 25
Pickle Dish 20
Sugar 40
Vases, various 15 - 35

NEAR CUT WREATH
Bowl, 8" - 9" 300
Rose Bowl 750
Tricorner Bowl 600

*All pieces very scarce, rare.

NELLIE BLY
Platter, rare 350

NELLY
Berry Bowl, lg. 35
Berry Bowl, sm. 15
Butter 55
Cake Stand 35
Celery Vase 20
Compote 30
Creamer or Spooner 20
Sauce 10
Shakers, ea. 15
Sugar 25

NEW CRESCENT
Bowls, various 20 - 45
Butter 60
Compote 40
Creamer 25
Grape Boat 35
Spooner 25
Square Bowl 30
Sugar 30

NEW ENGLAND CENTENNIAL
Goblet, rare 225
Lamp, rare 650

NEW ENGLAND PINEAPPLE
Bowl, 8" 90
Butter 275
Cake Stand 155
Castor Set, complete 280
Champagne 200
Compote, covered, 5" - 8" 300 - 600
Compote, open, 7" - 8½" 80 - 140
Cordial 200
Creamer 375
Cruet 195
Decanter, with and without stopper 200 - 375
Egg Cup 45
Goblet, 2 sizes 75 - 125
Honey Dish 25
Milk Pitcher 975
Mug, 2 sizes 300 - 400
Pitcher 1,300
Plate, 6" 100
Salt, master 60
Sauce, flat or ftd. 25
Spill 75
Spooner 70
Sugar 195 - 225
Sweetmeat 245
Tumbler, 2 sizes 100 - 135
Whiskey 200
Wine 165

NEW HAMPSHIRE
Basket 125
ruby stain 325
Biscuit Jar 90
ruby stain 260
Bowl, rnd., 6" - 9" 20 - 60
ruby stain 30 - 80
Bowl, sq., 6" - 9" 25 - 60
ruby stain 40 - 90
Breakfast Set 55
ruby stain 100
Butter 90
ruby stain 190
Cake Stand 100
ruby stain 200
Carafe 70
ruby stain 135
Celery Vase 50
ruby stain 100
Compote, covered, 6" - 9" 80 - 130
ruby stain 125 - 200
Compote, open, 6" - 9" 40 - 80
ruby stain 80 - 110
Creamer or Spooner 35
ruby stain 75
Cruet 90
ruby stain 235
Custard Cup 10
ruby stain 30
Goblet 40
ruby stain 125
Jam Jar, covered 70
ruby stain 150
Lemonade Cup 20
ruby stain 40
Mug, 2 sizes 35 - 50
ruby stain 70 - 90
Olive Dish 15
ruby stain 30
Pitcher, 3 styles 130 - 200
ruby stain 250 - 500
Plate, 8" 40
ruby stain 75
Relish Tray 20
ruby stain 40
Salt Shaker, 3 sizes 40
ruby stain 100
Sauce, rnd. or sq. 10
ruby stain 20
Sugar 50
ruby stain 80
Syrup 90
ruby stain 300
Toothpick Holder 25
ruby stain 90
Tumbler, 2 styles 20 - 25
ruby stain 75
Vase, 6" - 9" 20 - 50
ruby stain 50 - 70
Wine, 2 styles 20
ruby stain 50

NEW JERSEY
Bowl, 6" - 10" 15 - 50
ruby stain 50 - 80
Bowl, oval, 6" - 10" 20 - 60
ruby stain 45 - 85
Butter 85
ruby stain 200
Cake Stand 90
ruby stain 300
Celery Tray 25
ruby stain 50
Celery Vase 50
ruby stain 95
Compote, covered, 5" - 8" 60 - 120
ruby stain 90 - 200
Compote, open, 5" - 8" 30 - 60
ruby stain 50 - 100
Creamer or Spooner 50
ruby stain 95
Cruet 70
ruby stain 375

Fruit Bowl on Standard, 9½" - 12½". 40 - 65
ruby stain 50 - 125
Goblet 50
ruby stain 245
Milk Pitcher 100
ruby stain 300
Olive Dish 10
ruby stain 35
Pickle Tray 20
ruby stain 45
Pitcher, 2 styles 150
ruby stain 325
Plate, 8" - 12" 20 - 40
ruby stain 75 - 150
Shade, gas 75
ruby stain 195
Shakers, ea. 55
ruby stain 125
Sugar 55
ruby stain 150
Sweetmeat (High Butter) 100
ruby stain 300
Syrup 100
ruby stain 325
Toothpick Holder 60
ruby stain 225
Tumbler, 2 styles 20 - 30
ruby stain 100
Water bottle 60
ruby stain 200
Wine 40
ruby stain 100
*Add 10% for gilded pieces.

NEW MARTINSVILLE #169
Candlesticks, 7" 60

NIAGARA
Berry Bowl, lg. 35
Berry Bowl, sm. 10
Butter 55
Compote 30
Cracker Jar 30
Creamer or Spooner 20
Cruet 50
Cup 10
Jelly, hndl. 25
Mustard Jar 30
Plate 25
Sugar 25
Syrup 55

NICKEL PLATE'S RICHMOND
Bowl, master 60
Butter 140
Celery Vase 60
Cheese Dish 180
Creamer 50
Goblet 40
Milk Pitcher 100
Pitcher 90 - 125
Spooner 55
Sugar 90
Tumbler 40
Water Bottle 30
*Any ruby stained pieces found add 100%.

NOGI
Butter 40
Creamer or Spooner 15
Fan Tray 20
Goblet 30
Pickle Dish 10
Pitcher 60
Plate 20
Sugar 25
Tumbler 10
*Add 10% for ruby stained or gilded pieces.

NORTHERN STAR
Plate, 3 sizes 55
Sauce Bowl 30

NORTH STAR
Berry Bowl, lg. 30
Berry Bowl, sm. 10
Butter 55
Compote, stemmed, ruffled 35
Creamer or Spooner 20
Pitcher 70
Plate 25
Punch Bowl w/Base 110
Punch Cup 10
Tumbler 15
Sugar 25

NORTHWOOD NEAR-CUT (#12)
*Condensed list.
Berry Bowl, lg. 40
Berry Bowl, sm. 20
Butter 70
Celery Vase 30
Compote 40
Creamer or Spooner 25
Goblet 35
Nappy 25
Nappy, adv., rare 100
Pickle Dish 30
Pitcher 125
Shakers, ea. 30
Sugar 30
Toothpick Holder 45
Tumbler 25
Wine 25

NORTHWOOD'S GOOD LUCK
Bowl with Letterings
custard 350

NOTCHED BAR
Berry Bowl, lg. 25
Berry Bowl, sm. 10
Butter 40
Creamer or Spooner 20
Cruet 45
Oil Bottle 40
Pitcher 55
Shakers, ea. 25
Sugar 25
Tray 25
Tumbler 10

NOTCHED PANEL
Berry Bowl, lg. 35
Berry Bowl, sm. 10
Bowl, sq. 20
Butter 45
Creamer or Spooner 20
Relish 15
Shakers, ea. 15
Sugar 25
Toothpick Holder 20

NU-CUT #537
Jelly Compote 25

NU-CUT PINWHEEL (IMPERIAL)
Bowls 15 - 30
Salad Bowl 30
Vase 30

#9 BOOK
Match Holder 70
amber 90
vaseline 125
green/blue 120
milk glass 125

NURSERY RHYME BOWL
Bowl 45

NURSERY TALES (all miniature pieces)
Butter 100
Coaster 30
Creamer 40
Pitcher 70
Punch Bowl 85
Punch Cup 20
Spooner 40
Sugar 60
Tumbler 25

OAK LEAF
Bowl, oblong, lg. 65
Bowl, oblong, sm. 45
Decanter 85

OCTAGON
Berry Bowl, lg. 35
Berry Bowl, sm. 10
Bowl, 11" 40
Butter 55
Compote, lg. 45
Compote, sm. 35
Cordial 20
Creamer or Spooner 25
Goblet 30
Handle Nappy 35
Milk Pitcher 35
Pitcher, mid-size 45
Pitcher, standard 55
ruby stain 80
Punch Bowl 85
Punch Cup 10
Shakers, ea. 20
Sherbet 20
Sugar 25
Toothpick Holder 20
Tumbler 20
Vase, pedestal 30
Wine 15
Wine Decanter 45

O'HARA'S CRYSTAL WEDDING
Butter 75
Cake Stand 45
Celery Vase 25
Creamer or Spooner 25
Pitcher 95
Sugar 35
Tumbler 25

O'HARA'S DIAMOND
Bowl, covered, 5" - 8" 25 - 45
ruby stain 70 - 100
Bowl, open, 5" - 8" 10 - 25
ruby stain 50 - 85
Butter 55
ruby stain 140
Cake Stand 70 - 95
ruby stain 200 - 300
Celery Vase 50
ruby stain 85
Champagne 30
ruby stain 80
Claret 40
ruby stain 75
Compote, open, 5" - 8" 40 - 70
ruby stain 100 - 145
Condiment Tray 35
ruby stain 55
Creamer or Spooner 25
ruby stain 65
Cruet 60
ruby stain 175
Custard Cup 10
ruby stain 25
Dish, various 10 - 20
ruby stain 20 - 35
Goblet 30
ruby stain 75
Honey Dish 20
ruby stain 25
Lamp 120
Pickle Dish 15
ruby stain 25
Pitcher 125
ruby stain 185
Plate, 7" - 10" 25 - 40
ruby stain 50 - 80
Salt Dip 20
ruby stain 40
Salt Shaker 25
ruby stain 55
Sauce 10 - 20
ruby stain 30

Saucer ... 15
ruby stain ... 65
Sugar ... 45
ruby stain ... 105
Syrup ... 85
ruby stain ... 300
Tumbler ... 50
ruby stain ... 100
Water Tray ... 40
ruby stain ... 70
Wine ... 20
ruby stain ... 40

OHIO STAR
Banana Bowl, 3 sizes ... 55 - 90
Berry Bowl, lg. ... 65
Berry Bowl, sm. ... 30
Bowl, sq., deep, 6"x6" ... 85
Bowl, sq., lg., ruffled ... 100
Butter ... 165
Carafe ... 125
Card Tray Whimsey ... 100
Celery Bowl, 2 sizes ... 100 - 150
Cider Pitcher ... 115
Cider Tumbler ... 65
Cloverleaf Dish, 2 sizes ... 90 - 145
Compote, standard ... 85
sapphire ... 1,700
Compote, standard, ruffled, scarce ... 150
Compote, tall ... 225
amethyst ... 1,500
Cookie Jar ... 145
Creamer or Spooner ... 55
Cruet ... 200
Mint Dish ... 45
Pitcher, collar base, scarce ... 325
Pitcher, tankard, 9¼", rare ... 550
Plate, 3 sizes ... 45 - 90
Plate, sq., 5" ... 150
Plate, sq., 7" ... 175
Plate, sq., 9" ... 200
Plate, sq., 11" ... 250
Punch Bowl w/Base ... 1,200
Punch Cup ... 15
Rose Bowl Whimsey, stemmed ... 225
Rose Bowl, flat, 7" ... 135
Rose Bowl, flat, 9" ... 165
Shakers, ea. ... 375
Sherbet ... 65
Square Flat Dish, 5", 7" & 9" ... 65 - 125
Sugar ... 60
Syrup ... 375
Toothpick Holder ... 85
Tumbler ... 60
Vase ... 100
amethyst ... 1,500
Vase, sq. top, very rare ... 600
Vase, J.I.P. shape, very rare ... 850
Wine ... 125
*All pieces scarce, rare.
*Frosted pieces rare, add 25%.

OKLAHOMA VINEGAR CO.
Advertising Ale Glass ... 75

OLD COLONY
Berry Bowl, lg. ... 45
Berry Bowl, sm. ... 20
Butter ... 70
Creamer or Spooner ... 25
Pitcher ... 85
Sugar ... 30
Tumbler ... 20

OLD GLORY
Pitcher ... 75
Tumbler ... 15

OLD SANDWICH (HEISEY)
Ashtray ... 30
amber ... 40
green/blue ... 50
Basket ... 45
amber ... 60
green/blue ... 70
Bowls ... 20 - 40
amber ... 30 - 50
green/blue ... 35 - 60
Candlesticks, ea. ... 20
amber ... 30
green/blue ... 40
Champagne ... 25
amber ... 40
green/blue ... 60
Claret ... 20
amber ... 25
green/blue ... 35
Compote ... 40
amber ... 50
green/blue ... 65
Cup ... 10
amber ... 15
green/blue ... 25
Creamer ... 20
amber ... 30
green/blue ... 35
Cruet ... 65
amber ... 80
green/blue ... 95
Decanter ... 55
amber ... 70
green/blue ... 85
Finger Bowl ... 20
amber ... 30
green/blue ... 35
Goblet ... 25
amber ... 35
green/blue ... 40
Ice Pitcher ... 65
amber ... 80
green/blue ... 90
Juice Glass ... 10
amber ... 20
green/blue ... 30
Ketchup Bottle ... 35
amber ... 45
green/blue ... 50
Mug, 4 sizes ... 20 - 30
amber ... 25 - 40
green/blue ... 30 - 50
Parfait ... 15
amber ... 20
green/blue ... 25
Pilsner ... 20
amber ... 25
green/blue ... 30
Pitcher ... 70
amber ... 85
green/blue ... 110
Plate, 3 sizes ... 15 - 30
amber ... 20 - 35
green/blue ... 25 - 40
Shakers ... 20
amber ... 35
green/blue ... 40
Sherbet ... 15
amber ... 25
green/blue ... 35
Sugar ... 35
amber ... 45
green/blue ... 60
Sundae ... 15
amber ... 35
green/blue ... 40
Tumbler ... 15
amber ... 25
green/blue ... 35
Wine ... 10
amber ... 20
green/blue ... 30
*Add 10% for pink.

OLD STATE HOUSE (PHILADELPHIA)
Plate ... 85

OMNIBUS
Berry Bowl, lg. ... 35
Berry Bowl, sm. ... 10
Bowl, deep, 8" ... 25
Bowl, shallow, 9" ... 30
Butter ... 45
Celery Tray ... 25
Creamer or Spooner ... 20
Pickle Dish ... 15
Pitcher ... 75
Rose Bowl ... 30
Sugar ... 30
Tumbler ... 20

ONEATA
Butter ... 45
Cake Plates ... 20 - 40
Child's Table Set, complete ... 75
Creamer or Spooner ... 20
Cruet ... 40
Sugar ... 25
Wine ... 10

ONE-O-ONE
Bread Plate ... 40
Bread Plate, lettered ... 55
Butter ... 130
Cake Stand ... 165
Celery Vase ... 80
Compote, covered, 7" - 9" ... 90 - 140
Creamer or Spooner ... 50
Goblet ... 60 - 100
Hand Lamp, flat ... 90
Oil Lamp, standard ... 120 - 165
Pickle Dish ... 25
Pitcher ... 290
Plate, 6" - 9" ... 25 - 60
Relish Tray ... 20
Sauce, flat or ftd. ... 10
Shakers, ea. ... 40
Sugar ... 25
Toothpick Holder ... 65
green/blue ... 65
Tumbler ... 40
Vase ... 60
Wine ... 85

OPEN PLAID
Berry Bowl, lg. ... 35
Berry Bowl, sm. ... 10
Butter ... 55
Cordial ... 10
Creamer or Spooner ... 20
Pitcher ... 75
Plate ... 20
Salt ... 15
Shakers, ea. ... 15
Sugar ... 25
Syrup ... 65
Tumbler ... 15
Wine ... 10

OPEN ROSE
Bowls, various ... 10 - 40
Rose Bowl ... 50

OPEN ROSE (MOSS ROSE)
Bowls, oval, various ... 15 - 30
Butter ... 65
Cake Stand ... 150
Celery Vase ... 60
Compote, covered, 6" - 9" ... 80 - 160
Compote, open, 6" - 9" ... 70 - 140
Cordial ... 35
Creamer or Spooner ... 60
Egg Cup ... 35
Goblet, 2 styles ... 40 - 65
Milk Pitcher ... 200
Pickle Dish ... 20
Pitcher ... 225
Relish Tray ... 20
Salt Dip ... 35
Sauce ... 10

Sugar 70
Tumbler 65

OPPOSING PYRAMIDS
Bowls, various .... 10 - 30
Butter 55
Cake Stands, various .... 20 - 45
Celery Vase 20
Compotes, various .... 25 - 45
Creamer or Spooner 25
Pitcher 85
Shakers, ea 20
Sugar 40
Tumbler 15
Wine 10

OPTIC
Salt Dip 20

ORANGE PEEL
Bowl 25
Desert, stemmed 30
Punch Bowl 100
Punch Cup 15

ORANGE TREE (FENTON)
Bowl, 8½" 75
Punch Bowl, with base, rare
lime green 350
Punch Cup
lime green 50
Mug, scarce 55
green/blue 75
red 175

OREGON
Bowls, various, 7" - 12" .... 10 - 45
Bowl, covered, 6" - 8" .... 20 - 50
Bowl, open, 6" - 8" .... 10 - 35
Bread Plate 35
Butter, 3 styles .... 50 - 90
Cake Stand, 6" - 10" .... 50 - 95
Celery Vase 50
Compote, covered, 5" - 10" .... 50 - 90
Compote, open, various .... 30 - 55
Creamer or Spooner 40
Cruet 70
Goblet 50
Honey Dish 20
Horseradish, handle,
w/lid 80
Milk Pitcher 60
Mug 60
Olive Dish 15
Pickle Dish 15
Pitcher 85
Relish Dish 15
Salt, ind. 25
Salt, master 45
Sauce 10
Sugar 50
Syrup 100
Toothpick Holder 70
Tumbler 30
Vase 40
Water Bottle 70
Wine 80

ORIENTAL
Bowls, various .... 10 - 45
Butter 65
Celery Vase 20
Compote, covered 45
Creamer or Spooner 20
Goblet 35
Pickle Jar 25
Pitcher 70
Sugar 25
Tray 35
Tumbler 15
Wine 15

ORIENTAL POPPY
Pitcher, either size 350
Tumbler 45
sapphire 75

ORINDA
Berry Bowl, lg. 35
Berry Bowl, sm. 10
Butter 50
Celery Vase 20
Creamer or Spooner 25
Milk Pitcher 50
Pickle Dish 20
Pitcher 85
Shakers, ea. 20
Sugar 25
Syrup 55
Toothpick Holder 25

ORION THUMBPRINT
Bowl, oval, 11" 35
Butter 70
Celery Vase 30
Compote, covered 60
Compote, open 35
Creamer or Spooner 25
Goblet 45
Platter, oval (Daisy & Button cntr.) 40
Pitcher 85
Sauce 15
Sugar 30
Tumbler 20

ORNATE STAR
Berry Bowl, lg. 35
ruby stain 40
Berry Bowl, sm. 10
ruby stain 20
Butter 55
ruby stain 80
Celery Vase 20
ruby stain 30
Cordial 15
ruby stain 25
Creamer or Spooner 20
ruby stain 30
Goblet 40
ruby stain 60
Pickle Tray 15
ruby stain 25
Pitcher 70
ruby stain 125
Sugar 30
ruby stain 55
Tumbler 10
ruby stain 25
Wine 10
ruby stain 25

OUR GIRL/LITTLE BO-PEEP
Mug 50
amber 75
vaseline 90
green/blue 95

OVAL BASKET
Toothpick or Match Holder. 45
amber 65
vaseline 85
green/blue 70
blue slag 75

OVAL DIAMOND PANEL
Goblet 40
vaseline 85

OVAL LOOP
Bowl, oval, 5" - 10" .... 15 - 40
Bowl, rnd., 7" - 8" 25
Bread Tray 25
Butter 65
Candlesticks, ea. 25
Celery Vase 20
Compote, covered, 7" - 8" 50
Compote, open, 7" - 8" 35
Creamer or Spooner 20
Goblet 40
Milk Pitcher, 2 sizes .... 40 - 60
Pickle Jar 25
Pitcher, 2 sizes .... 50 - 80
Sauce, flat or ftd. 10
Shakers, ea. 20
Sugar 25
Sugar Shaker 40
Tumbler 20
Wine 15

OVAL MEDALLION
Bowls, various .... 15 - 35
amber .... 20 - 40
vaseline .... 25 - 50
green/blue .... 20 - 45
amethyst .... 30 - 65
Butter 65
amber 80
vaseline 130
green/blue 95
amethyst 110
Compotes, various .... 20 - 45
amber .... 25 - 50
vaseline .... 30 - 60
green/blue .... 25 - 55
amethyst .... 35 - 65
Creamer or Spooner 25
amber 30
vaseline 40
green/blue 35
amethyst 45
Goblet 35
amber 40
vaseline 50
green/blue 45
amethyst 60
Pickle Dish 20
amber 25
vaseline 30
green/blue 25
amethyst 35
Sugar 35
amber 40
vaseline 45
green/blue 40
amethyst 50
Wine 20
amber 25
vaseline 30
green/blue 25
amethyst 35

OVAL MITER
Butter 45
Celery Vase 20
Creamer or Spooner 20
Cruet 35
Goblet 20
Sauce 10
Sugar 25

OVAL PANEL
(AKA: OVAL SETT)
Berry Bowl, lg. 40
purple slag 50
Berry Bowl, sm. 20
purple slag 30
Butter 65
purple slag 100
Creamer 25
purple slag 40
Jelly Compote 30
purple slag 45
Novelty Bowl 40
purple slag 50
Pitcher 75
purple slag 135
Relish, 3 sections 35
purple slag 45
Spooner 25
purple slag 35
Sugar 40
purple slag 60
Tumbler 20
purple slag 25

OVAL WINDOW LAMP
- Oil Lamp ... 80
  - green/blue ... 165

OVERALL LATTICE
- Bowl, ruffled ... 25
- Butter ... 50
- Compote ... 30
- Creamer or Spooner ... 20
- Goblet ... 35
- Plate ... 25
- Sugar ... 25
- Wine ... 15

OWEN COIN BANK LAMP
- Oil Lamp ... 90
  - vaseline ... 235

OWL & POSSUM
- Goblet ... 150

OWL & THE PUSSYCAT
- Cheese Dish, rare ... 400

OWL ON A BRANCH
- Mug ... 55

PADDLE WHEEL
- Butter ... 50
- Celery Tray ... 30
- Celery Vase ... 25
- Creamer or Spooner ... 20
- Jelly Compote ... 25
- Pickle Dish ... 15
- Pitcher ... 70
- Punch Bowl w/Base ... 95
- Punch Cup ... 10
- Tumbler ... 15
- Relish ... 20
- Shakers, ea ... 20
- Sugar ... 25

PALING
- Bowls, various ... 20 - 40
- Butter ... 55
- Celery ... 30
- Creamer or Spooner ... 30
- Jelly Compote ... 35
- Pickle Dish ... 25
- Pitcher ... 65
- Shakers, ea ... 25
- Sugar ... 35
- Tumbler ... 20

PALISADES (LINED LATTICE)
- Vase ... 30
  - green/blue ... 75

PALM BEACH
- Berry Bowl, lg ... 40
- Berry Bowl, sm ... 15
- Butter ... 85
- Celery Vase ... 25
- Creamer or Spooner ... 25
- Cruet ... 60
- Jelly Compote ... 35
- Pitcher ... 125
- Plate ... 40
- Sauce ... 15
- Shakers, ea ... 25
- Sugar ... 30
- Tumbler ... 20
- Wine ... 20

PALMER PRISM (AKA: SCALLOPED FLUTE)
- Goblet ... 40
- Tankard Pitcher ... 70

PALMETTE
- Bowls, various ... 30 - 60
- Butter, various styles ... 90 - 110
- Cake Stand ... 300
- Castor Set, complete ... 265
- Compote, covered, 4 sizes ... 100 - 200
- Compote, open ... 70
- Creamer or Spooner ... 80
- Cup Plate ... 50
- Goblet ... 50
- Master Salt Dip, flat, rare ... 200
- Milk Pitcher ... 300
- Oil Lamp, 10" ... 125
- Pitcher ... 350
- Relish, scoop shape ... 25
- Shaker, lg ... 100
- Sugar ... 90
- Syrup ... 165
- Tumbler, 2 sizes ... 70 - 130
- Wine ... 125

PALM LEAF FAN
- Banana Bowl ... 65
- Bowls, lg ... 25 - 55
- Butter ... 70
- Cake Stand ... 60
- Celery Vase ... 40
- Compote ... 40
- Creamer or Spooner ... 40
- Cruet ... 70
- Goblet ... 50
- Milk Pitcher ... 70
- Pitcher ... 90
- Plates, various ... 20 - 35
- Sauce ... 15
- Shakers, ea ... 35
- Sugar ... 40
- Tumbler ... 35
- Vase ... 20 - 40
- Wine ... 60

PAMELA
- Compote ... 45
  - green/blue ... 75

PANAMA
- Berry Bowl, lg ... 40
- Berry Bowl, sm ... 15
- Bowls, various ... 10 - 30
- Butter ... 50
- Celery Tray ... 20
- Celery Vase ... 25
- Creamer or Spooner ... 25
- Pitcher ... 80
- Shakers, ea ... 15
- Sugar ... 30
- Toothpick Holder ... 30
- Tumbler ... 15

PANAMA ADVERTISING PIECES
- Rose Bowl, various advertisings ... 80
- Spittoon, rare ... 125

PANEL AND RIB
- Butter ... 45
  - amber ... 65
  - vaseline ... 95
- Creamer ... 25
  - amber ... 35
  - vaseline ... 65
- Pitcher ... 75
- Spooner ... 30
  - amber ... 40
  - vaseline ... 70
- Sugar ... 35
  - amber ... 45
  - vaseline ... 60
- Tumbler ... 25

PANELLED 44
- Basket, 2 sizes ... 50 - 80
- Bowls, various ... 20 - 50
- Bonbon, 3 legged ... 40 - 60
- Butter ... 90
- Candlestick ... 85
- Compote, open, various ... 35 - 65
- Creamer or Spooner ... 35
- Cruet ... 90
- Finger Bowl ... 40
- Goblet ... 40
- Lemonade Set ... 150
- Olive, hndl ... 15
- Pitcher ... 80
- Rose Bowl ... 45
- Shakers, ea ... 50
- Sugar ... 50
- Sugar Shaker ... 60
- Toothpick Holder ... 40
- Tumbler ... 45
- Vase (Loving Cup) ... 50
- Wine ... 25

*Add 100% for platinum stain and 75% for others.

PANELLED ANTHEMION
- Bowls, various ... 30 - 45
- Butter ... 65
- Celery ... 35
- Creamer or Spooner ... 35
- Jelly Compote ... 45
- Pickle Dish ... 35
- Pitcher ... 85
- Shakers, ea ... 30
- Sugar ... 45
- Tumbler ... 20

PANELLED CANE
- Bowls, covered, various shapes and sizes ... 35 - 95
- Bowls, various shapes and sizes ... 20 - 70
- Butter ... 75
- Butter, ftd ... 90
- Cake Salver, various sizes ... 45 - 60
- Celery ... 20
- Champagne ... 30
- Claret ... 25
- Compote, covered ... 70
- Compote, open ... 50
- Cordial ... 25
- Creamer or Spooner ... 20
- Cruet ... 45
- Egg Cup ... 50
- Goblet ... 25
- Jelly Compote ... 30
- Nappy, ftd., 4 sizes, no handle ... 20 - 35
- Pickle Dish ... 25
- Pitcher ... 110
- Salt, ftd ... 30
- Sugar, ftd., w/lid ... 30
- Wine ... 20

*Double prices for dark blue.

PANELLED CHERRY
- Butter ... 75
- Creamer or Spooner ... 30
- Goblet ... 35
- Mug ... 30
- Pitcher ... 85
- Sugar ... 35
- Syrup ... 65
- Tumbler ... 25

PANELLED DEWDROP
- Butter ... 60
- Celery Boat ... 20
- Celery Vase ... 25
- Cordial ... 15
- Creamer or Spooner ... 25
- Goblet ... 35
- Jam Jar ... 25
- Pickle Dish ... 15
- Pickle Jar ... 20
- Sauce, ftd ... 10
- Sugar ... 35
- Wine ... 15

PANELLED DIAMOND BLOCKS
- Berry Bowl, lg ... 35
- Berry Bowl, sm ... 10
- Butter ... 50
- Carafe ... 30
- Compote, covered ... 45
- Compote, open ... 30
- Creamer or Spooner ... 20
- Custard Cup ... 10
- Goblet ... 30
- Oil Lamp ... 75
- Orange Bowl ... 35
- Pitcher ... 70
- Sauce ... 10
- Sugar ... 25
- Syrup ... 60

Toothpick Holder 20
Tumbler 15
Vase 25
Wine 10

PANELLED DIAMOND CROSS
Bowl 25

PANELLED DIAMOND POINT
Berry Bowl, lg. 30
Berry Bowl, sm. 15
Butter 55
Creamer or Spooner 20
Goblet 30
Oval Platter 25
Pitcher 65
Sugar 30
Tumbler 10

PANELLED DIAMONDS
Goblet 40

PANELLED DIAMONDS & BOWS
Vase, scarce 45
red 125

PANELLED FISHBONE
Bowl 25
Bread Tray 35
Shakers, ea 20

PANELLED FORGET-ME-NOT
Bowl, covered 50
amber 70
vaseline 150
green/blue 100
Bread Tray 45
amber 55
vaseline 125
green/blue 70
Butter 60
amber 80
vaseline 200
green/blue 135
Cake Stand, 5 sizes 60 - 135
amber 70 - 145
vaseline 150 - 325
green/blue 100 - 135
Celery Vase 85
amber 125
vaseline 275
green/blue 200
Compote, covered, 3 sizes 90 - 130
amber 100 - 160
vaseline 250 - 375
green/blue 200 - 300
Compote, open, 3 sizes 40 - 60
amber 60 - 85
vaseline 150 - 225
green/blue 90 - 145
Creamer or Spooner 45
amber 75
vaseline 140
green/blue 90
Goblet 55
amber 100
vaseline 325
green/blue 250
Jam Jar 125
amber 200
vaseline 375
green/blue 300
Milk Pitcher 75
amber 135
vaseline 325
green/blue 250
Pickle Dish, boat shaped 30
amber 40
vaseline 100
green/blue 45
Pitcher 100
amber 165
vaseline 425
green/blue 300
Sauce, ftd. 15
amber 20
vaseline 90
green/blue 25
Sauce, flat 20
amber 25
vaseline 80
green/blue 30
Shakers, ea 95
Sugar 65
amber 90
vaseline 275
green/blue 135
Wine 100
amber 165
vaseline 300
green/blue 225

*Any other colors priced same as vaseline.

PANELLED HEATHER
Berry Bowl, lg. 35
Berry Bowl, sm. 10
Bowl, oval, ftd., 6½" 25
Bowl, salad, ftd. 30
Butter 55
Cake Stand 30
Celery Vase 20
Creamer or Spooner 20
Cruet 45
Goblet 35
Jelly Compote, covered 40
Pitcher 75
Sugar 30
Tumbler 15
Wine 10

PANELLED HEXAGONS
Bowls 15 - 35
vaseline 25 - 55
Butter 55
vaseline 80
Creamer 25
vaseline 45
Jelly Compote 40
vaseline 65
Pitcher 70
vaseline 135
Sugar 35
vaseline 50
Tumbler 15
vaseline 30

PANELLED HOBNAIL
Butter 45
amber 55
vaseline 90
green/blue 75
Compote, covered 50
amber 65
vaseline 80
green/blue 70
Compote, open 35
amber 40
vaseline 60
green/blue 50
Creamer or Spooner 25
amber 30
vaseline 40
green/blue 35
Goblet 30
amber 35
vaseline 45
green/blue 40
Pickle dish 25
amber 30
vaseline 40
green/blue 35
Pitcher 65
amber 80
vaseline 125
green/blue 95
Sugar 30
amber 35
vaseline 45
green/blue 40
Tumbler 15
amber 25
vaseline 30
green/blue 30
Wine 15
amber 25
vaseline 30
green/blue 30

*For opaque colors add 50% to crystal prices.

PANELLED HOLLY
Berry Bowl, lg. 40
Berry Bowl, sm. 20
Bonbon 25
Butter 65
Creamer or Spooner 20
Pitcher 150
Sugar 45
Tumbler 25

PANELLED HONEYCOMB
Creamer 65
Sugar 80

PANELLED IVY
Bowls, various 20 - 40
Butter 55
Celery 25
Creamer or Spooner 30
Goblet 35
Pitcher 70
Plate 30
Shakers, ea 25
Syrup 50
Tumbler 15
Vase 25

PANELLED JEWELS
Goblet 55
Wine 25
vaseline 70

PANELLED LATTICE
Butter 50
Creamer or Spooner 25
Goblet 35
Oil bottle 45
Sugar 30
Wine 20

PANELLED OAK
Berry Bowl, lg. 45
Berry Bowl, sm. 15
Butter 60
Celery Vase 35
Creamer, Spooner or Sugar 25
Pitcher 75
Tumbler 20

PANELLED OCTAGON
Butter 55
Creamer or Spooner 25
Sugar 30

PANELLED PALM
Berry Bowl, lg. 40
rose blush 65
Berry Bowl, sm. 10
rose blush 25
Butter 55
rose blush 90
Creamer or Spooner 20
rose blush 45
Pickle Dish 15
rose blush 30
Rose Bowl 30
rose blush 50
Shakers, ea 25
rose blush 50
Sugar 25
rose blush 60
Toothpick Holder 25
rose blush 50

PANELLED PLEAT
Berry Bowl, lg. 35

Berry Bowl, sm. 10
Butter 45
Creamer or Spooner 20
Goblet 35
Pitcher 60
Sugar 25
Tumbler 15

PANELLED PRIMULA
Bowls, various 20 - 45
Bread Plate 35
Butter 60
Celery 25
Cordial 25
Creamer or Spooner 30
Cup 20
Decanter 80
Goblet 40
Lamp 95
Pickle dish 25
Pitcher 90
Saucer 15
Sugar 40
Tumbler 20

PANELLED RIBBED SHELL
Bowl, lg. flat 50
vaseline 65
Bowl, sm. flat 25
vaseline 35
Bowls, covered 55 - 70
vaseline 65 - 110
Bowls, open 35 - 60
vaseline 50 - 85
Butter 75
vaseline 100
Compotes, covered 60 - 95
vaseline 75 - 135
Compotes, open 40 - 85
vaseline 60 - 100
Creamer or Spooner 40
vaseline 65
Milk Pitcher 70
vaseline 125
Pitcher 125
vaseline 250
Relish 35
vaseline 45
Salt Dip, individual 25
vaseline 35
Salt Dip, master 40
vaseline 50
Shakers, ea 50
vaseline 65
Tumbler 30
vaseline 40
Wine 25
vaseline 35

PANELLED STRAWBERRY
Berry Bowl, lg 65
Berry Bowl, sm. 30
Butter 90
Celery Vase 45
Creamer or Spooner 60
Goblet 70
Pitcher 100
Sauce, 3 sizes 10 - 20
Sugar 80
Tumbler 30

PANELLED SUNFLOWER
Basket, 3 sizes 30 - 55
Butter 45
Cake Stand 35
Celery Vase 20
Creamer, Spooner or Sugar 25
Cruet 45
Goblet 25
Honey Dish 20
Pickle Dish 20
Pitcher 65
Plate, 7½" - 8½" 15
Plate, 9½" - 10½" 25
Tumbler 15

PANELLED SWAN
Bowl, covered 55
Compote, covered 70
Goblet 35
Wine 20

PANELLED THISTLE
Banana Dish, ftd., 2 sizes 235 - 325
Basket 90
Berry Bowl, lg. 35
Berry Bowl, sm. 10
Butter 100
Cake Stand, 4 sizes 70 - 100
Celery Tray 35
Compote, open, 4 sizes 50 - 80
Creamer or Spooner 60
Cruet 90
Cup 25
Goblet 70 - 80
Honey Dish, covered, square 95
Milk Pitcher 65
Pitcher 100 - 225
Plates, 4 sizes 40 - 65
Salt Dip 25
Shakers, ea 70
Sugar 100
Toothpick Holder 70
Tumbler 50
Vase, 3 sizes 30 - 90

PANEL WITH DIAMOND POINT
Berry Bowl, lg 35
Berry Bowl, sm. 20
Butter 65
Cake Stand, 8" - 12" 30 - 50
Celery Vase 20
Cheese Dish, covered 60
Compote, covered 45
Compote, open 30
Creamer or Spooner 25
Goblet 25
Pickle Dish 15
Pitcher 70
Plates, 5" - 9" 15 - 35
Sauce 10
Sherbet 15
Spill Holder 25
Sugar 30
Tumbler 15
Wine 15

PANSY (IMPERIAL)
Bowl, very scarce 45
amethyst 150

PANTHER
Bowl, 5" - 9½", rare 75 - 175

PARKER & WHIPPLE CLOCK
Clock, 5", scarce 75
vaseline 165

PARROT (OWL IN FAN)
Goblet 45
Wine, rare 125

PARTY FAVOR
Basket 40
vaseline 75

THE PATRIOT SOLDIER
Plate, rare 350

PATTEE CROSS
Bowl, ruffled 25
Cake Stand 45
Compote 35
Olive Dish 20
Pitcher 75
Relish, 2 sizes 20
Syrup 65
Tumbler 15
Vase 25
Wine 25

PAVONIA
Bowl, 5" - 8" 15 - 30
ruby stain 30 - 60
Butter, 2 sizes 40 - 60
ruby stain 100 - 135
Cake Plate 25
ruby stain 50
Cake Stand, 8" - 10" 80 - 125
ruby stain 125 - 200
Celery Vase 30
ruby stain 75
Compote, covered, 5" - 10" 40 - 70
ruby stain 75 - 185
Compote, open, 5" - 10" 30 - 45
ruby stain 65 - 95
Creamer or Spooner, 2 sizes 30 - 40
ruby stain 80 - 90
Custard Cup 10
ruby stain 25
Dish, oblong, 7" - 9" 15 - 25
ruby stain 35 - 45
Finger Bowl w/Underplate 40
ruby stain 130
Goblet 40
ruby stain 55
Mug, hndl 30
ruby stain 60
Milk Pitcher 50
ruby stain 140
Pickle Dish 20
ruby stain 30
Pitcher, 3 sizes 60 - 70
ruby stain 100 - 175
Plate 15
ruby stain 35
Salt Shaker 30
ruby stain 40
Salt, ind. 15
ruby stain 35
Salt, master 25
ruby stain 50
Sauce, 3 sizes 10 - 20
ruby stain 20 - 30
Sauce, ftd., 3 sizes 15 - 25
ruby stain 25 - 35
Saucer 15
ruby stain 25
Sugar, 2 sizes 40 - 50
ruby stain 90 - 120
Tray, 2 sizes 50 - 60
ruby stain 85 - 100
Tumbler 25
ruby stain 50
Wine 30
ruby stain 40

*Add 10% for etched pieces.

PEABODY
Compote, small 80
Cup 55
Saucer 45

PEACH (NORTHWOOD)
Berry Bowl, lg. 45
Berry Bowl, sm. 20
Butter 55
Creamer or Spooner 30
Pitcher 75
Sugar 30
Tumbler 15

PEACOCK & GRAPE
Bowl, very scarce 45
green/blue 100
red 200

PEACOCK & URN (FENTON)
Bowl, very scarce 175
amethyst 400
Compote 65

PEACOCK AND URN (NORTHWOOD)
Banana bowl, large, 2 sides up custard 300
Berry, master custard 250
Berry, Sauce custard 90

Price Guide

PEACOCK AT THE FOUNTAIN
- Berry Bowl, lg., rare 125
- Berry Bowl, sm., rare 35
- Pitcher, rare 450
- Tumbler, rare 70

PEACOCK FEATHER (GEORGIA)
- Bowls, various sizes .... 20 - 45
- Butter .... 60 - 70
- Cake Stand .... 60 - 100
- Celery Tray 30
- Compote, covered, high, 6" - 8". 60 - 100
- Compote, covered, low, 6" - 8"... 25 - 45
- Condiment Set w/Stand 165
- Creamer or Spooner 70
- Cruet 65
- Decanter 90
- Jelly Compote 40
- Lamps, 5½" - 9" .... 75 - 200
- Mug 40
- Pickle Dish 20
- Pitcher 90
- Plate 40
- Relish Dish 20
- Sauce 15
- Shakers, ea 40
- Sugar 70
- Syrup 100
- Toy Table Set 200
- Tumbler 35

PEACOCK GARDEN
- Vase, 8", very scare to rare brown slag . 500

PEANUT LAMP
- Oil Lamp w/Matching Chimney, various styles & sizes .... 100 - 300

PEAS & PODS
- Decanter 45
  - ruby stain 65
- Tray 30
  - ruby stain 35
- Wine 15
  - ruby stain 20

PEEK-A-BOO
- Match hldr. 45
- Perfume bottle 55

PEEK-A-BOO PERFUME
- Cherub Perfume w/Stopper, very scarce . 95

PEERLESS
- Berry Bowl lg. 35
  - green/blue 60
- Berry Bowl, sm. 15
  - green/blue 25
- Bowl, sq. 30
  - green/blue 65
- Butter 55
  - green/blue 80
- Cake Stand 60
  - green/blue 75
- Celery 25
  - green/blue 35
- Clover Tray 35
  - green/blue 45
- Compote, 6½", covered 40
  - green/blue 60
- Cordial 20
  - green/blue 25
- Cordial Tray 40
  - green/blue 60
- Cracker Jar w/Lid 50
  - green/blue 70
- Creamer or Spooner 20
  - green/blue 35
- Cruet 55
  - green/blue 70
- Decanter, 2 sizes .... 45 - 60
  - green/blue .... 75 - 110
- Fruit Bowl, ftd. 80
  - green/blue 125
- Jelly Compote, open 30
  - green/blue 40
- Olive Dish, w/handle, 3 shapes .. 25 - 30
  - green/blue .... 35 - 55
- Salt Dip 30
  - green/blue 40
- Sugar 30
  - green/blue 45
- Toothpick Holder 40
  - green/blue 55
- Tray, rectangular 40
  - green/blue 65
- Vase, 6" - 8" 35
  - green/blue 40
- Vase, 17" - 18" 85
  - green/blue 110
- Whiskey Glass 25
  - green/blue 35
- Wine 20
  - green/blue 25

*Add 50% for amber and vaseline pieces.

PENELOPE
- Berry Bowl, lg. 35
- Berry Bowl, sm. 15
- Butter 55
- Creamer or Spooner 20
- Pickle Dish 15
- Punch Bowl 80
- Punch Cup 10
- Pitcher 70
- Sugar 25
- Tumbler 15

PENNSYLVANIA
- Berry Bowl, lg. 45
- Berry Bowl, sm. 15
- Biscuit Jar 85
- Bowl, round, 4" - 9" .... 10 - 50
- Bowl, scalloped, shallow, 4" - 9".. 10 - 35
- Bowl, straight-sided, 4" - 9" ...... 10 - 45
- Bowl, sq., 4" - 9" .... 10 - 50
- Butter, 2 sizes .... 50 - 90
- Butter, child's 125
  - green/blue 250
- Celery Tray 20
- Champagne, very rare 150
- Cheese Dish, covered 100
- Claret, very rare 135
- Compote, open 60
- Creamer 25
- Creamer, child's 50
  - green/blue 150
- Cruet 60
- Custard Cup, hndl. 15
  - green/blue 40
- Decanter, with & without hndls. .... 100 - 165
- Goblet 40
  - green/blue 75
- Ice Tub 50
- Jelly, hndl. 15
- Milk Pitcher 90
- Mug 40
  - green/blue 60
- Oil Bottle 60
- Olive Dish 15
- Pickle Dish, oval 15
  - green/blue 40
- Pickle Jar, w/lid 100
- Pitcher, bulbous or squat .... 90 - 125
  - green/blue .... 100 - 225
- Pitcher, tankard 150
- Plate, 7" - 8" 40
- Punch Bowl, flat 425
- Salt, ind. 10
- Salt, master 40
- Sauce, various 10
- Shaker, 3 sizes .... 35 - 45
- Spooner 45
- Sugar, 2 sizes .... 30 - 60
- Sugar, child's 100
  - green/blue 225
- Syrup, 2 styles .... 75 - 100
- Toothpick Holder (Toy Spooner) 50
  - green/blue 120
- Tumbler, 3 sizes .... 15 - 25
  - green/blue .... 25 - 60
- Water Bottle 60
- Wine 10
  - green/blue 40

*Add 10% to crystal prices for ruby stained pieces.

PENTAGON
- Butter 65
  - ruby stain 90
- Celery Vase 25
  - ruby stain 35
- Creamer 25
  - ruby stain 30
- Decanter 45
  - ruby stain 65
- Goblet 30
  - ruby stain 40
- Pickle Dish 25
  - ruby stain 35
- Pitcher 65
  - ruby stain 85
- Spooner 25
  - ruby stain 30
- Sugar 35
  - ruby stain 45
- Wine 15
  - ruby stain 20

PEQUOT
- Butter 60
- Castor Set 85
- Celery Vase 20
- Champagne 15
- Compote, covered 45
- Compote, open 30
- Creamer or Spooner 20
- Goblet 40
- Jam Jar 35
- Pitcher 85
- Sugar 30
- Tumbler 25
- Wine 15

PERKINS
- Butter 60
- Cake Plate, hndl., 12" 45
- Celery Vase 35
- Cracker Jar w/Lid 65
- Creamer or Spooner 25
- Cruet 50
- Pitcher 80
- Rose Bowl 40
- Sugar 30
- Tumbler 20

PERSIAN
- Berry Bowl, lg. 45
- Berry Bowl, sm. 15
- Butter 65
- Carafe 45
- Celery Dish 15
- Celery Vase 20
- Cheese Dish 65
- Claret 15
- Creamer or Spooner 25
- Cruet 50
- Cup 10
- Finger Bowl 20
- Jelly Compote 30
- Pitcher 95
- Salt Dip 15
- Sauce 10
- Shakers, ea 15
- Sugar 35
- Syrup 55
- Toothpick Holder 25
- Tumbler 20

PERSIAN MEDALLION
- Bonbon, handled 55

PETER RABBIT
- Candy Container ... 45

PETTICOAT (RIVERSIDE)
- Berry Bowl, lg. ... 35
  - vaseline ... 60
- Berry Bowl, sm. ... 15
  - vaseline ... 30
- Butter ... 95
  - vaseline ... 150
- Compote ... 70
  - vaseline ... 90
- Creamer or Spooner ... 35
  - vaseline ... 50
- Cruet ... 75
  - vaseline ... 95
- Hat Shapes, 3 Shapes ... 25 - 40
  - vaseline ... 45 - 65
- Match Holder ... 45
  - vaseline ... 55
- Mug ... 55
  - vaseline ... 70
- Mustard w/Lid ... 65
  - vaseline ... 85
- Pitcher ... 125
  - vaseline ... 200
- Salver ... 50
  - vaseline ... 75
- Shakers, ea ... 35
  - vaseline ... 55
- Spoon Tray ... 40
  - vaseline ... 55
- Sugar ... 50
  - vaseline ... 70
- Syrup ... 85
  - vaseline ... 135
- Toothpick Holder ... 55
  - vaseline ... 70
- Tumbler ... 25
  - vaseline ... 35
- Vase ... 40
  - vaseline ... 65

*Add 10% for gilded pieces.

PHEASANT
- Butter ... 245
- Compote, covered, low ... 225
- Creamer or Spooner ... 80
- Sugar ... 100

PHILADELPHIA 1876 CENTENNIAL
- Goblet ... 125

PICKET BAND
- Butter ... 55
  - green/blue ... 80
- Celery Vase ... 20
  - green/blue ... 25
- Compote, covered ... 40
  - green/blue ... 60
- Compote, open ... 30
  - green/blue ... 35
- Creamer or Spooner ... 25
  - green/blue ... 35
- Goblet ... 35
  - green/blue ... 50
- Pickle Dish ... 15
  - green/blue ... 20
- Shakers, ea ... 20
  - green/blue ... 30
- Sugar ... 35
  - green/blue ... 50
- Wine ... 15
  - green/blue ... 25

PICKLE VINE
- Pickle Jar w/Lid ... 55

PIGS IN CORN
- Goblet, rare ... 500

PILGRIM
- Bowls, various ... 20 - 40
  - ruby stain ... 30 - 50
- Butter ... 50
  - ruby stain ... 65
- Celery ... 25
  - ruby stain ... 30
- Creamer or Spooner ... 30
  - ruby stain ... 35
- Goblet ... 35
  - ruby stain ... 45
- Pickle Dish ... 25
  - ruby stain ... 30
- Pitcher ... 65
  - ruby stain ... 80
- Sugar ... 35
  - ruby stain ... 75
- Tumbler ... 15
  - ruby stain ... 25

PILGRIM BOTTLE
- Butter ... 65
  - amber ... 70
  - vaseline ... 125
  - green/blue ... 75
- Celery Dish ... 20
  - amber ... 25
  - vaseline ... 35
  - green/blue ... 30
- Creamer or Spooner ... 25
  - amber ... 30
  - vaseline ... 40
  - green/blue ... 35
- Cruet ... 60
  - amber ... 65
  - vaseline ... 90
  - green/blue ... 75
- Pickle Dish ... 20
  - amber ... 25
  - vaseline ... 35
  - green/blue ... 30
- Shakers, ea ... 30
  - amber ... 35
  - vaseline ... 45
  - green/blue ... 40
- Sugar ... 40
  - amber ... 45
  - vaseline ... 60
  - green/blue ... 55
- Syrup ... 95
  - amber ... 110
  - vaseline ... 295
  - green/blue ... 195

PILLAR
- Bowl ... 20
- Butter ... 45
- Celery Vase ... 15
- Creamer or Spooner ... 20
- Goblet ... 20
- Pitcher ... 60
- Sauce ... 10
- Sugar ... 25
- Tumbler ... 10

PILLAR AND SUNBURST

*Condensed list.
- Berry Bowl, lg. ... 30
- Berry Bowl, sm. ... 15
- Butter ... 45
- Creamer, Hotel ... 25
- Creamer, individual ... 20
- Creamer, regular ... 25
- Pitcher ... 65
- Spooner ... 30
- Sugar, hotel ... 30
- Sugar, individual ... 25
- Sugar, regular ... 30
- Tumbler ... 15

PILLOW ENCIRCLED
- Bowl, 4" - 8" ... 20 - 35
  - ruby stain ... 25 - 40
- Butter ... 55
  - ruby stain ... 80
- Cake Salver ... 35
  - ruby stain ... 50
- Celery Vase ... 20
  - ruby stain ... 30
- Compote, covered, 5" - 8" ... 25 - 45
  - ruby stain ... 40 - 80
- Creamer or Spooner ... 25
  - ruby stain ... 35
- Nut Bowl ... 20
  - ruby stain ... 30
- Pitcher, 2 sizes ... 80 - 95
  - ruby stain ... 90 - 165
- Shakers, ea ... 20
  - ruby stain ... 30
- Sugar ... 35
  - ruby stain ... 60
- Toothpick Holder ... 40
  - ruby stain ... 55
- Tumbler ... 20
  - ruby stain ... 30

*Add 10% for etched pieces.

PIMLICO (LOTUS LEAF)
- Butter ... 50
- Cake Plate ... 30
- Celery Vase ... 20
- Creamer or Spooner ... 25
- Goblet ... 35
- Pickle Dish ... 15
- Salt Dip ... 20
- Sugar ... 35

PINEAPPLE (AND BOWS)
- Bowl ... 40
  - Azure Blue ... 55
- Butter ... 65
  - Azure Blue ... 80
- Creamer ... 30
  - Azure Blue ... 40
- Sugar ... 40
  - Azure Blue ... 50

PINEAPPLE & FAN (Heisey)
- Berry Bowl, lg. ... 30
  - green/blue ... 45
  - ruby stain ... 65
- Berry Bowl, sm. ... 10
  - green/blue ... 20
  - ruby stain ... 25
- Butter ... 45
  - green/blue ... 60
  - ruby stain ... 90
- Cake Stand ... 35
  - green/blue ... 50
  - ruby stain ... 65
- Celery Vase ... 25
  - green/blue ... 35
  - ruby stain ... 40
- Creamer ... 25
  - green/blue ... 35
  - ruby stain ... 55
- Cruet ... 50
  - green/blue ... 70
  - ruby stain ... 85
- Custard Cup ... 20
  - green/blue ... 30
  - ruby stain ... 30
- Decanter ... 65
  - green/blue ... 80
  - ruby stain ... 90
- Goblet ... 25
  - green/blue ... 35
  - ruby stain ... 45
- Mug ... 30
  - green/blue ... 40
  - ruby stain ... 40
- Pitcher ... 55
  - green/blue ... 70
  - ruby stain ... 145
- Plate, 6½" ... 25
  - green/blue ... 35
  - ruby stain ... 40
- Punch Bowl w/Base ... 110
  - green/blue ... 150
  - ruby stain ... 225

- Punch Cup ... 10
  - green/blue ... 15
  - ruby stain ... 25
- Relish Jar ... 20
  - green/blue ... 30
  - ruby stain ... 35
- Rose Bowl ... 25
  - green/blue ... 35
  - ruby stain ... 40
- Spooner ... 25
  - green/blue ... 30
  - ruby stain ... 65
- Sugar ... 30
  - green/blue ... 35
  - ruby stain ... 70
- Tumbler ... 20
  - green/blue ... 25
  - ruby stain ... 35
- Wine ... 20
  - green/blue ... 25
  - ruby stain ... 30

PINEAPPLE & FAN (U.S. GLASS)

- Bowl, lg. ... 40
  - ruby stain ... 35
- Bowl, sm. ... 20
  - ruby stain ... 30
- Butter ... 65
  - ruby stain ... 75
- Cake Stand ... 45
  - ruby stain ... 55
- Celery Vase ... 30
  - ruby stain ... 40
- Creamer or Spooner ... 30
  - ruby stain ... 35
- Cruet ... 65
  - ruby stain ... 80
- Custard Cup ... 25
  - ruby stain ... 30
- Decanter ... 65
  - ruby stain ... 80
- Goblet ... 40
  - ruby stain ... 55
- Mug ... 40
  - ruby stain ... 50
- Pitcher ... 80
  - ruby stain ... 125
- Plate ... 30
  - ruby stain ... 40
- Punch Bowl w/Base ... 135
  - ruby stain ... 250
- Punch Cup ... 15
  - ruby stain ... 25
- Rose Bowl ... 30
  - ruby stain ... 40
- Sugar ... 35
  - ruby stain ... 40

*Add 25% to crystal prices for any emerald green.

PINECONE (FENTON)

- Bowl, very scarce ... 50
  - opaque red ... 150
- Plate, very scarce ... 85
  - opaque red ... 250

PINWHEEL & FAN

- Bowl, 4" - 5" ... 25
  - vaseline ... 65
- Bowl, 8" ... 50
  - vaseline ... 95
- Creamer ... 45
  - vaseline ... 70
- Jug, 3 Pt. ... 100
  - vaseline ... 135
- Puff Box ... 80
  - vaseline ... 10
- Punch Bowl ... 200
  - vaseline ... 375
- Punch Cup ... 15
  - vaseline ... 35
- Sugar ... 50
  - vaseline ... 75
- Tumbler ... 25
  - vaseline ... 50

PINWHEEL & FAN VARIANT

- Basket, rare ... 300

PIONEER #15

- Oil Bottle ... 70
- Puff Box ... 85

PIPE MATCH HOLDER

- Match/Toothpick Holder
  - milk glass ... 75

PISTOL

- Candy Container ... 60

PITTSBURGH FAN

- Butter ... 45
- Cake Stand ... 30
- Creamer or Spooner ... 15
- Goblet ... 30
- Pickle Dish ... 10
- Plate ... 15
- Sugar ... 20

PLAID

- Bowls, various ... 20 - 40
  - vaseline ... 35 - 60
- Butter ... 55
  - vaseline ... 80
- Celery ... 25
  - vaseline ... 45
- Creamer or Spooner ... 30
  - vaseline ... 40
- Goblet ... 40
  - vaseline ... 50
- Pitcher ... 85
  - vaseline ... 125
- Plate ... 40
  - vaseline ... 55
- Sugar ... 35
  - vaseline ... 45
- Syrup ... 60
  - vaseline ... 75
- Tumbler ... 25
  - vaseline ... 30
- Wine ... 20
  - vaseline ... 25

PLEAT & PANEL

- Bowls, covered ... 80 - 120
- Bowls, open ... 40 - 90
- Bread Tray ... 60
  - vaseline ... 250
- Butter ... 125 - 225
- Cake Stand, 3 sizes ... 80 - 175
- Candy Jar w/Lid ... 55
- Compote, covered, low and high ... 80 - 225
- Creamer or Spooner ... 40
- Lamp, various ... 135 - 300
- Marmalade w/lid ... 220
- Plate, sq. 5 sizes ... 35 - 100
- Relish ... 25
- Sauce, ftd. ... 15 - 30
- Shakers, ea. ... 35
- Sugar ... 125
- Syrup, very rare ... 800
- Waste Bowl, rare ... 80
- Water Tray ... 300

*For other colors add 75% to crystal prices.

PLEATED BANDS

- Goblet ... 45
- Pitcher ... 70
- Tumbler ... 20

PLEATED MEDALLION

- Butter ... 45
- Cake Stand ... 25
- Creamer or Spooner ... 15
- Cruet ... 40
- Pickle Dish ... 15
- Plate ... 20
- Sugar ... 20
- Toothpick Holder ... 25

PLEATED SKIRT

- Mug ... 30
  - green/blue ... 45
  - decorated alabaster ... 55

PLUME (ADAMS)

- Bitters Bottle ... 9
  - ruby stain ... 285
- Bowl, various, flat ... 90 - 135
  - ruby stain ... 200 - 265
- Bowls, various shapes and sizes . 35 - 70
  - ruby stain ... 80 - 110
- Butter ... 80
  - ruby stain ... 195
- Cake Stand ... 100 - 130
  - ruby stain ... 295 - 330
- Castor Set ... 200
  - ruby stain ... 500
- Celery Vase ... 50 - 65
  - ruby stain ... 100
- Compote, covered, 3 sizes ... 100 - 140
  - ruby stain ... 200 - 300
- Compote, open, various ... 45 - 70
  - ruby stain ... 80 - 160
- Creamer or Spooner ... 50
  - ruby stain ... 85
- Goblet ... 50
  - ruby stain ... 100
- Lamp ... 165
- Pitcher, 3 styles ... 90 - 135
  - ruby stain ... 300 - 450
- Sauce ... 20
  - ruby stain ... 35
- Sugar ... 80
  - ruby stain ... 160
- Syrup ... 100
  - ruby stain ... 300
- Tray ... 90
  - ruby stain ... 200
- Tumbler ... 30 - 40
  - ruby stain ... 60 - 90
- Waste Bowl ... 60
  - ruby stain ... 115

PLUME & BLOCK

- Berry Bowl, sm. ... 10
  - ruby stain ... 15
- Berry Bowl, lg. ... 25
  - ruby stain ... 35
- Butter ... 55
  - ruby stain ... 65
- Celery Tray ... 15
  - ruby stain ... 25
- Creamer or Spooner ... 20
  - ruby stain ... 30
- Pitcher ... 60
  - ruby stain ... 75
- Sugar ... 25
  - ruby stain ... 30
- Tumbler ... 10
  - ruby stain ... 20

PLUMS & CHERRIES (TWO FRUITS)

- Bowl, covered ... 90
- Butter ... 135
- Creamer or Spooner ... 50
- Pitcher ... 225
- Sugar ... 70
- Tumbler ... 35

PLUTEC

- Berry Bowl, lg. ... 35
- Berry Bowl, sm. ... 10
- Butter ... 60
- Cake Stand ... 40
- Celery Vase ... 20
- Compote ... 40
- Creamer or Spooner ... 20
- Decanter ... 50
- Goblet ... 45
- Nut Bowl ... 25
- Pickle Dish ... 15
- Pitcher ... 85
- Plate, 11" ... 25
- Sugar ... 25

- Syrup 60
- Tumbler 20
- Water Tray 30
- Wine 15

PLYTEC

- Berry Bowl, lg. 30
  - ruby stain 35
- Berry Bowl, sm. 15
  - ruby stain 20
- Butter 50
  - ruby stain 65
- Celery Dish 20
  - ruby stain 30
- Compote 30
  - ruby stain 40
- Creamer or Spooner 25
  - ruby stain 35
- Cruet 40
  - ruby stain 55
- Pickle Dish 20
  - ruby stain 30
- Pitcher 60
  - ruby stain 80
- Shakers, ea. 25
  - ruby stain 35
- Sugar 30
  - ruby stain 40
- Syrup 40
  - ruby stain 65
- Tumbler 10
  - ruby stain 20
- Vase 20
  - ruby stain 30

POGO STICK

- Butter 65
- Creamer 30
- Pickle Dish 25
- Spooner 35
- Sugar 45

POINTED JEWEL

- Bowls, covered 60 – 125
- Bowls, open 30 – 70
- Butter 85
- Cake Stand 125
- Celery Vase 60
- Cologne Bottle 90
- Compote, covered, 5 sizes 50 – 200
- Compote, open, various sizes 60 – 120
- Creamer or Spooner 35
- Cup 35
- Goblet 35
- Honey Dish w/Lid 200
- Milk Pitcher 145
- Miniature Table Set, 4 pcs. 475
- Pitcher 120
- Shakers, ea 70
- Sugar 70
- Syrup 125
- Tumbler 40
- Wine 25

*Add 50% for ruby stained.

POINTING DOG

- Mug 40
  - amber 55
  - green/blue 65
  - milk glass 60

POLAR BEAR

- Bread Plate 140
- Creamer 180
- Goblet 200
- Ice Bowl 165
- Pickle Dish 95
- Pitcher 1,100
- Sauce 85
- Sugar 235
- Tray 375
- Waste Bowl 125

POLKA DOT

- Compote, lg. 115
  - green/blue 165
- Pitcher
  - vaseline 225

POLKA DOT (AKA: INVERTED COIN DOT)

- Bar Bottle, 2 sizes 90 – 145
  - amber 100 – 165
  - vaseline 110 – 185
  - sapphire 200 – 225
- Bitters, bottle 110
  - amber 125
  - vaseline 145
  - sapphire 165
- Bowl, finger 35
  - amber 45
  - vaseline 65
  - sapphire 75
- Bowl, shell ftd. 95
  - amber 110
  - vaseline 150
  - sapphire 170
- Celery 40
  - amber 50
  - vaseline 70
  - sapphire 90
- Cheese Dish 100
  - amber 120
  - vaseline 145
  - sapphire 175
- Creamer or Spooner 60
  - amber 70
  - vaseline 90
  - sapphire 100
- Custard 30
  - amber 40
  - vaseline 60
  - sapphire 75
- Decanter 75
  - amber 85
  - vaseline 100
  - sapphire 125
- Jug, 6 sizes 50 – 135
  - amber 60 – 145
  - vaseline 70 – 165
  - sapphire 85 – 180
- Lemonade 50
  - amber 65
  - vaseline 80
  - sapphire 95
- Molasses Can, 2 sizes 80 – 100
  - amber 95 – 120
  - vaseline 110 – 150
  - sapphire 145 – 175
- Mustard w/Glass Top 100
  - amber 130
  - vaseline 150
  - sapphire 165
- Nappy, 2 sizes 20 – 40
  - amber 30 – 45
  - vaseline 50 – 80
  - sapphire 60 – 90
- Oil Cruet, 3 sizes 65 – 95
  - amber 70 – 110
  - vaseline 80 – 130
  - sapphire 90 – 140
- Salt, 2 sizes 35 – 45
  - amber 40 – 50
  - vaseline 60 – 70
  - sapphire 70 – 90
- Sugar 70
  - amber 80
  - vaseline 95
  - sapphire 130
- Sugar Sifter 85
  - amber 95
  - vaseline 120
  - sapphire 150
- Tumbler, 3 sizes 25 – 45
  - amber 30 – 50
  - vaseline 45 – 60
  - sapphire 55 – 70
- Vase 150
  - amber 165
  - vaseline 185
  - sapphire 225
- Water bottle 95
  - amber 110
  - vaseline 135
  - sapphire 165

POLKA DOT (GEO. DUNCAN & SONS)

- Butter 50
  - amber 95
  - vaseline 135
  - green/blue 110
- Bowls, ftd. 20 – 35
  - amber 25 – 40
  - vaseline 35 – 50
  - green/blue 40 – 65
- Bowl, finger 20
  - amber 35
  - vaseline 55
  - green/blue 50
- Celery Vase 20
  - amber 30
  - vaseline 60
  - green/blue 50
- Cheese Dish, covered 65
  - amber 85
  - vaseline 125
  - green/blue 100
- Champagne 20
  - amber 30
  - vaseline 50
  - green/blue 45
- Claret 15
  - amber 25
  - vaseline 40
  - green/blue 35
- Compote, covered 45
  - amber 95
  - vaseline 125
  - green/blue 90
- Creamer or Spooner 30
  - amber 45
  - vaseline 60
  - green/blue 55
- Cruet 65
  - amber 50
  - vaseline 90
  - green/blue 80
- Goblet 35
  - amber 40
  - vaseline 50
  - green/blue 45
- Sauces 15
  - amber 20
  - vaseline 30
  - green/blue 30
- Shakers, ea. 25
  - amber 60
  - vaseline 75
  - green/blue 60
- Sugar 40
  - amber 55
  - vaseline 70
  - green/blue 65
- Syrup 70
  - amber 100
  - vaseline 150
  - green/blue 115
- Toothpick Holder 35
  - amber 50
  - vaseline 65
  - green/blue 55
- Tumbler 25
  - amber 35
  - vaseline 45
  - green/blue 35

Water Bottles,
4 sizes ... 25 - 50
amber ... 35 - 65
vaseline ... 60 - 110
green/blue ... 50 - 85
Wine ... 20
amber ... 30
vaseline ... 35
green/blue ... 30
PONY (DUGAN)
Bowl, ice cream shape, rare
amethyst ... 200
POPCORN
Butter ... 75
Cake Stand ... 80 - 135
Cordial ... 45
Creamer or Spooner ... 40
Goblet ... 40 - 80
Pitcher ... 165
Sauce ... 15
Sugar ... 60
Wine ... 40
*Add 10% for raised husk pieces.
POPE LEO XIII
Plate ... 150
POPPY VARIANT (NORTHWOOD)
Bowl, 7", scarce ... 50
PORTRAIT
Goblet, rare ... 225
POST SCRIPT
Berry Bowl, lg. ... 45
Berry Bowl, sm. ... 20
Butter ... 65
Creamer or Spooner ... 25
Creamer or Sugar, Individual ... 20
Cruet ... 55
Goblet ... 40
Olive, hndl. ... 30
Shakers, ea. ... 25
Sugar ... 30
Wine ... 30
POTPOURRI
Cake Stand ... 125
Compote, deep, rnd. ... 75
sapphire ... 2,400
Compote (Salver) ... 75
Compote, goblet shape ... 100
Milk Pitcher, rare ... 600
Tumbler, rare ... 200
POWDER & SHOT
Butter ... 145
Castor Bottle ... 55
Celery Vase, very scarce ... 200
Compotes, covered ... 125 - 160
Creamer or Spooner ... 100
Egg Cup ... 65
Goblet ... 95
Pitcher ... 300
Salt, master ... 60
Sauce ... 25
Sugar ... 100
Tumbler ... 55
PREPAREDNESS
Plate, rare ... 400
PRESENT FOR A FRIEND
Novelty Book Toothpick or Match Holder . 65
vaseline ... 100
PRESIDENT McKINLEY ASSASSINATION
Pitcher ... 275
Tumbler ... 40
PRESSED DIAMOND
Berry Bowl, lg. ... 30
amber ... 35
vaseline ... 45
green/blue ... 50
Berry Bowl, sm. ... 10
amber ... 15
vaseline ... 20
green/blue ... 20
Bowl, finger ... 20
amber ... 25
vaseline ... 30
green/blue ... 35
Butter ... 55
amber ... 60
vaseline ... 120
green/blue ... 80
Cake Stand ... 80
amber ... 100
vaseline ... 165
green/blue ... 60
Celery Vase ... 20
amber ... 25
vaseline ... 35
green/blue ... 40
Compote, open ... 35
amber ... 40
vaseline ... 45
green/blue ... 50
Compote, covered ... 55
amber ... 60
vaseline ... 100
green/blue ... 90
Creamer or Spooner ... 25
amber ... 30
vaseline ... 40
green/blue ... 45
Cruet ... 70
amber ... 125
vaseline ... 165
green/blue ... 140
Custard Cup ... 10
amber ... 15
vaseline ... 20
green/blue ... 25
Goblet ... 30
amber ... 35
vaseline ... 45
green/blue ... 50
Pitcher ... 70
amber ... 75
vaseline ... 145
green/blue ... 100
Plate, 11" ... 25
amber ... 30
vaseline ... 50
green/blue ... 40
Salt Dip ... 20
amber ... 25
vaseline ... 30
green/blue ... 30
Shakers, ea. ... 25
amber ... 30
vaseline ... 35
green/blue ... 35
Sugar ... 40
amber ... 45
vaseline ... 80
green/blue ... 60
Tumbler ... 15
amber ... 20
vaseline ... 25
green/blue ... 25
Wine ... 15
amber ... 20
vaseline ... 35
green/blue ... 25
PRESSED LEAF
Bowls, oval, 5 sizse ... 15 - 40
Butter ... 100
Cake Stand ... 140
Compote, covered 6 sizes and
styles ... 70 - 100
Compote, open, 6 sizes and styles . 50 - 70
Cordial ... 25
Creamer or Spooner ... 80
Egg Cup ... 30
Lamp ... 110
Oval Dish ... 30
Pitcher ... 165
Sugar ... 90
Syrup ... 120
Wine ... 30
PRETTY MAIDEN
Novelty Toothpick or Match Holder ... 95
PRIDE
Berry Bowl, lg. ... 25
amber ... 40
vaseline ... 65
green/blue ... 45
Berry Bowl, sm. ... 10
amber ... 30
vaseline ... 50
green/blue ... 35
Butter ... 65
amber ... 85
vaseline ... 130
green/blue ... 95
Celery Tray ... 25
amber ... 35
vaseline ... 75
green/blue ... 50
Compote, tall, covered ... 80
amber ... 100
vaseline ... 195
green/blue ... 150
Creamer or Spooner ... 25
amber ... 35
vaseline ... 60
green/blue ... 40
Cruet ... 35
amber ... 65
vaseline ... 110
green/blue ... 70
Salt Shakers, ea. ... 25
amber ... 45
vaseline ... 65
green/blue ... 50
Sugar ... 25
amber ... 40
vaseline ... 70
green/blue ... 45
PRIMROSE (CANTON)
Berry Bowl, lg. ... 30
amber ... 35
vaseline ... 45
green/blue ... 55
milk glass ... 40
Berry Bowl, sm. ... 10
amber ... 15
vaseline ... 20
green/blue ... 30
milk glass ... 20
Bowl, flat ... 15
amber ... 20
vaseline ... 30
green/blue ... 40
milk glass ... 25
Butter ... 50
amber ... 55
vaseline ... 115
green/blue ... 105
milk glass ... 90
Cake Stand ... 100
amber ... 140
vaseline ... 200
green/blue ... 165
milk glass ... 155
Cake Plate, hndl. ... 35
amber ... 40
vaseline ... 50
green/blue ... 65
milk glass ... 40
Compote, covered, 6" - 9" ... 70 - 100
amber ... 80 - 125
vaseline ... 100 - 200
green/blue ... 90 - 165

milk glass ....70 - 135
Cordial 15
amber 20
vaseline 25
green/blue 35
milk glass 35
Creamer or Spooner 30
amber 45
vaseline 70
green/blue 60
milk glass 40
Egg Cup 35
amber 45
vaseline 70
green/blue 60
milk glass 50
Goblet 40
amber 55
vaseline 80
green/blue 65
milk glass 65
Lamp, finger size 200
Milk Pitcher 55
amber 65
vaseline 100
green/blue 90
milk glass 80
Pickle Dish 15
amber 20
vaseline 25
green/blue 35
milk glass 25
Pitcher 70
amber 95
vaseline 150
green/blue 160
milk glass 120
Plate, 4½" - 8" ....20 - 30
amber ....25 - 35
vaseline ....30 - 40
green/blue ....40 - 55
milk glass ....25 - 45
Platter, oval 25
amber 30
vaseline 45
green/blue 55
milk glass 35
Relish Tray 15
amber 20
vaseline 25
green/blue 35
milk glass 25
Sauce, 2 styles 15
amber 20
vaseline 25
green/blue 35
milk glass ....20 - 35
Sugar 55
amber 65
vaseline 100
green/blue 75
milk glass 85
Waste Bowl 25
amber 30
vaseline 35
green/blue 45
milk glass 35
Water Tray 40
amber 55
vaseline 80
green/blue 65
milk glass 55
Wine 15
amber 20
vaseline 25
green/blue 30
milk glass 30

PRINCE OF WALES PLUMES
*Condensed list.

Berry Bowl, lg 50
Berry Bowl, sm 30
Butter 135
Compote 75
Creamer, Spooner or Sugar 55
Jam Jar 60
Mustard Pot 70
Novelty Bowl 65
Pickle Dish 40
Pitcher 200
Plate 65
Shakers, ea 50
Sauce 25
Syrup 95
Toothpick Holder 150
Tumbler 40

*Add 10% for gilded pieces and 50% for ruby stain pieces.

PRISCILLA
Banana Stand 160
Biscuit Jar 200
Bowl, covered, 7" - 10" ....40 - 85
Bowl, sq. 50
Cake Stand, 9" - 10" ....80 - 140
Celery Vase 60
Compote, covered, 7" - 9" ....60 - 200
Compote, open, 5" - 9" ....50 - 100
Condiment Tray 40
Cracker Jar 65
Creamer or Spooner 35
Cruet 50
Cup 10
Donut Stand 40
Goblet 75
Jelly Compote, covered 40
Mug 35
Pickle Dish 15
Pitcher, 2 styles ....125 - 200
Plate 30
Relish Dish 15
Rose Bowl 40
Sauce, rnd. or sq. 15
Shakers, ea 30
Sugar 30
Syrup 120
Toothpick Holder 50
Tumbler 45
Wine 70

PRISCILLA (FOSTORIA)
Bowl, 8½" 60
green/blue 80
Butter 100
green/blue 200
Cake Stand 250
green/blue 525
Celery Vase 90
green/blue 125
Compote, covered 150
green/blue 210
Compote, open 75
green/blue 90
Creamer or Spooner 60
green/blue 80
Cruet 125
green/blue 250
Egg Cup 40
green/blue 70
Goblet 70
green/blue 100
Jam Jar 90
green/blue 165
Oil Lamp 125
green/blue 225
Pickle Dish 20
green/blue 30
Pitcher 165
green/blue 285
Sauce 10
green/blue 15
Shakers, lg. or sm 40
green/blue 70
Sherbet Cup 15
green/blue 25
Sugar 90
green/blue 120
Syrup 135
green/blue 385
Toothpick Holder 70
green/blue 200
Tumbler 60
green/blue 100
Vase 50
green/blue 60
Water bottle 90
green/blue 120

PRISM BARS
Berry Bowl, lg 30
Berry Bowl, sm 10
Butter 45
Celery Vase 20
Creamer or Spooner 15
Goblet 30
Pickle Jar 20
Pitcher 60
Relish 15
Sugar 20
Tumbler 10

PRISM WITH BALL & BUTTON
Creamer 25

THE PRIZE
Butter 70
Creamer or Spooner 20
Cruet 55
Goblet 60
Pickle Dish 20
Pitcher 90
Shakers, ea 15
Sugar 30
Syrup 45
Toothpick Holder 30
Tumbler 25

PROTECTION & PLENTY
Mug 50
Plate, 8½" 65

PSYCHE & CUPID
Castor Set, complete 145
Compote, covered 80
Celery Vase 45
Creamer or Spooner 45
Butter 85
Goblet 65
Jam Jar 50
Milk Pitcher 100
Pitcher 165
Sugar 60
Tumbler 35
Wine 30

PULLED LOOP
Vase, scarce 35
Bowl Whimsey, from vase, rare
amethyst 125

PUNTY & DIAMOND POINT
Berry Bowl, lg 45
Berry Bowl, sm 15
Bitters bottle 65
Butter 75
Creamer or Spooner 25
Cruet 50
Decanter 45
Pitcher 125
Platter 35
Punch Bowl 165
Punch Cup 15
Sauce 10
Shakers, ea 15
Sugar 35
Sugar Shaker 45
Toothpick Holder 35

Tumbler....... 20
Water bottle....... 40
Vase....... 25

PUNTY BAND
Butter....... 55
Cake Basket....... 40
Cake Stand....... 35
Candy Dish....... 25
Creamer or Spooner....... 25
Goblet....... 40
Mug....... 30
Pitcher....... 90
Salt Dip....... 10
Shakers, ea....... 15
Spoon Tray....... 20
Sugar....... 35
Syrup....... 45
Toothpick Holder....... 25
Tumbler....... 20
Wine....... 10

PURE PACK MUG
Mug....... 55

PURITAN (McKEE'S)
Bowls, various....... 25 - 60
Butter....... 40
ruby stain....... 80
Creamer or Spooner....... 20
ruby stain....... 30
Pitcher....... 70
ruby stain....... 105
Sugar....... 25
ruby stain....... 50
Toothpick Holder....... 30
ruby stain....... 45
Tumbler....... 15
ruby stain....... 30

QUADRUPED
Berry Bowl, lg....... 35
ruby stain....... 45
Bowl, mid size....... 15
ruby stain....... 20
Berry Bowl, sm....... 10
ruby stain....... 15
Butter....... 70
ruby stain....... 90
Compote, short stemmed....... 35
ruby stain....... 40
Creamer or Spooner....... 25
ruby stain....... 30
Hotel Creamer & Sugar....... 45
ruby stain....... 55
Jelly Compote....... 35
ruby stain....... 40
Pickle Dish....... 15
ruby stain....... 20
Pitcher....... 95
ruby stain....... 120
Relish....... 15
ruby stain....... 20
Shakers, ea....... 20
ruby stain....... 30
Sugar....... 35
ruby stain....... 40
Sundae Dish....... 20
ruby stain....... 25
Tumbler....... 15
ruby stain....... 20
Vase....... 25
ruby stain....... 30

QUARTERED BLOCK
Oil Lamp, 4 sizes....... 95 - 175

QUATREFOIL
Bowl, various....... 10 - 35
green/blue....... 20 - 45
Butter....... 60
green/blue....... 55
Compote, covered....... 55
green/blue....... 40
Compote, open....... 25
green/blue....... 30
Creamer or Spooner....... 20
green/blue....... 25
Goblet, rare....... 85
green/blue....... 95
Pitcher....... 80
green/blue....... 90
Shakers, ea....... 15
green/blue....... 20
Sugar....... 25
green/blue....... 30
Tumbler....... 20
green/blue....... 25

QUEEN
Basket....... 80
amber....... 100
vaseline....... 200
green/blue....... 165
Bowl, 8½"....... 30
amber....... 45
vaseline....... 45
green/blue....... 50
Butter, 2 styles....... 55 - 65
amber....... 60 - 70
vaseline....... 80 - 125
green/blue....... 70 - 120
Cake Stand, 3 sizes....... 40 - 80
amber....... 60 - 90
vaseline....... 95 - 135
green/blue....... 90 - 115
Cheese Dish, covered....... 70
amber....... 75
vaseline....... 100
green/blue....... 80
Celery Vase....... 30
amber....... 40
vaseline....... 40
green/blue....... 50
Claret....... 20
amber....... 40
vaseline....... 100
green/blue....... 90
Compote, covered....... 70
amber....... 80
vaseline....... 120
green/blue....... 115
Creamer or Spooner....... 30
amber....... 35
vaseline....... 60
green/blue....... 50
Cruet....... 60
amber....... 75
vaseline....... 90
green/blue....... 80
Goblet....... 35
amber....... 40
vaseline....... 60
green/blue....... 50
Milk Pitcher....... 40
amber....... 50
vaseline....... 80
green/blue....... 65
Oval Dish, 7" - 9"....... 20
amber....... 35
vaseline....... 55
green/blue....... 45
Pitcher....... 65
amber....... 70
vaseline....... 90
green/blue....... 80
Relish Dish....... 15
amber....... 20
vaseline....... 40
green/blue....... 35
Shakers, ea....... 30
amber....... 35
vaseline....... 50
green/blue....... 40
Sugar....... 35
amber....... 45
vaseline....... 60
green/blue....... 60
Tumbler....... 25
amber....... 35
vaseline....... 45
green/blue....... 40
Wine....... 20
amber....... 30
vaseline....... 45
green/blue....... 40

QUEEN ANNE
Bowl, covered, 8" - 9"....... 80 - 100
Butter....... 90
Casserole, 7" - 8"....... 125 - 155
Celery Vase....... 70
Compote, covered, high....... 135 - 165
Compote, covered, low....... 125
Creamer or Spooner....... 50
Egg Cup....... 40
Milk Pitcher....... 200
Pitcher....... 180
Plate....... 55
Sauce....... 15
Shakers, ea....... 75
Sugar....... 90
Syrup....... 300

QUEEN'S NECKLACE
Bowl, 10"....... 30
Butter....... 70
Cake Salver....... 40
Celery Vase....... 20
Cologne Bottle....... 40
Compote, open, 10"....... 35
Creamer or Spooner....... 30
Cruet....... 65
Lamp....... 85
Oil Bottle....... 40
Pitcher....... 100
Rose Bowl....... 25
Shakers, ea....... 20
Sugar....... 45
Syrup....... 70
Tumbler....... 20
Vases, 8" - 10"....... 20 - 35
Wine....... 20

QUILTED FAN TOP
Butter....... 55
Creamer or Spooner....... 20
Goblet....... 25
Plate....... 20
Pitcher....... 65
Shakers, ea....... 25
Sugar....... 30
Tumbler....... 15
Wine....... 10

QUINTEC
Berry Bowl, lg....... 30
Berry Bowl, sm....... 15
Biscuit Jar....... 35
Bonbon....... 20
Butter....... 50
Cake Stand....... 35
Celery Tray....... 20
Compote....... 35
Cracker Bowl, 6"....... 20
Cracker Jar....... 40
Creamer....... 25
Cruet....... 60
Decanter....... 40
Handled Bowl....... 25
Jelly Compote....... 25
Jelly Jar....... 35
Pickle Tray....... 25
Plate....... 25
Punch Bowl, handled....... 75
Punch Cup....... 15
Shakers, ea....... 20
Spooner....... 30

Sugar 35
Syrup 65
Whiskey 20
Vase, sm., pedestal 25
Vase, swung 35

RABBIT SITTING
Mug 70
amber 100

RABBIT UPRIGHT
Mug 60
amber 80
vaseline 100
green/blue 75

RACING DEER & DOE
Pitcher, very scarce 425

RAILROAD
Platter 90

RAINBOW
Berry Bowl, lg. 45
Berry Bowl, sm. 20
Carafe 60
Cigar Jar 40
Creamer or Spooner 25
Decanter 65
Goblet 40
Pitcher 85
Salt Dip 30
Shakers, ea 25
Sugar 30
Tumbler 25
Wine Tray 35

RAINDROP
ABC Plate 35
amber 40
vaseline 75
green/blue 50
Butter 45
amber 50
vaseline 70
green/blue 55
Cake Plate 35
amber 45
vaseline 70
green/blue 60
Celery Vase 15
amber 30
vaseline 55
green/blue 35
Compote, covered, high or low 35 - 50
amber 40 - 60
vaseline 55 - 75
green/blue 45 - 80
Creamer or Spooner 20
amber 25
vaseline 50
green/blue 35
Cup & Saucer 35
amber 40
vaseline 65
green/blue 45
Egg Cup 15
amber 40
vaseline 75
green/blue 45
Finger Bowl 15
amber 25
vaseline 40
green/blue 30
Miniature Lamp 45
amber 85
vaseline 100
green/blue 95
Pickle Dish 15
amber 20
vaseline 30
green/blue 25
Pitcher 50
amber 60
vaseline 85
green/blue 70
Plate, Dinner 20
amber 25
vaseline 40
green/blue 30
Relish Tray 15
amber 20
vaseline 30
green/blue 30
Sauce 10
amber 15
vaseline 20
green/blue 20
Sugar 25
amber 45
vaseline 75
green/blue 65
Syrup 65
amber 80
vaseline 125
green/blue 115
Tumbler 10
amber 15
vaseline 35
green/blue 40
Water Tray 30
amber 40
vaseline 60
green/blue 55
Wine 15
amber 25
vaseline 30
green/blue 35

RAMPANT LION (GILLINDER)
Compote, covered, 7" - 8" 150 - 170

RAM'S HEAD
Bowl, covered, 5" - 7" 175

RAM'S HEAD
Mug 45
vaseline 85

RANSON
Bowls, various 15 - 30
vaseline 30 - 70
Butter 55
vaseline 100
Creamer or Spooner 25
vaseline 45
Cruet 60
vaseline 90
Shakers, ea 35
vaseline 55
Sugar 35
vaseline 55
Tray 40
vaseline 50

RAYED FLOWER
Berry Bowl, lg. 30
Berry Bowl, sm. 10
Butter 45
Celery Vase 20
Creamer or Spooner 20
Custard Cup 10
Jelly Compote 25
Milk Pitcher 45
Pickle Dish 15
Pitcher 70
Shakers, ea 10
Sugar 25
Toothpick Holder 30
Tumbler 10

RAYED HEART
Bowl, 8" 35
Butter 65
Celery 35
Compote 40
Creamer, Spooner or Sugar 25
Goblet 35
Pickle Dish 25
Pitcher 75
Sauce, 4" 20
Tumbler 20

REAPER
Oval Platter, hndl. 70

REBECCA AT THE WELL
Compote, rare 800

RECTANGLE
Creamer 45
vaseline 90

RED BLOCK
Banana Dish 30
ruby stain 100
Bowls, oblong, 3 sizes 25 - 40
ruby stain 60 - 90
Bowls, rnd., 4 sizes 20 - 45
ruby stain 40 - 100
Bowls, square, 3 sizes 25 - 50
ruby stain 50 - 95
Butter 85
ruby stain 155
Cheese Dish, covered 120
ruby stain 375
Cologne Bottle 60
ruby stain 100
Creamer or Spooner 30
ruby stain 70
Cream Pot w/Lid 100
ruby stain 500
Cruet 55
ruby stain 200
Cup 25
ruby stain 65
Goblet 25
ruby stain 40
Lamp, 2 sizes 150 - 180
Lamp, miniature
w/Artichoke shade 175
Lamp, parlor size,
matching shade, very rare 675
ruby stain 4,800
Mug 20
ruby stain 40
Mustard Jar w/Lid 50
ruby stain 100
Pitcher, 2 styles 65 - 135
ruby stain 150 - 395
Plate, 10" 40
ruby stain 100
Rose Bowl, 2 sizes 40 - 50
ruby stain 80 - 120
Shakers, ea 45
ruby stain 165
Sugar 45
ruby stain 70
Syrup 65
ruby stain 225
Tumbler 20
ruby stain 45

REGAL SWAN
Master Salt 125

"REMEMBER ME "
Mug 65

RETICULATED CORD
Butter 55
vaseline 95
green/blue 90
Cake Stand, lg. 35
vaseline 45
green/blue 50
Celery Vase 20
vaseline 25
green/blue 30
Creamer or Spooner 25
vaseline 35
green/blue 45
Goblet 35
vaseline 125
green/blue 135
Pitcher 85

vaseline 150
green/blue 165
Plate 30
vaseline 40
green/blue 50
Relish 20
vaseline 25
green/blue 35
Sauce 10
vaseline 20
green/blue 25
Sugar 35
vaseline 45
green/blue 55
Tumbler 15
vaseline 35
green/blue 35

REVERSE DRAPERY
Bowl 25
Plate 55
Vase 30

REVERSE FAN & DIAMOND
Pitcher 85
Tumbler 20

REVERSE TWIST
Child's Cup 30

REXFORD
Basket 55
Bowls, lg. ..... 35 - 60
Bowls, sm. ..... 20 - 55
Butter 70
Cake Stand, 2 sizes ..... 45 - 65
Celery Vase 35
Compote, covered 55
Creamer or Spooner 30
Cup 25
Fruit Bowl, square, 9½" 35
Goblet 45
Honey Jar 45
Jelly Compote 50
Milk Pitcher 65
Mug 45
Nappy 30
Pitcher 90
Plate, various sizes ..... 30 - 55
Relish 30
Rose Bowl, 3 sizes ..... 20 - 50
Shakers, ea 30
Sugar Shaker 60
Sugar w/Lid 40
Sweetmeat w/Lid, 2 sizes ..... 65 - 80
Toothpick Holder 40
Toy Table Set, complete 110
Tray 45
Tumbler 30
Vase 35
Wine 25

*For ruby stained add 25%.

RIB BAND
Butter 55
Creamer or Spooner 25
Pitcher 80
Sugar 30
Tumbler 10

RIBBED ELLIPSE (ADMIRAL)
Berry Bowl, lg 45
Berry Bowl, sm. 15
Butter 65
Cake Plate 35
Compote 30
Creamer or Spooner 20
Mug, hndl 40
Pitcher 85
Plate 20
Sugar 30
Tumbler 20

RIBBED FORGET-ME-NOT
Bowls, various ..... 15 - 30
amber ..... 20 - 35
vaseline ..... 25 - 40
green/blue ..... 25 - 40
amethyst ..... 20 - 45
Butter 55
amber 60
vaseline 100
green/blue 85
amethyst 80
Cake Stand, 9" - 11" ..... 30 - 40
amber ..... 35 - 45
vaseline ..... 40 - 50
green/blue ..... 45 - 60
amethyst ..... 40 - 55
Celery Vase 25
amber 30
vaseline 40
green/blue 45
amethyst 40
Compotes, covered ..... 30 - 55
amber ..... 35 - 60
vaseline ..... 50 - 85
green/blue ..... 60 - 95
amethyst ..... 50 - 85
Compotes, open ..... 25 - 40
amber ..... 30 - 45
vaseline ..... 35 - 55
green/blue ..... 40 - 65
amethyst ..... 35 - 60
Creamer or Spooner 30
amber 35
vaseline 45
green/blue 55
amethyst 50
Cup & Saucer 25
amber 30
vaseline 40
green/blue 45
amethyst 40
Goblet 35
amber 40
vaseline 50
green/blue 60
amethyst 55
Mustard, hndl. 40
amber 50
vaseline 60
green/blue 55
Mustard w/lid 35
amber 40
vaseline 45
green/blue 50
amethyst 45
Mug 40
amber 45
vaseline 50
green/blue 55
amethyst 50
Aquatic) 50
amber 60
vaseline 95
green/blue 90
amethyst 80
Pitcher 85
amber 95
vaseline 150
green/blue 165
amethyst 155
Plates ..... 15 - 25
amber ..... 20 - 30
vaseline ..... 25 - 40
green/blue ..... 30 - 45
amethyst ..... 30 - 40
Salt, master 20
amber 25
vaseline 30
green/blue 35
amethyst 30
Sauce 10
amber 15
vaseline 20
green/blue 25
amethyst 20
Sugar 40
amber 45
vaseline 55
green/blue 65
amethyst 55
Toothpick Holder 40
amber 50
vaseline 65
green/blue 75
amethyst 70
Toy Table Set, complete 115
amber 145
vaseline 165
green/blue 180
amethyst 179
Tumbler 15
amber 20
vaseline 35
green/blue 40
amethyst 35
Water Tray (Herons, Storks or Wine 20
amber 25
vaseline 30
green/blue 35
amethyst 30

RIBBED LEAVES VARIANT
Mug 45

RIBBED PALM
Butter 160
Castor Set 200
Celery Vase 90
Champagne 165
Compote, covered, 6" 255
Compote, open, 7" - 10" ..... 190 - 240
Creamer 200
Egg Cup 55
Goblet ..... 45 - 60
Lamp 275
Pitcher 345
Plate, 6" 70
Salt, master 50
Sauce 20
Spooner 65
Sugar 135
Tumbler 100
Wine 70

RIBBON
Berry Bowl, lg 65
Berry Bowl, sm. 30
Butter 90
Cake Stand 290
Celery Vase 70
Champagne 225
Cheese Dish, covered 300
Cologne Bottle 135
Compote, covered, low,6" - 8" ... 80 - 100
Compote, covered, high, 6½" - 8½" ..... 40 - 60
Compote, open, dolphin, round, 2 sizes ..... 260 - 300
Compote, open, Rebecca At The Well, oval 800
Creamer or Spooner 65
Goblet 50
Milk Pitcher 100
Pickle Jar 300
Pitcher 135
Plate 70
Platter 100
Sauce 20
Shakers, ea 50
Sugar 80
Tumbler 60
Waste Bowl 85
Water Tray 400
Wine, rare 235

RIBBONS & OVERLAPPING SQUARES (VERRE D' OR)
- Bowl, lg.
  - green/blue 95
  - amethyst 105
- Bowl, sm.
  - green/blue 75
  - amethyst 85
- Bowl, square
  - green/blue 125
  - amethyst 150
- Compote
  - green/blue 80
  - amethyst 90
- Plate
  - green/blue 110
  - amethyst 120

RIBBON STAR & BOWS (NORTHWOOD'S VERRE D'OR)
- Berry Bowl, lg.
  - green/blue 65
  - amethyst 85
- Berry Bowl, sm.
  - green/blue 30
  - amethyst 40
- Compote
  - green/blue 75
  - amethyst 90
- Nappy
  - green/blue 40
  - amethyst 60
- Plate, lg.
  - green/blue 65
  - amethyst 85
- Plate, sm.
  - green/blue 40
  - amethyst 55

RIB OVER DRAPE
- Bowl, various sizes........ 15 - 30
- Butter 85
- Creamer or Spooner 40
- Ice Bucket 65
- Pitcher 135
- Sugar 55
- Tumbler 20

RICHARD WALLACE
- Compote 250

RINDSKOPF
- Creamer 45

RINDSKOPF GOOSEBERRY
- Tumbler, either 65

RING & BEADS
- Creamer 30
- Sugar, open 25
- Vase 30

RINGED CRANE
- Vase, 7", very scarce 125

RING NECK
- Oil Bottle 40
- Water Bottle 65

RING PUNTY, SAWTOOTH & EYE
- Lamp, marble base 250

RING TREE
- Ring Holder 65
  - vaseline 175
  - green/blue 225

RIPPLE
- Vase, squat 35
  - cobalt 100
- Vase, standard 30
- Vase, mid size funeral 60
  - sapphire 150
- Vase, funeral 75

RISING SUN
- Bonbon, ftd. 15
- Berry Bowl, lg. 35
- Berry Bowl, sm. 15
- Butter, 2 sizes .... 50 - 65
- Cake Stand 65
- Celery Vase 25
- Champagne 20
- Compote, covered or open .... 20 - 45
- Creamer or Spooner, 3 shapes 30
- Cruet 55
- Custard Cup 10
- Goblet 25
- Milk Pitcher 40
- Pickle Dish 15
- Pitcher 75
- Sauce 10
- Shakers, ea. 35
- Sugar, 2 shapes .... 40 - 50
- Toothpick 30
- Tray, for water set 35
- Tumbler 25
- Vase 20
- Wine 30

*Add 75% for stained or gilded pieces.

RIVERGLASS FLUTE
- Bowl, 5" - 9" .... 15 - 30

RIVERSIDE CABBAGE LEAF
- Berry Bowl, lg. 70
  - amber 90
- Berry Bowl, sm. 45
  - amber 60
- Butter 165
  - amber 190
- Celery Vase 55
  - amber 70
- Compote, covered 85
  - amber 100
- Creamer 50
  - amber 60
- Pickle Dish 45
  - amber 55
- Pitcher 165
  - amber 250
- Plate 60
  - amber 80
- Sauce 30
  - amber 40
- Spooner 65
  - amber 75
- Sugar 70
  - amber 85
- Tumbler 40
  - amber 60

RIVERSIDE COLONIAL
- Table Lamp, hndl., 3 sizes .... 225 - 300

RIVERSIDE ELK (DEER)
- Goblet 85
- Pickle Jar 65

RIVERSIDE'S COLUMNS
- Celery Vase, very rare 250
- Pitcher, very rare 625

ROARING LION
- Goblet, rare
  - vaseline 300
- Plate, 6½", rare
  - amber 125
  - vaseline 175
  - green/blue 135
- Plate, 12½", rare
  - amber 150
  - vaseline 250
  - green/blue 160

ROBIN
- Mug, 2 sizes and variations 50
  - amber 60
  - green/blue 65
  - opaque 75

ROBIN HOOD
- Butter 55
  - green/blue 65
- Celery Vase 20
  - green/blue 25
- Compote 35
  - green/blue 45
- Creamer or Spooner 20
  - green/blue 30
- Goblet 40
  - green/blue 45
- Jelly Compote 35
  - green/blue 40
- Milk Pitcher 60
  - green/blue 70
- Pickle Dish 15
  - green/blue 20
- Pitcher 85
  - green/blue 100
- Shakers, ea. 20
  - green/blue 35
- Sugar 30
  - green/blue 45
- Syrup, scarce 80
  - green/blue 95
- Tumbler 20
  - green/blue 25

ROBIN IN A TREE
- Mug 40
  - amber 50
  - vaseline 75
  - green/blue 65
  - amethyst 80

ROCKET
- Berry Bowl, lg. 40
- Berry Bowl, sm. 15
- Butter 65
- Cake Stand 40
- Compote 35
- Creamer or Spooner 20
- Pitcher 70
- Sugar 30
- Tumbler 15

ROMAN KEY WITH RIBS
- Bowl, 8" - 10" .... 60 - 95
- Butter 200
- Castor Set 250
- Celery Vase 20
- Champagne 115
- Compote, 8" - 10" .... 60 - 115
- Creamer 195
- Custard Cup 15
- Decanter, 2 sizes .... 185 - 210
- Egg Cup, handleless and with handle ... 60 - 200
- Goblet 70
- Jam Dish 135
- Milk Pitcher 1200
- Mustard Jar 150
- Oil Lamp 350
- Pitcher 900
- Plate, 6½" 60
- Relish Dish 50
- Salt, master 60
- Spooner 70
- Sugar 165
- Tumbler 130
- Wine 90

ROMAN ROSETTE
- Bowl, 5" - 8" .... 20 - 45
  - ruby stain 55
- Bread Plate, oval 45
  - ruby stain 90
- Butter 90
  - ruby stain 200
- Cake Stand, 2 sizes .... 120 - 145
- Castor Set, 3 bottles 225
  - ruby stain 300
- Celery Vase 45
  - ruby stain 125
- Compotes, covered, 5" - 8" .... 70 - 135
  - ruby stain .... 90 - 240
- Creamer or Spooner 25
  - ruby stain 80
- Egg Cup 55
  - ruby stain 150

Goblet 60
ruby stain 250
Honey Dish w/Lid 300
ruby stain 950
Jelly Compote 25
ruby stain 50
Milk Pitcher 80
ruby stain 300
Mug, 2 sizes .... 30 - 35
ruby stain .... 80 - 90
Pickle Dish 25
ruby stain 50
Pitcher 100
ruby stain 350
Plate 35
ruby stain 75
Shakers, ea 30
ruby stain 55
Sugar 65
ruby stain 130
Syrup 245
ruby stain 475
Tumbler 50
ruby stain 80
Wine 50
ruby stain 155

ROOSTER ABC
Plate 165

ROOSTER EGG CUP
Covered Egg Cup, very rare 375

ROPE & THUMBPRINT
Bowls, various .... 15 - 35
amber .... 20 - 65
vaseline .... 30 - 75
green/blue .... 25 - 55
Butter 45
amber 75
vaseline 125
green/blue 100
Celery Vase 25
amber 35
vaseline 45
green/blue 40
Compote, covered 65
amber 80
vaseline 200
green/blue 150
Compote, open 40
amber 50
vaseline 65
green/blue 55
Creamer or Spooner 30
amber 40
vaseline 55
green/blue 50
Cruet 55
amber 65
vaseline 90
green/blue 70
Lamps, various .... 65 - 100
amber .... 80 - 125
vaseline .... 100 - 275
green/blue .... 100 - 185
Pickle Dish 25
amber 35
vaseline 45
green/blue 40
Pitcher 70
amber 85
vaseline 150
green/blue 110
Sugar 35
amber 45
vaseline 75
green/blue 50
Syrup 60
amber 80
vaseline 95
green/blue 75
Toothpick Holder 25
amber 40
vaseline 65
green/blue 50
Tumbler 15
amber 25
vaseline 35
green/blue 25

ROSA
Oil Lamp 95

ROSE
Cake Plate, hndl 50
vaseline 70
green/blue 85
Candlesticks, ea. 40
vaseline 55
green/blue 65
Cologne 55
vaseline 65
green/blue 75
Compote 45
vaseline 55
green/blue 65
Console Bowl 35
vaseline 40
green/blue 50
Dresser Tray 40
vaseline 45
green/blue 55
Trinket Box 60
vaseline 75
green/blue 85
Trinket Tray 35
vaseline 45
green/blue 55

ROSE (& OTHER FLOWERS)
Berry Bowl, lg.
vaseline 70
Berry Bowl, sm.
vaseline 30

ROSE GARLAND
Bowl, 7¼" 70
vaseline 125
green/blue 100
chocolate 1,800
Bowl, covered, 4½" lid 65
vaseline 100
green/blue 85
Bowl, master 65
vaseline 100
green/blue 85
Bowl, sauce 35
vaseline 75
green/blue 65
chocolate 700
Butter 95
vaseline 145
green/blue 120
Celery Vase 55
vaseline 65
green/blue 55
Creamer or Spooner 65
vaseline 85
green/blue 75
chocolate 2,100
Egg Cup 40
vaseline 60
green/blue 45
Pitcher 100
vaseline 350
green/blue 275
chocolate 5,000
Salt, open, ftd. 45
vaseline 75
green/blue 60
Sugar 80
vaseline 95
green/blue 80
chocolate 1,000
Toothpick Holder 65
vaseline 85
green/blue 70
Tray 45
vaseline 90
green/blue 80
Vase, 6" 40
vaseline 90
green/blue 70

ROSE IN SNOW
Bitters Bottle 100
Bowl, covered, 8" - 9" 50
amber 75
vaseline 75
green/blue 85
Bowl, open, 8" - 9" 90
amber 165
vaseline 250
green/blue 200
Butter, 2 styles 60
amber 100
vaseline 180
green/blue 170
Cake Stand 100
amber 125
vaseline 250
green/blue 200
Compote w/Lid, high or low .... 85 - 100
amber .... 100 - 125
vaseline .... 175 - 235
green/blue .... 175 - 225
Compote, open 3 sizes .... 35 - 80
amber .... 75 - 140
vaseline .... 125 - 235
green/blue .... 100 - 175
Creamer or Spooner 50
amber 75
vaseline 125
green/blue 100
Dish, oval 15
amber 20
vaseline 30
green/blue 30
Goblet 40
amber 55
vaseline 95
green/blue 80
Jam Jar w/Lid 125
amber 200
vaseline 400
green/blue 290
Mug, 2 styles 55
amber 75
vaseline 125
green/blue 100
Pickle Dish 30
amber 80
vaseline 135
green/blue 100
Pitcher 145
amber 200
vaseline 365
green/blue 300
Plate, 5 sizes .... 25 - 50
amber .... 50 - 75
vaseline .... 50 - 125
green/blue .... 50 - 100
Platter, oval 65
amber 85
vaseline 125
green/blue 100
Sauce, flat or ftd. 10
amber 40
vaseline 65
green/blue 50
Sugar 50
amber 100
vaseline 145
green/blue 120

Sweetmeat w/Lid 100
amber 150
vaseline 265
green/blue 225
Toddy Jar w/Lid & Underplate 180
amber 265
vaseline 400
green/blue 345
Tumbler, scarce 55
amber 100
vaseline 140
green/blue 125

ROSELAND (LATE)
Berry Bowl, lg. 30
Berry Bowl, sm. 10
Pitcher 45
Tumbler 10

ROSE POINT BAND
Berry Bowl, lg. 30
Berry Bowl, sm. 10
Bowl, ftd. 25
Butter 45
Celery Vase 15
Compote 30
Creamer or Spooner 20
Pitcher 70
Sauce 10
Sugar 25
Tumbler 15

ROSES IN THE SNOW
Bowl, 9" 35
Plate, 11" 45
Oil Lamp, 10" 90

ROSE SPRIG
Biscuit Jar 175
amber 250
vaseline 400
green/blue 350
Bowl, seitz shape 30
amber 45
vaseline 50
green/blue 60
Cake Stand 100
amber 135
vaseline 200
green/blue 165
Celery Vase 60
amber 70
vaseline 100
green/blue 90
Compote, covered, 7" - 8" .... 80 - 100
amber .... 100 - 150
vaseline .... 125 - 225
green/blue .... 100 - 165
Compote, open, 7" - 8" .... 35 - 45
amber .... 50 - 65
vaseline .... 55 - 70
green/blue .... 60 - 75
Creamer or Spooner 50
amber 60
vaseline 65
green/blue 70
Dish, oblong 20
amber 25
vaseline 30
green/blue 35
Goblet 50
amber 55
vaseline 90
green/blue 80
Milk Pitcher 70
amber 80
vaseline 110
green/blue 90
Mug 60
amber 80
vaseline 100
green/blue 85
Nappy 20
amber 30
vaseline 35
green/blue 40
Pickle Dish 20
amber 25
vaseline 30
green/blue 35
Pitcher 75
amber 95
vaseline 135
green/blue 100
Plate, 6" - 10" .... 30 - 40
amber .... 35 - 45
vaseline .... 40 - 50
green/blue .... 50 - 70
Punch Bowl, ftd. 160
amber 175
vaseline 300
green/blue 265
Relish 20
amber 25
vaseline 30
green/blue 35
Salt (Sleigh Shape) 50
amber 70
vaseline 75
green/blue 80
Sugar 60
amber 70
vaseline 100
green/blue 90
Tray 50
amber 55
vaseline 80
green/blue 70
Tumbler 40
amber 45
vaseline 80
green/blue 70
Wine 60
amber 100
vaseline 130
green/blue 65

ROSETTE (MAGIC)
Bowl, covered 50
Butter 70
Cake Stand, 4 sizses .... 60 - 100
Celery Vase 40
Compote, covered, 3 sizes .... 60 - 80
Compote, open, 6 sizes .... 25 - 75
Creamer or Spooner 20
Fish Shaped Relish 35
Goblet 40
Jelly Compote 25
Milk Pitcher 55
Mug 20
Pitcher 80
Plate 25
Plate, hndl. 35
Shakers, ea. 35
Sugar 50
Tray 40
Tumbler 30
Wine 40

ROSETTE & PALMS
Banana Stand 45
Butter 75
Cake Stand 35
Celery Vase 20
Creamer or Spooner 25
Goblet 50
Pitcher 85
Plate, 9" 25
Relish Dish 20
Sauce 10
Shakers, ea. 15
Sugar 35
Tumbler 15
Wine 10

ROSETTE WITH PINWHEELS
Bowl, ftd. 35
Butter 70
Cake Stand, stemmed 45
Celery Vase 25
Creamer or Spooner 25
Cup, ftd. 20
Honey Dish, sq. 25
Jelly Compote 30
Pitcher 85
Sugar 30
Tumbler 25

ROTEC
Bowls, various .... 10 - 40
Butter 65
Celery Tray 20
Creamer or Spooner 25
Lamp, 2 piece, fixture dated 1907 125
Pitcher 75
Sugar 30
Tumbler 15

ROYAL
Butter 65
Creamer 30
Spooner 30
Sugar 35

ROYAL CRYSTAL
Bowls, 5" - 8", 3 shapes .... 15 - 35
ruby stain .... 30 - 65
Butter 60
ruby stain 120
Cake Stands, various .... 70 - 90
ruby stain .... 125 - 200
Candy Jar 60
ruby stain 70
Celery Vase 30
ruby stain 50
Cologne Bottle 45
ruby stain 100
Compote, 6" & 7" .... 35 - 45
ruby stain .... 45 - 55
Cracker Jar 95
ruby stain 125
Creamer or Spooner 40
ruby stain 40
Cruet, 2 sizes .... 50 - 60
ruby stain .... 100 - 130
Goblet 90
ruby stain 125
Milk Pitcher 80
ruby stain 140
Pitcher, 2 styles .... 100 - 120
ruby stain .... 160 - 200
Plate, 2 styles 35
ruby stain 40
Sauce, flat or ftd. 15
ruby stain 25
Shakers, ea. 40
ruby stain 60
Sugar 40
ruby stain 70
Syrup 80
ruby stain 145
Toothpick Holder 45
ruby stain 65
Tumbler 20
ruby stain 30
Water Bottle 70
ruby stain 160
Wine 40
ruby stain 60

ROYAL IVY (NORTHWOOD)
Berry Bowl, lg. 95
Berry Bowl, sm. 40
Butter 150
Creamer or Spooner 75
Jam Jar, covered 125
Lamp 600
Pickle Castor 110

Pitcher ... 250
Shakers, ea ... 65
Sugar ... 110
Syrup ... 165
Toothpick Holder ... 75
Tumbler ... 60

*Prices are for pieces that fade to pink, clear, or frosted. *Add 10% for amber craquelle pieces.

ROYAL JUBILEE
Basket, ftd.
vaseline ... 95
green/blue ... 75

ROYAL KING
Shot Glass ... 40
ruby stain ... 50

ROYAL LADY
(ROYAL)
Bread Plate, crying baby ... 70
Butter ... 165
Celery Vase ... 85
Cheese Dish ... 175
Compote, covered, 9" ... 175
Creamer or Spooner ... 100
Dish, oval, w/lid ... 125
Salt, master ... 35
Sugar ... 110
Tray ... 150

RUBY
Butter ... 70
Creamer ... 35
Spooner ... 30
Sugar ... 40

RUBY DIAMOND
Butter ... 75
Creamer or Spooner ... 30
Goblet ... 50
Pitcher ... 125
Sauce ... 10
Sugar ... 40
Toothpick Holder ... 50
Tumbler ... 20
Wine ... 15

RUFFLED EYE
Pitcher ... 85
amber ... 100
vaseline ... 400
green/blue ... 150
chocolate ... 700

SADDLE
Match Holder ... 45
amber ... 80

ST ALEXIS CLOCK SET
Candlesticks, ea.
vaseline ... 60
Clock
vaseline ... 150

SAINT BERNARD
Berry Bowl, lg ... 90
Berry Bowl, sm ... 45
Butter ... 200
Cake Stand ... 135
Celery Vase ... 60
Compote, covered, high, 7" - 8" .. 225 - 300
Compote, covered, low ... 160
Compote, open, low, 6" - 8" ... 60 - 90
Creamer or Spooner ... 55
Cruet ... 85
Goblet ... 60
Jam Jar ... 160
Pickle Dish ... 40
Pitcher, 2 styles ... 140 - 165
chocolate ... 400
Sauce ... 20
Shakers, ea ... 50
Sugar ... 130
Tumbler ... 40

ST CLAIR CLOCK SET
Candlesticks, ea.
vaseline ... 65
Clock
vaseline ... 150

ST. LOUIS ENCAMPMENT
Goblet, very scarce ... 250

ST LOUIS WORLD'S FAIR
Washington Hatchet
ruby stain ... 95

SALAMANDER
Vase, 10", rare ... 350
amber ... 375
green/blue ... 400

SALT LAKE TEMPLE PLATTER
Platter, very scarce/rare ... 350

SANDWICH SCROLL SALT DIP
Salt Dip ... 25
amber ... 35
vaseline ... 50
green/blue ... 40

SANDWICH STAR
Butter ... 900
vaseline ... 1,600
amethyst ... 1,300
Champagne ... 250
vaseline ... 400
amethyst ... 325
Compote, dolphin base ... 400
vaseline ... 650
amethyst ... 425
Cordial ... 275
vaseline ... 375
amethyst ... 450
Creamer or Spooner ... 175
vaseline ... 250
amethyst ... 375
Decanter ... 300
vaseline ... 425
amethyst ... 550
Goblet, very rare ... 1,500
vaseline ... 1,850
amethyst ... 1,200
Spill Holder, stemmed ... 225
vaseline ... 300
amethyst ... 375
Sugar ... 250
vaseline ... 325
amethyst ... 525
Wine ... 350
vaseline ... 425
amethyst ... 450

*All pieces very scarce to rare

SAWTOOTH
Bowl, covered, 6"&7" ... 60 - 80
Bowl, open, 6" - 12" ... 25 - 50
Butter ... 60
Cake Stand, 9" - 14" ... 80 - 130
Celery Vase ... 35
Champagne ... 40
Child's Table Set,
butter & creamer ... 125
Compote, covered, 6" - 10" ... 50 - 80
Compote, open, 6" - 10" ... 25 - 65
Cordial ... 25
Creamer or Spooner ... 55
Cruet ... 55
Decanter ... 60
Dish, oval, 5" - 7" ... 20 - 35
Egg Cup, open & covered ... 25 - 110
Gas Shade ... 40
Goblet ... 30
Honey Dish ... 20
Milk Pitcher, w/pressed or applied
handle ... 40 - 80
Oil Lamp, 4 sizes ... 100 - 165
Pitcher, w/pressed or applied
handle ... 50 - 160
Plate, 6½" ... 25
Pomade Jar ... 50
Salt, master, covered or open ... 60 - 20
Sauce ... 15
Tumbler ... 30
Water Bottle ... 125
Water Tray, 10" - 14" ... 60 - 80
Wine ... 15

SAWTOOTH BOTTOM
Butter ... 45
ruby stain ... 60
Compote, open ... 30
ruby stain ... 40
Creamer or Spooner ... 25
ruby stain ... 35
Goblet ... 25
ruby stain ... 35
Pitcher ... 70
ruby stain ... 90
Sugar ... 30
ruby stain ... 40
Tumbler ... 15
ruby stain ... 20
Waste Bowl ... 20
ruby stain ... 30
Wine ... 20
ruby stain ... 30

SAWTOOTHED HONEYCOMB
Bonbon ... 25
ruby stain ... 45
Bowl, master berry ... 40
ruby stain ... 150
Butter ... 60
ruby stain ... 200
Celery Vase ... 40
ruby stain ... 95
Compote, open ... 40
ruby stain ... 90
Creamer or Spooner ... 40
ruby stain ... 90
Cruet ... 70
ruby stain ... 260
Goblet ... 40
ruby stain ... 100
Milk Pitcher ... 60
ruby stain ... 160
Nappy ... 30
ruby stain ... 40
Nappy, adv., rare ... 75
Pitcher ... 80
ruby stain ... 190
Punch Bowl w/base ... 190
ruby stain ... 275
Punch Cup ... 20
ruby stain ... 40
Sauce ... 10
ruby stain ... 25
Shakers, ea ... 40
ruby stain ... 90
Sugar ... 60
ruby stain ... 145
Toothpick Holder ... 30
ruby stain ... 135
Tumbler ... 20
ruby stain ... 50

SCALLOPED FLANGE
Tumbler, 5 styles ... 15 - 40

SCALLOPED SIX-POINT
Bowl, 9", 2 shapes ... 35 - 50
Butter ... 65
Butter Pat ... 20
Cake Stand, 2 styles ... 80 - 110
Celery Tray ... 25
Celery Vase ... 35
Claret ... 40
Cocktail ... 60
Cracker Jar w/Lid ... 100
Creamer or Spooner ... 40
Cruet ... 60
Cup ... 15
Egg Cup ... 35
Goblet ... 40
Mustard, covered ... 35

Pitcher, 2 styles .... 90 - 120
Plate 25
Rose Bowl 50
Shakers, ea 35
Sherry 30
Sugar 35
Syrup 100
Toothpick Holder 50
Tumbler 25
Vase 25
Wine 20

SCALLOPED SKIRT
Berry Bowl, lg. 30
green/blue 45
amethyst 50
Berry Bowl, sm. 10
green/blue 20
amethyst 35
Butter 60
green/blue 80
amethyst 95
Creamer or Spooner 25
green/blue 40
amethyst 50
Jelly Compote 35
green/blue 50
amethyst 65
Novelty Bowls .... 15 - 35
green/blue .... 25 - 60
amethyst .... 30 - 70
Pickle Dish 15
green/blue 25
amethyst 35
Sugar 30
green/blue 45
amethyst 55
Toothpick Holder 40
green/blue 55
amethyst 65
Vase 35
green/blue 45
amethyst 55

SCALLOPED SWIRL
Berry Bowl 25
green/blue 45
ruby stain 40
Butter 55
green/blue 90
ruby stain 80
Cake Plate 35
green/blue 50
ruby stain 40
Celery Vase 25
green/blue 40
ruby stain 30
Compote 30
green/blue 45
ruby stain 40
Creamer or Spooner 25
green/blue 40
ruby stain 35
Goblet 40
green/blue 60
ruby stain 50
Pitcher 75
green/blue 165
ruby stain 135
Plate 25
green/blue 40
ruby stain 35
Sugar 40
green/blue 65
ruby stain 60
Toothpick Holder 30
green/blue 60
ruby stain 55
Tumbler 15
green/blue 40
ruby stain 30
Vase 25
green/blue 50
ruby stain 40

SCALLOPED SWIRL (YORK HERRINGBONE)
Bowl 20
ruby stain 30
Butter 55
ruby stain 75
Cake Plate 35
ruby stain 45
Compote 40
ruby stain 50
Creamer or Spooner 25
ruby stain 35
Pitcher 80
ruby stain 120
Shakers, ea 20
ruby stain 45
Sugar 35
ruby stain 55
Toothpick Holder, ruby stain 65
Tumbler 15
ruby stain 30
Wine 25
ruby stain 35

SCALLOP SHELL
Berry Bowl, lg 30
Berry Bowl, sm. 15
Butter 55
Celery Vase 25
Creamer or Spooner 25
Pitcher 80
Sugar 30
Tumbler 15

*For eched add 10%.

SCHEHEREZADE
Bowls, various .... 20 - 35

SCHRAFFT'S CHOCOLATE
Advertising Plate 85

SCROLL WITH CANE BAND
Butter 45
Celery Vase 15
Compotes, various .... 20 - 45
Creamer or Spooner 15
Cruet 45
Pitcher 75
Shakers, ea. 15
Sugar 20
Toothpick Holder 30
Tumbler 15

SCROLL WITH FLOWERS
Butter 55
Cake Plate, hndl. 40
Cordial 25
Creamer or Spooner 20
Egg Cup, hndl. 25
Goblet 50
Mustard, covered 35
Pitcher 70
Plate 40
Relish 25
Salt Dip, hndl. 25
Sugar 30
Tumbler 20
Wine 25

*All pieces very scarce to rare.

SECTIONAL BLOCK
Compote 40
Goblet 35
Stemmed Desert 30

SEDAN
Berry Bowl, lg. 30
Berry Bowl, sm. 10
Butter 45
Celery Tray 20
Celery Vase 35
Compote, covered 50
Compote, open 30
Creamer or Spooner 30
Goblet 30
Mug 30
Pickle Tray w/Double Handle 30
Pitcher 65
Relish Tray 20
Shaker 30
Sugar 35
Tumbler 10
Wine 10

SEITZ BATH
Novelty Bowl 75
amber 175
vaseline 280
green/blue 325

SENGBUSCH INK WELL
One Shape 35

SEQUOIA
Berry Bowl, lg. 35
Berry Bowl, sm. 10
Bowl, canoe shape 45
Brandy Tray 20
Butter 65
Butter Pat 10
Celery Boat 30
Celery Vase 20
Cheese Plate 25
Compote, covered or open 55
Cordial 10
Creamer or Spooner 20
Cruet 50
Decanter 45
Finger Bowl 20
Goblet 30
Nappy 20
Pickle Boat 20
Pickle Jar 35
Pitcher 90
Plate 20
Relish 15
Salt Dip 10
Shakers, ea 20
Sugar 30
Syrup 60
Tray 35
Tumbler 20
Wine 10

*For colors double price of crystal.

SERPENT WITH DIAMOND BAND
Vase, decorated serpent 225

SEXTEC
Berry Bowl, lg. 40
Berry Bowl, sm. 15
Berry Creamer 25
Butter 70
Celery Tray 25
Compote, tall 45
Creamer or Spooner 20
Cruet 50
Goblet 35
Nut Bowl, hndl. 25
Orange Bowl 45
Pickle Jar 35
Pitcher 65
Plate 25
Punch Bowl 85
Punch Cup 10
Relish Dish 15
Shakers, ea 20
Sugar 30
Syrup 45
Tumbler 15
Wine 10

SHASTA DAISY
Bowls, various
green/blue .... 40 - 95
amethyst .... 40 - 90
Compotes, various
green/blue .... 60 - 125
amethyst .... 55 - 110

Nappy
green/blue 60
amethyst 55
Plate, lg. or sm.
green/blue .... 65 - 95
amethyst .... 60 - 90

SHEAF & BLOCK
Berry Bowl, lg. 45
Berry Bowl, sm. 20
Butter 65
Celery Vase 20
Creamer or Spooner 25
Goblet 50
Pickle Dish 25
Pitcher 90
Shakers, ea 25
Sugar 30
Tumbler 20
Wine 15

SHEAF & DIAMOND
Bowl 30
Butter 75
Cake Plate 45
Creamer or Spooner 30
Pickle Dish 25
Pitcher 70
Sugar 35
Tumbler 15

SHEAF OF WHEAT
Platter 75

SHELL & JEWEL
Banana Stand 325
Bowl, 6" and 8" .... 30 - 80
amber 95
Bowl, oval, 7" and 8" .... 40 - 70
Butter 125
Cake Stand 225
Creamer or Spooner 40
Pitcher 50
amber 250
green/blue 375
Pitcher w/Stippled Foot, rare 235
Shakers, ea 50
Sugar 100
Tray 295
Tumbler 25
amber 75
green/blue 90

SHELL & TASSEL
Berry Bowl, 6 sizes; 6" - 12" .... 50 - 75
vaseline 325
Bowl, covered, 3 sizes .... 150 - 300
Bowl, 7½", shell shaped 450
Bowl, octagon shaped, 3 sizes; 7" - 10". 95 - 200
vaseline 500
Bread Plate 175
Butter, 2 styles .... 90 - 165
Cake Stand, 6 sizes .... 75 - 165
Celery Vase 125
Compote, covered, 6" 225
Compote, open, 6 sizes .... 50 - 125
Creamer or Spooner 75
Goblet, 2 styles .... 75 - 125
Ice Cream Tray 100
Jelly Compote 100
Mug 75
Nappy, with tab handle 100
Nappy, shell shaped with tab handle .. 135
Oyster Plate 475
Pickle Jar w/Lid 500
Pitcher, 2 styles .... 300 - 400
Plate, berry size 175
Plate: Tart & Fruit, shell shaped, 12". 450 - 600
Platter, sq. or oblong 100
Sauce, flat of ftd., 3 sizes .... 20 - 25
Shakers, ea., rare 225
Sugar 150
Tumbler, soda, 4 sizes .... 100 - 165
Vase 150

*Add 200% for other shapes in any color.
*Add 100% for pieces with frosted dog finials.

SHERATON
Berry Bowl, lg. 30
amber 40
green/blue 40
Berry Bowl, sm. 10
amber 15
green/blue 15
Bread Plate, oval 25
amber 40
green/blue 40
Butter 45
amber 65
green/blue 95
Celery Vase 30
amber 40
green/blue 45
Compote, covered, 7" 80
amber 100
green/blue 120
Compote, open 7", low and high 30
amber 45
green/blue 50
Creamer or Spooner 30
amber 40
green/blue 50
Dish, 8 sided or rnd. 30
amber 40
green/blue 40
Goblet 40
amber 50
green/blue 55
Milk Pitcher 50
amber 60
green/blue 70
Pitcher 65
amber 75
green/blue 90
Platter, oblong, 8 panels 35
amber 45
green/blue 50
Relish Tray 15
amber 20
green/blue 20
Sauce 10
amber 15
green/blue 15
Sugar 50
amber 55
green/blue 70
Tumbler 30
amber 40
green/blue 50
Wine 25
amber 30
green/blue 40

SHIELD
Bowl, sauce, 5" 10
Butter 60
Celery Vase 25
Creamer or Spooner 25
Flower Vase, 3 sizes .... 20 - 35
Goblet 25
Knife Rest 15
Pitcher 85
Sugar 30
Tumbler 15

SHIMMERING STAR
Berry Bowl, lg. 30
Berry Bowl, sm. 10
Butter 50
Creamer or Spooner 25
Pitcher 65
Shakers, ea 20
Sugar 30
Tumbler 10

SHOE BOOTIE
Novelty Shoe 35
vaseline 70

SHOSHONE
Banana Stand 70
green/blue 95
ruby stain 160
Bowl, various, 5" - 6" .... 30 - 35
green/blue .... 40 - 45
ruby stain .... 65 - 85
Bowl, various, 7" - 8" .... 40 - 50
green/blue .... 50 - 60
ruby stain ....80 - 100
Butter 70
green/blue 80
ruby stain 95
Cake Stand, 3 sizes .... 50 - 90
green/blue ....80 - 120
ruby stain ....140 - 195
Celery Dish 35
green/blue 80
ruby stain 110
Claret 30
green/blue 75
ruby stain 90
Compote, covered, 3 sizes .... 80 - 100
green/blue ....95 - 145
ruby stain ....160 - 210
Compote, open, 5¼" .... 20 - 25
green/blue .... 35 - 40
ruby stain .... 70 - 90
Creamer, 2 sizes .... 30 - 50
green/blue .... 40 - 50
ruby stain ....70 - 120
Cruet 65
green/blue 95
ruby stain 130
Goblet 80
green/blue 135
ruby stain 225
Horseradish w/Lid 50
green/blue 80
ruby stain 160
Ice Tub 50
green/blue 90
ruby stain 135
Pickle Dish 25
green/blue 35
ruby stain 50
Pitcher, 2 styles .... 60 - 100
green/blue ....130 - 165
ruby stain ....235 - 280
Plate, 7" 40
green/blue 70
ruby stain 155
Punch Bowl 235
green/blue 325
ruby stain 450
Punch Cup 20
green/blue 45
ruby stain 70
Salt, master 50
green/blue 80
ruby stain 240
Salt Shaker, ea 40
green/blue 60
ruby stain 100
Sauce 15
green/blue 20
ruby stain 30
Spooner 35
green/blue 45
ruby stain 120
Sugar, 2 sizes .... 50 - 60
green/blue .... 65 - 80
ruby stain ....130 - 160
Toothpick Holder 30
green/blue 80
ruby stain 175
Tumbler 40
green/blue 60

ruby stain ... 95
Wine ... 20
green/blue ... 35
ruby stain ... 80

SHRINE
Berry Bowl, lg ... 40
Berry Bowl, sm ... 20
Butter ... 90
Cake Stand ... 120
Celery Vase ... 70
Compote, jelly ... 25
Creamer or Spooner ... 40
Goblet ... 75
Mug ... 60
Pickle Tray ... 25
Pitcher, ½ gal. & 1 gal. (rare) ... 55 - 280
Platter ... 65
Relish Tray ... 20
Sauces ... 10
Shaker, 2 sizes, ea. ... 50 - 90
Sugar ... 90
Toothpick Holder ... 130
Tumbler, 2 sizes ... 40 - 60

SHUTTLE
Berry Bowl, lg ... 125
Butter ... 175
chocolate ... 1,600
Cake Stand ... 125
Celery Vase ... 100
Champagne ... 75
chocolate ... 2,000
Cordial ... 50
Creamer or Spooner ... 75
Creamer, tankard size ... 45
Cruet ... 90
Custard Cup ... 15
Goblet ... 90
Mug ... 50
chocolate ... 200
Nappy ... 50
chocolate ... 125
Pitcher ... 100
chocolate ... 4,200
Sauce ... 25
chocolate ... 100
Shakers, ea ... 200
chocolate ... 1,300
Sugar ... 125
Tumbler ... 85
chocolate ... 125
Wine ... 20

SIDE WHEELER
Bowls, various ... 15 - 35
Butter ... 55
Celery Dish ... 25
Creamer or Spooner ... 30
Goblet ... 30
Pitcher ... 80
Pickle Dish ... 25
Shakers, ea ... 25
Sugar ... 40
Syrup ... 60
Tumbler ... 15

SINGING BIRDS
Berry Bowl, lg ... 55
Berry Bowl, sm ... 15
Butter ... 95
Creamer or Spooner ... 30
Goblet, rare ... 550
Mug ... 100
Pitcher ... 250
Punch Cup ... 25
Tumbler ... 50
Sherbet ... 45
Sugar ... 50

SIX PANEL FINECUT
Bowls, various ... 10 - 45
Butter ... 65
Compote ... 35
Creamer or Spooner ... 20
Cruet ... 45
Goblet ... 35
Pitcher ... 75
Sugar ... 30
Sugar Shaker ... 40
Syrup ... 65
Tumbler ... 15

SIX-SIDED CANDLESTICKS
One Shape, ea. ... 20

SKILTON (EARLY OREGON)
Bowls, 5" - 8", 2 styles ... 20 - 40
ruby stain ... 40 - 80
Butter ... 80
ruby stain ... 175
Cake Stand ... 130
Celery Vase ... 40
ruby stain ... 85
Compote, covered ... 75 - 100
ruby stain ... 185 - 225
Compote, open ... 45
ruby stain ... 80
Creamer or Spooner ... 30
ruby stain ... 65
Dish, oblong, 3 sizes ... 10 - 20
Goblet ... 50
ruby stain ... 95
Milk Pitcher ... 75
ruby stain ... 175
Pickle Tray ... 15
ruby stain ... 30
Pitcher, 2 styles ... 75 - 100
ruby stain ... 200 - 235
Shakers, ea ... 40
ruby stain ... 90
Sauce ... 10
ruby stain ... 25
Sugar ... 50
ruby stain ... 100
Tray ... 75
ruby stain ... 375
Tumbler ... 30
ruby stain ... 60
Wine ... 40
ruby stain ... 65

SLASHED SWIRL
Berry Bowl, lg ... 25
Berry Bowl, sm ... 15
Butter ... 45
Creamer or Spooner ... 20
Pitcher ... 65
Sugar ... 30
Tumbler ... 15

SLEWED HORSESHOE
Berry Bowl, lg ... 40
Berry Bowl, sm ... 20
Butter ... 65
Compote ... 45
Creamer, Spooner or Sugar ... 25
Cup ... 15
Goblet ... 35
Ice Cream Tray ... 25
Novelty Bowl ... 40
Pickle Dish ... 25
Punch Bowl ... 165
Punch Cup ... 15
Under Plate, 32" ... 85
Wine ... 25

SNAIL
Banana Stand, 9" & 10" ... 200 - 265
ruby stain ... 700
Biscuit Jar w/Lid ... 375
ruby stain ... 1,100
Bowl, covered, 7" - 8" ... 120 - 140
ruby stain ... 290 - 320
Bowl, open, 7" - 10" ... 30 - 70
ruby stain ... 80 - 200
Butter ... 100
ruby stain ... 225
Cake Basket, 10" ... 200
Cake Stand, 9" - 10" ... 125 - 165
Celery Tray ... 35
ruby stain ... 60
Celery Vase ... 50
ruby stain ... 100
Cheese Dish, covered ... 150
ruby stain ... 295
Compote, covered 6" - 10" ... 100 - 200
ruby stain ... 300 - 400
Compote, open, 6" - 10" ... 60 - 125
Creamer, 2 sizes ... 50 - 70
ruby stain ... 90 - 125
Cruet ... 140
ruby stain ... 650
Custard Cup ... 35
ruby stain ... 60
Finger Bowl ... 70
ruby stain ... 100
Goblet ... 120
ruby stain ... 195
Jam Jar ... 250
Jug, 4 sizes ... 160 - 235
Milk & Cream Pitcher, 3 sizes ... 90 - 165
ruby stain ... 180 - 260
Pitcher, Water, ½ gal. ... 200
ruby stain ... 290
Pitcher, bulbous, qt. size ... 200
ruby stain ... 325
Plate, 5" - 7" ... 40 - 60
Relish ... 25
Rose Bowl, 3" - 7" ... 40 - 80
ruby stain ... 95 - 165
Salt, ind. ... 25
ruby stain ... 60
Salt, master ... 75
ruby stain ... 155
Sauce, flat or ftd. ... 20
ruby stain ... 40
Shakers, short & tall, ea. ... 60 - 70
ruby stain ... 100 - 120
Spooner ... 50
ruby stain ... 85
Sugar, 2 sizes ... 85 - 115
ruby stain ... 135
Sugar Shaker ... 125
ruby stain ... 340
Syrup ... 155
ruby stain ... 400
Tumbler ... 45
ruby stain ... 85
Vase ... 210

SNAKE DRAPE
Goblet ... 85

SNOW FANCY
Berry Bowl, lg ... 45
Berry Bowl, sm ... 20
Butter ... 75
Creamer or Spooner ... 20
Rose Bowl, 7½" ... 45
Sugar ... 30

SNOW FLAKE
Bread Plate ... 15
Butter ... 65
Celery Tray ... 25
Celery Vase ... 30
Condiment Set, complete ... 80
Compote, sm. ... 30
Compote, lg, 2 sizes ... 55
Compote, med, 2 sizes ... 45
Creamer or Spooner ... 25
Nappy, med, 2 sizes ... 35
Nappy, sm, 2 sizes ... 25
Oil Bottle ... 55
Pickle Dish ... 25
Pitcher ... 85
Shakers, ea ... 20
Sugar ... 35
Toothpick Holder ... 45

Tumbler 20
Vase, 6" - 8¼" 35

SOLAR
Bowls, lg. 45
Bowls, sm. 20
Cake Stand, 2 types 65
Celery Tray 40
Celery Vase 35
Compote w/Lid 75
Cruet 85
Custard Cup 15
Goblet 45
Jelly Compote 30
Milk Pitcher 55
Pickle Dish 25
Pitcher 125
Relish 25
Shakers, ea 25
Syrup 80
Tumbler 20
Vase 50
Water Tray 40
Wine 25

SOUTHERN GARDENS (VERRE D' OR)
Bowl, lg.
green/blue 100
amethyst 125
Bowl, sm.
green/blue 80
amethyst 100
Compote
green/blue 125
amethyst 165

SOUTHERN IVY
Berry Bowl, lg. 25
Berry Bowl, sm. 10
Butter 50
Creamer or Spooner 25
Egg Cup 35
Pitcher 75
Sugar 35
Tumbler 15

SOWERBY HOBNAIL
Handled Basket 65
vaseline 110

SPANGLED
Bowl, finger 70
amber 95
green/blue 100
rose 250
Creamer 90
amber 110
green/blue 120
rose 265
Globes 100
amber 130
green/blue 140
rose 300
Pitcher, 5 various shapes & sizes . 135 - 250
amber ..... 140 - 265
green/blue ..... 150 - 275
rose ..... 265 - 600
Salt 125
amber 140
green/blue 150
rose 225
Tumbler 135
amber 155
green/blue 165
rose 250
Vase, 3 various ..... 100 - 165
amber ..... 110 - 175
green/blue ..... 120 - 185
rose ..... 250 - 400

SPANISH-AMERICAN
Dewey Pitcher w/Cannonballs 85
Tumbler w/Cannonballs 45
Dewey Pitcher w/Bullets ..... 150 - 190
green/blue 300
Tumbler w/Bullets 100

SPANISH MOSS
Hatpin Holder 50

SPECIALTY
Butter 45
ruby stain 75
Creamer or Spooner 25
ruby stain 35
Goblet 35
ruby stain 55
Sugar 40
ruby stain 45
Toothpick Holder 45
ruby stain 60

SPILLS (VARIOUS MAKERS)
Spills, various shapes and sizes .. 20 - 65
vaseline ..... 40 - 85

SPIRAL DIAMOND POINT
Vase or Jar 45

SPIRALEX
Vase, 10" - 14", scarce 35
sapphire 150

SPIRALEX VARIANT
Vase, 5" - 8"
amethyst 100

SPIRALLED IVY
Butter 50
Creamer or Spooner 15
Pitcher 65
Sauce 10
Sugar 20
Tumbler 15

SPIREA BAND
Bowl, 8", flat or ftd. 25
amber 30
vaseline 40
green/blue 35
Butter 40
amber 50
vaseline 85
green/blue 65
Cake Stand, 4 sizes ..... 40 - 85
amber ..... 60 - 100
vaseline ..... 80 - 140
green/blue ..... 70 - 125
Celery Vase 30
amber 35
vaseline 55
green/blue 40
Compote, covered ..... 40 - 50
amber ..... 50 - 60
vaseline ..... 60 - 75
green/blue ..... 50 - 65
Compote, open ..... 35 - 45
amber ..... 40 - 50
vaseline ..... 45 - 80
green/blue ..... 50 - 70
Creamer or Spooner 25
amber 40
vaseline 50
green/blue 40
Goblet 30
amber 40
vaseline 50
green/blue 40
Jam Jar w/Lid 95
amber 120
vaseline 230
green/blue 210
Pitcher 50
amber 55
vaseline 90
green/blue 70
Platter, oval 35
amber 45
vaseline 45
green/blue 60
Salt, ind. & master ..... 20 - 55
amber ..... 30 - 85
vaseline ..... 60 - 200
green/blue ..... 50 - 150
Sugar 35
amber 45
vaseline 65
green/blue 40
Tumbler 20
amber 25
vaseline 40
green/blue 30
Wine 15
amber 20
vaseline 40
green/blue 30

SPITTOON
Spittoon-shaped Toothpick Holder 55
vaseline 135
green/blue 100

SPLIT WAFFLE
Bowl 30
amber 45
green/blue 50
amethyst 60
Individual Creamer 25
amber 40
green/blue 45
amethyst 55
Individual Sugar 25
amber 40
green/blue 45
amethyst 55
Syrup 50
amber 65
green/blue 70
amethyst 85

SPRIG (AKA: ROYAL)
Bowl, covered, 6" 50
Berry Bowl, lg. 40
Berry Bowl, sm. 25
Butter 70
Cake Stand, 3 sizes ..... 70 - 100
Celery Vase 40
Compote, covered, 6" - 8", low & high ..... 60 - 125
Compote, open, 7½" - 8½" ..... 75 - 125
Creamer or Spooner 30
Goblet 40
Honey Dish w/Lid, flat & ftd. .. 225 - 375
Mustard w/Lid 200
Pitcher 75
Sauce 15
Sugar 70
Wine, scarce 50

SQUAT PINEAPPLE
Berry Bowl, lg. 30
green/blue 45
Berry Bowl, sm. 15
green/blue 20
Butter 55
green/blue 85
Compote 40
Creamer or Spooner 25
green/blue 40
Cruet 65
green/blue 90
Pickle Dish 20
green/blue 30
Pitcher 75
green/blue 100
Shakers, ea 20
green/blue 30
Sugar 25
green/blue 35
Tumbler 15
green/blue 25

SQUIRREL
Mug 50

green/blue ... 130
opaque blue ... 175
Pitcher ... 400

SQUIRREL & STUMP
Match Holder ... 85

SQUIRREL IN BOWER
Bowl, very rare ... 475
Butter ... 350
Creamer or Spooner ... 145
Goblet, very rare ... 775
Oil Lamp ... 800
Pitcher ... 1,200
chocolate ... 900
Sauce ... 75
Sugar ... 225

SQUIRREL WITH NUT
Pitcher, scarce ... 350

S-REPEAT
Bowl, lg. ... 45
green/blue ... 90
Bowl, sm. ... 20
green/blue ... 30
Butter ... 85
green/blue ... 125
Celery Vase ... 25
green/blue ... 35
Compotes ... 25 - 50
green/blue ... 40 - 85
Creamer or Spooner ... 35
green/blue ... 45
Cruet ... 70
green/blue ... 95
Decanter ... 90
green/blue ... 150
Jelly Compote ... 35
green/blue ... 45
Pitcher ... 175
green/blue ... 250
Punch Bowl ... 200
green/blue ... 375
Punch Cup ... 15
green/blue ... 25
Shakers, ea., scarce ... 40
green/blue ... 65
Sugar ... 45
green/blue ... 60
Toothpick Holder ... 45
green/blue ... 65
Tray ... 50
green/blue ... 70
Tumbler ... 25
green/blue ... 40
Wine ... 25
green/blue ... 35
*Add 10% for gold decorated.

STAG & HOLLY
(FENTON)
Bowl, ftd., large, very scarce
amber ... 250
green/blue ... 75
red ... 200

STAR
Butter, very rare ... 350
amber ... 400
vaseline ... 450

STAR & CRESCENT
Berry Bowl, lg. ... 35
Berry Bowl, sm. ... 10
Butter ... 50
Creamer or Spooner ... 20
Cruet ... 55
Pickle Dish ... 15
Pitcher ... 65
Shakers, ea. ... 15
Sugar ... 25
Tumbler ... 10

STAR & DIAMOND
Bottle w/Stopper, 6"
vaseline ... 100

STAR & FILE
Bowl, 7" ... 20
Bowl, square ... 20
Butter ... 65
Celery Vase ... 35
Compote ... 40
Cordial ... 25
Creamer or Sugar ... 25
Custard Cup ... 15
Decanter ... 55
Ice Cream, stemmed ... 20
Juice Tumbler ... 15
Milk Pitcher ... 75
Pitcher ... 95
Relish, hndl. ... 25
Rose Bowl ... 50
Saucer ... 20
Tumbler ... 20
Wine ... 25

STAR & IVY
Cup ... 10
amber ... 15
green/blue ... 20
Plate, lg. ... 25
amber ... 30
green/blue ... 40
Saucer ... 10
amber ... 15
green/blue ... 20

STAR & NOTCHED RIB
Butter ... 50
Creamer or Spooner ... 20
Cruet ... 55
Pitcher ... 75
Shakers, ea. ... 15
Sugar ... 25
Tumbler ... 20

STAR & PUNTY
Cologne Bottle ... 60
Creamer ... 25
Lamp ... 95
Pitcher ... 85
Sugar ... 35

STAR & RIB
Butter ... 55
vaseline ... 95
Compote ... 65
vaseline ... 110
Creamer or Spooner ... 30
vaseline ... 45
Pitcher ... 80
vaseline ... 175
Shakers, ea. ... 15
vaseline ... 55
Sugar ... 25
vaseline ... 85
Tumbler ... 20
vaseline ... 35

STAR & THUMBPRINT
Bowls, various ... 40 - 70
Butter ... 95
Creamer or Spooner ... 50
Lamp ... 180
Pitcher ... 140
Spill Holder ... 50
Sugar ... 60
Tumbler ... 35
*All pieces rare.

STAR BAND
Berry Bowl, lg. ... 30
Berry Bowl, sm. ... 10
Butter ... 60
Celery Vase ... 25
Creamer, Spooner or Sugar ... 20
Pitcher ... 70
Tumbler ... 20

STARFLAKE & FAN
Bowl, 8½" ... 50
Compote ... 65

STAR IN BULL'S-EYE
Berry Bowl, lg. ... 35
Berry Bowl, sm. ... 10
Butter ... 50
Cake Stand ... 75
Celery Vase ... 25
Compote, covered ... 60
Compote, open, low ... 30
Creamer or Spooner ... 35
Cruet ... 60
Diamond-shaped Dish ... 20
Goblet ... 35
Nappy w/Advertising ... 60
Pitcher ... 70
Sugar ... 50
Toothpick Holder,
double or single ... 60 - 30
Tumbler ... 30
Wine ... 20

STAR OCTAD
Compote, stemmed ... 35
Pickle Dish ... 30
Salt Shaker ... 45

STAR OF DAVID
Berry Bowl, lg. ... 40
Berry Bowl, sm. ... 15
Butter ... 60
Compote ... 35
Creamer or Spooner ... 20
Cruet ... 45
Goblet ... 35
Hair Receiver ... 30
Pickle Tray ... 20
Pitcher ... 85
Sugar ... 25
Tumbler ... 20

STARRED HORSESHOE
Tumbler ... 25
Tumbler, with band ... 30

STARRED LOOP
Bowl ... 30
Cup ... 15
Pickle Tray ... 25
Pitcher ... 60
Shakers, ea. ... 20
Tumbler ... 15
Wine ... 20

STARRED SCROLL
Biscuit Jar ... 45
Bowl ... 35
Butter ... 70
Celery Vase ... 20
Creamer or Spooner ... 30
Cruet ... 50
Decanter ... 65
Goblet ... 35
Pitcher ... 90
Rose Bowl ... 30
Shakers, ea. ... 15
Sugar ... 35
Syrup ... 60
Tumbler ... 20

STAR ROSETTED
Bowl, 7" - 9", 2 styles ... 15 - 25
amber ... 20 - 30
vaseline ... 25 - 40
green/blue ... 35 - 60
Bread Plate ... 35
amber ... 40
vaseline ... 45
green/blue ... 55
Butter ... 45
amber ... 55
vaseline ... 75
green/blue ... 85
Compote, covered ... 50 - 70
amber ... 55 - 80
vaseline ... 65 - 85
green/blue ... 75 - 95

Compote, open 30 - 45
amber 35 - 50
vaseline 40 - 55
green/blue 45 - 65
Creamer or Spooner 35
amber 40
vaseline 45
green/blue 50
Goblet 40
amber 50
vaseline 60
green/blue 65
Pickle Dish 15
amber 20
vaseline 25
green/blue 30
Pitcher 85
amber 100
vaseline 160
green/blue 175
Plate 25
amber 30
vaseline 35
green/blue 40
Relish Tray 15
amber 20
vaseline 25
green/blue 30
Sauce 15
amber 20
vaseline 25
green/blue 30
Sugar 55
amber 60
vaseline 65
green/blue 70
Wine 40
amber 45
vaseline 50
green/blue 60

STARRY NIGHT
Bowl, 8" - 9½" 45

STARS & BARS
Butter 45
amber 55
green/blue 50
Creamer or Spooner 20
amber 30
green/blue 30
Jam Jar 35
amber 45
green/blue 40
Night Lamp 75
amber 85
green/blue 80
Pitcher 80
amber 95
green/blue 90
Tray 40
amber 50
green/blue 45
Tumbler 20
amber 30
green/blue 30
Shakers, ea 15
amber 30
green/blue 30
Sugar 25
amber 45
green/blue 40

STARS & BARS WITH LEAF
Butter 60
vaseline 80
Creamer or Spooner 35
vaseline 45
Pitcher 60
vaseline 115
Sugar 40
vaseline 55
Toy Table Set, complete 80
vaseline 100
Tumbler 20
vaseline 30

STARS & STRIPES (BRILLIANT)
Berry Bowl, lg 20
Berry Bowl, sm 45
Butter 65
Creamer or Spooner 20
Cup 10
Pitcher 85
Sauce 10
Shakers, ea 25
Sugar 25
Toy Table Service 100
Tumbler 20
Vase 20

THE STATES
Bowl, 9¼" 50
Butter 75
Celery Tray 30
Celery Vase 45
Compote, open, 2 sizes 40 - 80
Creamer or Spooner 40
Cup 15
Goblet 50
Ice Bucket 75
Nappy, 3 hndl. 40
Plate 40
Punch Bowl, w/base 185
Relish 25
Shakers, ea 30
Sugar 30 - 50
Syrup 85
Toothpick Holder, 2 kinds 50
Tray 35
Tumbler 40
Wine 40

STELLAR (SQUARED SUNBURST)
Berry Bowl, lg 35
Berry Bowl, sm 15
Butter 60
Celery Dish 25
Compote 35
Creamer, Spooner or Sugar 25 - 30
Pickle Dish 25
Pitcher 75
Tumbler 20

STERLING
Berry Bowl, lg 25
ruby stain 60
Berry Bowl, sm 10
ruby stain 25
Butter 50
ruby stain 80
Compote 35
ruby stain 55
Creamer or Spooner 20
ruby stain 30
Goblet 35
ruby stain 50
Pitcher 85
ruby stain 120
Punch Bowl 135
ruby stain 225
Punch Cup 10
ruby stain 15
Sugar 30
ruby stain 40
Toy Table Set 85
ruby stain 135
Tumbler 15
ruby stain 25
Wine 10
ruby stain 25

STIPPLED BAR
Butter 55
Creamer or Spooner 20
Plate 25
Pitcher 80
Sugar 30
Tumbler 15

STIPPLED CHAIN
Berry Bowl, sm 20
Berry Bowl, lg 45
Butter 55
Cake Stand 35
Celery Vase 25
Creamer or Spooner 25
Dish, oval 20
Egg Cup 15
Goblet 50
Pickle Tray 25
Pitcher 85
Relish Dish 15
Salt Dip, master 20
Sugar 30
Tumbler 20

STIPPLED CHAIN VT. (WITH CAT HANDLE)
Butter, rare 325
Creamer or Spooner, rare 100
Sugar, rare 175

STIPPLED CHERRY
Berry Bowl, lg 50
Berry Bowl, sm 20
Bread Plate, 9" 35
Butter 75
Creamer or Spooner 25
Pitcher 90
Plate, 6" 25
Sugar 35
Tumbler 25

STIPPLED DAISY
Butter, covered 60
Celery Vase 25
Compote, open 35
Creamer or Spooner 20
Pitcher 70
Relish 20
Sauce 15
Sugar w/Lid 25
Sugar, open 20
Tumbler 20
Wine 15

STIPPLED DART & BALLS
Bowls, various 20 - 35
Butter 60
Celery 25
Creamer or Spooner 30
Goblet 35
Pitcher 70
Relish Dish 25
Sugar 35
Syrup 55
Tumbler 20
Wine 15

STIPPLED FANS
Berry Bowl, lg 35
Berry Bowl, sm 20
Butter 55
Creamer 25
Pitcher 65
Spooner 25
Sugar 30
Tumbler 15

STIPPLED FORGET-ME-NOT
Bowl, 7" - 8" 40 - 65
Butter 120
Cake Stand, 9" - 12" 100 - 240
Celery Vase 80
Compote, covered, 6" - 8" 95 - 135
Compote, open, 6" - 8" 40 - 70
Creamer or Spooner 70
Cup 30
Dish, oval 30 - 50
Goblet 75
Milk Pitcher 120
Mug, toy 75

Mug, lg. ... 50
Oil Lamp ... 135
Pitcher ... 160
Plate, 6" & 7", baby face or star .. 75 - 30
Plate, 8" & 9", kitten or star ...... 40 - 110
Plate, plain, 8" ... 35
Relish, oval ... 25
Salt, master ... 60
Sauce, flat or ftd. ... 10
Sugar ... 80
Syrup ... 155
Toothpick Holder ... 135
Toy Set, butter & creamer ... 300
Tumbler ... 60
Waste Bowl ... 45
Water Tray ... 95
Wine ... 65

STIPPLED FORGET-ME-NOT WITH KITTEN
Plate, scarce ... 75

STIPPLED LEAF
Syrup ... 85

STIPPLED LEAF, FLOWER & MOTH
Butter ... 125
Creamer or Spooner ... 45
Decanter ... 140
Pitcher ... 300
Sugar ... 60
Tumbler ... 30

STIPPLED MEDALLION
Butter ... 55
Cake Plate ... 30
Compote, low ... 35
Creamer or Spooner ... 15
Egg Cup ... 15
Goblet ... 40
Plate ... 20
Sauce ... 10
Sugar ... 25

STIPPLED PEPPERS
Butter ... 65
Creamer or Spooner ... 25
Egg Cup ... 20
Pitcher ... 85
Salt, ftd. ... 20
Sauce ... 10
Sugar ... 35
Tumbler, ftd. ... 15

STIPPLED SANDBUR
Berry Bowl, lg. ... 35
Berry Bowl, sm. ... 10
Butter ... 45
Celery Vase ... 20
Compote, covered ... 40
Creamer or Spooner ... 20
Goblet ... 35
Pickle Jar ... 25
Pitcher ... 70
Sugar ... 25
Toothpick Holder ... 15
Tumbler ... 15
Wine ... 10

STORK & RUSHES (DUGAN)
Basket, handled, very scarce ... 75
Pitcher, scarce ... 200
Punch Bowl w/Base, very scarce 375
Punch Cup, very scarce ... 25
Tumbler, scarce ... 50

STOVE SHAKER
Shakers, ea. ... 95
vaseline ... 125

STRAWBERRY (NORTHWOOD)
Bowl, very scarce ... 200
Plate, rare ... 325

STRAWBERRY & CABLE
Berry Bowl, lg. ... 40
Berry Bowl, sm. ... 20
Butter ... 65
Creamer or Spooner ... 25
Goblet ... 25
Pitcher ... 80
Shakers, ea. ... 25
Sugar ... 30
Sweetmeat w/Lid, 2 styles ... 95
Tumbler ... 20
Wine ... 15

STRAWBERRY & CURRANT
Butter ... 100
Celery Vase ... 65
Cheese Dish w/Lid ... 125
Compote, covered, low & high . 120 - 165
Creamer or Spooner ... 50
Goblet ... 60
Milk Pitcher ... 65
Mug ... 70
Pitcher ... 80
Sauce, ftd. ... 10
Sugar ... 80
Syrup ... 165
Tumbler ... 35

STRAWBERRY & PEAR
Mug ... 15
amber ... 25
vaseline ... 50
green/blue ... 35

STRAWBERRY DIAMOND
Goblet ... 35
vaseline ... 70
Ice Bowl ... 45
vaseline ... 75
Pitcher ... 85
vaseline ... 175
Toothpick Holder ... 45
vaseline ... 85
Tray ... 60
vaseline ... 100
Tumbler ... 20
vaseline ... 50
Wine ... 20
vaseline ... 40
green/blue ... 55

STRIGIL
Berry Bowl, lg. ... 30
Berry Bowl, sm. ... 10
Butter ... 45
Celery Vase ... 15
Compote ... 30
Creamer or Spooner ... 15
Creamer, tankard size ... 25
chocolate ... 90
Egg Cup ... 20
Goblet ... 35
Pitcher ... 65
Sugar ... 20
Tumbler ... 10
Wine ... 15

STUDIO
Butter ... 65
Creamer or Spooner ... 25
Hair Receiver ... 40
Sugar ... 35

STUMP
Toothpick Holder ... 75
amber ... 110
green/blue ... 155

SULTAN
Lamp (bracket)
decorated opaque ... 325

SUMMIT (X-BULL'S-EYE)
Berry Bowl, lg. ... 40
Berry Bowl, sm. ... 15
Butter ... 55
Compote ... 30
Creamer or Spooner ... 20
Pitcher ... 75
Shakers, ea. ... 20
Sugar ... 25
Tumbler ... 20
Wine ... 15

SUNBEAM
Berry Bowl, lg. ... 45
green/blue ... 55
Berry Bowl, sm. ... 20
green/blue ... 25
Butter ... 65
green/blue ... 80
Carafe ... 35
green/blue ... 55
Celery Vase ... 25
green/blue ... 30
Creamer or Spooner ... 25
green/blue ... 30
Cruet ... 60
green/blue ... 75
Jelly Compote ... 30
green/blue ... 40
Pickle Dish ... 20
green/blue ... 30
Pitcher ... 95
green/blue ... 120
Sauce ... 15
green/blue ... 20
Shakers, ea. ... 20
green/blue ... 30
Sugar ... 30
green/blue ... 35
Syrup ... 55
green/blue ... 65
Toothpick Holder ... 20
green/blue ... 40
Tumbler ... 20
green/blue ... 25

SUNBURST
Butter ... 55
Cake Stand ... 30
Celery Vase ... 20
Compotes, various ... 20 - 55
Cordial ... 15
Creamer or Spooner ... 20
Egg Cup ... 15
Pitcher ... 75
Plates, various ... 15 - 35
Shakers, ea. ... 15
Sugar ... 25
Tumbler ... 20
Wine ... 15

SUNBURST (HEISEY)
*Condensed list.
Bowl, lg. ... 40
Bowl, sm. ... 20
Butter ... 60
Compotes, various sizes ... 25 - 50
Creamer, Spooner or Sugar ... 30
Cruet ... 50
Dessert ... 30
Oval Tray ... 35
Pitcher ... 70
Punch Bowl w/Base ... 125
Punch Cup ... 20
Salt Shakers, pr. ... 60
Tumbler ... 30

SUNBURST ON SHIELD (DIADEM)
Bowl ... 40
Breakfast Set ... 45
Butter ... 60
Celery Tray ... 25
Creamer or Spooner ... 20
Cruet ... 70
Pickle Tray ... 20
Pitcher ... 85
Shakers, ea. ... 20
Sugar ... 35
Tumbler ... 20

SUNFLOWER
Berry Bowl, lg. ... 45
amber ... 55
milk glass ... 65
Berry Bowl, sm. ... 20

amber 25
milk glass.... 40
Butter 55
amber 75
milk glass 125
Creamer or Spooner....25
amber 35
milk glass 60
Pitcher....85
amber 100
milk glass 150
Sugar....30
amber 45
milk glass 70
Tumbler....20
amber 30
milk glass.... 50

SUNK DAISY
Butter 60
Carafe.... 35
Compote.... 40
Cracker Jar 45
Creamer or Spooner.... 20
Goblet 40
Pitcher.... 75
Shakers, ea.... 15
Sugar 30
Toothpick Holder 20
Tumbler.... 20
Wine 15

SUNK DIAMOND & LATTICE
Bowl.... 30
Butter.... 65
Celery Vase.... 25
Compote.... 35
Creamer 25
Goblet 30
Pitcher.... 65
Plate 30
Spooner 25
Sugar.... 30
Tumbler.... 15

SUNKEN PRIMROSE
*Condensed list.
Banana Bowl....35
green/blue 45
ruby stain 65
Berry Bowl, lg....30
green/blue 35
ruby stain 45
Berry Bowl, sm....10
green/blue 15
ruby stain 20
Butter 65
green/blue 75
ruby stain 85
Compote....40
green/blue 45
ruby stain 55
Creamer or Spooner....30
green/blue 35
ruby stain 40
Lamp....70
green/blue 80
ruby stain 95
Pitcher....100
green/blue 120
ruby stain 145
Relish....20
green/blue 25
ruby stain 30
Salt Shaker....35
green/blue 40
ruby stain 50
Sugar....45
green/blue 50
ruby stain 60
Toothpick 45
green/blue 50
ruby stain 60
Tumbler....20
green/blue 30
ruby stain 35

SUNKEN TEARDROP
Berry Bowl, lg.... 35
Berry Bowl, sm.... 20
Butter 50
Creamer 25
Goblet 30
Pickle Dish 25
Pitcher.... 65
Shakers, ea.... 25
Spooner 25
Sugar 30
Tumbler.... 20
Wine 20

SUNK HONEYCOMB
Berry Bowl, lg.... 30
ruby stain 45
Berry Bowl, sm.... 10
ruby stain 15
Butter 50
ruby stain 80
Creamer or Spooner.... 25
ruby stain 35
Cruet 60
ruby stain 85
Decanter.... 45
ruby stain 60
Individual Creamer or Sugar.... 20
ruby stain 35
Jelly Compote.... 25
ruby stain 45
Mug.... 35
ruby stain 60
Shakers, ea.... 20
ruby stain 30
Sugar.... 35
ruby stain 50
Toothpick Holder.... 35
ruby stain 65
Wine 25
ruby stain 35

SUNK JEWEL
Celery Tray.... 30
Nappy 25
Pitcher.... 70
Tumbler.... 15

SUPERB DRAPE
Vase, lg., with ruffled top, rare.... 300

SURPRISE
Bowl, sq., 7", rare 65
Plate, 6", rare.... 50
Plate, 8", rare.... 80

SWAG WITH BRACKETS
Butter 165
Compote.... 55
Creamer or Spooner.... 90
Cruet.... 165
Pitcher.... 225
Salt Shaker.... 65
Sugar 150
Toothpick Holder (Age ?).... 100
Tumbler.... 55

SWAN
Compote, covered.... 100
Goblet 50

SWAN (BRYCE BROTHERS)
Mug....45
amber 55
milk glass 65

SWAN & EGRET
Mug.... 65

SWAN NAPPY
One Shape, 4½".... 75

SWAN ON POND
Butter 60
amber 70
green/blue 90
Creamer or Spooner....25
amber 35
green/blue 45
Goblet....35
amber 45
green/blue 60
Pitcher....85
amber 100
green/blue 145
Sugar....35
amber 45
green/blue 60
Tumbler....20
amber 30
green/blue 40

SWAN WITH MESH
Butter....150
vaseline 250
Compote, covered....110
vaseline 250
Creamer or Spooner....70
vaseline 125
Goblet 85
vaseline 150
Pitcher....280
vaseline 400
Tumbler.... 85
Sauce 25
vaseline 45
Sugar....165
vaseline 225
Wine 90
vaseline 125

SWAN WITH RING HANDLE
Mug....60
amber 75
green/blue 80
pink alabaster 100
Mug, advertising,
very scarce.... 125

SWAN WITH TREE
Bowl, dome based, rare.... 220
Goblet 120
Pitcher.... 350

SWEET SIXTY-ONE
Butter 75
ruby stain 125
Compote.... 50
ruby stain 75
Creamer 35
ruby stain 45
Pitcher.... 95
ruby stain 135
Spooner 30
ruby stain 45
Sugar.... 45
ruby stain 60
Tumbler.... 15
ruby stain 25

SWIRL & BALL (BEATTY & SONS)
Mug.... 50

SWIRL & BALL (McKEE)
Butter.... 75
Cake Stand 40
Candlesticks, ea.... 30
Celery Vase.... 20
Child's Mug.... 30
Cordial Set.... 95
Creamer or Spooner.... 20
Jelly, ftd.... 25
Plate, 6".... 20
Shakers, ea.... 20
Sugar.... 30
Syrup.... 65

SWIRL & CABLE
Bowls, various .... 25 - 40
Creamer, 2 sizes.... 30 - 40
Honey Dish 55

Jelly Compote 30
Mug 45
Pitcher, 2 sizes .... 70 - 85

SWIRLED COLUMN
Bowl, covered, ftd., 5" - 9" .... 25 - 45
green/blue .... 35 - 55
Bowls, flat or ftd., 5" - 9" .... 15 - 35
green/blue .... 20 - 45
Butter 70
green/blue 85
Cake Stand 45
green/blue 55
Celery, various .... 20 - 35
green/blue .... 25 - 45
Compote, open 45
green/blue 60
Compote, covered 65
green/blue 75
Creamer or Spooner 30
green/blue 40
Cruet 65
green/blue 75
Cup 15
green/blue 20
Egg Cup 30
green/blue 35
Goblet 40
green/blue 45
Mug 35
green/blue 45
Nappy, 5 sizes .... 25 - 45
green/blue .... 30 - 55
Plate 25
green/blue 35
Pitcher 95
green/blue 135
Salt Shakers, ea. 30
green/blue 35
Sugar Shaker 50
green/blue 60
Sugar 35
green/blue 40
Sugar Shaker 40
green/blue 50
Syrup 65
green/blue 80
Tumbler 25
green/blue 30
Wine 20
green/blue 25

SWIRL-STEM HOBSTAR
Vase, 11" 45

SWIRL HOBNAIL (MILLERSBURG)
Spittoon, very rare 1,500
amethyst 2,500

SWIRLED STAR
Berry Bowl, lg. 35
Berry Bowl, sm. 20
Butter 50
Creamer or Spooner 20
Sugar 25
Wine 20

SWORD
Novelty Pickle Dish 95

SYDNEY
Bowl, 6" - 8" 25
Butter 70
Celery Vase 35
Compote, open 40
Compote w/Lid 60
Creamer or Spooner 20
Pickle Dish, 6" - 9" 15
Pitcher 100
Shakers, ea 15
Sugar 40
Tumbler 15

SWORD & CIRCLE
Berry Bowl, sm. 15
Custard Dish 15

Tumbler 25
Tumbler, Juice 20

TACOMA
Banana Dish 55
ruby stain 130
Bowls, various .... 20 - 90
ruby stain .... 35 - 100
Butter 70
ruby stain 165
Cake Stand, 2 sizes .... 70 - 90
ruby stain .... 235 - 295
Celery Tray 25
ruby stain 65
Celery Vase 50
ruby stain 120
Compote, open, various .... 35 - 70
ruby stain .... 80 - 200
Cracker Jar 120
ruby stain 320
Creamer or Spooner 35
ruby stain 95
Cruet, 2 sizes .... 45 - 50
ruby stain .... 185 - 195
Decanter 100
ruby stain 285
Dish, oblong .... 20 - 30
ruby stain .... 100 - 120
Goblet 40
ruby stain 95
Pickle Jar w/Lid 100
ruby stain 200
Pitcher, 2 styles 90
ruby stain 240
Plate 20
ruby stain 35
Punch Bowl,
flat or w/base 100
ruby stain 250
Punch Cup 15
ruby stain 30
Salt, ind. 10
ruby stain 30
Salt, master 20
ruby stain 60
Sauce 10
ruby stain 20
Shaker, 2 styles 35
ruby stain 100
Sugar 50
ruby stain 155
Syrup 120
ruby stain 300
Toothpick Holder 30
ruby stain 200
Tumbler 25
ruby stain 70
Vase, 4 sizes, 2 styles .... 35 - 70
Water bottle 75
ruby stain 200
Wine 25
ruby stain 50

TANDEM DIAMONDS & THUMBPRINTS
Butter 75
Creamer or Spooner 25
Goblet 50
Pitcher 95
Sugar 35
Tumbler 20

TAPE MEASURE
Butter 70
Creamer or Spooner 20
Goblet 50
Pitcher 80
Sauce 10
Sugar 30
Tumbler 20

TAPPAN
Child's Table Set, complete 100
amber 150

TARENTUM'S LADDER WITH DIAMONDS
Berry Bowl, lg. 25
ruby stain 40
Berry Bowl, sm. 10
ruby stain 25
Butter 40
ruby stain 65
Creamer or Spooner 25
ruby stain 40
Pitcher 60
ruby stain 85
Sugar 30
ruby stain 45
Tumbler 15
ruby stain 20

TARENTUM'S MANHATTAN
Berry Bowl, lg. 30
Berry Bowl, sm. 10
Butter 65
Cake Stand 35
Compote, open 35
Creamer or Spooner 25
Cruet 70
Goblet 25
Oval Dish 20
Plates, 6" & 8" 20
Shaker 40
Sugar 30
Syrup 65
Tumbler 15

TARENTUM'S VICTORIA (QUESTION MARK)
Berry Bowl, lg. 30
amber 40
vaseline 55
green/blue 45
Berry Bowl, sm. 15
amber 25
vaseline 35
green/blue 30
Butter 55
amber 70
vaseline 85
green/blue 75
Celery Dish 25
amber 30
vaseline 40
green/blue 35
Compotes, various .... 25 - 40
amber .... 40 - 55
vaseline .... 55 - 70
green/blue .... 50 - 60
Creamer 25
amber 30
vaseline 40
green/blue 35
Cruet 50
amber 65
vaseline 80
green/blue 70
Dresser Tray 35
amber 45
vaseline 60
green/blue 50
Goblet 25
amber 35
vaseline 50
green/blue 40
Pickle Dish 20
amber 25
vaseline 35
green/blue 30
Pitcher 65
amber 75
vaseline 100
green/blue 85
Shakers, ea. 25
amber 30
vaseline 40
green/blue 35

Spooner ... 25
amber ... 30
vaseline ... 35
green/blue ... 30
Sugar ... 30
amber ... 35
vaseline ... 45
green/blue ... 40
Tumbler ... 15
amber ... 20
vaseline ... 30
green/blue ... 25

TARENTUM'S VIRGINIA
*Condensed list.
Berry Bowl, lg. ... 35
Berry Bowl, sm. ... 10
Butter ... 50
Celery Tray ... 20
Celery Vase ... 25
Compote ... 35
Cordial ... 15
Creamer or Spooner ... 20
Cruet ... 60
Egg Cup ... 15
Goblet ... 35
Jam Jar ... 25
Mustard Pot ... 25
Pickle Tray ... 15
Pitcher ... 70
Shakers, ea. ... 15
Sugar ... 25
Syrup ... 40
Tumbler ... 15
Wine ... 10

TARGET
Vase ... 30
sapphire ... 150

TEARDROP
Bowls, rectangular ... 15 - 40
Bowls, sq. ... 20 - 45
Butter ... 55
Candlesticks, ea. ... 25
Compote ... 35
Creamer or Spooner ... 20
Cruet ... 45
Goblet ... 50
Pickle Dish ... 15
Pitcher ... 65
Sugar ... 25
Tumbler ... 10
Wine ... 10

TEARDROP & TASSEL
Bowl, lg. ... 75
green/blue ... 170
Nile green ... 700
Bowl, sm. ... 65
green/blue ... 155
chocolate ... 200
Butter ... 85
amber ... 300
green/blue ... 240
chocolate ... 900
Celery Vase ... 45
Compote, open, 7½" ... 55
green/blue ... 300
teal ... 125
Compote, covered, 4½" - 7½" ... 80 - 165
green/blue ... 400 - 500
Nile green ... 300
Creamer or Spooner ... 55
amber ... 195
green/blue ... 175
chocolate ... 500
Goblet ... 90
green/blue ... 250
teal ... 95
Pitcher ... 100
amber ... 300
green/blue ... 245
Nile green ... 1,000
Relish, oval ... 65
amber ... 150
green/blue ... 190
Nile green ... 550
Salt Shaker ... 135
amber ... 295
Nile green ... 900
Sugar ... 90
amber ... 225
green/blue ... 200
chocolate ... 1,000
Tumbler ... 75
green/blue ... 180
Nile green ... 400
Wine, (2 varieties
from "Greentown") ... 150 - 200
green/blue ... 75
teal ... 120
green/blue ... 165 - 300
Nile green ... 325 - 400

TEARDROP FLOWER (NORTHWOOD)
Berry Bowl, lg. ... 30
green/blue ... 45
amethyst ... 45
Berry Bowl, sm. ... 15
green/blue ... 25
amethyst ... 25
Butter ... 70
green/blue ... 95
amethyst ... 90
Creamer ... 25
green/blue ... 40
amethyst ... 40
Cruet ... 65
green/blue ... 85
amethyst ... 80
Pitcher ... 75
green/blue ... 125
amethyst ... 110
Shakers, ea. ... 30
green/blue ... 55
amethyst ... 55
Spooner ... 25
green/blue ... 35
amethyst ... 35
Sugar ... 35
green/blue ... 45
amethyst ... 40
Tumbler ... 15
green/blue ... 25
amethyst ... 25

TEASEL
Berry Bowl, lg. ... 45
Berry Bowl, sm. ... 20
Bowl, Pedestal, 2 sizes ... 30 - 45
Butter ... 75
Cake Stand ... 35
Celery Vase ... 30
Compote ... 40
Creamer or Spooner ... 25
Cracker Jar ... 40
Cruet ... 65
Goblet, 3 types ... 40 - 60
Honey Jar, covered ... 55
Pitcher ... 100
Plate, 7" - 9" ... 35
Shakers, ea. ... 30
Sugar ... 35
Toothpick Holder ... 40
Tumbler ... 25

TEN-POINTED STAR
Berry Bowl, lg. ... 45
Berry Bowl, sm. ... 10
Bowls, ice cream shape ... 10 - 45
Butter ... 60
Cake Salver, stemmed ... 40
Compotes, 2 sizes ... 30 - 45
Compotier, 8" ... 55
Creamer or Spooner ... 25
Cruet ... 60
Milk Pitcher ... 45
Pickle Dish, rnd. or sq. ... 15
Pitcher ... 80
Plate ... 20
Plate, sq., 7½" ... 15
Sugar ... 30
Tumbler ... 20
Vase, 12" ... 25

TEN-POINTED STAR VARIANT
Milk Pitcher ... 55
Plate ... 30

TEPEE
Berry Bowl, lg. ... 50
ruby stain ... 90
Berry Bowl, sm. ... 20
ruby stain ... 55
Butter ... 60
ruby stain ... 135
Cheese Dish w/Lid ... 85
ruby stain ... 150
Creamer or Spooner ... 30
ruby stain ... 65
Cup ... 15
ruby stain ... 40
Goblet ... 40
ruby stain ... 95
Jelly Compote ... 35
ruby stain ... 60
Jelly, hndl ... 30
ruby stain ... 45
Plate ... 25
ruby stain ... 45
Shakers, ea. ... 30
ruby stain ... 70
Sugar ... 40
ruby stain ... 85
Syrup ... 80
ruby stain ... 165
Toothpick Holder ... 40
green/blue ... 165
ruby stain ... 80
Tumbler, 4 sizes ... 20 - 40
ruby stain ... 55 - 110
Water Bottle ... 70
ruby stain ... 185
Wine ... 20
ruby stain ... 65

TERRAPIN
Novelty Dish ... 85

TERRESTRIAL GLOBE
Covered Bowl on Stem, rare ... 3,500

TEUTONIC
Bowls, various ... 15 - 35
vaseline ... 25 - 55
Butter ... 45
vaseline ... 65
Celery ... 25
vaseline ... 35
Creamer or Spooner ... 25
vaseline ... 35
Goblet ... 30
vaseline ... 45
Pickle Dish ... 25
vaseline ... 35
Pitcher ... 65
vaseline ... 95
Shakers, ea. ... 25
vaseline ... 35
Sugar ... 30
vaseline ... 45
Syrup ... 55
vaseline ... 70
Tumbler ... 20
vaseline ... 30

TEXAS
Bowl, covered, 6" - 8" ... 90 - 155
ruby stain ... 185 - 265

Bowl, open, 6" - 9" ..... 55 - 80
ruby stain ..... 90 - 140
Bread Tray 80
ruby stain 175
Butter 140
ruby stain 285
Cake Stand, 9" - 11" ..... 125 - 300
ruby stain ..... 300 - 500
Celery Tray 45
ruby stain 75
Celery Vase 100
ruby stain 225
Compote, covered, 6" - 8" ..... 225 - 300
ruby stain ..... 350 - 475
Compote, open, 7½" - 9½" ..... 90 - 120
ruby stain ..... 200 - 325
Creamer, 2 sizes ..... 30 - 100
ruby stain ..... 50 - 225
Cruet 150
ruby stain 350
Goblet 100
ruby stain 235
Horseradish, covered 100
ruby stain 285
Olive Dish 20
ruby stain 40
Pickle Tray 35
ruby stain 90
Plate 65
ruby stain 150
Pitcher, 2 styles ..... 200 - 350
ruby stain ..... 425 - 650
Relish Tray 15
ruby stain 50
Salt Dip, master 100
ruby stain 200
Sauce, flat or ftd. 15
ruby stain 35
Shaker, hotel 100
ruby stain 225
Shakers, ea. 90
ruby stain 185
Spooner 95
ruby stain 235
Sugar, 2 sizes ..... 40 - 100
ruby stain ..... 60 - 200
Syrup 235
ruby stain 500
Toothpick Holder 45
ruby stain 150
Tumbler 85
ruby stain 160
Vase, 6½" - 10" ..... 30 - 60
ruby stain ..... 60 - 90
Water Bottle 165
ruby stain 300
Wine 60
ruby stain 140

TEXAS CENTENNIAL (AKA: ALAMO)
Butter, very rare 350
Coaster 80
Creamer 75
Pitcher 225
Plate 90
Sugar 90
Tumbler 50
*All prices scarce to very rare.

TEXAS STAR
Berry Bowl, lg. 45
Berry Bowl, sm. 10
Pitcher 75
Shakers, ea. 20
Tumbler 15

TEXAS START (SNOWFLAKE BASE)
Butter 60
Creamer or Spooner 20
Pitcher 80
Sauce 10
Shakers, ea. 20
Sugar 40
Tumbler 20

THEODORE ROOSEVELT
Platter 185

THIN RIB (NORTHWOOD)
Vase, 9" - 17" ..... 25 - 125

THIS LITTLE PIG WENT TO MARKET
Nursery Rhyme Plate 50

THISTLE
Berry Bowl, lg. 300
Berry Bowl, sm. 210
Butter 255
Cake Stand 235
Compote, covered, 6" - 8" ..... 200 - 300
Compote, open, 6" - 8" ..... 90 - 140
Cordial 85
Creamer or Spooner 100
Dish, oval 60
Egg Cup 90
Goblet 130
Milk Pitcher 225
Pickle Dish 40
Pitcher 300
Plate, lg. 95
Relish Tray 55
Salt, master 80
Sugar 145
Syrup 300
Tumbler, flat or ftd. ..... 80 - 135
Wine 125

THISTLEBLOW (PANELLED IRIS)
Berry Bowl, lg. 30
Berry Bowl, sm. 15
Berry Creamer & Sugar ..... 20 - 25
Butter 45
Celery Dish 20
Jelly, stemmed 35
Nappy 20
Pickle Dish 20
Pitcher 55
Punch Cup 15
Spooner 25
Sundae, stemmed 15
Sugar 25
Tumbler 15
Wine 20

THONGED STAR (IMPERIAL)
Berry Bowl, 5½" 15
Berry Bowl, 2 handled 15
Bowl, olive 15
Butter 35
Compote, 5" 20
Individual Creamer 15
Individual Sugar 15
Nappy, 6" round 20
Pickle Dish, oval with handle 20
Spoon Tray, oval 25
Vase, 6" 25

THOUSAND EYE
ABC Plate 45
amber 60
vaseline 75
green/blue 60
Bowl, 5" - 8" ..... 50 - 65
amber 70
vaseline 80
green/blue 70
Butter 70
amber 95
vaseline 165
green/blue 125
Cake Stand 40
amber 60
vaseline 125
green/blue 100
Celery Vase, 2 shapes 40
amber 50
vaseline 75
green/blue 50
Christmas Light 35
amber 40
vaseline 65
green/blue 45
Cologne 30
amber 40
vaseline 60
green/blue 45
Compote, high, 6" - 10" ..... 45 - 65
amber ..... 50 - 80
vaseline ..... 65 - 90
green/blue ..... 65 - 80
Compote, low, 8" 35
green/blue 135
Creamer or Spooner 30
amber 40
vaseline 70
green/blue 40
Cruet 95
amber 120
vaseline 175
green/blue 125
Dish, sq., 5" - 10" ..... 30 - 55
amber ..... 35 - 60
vaseline ..... 40 - 75
green/blue ..... 35 - 60
Egg Cup 50
amber 60
vaseline 100
green/blue 80
Goblet 45
amber 55
vaseline 75
green/blue 60
Honey Dish 75
amber 80
vaseline 100
green/blue 85
Ink Well 35
amber 70
vaseline 125
green/blue 90
Jelly Glass 20
amber 30
vaseline 45
green/blue 30
Lamp, 12" - 15" ..... 190 - 230
amber ..... 235 - 300
vaseline ..... 475 - 675
green/blue ..... 400 - 600
Milk Pitcher 90
amber 125
vaseline 165
green/blue 125
Mug, 2 sizes 25
amber 40
vaseline 65
green/blue 45
Pickle Dish 20
amber 25
vaseline 40
green/blue 30
Pitcher, 4 sizes ..... 75 - 110
amber ..... 85 - 125
vaseline ..... 135 - 225
green/blue ..... 95 - 165
Plate, 6" - 10" 30
amber 35
vaseline 50
green/blue 35
Platter 40
amber 45
vaseline 65
green/blue 45
Salt Dip, ind. 40
amber 50
vaseline 95
green/blue 75
Salt Dip, master 60

amber 50
vaseline 95
green/blue 75
Sauce 10
amber 15
vaseline 25
green/blue 20
String Holder 130
amber 175
vaseline 95
green/blue 165
Sugar 50
amber 55
vaseline 85
green/blue 75
Syrup 110
amber 125
vaseline 225
green/blue 165
Toothpick Holder, 3 types .... 20 - 35
amber .... 35 - 55
vaseline .... 75 - 95
green/blue .... 70 - 90
Tumbler 25
amber 50
vaseline 70
green/blue 60
Water Tray 60
amber 75
vaseline 95
green/blue 70
Wine 25
amber 30
vaseline 40
green/blue 35

THOUSAND EYE WITH FAN
Compote, stemmed
vaseline 110

THREADING
Butter 65
Celery Vase 20
Compote, open 35
Compote, covered 60
Creamer or Spooner 20
Goblet 30
Pitcher 90
Sauce 10
Sugar 25
Tumbler 15
Wine 10

THREE BIRDS
Pitcher, scarce 275

THREE DOLPHINS
Match Holder 60
amber 80
green/blue 95

THREE FACE
Biscuit Jar 3500
Butter 235
Cake Stand, 9" - 11" .... 350 - 500
Celery Vase, 2 styles .... 185 - 245
Champagne, solid stem 350
Champagne, solid stem w/saucer .. 1,800
Champagne, hollow stem, very rare. 4,200
Compote, covered, high, 7" - 9",
plain rim .... 250 - 675
*Compote, covered,
w/bidded rim .... 1,200 - 2,200
Compote, covered, low, 6" 950
Compote, open, high, 7" - 10",
plain rim .... 125 - 600
*Compote, open, w/bidded rim.. 1,000 - 2,800
Compote, open, low, 6" 300
Cordial 280
Creamer, with or without "face" . 150 - 250
Goblet 165
Jam Jar 300
Jelly Compote, huber panelled,
*ext. rare) 4,000
Milk Pitcher 2,250
Oil Lamps, several sizes,
plain & etched .... 350 - 1,200
Pitcher 1,000
Salt Dip, ind. 45
Sauce 45
Salt Shaker 65
Spooner 100
Sugar 190
Wine 290
*For decorated pieces add 10%.

THREE FRUITS (NORTHWOOD)
Bowl 75
Plate 125

THREE GRACES
Plate, 11½", rare 350

THREE-IN-ONE
Berry Bowl, lg. 30
ruby stain 65
Berry Bowl, sm. 15
ruby stain 25
Bowl, ftd., 6" - 7" 35
Bowl, ftd., 8" - 9" 20
Biscuit Jar 60
Butter 80
ruby stain 110
Cake Stand 55
Candlesticks, ea. 40
Carafe 60
Ketchup Cruet 90
Celery Vase 35
ruby stain 45
Compote, covered, 3 sizes 40
Creamer, spooner or sugar 25
ruby stain 40
Cruet 75
Fruit Compote 45
Goblet 25
Jelly Compote 30
Milk Jar, covered 85
ruby stain 95
Nappy 25
Pickle Dish, 7", 8" & 9" 25
Pickle Jar 35
ruby stain 60
Pitcher 165
Punch Bowl 325
Punch Cup 20
Shakers, ea. 30
Shot Glass 25
Syrup 65
Toothpick Holder 40
Tumbler 25
Vase, stemmed, 3 sizes 40
Whiskey Decanter 100
Wine Decanter 85
Wine Goblet 15

THREE PANEL
Bowl, 8½" - 10" .... 20 - 30
amber .... 25 - 35
vaseline .... 35 - 50
green/blue .... 30 - 45
Butter, 2 styles .... 75 - 100
amber .... 80 - 110
vaseline .... 100 - 140
green/blue .... 100 - 130
Celery Vase, 2 styles 40
amber 50
vaseline 80
green/blue 65
Compote, open, 7" - 10" .... 30 - 55
amber .... 45 - 65
vaseline .... 55 - 95
green/blue .... 50 - 80
Creamer or Spooner 25
amber 35
vaseline 50
green/blue 35
Cruet 125
amber 165
vaseline 255
green/blue 235
Goblet 35
amber 40
vaseline 60
green/blue 45
Milk Pitcher 70
amber 90
vaseline 130
green/blue 115
Mug, 2 sizes .... 20 - 30
amber .... 25 - 35
vaseline .... 35 - 50
green/blue .... 30 - 40
Pitcher 55
amber 75
vaseline 95
green/blue 80
Sauce 10
amber 15
vaseline 20
green/blue 25
Sugar 60
amber 60
vaseline 100
green/blue 80
Tumbler 30
amber 40
vaseline 60
green/blue 50

THREE PRESIDENTS
Goblet, rare 275

THUMBPRINT WINDOWS
Butter 65
Creamer 30
Spooner 30
Sugar 35

TIDAL (AKA: FLORIDA PALM)
Berry Bowl, lg. 30
Berry Bowl, sm. 15
Berry Bowl, lg., square 35
Berry Bowl, sm., square 20
Bowls, oval, various .... 15 - 45
Butter 60
Castor Set, complete 95
Celery Vase 25
Goblet 30
Pickle Dish 20
Pitcher 70
Plate 30
Spooner 25
Sugar 30
Tumbler 20
Wine 20

TIDY
Butter 65
Celery Vase 25
Compote 40
Creamer or Spooner 25
Goblet 55
Pitcher 95
Sugar 35
Tumbler 20
Wine 15

TILE (OPTICAL CUBE)
*Condensed list.
Bread Tray 30
Butter 60
Cake Stand 35
Celery Vase 20
Celery Tray 25
Compote, covered 45
Compote, open 30
Cordial 15
Creamer or Spooner 20
Cruet 50
Decanter 40
Goblet 45

Olive Dish 15
Pickle Dish 20
Pickle Jar 35
Pitcher 75
Shakers, ea 15
Sugar 25
Tumbler 15
Wine 15

TIPTOE (RAMONA)
Berry Bowl, lg. 30
Berry Bowl, sm. 10
Butter 45
Celery Vase 20
Compote 30
Creamer or Spooner 15
Pickle Dish 15
Shakers, ea 15
Sugar 20
Toothpick Holder 25

TOGO
Berry Bowl, lg. 35
ruby stain 45
Berry Bowl, sm. 10
ruby stain 20
Bowl, ftd., 7" 25
ruby stain 35
Bowl, ftd., 9" 30
ruby stain 40
Breakfast Set, 2 pcs. 40
ruby stain 60
Butter 60
ruby stain 90
Celery Tray 30
Creamer or Spooner 20
ruby stain 35
Cruet 55
ruby stain 85
Jelly Compote 25
ruby stain 35
Olive Dish, leaf shape 20
ruby stain 30
Pitcher, 2 styles 85
ruby stain 145
Plate, sq., 5" 15
ruby stain 30
Sugar 25
ruby stain 45
Tumbler 15
ruby stain 30

TOKYO
Berry Bowl, lg. 25
vaseline 35
green/blue 40
Berry Bowl, sm. 10
vaseline 15
green/blue 20
Butter 45
vaseline 75
green/blue 90
Compote 25
vaseline 40
green/blue 50
Creamer or Spooner 20
vaseline 30
green/blue 35
Donut Stand 35
vaseline 60
green/blue 75
Pitcher 75
vaseline 110
green/blue 135
Plate 25
vaseline 30
green/blue 35
Shakers, ea 20
vaseline 25
green/blue 30
Sugar 35
vaseline 45
green/blue 60
Syrup 45
vaseline 70
green/blue 85
Toothpick Holder 35
vaseline 50
green/blue 60
Tumbler 15
vaseline 25
green/blue 30
Vase 20
vaseline 35
green/blue 40

TOLTEC
Bar Sugar 25
ruby stain 30
Berry Bowl, lg. 30
ruby stain 35
Berry Bowl, sm. 15
ruby stain 20
Bowl, 8" flared 25
ruby stain 30
Butter 55
ruby stain 65
Celery, tall 25
ruby stain 30
Champagne Tumbler 25
ruby stain 30
Claret 20
ruby stain 25
Compote, lg. 40
ruby stain 50
Compote, sm. 25
ruby stain 30
Creamer, 2 sizes .... 20 - 25
ruby stain .... 25 - 30
Custard cup 15
ruby stain 20
Finger Bowl 20
ruby stain 25
Goblet 30
ruby stain 35
Jelly Bowl, 6" oval 25
ruby stain 30
Milk Pitcher 45
ruby stain 55
Nappy, handled 25
ruby stain 30
Oil Cruet 45
ruby stain 60
Pitcher 70
ruby stain 85
Plate, 9" 30
ruby stain 35
Shakers, ea 25
ruby stain 35
Sherbet 20
ruby stain 30
Spooner, 2 sizes .... 20 - 25
ruby stain 25
Spoon Tray 25
ruby stain .... 25 - 35
Sugar, covered 30
ruby stain 30
Sugar, open 25
ruby stain 35
Straw Jar, flat, 10½"x 4½" 60
ruby stain 75
Tankard Pitcher 75
ruby stain 85
Toothpick 30
ruby stain 35
Tumbler 20
ruby stain 25
Water Bottle 45
ruby stain 50
Whiskey Tumbler 25
ruby stain 30
Wine 15
ruby stain 20

TORPEDO
Banana Stand 340
Bowl, covered, 4" - 10" .... 75 - 100
ruby stain .... 110 - 200
Bowl, open, 4" - 10" .... 50 - 60
ruby stain .... 80 - 100
Butter 90
ruby stain 200
Cake Stand 160
Celery Vase 40
ruby stain 80
Compote, covered, 3 sizes .... 90 - 140
Compote, open, 3 sizes .... 40 - 60
Creamer or Spooner 70
ruby stain 80
Cruet 155
Cup & Saucer 60
ruby stain 75
Decanter 100
ruby stain 235
Finger Bowl 35
Goblet 60
ruby stain 90
Jelly Compote, open 45
Jam Jar 50
ruby stain 110
Lamp, 2 styles .... 85 - 120
Milk Pitcher, 2 sizes .... 90 - 155
ruby stain .... 125 - 235
Pickle Castor 140
ruby stain 250
Pitcher 135
ruby stain 235
Rose Bowl 75
Salt, ind. 30
ruby stain 50
Salt, master 65
ruby stain 80
Sauce 15
ruby stain 30
Shakers, ea 70
ruby stain 100
Sugar 90
ruby stain 140
Syrup 135
ruby stain 240
Tray, 10" - 12" .... 100 - 200
Tumbler 60
ruby stain 80
Wine 100
ruby stain 200

TOURING CAR
Candy Container 50

TREE
Butter 75
Creamer or Spooner 30
Pitcher 125
Sugar 35
Toothpick Holder 30
Tumbler 25

TREE BARK
Berry Bowl, lg. 25
Berry Bowl, sm. 10
Butter 40
Creamer or Spooner 20
Pitcher 45
Sugar 25
Tumbler 10

TREE OF LIFE
Bowls, oval or rnd. .... 40 - 60
Butter 165
Celery Vase 115
Champagne 125
Claret 110
Compote, covered 235
Compote, open, high or low .... 100 - 200
Creamer or Spooner 80
Epergne 500

Goblet ... 95
Milk Pitcher ... 200
Mug ... 100
Pitcher, applied hndl. & pressed hndl. ... 100 - 300
Plate, rnd. ... 60
Salt, master ... 40
Sauce ... 15
Sauce, leaf shape ... 10
Sugar ... 125
Toothpick Holder ... 75
Tumbler ... 75
Vases, several sizes ... 75 - 100
Water Tray ... 130
Wine ... 100
*For all colors double prices of crystal.

TREE OF LIFE WITH HAND (HOBBS)
Bowls, various sizes & shapes ... 50 - 75
vaseline ... 165 - 285
green/blue ... 195 - 375
Bouquet Vase ... 350
vaseline ... 500
green/blue ... 695
Butter ... 135
vaseline ... 250
green/blue ... 275
Cake Stand ... 300
vaseline ... 390
green/blue ... 450
Compote, 4" - 10" ... 40 - 85
vaseline ... 60 - 110
green/blue ... 100 - 200
Marine Green ... 200 - 350
Creamer or Spooner ... 70
vaseline ... 110
green/blue ... 150
Epergne, 2 sizes ... 325 - 400
vaseline ... 450 - 700
green/blue ... 550 - 800
Lamp, 3 sizes ... 135 - 295
vaseline ... 150 - 315
green/blue ... 250 - 575
Sugar ... 90
vaseline ... 150
green/blue ... 200
*All prices listed are for plain base.
*Add 50% for hand base/stem pieces.

TREE OF LOVE
Bowl ... 25
Butter or Cheese Dish ... 75
Compote ... 40
Creamer or Spooner ... 25
Cup ... 20
Plate, ruffled ... 30
Sugar ... 35

TREE STUMP
Bowl, covered, ftd. ... 65
Compote, covered, stemmed ... 90
Sauce, ftd. ... 20

TREE TRUNK
Vase, standard ... 30
sapphire ... 150
Vase, mid size funeral ... 100

TREFOIL FINECUT
Bowl, ruffled, rare ... 275
Bowl, ice cream shape, rare ... 350
Bowl, rnd., flared, rare ... 325
Plate, very rare ... 1,200

TRIPLE BAR & LOOP
Berry Bowl, lg. ... 25
Berry Bowl, sm. ... 10
Butter ... 45
Creamer or Spooner ... 25
Goblet ... 30
Pitcher ... 65
Sugar ... 30
Tumbler ... 15
Wine ... 10

TRIPLE THUMBPRINTS
Berry Bowl, lg. ... 45
Berry Bowl, sm. ... 15
Butter ... 85
Creamer or Spooner ... 25
Pitcher ... 125
Shakers, ea. ... 25
Sugar ... 40
Tumbler ... 30

TRIPLE TRIANGLE (U.S.GLASS & DOYLE & CO.)
Bowl, 6" - 10" ... 20 - 40
ruby stain ... 50 - 100
Bread Plate ... 35
ruby stain ... 80
Butter ... 55
ruby stain ... 100
Creamer or Spooner ... 35
ruby stain ... 70
Cup ... 20
ruby stain ... 45
Goblet ... 35
ruby stain ... 70
Mug ... 30
ruby stain ... 50
Pitcher ... 75
ruby stain ... 200
Sugar ... 50
ruby stain ... 135
Tumbler ... 25
ruby stain ... 60
Wine ... 20
ruby stain ... 50

TRIPOD STEM (ARCHED TRIPOD)
Butter ... 75
Celery Vase ... 25
Creamer or Spooner ... 30
Goblet ... 60
Pitcher ... 135
Sugar ... 40
Tumbler ... 30
Wine ... 20

TROPICAL VILLA
Compote, covered ... 165

TROUGH
Novelty Trough, 4 footed ... 35
green/blue ... 75

TROUT & FLY (MILLERSBURG)
Bowl, rare ... 600
Bowl, 2 sides up, very rare ... 800
Plate, very rare ... 1,400

TRUNCATED CUBE
Berry Bowl, lg. ... 45
ruby stain ... 80
Berry Bowl, sm. ... 15
ruby stain ... 20
Butter ... 70
ruby stain ... 125
Celery Vase ... 35
ruby stain ... 75
Creamer or Spooner ... 30
ruby stain ... 75
Cruet ... 60
ruby stain ... 120
Decanter ... 65
ruby stain ... 200
Goblet ... 45
ruby stain ... 80
Milk Pitcher ... 50
ruby stain ... 120
Pitcher ... 60
ruby stain ... 160
Sauce ... 15
ruby stain ... 25
Shakers ea. ... 25
ruby stain ... 60
Sugar ... 45
ruby stain ... 80
Syrup, 2 sizes ... 55 - 70
ruby stain ... 125 - 165
Toothpick Holder ... 30
ruby stain ... 70
Tumbler ... 25
ruby stain ... 50
Water Tray ... 35
ruby stain ... 65
Wine ... 20
ruby stain ... 40

TULIP
Butter ... 60
Celery Vase ... 25
Compote, high or low ... 30 - 50
Creamer or Spooner ... 20
Decanter ... 50
Goblet ... 45
Jug, pint ... 35
Jug, quart ... 50
Pitcher ... 85
Sugar ... 25
Tumbler ... 20
Wine ... 15

TULIP WITH SAWTOOTH
Barber Bottle ... 55
Butter ... 80
Celery Vase ... 40
Champagne ... 40
Compote, covered, 6" - 8" ... 125 - 165
Compote, open, 6" - 9" ... 60 - 85
Creamer or Spooner ... 75
Cruet ... 85
Decanter ... 100
Goblet ... 45
Honey Dish ... 15
Milk Pitcher ... 120
Pitcher ... 100
Plate, 6" ... 30
Salt, master, either edge ... 25
Sugar ... 50
Tumbler ... 40
Wine ... 30
*Nonflint pieces only.
*For olors double crystal prices.

TWENTIETH CENTURY
Berry Bowl, lg. ... 30
ruby stain ... 45
Berry Bowl, sm. ... 15
ruby stain ... 25
Butter ... 55
ruby stain ... 70
Celery Dish ... 20
ruby stain ... 30
Compote, open, lg. ... 40
ruby stain ... 60
Creamer ... 25
ruby stain ... 35
Cruet ... 60
ruby stain ... 75
Goblet ... 30
ruby stain ... 40
Jelly Compote ... 25
ruby stain ... 30
Pickle Dish ... 20
ruby stain ... 25
Pitcher ... 70
ruby stain ... 85
Spooner ... 25
ruby stain ... 35
Sugar ... 30
ruby stain ... 40
Tumbler ... 20
ruby stain ... 25
Wine ... 20
ruby stain ... 25

TWIGS (BEAUTY BUD)
Vase ... 25

TWIN CORNUCOPIA
Vase ... 100
amber ... 175

vaseline ... 200

TWIN CRESCENTS
- Butter ... 50
- Creamer or Spooner ... 20
- Pomade Jar ... 30
- Sugar ... 25

TWINKLE STAR (UTAH)
- Bowl, covered, 6" - 8" ... 25 - 50
- Bowl, open, 6" - 8" ... 15 - 35
- Butter, 2 sizes ... 40 - 55
- Cake Plate ... 25
- Cake Stand, 8" - 10" ... 35
- Celery Vase ... 20
- Compote, covered ... 45
- Compote, open ... 35
- Condiment Set, 3 pcs. ... 75
- Creamer or Spooner ... 20
- Cruet ... 60
- Goblet ... 45
- Pickle Tray ... 15
- Pitcher ... 80
- Sauce ... 10
- Shakers, ea. ... 15
- Sugar ... 25
- Syrup ... 60
- Tumbler ... 20
- Wine ... 10

TWINS (HORSESHOE CURVE)
- Berry Bowl, lg. ... 30
- Berry Bowl, sm. ... 10
- Bowl, 6½" ... 15
- Bowl, 10" ... 35
- Pitcher ... 65
- Plate, 7½" ... 35
- Rose Bowl, 7" ... 40
- Tumbler ... 15

TWIN SNOWSHOES
- Butter ... 65
- Cake Stand ... 35
- Celery Vase ... 20
- Compotes, various ... 20 - 55
- Creamer or Spooner ... 20
- Cruet ... 60
- Cup ... 10
- Pitcher ... 100
- Relish ... 15
- Relish, hndl. ... 20
- Sugar ... 30
- Toothpick Holder ... 25
- Toy Table Set ... 125
- Tumbler ... 25
- Wine ... 10

*For gilded pieces add 10%.

TWIN TEARDROPS
- Banana Stand, 2 sided turned up ... 50
- Bowl, 6" ... 15
- Butter ... 55
- Celery ... 25
- Cruet ... 65
- Goblet ... 40
- Jelly Compote ... 40
- Pitcher ... 75
- Plate, sq, 8" ... 35
- Plate, rnd, 10" ... 35
- Sauce ... 15
- Sugar ... 25
- Tumbler ... 15

TWISTED RIB
- Vase, 9" - 13" ... 25
- Vase, 7" squat whimsey, rare
  - amethyst ... 100

TWO BAND
- Butter ... 45
- Celery Vase ... 20
- Compote ... 30
- Compote, low, covered w/hndls. ... 45
- Creamer or Spooner ... 20
- Pickle Dish ... 15
- Pitcher ... 75
- Plate, hndl. ... 25
- Shakers, ea. ... 15
- Sugar ... 25
- Toy Table Set, complete ... 85
- Tumbler ... 15

TWO OWLS
- Compote, covered, lg. ... 250

TWO PANEL
- Bowls, 7" - 9" ... 20 - 45
  - amber ... 25 - 50
  - vaseline ... 30 - 55
  - green/blue ... 35 - 60
- Butter ... 60
  - amber ... 70
  - vaseline ... 100
  - green/blue ... 100
- Celery Vase ... 35
  - amber ... 55
  - vaseline ... 75
  - green/blue ... 65
- Compote, covered ... 70 - 90
  - amber ... 75 - 95
  - vaseline ... 130 - 165
  - green/blue ... 100 - 120
- Creamer or Spooner ... 25
  - amber ... 30
  - vaseline ... 45
  - green/blue ... 55
- Goblet ... 40
  - amber ... 45
  - vaseline ... 60
  - green/blue ... 55
- Jam Jar w/Lid ... 60
  - amber ... 80
  - vaseline ... 165
  - green/blue ... 140
- Milk Pitcher ... 50
  - amber ... 60
  - vaseline ... 130
  - green/blue ... 100
- Mug ... 30
  - amber ... 40
  - vaseline ... 50
  - green/blue ... 55
- Oil Lamp, tall, 3 sizes ... 80 - 100
  - amber ... 100 - 140
  - vaseline ... 160 - 225
  - green/blue ... 120 - 170
- Oil Lamp, finger style ... 701
  - amber ... 100
  - vaseline ... 165
  - green/blue ... 130
- Pitcher ... 70
  - amber ... 80
  - vaseline ... 165
  - green/blue ... 125
- Salt, ind. ... 30
  - amber ... 20
  - vaseline ... 35
  - green/blue ... 40
- Salt, master ... 25
  - amber ... 30
  - vaseline ... 50
  - green/blue ... 30
- Shakers, ea. ... 65
  - amber ... 85
  - vaseline ... 135
  - green/blue ... 110
- Tray, hndl. ... 80
  - amber ... 110
  - vaseline ... 165
  - green/blue ... 125
- Tumbler ... 35
  - amber ... 30
  - vaseline ... 75
  - green/blue ... 65
- Wine ... 20
  - amber ... 25
  - vaseline ... 35
  - green/blue ... 40

TWO POST
- Oil Lamp, 2 variations ... 175 - 225

U.S. COIN
- Ale Glass ... 335
  - frosted ... 500
- Bowl, covered, 6" - 9" ... 350 - 1,500
  - frosted ... 600 - 2,000
- Bowl, open, 6" - 9", various rims ... 300 - 1,000
  - frosted ... 325 - 1,300
- Butter ... 425
  - frosted ... 800
- Cake Stand ... 400
  - frosted ... 575
- Compote, covered, various ... 350 - 2,000
  - frosted ... 450 - 3,500
- Compote, open, various ... 300 - 900
  - frosted ... 375 - 1,200
- Celery Vase ... 250
  - frosted ... 400
- Champagne ... 2,000
  - frosted ... 4,000
- Claret ... 500
  - frosted ... 750
- Creamer ... 275
  - frosted ... 475
- Cruet ... 700
  - frosted ... 900
- Goblet ... 500
  - frosted ... 625
- Jam Dish w/Lid ... 175
  - frosted ... 275
- Milk Pitcher ... 600
  - frosted ... 850
- Mug ... 400
  - frosted ... 700
- Oil Lamps,
  - many shapes and sizes ... 400 - 725
  - frosted ... 400 - 900
- Pickle Dish ... 150
  - frosted ... 200
- Pitcher ... 700
  - frosted ... 1350
- Shakers, ea. ... 195
  - frosted ... 285
- Spooner ... 185
  - frosted ... 300
- Sugar ... 35
  - frosted ... 425
- Syrup ... 725
  - frosted ... 1,100
- Toothpick Holder ... 100
  - frosted ... 175
- Tray ... 475
  - frosted ... 750
- Tumbler; dollar or dimes in
  - base ... 125 - 300
  - frosted ... 150 - 350
- Waste Bowl ... 450
  - frosted ... 525
- Wine ... 500
  - frosted ... 700

U.S. GLASS #25,
(AKA, "LATE CRYSTAL")
- Berry Bowl, lg. ... 35
- Berry Bowl, sm. ... 15
- Butter ... 60
- Celery ... 20
- Compote, tall ... 45
- Compote, short ... 40
- Creamer, Spooner or Sugar ... 25
- Egg Cup ... 30
- Pitcher ... 75
- Sauce ... 15
- Shakers, ea. ... 25
- Tumbler ... 20
- Vase ... 30

U.S. GLASS #16046
- Vase ... 50

Price Guide

U. S. GLASS CROSS
Lettered Ashtray 100
U.S. GLASS LATE BLOCK
Berry Bowl, lg. 25
ruby stain 35
Berry Bowl, sm. 10
ruby stain 15
Bowls, various sizes & shapes 15 - 35
ruby stain 20 - 45
Butter 60
ruby stain 70
Celery Boat 25
ruby stain 35
Creamer 25
ruby stain 35
Cruet 60
ruby stain 75
Handled Relish 25
ruby stain 30
Horseradish Bottle 45
ruby stain 60
Ice Tub 65
ruby stain 80
Jelly Compote 30
ruby stain 40
Lamp 145
ruby stain 165
Mustard Pot 35
ruby stain 50
Pickle Dish 25
ruby stain 30
Pitcher 75
ruby stain 90
Punch Bowl w/Base 165
ruby stain 185
Punch Cup 10
ruby stain 15
Rose Bowls, various 15 - 35
ruby stain 20 - 40
Shakers, ea. 25
ruby stain 30
Spooner 35
ruby stain 45
Sugar Shaker 45
ruby stain 55
Sugar 40
ruby stain 50
Syrup 55
ruby stain 65
Water Bottle 45
ruby stain 50
U.S. GRANT-PATRIOT & SOLDIER
Plate, 11", sq. 85
U.S. LADY
Paperweight, frosted crystal 250
U.S. NURSERY RHYME
Butter 65
Creamer or Spooner 25
Pitcher 70
Sugar 35
Tumbler 20
U.S. REGAL
Basket 40
ruby stain 55
Berry Bowl, lg. 25
ruby stain 35
Berry Bowl, sm. 10
ruby stain 20
Butter 60
ruby stain 70
Creamer or Spooner 25
ruby stain 35
Decanter 55
ruby stain 65
Pitcher 80
ruby stain 90
Punch Bowl 110
ruby stain 130
Punch Cup 15
ruby stain 20
Sugar 35
ruby stain 45
Sugar Shaker 45
ruby stain 55
Toothpick Holder 40
ruby stain 55
Tumbler 15
ruby stain 25
Wine 10
ruby stain 20
U.S. RIB #15061
Berry Bowl, lg. 30
green/blue 45
Berry Bowl, sm. 15
green/blue 25
Butter 50
green/blue 75
Cake Stand 40
green/blue 55
Celery Tray 20
green/blue 30
Celery Vase 25
green/blue 30
Compote 35
green/blue 45
Creamer, Spooner or Sugar 20
green/blue 35
Desert 15
green/blue 25
Goblet 25
green/blue 45
Pickle Dish 20
green/blue 30
Pitcher 60
green/blue 80
Tumbler 20
green/blue 30
Wine 20
green/blue 25
*Add 10% for gold trimmed crystal pieces.
U.S. SHERATON
Berry Bowl, lg. 45
Berry Bowl, sm. 20
Bowls, ftd. 20 - 40
Butter 65
Creamer or Spooner 25
Cruet 45
Dresser Set, 3 pcs. 70
Jam Jar 30
Mayonnaise Plate 25
Miniature Lamp 65
Mustard Jar 25
Pin tray 20
Pitcher, 2 styles 70 - 95
Plate, sq. 20
Ring Stand 30
Sardine Tray 25
Shakers, ea. 20
Sugar 30
Sundae Dish 20
Syrup 55
Tea Tumbler 20
Toothpick Holder 20
Trinket Tray 30
Tumbler 25
U.S. WICKER EDGE
Compote 40
Fruit Bowl 35
UTOPIA OPTIC
Berry Bowl, lg. 30
ruby stain 45
Berry Bowl, sm. 15
ruby stain 25
Butter 55
ruby stain 70
Creamer or Spooner 25
ruby stain 40
Pitcher 65
ruby stain 80
Sugar 30
ruby stain 45
Tumbler 15
ruby stain 25
*For gilded add 10%.
VALENCIA WAFFLE
Berry Bowl, lg. 35
amber 40
vaseline 60
green/blue 55
Berry Bowl, sm. 15
amber 20
vaseline 25
green/blue 30
Bread Plate 30
amber 35
vaseline 60
green/blue 55
Butter 55
amber 60
vaseline 80
green/blue 90
Cake Stand 90
amber 100
vaseline 180
green/blue 200
Castor Set 130
amber 200
vaseline 350
green/blue 300
Celery Vase 35
amber 35
vaseline 55
green/blue 60
Compote, covered, high or low 70 - 100
amber 80 - 120
vaseline 100 - 130
green/blue 120 - 140
Compote, open, high 35 - 70
amber 40 - 85
vaseline 50 - 120
green/blue 55 - 130
Dish, oblong, 7" - 9" 20 - 35
amber 25 - 40
vaseline 25 - 50
green/blue 30 - 60
Goblet 40
amber 55
vaseline 70
green/blue 65
Milk Pitcher 70
amber 65
vaseline 140
green/blue 160
Pickle Dish 20
amber 25
vaseline 30
green/blue 35
Pickle Jar w/Lid 100
amber 130
vaseline 185
green/blue 200
Pitcher 95
amber 110
vaseline 200
green/blue 225
Relish Dish 20
amber 30
vaseline 35
green/blue 40
Salt Dip 20
amber 25
vaseline 60
green/blue 65
Sauce, flat or ftd. 10
amber 15
vaseline 20
green/blue 20

Shakers ea. 25
amber 35
vaseline 60
green/blue 55
Sugar 40
amber 50
vaseline 70
green/blue 75
Syrup 90
amber 110
vaseline 200
green/blue 175
Tumbler 20
amber 30
vaseline 50
green/blue 55
Water Tray 40
amber 40
vaseline 80
green/blue 60
VALENTINE (NORTHWOOD)
Berry Bowl, lg.. 45
Berry Bowl, sm.. 15
Bowl, square, 9", scarce 65
Bowl, 10" 50
Plate, 11" 85
VALENTINE (U.S. GLASS)
Butter 125
ruby stain 145
Cologne Bottle 100
ruby stain 130
Creamer or Spooner 65
ruby stain 80
Goblet 75
ruby stain 85
Pitcher 200
ruby stain 245
Sugar 75
ruby stain 90
Toothpick Holder 65
ruby stain 75
Tumbler 25
ruby stain 40
Wall Pocket Vase 85
ruby stain 95
VALTEC
Berry Bowl, lg.. 25
Berry Bowl, sm.. 10
Butter 45
Celery Vase 25
Cracker Bowl 25
Creamer or Spooner 25
Cruet 55
Pitcher 80
Plate 30
Sugar 30
Syrup 65
Tumbler 15
Vase 25
VEGETABLES
Relish Tray 65
VENETIAN
Berry Bowl, lg.. 50
Berry Bowl, sm.. 20
Breakfast Creamer & Sugar .... 25 - 30
Butter 85
Compote, 3½", 6 sided base 50
Compote, 6" 65
Compote, 9" squat 75
Creamer or Spooner 55
Lamp w/Shade 350
Giant Vase (rose bowl) 100
Pickle Dish, deep 40
Pitcher 180
Punch Bowl & Base, rare 300
Punch Cup, stemmed 30
Rose Bowl, 6" 75
Sherbet, hndl. 75
Spittoon Whimsey 120
Sugar 65
Tumbler 40
Vase, 6" 60
Vase, 9" 75
Vase, cylinder shape, scarce 80
VENICE
Berry Bowl, lg..40
amber 45
vaseline 55
Berry Bowl, sm..15
amber 20
vaseline 25
Butter 55
amber 65
vaseline 135
Creamer or Spooner 20
amber 25
vaseline 45
Goblet 45
amber 55
vaseline 65
Pickle Jar 25
amber 30
vaseline 35
Pitcher 85
amber 150
vaseline 225
green/blue 165
Sugar 30
amber 35
vaseline 60
Tumbler 20
amber 25
vaseline 45
green/blue 40
Tray 40
amber 65
vaseline 85
*Add 10% for etched pieces.
VENUS
Butter 85
Celery Vase 20
Compote, covered, 8" 65
Creamer or Spooner 35
Pitcher 125
Plate, crying baby 70
Shakers, ea. 25
Sugar 40
Tumbler 35
VERTICAL LEAF & RIB
Bowls, various .... 25 - 50
vaseline .... 35 - 60
Butter 60
vaseline 80
Cake Stand 45
vaseline 60
Compote 40
vaseline 55
Creamer or Spooner 30
vaseline 40
Pitcher 70
vaseline 125
Sugar 45
vaseline 60
Tumbler 20
vaseline 30
VICTORIA (RIVERSIDE)
Berry Bowl, lg.. 40
ruby stain 135
Berry Bowl, sm.. 15
ruby stain 25
Butter 80
ruby stain 250
Cake Stand 100
ruby stain 550
Celery Vase 40
ruby stain 225
Compote, 2 sizes .... 50 - 70
ruby stain ....150 - 300
Creamer or Spooner 30
ruby stain 135
Creamer, ind. 20
ruby stain 145
Cruet 70
ruby stain 385
Jelly 25
ruby stain 150
Pickle Dish 30
ruby stain 70
Pitcher 100
ruby stain 325
Sauce 15
ruby stain 40
Sugar 45
ruby stain 165
Syrup 90
ruby stain 525
Toothpick Holder 40
ruby stain 385
Tumbler 25
ruby stain 90
*Add 15% for amber stained pieces.
VICTORIAN LADY
Compote, very scarce 350
VIKING
Apothecary Jar 100
Bowl, covered, 8" - 9" .... 150 - 200
Bread Platter 80
Butter 100
Casserole w/Lid 250
Celery Vase 80
Compote, covered, high,
7" - 9" .... 130 - 290
Compote, covered, low, 9" 250
Creamer or Spooner 70
Cup, ftd. 75
Egg Cup 60
Epergne, 4 lily,
very rare 1,200
Jam Jar 160
Mug 200
Pickle Dish 50
Pitcher 200
Relish Tray 35
Salt, master, ftd. 60
Sugar 85
Vase, rare 125
V-IN-HEART
Banana Bowl, stemmed 45
Butter 50
Compote, 6" 25
Creamer or Spooner 20
Fruit Bowl 25
Pitcher 65
Sugar 30
Tumbler 15
VINTAGE BANDED (DUGAN)
Mug, very scarce
lime green 75
VIOLET BOUQUET (VERRE D' OR)
Bowl
green/blue 125
amethyst 135
Plate, 9"
green/blue 165
amethyst 175
VOLUNTEER
Plate, rare 450
WADING HERON
Pickle Jar w/Lid 95
green/blue 115
Pitcher 250
green/blue 335
Tumbler 55
green/blue 85
WAFFLE & BAR
Berry Bowl, lg.. 40
Berry Bowl, sm.. 20

Butter 55
Carafe 30
Celery Vase, flat or ftd 25
Cheese Dish, covered 60
Creamer or Spooner 20
Cruet 45
Ice Cream Tray 25
Sugar 25
Sugar Shaker 35
Tray, 7" - 8" 25

WAFFLE & STAR BAND
Butter 50
ruby stain 65
Compote 30
ruby stain 50
Creamer or Spooner 20
ruby stain 30
Nappy 25
ruby stain 35
Pickle Dish 20
ruby stain 30
Punch Bowl 95
ruby stain 150
Punch Cup 15
ruby stain 20
Rose Bowl 35
ruby stain 45
Sugar 25
ruby stain 40
Toothpick Holder 40
ruby stain 55
*Add 10% for gold trimmed crystal pieces.

WAFFLE BLOCK WITH ROSE CENTER
Square Bowl 25

WAFFLE WINDOW
Shakers, ea 30

WARRIOR (CONQUISTADOR)
Lamp, etched crystal, rare 650

WASHINGTON CENTENNIAL
Bowl, rnd., 7" - 9" .... 40 - 60
Bowl, oval, 7" - 9" .... 40 - 60
Butter, flat or ftd. .... 100 - 195
Cake Stand, 8½"x10' .... 70 - 100
Celery Vase 80
Champagne 190
Compote, covered, 7" - 8" .... 250 - 325
Compote, open, 7" - 10" .... 50 - 100
Creamer 120
Egg Cup, ftd 50
Goblet 80
Milk Pitcher 200
Pickle Dish, fish shape 35
Pitcher 280
Platter, lettered, 3 various .... 80 - 100
Salt, ind. 20
Salt, master 60
Sauce 15
Shakers, ea 100
Spooner 50
Sugar 100
Syrup 245
Wine 70

WASHINGTON HATCHET (LIBBEY)
Novelty 65
ruby stain 95

WATERFORD
Butter 70
Celery Vase 30
Creamer or Spooner 25
Double Relish 30
Goblet 45
Pickle Dish 25
Sugar 45

WATERLILY & CATTAILS (FENTON)
Bonbon 35
sapphire 75
Oval Footed Bowl, very scarce 125

WATERLILY & CATTAILS (NORTHWOOD)
Pitcher 90
green/blue 120
sapphire 150
Tumbler 25
green/blue 35
sapphire 45

WAVING QUILL (DUGAN)
Pitcher
green/blue 300
Tumbler
green/blue 40

WEBSTER FONT LAMP
Oil Lamp 125
vaseline 275
green/blue 200

WEDDING BELLS
Bowl, various shapes and sizes... 30 - 50
ruby stain .... 90 - 120
Butter 60
ruby stain 135
Celery Vase 25
ruby stain 70
Compote, covered, low or high.. 60 - 100
ruby stain .... 200 - 260
Creamer, applied handle 50
ruby stain 100
Cruet 65
ruby stain 200
Decanter 85
ruby stain 200
Pitcher, 2 styles .... 80 - 100
ruby stain .... 165 - 230
Punch Bowl, flat 235
ruby stain 675
Relish Tray 25
ruby stain 60
Shakers, ea 40
ruby stain 100
Sherbet 20
ruby stain 40
Spooner 50
ruby stain 95
Sugar 65
ruby stain 135
Syrup 135
ruby stain 400
Toothpick Holder 55
ruby stain 125
Tumbler 35
ruby stain 75
Whiskey glass 25
ruby stain 55
*Prices under ruby stained are for rose blush.

WEDDING DAY & AFTER
Plate
amber 100

WEDDING RING
Butter 245
Celery Vase 255
Champagne 200
Creamer, pressed & applied handles .... 85 - 200
Decanter, bar lip & w/stopper . 180 - 300
Finger Lamp 85
Goblet 135
Lamp, tall finger style 365
Pitcher, applied handle, rare 1,000
Spooner 100
Sugar 135
Syrup 300
Tumbler, 2 styles .... 80 - 120
Wine 65

WELLINGTON
Berry Bowl, lg 30
ruby stain 35
Berry Bowl, sm. 10
ruby stain 15
Butter 70
ruby stain 90
Creamer or Spooner 20
ruby stain 30
Goblet 25
ruby stain 45
Pickle Dish 15
ruby stain 25
Pitcher 80
ruby stain 130
Sugar 25
ruby stain 45
Tumbler 15
ruby stain 25
Wine 15
ruby stain 25

WELLSBURG
Bowls, various .... 15 - 30
Butter 70
Cake Salver 40
Creamer or Spooner 25
Mug 35
Pickle Dish 30
Pitcher 85
Punch Bowl 100
Punch Cup 15
Sugar 30
Syrup 65
Toothpick Holder 35
Tumbler 15

WESTMORELAND'S #98
*Condensed list.
Bowls, various .... 10 - 55
Butter 55
Celery 25
Creamer or Spooner 20
Pickle Dish 15
Pitcher 65
Sugar 20
Tumbler 10
Wine 15

WESTMORELAND'S #295
Creamer 30
Open Sugar 25

WESTMORELAND'S #750
Basket, 3" - 8" .... 20 - 65

WESTMORELAND'S DIMPLED DIAMOND
Child's Condiment Set, 4 pcs 85

WESTMORELAND'S SQUARE MUSTARD
Creamer 30
Sugar 25

WESTWARD HO
Bread Plate, deer & log cabin hndls. . 350 - 750
Butter 400
Celery Vase 250
Champagne, very rare 900
Compote, covered, 5" - 9" .... 250 - 400
Compote, open, low & high 5" - 8" .. 350 - 500
Compote, open, low, 9", rare 900
Compote, open, high, 9", rare 1,200
Creamer or Spooner 225
Goblet 365
Marmalade Jar 380
Milk Pitcher 600
Mug, 2 sizes .... 350 - 400
Pickle Dish 130
Pitcher 425
Sauce, 3" - 5" .... 45 - 85
Sugar 320
Wine, rare 800

WHEAT & BARLEY
Bowl, covered, 3 sizes .... 40 - 70
amber .... 60 - 90
vaseline .... 80 - 130
green/blue .... 70 - 100
Bowl, open, 3 sizes .... 20 - 35
amber .... 30 - 45
vaseline .... 40 - 60
green/blue .... 35 - 55
Butter 70
amber 80
vaseline 95

green/blue 95
Cake Stand, 3 sizes .... 60 - 100
amber .... 70 - 120
vaseline .... 90 - 145
green/blue .... 80 - 135
Compote, covered, 3 sizes .... 60 - 90
amber .... 70 - 120
vaseline .... 90 - 185
green/blue .... 85 - 165
Compote, open, 3 sizes .... 30 - 60
amber .... 35 - 70
vaseline .... 40 - 85
green/blue .... 50 - 90
Creamer or Spooner 35
amber 45
vaseline 80
green/blue 70
Goblet 40
amber 50
vaseline 60
green/blue 65
Milk Pitcher 50
amber 65
vaseline 90
green/blue 80
Mug 30
amber 35
vaseline 55
green/blue 50
Pitcher 80
amber 95
vaseline 135
green/blue 145
Plate, 7" - 9" 30
amber 35
vaseline 45
green/blue 40
Shakers, ea 40
amber 50
vaseline 85
green/blue 70
Sugar 35
amber 40
vaseline 65
green/blue 50
Syrup 120
amber 160
vaseline 235
green/blue 210
Tumbler .... 20 - 25
amber .... 30 - 35
vaseline .... 50 - 65
green/blue .... 40 - 50

WHEAT SHEAF
Basket, hndl 65
Compote, 5½" 50
Compote, 8" - 9" 70
Celery Vase 30
Cruet,
double hndl. 65
Decanter w/Stopper 150
Milk Pitcher 95
Pitcher, 3 sizes .... 95 - 145
Rose Bowl 65
Tray 40
Tumbler 35
Punch Bowl 200
Punch Cup 15
Sweetmeat w/Lid 85
Wine 25
Vase, 8", stemmed 45
*All pieces scarce.

WHEEL OF FORTUNE
Butter 45
Creamer or Spooner 15
Shakers, ea 15
Sugar 20

WHEELS
Berry Bowl, lg 40
Berry Bowl, sm 10
Fruit Bowl, 10" 50
Rose Bowl, 7½" 60
Tumbler 25

WHIRLED SUNBURST IN CIRCLE
Bowl 30
Butter 70
Creamer or Spooner 20
Pitcher 90
Sugar 30
Tumbler 20

WHIRLWIND
Bowls, various .... 20 - 40
Compote, lg. open 35
Pitcher 85
Shakers, ea 25
Tumbler 15

WHISK BROOM
Pickle Dish 40
amber 55
vaseline 95
green/blue 65

WICKER WORK
Basket, handled 45
amber 70
vaseline 85

WIDE & NARROW
Butter 55
Creamer or Spooner 25
Oil Lamp 95
Pitcher 65
Sugar 20
Tumbler 15

WIDE RIB (NORTHWOOD)
Vase, 7" - 13" .... 25 - 80
green/blue 45

WILDFLOWER
Basket, oblong with metal handle 100
amber 135
vaseline 165
green/blue 235
Bowl, rnd., 6½" 25
amber 35
vaseline 40
green/blue 45
Bowl, sq., 6" - 9" .... 20 - 40
amber .... 25 - 45
vaseline .... 40 - 70
green/blue .... 45 - 80
Bread Plate, oval 30
amber 35
vaseline 40
green/blue 45
Butter, 2 styles .... 50 - 70
amber .... 55 - 75
vaseline .... 75 - 95
green/blue .... 80 - 100
Cake Tray, oval 35
amber 40
vaseline 70
green/blue 65
Cake Stand 120
amber 135
vaseline 165
green/blue 175
Celery Vase 70
amber 90
vaseline 145
green/blue 140
Champagne 30
amber 40
vaseline 60
green/blue 70
Compote, covered, 7" - 8", high or low,
3 styles .... 70 - 120
amber .... 75 - 125
vaseline .... 100 - 165
green/blue .... 110 - 145
Compote, open, 3 sizes, scarce .... 60 - 120
amber .... 70 - 125
vaseline .... 100 - 140
green/blue .... 95 - 135
Creamer or Spooner 25
amber 40
vaseline 60
green/blue 55
Dish, sq., 6" - 8" .... 20 - 35
amber .... 25 - 40
vaseline .... 35 - 55
green/blue .... 30 - 50
Goblet 40
amber 50
vaseline 70
green/blue 80
Platter, 8"x11" 35
amber 40
vaseline 70
green/blue 70
Pitcher 80
amber 90
vaseline 150
green/blue 165
Relish 20
amber 40
vaseline 45
green/blue 50
Salt, master, turtle shaped 80
amber 95
vaseline 165
green/blue 145
Sauce, flat or ftd. 10
amber 15
vaseline 25
green/blue 30
Shakers, ea 35
amber 35
vaseline 65
green/blue 80
Sugar 45
amber 50
vaseline 70
green/blue 75
Syrup 125
amber 160
vaseline 265
green/blue 295
Tumbler 25
amber 40
vaseline 65
green/blue 75
Water Tray 90
amber 85
vaseline 190
green/blue 210
Wine 75
amber 85
vaseline 135
green/blue 150

WILDFLOWER (NORTHWOOD)
Compote 25
green/blue 40

WILD ROSE LADY'S MEDALLION LAMP
Oil Lamp w/Lady's Medallion 600

WILD ROSE LAMP (RIVERSIDE GLASS CO.)
Oil Lamp, 4 sizes .... 400 - 675

WILD ROSE WITH BOW KNOT
Berry Bowl, lg 50
Berry Bowl, sm 15
Butter 85
Creamer or Spooner 20
Cruet 60
chocolate 425
Pitcher 125
Sauce 15
Shakers, ea 20
Smoke Set on Tray 100
chocolate 900
Sugar 30

Toothpick Holder 30
Tray, Rect. 35
Tumbler 25

WILD ROSE WREATH
Mini Compote, gilded 50

WM. J. BRYAN
Tumbler 95

WILLOW OAK
Bowl, covered, 3 sizes .... 60 - 90
amber .... 70 - 100
vaseline .... 100 - 140
green/blue .... 100 - 130
Bowl, open, 3 sizes .... 20 - 40
amber .... 30 - 45
vaseline .... 50 - 80
green/blue .... 40 - 70
Butter 60
amber 70
vaseline 95
green/blue 85
Cake Stand, 2 sizes .... 60 - 70
amber .... 80 - 100
vaseline .... 100 - 130
green/blue .... 90 - 115
Celery Vase 45
amber 60
vaseline 80
green/blue 70
Compote, covered, 3 sizes .... 80 - 120
amber .... 90 - 130
vaseline .... 100 - 150
green/blue .... 100 - 140
Compote, open, 3 sizes .... 30 - 50
amber .... 35 - 55
vaseline .... 55 - 80
green/blue .... 50 - 70
Creamer or Spooner 40
amber 50
vaseline 60
green/blue 65
Milk Pitcher 60
amber 70
vaseline 125
green/blue 100
Mug 45
amber 50
vaseline 75
green/blue 70
Pitcher 70
amber 80
vaseline 135
green/blue 125
Plate, 3 sizes .... 30 - 50
amber .... 40 - 60
vaseline .... 60 - 90
green/blue .... 50 - 70
Sauce 15
amber 25
vaseline 35
green/blue 35
Shakers, ea. 40
amber 60
vaseline 80
green/blue 80
Sugar 45
amber 55
vaseline 80
green/blue 80
Sweetmeat w/Lid 90
amber 100
vaseline 135
green/blue 115
Tray 50
amber 60
vaseline 80
green/blue 70
Tumbler 40
amber 50
vaseline 70
green/blue 70
Waste Bowl 30
amber 50
vaseline 65
green/blue 65

WILTEC
Bonbon 30
ruby stain 45
Butter 65
ruby stain 95
Cigar Jar 50
ruby stain 65
Creamer or Spooner 25
ruby stain 30
Custard Cup 15
ruby stain 20
Flower Pot, scarce 60
ruby stain 85
Pitcher 85
ruby stain 150
Plate, 10" - 12" 35
ruby stain 40
Plate, 6" - 8" 25
ruby stain 30
Punch Bowl 100
ruby stain 195
Punch Cup 15
ruby stain 20
Sugar 25
ruby stain 55
Tumbler 15
ruby stain 25

WILTED FLOWERS
Basket 65
Bowl 40

WINDFLOWER
Bowl 30
ebony 75
Nappy, hndl. 75
Plate 125
*All pieces scarce.

WINDMILL SERVER
Dispenser & glass in nickel plated frame, rare 125
vaseline 325

WINDSOR ANVIL
Paperweight 55
amber 80
green/blue 95

WINGED SCROLL
Berry Bowl, lg. 35
green/blue 45
custard 60
Berry Bowl, sm. 15
green/blue 25
custard 35
Bonbon 20
green/blue 30
custard 40
Butter 80
green/blue 95
custard 135
Cake Stand 45
green/blue 55
custard 65
Celery Vase 25
green/blue 30
custard 45
Cologne 60
green/blue 75
custard 90
Compote, high standard 45
green/blue 50
custard 75
Cup 10
green/blue 20
custard 30
Creamer or Spooner 20
green/blue 30
custard 45
Cruet 70
green/blue 85
custard 120
Humidor 65
green/blue 80
custard 140
Olive Dish 20
green/blue 30
custard 45
Pickle Dish 20
green/blue 30
custard 45
Saucer 10
green/blue 20
custard 35
Smokers Set 75
green/blue 90
custard 125
Sugar 35
green/blue 45
custard 65
Syrup 85
green/blue 110
custard 165
Toothpick Holder 35
green/blue 45
custard 75
Trinket Box 40
green/blue 50
custard 80

WINTER CABBAGE
Bowl, ftd. 35

WISCONSIN
Banana Stand 160
Bonbon 45
Bowl, covered, 6" - 8", 2 shapes . 100 - 125
Bowl, open, 6" - 8", 3 sizes .... 50 - 80
Butter, 2 sizes and styles .... 125 - 230
Cake Stand, 6½" - 11½" .... 75 - 150
Celery Tray 50
Celery Vase 85
Compote, covered, 5" - 8" .... 90 - 160
Compote, open, 6" - 8" .... 50 - 80
Condiment Set, w/tray, 5 pcs. 275
Creamer or Spooner 60
Cruet 200
Cup & Saucer 75
Custard Cup 40
Goblet 125
Jelly Dish, covered or open .... 55 - 90
Jam Jar 225
Milk Pitcher 135
Mug 80
Mustard Jar 160
Oil bottle 230
Pickle Dish 35
Pickle Jar 70
Plate, 5" - 7" .... 40 - 55
Preserve Dish, 6" - 8" .... 60 - 75
Pitcher, 2 sizes .... 150 - 175
Relish Tray 50
Saucer, stemmed 30
Shakers, ea., 2 shapes .... 80 - 100
Sugar 100
Sugar Shaker 130
Syrup 265
Toothpick Holder 65
Tumbler 80
Vase, 6", rnd. 65
Wine 90

WOLF
Mug 75
amber 85
vaseline 130
green/blue 110

WOODEN PAIL (AKA: OAKEN BUCKET)
Butter 85
amber 110

vaseline 165
green/blue 165
amethyst 250
Creamer or Spooner 50
amber 65
vaseline 90
green/blue 80
amethyst 145
Ice Bucket 70
amber 90
vaseline 100
green/blue 100
amethyst 175
Jelly Bucket 30
amber 60
vaseline 60
green/blue 75
amethyst 90
Pitcher 100
amber 125
vaseline 235
green/blue 185
amethyst 250
Sugar 60
amber 70
vaseline 125
green/blue 100
amethyst 175
Sugar Pail, open 55
amber 60
vaseline 100
green/blue 85
amethyst 125
Toothpick Holder, 3 sizes .... 20 - 45
amber .... 25 - 50
vaseline .... 25 - 50
green/blue .... 30 - 65
amethyst .... 40 - 85
Toy Table Set 200
Tumbler 40
amber 45
vaseline 60
green/blue 50
amethyst 95

WYOMING
Bowl, 2 sizes .... 40 - 70
Butter 265
Cake Stand, 3 sizes .... 80 - 130
Cake Plate 60
Compote, open, 3 sizes .... 50 - 85
Compote, covered, 3 sizes .... 100 - 165
Creamer, open and covered .... 45 - 95
Goblet, rare 425
Milk Pitcher 125
Mug 75
Pickle Dish 35
Pitcher 180
Sauce 25
Shakers, ea 125
Sugar, open 70
Sugar w/lid 165
Syrup 265
Tumbler 75
Wine 130

X-LOGS
Bowl, oval 25
Butter 55
Cake Stand 35
Creamer or Spooner 20
Goblet 40
Mug 25
Pickle Dish 15
Sauce 10
Shakers, ea 25
Sugar 25
Wine 20

X-RAY
Berry Bowl, lg 45
green/blue 55
amethyst 70
Berry Bowl, sm. 20
green/blue 50
amethyst 60
Butter 65
green/blue 125
amethyst 165
Celery Vase 30
green/blue 55
amethyst 90
Compote, covered 80
green/blue 145
amethyst 200
Compote, open 35
green/blue 65
amethyst 85
Creamer, 3 sizes .... 20 - 40
green/blue .... 40 - 60
amethyst .... 60 - 90
Cruet 65
green/blue 180
amethyst 250
Plate, bread size 35
green/blue 65
amethyst 85
Sauce dish 15
green/blue 30
amethyst 40
Shakers, ea 25
green/blue 70
amethyst 100
Sugar 40
green/blue 55
amethyst 75
Syrup, rare 235
green/blue 300
amethyst 450
Toothpick Holder 40
green/blue 65
amethyst 95
Tray, clover leaf 50
green/blue 85
amethyst 125

YALE
Berry Bowl, lg 30
Berry Bowl, sm. 15
Butter 45
Cake Stand 30
Celery Vase 20
Compote, covered 35
Compote, open 25
Creamer or Spooner 20
Goblet 35
Pitcher 85
Relish, oval 15
Sauce, flat or ftd 10
Shakers, ea 20
Sugar 25
Syrup 65
Tumbler 20

YOKE & CIRCLE
Berry Bowl, lg 35
Berry Bowl, sm. 15
Butter 55
Celery Dish 20
Compote, open 35
Creamer or Spooner 25
Goblet 35
Jelly Compote 25
Milk Pitcher 50
Mustard Jar 35
Nappy, hndl. 25
Pickle Dish 20
Pitcher 70
Plate 30
Rose Bowl 25
Tumbler 20
Shakers, ea 30
Sherbet 20
Sugar 30

YORK
Banana Bowl 35
Bowl, sm. 15
Plate 20
Rose Bowl, rare 100

YUTEC
Berry Bowl, lg 30
Berry Bowl, sm. 10
Butter 60
Cordial 15
Creamer or Spooner 20
Pickle Dish 15
Pickle Dish, "hub" advertising 40
Pitcher 75
Punch Bowl 95
Punch Cup 10
Relish Tray 15
Sugar 25
Tumbler 15
Wine 10

ZIG-ZAG BAND
Bowl, covered, 7" with squirrel finial 125
Creamer 40
Sugar 65

ZIPPER
Bowl, 7" 20
Butter 65
Celery Vase 35
Cheese Dish, covered 75
Compote, covered .... 60 - 75
Creamer or Spooner 40
Cruet 65
Dish, oblong 25
Goblet 40
Jam Jar 65
Milk Pitcher 55
Pitcher 100
vaseline 300
Relish Tray 20
Salt Dip 15
Sauce, flat or ftd 10
Sugar 45
Tumbler 30
Vase, stemmed 35
Wine, very scarce 45

*For any color in any pieces, add 300% to crystal.

ZIPPER CROSS
Butter 65
Compote 45
Creamer or Spooner 25
Mug 35
Sugar 35

ZIPPERED CORNER
Bowl 35
Butter 60
Creamer or Spooner 25
Pickle Dish 15
Sugar 35
Syrup 55

ZIPPERED DANDELION
Oval Bowl 45
vaseline 80

ZIPPERED HEART
Berry Bowl, lg 25
Berry Bowl, sm. 10
Bowl, sq 35
Butter 75
Candleholder from Punch Cup 75
Celery Vase 45
Creamer or Spooner 25
Creamer or Sugar, sm. 20
Custard Cup 10
Finger Bowl & Plate 40
Fruit Bowl, 12" 85
Jelly Compote 30
Mayonnaise & Plate 40
Nappy 25

Nut Bowl, 2 sizes 30
Orange Bowl, 12" 85
Pitcher 225
Pitcher, sm. 75
Punch Bowl 165
Punch Cup 10
Rose Bowl Whimsey, rare 100
Rose Bowl, 2 sizes .... 65 - 125
Sherbet 15
Spoon Tray, hndl. 25
Sugar 30
Tumbler 30

ZIPPERED WINDOWS
Wine 20

ZIPPER LOOP
Hand Lamp 75
Lamp, lg. 165
Lamp, med. 125
Lamp, sm. 145

ZIPPER SLASH
Banana Dish 30
ruby stain 45
Berry Bowl, lg. 30
ruby stain 40
Berry Bowl, sm. 10
ruby stain 20
Butter 65
ruby stain 80
Celery Vase 20
ruby stain 35
Compote, covered 45
ruby stain 70
Compote, open 30
ruby stain 40
Creamer or Spooner 20
ruby stain 30
Cup 10
ruby stain 15
Jelly Compote 25
ruby stain 35
Pitcher 85
ruby stain 125
Sauce, ftd. 10
ruby stain 15
Sherbet 15
ruby stain 25
Sugar 30
ruby stain 45
Toothpick Holder 25
ruby stain 45
Tumbler 20
ruby stain 25
Wine 10
ruby stain 25

*Add 10% for frosted or amber stained pieces.